Horizons In Buddhist Psychology

Practice, Research And Theory

Edited by
Maurits G.T. Kwee, Kenneth J. Gergen
& Fusako Koshikawa

Taos Institute Publications
Chagrin Falls, Ohio
USA

HORIZONS IN BUDDHIST PSYCHOLOGY

For the Japanese guardians who brought the torch of Chan/Zen to the West and Dr. Yutaka Haruki,
Emeritus Professor of Waseda University, Tokyo,
and Founder of the Transcultural Society for Clinical Meditation.

COVER PHOTO: Jack Thewlis

FIRST EDITION
Copyright © 2006 Taos Institute

In collaboration with the TSCM Editorial Board:
M.G.T. Kwee, K.J. Gergen,
F. Koshikawa, Y. Ishii, C. P. Bankart,
R. Kawano, G. Sugamura,
and M.K. Taams

Taos Institute Publications
Chagrin Falls, Ohio

ISBN: 0-9712312-6-5
LCN: 2006932019

PRINTED IN U.S.A.

 **Introduction To**
Taos Institute Publications

The Taos Institute is a nonprofit organization dedicated to the development of social constructionist theory and practices for purposes of world benefit. Constructionist theory and practice locate the source of meaning, value, and action in communicative relations among people. Chief importance is placed on relational process and its outcomes for the welfare of all. Taos Institute Publications offers contributions to cutting-edge theory and practice in social construction. These books are designed for scholars, practitioners, students, and the openly curious. The **Focus Book Series** provides brief introductions and overviews that illuminate theories, concepts, and useful practices. The **Books for Professionals Series** provides in-depth works, which focus on recent developments in theory and practice. Books in both series are particularly relevant to social scientists and to practitioners concerned with individual, family, organizational, community, and societal change.

Kenneth J. Gergen
President, Board of Directors
The Taos Institute

For information about the Taos Institute visit: www.taosinstitutepublications.net

Taos Institute Publications

Focus Book Series

The Appreciative Organization, (2001) by Harlene Anderson, David Cooperrider, Kenneth J. Gergen, Mary Gergen, Sheila McNamee, and Diana Whitney

Appreciative Leaders: In the Eye of the Beholder, (2001) Edited by Marge Schiller, Bea Mah Holland, and Deanna Riley

Experience AI: A Practitioner's Guide to Integrating Appreciative Inquiry and Experiential Learning, (2001) by Miriam Ricketts and Jim Willis

Appreciative Sharing of Knowledge: Leveraging Knowledge Management for Strategic Change, (2004) by Tojo Thatchekery

Social Construction: Entering the Dialogue, (2004) by Kenneth J. Gergen and Mary Gergen

Dynamic Relationships: Unleashing the Power of Appreciative Inquiry in Daily Living, (2005) by Jacqueline M. Stavros and Cheri B. Torres

Appreciative Inquiry: A Positive Approach to Building Cooperative Capacity, (2005) by Frank J. Barrett, Ph.D. and Ronald E. Fry

Books for Professionals Series

SocioDynamic Counselling: A Practical Guide to Meaning Making, (2004) by R. Vance Peavy

Experiential Exercises in Social Construction – A Fieldbook for Creating Change, (2004) by Robert Cottor, Alan Asher, Judith Levin, and Cindy Weiser

Dialogues About a New Psychology, (2004) by Jan Smedslund

Therapeutic Realities: Social Construction and the Therapeutic Process, (2006) by Kenneth J. Gergen

Horizons In Buddhist Psychology, (2006) edited by Maurits G.T. Kwee, Kenneth J. Gergen and Fusako Koshikawa

For on-line ordering of books from Taos Institute Publications visit
www.taospub.net or www.taosinstitutepublications.net

For further information, write or call:
1-888-999-TAOS, 1-440-338-6733, info@taosinstitute.net or
taosinstitute@alltel.net

Table Of Contents

Preface

Yutaka Haruki
Emeritus Professor of Psychology, Waseda University

In the days when transportation and communication systems were not so developed as they are today, there were diversified cultures throughout the world. Meanwhile, however, the culture of an influential country in a given area overpowered the cultures of other countries, albeit on a scale less than global, and succeeded in making the different cultures identical. The development process of cultures from diversification to unification at one time and from unification to diversification at another may have contributed to the making of history.

We may be living in the period marked by a rising tendency towards unification. In the past we have been dominated by the cultures of countries which are strong militarily, politically, and economically and the same situation still continues to exist today. The culture known as "science" which has become the basis for producing such power has in and of itself become more global in nature than regional. For instance, philosophy is wisdom to trace the source of knowledge and its turnout ought to be applicable anywhere in the world. Today this is not the case, however. Though science used to be the European culture, the universality of science — for instance, the law of gravity is applicable at any place in the world — is replacing cultural diversification with the trend towards unification of the world's cultures.

Psychology is not an exception. Psychology started out as science and its knowledge is considered universal. It may be true that Hermann Ebbinghaus' forgetting curve is not regional. Generally speaking, any knowledge in the basic field of psychology is universal. What about the situation in the field of psychotherapy? With a variety of factors interrelated in a complex way, there is no simple way of explaining matters related to the universality of the theory and technique of psychotherapy as opposed to knowledge in the basic field. To take up some example cases, in Japan, Rogers' client-centered therapy draws attention as the basis for psychotherapy and counseling in Japan and it is the most widely practiced method among the therapists. Behind this situation is the Japanese culture which exhorts the attitude of accepting others instead of self-assertiveness in our relationship with others. There is a saying "Be a good listener and a poor talker" in Japan. A good listener will win the respect of other people. It is behind this cultural background that Rogers' counseling technique is the most popular. In contrast, psychotherapy focused on cognitive persuasion seems to be gaining wide acceptance in western countries. This may show that each type of psychotherapy differs from another depending on the country's culture.

Psychotherapy has developed as a science in Western cultures and it is also beginning to be well accepted today in Japanese society. Until recently, however, religion has been playing a vital role in Eastern countries as a method of addressing psychological problems. In Japan Buddhism has been playing the role. The Buddha's thoughts and his method of leading people are considerably different from the teachings of Christianity, which attach importance to faith in the only God. The Buddha teaches the importance of self-reflection based on a philosophical outlook on the world (Buddhism), and it also teaches the method of addressing the problems of basic sufferings of mankind such as the difficulty of going on living, aging (fear of getting old), illness (fear of illness), and death (fear of death). What Buddha did was to probe thoroughly into the root causes of human sufferings and to come up with the method of addressing these problems. These characteristic qualities of Buddhism may naturally attract attention of psychotherapists in Western countries. The question is what they seek in Buddhism (in relation to psychotherapy). We may expect clarification of this point as the comparison study of these two progresses. It would not be productive just to point out the similarities between the two. We might expect them to clarify whether Buddhism has anything to offer by way of complementing Western psychotherapy. What always comes up as a problem when there is an attempt to incorporate Buddhism in psychotherapy is that the scientific psychotherapy demands demonstration of the therapeutic effect of Buddhism and its universality. There will be no simple answer for the question of whether Buddhism has such a quality. For instance, Zen meditation has been subjected to scientific tests for verification, but reliable data have yet to be obtained.

It is also necessary to think of the limits to the cultural distinctive qualities. For instance, Buddhism often contains physical training. In Western culture, however, the dualistic theory with regard to mind and body is predominant with the penchant for making light of the body and for making much of the mind. What sets Western culture apart from Eastern culture most vividly are matters related to ego or self. In Western countries, establishment of "self" is regarded as being of the greatest value. In contrast, Buddhist followers aim at non-self. It is practically impossible for Westerners to understand this Buddhist thought. Looking back on the past, we find that a conflict among different cultures very often gives birth to a new culture. It is a matter of our great interest to find out what kind of innovation is due from a conflict between psychotherapy as science and Buddhism. In this case, the focus will be on the question of what aspects of Buddhism will make psychotherapy innovative. Granted there are certain cultural limits, what is important will be to find out what aspects of Buddhism are universal and will be able to stand scientific verification.

It is very gratifying that some Western psychotherapists have begun to show interest in Buddhism. However, the hardest part has yet to come. First and foremost, it is important to understand Buddhism and then to clarify the similarities and dissimilarities between psychotherapy and Buddhism. If there is something that can be incorporated in psychotherapy, it will open the way for inventing a new type of psychotherapy. It will be a highly time-consuming project and the project has just gotten underway.

Acknowledgments

This work is made possible through the collaborative efforts of numerous individuals and groups. Foundational to this project have been the efforts of the Transcultural Society for Clinical Meditation (TSCM), established by Emeritus Professor Yutaka Haruki. The present work would not be possible without the efforts of its Buddhist-Psychology-Cognitive-Behavior-Therapy connecting pioneers Padmal de Silva, Yutaka Haruki, Maurits Kwee, William Mikulas, Deane Shapiro Jr, and all its collaborators and presenters during its 9th convention within the 5th International Congress of Cognitive Psychotherapy. Special thanks are due to C.P. Bankart for his cogent remarks and editing syntax of several chapters. Finally, special appreciation must be expressed to Tim Beck and the 14th Dalai Lama for allowing their conversation to be included here. This book has been made possible by a generous grant of the Advanced Research Center for the Human Sciences, Waseda University, Tokyo, Japan, through Prof. Yasutomo Ishii. Our genuine appreciation is expressed to all.

Maurits G.T. Kwee
Kenneth J. Gergen
Fusako Koshikawa

Foreword

Jan Beskow & Astrid Palm Beskow

Conveners of the 5th International Congress of Cognitive Psychotherapy, Gothenburg, Sweden, 2005

Our grandson, 16 months old, is playing on the carpet. He is smiling and full of energy. He stretches out his hand as quick as lightning and grips one thing after the other. Then he lets it go, it falls down on the carpet, as rapidly as he took it. Children are really different from adults! But perhaps not so much as we may think. In fact, they act similarly to adults. Rapidly we focus our attention on one thing, trying to grasp it mentally. Sometimes we keep it for a while but often we equally rapidly let it go.

Projections. "Everything is projection" said our friend Maurits Kwee. I, Jan Beskow, can perceive this mental gripping as an act of projecting attention in order to grip a bit in the outer and/or inner flow of perceptions, feelings, and cognitions. Interacting with it for a shorter or longer while and then letting it go. Behind the gripping there is always a choice, a wish. What we are doing is constructing our inner world, just as the little boy did so eagerly. For me this is probably the first step on the way of understanding that "everything" is projection. On Sunday the 12th of June HH the 14th Dalai Lama met the Swedish archbishop K.G. Hammar in a conversation entitled "Looking for meaning in the present world." HH told us that once when he gave a lecture in Australia, one of the hosts remarked that he seemed to be "a good Christian." A bit later in the conversation the archbishop replied: "If so, I am perhaps a small Buddhist." Certainly all humans have a rich basis of common images and values. Bridges may thus be built on a basis of many similarities.

Bridges. Since decades, ideas from Buddhist Psychology have influenced cognitive psychotherapy in the form of "mindfulness." More recently it has been used to postpone relapses in depression and integrated into new forms of cognitive behavioral therapies. In addition, The Dalai Lama has been deeply involved in conversations with leading scientists in the Mind and Life Organisation <www.mindandlife.org>. The invitation of spiritual and scientific leaders to conversations at a world congress in cognitive psychotherapy has never happened before. Certainly it is a big step and consequently an adventure. It was an effort to bridge some of the gaps between humanistic and natural scientific perspectives but also between the psychological knowledge in the West and the East. Certainly it was a test of the broad-mindedness of cognitive scientists and therapists.

Conviviality. A congress is not a thing, nor an event. It is a process or rather a confluence of many processes, intensively confronting each other during a few days. One of these pre-congress processes was our work at the Center of Cognitive Psychotherapy and Education in Göteborg with the concept of "conviviality." Literally, this old Latin word means living together. But it has also references to *convivium*, that is, a real feast. Our primary connotation is respect for the legitimacy of each other,

Contributions. In elaborating this adventure it was continuously re-assuring to discuss the development of the congress concept with old friends in the International Association of Cognitive Psychotherapy, IACP, such as Arthur Freeman, Paul Salkovskis and Robert Leahy, who poured out their rich experience. The next contributing old friend was Michael Mahoney, who brought in the constructivist perspective. He proposed that the congress could be a confluence between IACP and the Society for Constructivism in the Human Sciences, SCHS. In that way we got in contact with Maurits Kwee from the Transcultural Society for Clinical Meditation, TSCM. He, and his wife Marja Taams, played a major role as organizers of the symposia and workshops in Buddhist Psychology and as initiators and editors of this book. After the opening ceremony on Monday the 13th the founder of cognitive psychotherapy professor Aaron Beck met the Dalai Lama in an 1-1/2 hours conversation, the "Meeting of Minds." They shared emotions and thoughts about the hostility of our time and the possibilities of supporting human growth and peace. These two introductory events seemed to set the emotional standard of the whole congress, characterized by friendliness and good atmosphere, indeed a feeling of conviviality. Now we know that most clinicians and scientists in cognitive psychotherapy were really ready to combine their old knowledge and experiences with new impressions. There seems to be a longing for a comprehensive structure capable of including global similarities and variations in feelings and cognitions.

New bridges. Modern psychotherapy has developed in two waves: behavioral psychotherapy and cognitive or Cognitive-Behavior Therapy. "The third wave" so richly represented at the congress, is experimenting with new approaches. Many of them tried to integrate mindfulness in various ways. The clinical effects reported were good but more scientific evidence is necessary. In CBT the border between normality and pathology has always been fleeting. Efforts to build resilience in persons by exploring their talents for further development erased this border even more and are a further similarity to Buddhist Psychology. The bridge between West and East at the congress finally consisted of three parts, elaborated in many invited addresses, symposia, round tables, posters and workshops: On the West side, the first two waves of CBT; on the East side, Buddhist Psychology in traditional and newer forms, and between them the experiments of the third wave including mindfulness.

The future. The congress in Göteborg was a confluence of many processes. The work done is now freely flowing forward in many big and small brooks in all the delegates in their more than 40 home countries. Discussions also followed at the post-congress constructionist workshop with Kenneth and Mary Gergen at Ellös, North of Göteborg. The congress is further being followed up by a DVD-film of "A Meeting of Minds," which is available at the Center, info@cognitivterapi-gbg.se,. Profits are divided between Tibetan Charity and the Foundation for Research in Cognitive Psychotherapy, initiated by the Center. This book is also a major contribution to the post-congress work. Hopefully it will be read as an inspiring source of new experiences, new clinical techniques, and more clinical research, all making cognitive psychotherapy richer and more effective.

Foreword

Michael Mahoney

Convener IX World Congress on Constructivism

Spirituality and psychotherapy share much. They share a lineage that is ancient, and they share a commitment to compassion. As we celebrate contemporary dialogue on the deep resonance of spirituality and psychotherapy, it is worth reflecting on that legacy and that shared commitment.

Existential philosopher Karl Jaspers was among the first to recognize a near-global shift in human consciousness that dates back to approximately 600 BCE. Contemplation began to take the forms that we now recognize in both philosophy and the major world religions. As is so often the case in developmental processes, this emergence was characterized by differentiation. In Asia and the Middle East, the emphasis was on the human connection to the infinite and eternal. Taoism and Hinduism begot Confucianism and Buddhism. Zoroastrianism marked the foundations of what would later find expression as Judaism, Christianity, and Islam. On the other side of the differentiation emerged the western tradition now known as philosophy. Defined as love of wisdom by Pythagoras, all philosophy begins in awe. This was first noted by Aristotle. When the rationalist tradition in philosophy merged with empiricism in the 17th century, the result was what we now call science. Modern textbooks suggest that psychotherapy was a 20th century differentiation of science, but its roots go back much further in time. Psychotherapy shares a legacy that can be traced back to philosophy and spiritual wisdom traditions. Although philosophy is sometimes stereotyped as abstraction, its heart lies in the pursuit of meaning in life. Consciously or otherwise, every practitioner of psychotherapy is an applied philosopher and every philosopher is implicitly a life counselor.

The chapters in this volume are welcome expressions of an integral and emergent dialogue. Thirty-five years ago, Aaron T. ("Tim") Beck and I were privileged to participate in what was then called "the cognitive revolution" in psychology and psychotherapy. It represented the opening of scientific psychology to the contributions of the cognitive sciences. It was, in a sense, the re-opening of psychology to the inner realm of the mind. We now share the privilege of participating in an even more significant contemporary opening — the opening of psychology and psychiatry to the human heart. Here, at last, there is an expansion of dialogues between mental health professionals and practitioners of the world's spiritual wisdom traditions. This opening and these dialogues reflect a return to ancient sources and the deepening of our collective global appreciation for the intimate synergy of mind, body, and spirit. They are also a celebration of our growing sense of wonder and responsibility at how deeply and complexly we are all connected — connected to all the parts inside ourselves, connected to each other, connected to this little blue planet that sustains us, and connected to the timeless and spacious mysteries that dance the cosmos.

Like the conference itself, this volume begins with a delightful dialogue between two wise beings who have committed their lives to compassion and the reduction of human suffering — His Holiness the Dalai Lama and Aaron Beck. In a spectrum of later presentations — regenerated here as chapters — there is a mindfulness and a "bodifulness" that bids us integrate and connect. We are, perhaps, just beginning to make some vitally important connections that will serve future generations. In honor of that process, I close with a poem:

Connecting

Minding body, minding heart
May our meeting be a start.

Let us follow, let us lead
Let us serve love's higher need.

Labile labels need not hide
All we share of life inside.

Those who seek our counsel wise
Let them see compassion's eyes.

We all suffer, we all strive
Keeping children's hopes alive.

Mind and body, heart and soul
May connecting make them whole.

May our efforts never cease
Till all beings enjoy peace.

General Introduction:
Toward A New Buddhist Psychology

This work finds its most immediate origins in the 5th International Congress of Cognitive Psychotherapy held in Gothenburg, Sweden, in June, 2005. Its scientific program was organized by Dr. Astrid Palm Beskow, president, and Prof. Jan Beskow, secretary. The event took place in confluence with the 9th World Congress on Constructivism, headed by Prof. Michael J. Mahoney. Informally the convention also hosted the 9th conference of the Transcultural Society for Clinical Meditation (founded by Prof. Yutaka Haruki). It was a historical event in many respects. According to history, in 1904 the Sri Lankan monk Dharmapala gave a lecture at Harvard on not-self after which William James, founder of American psychology, allegedly said to the audience: "This is the psychology everybody will be studying 25 years from now." Now, 101 years later, we have witnessed a full welcoming of Buddhist teachings and practices by an entire congress of professional psychologists.

This vital collaboration was most dramatically symbolized at the very opening of the meetings. Over two thousand participants were treated to a public dialogue between the 14th Dalai Lama (Dr. Tenzin Gyatso) and Prof. A.T. Beck, founding father of Cognitive Therapy. Their exchange of views on commonalities and differences in psychological orientations is featured as the first chapter of this work. The remainder of the volume is composed primarily of chapters growing from presentations at the Gothenburg meetings. For further depth we have also included additional chapters commissioned after the meetings. This volume reflects a genuine East-West collaboration; contributors converge from twelve different nations. All are concerned with the integration of Buddhist teachings and scientific psychology by exploring the possibilities of merging practices of therapy, research methods and theory. Our chief hope in this volume is that this communion may enrich practices for the positive transformation of individuals and societies.

Toward a New Buddhist Psychology

"Buddhism" is a modernist term inherited from the 18th century European era of Enlightenment. Meant as a translation of the Buddha's Dharma (a systematic way to teach a practice on a certain understanding of life through meditation in action), Buddhism is a container that has been variously filled with almost everything related to the Buddhist teachings for more than 2500 years. Historically, it came to mean, among other things, a philosophy, a metaphysics, and a religion, or some amalgam of these combined with atavisms derived from regional cultures like Bon (Tibetan Buddhism) or Taoism (Chan/Zen Buddhism). The existence of a large body of Buddhist scriptures — estimated to be 60 times larger than the bible — in Pali (Theravada/Hinayana), Sanskrit (Mahayana), Tibetan (Vajrayana/ Tantrayana), and in Chinese, has made it impossible for one person to read and fathom them all in a lifetime. In the course of history many denominations and sects have come into being, selecting and adapting various materials and practices to serve various local needs and values. Unsurprisingly, many of these communities started to claim their own proprietary truth around a certain sutra. These competitions eventually lead to rivalry and fragmentation down the ages, some of which we will take up in the pages of this book. Unfortunately, however, this has meant both a distancing of groups that might otherwise stand to enrich each other, and in some cases a degeneration and disappearance of Buddhist teachings and practices

Our effort in the present work is to regenerate and rejuvenate these Buddhist teachings as a transcultural and unifying psychology. Although there are important differences in emphasis and content in the jungle of schools, denominations, and sects resulting from 2500 years of Buddh-*isms*, we emphasize here what we take to be various themes intrinsic to all. The hope for a unifying Dharma is not new (see, for example, Goldstein, 2002). However, our specific hope in this work is not only to locate unifying themes, but to inject a vitality that enables them to flourish in a globalized world. In our view, this first means finding means of linking East and West, and second of traversing the historical planes of pre-modern, modern, and post-modern. In effect, we press toward a Buddhist teaching that is apt for the 21st century.

The possibility of bridging eastern and western traditions is already in active motion. As will be evidenced in later chapters, western scientists and practitioners have become increasingly drawn to the potentials inherent in the Buddhist traditions. We view developments in psychology, and particularly within the domain of therapy, as a particularly fertile field for unification. This is so because at the heart of both the Dharma and the therapeutic mission is practice, that is, action in the world for the alleviation of suffering and the realization of positive human relationships. We generally avoid the term Buddhism — reserving its use to denote the traditions of the past — and consequently speak about Buddhist Psychology. More specifically we propose a New Buddhist Psychology (NBP) to delineate a movement in Buddhist teachings that, by including western psychology, go beyond the major traditions of Theravada and Mahayana.

The advantages of a New Buddhist Psychology are many. Western psychology brings to the table the broadly employed discourses of science. It invites one to view Buddhist practices, then, in both biological and social contexts. It opens the possibility carrying out systematic, empirical research on the efficacy of practice. And it invites open and reflexive dialogue on such practices, their potentials and implications. It is just such dialogue that can also bring about creative amalgamations, and new practices that speak to the unfolding predicaments of cultures in motion. At the same time, western psychology is challenged not only to expand its repertoire of practices, but as well its theoretical vocabulary, and its traditional presumptions. In particular, presumptions of mental illness, cause and effect, and mental mechanics are opened for further deliberation. In effect, we strive for an orientation that dialectically connects social, clinical, and neuropsychology to the Dharma in order to generate effective practices for all people. We hope for a Dharma that invites and guides professional practice, and in which research is meant to improve the practice of action, and theory serves the enrichment of dialogue.

Bridging History: The Constructionist Connection

It is one thing to press toward a vision of the Dharma that brings together East and West, thus moving toward pan-cultural inclusion. However, another way of viewing the adequacy of NBP for the challenge of 21st century globalization, is in terms of history. Cultural variations invariably earmark differences in historical developments. In this sense, Buddhist teachings largely bear the marks of what may be viewed as Traditional or Pre-modern history. They grew into form and presence prior to the rise of science, secularist materialism, democracy, and a belief in infinite progress through technology — all marks of what is often viewed as Modernism. In this sense, psychological science is a child of modernist history, as evidenced in its firm commitments to the observable world, scientific research, and continuous strides in the understanding and treatment of human suffering. Yet, as many see it, the global flows of information, peoples, technology, goods, and entertainment, bring forth a new Zeitgeist. In what is commonly viewed as an emerging period of Postmodernism, we are increasingly sensitized to the existence of multiple truths, rationalities, and values. Western science is based on a particular array of assumptions and values lodged within a particular time in history. This does not render its truths invalid so much as revealing them to be of a particular and delimited kind, one among many as opposed to an unquestioned ultimate.

Within the postmodern sphere this heightened sensitivity to the social basis of beliefs about the real, the rational and the good is generally viewed as *social constructionist*. Social construction places the primacy in reality construction not within individual minds but within relationships. Meaning is not a solipsistic matter, but it resides in social negotiation, collaboration, and agreement. In this sense individuals owe their private meanings to their existence in a history of relationship. This includes the meaning of the self. Such revolutionary and radical stance toward permanence is deeply resonant with the Buddhist viewpoint that we should not mistake our conventions of understanding for transcendental truth. As humans we construct the world and the self but these constructions are often the root of suffering. We may live by our constructions, but we also die by them. Whether we call it "no mind" or "deconstruction," the potential for liberation is essential for human well-being.

We shall have more to say about the relationship between Buddhist and social constructionist thought as the volume proceeds. Most important for now, this affinity in orientations provides us with a means of bridging history. That is, in their postmodern stance, they do not eliminate the beliefs of any period of history. No person, profession or culture is transcendentally wrong in its constructions of existence; all contain validity for those who live within their frame. Thus, all are invited to participate in the dialogues from which the future is molded. In effect, we may hope for a New Buddhist Psychology that not only entwines the Dharma with modern psychological inquiry, but will be enriched by all those who wish to enter the conversation.

Organization of the Book

Informed by the preceding, we have organized the present volume in the following way: We begin with what may be regarded as a historical landmark, the dialogue between the 14th Dalai Lama (Dr. Tenzin Gyatso) and Prof. Aaron Beck, a major figure in the development of cognitive therapy. The account not only includes their thoughts on similarities and differences in approach, but the relationship of Buddhism to science, imagery and visualization, and educating the public. Appended to the account of this engaging exchange are Beck's later reflections on the dialogue.

The remainder of the volume is divided into four sections. In Part I we feature a variety of cutting edge contributions to the use of Buddhist practices and their therapeutic modifications for purposes of human change. Eight practitioners describe in illuminating detail the practices they employ in eliminating anger, increasing compassion, treating excessive grief, developing social skills, reducing anger, controlling obesity, treating post-traumatic stress disorder, augmenting positive emotions, and bringing about an enhanced sense of well-being. It is important to note that this placement of practices toward the beginning of this volume first represents the Dharma's emphasis on practice as opposed to theoretical musing. Both Buddhist teachings and social construction caution against relying on theory as a picture or map of what is the case, and emphasize placing human action in the forefront of concern.

Part II features chapters that illuminate the landscape of contemporary research in Buddhist psychology. The majority of these studies are essentially concerned with the outcome of Buddhist practices, or variants thereof, on problems typically challenging the psychotherapist. Ten different studies are featured in this section, and they variously demonstrate the efficacy of Shikanho, a cognitive-behavioral method for alleviating feelings of negativity; the effects of a mindfulness training program on reducing stress; the effects of a mindfulness-based stress reduction program in treating emotional disorders; the efficacy of Zen meditation in reducing depression; the utility of a sensory awareness seminar on professional functioning; and the efficacy of combining Tai Chi and Zen meditation in reducing anxiety. In effect, while the chapters in Part I offer a broad range of practice possibilities, the contributions in Part II build substantial confidence in the efficacy of such practices for human change.

In Part III, we include theoretical reflections on Buddhist traditions and practices and their various relationships with western psychology. These chapters first of all explicate more fully the relationship between social constructionist thought and central ideas in the Buddhist tradition. However, the stronger emphasis of this section as a whole is on the ways in which Buddhist ideas and practices either parallel, augment, or are in tension with central movements in western psychotherapy. In opening this relationship to both constructive and critical analysis, we create avenues to new departures in practice. These contributions also set the stage for the more fully elaborated theoretical offering in Part IV.

In Part IV, a single, comprehensive essay is featured. This essay, by Maurits Kwee and Marja Taams, is an attempt to collect the major strands of thought in the Buddhist tradition and to integrate them more fully with central tenets in western psychology. In doing so the authors also draw together much of the work included in this book. This integrative attempt is most useful, as well, in furnishing a rich historical background that enables the reader to appreciate the many variations in Buddhist beliefs and practices, and where they both resonate with and differ from the western psychological orientation.

Does this volume succeed in bringing about an integration across cultures and time? By blending social construction with a New Buddhist Psychology we certainly hope we can make a contribution to fitting the Dharma for the 21st century. At the same time, if reading evokes more questions than answers, we might say the book has done a good enough job of serving the Buddhist teaching. If reading this book is like throwing a million little bits and pieces into the air and letting them fall into a curious and provocative mosaic, we have proceeded at least minimally toward our goal. More hopefully the present effort will serve as a catalyst to creating a vision of an East/West/North/South communion that is not only diagnostic, therapeutic and prophylactic, but above all provides new ways of being-in-the-world that are salubrious, sublime, and sane.

1

Himalaya Buddhism Meets Cognitive Therapy: The Dalai Lama And Aaron T. Beck In Dialogue

Photo courtesy of Aaron T. Beck.

This chapter, written on behalf of the Transcultural Society for Clinical Medita-
tion, is an edited and narrated report on a public dialogue between Dr. Aaron T.
Beck, a psychiatrist and the founding father of Cognitive Therapy, and Dr. Tenzin
Gyatso aka the 14th Dalai Lama, leader of the Tibetan people and head of state in
exile. The two scholars exchanged ideas in an open atmosphere during a conver-
sation that was at the opening of the joint 5th International Congress of Cognitive
Psychotherapy 2005 (conveners: Drs. Astrid Palm Beskow and Jan Beskow) and
IX World Congress on Constructivism (convener: Dr. Michael J. Mahoney), held
in Gothenburg, Sweden. Dr. Astrid Palm Beskow, assisted by Dr. Paul Salkovskis
on stage, hosted the unique Meeting of Minds session. This dialogue between
Cognitive Therapy's leading proponent and the alleged reincarnation of the
Bodhisattva of Compassion (Avalokiteshvara) is historical by any standard. It
was a litmus test of a proposition that Dr. Gyatso has said on several occasions,
"If the words of the Buddha and the findings of modern science contradict each
other, then the former have to go (The Boston Globe, 9/14/03). We find here a
strong echo of the Buddha's Charter for Free Inquiry (Anguttara Nikaya, III 65)
that counters the decrees of blind faith, fanaticism, dogmatism, bigotry, personal-
ity cult, and intolerance. It was in this spirit that the two giants explored the
interface between therapy and meditation.The two discussed issues of human
concern and particularly commonalities and differences of their disciplines. This
report is complemented by Dr. Beck's reflections on this public dialogue and the
narrators" introduction and comments.[1]

Setting the Stage

The event starts by Dr. Beck's waiting for Dr. Gyatso,[2] who soon enters the stage of the Göteborg Convention Centre that is filled with psychologists/cognitive-behavior therapists. Dr. Gyatso, wearing a scarlet robe, accompanied by his personal interpreter (a Tibetan Buddhist monk), walks forward up the stairs, shakes Dr. Salkovskis' hand, Dr. Beck's hand with both hands, bows deeply, and laughs with a radiating joy, and shakes Dr. Astrid Palm Beskow's hand again with both hands. While slightly bowing, he kindly greets the audience with a big smile and his typically held hands (stretched fingers and palms flat against each other in front of his head), which he also did gracefully in between the hand shaking. Thus, they all sit in easy-chairs in front of the public from the left to the right: Drs. Palm Beskow, Beck, Gyatso, the interpreter slightly behind, and Dr. Salkovskis. Dr. Palm Beskow opens the session by saying: "And now is the most exciting moment in our lives... Dr. Beck is going to start." Dr. Beck takes over the torch and reiterates: "This is a very exciting moment for me and I am honored to be able to chat with one of the great world leaders of time and I really treasure the opportunity to discuss the cognitive approach to people's problems with you." Dr. Gyatso: "It is a great honor having this meeting with a senior respected and experienced scholar (bowed with hands" clasped in greeting). In my tradition in the monasteries, there is seniority; the younger one must respect to the older one" (the younger Dr. Gyatso[3] bows again to pay his respect to Dr. Beck; they both laugh in a heartfelt way, the audience laughs in synchrony and applauds; this breaks the ice). In a relieved atmosphere Dr. Beck demurs: "So we want to start with negative thoughts?"

Buddhism and the Science of Psychology

Dr. Beck's remark prompts a monologue on Dr. Gyatso's side about similarities with science and psychology, which provides a framework: "Modern scientists who are dealing with the mind (show) many similarities because the Buddhist system is not just prayer or devotion (but also includes) 'analytical meditation.' " That means analyzing external events; many events (are) actually a human creation, (thus) as far as human movement is concerned, the ultimate factor is motivation. So, first (it) starts here (Dr. Gyatso, who abundantly gesticulates while talking, pointed at his heart; Dr. Beck nods) or combined here and here (pointing also at his head), then (there are) actions, verbal actions, physical actions, mental actions. (These) actions make (the difference) in the external things. So, in the Buddhist tradition, whenever a problem that we do not want (and) actually (wish) to overcome, then just prayer (or) sitting meditation will not work. We must analyze the sources of these problems, we (will have) to go into the mind; (it is) the mind that is (then) important, therefore some people describe Buddhism as the science of mind. I think that is true. The Buddhist (approach) is using mind (or rather) valid mind (to) transform emotion(s); usually those emotions which (are) beneficial to oneself as well as to others (I call) "valid." These are valid because we (all) want happiness, satisfaction, and peace. (Those) mental elements, which ultimately bring peace, happiness, satisfaction (are) "valid"; those negative or harmful emotions, such as hatred and anger not only destroy one's own peace of mind but also create (a) negative or unhappy atmosphere. (It) creates pain and (more) suffering (to) oneself as well as to others. These (I call) "not valid."[4]

Now (we) utilize positive emotions as a countermeasure for negative emotions, (as) a way to transform our emotions; not through drugs or injections but (by) utilizing our own minds. In Buddhism — like in many other ancient Indian non-Buddhist traditions — there (exists) very detailed explanations about the world of mind. This is a vast subject; there are so many different categories of mind or thoughts and emotions. (Also) there are different levels (of mind), grosser levels and more subtle (levels). (For instance,) this moment we are (on) a gross level of mind, when we are dreaming we are on a subtle level of mind; (another) mental state is deep sleep without dreaming. (Like) modern science's studying and trying to seek reality (of) the emotional mind, (Buddhism) investigates and (also) tries to find the reality of mind (our mental worlds); (it has done this throughout its long history along with other ancient traditions)."

Dr. Gyatso continues: "(There) are many similarities (which) according to my own experience of more than 16 or 17 years that I (foster) meetings and dialogues (to exchange ideas for many days) with scientists on four fields: cosmology, neurobiology, subatomic/quantum physics, and psychology. In these four fields (we have found to share) common grounds. The Buddhist literature (offers) many explanations to questions (concerning) these four fields. (Take) the field of cosmology, some of the descriptions in the Buddhist literature (are) now outdated. Modern scientific findings are much more reliable and (precise). In the Buddhist Sanskrit or Mahayana tradition, there is a quotation of the Buddha that roughly states.[5] 'My followers should not accept my teaching out of devotion, faith, or respect but rather out of investigation or experimentation.' Therefore, we have some liberty to investigate even the Buddha's own words; we have the liberty to say that (for instance) the Buddhist literature that describes the world (like) geography and (astronomy) — the distances from the earth to the moon or the sun and other planets — are a disgrace (laughs). This is the greatness of the Buddhist way of thinking: (it is about investigation), not blind faith, Therefore, (I have) meetings with scientists and as a result, we learned many useful things from scientific findings. We need some modifications in some of our ancient beliefs and concepts. In the field of psychology, I think Buddhist Psychology seems to be more advanced, but still I don't know. You have to judge (both laugh). According to my conversations with modern psychologists, it seems that the Buddhist tradition is more systematic and (provides) more detailed explanations. (Thus), modern scientists find some usefulness about Buddhist explanations on mind, thoughts, emotions, and particularly on the method or way to transform the mind or emotions (Dr. Beck said: "Right.") So, no doubt there are many similarities (Dr. Beck tries to come in between by saying: "Actually I have a suggestion"; but Dr. Gyatso abruptly interrupts). Actually I saw your book *Prisoners of Hate* that is almost like Buddhist literature (Dr. Beck laughs, the audience applauds, and Dr. Gyatso laughs in his characteristic way)."

Similarity to Cognitive Therapy's Centerpiece

Dr. Beck replies that "the book is about 1500 years late. Now, we analyze in a very special way; just to start with anger, if one of my colleagues says something, I (could) maybe think: 'he is putting me down, he is insulting me' " I get that thought, "he is not showing me respect," so that is the thought and then I feel I have been wronged by him, that's very important in anger. I have been wronged, he has done me wrong — that is my wrong thinking — but I think he has done me wrong and then I think I am the victim, he has made me into a victim and then I get angry and want to punish him. But, I have learned from experience, this is personal experience rather than science shows that 90% of the time I am wrong; that's the negative thinking that comes in. So then I start to analyze and think: "Is there some explanation as to why he said what he said? Maybe he does not feel well, maybe I did not hear him right, (or) maybe what he says is correct." When I start to think about this, when I think (thus) my anger goes away or I may feel that maybe he is in some pain himself and then, that is compassion, he won't have said that to me unless something is really hurting him. I think if something is hurting him, then I understand; and as soon as I get understanding, I no longer feel angry; the anger goes away out there.

Dr. Gyatso's response: "I think the Buddhist approach to these negative emotions is almost the same. Negative emotions, firstly (should be demarcated). What is negative and positive? From a Buddhist viewpoint there is no absolute negative or positive, things are relative (Dr. Gyatso addresses his interpreter in Tibetan, who translates: 'It is only from a relative point of view that we can talk about what is positive and what is negative; it is always a comparison, there is no absolute entity.') By nature we have cognitive experience, with (cognition comes) the experience of feeling, feelings of pain, joyfulness, or pleasure; by nature we, (being also) animals, want happiness or joyfulness and do not want pain. Since we want happiness, satisfaction, or hope (and) do not want suffering or pain, those things, which cause pain and suffering including pain and suffering themselves are negative. Those things, which ultimately bring happiness, joyfulness, satisfaction are positive. In terms of emotions, some emotions may bring temporary satisfaction, but are in the long run harmful. Between temporary and long term, (the latter) is more important because its effects and consequences are more serious than the short term ones. Those emotions, which not only bring temporary, but also long run benefit are positive; those emotions that bring temporary satisfaction, but are in the long run harmful are negative. Someone who feels temporary uneasiness (to feeling) in the long run beneficial, that is positive. Now the question is (how to deal with) afflicted emotions, such as anger or hatred? For example, when I loose my temper and am angry at someone, I would use some harsh words and look with (bulged) eyes. I would feel satisfied because I have done something, I have responded, but then after some time when the anger (has) cooled down, I feel ashamed (guilty/contrite) that I have done something wrong. That means that the anger, although bringing temporary satisfaction, it is in the long run shameful and uncomfortable."

Dr. Gyatso continues: "Why do these things happen? Exactly as you mentioned, when all these negative emotions fully develop, one cannot see reality; much of it is mental projection. There might sometimes be some basis, whether bad or good, but the moment negative emotions develop, there is exaggeration of the good or the bad. Good means here that there is something beautiful that leads to attachment, which also results in a negative emotion; one exaggerates the positive-ness of the object. Then, there is negativity or ugliness of something you do not want, leading to a rejection/pushing out of hate or anger. There may be some basis, but then again through mental projection there is an exaggeration of 100% negativity, fully developing anger or hatred, and rejection. On the other side, there may be some basis, some good thing, but when it is still (a) mental projection of something 100% good then there is attachment. Both attachment — wanting to be near or come close to an object — as well as anger, distance, rejection, repulsion, both are essentially misconceptions, unrealistic mental projections and exaggerations.[6] As you (have) mentioned, 90% or (even) 100% (is exaggerated), a very important point. Usually, when these negative emotions develop, the whole (self/mind) becomes an embodiment (of the emotion). That is why these disastrous things happen, (but) we do not (always) know (the reason). What is important here is that through some training eventually we have the ability — when these negative emotions develop — to try to separate (one's) self (and to be) like a watcher, an observer of negative emotions (like) anger. At some occasion, I myself — when some anger comes — try to separate myself, (to be able) to see the anger (and) sometimes when a strong anger (arises), there is a bit of warmth here (points at his chest); I can feel the anger's 'blessing.' As soon as seeing the ugliness of the anger, (at that) same time — the anger is still there — (when looking at it while being) separated (from it), (its) intensity automatically goes down."

Exploring Further Similarities

Dr. Beck comes back: "We have a word for the separation from anger, interestingly we use 'distance': we try to put it at a distance from self; that is another point of similarity (Dr. Gyatso nods). The other point of similarity is attachment, you talk about attachment — we are talking about too much attachment — (and) we see that not only people (are) getting too attached and too dependent on people and then loosing (their) own freedom, but we also (can) become too attached, dependent, addicted to drugs, success, or material things, and those don't bring us happiness, they make a momentary pleasure; but then (they) still want more and we find that people put their attention on these kind of worldly things: fame, fortune, money, and so on. Once they keep thinking about it, they are never satisfied because as soon as they get it, they still want more and more. Some of the unhappiest people that I have known have had the most money, the most success, and sometimes the most fame, but they are not happy; momentary pleasure yes, but long range contentment, happiness, not at all."

Dr. Gyatso responds: "That's true. The Buddhist literature says on discontentment that it is one kind of suffering. The person who is discontented always feels that something is wrong, never gets satisfaction, always wants more and more, want, want, and want (addressing his interpreter in Tibetan, who then says: 'Those who are discontented are the real poor people; they are suffering from poverty.') They never get satisfaction. The opposite is contentment; if you have contentment then in reality or on the mental level you are really rich. 'I have everything,' (with) that kind of contentment you (will) have the real and complete satisfaction. (In addition) discontentment leads to the unnecessary or impossible effort (due to) too much expectation; eventually in most cases too much effort and attempts (result) in failure. (Also one will meet) more obstacles and (there will be) more anger and more worry. Discontentment will also bring (along) jealousy. Someone (who is) contented seeing someone else having all facilities, would (think/feel) 'very good.' (However), if discontented, you want more and more (and if) your neighbor gets something good, you feel jealous.7 Discontentment brings more negative emotions and as a result eventually you (will) loose your peace of mind and sometimes even suicide (is possible), isn't it?"

Dr. Beck: "You mention pain and suffering and we make a distinction between pain and suffering. In this way that if a person has pain, say in the joints, in the arms, legs that they get from arthritis, they can suffer all the time because they think about it; their attention goes to their arms and legs and they think: 'Why me? Why has fate chosen me? This is terrible! I can never have an enjoyable life! I have no control over my life! I am just doomed!' There have been scientific studies showing that people who have some kind of medical disability (and) have thoughts like that suffer much more than people who have positive thoughts. Some people who have positive thoughts think: 'Oh well, this gives me a greater perspective, I now can see things from a different point of view; things that seem so important to me before are not so important. The pain that I have maybe brings me closer to my family and the pain will then lead me maybe to do things that I never did before.' Those people have minimal suffering. Now you used the word separation before; there have been some studies done in London, England, where they show that people who are able to separate themselves, who do not see the pain as part of them, suffer much less than those who actually see the pain is me. So some persons will say 'My back aches' and they feel great suffering, others would just say 'It aches,' it meaning something separate from themselves, and they don't suffer as much. It is interesting how just the separation, the distancing as we say, can actually reduce suffering."8 Dr. Gyatso: "I see. This is new (to me). I will try, sometimes (I have) some itching; usually I get some trouble here (scratches his right arm and points at the back of his head and laughs), always some trouble, now (for) more than fifty years, always itching like that. I will try something else. I don't know, hahahaha."

Relativity and Common Sense

Dr. Gyatso continues: "Now, (if) some negative thing happens, (like) physical pain or a tragic experience — a loss of a family (member) or a dear friend or (getting) a lot of baseless criticism — it is very helpful to look at the negative thing, which causes (the) anger or sadness and to look at (it) from a (relatively) wider perspective. That (can) really make a big difference. If some unfortunate thing happens and if you look closely or narrowly then that unfortunate thing becomes huge and immense. The more of that kind of impression, the more unhappiness; but if you look at it from a wider perspective, then it is (only) one unfortunate thing (amidst) a vast world of many events. There is a Buddhist teacher who mentioned that if you come across criticism, then think that there are also people who are praising you. So, if you (only) look at the criticism, there is more anger and unpleasantness, but if (you would think) at the same time: 'Oh, OK it does not matter, there are some other people who praise me.' Then the mental level would be more balanced; someone says bad things to me, but it does not matter, there are others who praise me. (It also occurs that) someone who is praised becomes too much attached and thinks 'I am bright,' (this person is advisably heedful that) there are people who are criticizing (too). So, (we need) to look broadly. People would ask me with reason why the world is declining. Usually I respond, I truly feel obviously there are sad things — certain events like Iran or terrorism, and this sort of things — but if you look overall during the 50s and 60s there were two blocks with nuclear weapons were ready to shoot each other, then the whole group (of countries) was in a state of danger. Now today, the desire for peace, the spirit against violence, is big; if we look from a broader perspective, then today's world is much better than the mid of the previous century. It is important to look more holistically, that is very important and useful. And, as I mentioned before, things are relative; so if you look with a positive view than you can see this positive, negative, positive, negative (constantly alternating). If you (only) focus on the negative then (the) mind will become more worried, and there is more unhappiness."

Dr. Beck: "Your holiness, the question is how we focus our attention. People who get depressed said that they see the glass of water half empty, somebody else sees the glass — it could be milk or wine — as half full. So, it is a question of where you focus your attention to largely; if you focus it on the negative that is all you are going to see, if you focus it on the positive you see much more positive. Now, we also believe that much of this type of negative thinking or negative thought actually comes from a self-centeredness — egoism or egocentricity — and so the more they focus on the self, it could be their pain or the attachment or other people's criticism, the more they focus on that actually the worse they feel. They have to get away from focusing on me, me, me, my pain, my desires, my attachments, and (not) to see themselves as a part of the whole human structure. Where I think it comes to bigger problems, that I want to mention to you, has to do with what we call group egoism, when we then extend our own ego to the whole group and we start to think the group is right, just as I would think 'I am right,' now I think 'My whole group is right,' as soon as I think (that) it means that the other group is wrong and we are better than them and they are worse than us; and if there is any conflict at all, then we see ourselves even more so as all good and all right and they are all bad, and pretty soon we start to dehumanize them, they are not real anymore, they have just become like robots and then they become demons. Once there are demons we have to deal with them, so it seems to me that a major problem in the world is stemming from the self-centeredness that each individual has, but then extends that self-centeredness or egoism to his entire ethnic group or political group or racial group. I was wondering what you thought of that formulation?"

On the Self and Others

Dr. Gyatso: "I think this is quite complicated. My understanding of English words is not profound and may not be very correct and when I (am) explaining to others without a proper translation, then within my own limited vocabulary, I (would) use certain words. Now, the concept of (I/self): the self is there, although there (had been) a lot of discussions (on) what is (the) self (during) the last 2-3000 years.[9] (Dr. Beck: 'And we do not know yet.') So that is something different and here now the self is there. Also the self is the center of the whole universe, (which) is a fact. Who designates: I (and) self? Like East, West, North, or South, from where is (a) direction counted? It is from the viewpoint of the person. There (is) no absolute East or West or North and South, so it must be (existing) through comparison; therefore, the self is the center of the whole universe. The self is there and (is) important. (Furthermore), it is a basic right to gain something good for the self.

"But now, (on) the illusion or misconception (of the self in particular); when we were young, although the feeling of self, the importance of self is there, but the reality is very obvious: the maximum benefit to self depends on someone else's care (and others" affection is appreciated). Now we are grown up (and) feel independent (chuckles) and think 'My existence does not depend on others,' then there is a (subsequent) misconception 'I am superior, I can bully and exploit others.' There is no respect any longer for the other; thus, the misconception leads to (helped by the interpreter) a radical state of the self. I think the self goes extreme. Now, without loosing (or) forgetting self, the human self according to reality is part of humanity (Dr. Beck murmurs that he agrees) and furthermore (the) human being is a social animal, therefore no matter (whether) one single human being is very powerful, very smart, and intelligent, without other human companion, it is very difficult to survive (Dr. Beck agrees: 'Lonely'), isn't it?" Dr. Gyatso: "Without any other human beings, (if one is just by) oneself, even in a big city (where there are) a lot of human beings, one can be feeling loneliness, that is also suffering isn't it?" Dr. Beck: "Yes."

Dr. Gyatso continues: "(Thus), without any human brothers and sisters, just a single person remaining there, I think (s/he) will die very soon. That is very clear. So, therefore since we (as) human (selves) (are) part of humanity and if (humans) are social animals, the interest or benefit (of) oneself depends entirely on others. My success or my future depends on them. So, in order to have a better future and a successful life, I have to take care of the other side. Without loosing or forgetting the importance of self, (we need to remember that) the importance of self's future depends on other selves, therefore the other self is equally important as oneself. So the egoism (or rather) the feeling of self itself is not necessarily wrong, but (if) the feeling of self goes extreme, then it will bring a lot of disaster. Similarly, (if) the self is in the center of the universe, then the world or your neighbor, my neighbor (I will be) friendly (with), (make) friendship (with), (there will be a) sense of caring, then (there is in) my town friendship (and) respect, (due to) regarding (it as a) part of myself; then (the same applies to) my nation, (my) humanity, my continent, my world, my planet. I think (it need) not necessarily go wrong, (does) it? OK, so (in) my positive way the whole universe is considered (as) a part of mine (that I take care of), but if you make a distinction in 'we' and 'they,' (then) they have (got) nothing to do with our own fortune or future, (which is wrong). That is why I always tell people (that) the very concept of war (throughout) human history (comes because) in ancient time each country (was) more or less independent, self-sufficient, not depending on neighbors. In (those) circumstances the concept of war comes (in that) the destruction of your neighbor, your enemy, is the victory of yourself; but now today that (is) no longer reality. All neighbors are part of (themselves altogether). So destruction of your neighbor is (a) destruction of yourself. The concept, one side's victory and the other side's defeat (has become) unrealistic. The entire world/humanity is ours, belongs to 'us,' is 'we.' So, that is usually my way of approach. (Dr. Beck: 'That's good.') Is this wrong or right, please tell me?" Dr. Beck replies: "I think you are on the right track." (They both laugh touchingly, which radiates affection and sympathy for each others' ideas to the applauding audience. The atmosphere is excellent.)

On Imagery and Visualizing

Dr. Beck continues: "I like to add one more thing. That is when we think of somebody as being opposite, against us, we actually get a mental image. People don't realize that. We ask them when we are doing therapy and it turns out that when they are angry at somebody else, they actually have an image of that person, sometimes seeing this person as an ape and sometimes with horns (Dr. Beck points at his head; both laugh.) We see that from one individual to another individual, but it is also between countries, nations, ethnic groups; they tend to have a kind of mental image of the other people as some way subhuman — that is not (per se) bad, all life is precious — but they see them in a really negative way and (in) much of the propaganda they would have pictures. Let's say the Germans would have pictures of the Russians and they would show the Russians during World War II as looking like wild beasts; then of course the people found it is OK to shoot at wild beasts, because they are not human beings anymore. But we also think in terms of positive imagery; we see people who let's say have a fear of other people. Sometimes, as an example of a student, a youngster who is going to go to school and he had a picture in his mind of all of the other students looking at him. They were very big and he was very small in this image and what we did, we had him picture himself as superman. He had an image of himself as superman, and as soon as he had a picture of himself as superman, he saw the other students as small and he was big and he was able to go to school. I just wanted to add that little bit, (that) these images are very important."

Dr. Gyatso: "That's right, that's right (thinking for a while). I think that all those negative emotions, for example two main negative emotions, attachment and hatred." (Dr. Gyatso says something in to his interpreter, who then speaks for Dr. Gyatso: "Your point is very valid in terms of how you imagine things; let's take the example of two strong negative emotions like hatred and attachment. In the case when we develop attachment we tend to see that object as something attractive, pleasing, and close to your heart. Now the key question is whether that attractiveness that you see in the object is there in the object itself or is it something that you imagined. If it is something there in the object, then everybody who looks at the object should be able to see that object as pleasing, as wonderful, as attractive, but this is normally not the case. It is only you who are seeing that object as something special and attractive. So, this clearly shows that this is what you have exaggerated, what you have imagined.") Dr. Gyatso picks up the thread: "That is not objective, but actually a mental projection; a mental projection (upon) a mental projection creates some kind of beautiful image in our mind, and so attachment develops. Similarly, anger comes (through) a negative image (that is) actually a mental projection."

Dr. Beck: "Actually, what we find is that if we get a negative image of somebody else, and it stays on and on, we start to attack the other person, but actually we are attacking the image. We are not attacking — in our own mind we think we are attacking a real person, if I can explain this, by attacking this image of the person we are actually entering a person who may be nothing like the image. So the more we have the negative image of the person, the more we are going to attack him, but it is always the image that we are having that is bothering us, not the real person. So, we talked about delusion before (in a private talk; Dr. Gyatso says: 'Yes.'), in a way a lot of hatred is based on a delusion; a delusion can be based on a real image like we see each other right now."

Dr. Gyatso: "Absolutely, very right. So, I think it is similar; (in) the Buddhist concept all these negative emotions (are) based on ignorance, on misconceptions. The appearance is not the reality. There is always a big gap between the appearance and the reality. Then, due to one's own mind the appearance is further more exaggerated, (thus) certain kind of image comes (up) and the anger, attachment, and these things happen, (which are) actually deeply rooted (in) misconception. So all these negative events on this planet now today, I think many of this misfortune or unfortunate events (are) ultimately due to the wrong image (of) the group or in individuals' minds according to their own imagination or on the bases of their image, and then carry some decision or action."

Analytical Meditation

Dr. Beck: "Your holiness, just apart for one moment, you mentioned about the broad perspective before and I think much of the unhappiness that individuals have is because they lose perspective and I thought I give you an example. Some time ago I was asked to consult by a professor of physics and he thought that he had made a very great discovery, which might give him the Nobel prize (Dr. Gyatso becomes visibly positively affected in his facial expression), he got passed over, he did not get the Nobel prize, and so he was depressed. And so I said, 'How important part of your life was this prize' and he said: 'A hundred percent.' So, I asked him, 'Do you have a family?' and he said, 'Oh yes' and I said, 'How important is your family to you?' so he said: 'Well, my wife twenty percent' (Dr. Beck chuckles). So, then that is eighty percent now for the prize and I said, 'Do you have children?' and he said, 'Yes, I have three children' and I said, 'How important are they to you?' and he said, 'Oh, I guess they are about forty percent.' (Both chuckle.) So we are beginning to get around (both laugh) and I said, 'Do you get to see your children very much?' and he said, 'No, I have so much time working on my physics project, that I really haven't spent much time with them' and I said, 'How do you feel about that?' and then he started to weep and I said, 'Why are you weeping?' He said, 'It reminded me when I was growing up that is just the way my father was to me and now I suddenly realize what I am missing out on. My father missed out on it, I am missing out, and of course my children are missing out.' So I said, 'How important are your children to you now?' and he said, 'Eighty percent.' (Dr. Gyatso laughs.) I said, 'Where does that leave your wife?' (Dr. Beck is amused; both laugh.) Anyhow, he left the office and he was not depressed anymore." Dr. Gyatso: "Wonderful." (Both laugh and the audience applauds.)

Dr. Gyatso (laughs): "Very wise, I think that method we call exactly analytical meditation." Dr. Beck: "Oh really!?" (The mood becomes joyful if not exuberant.) Dr. Gyatso: "Now in this case, a second person (might) utilize analytical meditation and make clear to that person, then all his emotions, which are based on misconception (would) then change; wonderful, very good." (The audience laughs elated.) Dr. Beck: "So how long have you known about the analytical..." Dr Gyatso (overrides this question): "So you should get the Nobel peace prize." Dr. Beck looks at the interpreter, who repeats what has been said, then laughs. Dr. Gyatso: "Because someone depressed due to (a) loss of opportunity of receiving the Nobel peace prize, (was given by) you a sort of a new life, wasn't it? (A hilarious Dr. Gyatso gives Dr. Beck a pet on his arm.) Great work!"

Dr. Beck: "And so we can do the same thing with pain too. We see how important the pain is and then we get to the other things in their lives, which they had given up on and they realize they can still get much satisfaction and pleasure, but they forgot about that, because they are so preoccupied, the attention is all on the

pain." Dr. Gyatso: "Absolutely, very right." Dr. Beck: "So that's all analytical meditation; how long have they been doing analytical meditation; how long since they
have discovered analytical meditation, 2500 years ago?" Dr. Gyatso: "Oh, no, no,
no. I think, even before Buddhism, this analytical meditation (was) already there;
it is nothing special, it is utilizing human intelligence properly." Dr. Beck: "We
discovered it thirty years ago." (Both laugh heartily.)

Dr. Gyatso (scratching on his forehead): "I think (on) human intelligence (that)
actually the purpose of education (is) narrowing the gap between reality and appearances. Through education, proper education, this gap between appearances
and reality (can) be reduced. So, whether good or bad, it is very important to deal
with realistically, then (it will be) much easier to overcome the problems and (the)
things that you want can be achieved, but we often base our actions on appearances, not reality.[10] Particularly, now today I feel the world (has) much changed, I
think firstly due to the population, economy, environmental issues, and many new
developments; due to these developments now the reality (has) much changed,
(there is) a new reality, but our human thinking and (conceptualizing) still (follow)
the old patterns. I think some of our activities may not go well with the new reality,
that's why sometimes unnecessary problems happen. Therefore, analytical meditation means analyze reality (to) then accordingly act."

After a short silence Dr. Gyatso continues: "Another thing, I believe (that)
like external matters our internal mind world — particularly the emotional world
(that is) by nature contradictory — (will) always (harbor) contradictory things.
Without contradictory forces we cannot change, but because of the contradictory
forces if (there is) something bad for us, then try to find the opposite force and try
to increase that then this will reduce. The thing (that) we do not want, will not just
go away, but we have to find the opposite force. Similarly, in our emotions (like)
anger, even though we realize anger is bad (and despite) some impact (of this),
still anger will not go easily. We have to find out the opposite force, the
counterforce, of anger, that is loving kindness. The more the loving force increases, the (more) anger will reduce. Similarly, ignorance and awareness are two
opposites; the more awareness comes (in), (the more) ignorance (gets) reduced.
So, analytical meditation means trying to know reality, bringing (in) awareness
that reduces misconception."

Educating the Public at Large

Dr. Beck: "You use the word contradictory force; we use the word contradiction
quite a bit. Because (if) somebody will come in and say, 'I went to a social event,
a conference, I guess nobody likes me because nobody talked to me.' So, we say:
'OK, what is the evidence?' and he, 'Well, I was in a big room and nobody came
over to say hello.' So then I say: 'Is there any contradictory evidence, anything else
that happened?' 'Oh yeah, I guess on the way in somebody did talk to me, but I

forgot about that' and then I said, 'And how about earlier?' 'I guess when I was at the bar having a drink somebody talked to me.' So as soon as they bring in contradictory evidence, that's very important, then the conclusion goes away (and) they come back to reality." Dr. Gyatso (exclaims): "Yes, that's right, that's right!" Dr. Beck: "That's why contradictory forces are so really important, otherwise people will come to a conclusion and then they"ll look for evidence that supports the conclusion. But you have to teach them to contradict their conclusion, to find contradictory evidence. That is education too; much of therapy is just education." (Dr. Gyatso: "Yes, that's right.") The big question is how to educate the mass of the world, (how) to do that (chuckles)." (The audience chuckles too.)

Dr. Gyatso: "I think in modern education — my view since several years - it seems in modern education (there is) sufficient attention paid to brain development (and) knowledge, but not equal attention has been paid (to educate) warm-heartedness. I think (when) almost a thousand years ago on the European continent the separate education institutions started (that) at that time as far as moral ethics is concerned the church (has taken) the full responsibility and also (the) family. At that time the separate newly developed education institutions (were) only responsible for the education of brain development. Now, time (has) passed and the influence of the church (has) declined and the family values are also in difficulties, still the newly developed education institutions only take care of brain development (Dr. Beck nods agreeing) and eventually nobody pays attention to/ takes care of the moral-ethic (part). So, modern education seems not to be complete. Now, again, there are two views; one opinion is that moral ethics must be based on religious faith and this moral ethics has now narrowed. Another view (is) that moral ethics can be taught and sustained through our awareness, through our analytical meditation (chuckles) (and) even (be) helped by scientific findings, as in your sort of experiment without involving religious faith. That is what I usually call 'secular ethics.' Secular here means — according to Mahatma Ghandi — not a rejection of religion, but (a) respect for all religions and (thereby there is) also no discrimination whether one is a believer or a non-believer. That is the spirit of secular, so (then) irrespective whether (one is) a believer or a non-believer (one can) make clear the importance of moral ethics (to everybody). (Otherwise, if moral ethics involves religious faith, it will come into conflict with the education system — which has generally a more secular basis — with their according principles of secular education. So, I feel, I don't know whether I am correct or not, but I feel we need (a) secular way to approach moral ethics; that I think can (be) promoted (by) scientific findings (and can be combined with) (one's) own experience, helped by these findings. Then, I think we should have more (some of) a program for education from the kindergarten (onward) and (teach) the best response to conflict, (which) is dialogue, not violence, not showing force; because the other is also part of me, part of we, we have to solve (conflict) through the human way, not (through) the violent way. The promotion of peace (goes along with) the promotion of the spirit of dialogue, (these two) must go together. So, this is one way in the educational field.

"Then, (we have) the media people. I think, usually the media (looks at his watch), (now this is going to be) a bit too long." Dr. Beck says: "Two minutes (and laughs)." Dr. Gyatso switches: "My fundamental belief is — and I actually want to see your view — my fundamental belief is (that) human nature is gentleness, because the way we come, from (the) mother's womb and than entirely depend on mother's milk, which means that our life begins within the human affection (and) compassion. (Dr. Beck murmurs and demurs.) So, without that we cannot survive and also according to medical science after birth the next few weeks simply the mother's physical touch is the crucial factor for (a) proper development of the brain.[11] This physical element (points at his arm) needs someone's affection. Our life starts like that (and) till our death the human compassion or affection (is in our) whole life something very important, a key factor (whispered by the interpreter). Anger and aggressiveness are also a part of our life, but (they) occasionally come, (they are) not a dominant force. The dominant force is human affection; that is my view. What is your view?" (The audience and Dr. Beck chuckle.) Dr. Beck: "My view is that people are basically good, to start with; the core is good, but, and it is a big but, it gets poured on there by what you call negative thinking, we call it errors in thinking. First, we start to misinterpret other people's behavior, so that puts a negative layer around the positive. Then we get misconceptions, we hear that this other ethnic group is bad (because) two thousand years ago they invaded our country, so they are bad, that makes another layer. And then we start seeking for things to give us immediate pleasure rather than contentment and so we get dissatisfied, that's another layer. Then we get angry at other people because they have more than we have. So, in the end this core is covered up. What we can do in therapy is that we get through (the layers and to) the core. So, I think that we can be successful in doing treatment and I would hope that there will be some way of doing this on a very large scale. Perhaps the project that you propose will get taken up some day and actually public schools are trying to introduce subjects like you just described to help the students out. Education is the final answer."

Dr. Gyatso: "Very good; so I am very glad (that) in principle an elder scientist blesses my view. Thank you very much (shakes Dr. Beck's hand)." Dr. Beck murmurs: "Would you like to have a question for you?" Dr. Gyatso: "Oh yes (but picks up a thread he left unfinished before). So the conclusion, the media has a great (and) important role for promoting these insights. Usually, the negative things, murder or scandal, (etc.) become news; again now, these things become news, why? In the human mind, murder, killing, bullying, abuse, these are something shocking, so (these) become news. On the other hand, news (about) a mother taking care of her own child (giving her milk), these things (are) not news, (because) that is something normal, isn't it!? (Dr. Beck agrees.) The kindness or action of kindness (and) compassion we take for granted, (that) is (no) news. Something bad, killing, bullying, or raping does become news. This also shows our basic nature, gentleness and positive things we take for granted. Anyway, the media people usually (have) more enthusiasm or report on the more negative things, so that the public sometimes (gets) the feeling (that) human nature is bad, the world is bad. I think (it is) important to make (a) clear presentation in a more balanced way; there are bad things, but there is always (a) basis (for) hope because such and such wonderful things (are) also there. There are negative things, but equally (a positive) counterforce (is) also very much in living; so the only thing is we must broaden these positive things so that the negative things can (be) reduced. Otherwise, the feeding of the public mind (will be all) with negative things and (some people) will lose hope."

In Closing

Dr. Salkovskis concludes: "I am going to say a few words. It was an extraordinary meeting and the good news is that we had a meeting of minds. What kind of meeting was it? Well, at one level it was the meeting of two great thinkers; one thinker from the West and one thinker from the East. At another level it was the meeting of a monk and a doctor, and monks and doctors have different functions, but their minds can meet. At another level, I think, what we have was the meeting of two human beings who have in common that they care more for other people than that they even care for themselves. I think these are fantastic things. And what came from this meeting? Well, Mahatma Ghandi, we mentioned, once answered a question; the question was what did he think of western civilization and he said he thought it would be a good idea (the audience and Dr. Beck laugh and applaud). The issue that, I think, you referred to was the issue of values of the fact that western civilization sometimes, as you both have said, neglects values. At the same time, it is not possible, as you said yesterday, your holiness, to be concerned about moral ethics and values if you are starving, if you are hungry, and that is partly what western society offers. So, we need the development and what we are seeing I think today in terms of the people here is the development of some questions about motivation, about the seeking for compassion, the motivation to reduce suffering, and that I think is one of the things that we are beginning to hear. It is one of the things that modern psychotherapy and analytical meditation have in common and is moving towards. I think everyone here must welcome that. Everyone here I think also today will leave questioning their motivation, questioning how they can deal with suffering, because in the end there is an important I: what can I do? And that I believe you have both given us something. Tim, you are a scientist and you, you are a monk and science sometimes can be empty and sometimes spirituality gives you no food and I hope what we are seeing is the emergence of not an empty science, but of a Buddhist science and a cognitive science, which will give us a lot of hope for the future. And finally, just to show what a difference one person can make, I would just like to point out to you that Astrid Palm made today happen and as a result of Astrid's motivation, which is about reducing suffering, about caring for other people, compassion, we have fourteen hundred people here that come to hear two human beings meeting together in their minds. I like to thank you all. Thank you!" (Applause, Dr. Beck stands, Dr. Gyatso smiles abundantly and greets with his Buddhist gesture; the audience gives a standing ovation, all are standing on stage.)

Dr. Gyatso: "Some music?" Dr. Astrid Palm Beskow: "We would like, all of us, to wish you a wonderful coming birthday with a song." (The jazzy band plays/ sings "happy birthday"; Dr. Gyatso grabs to hold Dr. Beck's hand and with the other hand he holds Dr. Salkovskis" hand; he is offered flowers.) Dr. Gyatso: "Thank you, thank you very much! So, thank you very much for your beautiful expression to me; I really enjoy this meeting. Of course this morning we also spend some time, with him (still holding Dr. Beck's hand and flowers), (and we had a) really meaningful discussion. And now here it was also a very, very great inspiration (with) that large number of people here showing your warm feeling towards us and with these flowers towards me for an occasional birthday. As a Buddhist monk (looks at Dr. Beck), I always feel (every) early morning (is) something like (a) birthday, a new birthday, isn't it (addressing the audience)? (In the) morning everything (is) very fresh, (there is) alertness (in) my mind; (at) that time I (am) usually shaping my mind; the rest of the day I should utilize (in) a meaningful way. So, I want to tell you the best birthday gift. Please try to strengthen your warm-heartedness and be a compassionate person, so that not only you (as an) individual self becomes a happier person, but also your family, especially your children; (thus) we will get maximum benefit. And through that way, I think, we can change the atmosphere of our homes; (and from) within the home, within the community, within the society, within the national level, (and on a) global level. I always believe (that) every individual has some kind of ability to contribute for a better world. All have, I think, (the) same opportunity, so please give me that in your mind. And I also want to extend my share to each one; each one has a birthday, so I would like to say, happy birthday to all of you. Thank you!" (Dr Gyatso laughs gratefully while holding flowers in one hand and with the other hand also still touchingly holding Dr. Beck's hand that he joyfully brings to his cheek.) Dr. Beck says: "Thank you so much, thank you!" (the audience laughs and applauds.)

Dr. A.T. Beck's Reflections on the Dialogue

Judy Beck and I met with the Dalai Lama initially in his private drawing room in the hotel for an informal discussion a couple of hours prior to the actual public dialogue. Also attending were Paul Salkovskis, Astrid Beskow, and a number of his own representatives, including his long-time interpreter. Initially, I presented

HH with a copy of *Life* magazine from 1959, which had a cover picture of him receiving bouquets from his American supporters after his escape from Tibet to the US. He seemed pleased to see this much younger picture of himself. I also presented him with a hard copy of *Prisoners of Hate*. He seemed taken by the title, which epitomized his own view that hatred imprisons the people who experience it. He then remarked that there must be six billion prisoners in the world! On a personal level, I found him charismatic, warm, engaging, and very attentive to what I had to say. At the same time, he seemed to maintain an objective detachment not only with me but also with the members of the entourage. He also impressed me with his wit and wisdom and his ability to capture the nuances of very complex issues.

The dialogue was held at the Göteborg Convention Center at the International Congress of Cognitive Psychotherapy. In keeping with his expressed wish, I started the dialogue. I began to recite the dozen or so main points of similarity between Tibetan Buddhism and CT (listed below). After I recited four or five similarities, he interrupted with the statement that they were as many items as he could absorb at one time. My main challenge in the dialogue was to inform him about the cognitive approach to human problems without in any way taking away from the broad philosophy and psychology of Buddhism. My strategy was to find appropriate points in his discourse where I could introduce cognitive concepts that were relevant in some way to his train of thought. I tried to represent the cognitive approach as a valid system or discipline in its own right that overlapped but also was complementary to Buddhism. I also had to be conscious of my choice of words. Although His Holiness is quite fluent in speaking English, he is not familiar with more technical words, especially those for which there are no Tibetan equivalents. For example, he used the term "negative thoughts," which I repeated in preference to the more technical (and precise) cognitive terms, such as self-defeating thoughts or dysfunctional cognitions.

Among the points that I brought up, which he then expanded on from his own vantage point, were that both systems use the mind to understand and cure the mind. Acceptance and compassion were key similarities. Also, in both systems, we try to help people with their over-attachment to material things and symbols (of success, etc., something we call "addiction"). I gave a case example of a depressed scientist who was so attached to success (in this case, specifically winning a Nobel Prize) that he excluded everything else in his life, including his family. I had used a typical cognitive strategy to give the patient perspective. In the course of a single session, he changed his beliefs and got over his depression (at least temporarily). The Dalai Lama's response to this anecdote was, "You should get the Nobel Prize for Peace." Another point that I brought up was our distinction between pain and suffering. I suggested that much of people's suffering is based on the fact that they identify themselves with the pain. People who are able to separate ("distance") themselves from the pain and view it more objectively had significantly less distress (as pointed out by Tom Sensky's group in London). HH seemed taken with this concept and then said in an amusing way that maybe he could use this notion to help himself with his chronic itch. (This half-serious comment, of course, evoked a large amount of laughter from the audience.) He later referred to CT as similar to "analytical meditation."

I asked HH how he thought that his message could really take root in the world. He then expanded on his ideas that education had to be the answer. He also expressed his own philosophy, which he described as secular ethics. Although people of different faiths could embrace the values that he expressed, such as total acceptance of all living things, he did not feel that religion was a necessary instrument for this. He appeared to echo what is also the essence of the cognitive approach, namely self-responsibility rather than depending on some external force to inspire ethical standards. Since I believe that CT also regards unethical and morally destructive behavior as a cognitive problem and thus would advocate a "cognitive morality," I later was able to get this point across but in different words. When he asked me for my view of human nature, I responded that I agreed that people were intrinsically good but that the core of goodness was so overlaid with layer after layer of "negative thoughts" that one had to remove the layers for the goodness to emerge. He expressed the belief that positive thinking (focusing on positive and good things) was the way to neutralize the negative in human nature. My position was that the best way to reach this goal was to pinpoint the thinking errors and correct them. After we concluded the dialogue, Paul Salkovskis gave an outstanding summation of the topics that we had covered.

Since Astrid Beskow (the prodigious organizer of the event) discovered that by coincidence this was his birthday, there was a short birthday celebration during which he was then given a large bouquet. He then gave Astrid, Paul, and my self a Buddhist prayer shawl. I later learned from an intermediary that he enjoyed the dialog and that he would think about several points that I raised. All in all, it was a thrilling experience for me and, from what I heard from several of the attendees, also for the audience.

Similarities between CT and Buddhism

From my readings and discussions with HH and other Buddhists, I am struck with the notion that Buddhism is the philosophy and psychology closest to CT and vice versa. Below is a list of similarities that I suggested to the Dalai Lama in our private meeting. Of course, there are many strategies we use such as testing beliefs in experiments and formulating the case that are not part of the Buddhist approach.

I. Goals: Serenity, peace of mind, relief of suffering
II. Values:
    (1) Importance of acceptance, compassion, knowledge, understanding
    (2) Altruism vs. egoism

(3) Universalism vs. groupism: "We are one with all humankind"

(4) Science vs. superstition

(5) Self-responsibility

III. Causes of distress:

(1) Egocentric biases leading to excessive or inappropriate anger, envy, cravings, etc (the "toxins") and false beliefs ("delusions")

(2) Underlying self-defeating beliefs that reinforce biases.

(3) Attaching negative meanings to events.

IV. Methods:

(1) Focus on the immediate (here-and-now)

(2) Targeting the biased thinking through (a) introspection, (b) reflectiveness, (c) perspective-taking, (d) identification of "toxic" beliefs, (e) distancing, (f) constructive experiences, (g) nurturing "positive beliefs"

(3) Use of imagery

(4) Separating distress from pain

(5) Mindfulness training

---

1. Responsibility for this report's content and its introduction lies with the TSCM (Drs. Marja Taams and Maurits Kwee). This narrative transforms the verbatim into written language that intends to concisely catch the meaning of the uttered phrases. Parentheses indicate whenever the extended spoken words have been shortened and/or substituted with different wording to improve grammar and syntax, to delete irrelevant asides in favor of a compact message, or to make full sentences. This dialogue is accompanied by several explanatory footnotes by the narrators" commentary and background information. The full conversational session is also available on DVD (to order, email: info@cognitivterapi-gbg.se).

2. To avoid role confusion, we prefer to use the name Dr. Tenzin Gyatso (being 17 times doctor *honoris causa* of many universities in the world the title is well deserved) throughout this transcript. During the dialogue Dr. Gyatso performed in his capacity as a scholar and Buddhist specialist of the mind (and its biological, psychological, and social correlates).

3. Dr. Gyatso was born in Takster to a peasant family on July 6th, 1935; he was named Lhamo Dhondrub and was recognized as the 14th Dalai Lama at the age of two.

4. Dr. Gyatso applies the qualification terms "valid" and "invalid," where cognitive therapist would use "functional" and "dysfunctional"; rational emotive behavior therapist would use "rational" and "irrational."

5. Dr. Gyatso refers to the Buddha's exposition to the clan of the Kalamas, which is based on Theravada sources (Kalama Sutta; Anguttara Nikaya III, 65) also known as the Buddha's *Charter of Free Inquiry*, a TSCM extended summary of which reads: "Don't believe on rumors or hearsay, because it's reported to be good, ancient, or practiced by tradition... because it is written in the scriptures or because of logic, inference, or metaphysics... because the speaker appears believable or you are shown the testimony of an old sage... don't believe in what is fancied, because it's extraordinary, it must have been inspired by a god or other fancy being... because of presumption or custom of many years inclines you to take it as true... just because of someone's reputation and authority or because s/he is a teacher." The essence of this discourse is to accept only what you can perceive as valid, to rely on your own efforts, and to be a light unto yourself.

6. Dr. Gyatso is talking here about what we have coined "the Buddha's psychopathology": ignorance (on the working of the mind and emotions, leading to an illusory/delusional view of the world and self), greed, and hatred; the latter two are based on the root proclivities of attraction and rejection, usually studied in relational dynamics and in economic psychology. It is partly connected to the fight-flight, approach-avoidance, and frustration-aggression topics studied in experimental psychology.

7. Dr. Gyatso refers here to one of the Brahmaviharas (the basic Buddhist social values to contemplate on) that fill a possible horror vacuum of "emptiness." These "divine" abidings are: equanimity, kindness, compassion, and joy, which are to be aggrandized immeasurably. The immeasurable of shared joy based on empathy-sympathy is the Buddhist antidote against jealousy.

8. This view of thoughts and feelings as weather conditions, like "it aches" instead of "my back aches" was already put forward in the Burmese Theravada tradition of mindfulness and curiously enough also by William James (1842-1910), father of American psychology and Radical Empiricism. The latter proposed "Experience-only" that is to witness pure experience (direct, preconceptual, and unreified) by simply monitoring, like for instance "it thinks" as we say "it rains" or "thinking goes on" (Shaw, 1987), which is not different from Dr. Beck's distancing. Although he was knowledgeable about the latest in Buddhist scholarship and had been exposed to the Pali Text Society's translations through his neighbor, friend, and colleague at Harvard the buddhologist C.R. Lanman, and even borrowed metaphors like "the stream of consciousness" (Ferarri, 2002), it is unknown how much James was inspired by Buddhist thought.

9. Here it seems that Dr. Gyatso would like to avoid the hairsplitting discussions down the ages on the Buddha's "not-self" (6th c BCE), Nagarjuna's "non-self" (2nd c), or Asanga's "Buddhanature" (4th c) (see Chapter 2) and be actual/practical instead.

10. It seems that Dr. Gyatso is referring here to a quintessential Buddhist theme already raised by the Buddha and worked out by Nagarjuna; both contend that in practice one might discern a provisional reality, which is the conventional reality of the householder

that talks as if a self is there versus the ultimate reality of biopsychological awakening (impermanence and emptiness of non-self that no words can describe) and of social/ interpersonal awakening (human are "interbeings" or relational selves indicating that we are not independent from each other). We are interconnected, conditioned, and predicated upon each other in a matrix or web-like structure poetically evoked in the pinnacle of Mahayana, the Avatamsaka (Flower Garland) Sutra (a Sanskrit scripture on universal cooperation and mutual interpenetration, ascribed to Nagarjuna; Cleary, 1989). We are interwoven in other-dependence, in numerous strands of existence (the ultimate reality of things as they are) to be experienced directly in the preconceptual phase of awareness, which hence is impossible to formulate.

11. Dr. Gyatso, who also on other occasions points at this research, probably refers to studies by Harvard's Mary Carlson (neuroscientist/psychologist), a student of Harry Harlow (1906-1981), who conducted classic experiments in the 50s and 60s that brought a new understanding of human behavior: contact comfort is an essential condition for a normal development.

Part I

Practices For
Well-being

Introduction

Dharma is a word that usually refers to a teaching system. There is no English equivalent for Dharma because it carries several meanings; we take it here to be the Buddha's way to teach meditation in action, based on the Buddhist understanding of life and its predicaments. Buddhadharma means the Buddha's Dharma (following the footsteps of the historical Buddha Gautama who lived probably 563-483 BCE), while the Buddhist Dharma adds the teachers' creative musings over the centuries. The term Dharma does not refer to lectures poured into students' heads, but to learning through experience, typically through a teaching method realized in practices. Thus, the Dharma indicates a method that emphasizes first doing and experiencing, studying whether it worked, and then thinking and theorizing; this boils down to what we would call a seminar, practicum, workshop, coaching, or clinical training. The Dharma is primarily on the practice of living a liberated life by practicing what one teaches and teaching what one practices. The metaphor of the Way/Tao (Japanese, Do) also aptly indicates the guiding principle in the Dharma to see and infer the Buddhist way.

The Buddhist guidance is succinctly formulated in the 4-Noble Facts on the profound experiences that existence implies: suffering/dis-ease, impermanence/imperfection, not-self/emptiness, and a way out: the 8-Fold Path. The latter includes right mindfulness, concentration, understanding, intention, effort, action, speech, and livelihood, all of which enhance karma (intentional behavior) for the benefit of all beings. For this mind/speech/body-change practice, psychology is the term that most completely fits the spirit of what we infer the Buddha might have meant. The first to explicate the Buddha's teaching as a psychology (in 1900) was Caroline Rhys Davids, who was also one of the first to use the term "mindfulness" to refer to Buddhist meditation. As an applied psychology the Dharma teaches how the mind can change itself through behaving-thinking-feeling differently.

What awakens/liberates is meditation, a practice wherein one first neutrally observes from now-to-now internal phenomena — specified as perceivables/imaginables/knowables (*dhammas*) — as to transparently see that all things' impermanence leaves the truth as contended by science and religion or even by the Dharma itself as only a provisional or constructed reality, without essential substance or inherent existence. Expressed in the Buddha's way, it is neither the absence, nor the presence of something. Nihilism and solipsism can be safely discounted. Having attained the profound insight of the emptiness/non-selfness of beings — by realizing the illusory quality of things — one is prepared to strive for *bodhicitta*, a condition in which all beings are awakened. The practices of kindness, compassion, and joy go in tandem with the metavision of ultimate relatedness, *interbeing* for many Buddhists, *relational being* in the constructionist case.

There are, of course, many variations in the means for attaining these ends. As we see it, a New Buddhist Psychology would be open to all forms of practice, subjecting all to both empirical exploration and theoretical deliberation.

It is in this spirit that we introduce in Part I of this book, the work of eight practitioners, each of whom broadens the horizons of practice in significant ways. In Chapter 2, Padmal de Silva compares a range of practices common to the Buddhist and cognitive therapy traditions. He expands on the ways in which Buddhist practices can be used, for example, in eliminating anger, increasing compassion, treating excessive grief, developing social skills, and reducing anger. In the following chapter, Peter Bankart intensifies the focus on working with anger, and demonstrates how a combination of meditation and yoga not only reduce anger, but kindle an appreciation for the wellbeing of others. In Chapter 4, Jean Kristeller and James Jones demonstrate the efficacy of mindfulness meditation as a means of controlling obesity. As they see it, this practice may also be used in a wide range of settings in which behavior control is desired. Dennis Tirch and Richard Amodio (Chapter 5) then turn to the possibilities of integrating meditation practices with cognitive-behavioral therapy. As they see it, in the case of post-traumatic stress disorder, different blends of practices may be useful in treating individuals with specific needs. Herman Kief (Chapter 6) then adapts practices taken from the Zen tradition to cognitive-behavioral therapy. By exploring the implications of paradoxical questioning, as exemplified in the koan, he finds an unburdening of clients' problems. In the following chapter, Paul Soons explores ways of combining Buddhist practices with those used in Rational Emotive Behavior Therapy. Of special importance are Buddhist practices that replace negative emotions with positive emotions, and that directly develop happiness through augmenting positive emotions. Adeline van Waning then takes up the problem of cognitive distortions, as understood and treated in both the Buddhist and Western traditions (Chapter 8). Favored are practices in which these approaches are used to complement each other. In the final contribution to Part I, Noriko Kubota describes practices employed in Dosa therapy. Here the focus is on slow, intentional and smooth bodily movements, that not only have a relaxing effect, but create an enhanced sense of well-being.

As a whole, these contributions represent a rich panoply of possibilities. They demonstrate that the Buddhist contribution to human change is multi-hued, and not reducible to a single, canonized method. Rather, these contributions suggest that the Buddhist tradition invites continuous innovation in practices for enhancing human well-being.

2

Buddhist Psychology: Theravada Theory And Practice

Padmal de Silva

Buddhist Psychology (BP) has many aspects. One focus is on the personal development leading to a liberated state. An equally important aspect is the consideration of dealing with day-to-day life, with the aim of promoting smooth and adaptive functioning. This aspect is linked to the ultimate goal of achieving a liberated state, but one is encouraged to work on adaptive functioning even if one is not committed to this ultimate goal. This chapter discusses BP as found in the Theravada Buddhist teaching. Some basic notions are considered first, including the Buddhist theory of motivation. It then explores the practical aspects of BP, which have a relevance to therapeutic work. In promoting adaptive, skilful functioning much of the Buddha's teachings focus on meditation. Its large array of strategies has several parallels with present-day Cognitive-Behavior Therapy. Numerous examples are found in the Buddhist canonical texts and the commentaries. These are of a clearly behavioral nature, while others are cognitive or cognitive-behavioral. Some of the similarities are highlighted and discussed with textual references, and also with comparisons to present day psychology. A selection of Buddhist techniques is made, which includes tactics for eliminating anger and developing kind feelings, ways of reducing attachments, using aversive strategies for controlling problematic behaviors, ways of dealing with excessive grief, developing social skills, and the reduction of fear/anxiety. The contribution BP can make to preventive work in mental health is attended to in the final part.

This chapter aims to provide a descriptive and analytical account of Buddhist Psychology (BP). It does not attempt a comprehensive review of the subject; the literature is too vast to permit a comprehensive review in a single chapter. What is presented here is essentially a selective account of the psychological notions found in *Dhamma* or *Dharma* (the Buddhist teaching that is mainly practical). Only some of the major concepts are discussed here. Some practical aspects of BP that have a relevance to therapeutic practice are also reviewed. This chapter is selective in another way. It is confined to Theravada and does not deal with later developments of Mahayana that includes Zen. (For an account of Theravada, see Gombrich, 1988; for a discussion of the different schools, Guruge, 1999; Harvey, 1990; Kalupahana, 1976).

The Theravada Literature

The literature of Theravada is in the Pali language, and consists of:
   (A) The original Buddhist canon that was put together soon after the Buddha's death and committed to writing in the first century BCE. It comprises three parts:

   (1) *Sutta Pitaka*, which contains the discourses of the Buddha on various occasions throughout his preaching life;
   (2) *Vinaya Pitaka*, which contains the rules of discipline for the monks and nuns; and
   (3) *Abhidhamma Pitaka*, which contains highly systematized philosophical and psychological analyses, which were finalized in their present form about 250 BCE. The individual books of the canon are listed in Table 1.

   (B) The early Pali commentaries on the canon that were in their present form by the end of the 5th include major texts such as *Sumangalavilasini, Papañcasudani*, and *Dhammapadatthakatha*, which are commentaries on specific parts of the canon.
   (C) Other Pali texts of the same period which are best described as expository and interpretive works. The early expository and interpretive texts include, among others, *Visuddhimagga, Milindapañha,* and *Nettippakarana*.

Table 1: Individual books of the Buddhist canon

Vinaya Pitaka	*Patimokkha*	*Abhidhamma Pitaka*	*Dhammasangani*
	Khandhaka		*Vibhanga*
	Parivara		*Dhatukatha*
			Puggalapaññatti
Sutta Pitaka	*Digha Nikāya*		*Kathavatthu*
	Majjhima Nikaya		*Yamaka*
	Samyutta Nikaya		*Patthana*
	Anguttara Nikaya		
	Khuddaka Nikaya		

Problems of Translation

The entire canon, and most of the commentaries and expository works, have been translated into English and published by the Pali Text Society, founded in London in 1881. However, the English versions are often beset with problems of translation and interpretation. Perhaps it is worth illustrating this problem with examples. A major example is the term *dukkha* (Sanskrit *duhkha*), translated by many as suffering. This has led to the Dharma being described as essentially pessimistic, as *dukkha* is stated as characterizing all existence. Some authors have offered alternative translations such as unsatisfactoriness, disharmony, and painfulness (Gunaratna, 1968; Matthews, 1983). None of these offers a precise rendering of the original term, and Rahula (1967), among others, leaves the term untranslated. Another example is the very challenging term *papañca* (Sanskrit *prapañca*; derived from *pra + pañc*, to spread out). In his book, *The Principles of Buddhist Psychology*, Kalupahana (1987) consistently translates this as obsession. This is inaccurate, although the official *Pali-English Dictionary* of the Pali Text Society (Rhys Davis & Stede, 1921-1925) does offer obsession as one rendering of this word. *Papañca* is a key term in BP, and has been variously translated as impediment, conceptual proliferation, manifoldness, diffusion, complex, and imagination, among others. It should be clear from these examples that the problem of translation can be a major obstacle to one's understanding of Theravada or indeed any other ancient system of thought. For this reason, the material in this chapter is drawn from the original Pali texts.

The Buddha's Teaching

The Buddha (the word, derived from the root *budh*, to know, to comprehend, literally means the awakened or enlightened one) lived in the foot-hills of the Himalayan range of mountains in Northern India from 563 to 483 BCE. (For excellent accounts of the Buddha's life, see Kalupahana & Kalupahana, 1982; Schumann, 1989). The main teachings of The Buddha are contained in the Four Noble Truths. (See Gowans, 2003; Guruge, 1999; Harvey, 1990; Rahula, 1967; Saddhatissa, 1971). These are: (1) that life is characterized by suffering and is unsatisfactory (*dukkha*); (2) that the cause (*samudaya*) of the suffering is craving or desire (*tanha*); (3) that this suffering can be ended (*nirodha*), via the cessation of craving or desire — this is the state of *Nibbana*; and (4) that there is a way (*magga*) to achieve this cessation, which is called the Noble Eightfold Path (*Samyutta Nikaya V*). The Noble Eightfold Path is also called the Middle Path, as it avoids the extremes of a sensuous and luxurious life on the one hand and a life of rigorous self-mortification on the other. The eight aspects of the Path are: right understanding; right thought; right speech; right action, right livelihood; right effort; right mindfulness; and right concentration. The person who undertakes a life based on this path, renouncing worldly attachments, hopes eventually to attain the *arahant* state, which may be described as a state of perfection; the word *arahant* literally means the worthy one. This state marks the attainment of *Nibbana*. Other major teachings of the Buddha include the negation of a permanent and unchanging soul (*anatta*), and the notion of the impermanence of transience of things (*anicca*) (*Majjhima Nikaya I*). The notion of a God is excluded. There is no creator or a supreme being who rules and purveys the universe. Thus there is no absolutism in either the form of an eternal God or an unchanging universe, or an unchanging soul.

For the laity, the vast majority of people who did not renounce worldly life to devote themselves to the immediate quest for *Nibbana*, the Buddha provided a sound and pragmatic social ethic. They were expected to lead a life characterized by restraint and moderation, respecting the rights of others and being dutiful to those around them. Such a restrained and dutiful life was considered not only to be a necessary prerequisite for one's ultimate religious aim; it was also valued as an end in itself. For example, the Buddha advised his lay students to abstain from alcoholic beverages because alcohol indulgence could lead to demonstrable ill-effects such as loss of wealth, proneness to socially embarrassing behavior, unnecessary quarrels, disrepute, ill-health and eventual mental derangement (Sigalovada Sutta, *Digha Nikaya III*). This empirical and pragmatic approach is a prominent feature of the Dhamma's ethical stance. Detailed discussions of its ethics are available in Kalupahana (1995), Keown (2000) and Saddhatissa (1970).

The Psychology of the Buddha: Some Basic Notions

The interest shown by modern scholars in BP is understandable in view of the fact that there is a great deal of psychological content in the Dhamma. Some parts of the canonical texts, as well as later writings, are examples of explicit psychological theorizing, while many of the others present psychological assumptions and much material of psychological relevance. For example, the *Abhidhamma Pitaka* contains a highly systematized psychological account of human behavior and mind, and the translation of one of the *Abhidhamma* books, the *Dhammasangani*, was given the title *A Buddhist Manual of Psychological Ethics* by its translator, Caroline Rhys Davids, when it was first published in 1900. The practice of the Dhamma, as a "religion" and as a way of life, involves much in terms of psychological change. The ultimate goal of the *arahant* state both reflects and requires major psychological changes. The path towards the achievement of this goal, the Noble Eightfold Path, involves steps which can only be described as psychological. As the goal is attainable essentially through one's own efforts, it is not surprising that it has much to say about one's thinking and behavior. As noted above, there is no God one can turn to for one's salvation. Nor did the Buddha claim to be able to ensure the attainment of the goal. On the contrary, the Buddha explicitly stated that he was only a teacher who could show the way and that the actual task of achieving the goal was up to each individual's efforts. As a much-quoted passage in the *Dhammapada* (part of the *Khuddaka Nikaya*) says: "The task has to be accomplished by you. The Enlightened One only teaches the way."

Motivation

Among the Dhamma's main psychological aspects is motivation. Perhaps the most logical starting point in a discussion of BP is the theory of motivation. What drives people in their behaviors? What motivates human action? The unawakened person's behavior, it is said, is governed and driven by *tanha* or craving, which is given as the cause of suffering/un-satisfactoriness in the Second Noble Truth. *Tanha* is classified into three basic forms: *kama tanha* (craving for sensory gratification); *bhava tanha* (craving for survival or continued existence); and *vibhava tanha* (craving for annihilation) (*Samyutta Nikaya V*). Like Freudian theory, this account of motivation may be seen as a primarily reductionist one: all actions have as their source a small number of drives. While craving is seen as the source of suffering, the term *tanha* is not exclusively used in a negative sense. There are several instances in the literature where it is acknowledged that one can also develop a *tanha* for the cessation of suffering. Thus *tanha* can take the form of or can be turned into, a desirable force. For example, the expository text *Nettippakarana* says: "Here, craving is of two kinds, wholesome and unwholesome. While the unwholesome kinds go with the unsatisfactory worldly existence, the wholesome kind leads to the abandonment of craving." In a further analysis of motivation, three factors that lead to unwholesome, or undesirable, behaviors are identified. These are: *raga* (passion or lust); *dosa* (hatred or malice); and *moha* (delusion or false belief) (e.g. *Anguttara Nikaya I, II*). All unwholesome action is seen as deriving from a set of fundamental roots. In fact, the texts explicitly refer to these as roots (*mula*). They are called *akusalamulas* — unwholesome or unprofitable roots. It is not made explicit whether these always operate at a conscious level.

On the other hand, certain clearly non-conscious factors also have a part to play in determining behavior. One such group of factors mentioned is *anusaya*, translated as latent tendency, latent bias, predisposition, and latent disposition. The Pali Text Society Dictionary adds that these meanings are always in bad sense (Rhys Davids & Stede, 1921-25, p. 44). The term itself (from *anu* + *si*, to lie down, lie dormant) indicates that these are non-conscious factors. These dispositional factors are part and parcel of one's personality, acquired through past experience, and they play their part in influencing one's behavior and contribute to the perpetuation of the cycle of suffering. Seven types of *anusaya* are often mentioned. The list given in *Samyutta Nikaya V* is as follows: tendency to want pleasure; tendency to anger or disgust; tendency to speculation; tendency to doubt; tendency to conceit; tendency to want continuous existence or growth; and tendency to ignorance. Another group of factors which are non-conscious and which influence one's behavior are the *asavas* (Sanskrit *asravas*, from the root *sru*, to flow; or ooze). This term has been translated as influxes, biases, and cankers. These are factors that affect the mind so that it cannot rise higher. It is said that they intoxicate and bemuddle the mind (Rhys Davids & Stede, 1921-25, p. 115). They color one's attitudes and thwart ones insight. In one's endeavour for self-development, one has to excise them, and this is done through wisdom. The influxes are described as arising from different factors: sensuality, aggression, cruelty, body, and individuality are given in one account (*Digha Nikaya III*). Other lists include, among others, gain, loss, fame, disrepute, and even intentions (*Anguttara Nikaya IV*).

Motives for good, or wholesome, actions are usually expressed in negative terms. The most consistent account is the one which gives *araga* (non-passion, or absence of passion), *adosa* (non-hatred or absence of hatred) and *amoha* (non-delusion, or absence of delusion) as the roots of good action — the opposites of the roots of unwholesome behaviors (*Anguttara Nikaya I*). Occasionally, they are described in clearly positive terms — as *caga* (renunciation), *metta* (loving kindness) and *pañña* (wisdom, understanding) (*Anguttara Nikaya III*). It is stated that one must strive to develop these in order to combat their opposites.

Perception and Cognition

Perception is based on 12 gateways or modalities (*ayatana*), 6 of these being of 5 sense organs plus the mind, or inner sense, and the other six being the objects of each of these (*Samyutta Nikaya II*). The status of mind (*mano*) is special. It has the ability to reflect on the objects of the other senses so in this way it is linked to the activity of all the senses (Kalupahana, 1987). Each combination of sense organ and its objects leads to a particular consciousness (*viññana*) — for instance, visual consciousness arises because of the eye and material shapes. When consciousness is added to each of the pairs of modalities, one gets 18 factors of cognition, referred to as *dhatus*, or elements. These are presented in Table 2. It is said that the meeting of the sense organ, object, and consciousness (e.g. eye, material shape, and visual consciousness) constitutes contact; because of this contact feeling arises, and what one feels, one perceives (*Majjhima Nikaya I*).

Table 2: The 18 factors of cognition

Sense Organ	Object	Consciousness
eye	material shapes	visual consciousness
ear	sounds	auditory consciousness
nose	smells	olfactory consciousness
tongue	tastes	gustatory consciousness
body	tangibles	tactile consciousness
mind	mental objects	mental consciousness

This is a relatively straightforward account of perception. However, the Buddhist exposition goes beyond this. The account continues: "What one perceives, one reasons about. What one reasons about, one turns into *papañca*. What one turned into *papañca*, because of that factor, assails him in regard to material shapes recognisable by the eye belonging to the past, the future and the present..." (*Majjhima Nikaya I*).

It will be recalled that the term *papañca* was cited in the third paragraph as an example of a term posing particular difficulties for the translator. In this passage, the verbal form *papañceti* is used. Thus, the final stage of the process of sense-cognition is *papañca*. An examination of the use of the term in various contexts related to cognition shows that it refers to the grosser conceptual aspect of the process, as it is consequent to *vitakka* (reasoning). Once an object is perceived, there is initial application of thought to it, followed by *papañca*, which in this context is best taken to mean a tendency to proliferation of ideas. As a result, the person is no longer the perceiver who is in control, but one who is assailed by concepts generated by this prolific tendency. The person is overwhelmed by concepts and by linguistic conventions. One's perception is, in this way, open to distortion and elaboration due to the spontaneous proliferation of thoughts. This proliferation is said to be linked to *tanha* (craving), *mana* (conceit) and *ditthi* (dogma or rigidly held views) (*Maha Niddesa I*). They are all bound up with the notions of "I" and "mine." This marks the intrusion of the ego into the field of sense perception. In BP, there is no self (*atta*; Sanskrit *atman*), but the delusion of self affects all one's behaviors (*Sutta Nipata*). One of the aims of personal development is to enable oneself to see reality as it is, without the distortions arising from the various factors that characterize the unawakened person's functioning. A major aspect of reaching the state of *arahant* is indeed the freeing of one's perceptions from these distorting influences. When one reaches this state, one's perceptions become free of such distortions and allow a direct appraisal of the objects.

Therapeutic Aspects of Buddhist Psychology

It was noted above that the attainment of the *arahant* state required personal development based on both restrained and disciplined conduct and meditative efforts. This explains why meditation is given a key place in Buddhist texts. Meditaion provides a means to personal development. In addition to numerous canonical discussions, large sections of Buddhaghosa's *Visuddhimagga* are devoted to a consideration of this subject in great detail. It is significant that the Pali word for meditation, *bhavana*, etymologically means development or cultivation. As there is a large body of literature on this subject, only a few brief comments will be made here. (Detailed discussions are available in Bronkhorst, 1993; Pradhan, 1986; Sole-Leris, 1986; Vajiranana, 1978; see also Kwee, 1990, Kwee & Holdstock, 1996). Two forms of meditation are prescribed: the first is called *samatha* (tranquility), and the other, *vipassana* (insight). While further forms of meditation have been developed in later forms of the Dhamma, *samatha* and *vipassana* represent the earliest Buddhist techniques, dating back 2500 years. It should be noted that meditation of the *samatha* type is also found in some other ancient Indian systems, while *vipassana* is uniquely a Buddhist development (Nanamoli, 1975; Rahula, 1967). The word *samatha* means tranquility or serenity. *Samatha* meditation is aimed at reaching states of consciousness characterized by progressively greater levels of serenity and stillness. It has two aspects: (a) the achievement of the highest possible degree of concentration; and (b) the progressive calming of all mental processes. This is done through increasingly concentrated focusing of attention; the mind withdraws progressively from all external and internal stimuli. In the end, states of pure and undistracted consciousness can be achieved. The *samatha* meditation procedure starts with efforts of concentrating the mind of specific objects and progresses systematically through a series of states of what are called *jhanas* or mental absorption (*Visuddhimagga*).

Vispassana, or insight meditation, also starts with concentration exercises using appropriate objects on which one focuses. In this procedure, however, once a certain level of concentration is achieved so that undistracted focusing can be maintained, one goes on to examine with steady, careful attention and in great detail all sensory and mental processes. Through this contemplation, one becomes a detached observer of one's own activity. The objects of this contemplation are classified as fourfold: body, sensations, mental states, and "mental objects" (e.g. various moral and intellectual subjects). The aim is to achieve total and immediate awareness or mindfulness of all phenomena. This leads — it is claimed — eventually to the full and clear perception of the impermanence of all things and beings (*Majjhima Nikaya I*; *Samyutta Nikaya V*). It is held that *samatha* meditation by itself cannot lead to enlightenment (awakening or perfection); *vipassana* meditation is needed to attain this goal. While the former leads to temporarily altered states of consciousness, it is the latter which leads to enduring changes in the person and paves the way to achieving the *arahant* state.

Benefits of Meditation

The meditative exercises of both types, when properly carried out and developed, are claimed to lead to greater ability to concentrate, greater freedom from distraction, greater tolerance of change and turmoil around oneself, and sharper awareness and greater alertness about one's own responses, both physical and mental. They would also lead, more generally, to greater calmness or tranquility. While the ultimate goal of the *arahant* state will require a long series of regular training periods of systematic meditation coupled with major restraint in one's conduct, the more mundane benefits of meditation are available to all serious and persisting practitioners. From a practical perspective, Buddhist meditation techniques may be seen as an instrument for achieving certain psychological benefits. Primarily, meditation would have a role as a stress-reduction strategy, comparable to the more modern techniques of relaxation. There is a substantial literature in present day clinical psychology and psychiatry which shows that meditation can produce beneficial effects in this way (e.g. Kwee, 1990; Shapiro, 1982; West, 1987). Studies of the psychological changes that accompany meditation have shown several changes to occur which, together, indicate a state of calmness or relaxation (Woolfolk, 1975). These include: reduction in oxygen consumption, lowered heart rate, decreased breathing rate and blood pressure, reduction in serum lactic acid levels, increased skin resistance, and changes in blood flow. These peripheral changes are generally compatible with decreased arousal in the sympathetic nervous system. There are also certain central changes, as shown by brain wave patterns. The amalgam of these physiological changes related to meditation has been called the Relaxation Response by Benson (1975).

Interestingly, the Buddha himself advocated meditation for what we would today call clinical problems. For example, he advocated that meditation be used to achieve trouble free sleep and as a way of controlling pain (*Vinaya Pitaka I*; *Samyutta Nikaya V*). It is perhaps worth dwelling briefly on the use of mindfulness (a form of *vipassana*) meditation for pain control. Kabat-Zinn and others (1985) reported that 90 chronic pain patients who were trained in mindfulness meditation in a 10-week, stress-reduction program, showed significant reduction in pain and related symptoms. A control group of patients not receiving the training did not show such improvement. The rationale for selecting this strategy for the treatment of pain is explained as follows: "In the case of pain perception, the cultivation of detached observations of the pain experience may be achieved by paying careful attention and distinguishing as separate events the actual primary sensations as they occur from moment-to-moment and any accompanying thoughts about pain" (p. 165). In another paper, Kabat-Zinn (1982) has given an even more detailed account of the rationale for using mindfulness meditation for pain control. He shows how mindfulness meditation can enable one to focus on sensations as they arise, rather than attempt to escape from them. It helps to recognize the bare physical sensation, unembellished by psychological elaboration. One learns to observe these psychological aspects as separate events. This uncoupling has the effect of changing one's overall experience of pain. To quote: "The nociceptive signals (sensory) may be undiminished, but the emotional and cognitive components of the pain experience, the hurt, the suffering, are reduced" (p. 15).

It is this detached observation of sensations that mindfulness meditation, as described in the Buddhist texts, helps one to develop. This makes such meditation a particularly well-suited strategy for pain control. In fact, the references in the texts to pain control by mindfulness meditation appear to make this very point. For example, it is stated that the venerable Ananda, the Buddha's personal assistant, once visited a householder named Sirivaddha who was ill. On hearing from the patient that he was in much pain, and that his pains were getting worse, Ananda advised him to engage in the meditation of mindfulness. Similarly, it is recorded that the Buddha himself visited two ailing monks, Mogallana and Kassapa, who were in pain, and advised each of them to engage in mindfulness meditation. Perhaps the most impressive and most explicit — in terms of the rationale for this use of meditation — is the account given of the venerable Anuruddha. He was sick, and was grievously afflicted. Many monks who visited him, finding him calm and relaxed, asked him how his "painful sensations evidently made no impact on his mind." He replied: "It is because I have my mind well-grounded in mindfulness. This is why the painful sensations that come upon me make no impression on my mind." The implication is that meditation can reduce or block out the mental aspect of the pain (e.g. while the physical sensations may remain intact, one's vulnerability to subjectively felt pain is reduced). The above accounts are all from the *Samyutta Nikaya*, which states this position quite explicitly in a different passage: "The untrained layman, when touched by painful bodily feelings, grieves and laments... and is distraught... But the well-trained disciple, when touched by painful bodily feelings, will not weep, nor grieve, nor lament... nor will he be distraught... The layman, when touched by painful bodily feelings, weeps... He experiences two kinds of feeling: a bodily one and a mental one. It is as if a man is hit by one arrow, and then by a second arrow; he feels the pain of two arrows. So it is with the untrained layman; when touched by a painful bodily feeling, he experiences two kinds of feeling, a bodily one and mental one. But the well-trained disciple, when touched by a painful bodily feeling, weeps not ... He feels only one kind of feeling: a bodily one, not a mental one. It is as if a man is hit by one arrow, but not by a second arrow; he feels the pain of one arrow only. So it is with the well-trained disciple; when touched by a painful bodily feeling, he feels but one feeling, bodily pain only" (*Samyutta Nikaya IV*).

The view of pain contained in this account is abundantly clear: physical pain sensations are usually accompanied by psychological correlates, which are like a second pain. The disciple who is trained (in mindfulness), however, sees the physical sensation as it is, and does not allow himself to be affected by the psychological elaboration of pain. Thus his experience is limited to the perception of the physical sensation only. It is this account of pain that provides the rationale for the instances cited above, where those in pain are advised to engage in mindfulness meditation.

Behavior Modification Strategies

The literature of Theravada also contains a wide range of behavior change strategies other than meditation, used and recommended by the Buddha and his disciples, which can be described as behavioral. This aspect had been neglected by modern researchers until very recently. It is only in the last 25 years that these behavioral strategies have been highlighted and discussed (e.g. de Silva, 1984; Mikulas, 1981). They are remarkably similar to several of the established techniques of modern behavior therapy. Thus, if BP is akin to modern humanistic, transpersonal and existential psychologies in view of its emphasis on the individual, his problems and anxieties, his predicament, and his development through personal effort, it also has a clear affinity to present-day behavioral psychology in view of these explicitly behavioral techniques. The ways in which the overall approach of behavior modification and that of the Dhamma may be seen as broadly similar have been discussed by Mikulas (1981). Some areas of similarity highlighted by Mikulas are: the rejection of the notion of an unchanging self or soul; focus on observable phenomena; emphasis on testability; stress on techniques for awareness of certain bodily responses; emphasizing the here and now; and dissemination of teachings and techniques. Given this broad similarity, and the general Buddhist empiricist/experientialist attitude, it is not surprising that specific behavior change techniques were used and recommended in Theravada. This empiricist/experiential approach is exemplified by the Kama Sutta (*Anguttara Nikaya I*), in which the Buddha advises a group of inquirers not to accept anything on hearsay, authority or pure argument, but to accept only what is empirically and experientially verifiable. It is also entirely consistent with the Dhamma's pragmatic social ethic, which recognizes the importance of behaviors conducive to one's own and others' wellbeing as a goal in its own right. Behavior changes, both in oneself and others, were to be affected through the use of specific techniques.

The range of behavioral strategies found in the Theravada literature is wide. When these are described using modern terminology and listed together, they look like the content page of a modern behavior therapy manual! The strategies include: fear reduction by graded exposure and reciprocal inhibition; using rewards for promoting desirable behavior; modeling for inducing behavioral change; the use of stimulus control to eliminate undesirable behavior; the use of aversion to eliminate undesirable behavior; training in social skills; self-monitoring; control of intrusive thoughts by distraction, switching/stopping, incompatible thoughts, and by prolonged exposure to the unwanted intrusions; intense, covert, focusing on the unpleasant aspects of a stimulus or the unpleasant consequences of a response, to reduce attachment to the former and eliminate the latter; graded approach to the development of positive feelings towards others; use of external cues in behavior control; use of response cost to aid elimination of undesirable behavior; and use of family members for carrying out behavior change programs. In addition, there are also cognitive and cognitive-behavioral techniques. Since details of these strategies have been discussed in previous publications (de Silva, 1984, 2001, 2002), which also give references to the original texts, a full discussion will not be undertaken here. It will be useful, however, to cite an example of the Buddhist approach and indicate its similarity to Cognitive-behavior Therapy (CBT).

For the control of unwanted, intrusive cognitions which particularly hinder one's meditative efforts and can therefore be a major problem for a Buddhist, several strategies are recommended. These are presented in a hierarchical fashion, each to be tried if the preceding one fails:

(1) *Switch to an opposite or incompatible thought.* The first is to reflect on an object which is associated with thoughts which are the opposite of the unwanted thought. This means that, if the unwanted cognition is associated with passion or lust, one should think of something promoting lustlessness; if it is associated with malice, one should think of something promoting loving kindness; and if it is something associated with delusion or confusion, one should think of something promoting clarity. This exercise of switching to a thought incompatible with the unwanted one "like a carpenter getting rid of a coarse peg with a fine one" is claimed to help eliminate the unwanted intrusion.

(2) *Ponder on harmful consequences.* If, however, the unwanted thought still keeps arising, one is advised to ponder on the perils and disadvantages of the thought; that is, to consider its harmful consequences. His would help one to rid oneself of the thought in question, "like in the case of a young man or woman, who is eager to look nice and clean, who would be revolted and disgusted if he/she finds the carcass of a snake around his/her neck and would immediately get rid of it."

(3) *Ignore and distract.* If that, too, fails, the technique of ignoring an unwanted thought is recommended. One is to strive not to pay attention "like a man who closed his eyes or looks in another direction in order not to see a visual object that he does not wish to see." It is suggested that various distracting activities may be used in order not to pay attention to the unwanted cognition. These include: recalling of a doctrinal passage one has learned, concentrating on actual concrete objects, and engaging in some unrelated physical activity.

(4) *Reflect on removal of causes.* If the problem still persists, then a further strategy is recommended. This is to reflect on the removal or stopping of the causes of the target thought. This is explained with the analogy of a man walking briskly who asks himself "Why am I walking briskly?," then reflects on his walking and stops and stands; then reflects on his standing and sits down, and so on.

(5) *Control with forceful effort.* If the foregoing strategies fails, then a fifth method is advocated, which is forcefully to restrain and dominate the mind. This use of effort is likened to "a strong man holding and restraining a weaker man." One is to use the "effort of one part of the mind to control the other."

The above account is based on the *Vitakkasanthana Sutta* of the *Majjhima Nikaya* and its commentary, *Papañcasudani*.

The similarities between some of these Buddhist strategies and the techniques used for unwanted intrusions and related problems in CBT are only too obvious (de Silva, 2001). Thought-stopping, thought-switching, distraction (de Silva & Rachman, 2004; Rachman & Hodgson, 1980; Wolpe, 1958), and covert sensitization (Cautela, 1967), are all foreshadowed here. It will have been noticed that the currently widely used technique of exposure/habituation training — that is, instructing the client to exposure himself to the thought repeatedly and/or for prolonged periods (Rachman, 1978) — is absent from this account. However, a parallel of this is found in the *Satipatthana Sutta*, also part of the *Majjhima Nikaya*, and the *Mahasatipatthana Sutta* of the *Digha Nikaya*. These discourses outline the important meditation technique of mindfulness, which was referred to earlier. Mindfulness training is not simply a formal method of meditation but is a general self-improvement skill, with the person training him/herself to be aware of his/her body and bodily actions, of feelings and sensations, and of thoughts and ideas, as they happen. In developing mindfulness or total/immediate awareness — one might say continuous monitoring — of one's thoughts, one is advised to be alert to all thoughts that arise, including unwanted ones. If an unwanted thought arises, one is advised to face it directly and continuously, to look straight into that thought and dwell on it. It is said that then, gradually, that thought will lose its intensity, and will disappear (Gunaratna, 1981). The similarity between this and the habituation training paradigm of present-day therapists needs no comment.

Similar comparisons can be made between most of the other strategies found in the Buddhist texts and those established in present day CBT (de Silva, 1984, 1986, 2002; Mikulas, 1981, 2002). The significance for the presence of these techniques in the Buddhist texts is manifold. Firstly, it reflects the fact that the Dhamma is not only concerned with one's endeavors to achieve the ultimate religious goal by a process of self-development. As noted earlier, it also has something to offer in the area of day-to-day management of behavior problems, often as a goal in its own right, for reasons of one's own and one's fellow beings' benefit and happiness. Thus, these techniques are applicable irrespective of whether or not one has committed oneself to a life devoted to the aim of personal development and, ultimately, the state of *arahant*-hood. Secondly, these are well-defined, easy to use, and — above all — empirically testable. Indeed, the Buddhist approach is one of trying out various strategies until one that is effective is found. As seen above, the Vitakkasanthana Sutta offers the disciple five different techniques for dealing with unwanted, intrusive cognitions, each to be tried if the preceding one fails to produce the desired results. The Buddha's advice to the Kalamas, noted in a previous paragraph, reflects and embodies this approach. He said: "Do not accept anything from hearsay, because of tradition, or because of the reputation of a teacher. Accept what you can see for yourselves as valid...

When you have verified for yourselves that this is wholesome and that is not, this is blameless and that is blameworthy, this is conducive to well-being and happiness and that is conducive to suffering and illness, then you will choose this as your practice and reject that" (*Anguttara Nikaya, I*). Indeed, the Buddha's own quest for enlightenment followed this path: having tried out various methods and teachings available at the time, the rejected all of them as each failed to lead him towards his goal and help him develop his own path. Thirdly, the techniques are for use on oneself as well as for influencing the behavior of others; numerous examples are found for both types of use.

Relevance of Buddhist Behavior Change Strategies

From a practical perspective, the relevance of Buddhist behavior change strategies seems abundantly clear. A range of defined techniques is available for use with common behavioral problems. The fact that the strategies are closely similar to modern behavioral therapeutic techniques has the implication that their validity and utility are already established, as many of the latter have been subjected to rigorous clinical and experimental investigation. There is a strong case, too, for those Buddhist strategies that, so far, have no counterpart in modern behavior modification, to be empirically tested using clinical and experimental research methods. If grounds are then found for considering them clinically useful, they can be fruitfully incorporated into the repertoire of techniques available to the present day therapist. It can also be argued that these techniques will have particular relevance to the practice of therapy with Buddhist client groups. One of the problems arising in using methods derived from western science with client populations of a different cultural background is that the techniques offered may seem alien to the indigenous population. Thus, they may not be readily accepted or, if accepted, the compliance with therapeutic instructions may be poor. These cultural difficulties in therapy and counseling have been fully recognized in the literature (Kazarian & Evans, 1998; Lloyd & Bhugra, 1993).

On the other hand, if the techniques that are used and offered, although they may be an integral part of a western psychological system, are shown to be similar to ideas and practices that were accepted historically by the indigenous culture, then they would have a greater chance of gaining compliance and success. How a behavioral treatment program was successfully devised for a Hindu patient, which included the Hindu religious concept of karma yoga, has been described by Singh and Oberhummer (1980). Similarly, therapeutic packages that include traditional Zen practices have been used successfully with neurotic patients in Japan (Kishimoto, 1985). It is likely that modern therapeutic strategies will be more readily acceptable to Buddhist client groups if their similarities with those found in early Buddhist literature, and the use of the same or similar techniques by the Buddha and his early disciples, are highlighted. The use of meditation techniques as a stress-reduction strategy with Buddhist groups in several places provides an example of this phenomenon. A case in point is the use of Buddhist meditation in a psychiatric setting in Kandy, Sri Lanka (de Silva & Samarasinghe, 1998). Mikulas (1983) has commented on the favorable reception accorded to the ideas and techniques of behavior modification in another Buddhist country, Thailand.

Mental Health: Prevention

Numerous examples relevant to psychological prophylaxis and health promotion can be cited from the Buddhist texts, both in the original canon and in the subsequent literature. The value of some of these has come to be recognized in today's professional and academic circles (cf. de Silva, 2005). The idea of prevention has its roots in public health, where the concern with infectious diseases is a major factor. This gradually came to be extended to the area of mental health, mainly through the work of Caplan (1964). It was recognized that, along with the traditional focus on remediation or therapy of psychological disorders, attention also needed to be paid to the prevention of such disorders. The work has included identifying possible causes (i.e. risk-factors, early intervention, and work on how to help individuals equip themselves with strategies for coping with risk factors including common stress situations).

Broadly, three types of prevention have been recognized and guided much of the research and practice (Albee, 1982; Caplan, 1964). These are: primary; secondary; and tertiary prevention. Primary prevention is designed to prevent the development of new problems, and thus is the most radical and ambitious of the three. Secondary prevention seeks to intervene early when problems begin to appear and prevent them turning into more serious difficulties or dysfunctions. It also includes endeavors to avoid relapses of problems or disorders that have been got over; in other words, to prevent further episodes. Tertiary prevention has as its aim the reduction of long-term disabilities and serious negative effects that may emanate from a disorder that someone is afflicted by. In mental health practice, work has been done in all these ways with a variety of psychological problems, including individual work as well as community-based interventions.

Buddhist Aspects Relevant to Primary Prevention

There is much in the Dhamma that deals with primary prevention, along with the overall promotion of positive psychological health. This latter is in fact a more ambitious aspect of prevention, in that it tries more than simply to stall the development specific psychopathology; it aims to make one, overall, a more contented, more stable person, who is as a result less prone to developing psychological problems. This is a particularly valuable Buddhist contribution to the area of prevention, and there are many aspects that exemplify this. Some of these are discussed below.

Developing loving kindness: The Buddhist emphasis on the development of positive regard and loving kindness, and the corresponding reduction/elimination of anger/hatred, may be cited as an example of its contribution to the promotion of positive psychological health. In one's Endeavour to develop loving kindness (*metta*), a gradual and hierarchical series of steps is recommended. The ultimate step of this Endeavour is to develop loving kindness towards all beings. The interim steps include training oneself to have feelings of loving kindness towards liked and admired individuals, towards friends, towards persons about whom one is neutral, and towards one's enemies. This training, it is said in the *Visuddhimagga* and elsewhere, helps one to conquer anger and malice, and all the negative consequences that follow from them (Aronson, 1980). One is enabled to interact with others with a positive frame of mind. A useful recent discussion of the relevance of loving kindness to day to day life is given in Mikulas (2002).

Controlling lust and desire: The Buddhist approach to the control of problematic lust and desire is a further area worth highlighting. There are many discussions in the Theravada Buddhist literature which describe ways of meditating on or being aware of and alert to the aversive or unpleasant aspects of the stimuli that bind one and cause strong attachments and/or lust. The contemplation of *asubhas*, or the aversive — loathsome — properties of stimuli, is emphasized clearly in the literature. Examples include the contemplation on the repulsive and unattractive aspects of food, the aim being to develop the attitude that food is for essential nutriment, not for greed or gluttony. The aversive aspects of the human body are the subject of another meditative exercise, this being part of the wider meditation on the contemplation of the body. The disciple is encouraged to focus on the various parts of the body — given as thirty-two— in a sequence. The focus is on the true, loathsome and perishable, nature of them. This process also includes mental images which highlight the loathsomeness of the body. The aim is to reduce undue and unwholesome attachment to the human body, one's own and others." The value of this form of contemplation is explicitly stated in several places. The *Majjhima Nikaya I* says: "Cultivate, Rahula, *asubhabhavana*; for, when you cultivate it, the passion of lust will cease." And in the *Anguttara Nikaya IV* it is said: "Meditation on *asubhas* should be practiced for the destruction of lust."

Recognition of impermanence: The Buddhist emphasis on *anicca*, or impermanence, can also be seen as a potential contribution to the promotion of psychological health. The *anicca* perspective helps one to recognize, and constantly bear in mind, the essential transientness of phenomena. Nothing is permanent or everlasting. All that one loves, desires, and cherishes perish in the end, things change; they do not stay the same. One's loved ones pass away. Success may give way to failure. Fame may turn into ill-repute. Beauty fades. The firm grasping of the inevitable, impermanence of things — including people — helps to create a perspective where one can handle losses of all kinds, including bereavement, without undue devastation, and with a sense of equanimity. This leaves little room for abnormally prolonged or pathological grief reactions. The *anicca* perspective also helps, in a wider sense, to keep one's desires and lusts from getting out of control. What one desires and lusts after, are essentially impermanent and perishable things. Recognition of this helps one to control the lust, and to place natural human desire in proper perspective. As noted in an earlier paragraph, in the Vitakkasanthana Sutta of the *Majjhima Nikaya* advice is given on how to remove or control unskillful cognitions which are based on desire (*chanda*). These unskillful thoughts should, it is said, be countered by skilful thoughts, which focus on matters that do not promote, indeed inhibit, desire. One of the ways to do this is to contemplate on the impermanence of the object. This is compared to an expert carpenter getting rid of a coarse peg, on a plank, with a fine one.

The four sublime attitudes: The development of the four sublime moods — or sublime attitudes (*brahmaviharas*) — is considered a major part of one's personal development. These have been briefly discussed in an earlier paper (de Silva, 2000), and a fuller analysis is available in Aronson (1980). The four are *metta* (loving kindness), which has already been referred to; *karuna* (sympathy); *mudita* (congratulatory benevolence/shared joy); and *upekkha* (equanimity). These key Buddhist concepts are worth close study, as they reflect a major aspect of BP. These are mental attitudes or higher sentiments that one is encouraged to develop. They are considered to be indispensable for person/spiritual development (see Vajiranana, 1975). Detailed discussions of these are available in the early texts, including the *Visuddhimagga*. These sublime moods, when developed, can transform one's overall attitude to one's fellow-beings and to life in general, and contribute significantly to one's own psychological well-being. Loving kindness is free of lustful attachment. Its manifestation is the feeling of love and friendliness, and the removal of hatred. Sympathy is an emotion conducive to the removal of pain or suffering of others. It refers to feelings for those in distress. Congratulatory benevolence (the term *mudita* has also been translated as "sympathetic joy") refers to rejoicing at others' happiness, success, and prosperity. The absence of envy and jealousy, two negative emotions, are said to be its essence. It is worth nothing that both *karuna* and *mudita* involve, and are marked by, a strong sense of empathy. One feels for others and with others, in their distress and in their joy, not simply as an outsider but also through a perspective of sharing the distress or the joy. This is an area of BP which requires further elucidation and analysis, as it has, potentially, a major contribution to make to a human psychology of wellbeing. The fourth sublime mood, equanimity, refers to the development of a neutral, stable and balanced attitude which enables one to remain calm and unruffled, unaffected by attraction or repulsion, and not subject to elation or depression. It is also marked by impartiality or lack of bias in one's dealings with others. Thus it promotes acceptance. In the hectic and competitive present-day world, such an attitude can have a substantial hearing on whether one succumbs to the upheavals around one, or succeeds in remaining calm and stable despite the changes around one. The events around one are un-predictable; in this context of unpredictability, one can retain a sense of stability through the cultivation of u*pekkha*.

Hindrances: Another aspect of Buddhism that has relevance to the cultivation of psychological well-being is that of hindrances to one's psychological development. In BP it is stated that one's efforts at such development are hindered by various negative factors. Various discussions of these are found in both Canonical and commentatorial texts, including the Samaññaphala Sutta of the *Digha Nikaya*. Five main barriers or hindrances (*ninaranas*) to psychological progress are listed. These are: (a) sensory desire; (b) malice, or ill-will; (c) sloth and torpor; (d) restlessness and worry; and (e) skeptical doubt, or perplexity. These are described as hindering one's efforts in meditation, and — more generally — hindering one's personal/psychological development. The texts repeatedly stress the need to overcome these hindrances in order to achieve psychological development. It is stated that sensory desire (*kamacchanda*; i.e. desire for pleasurable sense experiences) is likened to being in debt. If a man is filled with sensory desire for a certain individual, he will be full of craving for that object of desire be strongly attached to her. Even if spoken to rudely by that individual or harassed or beaten, he will bear it all. In that way, sense desire is like being in debt. When he overcomes this sense desire, he is no longer attached and bound to the object of his desire. Even if he sees divine forms, passion will not assail him. This is like one who has freed himself from this debt who no longer feels any fear or anxiety when meeting his former creditors. Ill-will (*byapada*) is compared to suffering from a bilious disease which makes everything, even honey and sugar, taste bitter. One feels irritation and harassment even at those who wish him well. Getting over this ill-will is like being cured of the illness and one can once again appreciate the taste of honey and sugar. One is able to appreciate the value of advice, and respond positively. Sloth and torpor (*thina-middha*; mental and physical laziness or inertia) is compared to being in prison. The person is trapped in his passive, inactive state. Overcoming sloth and torpor is likened to being set free from prison. He is no longer passive and inactive; he can engage in activities, just as a freed prisoner can participate in, and enjoy, festivities outside jail. Restlessness and worry (*uddhacca-kukkucca* — i.e. the mood fluctuating between phases of overexcitement, with a flurry of thoughts, and a low state of unease, guilt or worry) is compared to being a slave, having no independence. Getting over restlessness and worry is compared to becoming a free man again, able to do what he likes. Finally, skeptical doubt or perplexity (*vicikiccha*) is likened to the state of a traveler in a hazardous territory where he gets anxious and nervous at the slightest noise or sound. He will go a few steps and then stop. He may even turn back completely. The person assailed by perplexity or skeptical doubt is similarly hindered. The overcoming of skeptical doubt is compared to strong man, in company and well prepared, walking through a difficult territory and reaches his destination.

The above descriptions are based on the Samaññaphala Sutta of the *Digha Nikaya* and its commentary in the *Sumangalavilasini*. In meditation, these hindrances are seen as the major obstacles to one's progress. In the wider context of one's day-to-day life, again one is seriously affected and held back by these. They are, in a very real sense, hindrances to psychological health. Overcoming these is a significant step in achieving psychological development, not just in a religious or spiritual sense, but also in the sense of general psychological health and wellbeing. Systematic meditative exercises help one to overcome these, including some that have already been noted. Constant alertness to the operation of these factors is also considered an effective way of guarding against the negative impact of these on one's psychological development and wellbeing. The Buddhist texts also give very specific, practical advice on how to overcome these hindrances. As an example, it is worth nothing here the steps recommended in the texts for overcoming the hindrance of sense desire. It is stated that there are six things conducive to this. These are: (a) Learning how to meditate on impure or loathsome (*asubha*) objects. We have already discussed this in brief in an earlier section. (b) Devoting oneself to the meditation on such aversive stimuli (*asubha bhavana*). This includes focusing on the aversive aspects of the human body. Again, we have noted this briefly in an earlier section. (c) Guarding the sense doors. (d) Moderation in eating. (e) Noble friendship. The reference here is to such friends who have experience and who can be a model and help the person. (f) Suitable conversation. It is said that one should engage in conversations that deal with the overcoming of sensory desire, and more generally in conversations that help advance one's progress in personal development. Similar steps are recommended for overcoming the other four hindrances. As can be expected, meditation on loving kindness is one of the steps recommended for the task of overcoming ill-will. Regular practice in this meditation is considered a powerful way of doing this. This can be easily incorporated into one's daily routine, and does not require setting aside a great deal of time.

Ideal state: An important topic that needs to be addressed at this point is that of the Buddhist ideal, which was mentioned in passing in an earlier paragraph. The attainment of Nibbana means that the person has reached the ultimate state of personal development that of the *arahant* state. An *arahant* is one who has conquered the negative, maladaptive factors called the *asavas* (influxes or biases; see above). There are several detailed discussions of *asavas* in the texts (e.g. Sabbasava Sutta of the *Mijjhima Nikaya*). These are the bias of sensual desire (*kamasava*), the bias of the desire for permanent existence (*bhavasava*), the bias of dogmatic views (*ditthasava*), and the bias of ignorance (*avijjasava*). Those who have destroyed and conquered these *asavas*, it is said, have freedom from "mental disease." The implication of this and similar references is that those who have not attained personal development to this high degree are not immune from psychological ill-health. Does this mean that, short of this perfect or worthy state, there can be no psychological health or well-being? This is not the case. Indeed, the Dhamma extols virtues at all levels, and recognizes their benefits. Buddhist texts speak about the life of a good or righteous householder — that is someone who leads a lay life, with duties and obligations (see Sigalovada Sutta of the *Digha Nikaya*). He has not renounced ordinary life for the purpose of seeking *arahant*-hood. He practices virtuous living, engages in contemplative meditation as he can, resists from gross misconduct, discharges his duties and responsibilities diligently and develops a benevolent attitude to the world and to those around him. This life is described as harmonious living or righteous living (*sammacariya, dhammacariya*). Such a person displays a clear dimension of mental health. Thus the Dhamma does not take the position that only those who have renounced a lay life can achieve psychological wellbeing. Indeed, much of Buddhist ethics is based on the value placed on a harmonious lay life (see Guruge, 1999; Kalupahana, 1995). The value of psychological health in promoting social well-being is clearly emphasised (see de Silva, 2004).

Secondary Prevention: An Example

In the above section, we have discussed Buddhist ideas and practices which are geared towards the primary prevention of psychological disorders, including the more positive aim of cultivating sound, stable mental health. Some Buddhist ideas and strategies are also relevant to the other forms of prevention. The best example to date how BP can contribute to secondary prevention comes in the work of a team of present-day psychologists who have used mindfulness meditation as a way of preventing relapse in those with a history of depression. Segal and others (2002) have reported the results of a large clinical trial. In this trial, Mindfulness-Based Cognitive Therapy (MBCT), carried out in a group setting, was shown to be a cost-efficient psychological approach to the prevention of relapse/recurrence in recovered, depressed patients who have a history of recurrent episodes. This is secondary prevention *par excellence* evidenced by a large, multi-centre study, which involved a substantial number (145) of patients. Why was mindfulness meditation applied in this context? As pointed out by the authors, increased mindfulness is relevant to the prevention of relapse of depression as it allows the early detection of relapse-related patterns of negative thinking, feeling and physical sensations, so that they can be "nipped in the bud." Further, entering a mindful mode of processing at such times allows disengagement from the relatively automatic-ruminative thought patterns that would otherwise promote the relapse process. A full discussion of this rationale is given by Segal and others (2002). This impressive contemporary piece of work shows the relevance of BP in a major clinical area, aiding and promoting secondary prevention. There is clearly scope for further work along these lines, using specific Buddhist strategies for preventive purposes in well-controlled clinical trials.

Conclusion

This chapter reviewed some basic notions in BP, focusing on motivation/emotion, behavior, and cognition. Some practical aspects of the Dhamma, which are relevant to psychological treatment, were also discussed with emphasis on meditation and on cognitive-behavior change strategies. Finally, the value of Buddhist notions and practices in the prevention of psychological disorders was commented on. Clearly there is a need and much scope for further empirical research in these areas.

3

Mindfulness, Compassion, And Wisdom: Working With Anger

Peter Bankart

My preliminary work applying mindfulness practice to helping young men achieve greater control over their lives has produced encouraging results. What I have found is that when young men are asked to practice a regular program of meditation, yoga and cognitive-behavioral self monitoring, angry impulses and thoughts spontaneously emerge as objects of meditation and reflection. In the natural mindful process of discovering the creative potential inherent in their own consciousness the men I work with appear to learn not just to avert and subdue their anger, but also to transform it into greater awareness of and concern for the wellbeing of others. What I perceive to be happening is that meditation and yoga lead my subjects to discover within themselves a wellspring of compassion that they had previously ignored, misdirected, or misinterpreted. This compassion opens a sort of cognitive gap that mediates between provoking situations and the active choice of how to respond to emotional challenge. Something akin to wisdom enters this gap and begins to transform the ignorance of greed, hate, and delusion into a deeper appreciation for interconnection and the wellbeing of others.

Anger, along with greed and delusion, has long been recognized in Buddhist teaching as one of the three poisons that contaminate human minds and corrupt the physical body (Martin, 2000). As with a great many other Buddhist truths, however, western mental science has only recently begun to recognize the global corrosive power of anger. The scientific literature on anger confirms that it is a powerful and destructive emotion that can lead to disrupted human relationships, catastrophic health problems, and chronic clinical depression (Sapolsky, 1998, 2004). So I am inspired anew to urge my colleagues to explore the wisdom that Eastern philosophy and practice bring to bear on Western therapeutic practice (Bankart et al., 1992; Bankart, 2000a).

Perspectives on Anger

Hogan and Linden (2004) have documented that the physiological effects of chronic anger are reflected in elevated blood pressure and chronic hypertension, finding that anger response styles accounted for 23% of the variance in resting blood pressure readings for men (and a statistically non-significant 9% in women). Richards and others (2000) have documented increased levels of total serum cholesterol and low-density lipoproteins in men who were angry, frustrated, and felt unfairly treated. Anger also appears to significantly increase in people who have substantially depleted serotonin levels as a result of abusing so-called party drugs like MDMA (Bond et al., 2003). Moreover these harmful biological correlates of anger are substantially mediated by rumination that serves to prolong angry feelings and provoke the tendency to behave aggressively. Not too surprisingly angry people who attempt to suppress their ruminations experience substantially higher levels of hypertension and elevated blood pressure (Hogan & Linden, 2004).

In 2002 Troisi and D'Argenio reported that among a sample of young male military recruits referred for psychiatric evaluation, anger-based depression accounted for almost 85% of the non-neurological or psychotic psychiatric problems that were diagnosed. They also reported that there was a direct link between levels of chronic anger and what they called insecure attachment. Insecure attachment was characterized by avoidant and anxious interpersonal styles, a finding which was supported by Hogan and Linden (2004) who described their angry hypertensive subjects as high in avoidance and very low in support seeking. Angry people, and especially angry men, are mighty low in what Buddhists call loving-kindness, and they are low in that regard both toward others and toward themselves.

From a developmental perspective, according to Del Vecchio and O'Leary (2004), anger is often linked to chronically low-self esteem, poor cognitive and social skills, lack of engagement with others, impatience, and chronic substance abuse. Angry men show a unique pattern of asymmetrical left frontal lobe activation that reflects impaired neurological processing and which may make self-control particularly challenging when an angry person is stressed (Harmon-Jones, 2004). This, in turn, makes chronic (trait) male anger particularly problematic because it becomes linked to a wide variety of impulsive negative behaviors including child abuse, spouse abuse, road rage and even murder. Del Vecchio and O'Leary estimate that 94% of the time anger is directed at other people, with family members, friends, and coworkers being the most likely outlets for an angry person's aggression. Of course anger, manifest or not, is also directly related to depression, especially in men (Cochran & Rabinowitz, 2000). As they report, angry men tend to withdraw from sustaining social contacts and exhibit "a male tendency to externalize problems, discharge uncomfortable dysphoric affective states ... and self-medicate mood difficulties with mood altering substances" (p. 85).

The Buddhist Perspective on Anger

From a Buddhist perspective, anger is a manifestation of the break down of compassion, reflecting not just a failure of sufficient inhibition, but a fundamental loss of what it means to be a connected, aware and interdependent co-originating being. The problem of anger is located at the center of Buddhist concern for human well-being. Buddhist teaching recognizes anger as one of the three great destructive fires, along with greed and delusion, as the source of human suffering. Intense social and emotional isolation is the ultimate cause of an angry person's distress. This emotional affliction is rooted in an alienating preoccupation with selfish desire that derives from an unenlightened understanding of self and the world. Thurman (1999) summarized the Buddhist perspective on the connection between powerful negative emotions and suffering as follows:

> One of the great sources of our suffering is hatred, and all of its variation: resentment, anger, bitterness, dislike, irritation, aggressiveness, hostility. Hate is very powerful. When we are gripped by hatred we go into a rage and become completely out of control. We smash up our own beloved body and commit suicide. We smash up people whom we love, wives, husbands, children, parents. Rage can turn us into a complete maniac or demon — temporarily. It's one of the most dangerous kinds of energies, very difficult to control. Any force we can marshal within ourselves to prevent and forestall the explosive moment of rage is really beneficial. (Thurman & Wise, 1999, p. 76)

The social and emotional isolation and alienation of angry people, from a Buddhist perspective, is the root cause of an angry person's distress — a problem rooted in preoccupation with the self and the impossible desires of an unenlightened understanding of the self and the world. The challenge for the therapist, from this perspective, is to help the angry one to awaken from the illusion that desires can be satisfied, obstacles eradicated, and suffering eliminated through the application of force, and to recognize that the elimination of this monstrous suffering can only be achieved though the realization of compassionate regard for self and others. Moreover, as the Buddha taught, the most effective way to reduce anger is to adopt a Right View of causation; one must make a concentrated study within oneself of the thoughts, feelings, and actions that make anger come and that make anger go away (Levine, 2000).

Thus, much anger can be seen as the product of what Shakespeare might have called "a mind diseased." But in addition, as Aristotle (1960) observed, "anger is always attended by a certain pleasure arising from the expectation of revenge" (p. 93). Indeed, The Iliad, Homer's epic "song" of the anger of both gods and men reminds us that much anger is about coercing compliance from those who have made the serious error of disagreeing with us. The second Noble Truth that the Buddha taught was that our suffering is directly tied to our constant and sometimes quite intense desires. We pursue these desires in ways that often harm and degrade others. The effects of our pursuit of desires on others are usually obvious. The effects on our own wellbeing are often more subtle but can certainly be equally corrosive and self-destructive. It is not that the angry person's desires are fundamentally any different than our own or anyone else's, but that living so intensely with desires one has lost any real awareness of the suffering his desires have caused — both in oneself and in the people one loves.

A Cognitive-Behavioral Approach to Anger

As Novaco (2004) suggests, it is easy and common for clients to become quite attached to their anger and actively resist any efforts to identify anger as a focus of therapeutic treatment. Rather than admonishing angry clients, Novaco recommends helping them replace angry thoughts with positive self-statements; helping them buy some time while their autonomic nervous systems cool off; encouraging them to discover the paths to mature happiness that are available to them — a resolution of the endless suffering that is the price we pay for our unrelenting desire to be right, invulnerable, and in control. Albert Ellis might observe that all this angry suffering is the price we pay for spending much of our waking lives thinking, talking, and interacting with others as if we were Moses. From a mindfulness perspective, as Kabat-Zinn (1994) has remarked, "anger is the price that we pay for being attached to a narrow view of being right (while) the collective pain we cause others and ourselves bleeds our souls" (p. 242).

In counseling with young men I am consistently struck by how much anger is directly connected with absolutist rules about "right" and "wrong" — views that are justified by an extensive catalog of abstract principles and standards about the acceptable definition of proper human conduct, a great deal of which is defined by rigid sex-specific cultural norms. Thus the angry young man not only sees himself as the last bastion of what is right and proper and acceptable, but also as the pinpointed target of a myriad of moral infractions that he encounters on a daily, if not hourly, basis. Scratch the surface of any young man's anger, in my experience, and you will find the wildly beating heart of an enraged defiant victim. This is the root of what Thomas (2003) has termed "justified anger." Indeed, Aquino and others (2004) found that perceptions of victimization are frequently the root of overt anger manifested by employees with a hostile attribution style. Closely related to the idea of justified anger is the concept of "unrealistic anger" defined as the negative emotion experienced from going through the process of "trying to assert control over something that does not need correcting or that cannot be corrected" (Sapolsky, 1998, p. 334). Unrealistic anger provokes all of us, but especially young men, into a self-perpetuating series of emotional battles that is biologically dangerous and, over time, even lethal. Thus we can see how deeply the corrosive power of anger is fed by an emotional core of craving, aversion, and ignorance that are the central focus of a Buddhist approach to understanding human suffering.

Yet justified and unrealistic anger are deeply socialized into young men as masculine virtues by a culture that glorifies strength and violence, and that at the same time is deeply distrustful of authority and convention. Anyone who works intimately with young men who has not forced herself to watch repeated screenings of the film *Fight Club* is at risk of not fully being aware of the pervasive importance of this highly resilient strand in American boys' masculinity training. This is why I have argued (Bankart, 2000b, 2002) that it is essential in therapeutic work with young men for the therapist to offer her clients a sort of mindful psychological buffer zone, a place for introspection, where a young man can retreat from the rhetoric of testosterone, demanding respect and maintaining face, as well as defending against any appearance of weakness or uncertainty. I have found and in practice have come to believe that mindfulness practice can and often does provide a sanctuary for young men, and especially angry young men where they can take stock of themselves and their relationship to the world. Most importantly, perhaps, they can take stock of their relationship with a whole variety of authoritarian teachings, and begin the process of sorting out and owning what is true, important, and real. By adopting a mindful orientation toward their personal experience they will almost certainly experience a wide range of beneficial emotional, psychological, interpersonal, and spiritual effects, as did the highly competitive medical and premedical students who were introduced to mindfulness meditation by Shapiro and others (1998).

Opening the Cognitive Gap

Working with angry young men is not for the faint-hearted, however! Indeed the use of mindfulness practices can release a whole array of demons (Bankart, 2000b, 2001) that need to be grappled with in a safe and serious place. It involves confronting powerful and often uncharted emotions, and grappling with those emotions in a deliberate and constructive way (Greenberg, 2002). It is often the case that my clients and students come to resist the difficult, frustrating, and serious work of laying a claim to a sustainable view of the self and the world. It is frequently necessary to offer a gentle or sometimes not so gentle *gaman suru*[1], an uncompromising request that the student exerts what Buddhist teachers call Right Effort (Bankart, 2003) in his quest for enlightenment. It is essential that the angry client not feel preached to or lectured to; it is essential that his anger be approached in a collaborative effort with empathy, compassion, and with your loving-kindness. This is not just some Buddhist sentimentality, but one of the main findings of researchers who work with angry and violent offenders (Taft et al., 2003).

Levine (2000) admonishes that successful control over anger comes directly from learning to be mindful. He advises us to learn to pay close attention to our inner emotional states. He advises that it is necessary to pay attention to the subtle beginnings of irritation, displeasure, and annoyance; to become aware of the clenched fist, the locked jaw, the pounding heart. He also counsels that one must become aware of the manner of one's speech especially sarcasm, criticism, put-downs, and other violations of the Buddha's teachings about Right Speech. As Kristeller and Johnson (2003) point out, in order for a person to get in touch with his capacity for empathy, compassion, and altruism it is necessary first for that person to disengage from his usual preoccupation with self-reinforcing, self-defeating, and self-indulgent behaviors and reactions. He needs, perhaps through the practice of mindfulness, to become intimately aware of his habitual reflexive patterns of experiencing stress, disagreement, challenge, and disappointment. As Kornfield (1993) wisely put it, he needs to begin the process of confronting the self-protective anger in himself by experiencing a measure of self directed compassion — he needs to open his mind by first opening his heart. He must discover new ways of understanding and meeting his most fundamental needs — essentially a process of creating human meaning, which is a necessary precursor to his ability to manage his emotions and negotiate a successful resolution to interpersonal conflicts (Griffith & Graham, 2004). To put it succinctly, he needs to begin thinking very deliberately about forgiveness (Coyle & Enright, 1997), and how to establish, build, and enhance significant intimate human relationships (Carson et al., 2004). He needs to discover that compassion is not about weakness — but is, in fact, the product of great inner strength, courage, and power (Noll, 2004).

This is a process described by any number of Buddhist teachings; indeed it is probably the central theme of most of them. Among my favorites is a passage in *Meeting the Monkey Halfway* (2000) by A. S. Bhikkhu who asks the reader to direct loving-kindness to one's self, to one's feelings, moods and perceptions in order to experience love. Here is what Bhikku says about anger.

> *Undercut the power of anger by seeing it in the present. Look intently into all its aspects and it will loose its power. Discard every layer of anger, look into your reactions in relation to the offender. Why are you angry? What do you wish to do with this anger? How far and in what direction do you want to go with it? How significant is this in your life? Is this anger worth jeopardizing your well-being? Is it worth all the time you are spending on it? The exercise of questioning your way through your anger will effectively force you into facing the realities of that moment. It will also give you the opportunity to answer those questions honestly. At the end of your investigation, you can be sure that you have lost the momentum of that anger and, therefore, have regained control over your otherwise runaway emotions. This is one of the great escapes from suffering.* (p. 73)

I think Bhikkhu's point is wonderfully illustrated in a short news item in the *New York Times* a while back. The story reported that an executive left his New York City hotel and got in a cab headed for a very important meeting. The cab driver said he knew a shortcut across town and took his passenger down a series of narrow alleys that avoided the congestion of midtown Manhattan. Halfway down one alley the cab found itself behind a city garbage truck whose crew was loading a huge mountain of trash — at a not very fast rate. The cab driver, exercising his legendary New York cab driver's impatience, began blasting his horn, which of course accomplished very little except to upset his passenger and the sanitation workers, who now staged a work slow-down. The cab driver began to back up, but was almost immediately blocked by two other cabs. They had come down the same alley and were now equally stuck and now joined in the blasting of horns. Here's where the story gets interesting. The business man calmly removed his suit coat, got out of the cab, and started helping load the trash into the garbage truck. Thus, he not only made the world a slightly better place, but he also solved the problem of his desire to get to his meeting in a timely fashion. His suffering was diminished in a most effective way.

Mindfulness and Compassion

In my work with young men and their angry suffering it is tempting to try to graft myself onto their thought processes as a sort of gigantic surrogate frontal lobe. Yet, this approach teaches them very little and frustrates me to no end. The more important and effective task is to help these men discover ways to discover the potential for wisdom that exists within their own consciousness. The goal is not just to subvert and subdue anger, but to help them open up to experience and to understand the choices that difficult situations call on them to make. Mindfulness practice is structured as a set of exercises whereby my clients come to develop significant skills as an observer of their own mental and emotional processes. Mindfulness invites a patient, accepting awareness of a person's own attentional processes on purpose, in the present moment, and non-judgmentally without succumbing to the flood of likes and dislikes, opinions, prejudices, projections and fantasies which usually contaminate our moment to moment consciousness. As Levine (2000) put it, mindfulness means learning to pay attention on purpose, in the present moment, for the sake of greater awareness, clarity and acceptance of present-moment reality.

By practicing mindfulness the client becomes aware of just how clouded and distorted his awareness of the world (and himself) has become. He becomes intrigued with the process of sorting it all out, non-analytically and non-judgmentally. He discovers how constraining his automatic assumptions have been; how distorting of reality his unawareness has been. He comes to glimpse how little of his mind he has been using in his day to day life. As it deepens one's awareness, mindfulness practice offers unlimited opportunities to live one's life in the present moment, to make deliberate and informed decisions, and to take full and complete responsibility for one's speech and deeds. The openness that unfolds through the practice of mindfulness allows one to be more careful and more precise about one's intentions, perhaps to recognize the selfish and instrumental nature of many angry displays. In practicing mindfulness we can actually begin see and experience the truth in the observation shared by both the Buddha and by Cognitive-Behavior Therapy that "we are what we think" and that our angry thoughts create a hostile world around us. As a therapist, however, I think that this understanding about anger by itself is incomplete if it is recognized in an interpersonal vacuum. That is why the principle of compassionate engagement is also so important.

Compassion is the wellspring of Buddhist ethics (Bankart et al., 2003; Khong, 2003; Ragsdale, 2003). Compassion connects every human being with every living thing; it is the true-north of one's moral compass and it is the highest calling of the human heart. In traditional Buddhist teaching (e.g. Gunaratana, 2002) compassion is understood to arise spontaneously as a product of the exercise of morality, mental discipline, and wisdom. But based on my clinical work with western clients, I think I am in essential agreement with Alfred Adler that compassion is often a human faculty that in a highly agentic and individuated culture needs to be explicitly addressed and awakened in the therapeutic context. In general, the issue of compassion comes up in two ways in therapy. The first is that compassionate concern for the self and others is an essential requirement for mental health and wellbeing. The second is that compassion must be awakened and nurtured in human beings. This awakening and nurturing is probably the single most important function of parents and teachers, and is the primary mission of psychotherapists of all stripes. Any therapeutic process that hopes to address male anger must be deeply rooted in an ethic of compassion if it is to have any meaningful probability of achieving its goals. The data on this point are abundantly clear and seem to me to be completely irrefutable (Hubble et al., 1999).

Conclusion

In conclusion, it is the thesis of this paper that if, as Brown and Ryan (2003) have documented, mindfulness and being fully present are directly related to psychological wellbeing — then significant evidence of non wellbeing and stress in the form of anger and angry arousal should lead us to invite our clients to explore the emotional core of craving, aversion, and ignorance that are perpetuating their suffering. In mindfulness work, the angry impulse itself becomes an object of meditation and thus a wellspring for the growth of wisdom, compassion, and interconnectedness. By focusing on the creative potential inherent in their own consciousness, clients learn not just to avert and subdue their anger, but also to transform the consuming fires of greed, hate, and delusion into a deeper appreciation for the well-being of others. The men I have worked with who have sincerely and successfully engaged this process report that the greatest benefit of their practice is that they no longer have to be eternally vigilant, never certain if their emotional impulses will overwhelm their ability to act with reason and awareness. As one of my recent students wrote: "These days, when I start to get angry (usually at my sister), I tend to think about situations and how it's not a big deal. After reflecting for a moment, I just deal with it; and freak her out by being kind!" Mindfulness training thus appears to offer young men an opportunity to engage the world with a significantly greater capacity for empathy, especially in situations where they had previously experienced only reflexive competitive self-interest. Compassion thus becomes the ally of reason in guiding a young man through sometimes difficult emotional terrain by opening a sort of "cognitive gap" between impulse and action. This gap, I believe, is the place where mature wisdom can take root; and this wisdom begins the transformation of ignorance, greed, hate, and delusion into a deeper appreciation for interconnection and concern for the wellbeing of others and of our own.

---

1. A phrase heard numerous times a day in Japan; it translates roughly as "Do your best, keep trying, and never be a quitter."

4

A Middle Way: Meditation In The Treatment Of Compulsive Eating

Jean Kristeller & James Jones

Understanding and engaging in the processes of eating from a Buddhist meditative perspective has proven to be a particularly powerful means for exploring the potential of mindfulness meditation as a therapeutic tool and as a path to wisdom in every domain of human functioning. The process of eating and our relationship to food and our bodies can be seen as engaging a wide range of physiological and psychological conditioning. If meditation is conceived as a way to disengage ourselves from the wheel of samsara, from the bounds of endless conditioning, while allowing a full engagement with life in the moment, then examining how we relate to food brings us right up against many of these issues. Examining these processes in relation to such a common, universal, everyday experience as eating may be valuable in understanding the power of the meditative process in creating wisdom in other areas as well.

In the Noble 8-fold Path the Buddha provided direction on how to live one's life without constantly being caught in conditioned desires and cravings of life, in order to find release from *dukkha*, or suffering. The Buddha assuredly meant for his teachings to be taken into the day-to-day activities of one's life. The Noble 8-fold Path is a way to the cessation of suffering by "rightly" engaging in ordinary human activities such as speech, action, and livelihood. In addition to these ordinary activities of daily life, the Buddha also spoke to engaging the appropriate attitude (right view or understanding), motivation (right intention), and means (meditation practice and mindful awareness) to achieve this disengagement from conditioned desires and patterns. Furthermore, right view and right intention were then recognized to form together the essence of "wisdom" (*panna*, Pali; *prajna*, Sanskrit) (Lopez, 1995; Williams, 1989).

Unwise eating. One of the most fundamental daily needs of the human being is to consume food. Eating is also a source of pleasure and thus attachment. It engages the senses, conditioned preferences, aversions, personal choices, judgments and social decisions many times over the course of the day. Patterns and habits around food and eating are established early in life and represent one of the most universal experiences, culturally embedded yet highly personal. Being in "right" relationship to food was one of the core struggles of Gautama Buddha, as he came to the realization that the strict asceticism of the yogic path was not the road to enlightenment, and as he began to preach the "middle way." In our contemporary culture, food is plentiful, and the opportunities for indulgence so pervasive that virtually everyone struggles to find a balance, if not in regard to quantity of food, then in regard to the types and quality of the food we choose. Although almost all of us could identify ways in which we might make wiser or healthier choices about the foods we decide to eat, the individuals with whom we[1] work in our MB-EAT (Mindfulness Based Eating Awareness Training) treatment program are in almost constant distress in regard to their eating, to food and to their bodies. They suffer from a pattern of compulsive overeating that occurs several times a week and about which they experience a sense of loss of control and substantial depression. They are often seriously obese and have generally gone on many diets, sometimes successfully, but then regain the weight either slowly or quickly after the diet ends. Everyone entering our program craves and loves food, yet they have also created a relationship to eating that they distrust, if not hate. The wheel of life is severely out of balance.

In working with eating problems, we draw the distinction between appropriate — and balanced — use of food and the compulsive patterns that are out of control. Therefore, we are conceptualizing right intention in relation to eating as a motivation to use food wisely, which may include the incorporation of pleasure, moderate desire, and moderate attachment, consistent with a "middle way." The focus on habitual attachments and the means of detaching from them is very important in the application of Buddhist teachings to psychotherapy and especially to the treatment of eating disorders. The Buddha recognized that our thoughts — and our behaviors — are conditioned, that they are very powerfully linked to seeking pleasure or avoiding pain in a way that protects the immediate needs of the self, but which may distort or cloud more enduring needs. In the context that we are exploring here, that of recovery from an addictive or compulsive behavior, we do not mean transcendent or ultimate needs, but rather the very important distinction between immediate cravings, such an urge to eat an entire box of chocolates, as compared to savoring one or two and then eating healthier foods. Engaging or meeting these enduring needs assumes two principles: that they can be accessed by self-observation, as occurs in mindfulness meditation practice, and that engaging them reflects a more balanced wisdom.

Contemporary Cognitive-Behavior Therapy. CBT techniques are also based on the understanding that much of what we experience is conditioned and responsive to experience and to the seeking of pleasure and avoidance of pain or discomfort. Learning theory, in which our attachments and desires are primarily seen as learned behaviours, has contributed substantially to development of effective therapeutic interventions, including treatment of obesity and eating disorders (Fairburn,

1995; Agras et al., 1997; Wilfley et al., 2002). Self-monitoring, used within CBT to help identify conditioned patterns, is nevertheless experienced by many as a burdensome task that is rarely continued outside the therapeutic context, in contrast to mindful awareness, which can be incorporated into moment to moment experience and does not carry the same sense of burden to the individual. In CBT, self-monitoring is then used to inform a plan for changing triggers or substituting alternative behaviors. While CBT has been shown to have considerable value in treating eating disorders and obesity, it is generally not viewed as cultivating wisdom, but rather serving to assist with the substitution of more functional but parallel behaviors or responses. This may result in efforts to simply push away patterns of overeating, overindulgence, and over-attachment through overly rigid adherence to structured diets, efforts that may increase a sense of control but provide little balance. These alternatives may be experienced as forced, and as requiring continued effort, rather than emerging from inner experience and therefore are difficult to sustain. Often the person experiences a struggle in creating this shift, rather than a sense of freedom or awakening of awareness.

The use of mindfulness meditation, conversely, appears to assist the individual in becoming aware of how the conditioned mind reacts and then, with purpose, disengage the reactive mind, producing a sense of stillness and clear awareness. Our constructed meanings and habitual patterns associated with eating are a natural target for such meditative interventions. Meditation practice is a powerful tool for cultivating this awareness and the ability to be non-reactive. Although we will primarily be drawing on the tradition of mindfulness or insight meditation in this paper, concentrative meditation also serves to cultivate a still mind, and informs our work. We will argue in this paper that wisdom, in relation to everyday types of activities, emerges from this still awareness. Therefore, stilling the mind allows the emergence of right action and right thought, resulting in balance rather than imbalance and distress (*dukkha*).

This is an important difference between meditation based approaches and CBTs or structured dieting, which seek to directly modify the content of a person's cognitions and behaviors. Mindfulness meditation focuses less directly on the contents of our thoughts and feelings and more on our relationship to them. Over time meditation modifies how we relate to our thoughts and feelings more than the contents of those thoughts and feelings. It is our contention that by changing our relationship to the contents of our minds, we will affect a modification our thoughts and feelings and actions themselves. And in addition we argue that the success of meditation-based interventions like the MB-EAT programs demonstrates this. In addition we propose that this change in thought and behaviour is due in part to the accessing of a deeper wisdom through the practice of meditation that can be engaged across the full range of human experience and behavior.

Translating the Middle Way into a Wise Relationship with Eating: A Multi-Domain Model of Meditation

Considering how meditation may be used to treat disordered eating brings up the question of how these therapeutic effects may occur. Numerous models (Benson, 1975; Austin, 1999; Orme-Johnson, 2000; Kornfield, 1993; Rubin, 1996; Teasdale, 1999) have addressed the mechanisms of the effects of meditation within contemporary understanding psychology and neurophysiology. When reviewing the meditation literature, there is nevertheless some risk of falling into trap of the "six blind men and the elephant" analogy, with some claiming meditation is fundamentally a relaxation technique, others that it functions through a change in relation to self, or through cultivation of compassion, or through spiritual awakening. A wide range of meditation effects has in fact been very well documented (Murphy et al., 1999), but different types of effects are often treated somewhat separately from a conceptual perspective.

Rather than arguing that each of the types of effects we observe in our treatment program occurs through separate mechanisms, for the remainder of the chapter I will be proposing that a multi-domain model of meditation is the most useful, not only in integrating the traditional and contemporary meditation literature, but in understanding how a set of relatively simple cognitive processes can produce such a wide range of powerful experiences in regard to disordered eating. The multi-domain model (Kristeller, 2004) proposes that the cognitive processes involved in meditative practice, of focusing attention and awareness, and disengaging analytic thought and self-judgment, have impact across all domains of human functioning, because every domain is sensitive to conditioning processes that are suspended or reorganized through the practice of meditation. Even though the domains of functioning can be defined in different ways, it is useful to organize the impact of meditation around the following six: cognitive, physiological, emotional, behavioral, relation to self and to others, and spiritual. While effects in one domain clearly must interact with those in others, these are also areas of functioning that are seen within contemporary psychology to engage somewhat distinct processes. Furthermore, the order of the domains is not arbitrary, but neither are they intended to be hierarchical. Consistent with a model that views meditation as fundamentally a cognitive process (Bishop et al., 2004), cognition is placed first. The remainder are ordered to some degree by the ease by which individuals report experiencing them (i.e., virtually everyone reports a sense of physical relaxation after meditating), but given that such experience is highly sensitive to context (e.g., a spiritual context or a loving-kindness meditation), the order of the domains is neither fixed or linear (see Kristeller, 2004, for a more detailed overview).

Although eating can be viewed as a fairly primitive behavior — after all, even the lowest organisms consume nutrients — in truth, the process of eating engages all these domains: how we think about food, our physical reactions, the meeting of emotional needs, our actual eating behavior, our sense of self-identify and social needs, and even spiritual values, such as ritual use of food — or negatively, in the use of eating and the body as misdirected ultimate goals. Paradoxically, the extent to which eating could be reduced to relatively simple components makes apparent the sheer complexity of the conditioned and constructed elements that are layered on top of our basic needs for nutrition. In a food abundant society, with almost an infinite variety of choice, patterns become established that are extremely difficult to disengage. That is why changing our relationship to eating can serve as a good model for the potential of meditation as a means to self-regulation in a variety of domains. After reviewing the fundamental structure of the MB-EAT program, I will return to review the relationship of the therapeutic process in regard to the multi-domain model.

Using Meditation in Therapy: An Example from Treatment of Eating Disorders

Eating is immediate, compelling, and laden with conditioning and meaning, and therefore serves as a good path into mindful self-awareness, yet surprisingly little research has been carried out using meditation-based interventions for treatment of eating disorders or obesity. However, the first exercise that Kabat-Zinn (1990) uses in the widely respected MBSR (Mindfulness-Based Stress Reduction) thera-peutic meditation program at the University of Massachusetts Medical Center is the raisin meditation. The goal of this meditation is to eat this small, dried piece of fruit as mindfully as possible — as if one has never eaten a raisin before. The MBSR program uses this exercise to illustrate how mindful awareness can be brought to every aspect of daily life, and as a way to de-mystify the process of mindfulness meditation that will be introduced to participants over the following two months. While I (JK) was working at the University of Massachusetts Medical Center, I was strongly influenced by this approach. I had already been developing a meditation-based intervention for compulsive eaters before I went to UMMC that drew on mantra meditation and relaxation techniques, combined with CBT. This intervention was informed by principles of self-regulation (Schwartz, 1975; 1979; Carver & Scheier, 1981), evidence from sensory deprivation research (Suedfeld & Kristeller, 1982; Kristeller et al., 1982), and the growing understand-ing that chronic dieters and compulsive eaters were disengaged from internal self-regulatory systems of eating control and overly influenced by external cues, belief systems, or emotional signals that had become automatic and habitual in their lives (Rodin, 1981; Kristeller & Rodin, 1989) As I continued to develop this work, I came to feel that mindfulness meditation provides a powerful complement to these approaches (Kristeller, 2003), and over the last decade this program has developed into the MB-EAT program, which integrates various meditation techniques, in-formed by knowledge drawn from experimental and clinical psychology.

The MB-EAT is a 9-week program for individuals with Binge Eating Disorder (BED). In addition to teaching basic mindfulness meditation techniques, it includes a number of focused meditative exercises that engage experiences of hunger, satiety, eating awareness and appreciation, recognition of the distorted thoughts that often accompany urges to eat, and the pervasive sense of self-loathing that individuals with compulsive eating problems often report. In our first study with 18 overweight women who met criteria for BED — that of eating excessively large amounts of food and feeling out of control, generally several times per week — we found that this program significantly decreased frequency and intensity of binging, improved mood, and increased a general sense of self-control and self-worth (Kristeller & Hallett, 1999). We have recently completed a study further evaluating this intervention with obese men and women. All are at least 30% overweight, with an average weight of about 240 lbs.; some participants have weighed over 300 lbs. for most of their adult life. Their average age is about 45, and some are over 60 years old. Almost all have a history of trying numerous diets; and many have given up hope of ever having control over their eating. While some are seriously depressed or on medical disability due to their weight, others hold down highly skilled jobs. Quite a few are teachers, nurses or other professionals. The current treatment program uses a number of meditation-derived practices designed to increase mindfulness. First is training in basic mindfulness meditation techniques — both breath-anchored sitting meditation for about 20 minutes per day, and "mini-meditations." Mini-meditations take from a few seconds to a few minutes, and provide a means to bring focused awareness into the everyday environment. Another element is re-engaging the body through focused breathing, body awareness and simple yoga movements. Often these individuals hate their bodies, feeling both disconnected from them and totally defined by them at the same time. Meditative breathing serves as both a relaxation component and as an important means (Haruki & Takase, 2001; Lehrer et al., 1999) of re-regulating the balance of the autonomic nervous system. It increases awareness of basic physiological processes in a way that is not threatening. In addition, different focused meditations are used during each week of treatment. These guided meditations ask participants, in the safe space of the group, to engage focused attention in relation to their experience of food, hunger, feeling full, thoughts about food and eating, and emotions. About half of the guided meditations involve use of actual food, expanding the simple raisin meditation to chocolate cake, cheese, crackers — and a whole meal that participants create themselves. Also important is a forgiveness meditation that raises issues of anger and hurt toward both themselves and to others, and teaches the ability to accept these feelings non-judgmentally. Finally, we engage in what might be called "spiritual wisdom," in which patients are asked to find an inner place of peace and awareness that can connect them to a higher purpose, values and strength. Again, this is based on the Buddhist teaching that there is an inherent process of wisdom within all of us that we can access.

The following represents a focused meditation on the experience of eating (note: the pauses indicated are extended for the length of 3-4 breaths):

> *Centering yourself in your chair, in your body, gently close your eyes and bring your attention to your breath. Be aware of your breath moving in, flowing down toward your stomach, flowing out again through your nose... Relax your stomach, being aware of the gentle movements up and down... Now bring yourself into awareness of a recent time when you were planning to eat... Experience it in the present... What are you planning to eat? What does the food look like?... How did you choose this food?... Notice the feelings you are having, the thoughts... Are you experiencing hunger?... How do you know?... What does that feel like?... How much hunger are you feeling?... Now imagine yourself beginning to eat as you usually do. What is your mouth doing?... How fast are you eating?... What are your thoughts?... Continue eating as you usually would... You have now eaten most of the food. How full are you?... How do you know?... What are your thoughts?... What are your feelings?... What do you want to do now?... What is your breath doing?... Now bring your attention back to your breath. Take a few slow, deeper relaxed breaths... Bring your awareness back to the feeling of sitting in your chair... Bring yourself back into the space of the room, and gently open your eyes.*

This example (which combines components of several guided meditations that would used separately in our actual treatment program) is illustrative of several of the domains mentioned above: physical experience, thoughts, and emotion. Another aspect of the meditation is important to note. Whereas this may appear to be a type of guided imagery or even hypnosis, care is taken to be non-directive as to the nature of the experience that may arise or to the interpretation of that experience. No meaning is imposed from without; rather the message is given repeatedly that wisdom can be found within, once the nature of the mind is simply observed, rather than reacted to, and once these patterns of reaction are disengaged. This is clearly consistent with the idea of an inherent wisdom found in many schools of Buddhism (Williams, 1989; Gethin, 1998). What is being taught are ways of looking for and listening to that wisdom.

Meditation as a Path to Wise Eating Across the Six Domains

Previously, meditation has not been systematically studied as an intervention for eating disorders, although it has been applied to treatment of many of the elements that that are characteristic of such problems, including anxiety (Kabat-Zinn et al., 1992), depression (Teasdale et al., 2000), addictions (Marlatt & Kristeller, 2000; Gelderloos et al., 1991), and obesity (Bauhofer, 1983). Dialectical Behavior Therapy, which draws on principles of mindfulness, has also been shown to be effective in treating binge eating disorder (Telch, Agras, & Linehan, 2001). The mechanisms posited to be involved in maintaining compulsive eating and binge eating disorder — an alternative means for relief from distress, personal empowerment/sense of perceived control, a heightened ability to resist impulsive urges, a deconditioning of habitual behavioral patterns — are all applicable to the compulsive aspects of BED, including elevated anxiety and dysphoria, distorted and reactive thinking patterns, and severely disturbed awareness and use of normal physiological cues related to food intake. Our treatment program appears to produce effects across each of the six domains of functioning; our more encompassing goal is to lead the individual to recognizing a deeper sense of wisdom with which to construct new experience.

Meditation and cognition. Meditation is arguably fundamentally a cognitive process, which can be defined as learning to shift and focus the attention at will onto an object of choice, whether on the body or in the mind, and to disengage usual conditioned reactivity or elaborative processing (Bishop et al., 2004). In mindfulness or insight meditation, the role of "bare attention" may be one of the most powerful aspects of meditation practice for individuals whose conscious mind is habitually caught up in thoughts and reactions to those thoughts. The mind is designed to construct meaning out of experience and that constructed meaning is encapsulated by conscious thoughts; Buddhist psychology acknowledged the degree to which conditioned desires distort perception. One of the initial effects of meditation is acute awareness of the "monkey mind," the continuous jumping of the thought from one point to another; this is one of the metaphors often brought into contemporary usage from the classical texts (Bodhi, 2000). Compulsions and obsessions, such as occur in eating disorders, are often powerfully directed by such thoughts, which the individual experiences as both uncontrollable and as an inherent aspect of self. Experiencing that these thoughts are "just" thoughts — that they can be separated from the reactions they normally trigger; that they need not be responded to — can be extremely powerful in returning a sense of control to the individual. In his work with depression, Teasdale and colleagues (1999, 2000, 2002) suggest a model in which mindfulness meditation allows the individual to interrupt cascades of negative thinking that otherwise contribute to psychobiological disregulation and relapse into major depression. In our treatment program, we begin to train the skills of mindfulness immediately, both in relation to eating, first with the raisin meditation and then with more complex eating experiences, that interrupts the cascades of reactions around eating, while providing training and experience in general breathing awareness mindfulness meditation. We also introduce the concept that thoughts are just thoughts and that one can cultivate control of the process and movement of thoughts as one develops control over attention. One of our patients offered a contemporary metaphor. She regularly used a local indoor shopping mall for walking exercise. When she was mall walking, she might notice new displays in store windows, but she kept herself from stopping or going into the store, and continued her walking. She noted that this was like mindfulness meditation; she could be aware of intrusive thoughts, but she didn't need to pursue or react to them. After only a few weeks of practice, participants in the MB-EAT program report increased awareness of habitual patterns of reacting to triggers for overeating and are able to experience an increasing ability to sustain moments of detached observation, realizing that they do not need to follow every thought or urge that arises.

Meditation and physical response. In the physical realm, food and eating, in contrast to other addictions, are necessary to basic survival and life. The body contains numerous natural feedback signals for hunger and satiety for initiating and terminating eating, from the mouth to the gut. These signals are sensitive to blood sugar levels (you will salivate more to a food if you haven't eaten for a while), levels of fat deposits (individuals who are starving will almost always over-eat), and hormonal feedback from individual cells of the muscles, fatty tissue and the liver. At the same time, these signals are highly conditionable and elastic, allowing for overload and flexibility to a degree that other physiological systems, such as our need for sleep or water, do not have. While most of us ignore or override our hunger and satiation signals on occasion, individuals with eating disorders, whether binge eating, bulimia or anorexia, appear to be particularly disengaged from this physiological feedback (Hetherington & Rolls, 1988; Hadigan et al., 1992). Meditation may therefore be particularly well suited to treating such problems. Unlike other compulsive behaviors in which abstinence is possible (such as smoking, drugs or alcohol), abstinence is not a possibility. Moderation and flexibility must be learned, and mindfulness meditation techniques may be particularly valuable for reconnecting the mind and the body and increasing awareness of some of the physiological processes going on in our bodies. Biofeedback operates under the principle of self-regulation (Schwartz, 1975, 1979) which posits that physiological functioning can be re-regulated simply by heightening awareness of the appropriate physiological signals. Meditation has been shown to be as effective or more effective in promoting control of even basic autonomic physiological systems such as heart rate (Cuthbert, 1981), and has been well documented to lower blood pressure and promote a sense of relaxation by disengaging the hyper-reactivity (fight or flight response) that accompanies anxious reactions (Benson, 1975; Schneider et al., 1995). Individuals in the MB-EAT program often express surprise at how much more sensitive they become to the physical experiences that signal hunger in contrast to emotional experiences, and to experiences of satiety at moderate levels, both in regard to the taste of food and to feelings of fullness.

Meditation and emotion. Meditation was popularized as a stress management tool in the US in the 1960s and 1970s, first by the introduction of Transcendental Meditation (TM) by the Maharishi Mahesh Yogi (1966) and then by Benson (1975) through his more secularized version of TM which he labeled the "relaxation response." Literature reviews (DelMonte, 1987) and meta-analyses (Eppley et al., 1989) have supported the value of meditation in decreasing both state and trait anxiety in the general population. Research by Kabat-Zinn and associates (1992) was one the first to establish the effectiveness of an 8-week mindfulness meditation program in significantly lowering the anxiety, panic symptoms, and level of dysphoria of individuals with documented anxiety disorders, effects that remained after three years of follow-up (Miller et al., 1995). Teasdale and others (2000, 2003) recently completed a randomized clinical trial using mindfulness meditation that substantially reduced relapse in individuals diagnosed with chronic depression. In the case of eating disorders, meditation may provide a particularly powerful way of re-regulating the emotional value of eating. We take a "middle way," in contrast to the many approaches to dieting and weight control that explicitly or implicitly convey the message that eating in response to emotional needs is inappropriate. This is linked to a common misperception that only individuals with eating problems eat in response to stress or for other emotional reasons. In fact, for most individuals, and in virtually all cultures, food is integrally linked to meeting emotional and non-nutritive needs (Rozin et al., 1999; Kristeller & Rodin, 1989). Food is used for celebration and for comfort. Our preference for sweet and high fat foods is biologically and genetically based, then shaped by our associations between feeding and nurturing as infants and children, and further determined by repeated exposure and cultural patterns. As our concern about weight and dieting increases, our emotional relationship to food may take on a love-hate dimension, with food coming to represent uncontrollable and overwhelming urges. The Buddha linked overeating to other sensual indulgences (*Majjhima Nikaya XVI* 11). Some of this emotional conflict is driven by investing in excessively stringent and inappropriate "rules" of food intake (i.e., fad diets) or extreme restriction that has little relationship to actual needs for food as an appropriate source of satisfaction. Diets and nutritional programs generally provide little or no guidance for how to manage emotionally linked eating. Mindfulness meditation practice appears to provide a way to bring this pendulum back into balance. Emotional associations to food are powerfully conditioned, and meditation may allow for a gentler and more effective disengagement from dysfunctional conditioning than simply taking on a new set of externally constructed and imposed rules. Thus, meditation goes beyond simple relaxation and stress relief to transform our relationship to our emotional life itself and to the emotions associated with eating. At the end of treatment, participants in our MB-EAT program are in general less depressed and less anxious. Yet they also note that they are drawing more pleasure and satisfaction from what they are eating, at the same time being able to better resist indulgences that their "wiser" mind recognizes as harmful or excessive. They seem to have been able to separate emotional "wanting" of food from how much they like food, a distinction that actually appears to have different underlying neurophysiological processes involved (Berridge, 2004). One could interpret this as being more in the moment with the actual experience of eating, rather than engaged in the associated attachments and desires.

Meditation and behavior. What is "right" action? How does meditation practice promote this? Participants in our treatment programs (Kristeller & Hallett, 1999; Kristeller et al., 2004) report profound differences between their ability to change their eating patterns through using mindfulness techniques in contrast to using a prescribed "diet." First, they find that their meditation practice allows them to simply observe their own behavior in more helpful ways, as illustrated by something as simple as paying attention to eating a raisin. They are able to be in the moment with their eating rather than being caught up in the constructed associations, both positive and negative, that food and eating engender. By learning to disengage from emotional and cognitive compulsions, they can see eating as just eating, and food as just food. Therefore, they can experience an urge to binge without having to act on it. Marlatt and Kristeller (1999) refer to this as "surfing the urge." Not only does the experience change, but behavior follows. About half way through the program, the homework assignment is to have a meal at an all-you-can-eat buffet. Going to such a buffet is a frequent indulgence for many binge eaters; it is a socially acceptable way to overeat, yet all of our program participants recognize it as problematic, and no diet program ever recommends doing this. So people react with surprise and often anxiety at being challenged to do so. Yet they go — and return with a greater sense of control that comes from a new sense of inner wisdom. They find they can use their new skills of mindfulness and awareness to make choices that are satisfying but not excessive. This greater sense of inner control also transfers to more ordinary triggers for binging. Both of our studies to date (Kristeller & Hallett, 1999; Kristeller et al., 2004) show a decrease in frequency of binge eating from more than every other day, to about once per week, and the size of binges substantially decreased.

Improved self-concept and relation to others. A somewhat more elusive effect of mindfulness meditation is to improve self-concept and self-acceptance, areas that are often disturbed in individuals with compulsive eating problems. Bono (1984) found that a group of novice TM meditators appreciably improved their self-concept in relation to a group that simply sat and relaxed for the same length of time. A more recent study (Easterlin & Cardena, 1998) found that more experienced meditators reported a higher sense of "acceptance" when under stress than did less experienced meditators. Kornfield (1993) has written eloquently of meditation as a path to loving kindness and to opening the heart. Carson and his colleagues (2004) found that a loving kindness meditation program improved relationships between married couples, even when the quality of the relationship was already high. Several elements of our program are designed to contribute to the process of engaging relationship to self in a healthier way. As the group progresses, meditation is focused less on food per se, and more on the types of cognitions and emotions surrounding eating out of control. Many of these involve becoming aware of self-hatred and disgust, particularly in relation to their bodies, but also more generally. Individuals become detached from their craving of food and compulsive eating because they recognize their compulsive thoughts about eating as ephemeral, rather than as parts of "self." The experience of the group meal, eaten partly in silence, common to contemplative traditions, is also compelling for many of our participants. They both appreciate the social pressure to overeat and the distraction that social conversation contributes, but also gain an appreciation for the social engagement and the challenge to maintaining mindful eating when surrounded by friends or family. In keeping with contemporary applications of Buddhist teachings to therapeutic usage (i.e., Kornfield, 1993; Carson, 2004), meditation also appears to promote the ability to re-engage parts of the self that are more loving and appreciative of others, once negative preoccupations with self have been disengaged (Kristeller & Johnson, 2005). For example, group members often express powerful feelings of connectedness to each other, a connection that is not as evident in our control treatment groups (who use an educationally oriented approach but have about as much group discussion and sharing).

Meditation and spiritual growth. Although meditation practice is traditionally identified with spiritual and religious goals, virtually all of the contemporary empirical research on meditation, at least in the U.S., has attempted to secularize meditation practice and document effects across other areas of functioning as noted above. However, attention to spirituality as an appropriate and meaningful focus for therapeutic engagement has been growing rapidly, both in general and in relation to meditative practice (Sperry, 2001; Marlatt & Kristeller, 1999). Measures of spiritual well-being that can be used outside of particular religious belief systems are being developed (e.g., Peterman et al., 2002); use of these is beginning to document increases in spiritual growth in response to meditation practice even without an explicit focus on this aspect of experience. A recent randomized study (Shapiro et al, 1998) with medical and premedical students showed substantial and consistent changes across all measures of well-being, including increased spirituality, in those participating in a 7-week mindfulness meditation program. Similar effects have been documented with medical populations (Kristeller et al., unpublished). In the final session of the MB-EAT program, we explicitly call on participants to identify or access what they have experienced as a sense of spiritual or religious strength. This often is identified as a higher — or deeper — connection to a power that enables disengagement from the conflicts related to food, which leads to wiser choices. Throughout the program there is no explicit teaching or indoctrination about spirituality. Rather, these new perceptions and awareness, which some participants themselves identify as spiritual, arise naturally in the course of their meditative explorations. In this way, and in keeping with some aspects of Buddhist teaching, the previously described effects of meditation (increased awareness of physiological cues, transformed relationship to habitual thoughts and feelings) may be seen as preparing the way for the development of spiritual wisdom in that an increased ability to suspend preoccupation with eating and dieting allows engagement of the spiritual domain.

The Experience of Practice

Traditionally, meditation was discussed in terms of two complementary goals: stillness (*Samatha*) and insight and mindfulness (*Vipassana*), which were usually understood to operate sequentially (Gethin, 1998, pp. 174-175). In our program, we introduce the experience of mindfulness immediately, but use the focus of the breath, body experiences, and the experience of eating as ways to cultivate stillness and one-pointedness. Almost immediately, our participants note the difficulty of quieting the mind and staying with the breath during the mindfulness sitting meditation, but they find it much easier to stay attentive to their experiences of eating. Therefore, the broader scope of their practice is inherently somewhat limited. Yet they also frequently comment on a growing ability to cultivate broader awareness, of being aware of greater insight into other areas of their life, and of being able to find a place of inner calmness. In the traditional practices, cultivating such an ability for detached awareness is assumed to take extended, committed periods of practice. However, much of the research on the therapeutic uses of meditation (Kabat-Zinn et al., 1992; Teasdale et al., 2002) suggests that valuable effects can be obtained within 8 weeks of practice; this is consistent with our experience.

In respect to the traditional basis of practice, we are careful to avoid all direct exploration or discussion of our program in terms of Buddhism or Buddhist principles (such as "no-self"). Virtually all of our group participants are Christian or Jewish in background, and most are actively involved in religious practice within these traditions. When we first introduce them to the concepts involved in the MB-EAT program, we do so in a private orientation session in which we inquire into any concerns they might have about learning or practicing meditation. We have found this to be particularly important in religiously conservative communities. We discuss meditation as a way of engaging the mind and we frame it as a psychological practice involved in finding "inner" wisdom. We also point out that most religious traditions, including Christianity and Judaism, have developed meditative-type practices because they are helpful in managing difficult or painful experiences and in finding sources of strength (Goleman, 1988; Gross & Muck, 2003). We are quite careful to express respect for whatever religious or spiritual tradition the participant may have. These approaches appear to reassure our participants and leave them open to engage with the practices required in the program.

The Cultivation of Wisdom

The concept of wisdom is increasingly being examined as a psychological construct (Sternberg, 1990, 1998; Boltes & Staubinger, 2000), but often in a more limited way than within early Buddhist psychology. From a psychological perspective and in keeping with the notion of inherent wisdom found in many schools of Buddhism (Williams, 1989; Gethin, 1998), we propose that wisdom is an emergent process that occurs when the habitual, generally self-protective reactions of the conditioned mind are suspended, allowing integration of more complex processing to occur. This can be seen as parallel to the traditional categories of stillness and insight. Stillness involves suspending the mind's habitual patterns; insight refers to the more complex, creative, and deeper levels of processing that emerge. This type of wisdom can therefore occur within any domain of functioning and need not entail intellectual processing, as is often implied in Western concepts of wisdom. Often, while meditating, the result of this process is experienced as a sense of knowing — a sense of realizing a true or wise perspective on a problem, or source of suffering, for oneself. The actual content or problem solved may not be profound (i.e., what to eat at a meal), but the solution is experienced as balanced and unconflicted. This is in keeping with the emphasis in Zen on elevating mundane and ordinary aspects of life to expressions of wise action such as occurs in the Japanese tea ceremony or flower arranging. To the extent that insight into how to create balance or solve a problem involves disengagement from habitual patterns and seeing the problem in a larger perspective, it is in continuity with the Buddhist concepts of insight, wisdom, and spiritual growth (Kornfield, 2000).

Craving often reflects movement toward an ephemeral source of satisfaction, which then quickly leads to distress once the initial pleasure is gone. In working with eating problems, we draw the distinction between appropriate — and balanced — use of food and the compulsive patterns that feel out of control. This focus on habitual attachments and the means of detaching from them is very important in the application of Buddhist teachings to psychotherapy and especially to the treatment of eating disorders. Individuals become detached from their craving of food and compulsive eating because they recognize their compulsive thoughts about eating as ephemeral, rather than as parts of self. In addition, Buddhism teaches that since we desire hedonic pleasure, security, power, affiliation and other such things, we see reality (including the reality of who we are) as more stable than it really is. Intending to end craving is a part of wisdom, because the state of detachment is the state of clear perception and knowing and wise acting. In order to perceive reality without the clouding effects of compulsive desire, the individual must be able to be aware of how the conditioned mind reacts and then, with purpose, disengage the reactive mind, producing a sense of stillness and clear awareness. Meditation practice is a powerful tool for cultivating this awareness and the ability to be non-reactive. In our experience wisdom, as we understand it, emerges from this still awareness. Therefore, stilling the mind allows the emergence of right action and right thought, resulting in balance rather than imbalance and distress, not only within what is considered spiritual experience, transcendence or enlightenment, but across all domains of one's experience. This result of meditative practice — being able to disengage from one's feelings and thoughts — has powerful psychotherapeutic effects.

In the traditional practices, cultivating an ability for detached awareness is generally assumed to take extended, committed periods of practice. Yet in our experience and that of others adapting meditation practice for therapeutic purposes, substantial and sustained effects can be evident within two months of practice. While such effects may not be as pervasive and profound as those experienced by more experienced practitioners, they are often strikingly powerful in regard to producing therapeutic effects. Contemporary psychotherapeutic research is finding that even beginning meditators, with only a few weeks practice, can begin to experience a detachment from conditioned associations and reactions (Kabat-Zinn, 1990; 1992; Teasdale et al., 2002; Kristeller & Hallett, 1999), and may even experience moments of inner stillness. In much of Buddhism, wisdom is not a set of concepts or a philosophical-religious doctrine. Wisdom, rather than coming from reading inspired books or listening to enlightened teachers, emerges as a result of practice. Wisdom is a process of transformation that puts the practitioner in a psychological and spiritual position to experience reality clearly and calmly. Much Buddhist thought suggests that as one clears away compulsive patterns of thinking and acting, wiser decisions are made. Our research (Kristeller & Hallett, 1999; Kristeller et al., 2004) on using meditation in the treatment of eating disorders illustrates this process. Rather than challenging compulsive eaters to change their behavior, we give them the tools to observe the self more gently, and more fully, particularly in regard to those situations that trigger mindless eating or that override natural signals to stop eating. The results of this treatment program are evidence for the notion of an inherent wisdom that emerges when compulsive thoughts or urges are mindfully observed, rather than being engaged with or reacted to.

Thus much Buddhist Psychology has a great deal in common with contemporary applied psychology. In this article and in our psychotherapeutic work we are drawing on those schools of Buddhism that suggest human beings posses an inherent wisdom that is hidden by our conditioned desires and cravings. Buddhist Psychology also posits that it is over-engagment with distorted views of self that leads to suffering. Through the practice of mindfulness and the other aspects of the 8-Fold Path, we can uncover that inherent wisdom that is our natural legacy. The claim that transformation comes through experiential insight, leading to changes in behavior, echoes the presuppositions found in many psychotherapeutic systems, including self-psychology (see Brazier, 1995; Epstein, 1995; Rubin, 1996) and cognitive behavioral approaches (Teasdale et al., 2000; Kwee & Ellis, 1998). The question at the interface of Buddhist teachings and clinical psychology is how the early Buddhist theory of mind and the system of practices might be applied to the treatment of specific disorders. MB-EAT is one example of this application. The multi-domain model of meditation presented in this chapter provides a way to understand psychologically some of the connections between the practice of meditation and the development of wisdom. If wisdom is understood as a process of discovering perspective and balance, rather than as a set of philosophical constructs, or as simply an intellectual attainment of a higher understanding, then it becomes possible to wisely and mindfully engage each of these psychological domains (cognitions, feelings, behavior, physiology, sense of self, and the spiritual). Wisdom is primarily a process, not a set of external concepts or rational perspectives. It involves, among other elements, the capacity to see clearly, face reality, and make more balanced decisions. Buddhist thought suggests that as one clears away compulsive patterns of thinking and acting, wiser decisions are made. The MB-EAT program illustrates this process. Rather than admonishing or challenging compulsive eaters to change their behavior or giving them specific diets to follow, we give them the tools to observe the self more gently, and more fully, particularly in regard to those situations that trigger mindless eating or that override natural signals to stop eating. The results of this treatment program are evidence for the notion of an inherent wisdom that emerges when compulsive thoughts or urges are mindfully observed, rather than being engaged with or reacted to.

Mindfulness meditation facilitates this wiser engagement with our psychological life by training us to approach our experiences and challenges within each of these domains from a more disengaged position, stilling the mind so a deeper and more balanced perspective can emerge. Mindfulness meditation is far more than a technique for achieving relaxation or countering stress; it can most substantially be considered a means to a deeper exploration of the mind and to discovering inherent wisdom.

---

1. The MB-EAT program was developed by JK, the first author; JJ, the second author, has consulted to the program and uses related approaches for treating compulsive eating problems in his private practice.

5

Beyond Mindfulness And Post-Traumatic Stress Disorder

Dennis Tirch & Richard Amodio

Over the course of the past few years, eastern psychological concepts and meditation practices have been integrated into Cognitive-Behavior Therapy (CBT) with increasing frequency. The practice of mindfulness, drawn from Buddhist meditation practices, has generated a strong current of interest, resulting in a great deal of recent research activity and consideration (Germer et al., 2005). As this discussion has gained in momentum, mindfulness has often been referred to as a specific technique, which can be used to treat particular symptoms while its psychological foundations have not been thoroughly discussed. This chapter describes the development and implementation of an "experientially-based' CBT for the treatment of Post-Traumatic Stress Disorder (PTSD). The CBT Center at the Bedford Veterans Affairs Medical Center offers a therapy group to Vietnam veterans. They are taught techniques and concepts drawn from Buddhist traditions. The authors did not seek to simply adapt current mindfulness-based methods to work with PTSD, but to review a wide variety of Buddhist and western psychological sources, reconsider the nature of the disorder and its treatment, to tailor the approach to the needs of specific individuals. A session-by-session description of the pilot group-protocol is explained, describing each technique and potential obstacles that clients may encounter in treatment. One case illustrates the progress and challenges a veteran encountered during the group.

The dialogue concerning the potential use of meditation in concert with western mental health treatment has been growing for over 30 years (Kwee, 1990). Since the mid to late 90s, eastern psychological concepts and meditation practices have been integrated into Cognitive-Behavior Therapy (CBT) with increasing frequency (Germer et al., 2005). This confluence of CBT methods and meditative disciplines has become such a strong force in the arena of evidence-based therapy that it has come to be indicated as a "third wave" (Hayes, 2004). Dialectical Behavioral Therapy (DBT) (Linehan, 1989), Acceptance and Commitment Therapy (ACT) (Hayes et al., 1999), Mindfulness-Based Stress Reduction (MBSR) (Kabat-Zinn, 1990), and Mindfulness-Based Cognitive Therapy (MBCT) (Segal et al., 2002) are currently the most widely practiced and researched applications of this new generation of treatments. Each of these methods emphasizes mindfulness, a practice containing an essence of Buddhist meditation, as a central element in the training.

Kabat-Zinn's (1990) definition of mindfulness is "paying attention in a particular way: on purpose, in the present moment, and non-judgmentally" (Segal et al., 2002, p. 121). In the discussion concerning these new generation therapies, mindfulness is often referred to as a specific technique that can be used to treat particular problems and symptoms, such as a difficulty tolerating uncomfortable emotions. As yet, the original foundations of mindfulness have not been considered in detail. Having awakening/enlightenment as the ultimate state, mindfulness and other Buddhist techniques aim far more than merely reducing psychological disorders. No doubt, clinical psychologists target secular aims based on scientific grounds even if inspired by Buddhist sources. Dimidjian and Linehan (2003, p. 167) suggested that "it is possible that relinking mindfulness with its spiritual roots may enhance clinical practice." Similarly, Hayes (2002, p. 105) asserted, "Combining these two great traditions, spirituality and science, promises a leap forward in our understanding of human suffering, but only if psychological scientists keep their eye on the development of a coherent and progressive discipline, not merely the acquisition of a few new clinical maneuvers." In exploring Buddhist source materials for tools to use in combination with CBT, reducing emotional suffering is the aim rather than enlightenment. Supernatural assumptions are in the pristine Buddhist teaching anathema.

Post-Traumatic Stress Disorder, (PTSD) has not yet been the target of an evidenced based method that combines CBT and Buddhist tenets. Several of the phenomena involved in PTSD, such as thought suppression (Ehlers & Clark, 2000), hyperarousal (Van der Kolk, 1996), and experiential avoidance (Follette et al., 2004) may be well suited to treat with mindfulness/acceptance-based interventions. Thus, a shift in clients' thinking and feeling may be accomplished resulting in the correction of the negative information processing typical for PTSD. In the summer of 2002, the CBT Center at the Bedford Veterans Affairs Medical Center started to offer a Buddhist-informed CBT training group to Vietnam-era "heavy combat" veterans. We developed a pilot protocol for this group that did not seek to simply adapt current mindfulness-based protocols to work with PTSD, but to review a range of Buddhist and western ideas, to consider the nature of the disorder and its treatment, and to tailor the approach to the specific needs of the population. The service, described as a Course in Well-Being, was offered as a part of a larger PTSD treatment program, which involved peer support groups, individual CBT sessions, additional psychodynamic processing, and CBT skills training. This chapter describes the central elements of this "experientially-based" CBT method and examines some foundations of the Buddhist teaching, which understanding may enhance treatment's effectiveness as exemplified by a group CBT for PTSD. A brief session-by-session description of the pilot group is provided, including a case illustration describing the progress and challenges one heavy combat veteran encountered during his participation in the group.

The PTSD and attentional training

According to Ehlers and Clark (2000, p. 320) clients develop ongoing PTSD only when they "process the traumatic event and/or its sequelae in a way that produces a sense of serious current threat." Several factors are hypothesized as being involved in this exaggerated expectation of present danger. Within this cognitive model, excessively negative appraisals of the event, of the symptoms arriving after the event, or of the clients themselves are viewed as maintaining the ongoing PTSD. Ehlers and Clark (2000) suggest that traumata fragment memories, such that these are poorly elaborated and improperly incorporated into an autobiographical memory base. One function of autobiographical memory is the organization of an appropriate retrieval route and the inhibition of spontaneous recollection on the basis of sensory triggers. Persons with PTSD are subject to highly distressing intrusive memories of their trauma through the spontaneous recollection and reliving of horrifying events. These are mostly triggered by sensory stimuli that cause a flood of misery.

PTSD clients employ maladaptive strategies in dealing with troubling intrusive thoughts by attempting to take conscious control over their symptoms. One chief strategy is thought suppression; it is the attempt to actively not think about horrendous events and to push away memories/ideas about these experiences. Ehlers and Clark (2000) suggest that thought suppression only serves to increase the frequency of intrusive thoughts; it can be viewed as a variant form of experiential avoidance. Hayes (1996) postulates that experiential avoidance is a central mechanism that contributes to suffering in psychological disorders. Thus, trauma survivors' attempts to escape from emotionally difficult memories by banishing anxiety provoking thoughts and running from their feelings backfire. Distress becomes exacerbated as such reactions actually increase the frequency of those mental events and support one's excessively negative appraisals. Addressing PTSD by an integrative — mindfulness and acceptance informed — CBT, Follette and others (2004) point at experiential avoidance as the key target for intervention. Van der Kolk and others (1996, p. 419) suggest a general approach to PTSD treatment: clients should be assisted in the "integration of the alien, the unacceptable, the terrifying, and the incomprehensible into their self-concepts." Compatible with this notion is the use of mindful, accepting awareness, whereby the client learns to sit with their pain rather than to flee in experiential avoidance. Applying meditation to trauma survivors, Urbanowski and Miller (1996, p. 170) contend that mindfulness trains PTSD patients in developing an "exploratory stance towards whatever mind-object presents itself in a given moment" and distinguish two types of training. The first, concentration meditation is largely associated with the Zen tradition. It involves the focusing of attention on and persistently redirecting attention to a single (inner) object with a "laser beam" quality. The second, mindfulness meditation, can be considered a "spotlight quality" of attention. Through this practice, the meditator learns to observe mental events merely as the contents of consciousness, and to approach these events from an open and accepting stance. Miller (1993) raises the concern that traumatized clients may find certain forms of meditation particularly distressing due to the possibility that vivid, possibly repressed or poorly remembered, material will surface during the practice. Thus, clinicians training trauma survivors to meditate should be prepared to address the potential of difficult material that may arise as they engage their thoughts, feelings, and memories through the meditative process. Accordingly, Germer (2005) admonishes clinicians working with PTSD patients that mindfulness training needs to be conducted carefully. He describes "attention regulation," a "wisdom skill," which should be a component of such training. This involves training PTSD clients in how to regulate the degree to which their attention is directed outward as opposed to inward, thereby addressing the central question, "Can the patient experience the pain without being overwhelmed?" (p. 171). A similar modulation of focus, intensity and direction of attention, is the central feature of the meditation training component of the Bedford course.

Continual awareness techniques

During the course, all meditative techniques are presented to the group as "awareness based exercises." The veterans are taught to view their attention as behaving along a "continuum." The primary operative variable in this continuum is the degree to which awareness is focused and controlled, or open and accepting. One end of the continuum involves an increasingly narrow focus of attention, greater concentration, and an active, containing awareness. This is the sort of awareness attained through concentration meditation. The other end of the continuum describes an increasingly wide focus of attention, a mindful, non-judgmental stance in the observation of the contents of consciousness, and a flowing, receptive attitude regarding internal stimuli. This awareness is aimed at in mindfulness. The continuous model of attention contends that awareness can be successfully cultivated and deployed along the length of the continuum in accordance with the individual need in a given situation. Thus, the clients and group facilitators discuss the range of meditative methods employed as "continual awareness techniques." The continuum from concentration to mindfulness can be thought of as a conscious way to choose to be with experience. As clients' experience is intense and more difficult to simply witness and feel, they can move their attention intentionally along the continuum. — for example, toward concentrated attention that progressively structures more by narrowing attention. This end of the continuum may even offer complete distraction from current distress and provide absorption in some other attentional focus. Thus, clients are instructed in intentional distraction to raise affect tolerance, such as holding onto an ice cube or running their thumb along the edge of a comb. These techniques of distress tolerance are adapted from Linehan's DBT. Intentional distraction is meant as an adaptive response, because it is a consciously chosen and not simply an automatic reaction. Hence, clients are trained in increasing their sense of self-control, a mechanism considered to be an essential therapeutic aspect of Zen (Shapiro, 1992). Moving toward the mindfulness end of the continuum, one simply witnesses and gradually allows feelings to be experienced fully. In the framework of CBT, this intends to release the arising conditioned patterning that eventually results in a weakening/uprooting of the unwanted conditioned responses. This (un)learning view is in accord with earlier observations that mindfulness is a form of prolonged exposure to uncomfortable sensations in the absence of terrible consequences leading to extinction of the emotional response to such experiences (e.g. Kabat-Zinn, 1982).

To disidentify with thoughts and thinking is a central skill that Buddhist meditation aims to develop. Clients are taught to mindfully notice thoughts as they arise and to simply observe them without evaluating. This creates "distance to thinking and enhances treating thoughts" contents as hypotheses. Clients are encouraged to discover this while working in the individual and group CBT sessions. They may choose whether or not such thoughts are rational and adaptive, and to subsequently retain or re-structure their thinking. By training themselves in accepting and making space for thoughts as they pass through awareness, they are actually remedying the disruption of thought suppression. Mindfulness and other Buddhist practices are a means to lessen attachment to the "self" that is considered to be an abstraction, a word and not the thing, thus an illusion. Disattachment results from a change in self-identifications and from an expansion of awareness that incorporates the interconnectedness of the referents of self: thinking-feeling-behaving. Ways of construing one's self are questioned; how one relates to the world is discussed. The Buddhist view is reflected in the teaching of the two realities and of empathic compassion.

Two realities. According to the Madhyamaka teaching of Nagarjuna (2nd century), reality can be seen from two perspectives. One is the conditioned representation of reality, subjectively constructed in each individual's mind. The second is the nature of things as they "are" devoid of perceptual processing and cognitive interpretation, which is neither objective nor subjective. While we may experience ourselves as separate beings with a consistent sense of self, Buddhist Psychology (BP) contends that this is an illusion (Price & Mou-Lam, 1990). From the Buddhist perspective of "dependent origination" and "karma" (intentional action) all phenomena arise as the result of the interplay of numerous cause-and-effect relationships. All things in the world are not only interrelated, but also impermanent; and always being in a state of change, they lack "inherent existence." In other words, "Upon examining the ultimate nature of reality, Buddhist philosophers have concluded that things lack inherent existence that is they do not have self-defining, self-evident characteristics. This is because if we search for the essence of matter in whatever object it may be, we discover that it is unfindable" (Dalai Lama et al., 1991, p. 23). In order to demystify this perspective, one might consider the assumptions of string theory in quantum physics, wherein matter, ultimately, can be reduced to energy and movement (Greene, 1999). Similarly, the "two realities" working hypothesis can be viewed through the neural network and neuroscientific paradigm, which explains all human phenomenology as arising from spreading activation across a vastly complex network of nodes (LeDoux, 2002; Tirch, 1993).

The "two realities" model has implications for understanding the concept of self. The self is an important construct, since a cohesive and well-integrated sense of self enables one to adapt and function well in the world. However, in BP, there is no referential entity that is enduring, unchanging, or otherwise substantial that corresponds to our experience of self. The sense of solidity or continuity of having a subjective self is due to factors such as familiarity, frequency, and patterning of cognitive and affective processes with which we — unaware and unawakened — erroneously identify. Self is thus an illusion. Mindfulness serves the pursuit to gain a pervasive insight (intuitive realization) in the inherent insubstantiality of all phenomena by seeing "things as they are" (as impermanent momentary manifestations that arise and pass away). The two perspectives of Buddhist and western psychology regarding the self can be reconciled if we understand: (1) the psychological self to be a necessary aspect of daily conventional and functional existence, while (2) the ultimate nature of self is an interdependent and synergetic flux of sensing, imaging, thinking, emoting, and behaving, which is, because of its impermanence, empty of self. On this ultimate level we are not a self, but a not-self. Any attempt to grasp the constantly changing self is doomed to fail. Buddhist meditation is simply a method of retraining perceptual habits by cultivating selective attention and an accepting awareness.

Compassion. A Buddhist view of the self stresses an interdependent nature of existence, suggesting that all phenomena are inextricably interwoven. It asserts that the contemplative experience of this great sense of connection will eventually result in an arising an altruistic aspiration to work towards the alleviation of suffering for all beings. This arising motivational imperative, known as *bodhicitta* (awakened heart) (Chödrön, 2003), is a major foundation of Buddhist practice. Buddhist techniques to develop compassion have been employed and refined for more than 2500 years, while only recently psychology and neuroscience have involved the study and practice of developing compassion. Particular changes in cortical activity have been noted in persons who have meditated upon compassion for many years (Goleman, 2003). These changes involve relatively greater rates of activation in the left cortical areas that involve the regulation of the amygdala. It happened that innovative studies have discovered amygdala activation in high levels of anxiety and in PTSD (LeDoux, 1996). Thus, experienced meditators may be training themselves in the development of a particular skill set that allows them to abide in a state of active compassion, while reducing their experience of destructive emotions and regulating brain structures.

Recently, Wang (2005) describes a compassion-oriented sense of self as a "species-preservative" perspective as opposed to that of a "self-preservative" system. In a thorough examination of the neuroscientific underpinnings of compassion, she explains compassion as a unique human phenomenon, which is a "complex social behavior that appears to emerge from the development of an enlarged neocortex and from the critical role of caretaking in the young, especially by the mother" (p. 78). Such formulation resonates with the Vajrayana visualization on developing compassion that all beings are one's mother. Drawing on Buddhist views Gilbert (2005) developed a specific training to access "compassionate mind" in psychotherapy.

Continual awareness in practice

Buddhist meditation comprises a wealth of different practices, ranging from simply sitting to complicated visualizations and esthetic practices such as flower arranging or physical exercises such as martial arts and archery. In fact any cognitive-behavioral-emotional activity can become a meditation. During the course we choose to present basic awareness practices that can be thought of as roughly representing particular points along the continuum of awareness. These form the basis of subsequently developed individualized meditations and coping strategies for each of the veterans. The six central continual awareness techniques are the following.

Walking meditation. This activity took place outdoors on the wooded VA grounds. Veterans are instructed to simply bring attention to their body moving through space, walking at a normal and relaxed pace. They are then sequentially asked to bring attention to the experience and movement of various body parts: legs, arms, torso, and head. Afterwards, as a means of facilitating and maintaining a relatively narrow focus upon the body, they are told to particularly notice the experience in/movement of each leg as they walk. Other instructions involve having the eyes slowly scan the environment, focusing upon approaching objects, such as trees along the path, and feeling the body weight as experienced through the foot contacting the ground.

Sensory awareness. In this exercise, veterans were seated in chairs as they practice bringing attention to the physical sensations in various body parts. Eyes are open and generally focused upon the area of the body being addressed. The instruction is to take several relaxed full breaths into the abdomen and feel the contact of the body with the physical environment, for example buttocks and back pressing against the seat and back of the chair, forearms resting on the chair arms, and feet resting flat on the floor. Next, they press and release the thumb of one hand into the palm of the other, moving the pressing thumb across the palm and each finger. While doing the movement, they simply notice the sensations in the hand being massaged. Then they rest their hands back in the lap or on the arms of the chair as they bring attention to both hands simultaneously, noting any differences in sensations between the hands. The same instructions are then repeated with regard to massaging the other hand. This same protocol involving the massaging and noting of sensation was then applied to each forearm (wrist to elbow) and then to each bicep (elbow to shoulder). Once familiar with the basic sensory awareness practice, we incorporate awareness of breathing into the exercise. Specifically, after massaging each body part and still with arms resting on the lap or on the arms of the chair, they focus attention on the sensations in the hand, forearm, or biceps, as well as on experiencing abdominal breathing. They allow their attention to encompass the expansion and contraction in the abdomen. The exercise is to learn that awareness can be either broadened to include a large scope of experience or narrowed to a limited field of attention.

Standing meditation. A variation on a martial arts exercise, this practice focuses on the breath while coordination the movement of the arms with each inhalation and exhalation. It begins by standing with the feet shoulder width apart (the knees relaxedly bent, not locked), feeling the feet firmly planted on the ground, and bringing attention to a small point 2-3 inches below the navel. We suggest that veterans initially place a hand on this point below the navel to facilitate their focus on this portion of the abdomen, while witnessing each inhalation and exhalation; we also suggest the image of the feet as being deeply rooted down into the ground. After several minutes, they are shown a simple movement of the arms that involves reaching the hands horizontally outward in front of the chest (palms facing away from the chest) on the exhalation and then drawing the hands back to the chest (palms facing downward) on the inhalation. The hands remain close to each other throughout the cycle of the movement, while the elbows bend outward as the hands come close to the chest and straighten as the hands reach outward. Breathing is slow and deep, both on the inhalation and exhalation, which necessarily keeps the coordinated arm movements somewhat slow. Eyes are open with a relaxed "straight ahead" gaze, not focusing on anything in particular. The arms are moved in a relaxed and effortless manner, with as little muscular tension as necessary; similarly the torso is relaxed. The legs are actively engaged as described.

Having the lower half of the body actively engaged while simultaneously keeping the upper body light and relaxed, an aspect of Tai Chi Chuan, may be particularly useful for trauma survivors. We speculate that the grounding and strength experienced in the lower body facilitate the experience of safety and control. This may then serve as a foundation to focus attention toward as well as to more easily relax into other aspects of experience: the witnessing of the breath and the slow effortless movement of the arms. Another relevant aspect, probably particularly applicable to the veterans is that the tendency toward hypervigilance and hyperarousal can be channeled into the active engagement of the lower body. The conscious intention to actively engage the lower body may serve to temporarily replace the chronic generalized and diffuse hypervigilance, hence allowing them to shift from a tense hyperarousal to an alert yet comparatively relaxed attention in the present moment. If trauma-related hypervigilance, at least in part, is an attempt at remaining safe (though conditioned from the past and chronically superimposed upon the present moment), it may be useful for them to learn another means to both establish a sense of safety (particularly experientially in the body) and to remain relaxedly alert in the present moment.

Sitting meditation. In this exercise, veterans learn to bring attention to the experience of breathing, emphasizing focus at a contact point upon the outer abdomen. The exercise begins with sitting comfortably upright in the chair, feet flat on the ground, and arms resting by the sides or on the chairs arms. Attention is directed to the body's position. We encourage an upright yet relaxed posture that would minimize muscular tension or stress during the sitting. Eyes are open and relaxedly gazing either straight ahead or comfortably downward to the floor. They then place one hand on the abdomen, 2-3 inches below the navel. They then begin abdominal breathing by dropping the breath into the abdomen, allowing the inhalation to be naturally full without forcing it, resulting in a slow relaxed exhalation. The hand on the abdomen is a focus point as they are instructed to place attention at the interface of the hand and the abdomen while experiencing expansions and contractions of the breath. After several minutes of abdominal breathing, they relax the breath and allow it to return to normal while keeping attention on the interface of the hand and abdomen. The rest of the exercise involves having them rest their attention on the focal point at the abdomen while observing expansions and contractions of normal breathing, and instructing them to return attention to the focal point whenever they realized being distracted. We attempt to normalize the arising of a whole range of potentially distracting phenomena (such as thoughts, sounds, other sensations, emotions, etc.), repeatedly suggesting that the nature of the mind tends to be busy and distractible. We encourage them to simply return attention to the breath rather than attempting to change or stop thinking or suppress distractions. Throughout, we remind them to allow the full range of potential distractions in the body-mind to exist while keeping the attention on the breath.

Making space meditation. This brings awareness to the experience of breathing, but with a field of attention that is broader than in the sitting meditation. The exercise starts exactly in the same manner as the previous one. Veterans establish a comfortable upright seated position, place a hand 2-3 inches below the navel, and begin abdominal breathing as described above. After several minutes, they are instructed to remove the hand from the abdomen and allow the breathing to return to normal. They are told to allow attention to rest on the whole abdomen (from the bottom of the rib cage to the base of the pelvis), while observing the cycles of inhalation and exhalation. In contrast to the sitting meditation with a relatively narrow focus of attention upon the interface of the hand and lower abdomen, in this exercise they are instructed to witness the breathing experience throughout the abdomen. Specifically, they are told to bring attention to the salient sensations related to each inhalation and exhalation in the abdomen. Typically, they attend to the general experience of the abdomen expanding and contracting, like a beach ball being inflated and deflated. In addition to this general instruction, they are told to simply allow or "make space" for any other sensations of which they might be aware within the abdomen. These sensations can be experienced as pleasant, unpleasant, or neutral, but in any case the instruction is to simply allow the sensation to be present, witnessing both the particular sensation as well as the abdominal experience of breathing. Thus, they are instructed to maintain, whenever relevant, a dual attentional focus encompassing the ongoing breathing experience and any other particular abdominal sensation. As in the previous meditation, they are to simply return attention to the abdomen whenever realizing distraction. Again, they are encouraged to simply shift attention back to the abdomen rather than trying to push away or change the source of distraction.

Loving kindness meditation. This contemplative awareness technique has its origins in the Theravada tradition from some 2500 years ago. As described by Kornfield (1993) this meditation consists of sitting in a comfortable, meditative posture, and inwardly reciting phrases such as: "May I be filled with loving kindness, may I be well, may I be at peace" (p. 20). While affirming, meditators visualize themselves as a gentle and innocent child, surrounded by love and compassion. Thus, the cultivation of compassion begins with directing this positive affect towards oneself. Given the overly negative self-evaluations that PTSD veterans present, this self-directed loving-kindness seems to be an appropriate training to access their "compassionate mind."

The above six meditations along the awareness continuum are described in the manner in which we teach them. However, each of these practices can be significantly modified and tailored to optimally address therapeutic objectives and personal inclinations. In actuality, veterans are encouraged to experiment with these techniques outside of the group and report their experiences. Several of these variations are presented in the following case example.

Case example

The participation of one of the heavy-combat veterans and his responses to the course are illustrated below. A session-by-session description of the group is alternated with material relating to the case example (in italics) whose I.D. is made anonymous.

Christopher, a 51 year divorced Caucasian, had been exposed to multiple traumatic events during his tours of duty in Vietnam in the late 60s. Frequently involved in heavy combat, he had repeatedly witnessed the violent deaths of his fellow soldiers and had faced his own potential death many times. He developed PTSD soon after his return, over 30 years ago. Nightmares, fear of crowds, flashbacks, and intrusive thoughts about the trauma he endured were prominent among his symptoms. These caused him extreme distress. He had tried desperately to avoid thinking about, or remembering Vietnam, for decades. Over the years, he had become dependent upon heroin, alcohol, and other drugs, as he attempted to avoid his memories, and self-medicate. The cost of his addictions was grave. Christopher had lost many jobs, become estranged from his ex-wife and children, and had lived on the streets at times. He did not seek out any treatment for 25 years following his military service. Although he was aware that he could receive psychiatric services through the veterans affairs system, his distrust of the government and his feelings of humiliation regarding his symptoms prevented him from connecting to services. When he presented to participate in the Course in Well-Being for Trauma Survivors, he had been clean and sober for 5 years and had been in long-term supportive group psychotherapy for PTSD for 2 years. Christopher was living in a working class neighborhood and earned a modest living working as a graphic designer for internet-based companies.

Session-by-session group description

Session 1. During the first session facilitators presented an orientation to the concept of meditation techniques and emphasized the importance of committed practice as homework exercises. Next, the group leader introduced a number of brief, gentle stretching exercises derived from Tai Chi and Chi Kung. These exercises prepare for the bodily experience of prolonged sitting. Subsequently, the participants took part in the first meditation exercise, a five-minute concentration on the breath, presented as the "sitting meditation — outer abdomen" exercise described earlier. Veterans were generally surprised by the relaxing potential of such simple technique. A good portion of the first session was spent in reviewing the two truths and in practicing a perspective akin to what Linehan (1993) describes as dialectical reasoning. In this way, they can work to recognize the importance of a "relative perspective," while acknowledging the possibility of a broad sense of self and accepting the limitations of their own present contextual understanding.

After the initial instruction and brief sitting meditation, Christopher reported feeling relaxed and asked many questions, which the group facilitators addressed in turn. He expressed concern about the possibility of falling asleep during a meditation and then having a nightmare. The facilitators emphasized that the aim of the practice is the cultivation of relaxed alertness, rather than semi-conscious drifting of attention or sleep. It was explained that there is no end in mind in this practice and, indeed, that this is a practice of "being" rather than "doing." This meaning was readily absorbed by Christopher and his fellow group members. Although skeptical, he reported he was encouraged by the notion that some of his beliefs and painful thoughts are just thoughts and beliefs, not an absolute reality.

Session 2. The second session began with a ten-minute practice of the sitting meditation presented last week and a review of the homework. They were encouraged to report the range of experiences they had and to also discuss obstacles and challenges faced in the practice. Then, the facilitators discussed wellness (based upon the Buddhist idea of compassion and a sense of self that is broader than ego identifications) and disattachment (to disidentify from conditioned and limited perspectives alleviates suffering). In an open discussion members reflected that suffering may be related to the degree to which someone is not able to accept reality on its own terms. They considered how different areas of their lives might be changed for the better, if they adopt an attitude of acceptance. These domains of wellness discussed include physical, mental, emotional, perceptual, and "spiritual" (loving kindness / compassion) domains. At this session's end, facilitators guided the participants through the sensory awareness exercise that attends bodily sensations (ca. 15 minutes).

> *Christopher reported that he had found it difficult to sit alone for even the five-minute meditation exercise during the past week. He noted that turning his attention inward, on two occasions, brought him into contact with highly disturbing memories and ideation concerning past traumatic events, which he had tried very hard in the past to forget. He was concerned that these techniques might be too much for him. Nevertheless, on one of these occasions he was able to stay with his experience and view it from the observational stance, resulting in anxiety and fear gradually subsiding. At the outset of the session, he reported he felt better doing the meditation in the group's presence. He views his fellow veterans as brothers and that their presence in the room is soothing.*

Session 3. The group again began with a review of the homework; experiences, and obstacles encountered during daily practice. The sensory awareness exercise was again presented, however, now attention is expanded to include a dual focus on the awareness of breathing and of body sensations. In the discussion, they were asked to consider emotions they find either constructive or destructive. This led to an open exchange about core beliefs and judgments about their own emotions. Then they came to talk about traditional views of manliness and their own beliefs about emotions. Many shared the belief that emotions are a sign of weakness; that is why they sought to rid themselves of emotions through distraction, substance abuse, or isolation. Several saw aggression as the only acceptable emotional mode for a male. Subsequently, mindfulness was introduced, which includes the metaphorical instruction of making space. They were also trained in labeling and observing affective and cognitive phenomena, and in returning to a state of even hovering attention. Then, the idea was introduced that awareness can be rated on a continuum of attention, ranging from focused concentration to an open/accepting mindfulness. A 20 minute meditation was presented, which began with concentration on the breath and focusing attention on the outer abdomen. About 10 minutes into the exercise, the facilitators transitioned to the making space meditation that expands attention on the breath and the entire abdomen, consequently incorporating a wider field of experience.

> *Christopher reported dedicated and regimented compliance with the homework assignments: the sensory awareness and the concentration sitting meditation (outer abdomen). He was better able to tolerate the anxiety encountered during the sitting, reporting that that seems lessened this week. Moreover, he had come to realize having often experienced periods of intense emotion/anxiety during his daily life, which he had learned to suppress by engaging in emotional avoidance such as looking at internet pornography or "losing himself" building web pages. As he became more aware of this tendency and instead allows himself to stay with these experiences, he tended to become less upset with the experiences and to be less judgmental of himself.*

Session 4. Veterans returned to the group with many observations regarding the implementation of their meditative practices. The facilitators again presented last week's exercise, which begins with concentration and then shifts to mindfulness by embodying making space. After a brief review of the making space instructions, the facilitators used the next 10 minutes for a period of silent meditation. The remainder of the group material focused on cultivating compassion. Everyone was then encouraged to recall experiences where they had received or given unconditional love and acceptance. Each member, in turn, contributed some recollection of the power and poignancy of the experience. This was extended to a discussion regarding the possibility of intentionally experienceing compassion for oneself. The group then took part in the guided loving kindness meditation described earlier.

> *Christopher reported that he found the concentration focus more comfortable than the more mindfulness component of the meditation, stating that it is less distressing to focus concentration more narrowly on his breath sensations than to adopt a more open/receiving attitude towards experience. Concentration meditation reminds him of the stillness and precisely directed attention that he employed while sitting in the jungle as a sniper. He became tearful with remorse upon remembering the violent nature of the task involved in sniping, but was able to allow this emotionality and to continue discussing his appreciation of the quiet stillness experienced during the concentration. Compassion seemed to imply weakness or femininity to him at first (as it did for many veterans). Beyond this concern, there is so much guilt and shame that it seemed impossible to direct loving kindness to oneself. After actively engaging in the exercise in accessing a compassionate mind, Christopher was struck by how pleasant and relaxing it was to visualize himself as the source and recipient of unconditional love and acceptance.*

Session 5. The veterans focused on acceptance and overcoming guilt and negative self-talk through the use of cognitive-behavioral thought challenging techniques. They observed negative automatic thoughts arising during states of intense emotion and learned to challenge them together using cognitive therapy techniques. However, the emphasis in challenging was upon: decentering, making space for their emotional response, identification with an observing self, and self-validation. Group facilitators then proceeded to instruct them in a visualization practice designed to facilitate self-forgiveness and accessing a compassionate mind. This technique is based on *Sange-Mon*, a Japanese Tendai Buddhist practice (Hayes, 1992). During the exercise, participants enter a basic meditative state and visualize the previous day, particularly a happening they would like to have handled differently. They are then encouraged to visualize making the preferable choice and behaving accordingly, and to visualize the outcome of the changed behavior, allowing themselves to consider a potential positive result. Subsequently, they visualize receiving compassion, forgiveness, and unconditional acceptance. The session concluded with the standing meditation, practiced for 15 minutes.

> *This week had been a bad for Christopher. Problems negotiating visitation of his teenage children with his ex-wife and arguments with his parents, had led him to abandon practice for a few days. Furthermore, it was very difficult to practice the meditation on loving kindness, owing to remorse for past substance abuse, failure in marriage, and survivor guilt associated with heavy combat trauma. The Sange-Mon exercise in session 5 was helpful, but he could not bring himself to forgive, only to accept or deal with past negative behaviors. Group members' feedback to Christopher was that even this represented progress.*

Session 6. The session began with a review of observations concerning the weekly practice. The facilitators made a distinction at this point between observation, description, and judgment. The veterans were encouraged to report observations, but to refrain from making judgments/evaluations regarding their experience. This, understandably, proved difficult, but provided insight into the bare attention involved in mindfulness. After an initial 15 minute practice of the standing meditation, emphasizing the experience of grounding their awareness in their body, they were guided through a group imaginal exposure to one manageable traumatic memory, during which they used visualization similar to the Sange-Mon procedure to change the way in which they had construed the situation, and to visualize an alternative outcome. Excessively negative appraisals of the self and the situation, as well as lack of meaning and disempowerment, were changed in the visualization in order to imbue the situation with a sense of significance and a broader perspective. A brief discussion of the emotional experiences evoked by the visualization was conducted, immediately followed by instruction and practice of the previously described normal walking meditation exercise. The veterans responded particularly positively to the opportunity to walk in nature around the lovely wooded grounds of the veterans' hospital campus.

> *Christopher reported having gotten a lot out of the walking meditation. He told the group that he was beginning to understand that meditation was not just an exercise, but an approach to living and being alive in the present. He speculated that someone could be meditating "while they were working on the docks or scaling a fish." He told the group that while he engaged in the walking, he had begun to experience some images of traumatic experiences. He reported that he then employed a narrow concentrated focus upon a tree, particularly focusing on the green quality of the leaves. As he focused his attention towards observing the color of the tree, he also engaged in abdominal breathing in an attempt to effectively cope with agitation and anger that was suddenly triggered. He reported that his activity allowed him to get the necessary "distance" from the distressing emotions, gradually returning to his baseline level of arousal. He reported that the emotion triggered was particularly charged and hence his strategy seemed to allow him an optimal distance from his experience, without engaging in active thought suppression or experiential avoidance. With regard to the imaginal exposure to the trauma, Christopher reported that the focus on body sensations, breath, and the experience of being grounded in his body were useful in helping him sit through the experience. He noted that during past traumatic re-experiencing episodes, he often felt swept away by the content of his thoughts and the intensity of his emotions. Having a more tangible focus on his body, particularly the experience of being rooted and grounded, provided him with a more safe and secure foundation from which to approach the trauma. Consequently, he also reported that while uncomfortable during the exercise, he sensed himself as more in control than other times in his life when traumatic re-experiencing occurred.*

Session 7. This group began with a review of the homework in imaginal exposure to traumatic material; challenges and progress were discussed. Veterans reported some surprise at the manner in which their appraisals and understanding of a situation had changed through the exercise. This session's theme was impermanence and not independent origination; more simply put the group discussed how all things are ultimately interconnected and that all apparently separate phenomena ultimately come to an end. Although this may seem overly heady at first, most of the veterans readily engaged in a discussion of these ideas. Impermanence was particularly interesting to several veterans, who are encouraged by the idea that they had not been given a life sentence of PTSD. Also core beliefs and schemas regarding oneself, the future, and the world were reviewed. They then engaged in a 20 minute making space meditation; however, they could return attention to the outer abdomen at any time they needed a more concentrated/containing focus.

During this session, Christopher reported that although he was still much more comfortable with concentrated awareness, he had been experimenting with opening awareness to encompass a wider range of somatic phenomena in the torso. He seemed to have deepened his understanding that one can modulate the focus of attention to respond to arising experience at best. Yet, he continued to be hesitant to push with regard to opening too much to arising experience. He also continued to utilize concentration and breathing techniques to manage emotionally charged situations in daily life, reporting increased confidence to utilize techniques when needed.

Session 8. This final session again reviewed the homework material and integrated what has been discussed. The group began with a 30 minute meditation during which the facilitators encouraged the veterans to direct attention to the sounds in the room. Their attention was at times more focused and concentrated, and at times more open, mindful, and non-directional. They were also directed to move attention along a continuum of inner to outer orientation by at times devoting almost total attention to the sounds themselves, and at times directing attention to their own thoughts, emotions, and body sensations, which arose in response to sounds arising in the room. Non-attachment and letting go were discussed. They reviewed their experience of the facilitator, techniques, and group process, and were encouraged to report their feelings in the present moment and to discuss their observations. The theme of non-attachment to phenomena was extended to the trauma and to the emotional responses to traumatic events. Attachment to labels and roles were discussed, reflecting upon the nature of grasping to one's identity as a veteran, as a man, as a soldier, or even as a veteran with PTSD.

Christopher expressed satisfaction with his participation for the duration of the group. He also expressed appreciation for being able to participate in the group with fellow combat veterans, noting that they shared a bond that helps create a useful safe container for his experiences. He also shared that although he knows he will continue to experience PTSD distress and challenges, he is pleased to have learned useful skills that he expects to continually apply in his daily life. Christopher and the other group members stated that the various issues discussed along with the awareness exercises help to contribute to having a broader perspective of themselves and their experiences.

Concluding remarks

The course was conducted as an adjunctive intervention, supporting the veterans' involvement in other empirically supported treatments. The authors favored this approach, as it allowed them to explore new methods with the confidence that the clients remained in receipt of reliable, ongoing clinical services. The group was conducted as a pilot, to explore possible use of meditative varieties such as mindfulness, known to be efficacious in a variety of previous applications (Baer, 2003). Techniques were modified in accordance with current perspectives on the treatment of PTSD (Ehlers & Clark, 2000) in an attempt to address the challenges that patients with PTSD present, including containing and modulating affect, experiential avoidance, and overly negative evaluations of themselves and their experience. The authors turned to original Buddhist sources, which form the foundation of current applications of concentration and mindfulness, to find inspiration for discussing issues and innovating techniques, from which to build this pilot protocol. Specifically, continual awareness techniques were designed to be able to be modified in order to achieve either affect regulation (modulation) or affect tolerance (containment). Some basic Buddhist tenets were presented in order to facilitate a perspective upon reality and the self consonant with challenging the veterans' relationship to their thoughts, while leaving room for challenging those thoughts when they are deemed irrational. Techniques were provided to access a compassionate state of mind; such a state has been promising to potentially assist individuals in coping with anxiety (Wang, 2005; Gilbert, 2005; Goleman, 2003).

Ultimately, the goal of this pilot protocol's design and implementation was to develop a foundation for a new empirically validated treatment for the treatment of PTSD, which would build upon the advances of CBT's third wave, while mining Buddhist and related spiritual sources for treatment innovations. This pilot treatment was conducted on three separate occasions with relatively small groups of 4 to 12 veterans each. The small sample size and lack of experimental design excluded quantitative analysis in our explorations during these initial groups. The authors are currently developing a multi-site study to examine the effectiveness of this intervention using thorough statistical analyses. This chapter is offered as a description of innovative ideas and techniques as they are being developed and preliminary tested in the clinic.

6

Zen Meditation As A Source For Therapeutic Practice

Herman Kief

Having read Hirai's Zen Meditation Therapy, *this author explored and discovered the powerful psychotherapeutic possibilities of Zen. Many Buddhist meditation techniques can be adjusted for therapeutic use. I have innovated with up to 10 Zen Buddhist inspired cognitive-behavioral techniques, some of which are elaborated in this chapter. To give an example, instead of a traditional mantra, a client repeats an affirmation on assertiveness while exhaling during 20-30 minutes. In this manner, one might well overcome self-doubt about the statement. After a few days (or sometimes weeks) the statement might become a conviction even for the most subassertive. Another intervention looks at the client's problem or symptom as a koan. This is a technique often in the form of a paradoxical question (e.g. what is the sound of one hand clapping?). If a complaint is treated and studied like a koan, it can be handled accordingly. The client repeats a question on her/his complaint every time s/he exhales; out of the unconscious mind answers surface. Analogous to the Zen master's checking of the student's answers in a* dokusan *(private meeting), the Zen-therapist discusses the bubbling answers in an individual session. (E.g. why do I drink too much wine? why don't I ever listen to my wife? what makes me depressed?) Subsequently, client and therapist scrutinize insights and interpretations, and the functionality of the complaint might reveal itself. Thus, the koan-like question "Why do I need alcohol?" might accrue the answer "Because I feel lonely." This leads to a new question "What makes me feel lonely?" Answer: "The state of my marriage," etc. This goes on until the client gains insight, feels unburdened/relieved, or might we say "becomes enlightened"?*

This chapter presents a new method of psychotherapy that I as a full time clinical practitioner have developed from the 90s onward, based on a few seemingly non-related events relating to koans. Before studying koans, I suffered from a grave personal loss of somebody I loved and still love, which I got over through practising a bereavement meditation based on Thich Nhat Hanh's method as described in his book *The Miracle of Mindfulness* (1996). This is mainly about how to stay in the present reality, whether eating a raisin, playing with kids, or washing the dishes. Mindfulness helped me to heal my grief and find refuge in Buddhist teaching. This is how my interest in Zen was born.

Professionally, three subsequent events led me to develop Zen-based therapy tools. The first was that after one year of arduous Zen training I "was told by my Zen teacher that I had solved" my first koan (indeed, the sound of one hand clapping). It gave me a tremendous boost in my personal development. The second event was that I re-read a tiny book written in 1977 by a Japanese psychiatrist, Hirai; with the intriguing title *Zen Meditation Therapy*. In this book he elaborates upon a number of physiological effects of Zen meditation (such as blood pressure, heartbeat, and galvanic skin response during the steadiness in the sitting-posture when practicing zazen). Hirai made a casual remark about one of his subjects, to whom he suggested, that while waiting for the train on the platform of the Tokyo railway station he should repeat a positive statement about achieving some positive result. I suddenly realized that this technique could be used therapeutically. A repeated statement like this can be regarded as a mantra, a power-laden syllable or sentence, which enables someone to see the reality of the present moment. I will elaborate on this potentially powerful therapeutic technique later. The third event relates to clinical hypnosis, the practice of which I was trained in by Zeig (1985). He taught me to apply therapeutic paradoxes based on the work of the American psychiatrist and hypnotherapist Erickson who is in my view a Buddha. In his teaching a symptom can be considered a paradox: a client does something, while at the same time not wanting to do it; for instance, an obsessive-compulsive behavior. Haley (1985, p. 138) noted in a conversation with Erickson: "You know, Zen... is that everyone gets caught up in neurotic patterns, the wheel of life, and you can suddenly, by dealing with right now, get out of it. It strikes me that that is similar to your attitude about therapy."

In those days in 1995, I talked with my Zen coach and he strongly encouraged me to go on with this work. He suggested that I use the format of his Zen-lessons, which I did. Thus, I started to do Zen inspired group psychotherapy.

Zen Buddhist Inspired Group Therapy

The original Zen group session that I usually participate in is typically structured as follows:

(1) Gathering
(2) An introductory lesson about a particular subject of the Buddhist teaching *Dharma*) in general or Zen in particular also called *teisho* (Dharma talk)
(3) Buddhist scripture/*sutra*-recitation, especially from the Heart Sutra (of which is famous the fragment "emptiness is form, form is emptiness"
(4) First sitting meditation exercise (25 minutes)
(5) Walking meditation (*kinhin*) with the possibility to go the toilet (5 minutes)

(6) Second sitting meditation exercise (25 minutes) during which each group member has a brief individual/private interview with the Zen teacher (*dokusan*). The meditation process, progress or stagnation, is discussed during this strictly formal meeting that ends with a personal note and an instruction

(7) A simple tea ceremony

(8) Opportunity to ask questions in the group

(9) Formal closing, washing the tea cups, cleaning the pillows, etc.

Each of the above format's elements are used in my own open therapy groups that I conduct with eight clients who suffer from a variety of neuroses. Needless to say, I do not apply such strict format. As a matter of course I do therapy as usual using evidence-based techniques in an eclectic manner. Although I keep a Buddha statue in my group therapy room, neither Buddhist teaching nor Zen is a predominant subject matter. I might bring it up advertently, but usually Buddhist views come naturally to the fore while discussing a variety of the clients' symptomatology and problems of living. Depending on the clients' level of understanding even difficult issues like "having thoughts without a thinker" (Epstein, 1995) can be discussed and used in therapy.

I have created and adapted up to 10 Zen Buddhist inspired therapeutic techniques, some of which are presented here. I had the privilege to discuss these in a personal communication with Prof. Yutaka Haruki at a conference in Kathmandu, Nepal, several years ago. We came to the conclusion that according to Ockham's razor, the common denominator of the supposed working mechanisms and therefore most appropriate label for these clinical tools is "cognitive-behavioral."

Buddhist Meditation and Psychotherapy

In a lecture called Zen and the Art of Psychotherapy, Haley (1994, p. 56) contended that,

> Zen Buddhism is apparently the oldest continuing procedure, in which one person sets out to change another. For at least 700 years, Zen masters have responded in a one to one relationship with someone who wishes to change.

What struck me in books and articles about the therapeutic use of meditation is the fact that traditions stick strongly to their own particular form and content. To give an example, there is some evidence that mantras can be effectively used to decrease tobacco, alcohol, and drug abuse (Gelderloos, 1990). However, as far as I know, nobody thought of the rather obvious idea to apply mantras therapeutically in areas of psychological disorder other than substance abuse. I wonder whether this kind of "profanation" may be sacrilegious. This certainly would not refer to

Zen in which nothing is considered sacred. Thus, the Zen one liner "If you meet the Buddha on the road, kill him!" dismisses any clinging to a guru. In fact, I discovered later that this is a title of a book that describes in a funny but poignant pilgrimage of psychotherapy clients toward independence, responsibility, and freedom (Kopp, 1972).

No doubt, Zen meditation has a healing outcome on many kinds of psycho-physiological anomalies — like enhancing the EEG alpha rhythm, lowering the GSR, decreasing the body's energy need, calming the heartbeat and blood pressure, and many other effects — such that the term "perennial" psychophysiology was coined (Austin, 1998). Zen teaches discipline, enhances concentration, and especially raises attention. It reminds me of a little story about Ikkyu (1394-1481), a Japanese Zen master (Beck, 1993). Asked about Zen's highest wisdom, he made calligraphy of *attention* on the board. "Isn't there something more profound?" the student asked. Ikkyu said "Yes, there is!" And again he wrote *attention*. "Is that all, isn't there anything more?" Ikkyu retorted "Yes, there is!" And once more he wrote *attention.* Now the board signals *attention, attention, attention.* Perplexed the student asked "What does attention mean anyway?" Ikkyu replied "Attention means attention!" The lecture is clear enough: Zen requires attention in the beginning, the middle, and the end of practice. In fact, attention is the key to awakening. Meditation's content does not seem to matter much; a mantra, koan, breath, sight, sound or the words Cup-A-Soup are only springboards for attention in the present moment. What one attends, one needs to attend in neutral observation.

If one refrains from judging and evaluating, one will experience that feelings and thoughts come and go. Thus, even delusions and "mystical" images (*makyo*) are not to be clung on to. A very good example is given by Dogen Zenji (1200-1253), the founder of the Soto School of Zen in Japan (Cleary, 1992). A student told Dogen that during meditation he had a beautiful vision of a golden light from which emerged a shining golden statue of the Buddha. He asked what the master thought of that. Dogen replied "Good, very good! Really beautiful! And if you continue your mediation tenaciously, it will disappear by itself." This method might probably not be enough to deal with psychosis, but in combination with neuroleptics one can come a long way. Or, as one of my patients remarked: I can make a difference between my visions and reality.

You Can Only See It, When You Have Known It

This paragraph's title paraphrases a famous Dutch soccer player and wisdom oracle: Johan Cruyff. Only when insight rings one's bells, is one able to see an issue from a different perspective. The moment I understood that every component of Zen meditation training can (and perhaps should advisably) be used in psychotherapy, I applied this insight in my clinical practice, and never stopped contemplating about and figuring out how and where to formulate their parallels. Below is an elaboration on some of these analogies for technical innovation. The initial step is to first have the meditative insight bells ring in order to be able to see it. This implies education, also called Dharma talk or *teisho* in Japanese, during which a *Roshi* (Zen master) expounds a theme of the Buddhist teaching. Thus analogously, I start every group session that I conduct with a psycho-education; this is a lecture wherein I mostly inform my clients about the psychological disorders and emotional problems of living they suffer from. Specifically, this can be about the various kinds of depressions, anxiety disorders, phobias, or even psychosis (as I am also a psychiatrist prescribing medication). Psycho-education makes an essential contribution to the treatment of schizophrenia, major depression, and other complex biopsychosocial conditions. To start with psycho-education gives rise to discussion on relevant themes between the clients in the group right away. Besides psycho-education, two Zen inspired techniques that I most frequently apply are based on the meditation tools: mantra and koan. As a matter of course, before I actually start to implement these techniques a psycho-educational, teisho-like, explanation precedes the intervention, comprising what is written below.

The Mantra as a Therapy Tool

According to the dictionary the Sanskrit word mantra or mantram (Kohn, 1991) is a power laden syllable or series of syllables that in some (popular) forms of Buddhist practice manifest certain cosmic forces and aspects of the Buddha's positive powers. Continuous repetition of mantras is practised as a form of meditation in many Buddhist schools, for example, in the Pure Land School where the Buddha of the western paradise (*Amida*) is revered and the mantra *namu-amida-butsu* is repeated to awaken one's gratitude. There is even an esoteric school in Japan based on mantras known as *Shingon* (true word), which is congenial to the Vajrayāna, the Diamond vehicle of the Tibetans, wherein mantras play a considerable role. In this tradition the mantra is defined as a means to protect the mind. Tradition holds that thanks to the vows of the Buddhas/Bodhisattvas a miraculous force resides in the mantras, so that by pronouncing them one may acquire merit. Etymologically, mantra links with *manas* meaning mind and *trâna* or *tra* meaning protection or tool, so that mantra might mean a tool/technique protecting the mind. In the Buddhist teaching the correct vibration/sound of a mantra (mostly through chanting) is able to deliver the mind from illusion and attachment. For instance *Om gate gate paragate parasamgate bodhi swaha* is a mantra derived from the Heart of the Perfection of Wisdom Sutra, meaning gone, gone, gone to the beyond, arrived safely at the other shore in awakened state, hail.

The shortest and most well-known mantra is *Om* (or aum, shortly meaning: hail), thought by the Brahmins to be the sound the universe vibrated when it was created. In the Tibetan Buddhist tradition the six syllables mantra of Chenrezig *om mani padme hum* (hail the jewel in the lotus) is commonly practiced to relieve negative karma, accumulate merit, help rescue from the sea of suffering, and achieve Buddhahood. One should not seek for Buddhahood outside of oneself; the essence for awakening is within. All beings naturally have the Buddha nature in their own being. *Om* (hail) stands for one's impure body/speech/mind that can be transformed into the noble body/speech/mind of a Buddha. *Mani* (jewel) symbolizes method and compassion/love that are able to transform the poverty of solitary awakening into the altruistic intention to end suffering for all sentient beings. *Padme* means lotus or wisdom. Growing out of the mud, but never being stained and always pure, lotus indicates the quality of wisdom, which is nondual and beyond contradiction. The last syllable, *hum* indicates inseparability that refers to the indivisible unity of method and wisdom. This suffices the background information on the origin of the Buddhist mantra.

Psychologically, it is possible to give a mantra such specific wording that it becomes therapeutically active. I illustrate with clinical examples of the individual problems for which prescribe a personalized mantra. Regularly, I meet clients who do not feel welcome to be on planet earth — because their parents bluntly said so — and they have carried this burden ever since; e.g. a mother said to her third child: "Your father and I only wanted two children." In another case a parent said: "The only reason we have got you was because during the War we could not get reliable contraceptives." A father allegedly expounded: "Rob, the only reason I married your mother was because of you sneaking out of my rubber." On a subtle note, but repeatedly communicated, one client got the message as a child that he is a good-for-nothing (e.g. "There is always something wrong with you, your clothes, your shoes, your attitude, and your friends! Why is it I always have to correct you? Keep your stupid mouth shut!"). A grown-up would be able to respond to such statements with: "Good question, mother, why do you always have to correct me?" or "Will you please stop correcting, I know what I am doing?" But a child dares not give such clever or assertive response. Being in an important emotional relationship s/he gets caught in what Bateson (1972) has called a "double bind": an interpersonal paradox impossible to comment about or withdraw from usually leading to extreme frustration and inappropriate behavior. A child thus imprinted by a "toxic parent" (Forward, 2002) will develop a poisoned self-concept/image and seek therapy later in life. In such instances I have found strong indications that the mantra is a highly effective therapeutic tool.

In my Zen-inspired therapy, I then prescribe such clients an ego-strengthening mantra as an antidote, like: "I am okay, I am a good person, I did the best I could, I have the right to exist, I am loveable," or kindred texts that can be found in Shapiro (1997). Working with affirmations is not entirely new as Norman Vincent Peale described in his early book *The Power of Positive Thinking*. Before him Emile Coué at the turn of the 19th/20th century also proposed to repeat "Every day, in every way, I am getting better and better" in the framework of autosuggestion. Using self-hypnosis might help the client believe the affirmations, but may also sound disingenuous if the client is used to thinking the opposite of himself. As speaking out loudly does not seem to work, the quintessential question is: how to make the disbeliever believe and embody the new statements on her/him self? I have found that meditative repetition has a tremendous power in getting one's life mantra ingrained. This implies making use of the breath by subvocally repeating the mantra every time one breathes out. On the average one breathes 10 times every minute, so within one meditation period of 25 minutes one may be able to silently say about 250 times a firm powerful self-confirming statement to oneself. After a couple of days or weeks this works out and the mantra will come to life, so to speak, or as one of my clients puts it: "In the beginning I said to myself 'I am okay'; but now I say it from deep inside myself." Here is the instruction that I give:

(1) Sit in a comfortable meditation position, with your back straight and your feet flat on the ground, if you wish you may close your eyes... and breath naturally... just note how you breath... long or short, deep or shallow...

(2) Look for peace inside yourself... and if peaceful, observe what influences your serenity: thoughts, feelings, sights, sounds, or other sensations, etc.
- How do you experience this feeling of peace? ...
- What is disturbing your feeling of peace? ...
- What increases your inner peace? ...
- What decreases your inner peace? ...

(3) Let go now... and contemplate about what you have learned about yourself in the past few minutes... which thoughts did disturb you...?

(4) Construct one short sentence, as a positive affirmation countering the thoughts disturbing your inner peace... and open your eyes

(5) Now write this sentence down... and be sure you start with "I..." when you are finished, take your comfortable meditation position again, and close your eyes... investigate how you breathe and feel now, at this moment, from moment to moment... repeat silently your own private mantra, every time you breathe out, and go on so doing until the bell tolls....

(6) Now examine your inner space... and find out whether you might experience the slightest change for the better... when you had any positive experience, and you do wish to share it with us... that can be done... open your eyes now...

The Koan as a Therapy Tool

The koan is the most enigmatic meditation method in Zen (Chan in Chinese, which is a blending of the Early Buddhist Teaching and Taoism). The Japanese word koan stems from the Chinese *kung-an* (public case record), a metaphor, originally

meaning jurisprudence to be used for future similar instances. In Zen, koans indicate a sudden awakening experience of a student due to a master's transmission of
a kind of mind boggling riddle that cannot be resolved or defied by logic. A koan
contains what we in the West would call a paradox that in Greek means "beyond
thinking." It is usually an anecdote/dialogue between two masters or a master and
a student, which is self-contradictory or essentially absurd, that needs to be "dissolved" (i.e. beyond words). The question posed in a *mondo*/Q&A koan, has no
answer. The only way out is to "blast the fetters of the mind," thus shaking off all
abstractions, cognitions, and images that are considered to be reified illusions (including the self) and eventually awaken in *kensho* or *satori* (enlightenment). By
conceptualizing or naming a thing, we think that we really know what we are
talking about. In the West, Korzybski (1933) already pointed out in his General
Semantics that the map is not the territory; the menu card is not to be swallowed.
Mathematics, physics, and even quantum mechanics are, though precise abstractions, not the real thing. The Zen Buddhist teaching is about coming back to senses
in order to "see things as they really are" (i.e. without conceptualizing). Such a
way of working might be a relief for professionals who work mostly with highly
abstract concepts like DSM diagnoses.

First compiled in the 10th century, there are 1700 koans extant of which a few
hundred are in use. To elucidate, when asked "What is Buddha?" many masters
answered in a baffling koan. Ma-tsu (8th century) answered "This very mind," but
to another student he said: "Not mind." Yun-men (9-10th century) answered with
"Dried dung." For Dong-shan (10th century) the Buddha is three pounds of flax.
The absolute koan champion was Lin-chi (9th century). His name transcribed into
Japanese reads Rinzai, which is also a name for one of the two main Zen schools in
Japan. The essence of his tangential Zen teaching sounds as follows:

> *Followers of the Way, there are certain baldheads who turn all their efforts in-*
> *ward, seeking in this way to find some otherworldly truth. But they are completely*
> *mistaken! Seek the Buddha and you'll lose the Buddha. Seek the Way and you'll*
> *lose the Way. Seek the patriarchs and you'll lose the patriarchs. Can't stop the*
> *thoughts arising and disappearing in your mind, True awareness shining bound-*
> *lessly, you must focus on the one that doesn't move. To realize there are neither*
> *forms nor names, nothing to pursue, Sword of Wisdom has been used, must hurry*
> *to hone it... Followers of the Way, if you wish to attain the view that is in accord*
> *with the Dharma, just do not let yourselves be deceived. Whether you face the*
> *inside or the outside, kill whatever you encounter. If you encounter the Buddha,*
> *kill the Buddha. If you encounter a patriarch, kill the patriarch. If you encounter*
> *your parents, kill the parents. If you encounter a relative, kill the relative. Only*
> *then will you attain release....* (Chine, 1984, p. 390; cited from Watson, 1993)

Indeed, Zen's splendor is reflected in metaphors that are terse, radical, iconoclastic, and perplexing conundrums with a nimble wit. His puzzling expressions are

easy to understand and an excellent meditation device for those who uncompromisingly wish to liberate themselves from the shackles of I-me-mine/self. Rinzai Zen applies up to 30 from their stock of 700 koans to develop students over many years to shake them free of mental fetters. Wu-men (13th century) who edited the Gateless Gate (*Wu-men kuan*) that consists of 48 frequently used koans explained that satori comes only after thinking has been exhausted that is when one has embodied the insight that the mind cannot grasp itself <u>www.ciolek.com/ WWWVLPages/ZenPages/KoanStudy.html</u>>. Then one is able to respond in Zen's "trigger-fast and razor-sharp" style (Chan's *chi-feng*). If you do not kill the Buddha, he will only stand in your way. This style is to delete binaries (me and the Buddha or subject vs. object) by negating opposites in any appearing coincidental instance that is neither affirmed nor rejected and thus practicing the silent transmission from mind to mind. Lin-chi developed the koan to convey the message that language, concepts, and logic fall short to fathom the ultimate. The following six are much practiced koans: Has a dog Buddha-nature or not? Mu!; What is your original face before your parents were born?; What is the sound of one hand clapping?; What is the color of the wind?; What is the value of a bucket without a bottom?; Can you catch my fan without using your hands?

Taking the western view of the paradox as the quintessence of Zen, psychotherapy can profit from it. In fact, the paradox has been used in therapy, as in paradoxical intention (cognitive paradox; Frankl) and paradoxical therapy (relational paradox; Erickson). In their early work Haley (*Strategies of Psychotherapy*) and Watzlawick (*Pragmatics of Human Communication*), suggested that a symptom is a paradox too. If a person emits anomalous behavior, like for instance an obsessive-compulsive act of controlling, s/he denies doing it at the same time. The therapist will often be told that it happens spontaneously. In paradoxical therapy, instead of getting rid of the symptom behavior, it is prescribed. The therapist requests that the client act on his compulsion deliberately and on purpose. Name the symptom behavior, and it is prescribed in the framework of making things better by making them worse. Thus, an agoraphobic person will be asked to walk around for at least three-quarters of an hour in the name of "exposure." At the same token, a depressed passive individual might be asked to raise and monitor activities like running. On the basis of my combined interest in therapy, Zen, symptoms, koans, and the paradox, I have constructed the following syllogism: *a symptom is a paradox; a koan is a paradox; ergo, a symptom is a koan.* This implies that one can study and handle symptoms in therapy in the same way as one works with koans. While in *Zendo* (the hall of Zen) I use to do this by silently repeating the prescribed koan question every time I breathe out in order to fill my whole expiration with it, in therapy I first generate the idiosyncratic questions and then prescribe it along with the breathing. Here are a few examples from my daily practice:

- Why do I drink so much (alcohol)?
- What makes me feel so lonely?
- What makes me so tense?
- What (or often who) "gives" me headaches?
- Why am I always so insecure?

The answers that pop up and appear on the screen of consciousness, only by repeating the question, are often surprising to both therapist and client. One does not seek for an answer. One only repeats the question and tries as best as one can to ignore distracting thoughts.

The answers are checked in *dokusan*, the private meeting with the Zen master/ Zen therapist in a room apart from the meditation room / group session room. A Zen therapy dokusan is as the original one utterly formal. For instance, the therapist asks: "What is your koan?" Client: "Why do I drink so much?" Therapist: "Good, and what is your answer?" Client: "Because only then I do not feel so lonely." Therapist: "That is a very good answer. Now I'll give you a new koan, what makes me feel so lonely?" In this way several layers of the behavioral problem are peeled off, until the client gets real insight in its roots and overcome it in the end, combined with "meditative drinking." The instruction might be combined with a mantra or other meditations like mindfulness, which is the common basis for all Buddhist meditations. Therapeutic dokusan is also a magnificent opportunity for motivating, reinforcing, and shaping the client in a good old fashioned way of operant learning. Thus, the therapist responds to the client with stimulating remarks like "very good!," "you are very close!," "this is a very good answer!," or "you can find more information if you continue this line of thinking!." This kind of comment will increase the client's trust in his own feelings, capacities, and possibilities. To elucidate the therapeutic koan technique that I have developed, here are its instructions:

> (1) Sit in a comfortable meditation position, with your back straight and your feet flat on the ground, if you wish you may close your eyes... and breath naturally... just note how you breath... long or short, deep or shallow...
>
> (2) Meditate or rather contemplate a couple of minutes on a difficult problem of your choice or choose one from your individual symptoms list sheet...
>
> (3) Produce a question on it, formulate a one liner, begin with "what" or "why," and for the sake of this exercise: write this question down...
>
> (4) When you are finished, take your comfortable meditation position again, and close your eyes... investigate how you breathe and feel now, at this moment, from moment to moment...
>
> (5) Now, repeat the question during a few minutes... every time you exhale, and be aware of the answers that spontaneously pop up in your mind...

(6) After the bell rings, open your eyes… and write down the answers that seem correct to you or true for you… and think it over… also what about them that you wish to discuss with me, in the group or privately…

Concluding Remarks

Even though Zen inspired techniques are made apt here to be applied for therapeutic purposes, the rationale that I gave above is more of an apology for the ideas that have been inspired by Zen in my practice than as a direct claim that I use Zen per se in working with my clients. After all therapy is not meditation; they each serve different purposes. The way I use Zen, clients must be a little bit knowledgeable about it, not only to assuage symptoms, but also as a prophylaxis over the long term. Fortunately, Zen has become a household word thanks to the media that treat Zen as an almost normal western phenomenon. The real understanding of Zen, however, comes with one's own practice. It is nearly impossible to teach someone to fish by reading books on fishing instead of actually holding a rod in the hand. If mere training is the secret, it would imply that awakening is warranted to come gradually. But, to awaken also means to open one's inner eyes from an unconscious life that is a sudden happening like awakening in the morning from a deep sleep. I am reminded of a story about the novice who asked, "How long will it take to achieve enlightenment if I meditate for two hours a day?" The abbot answered, "10 Years." "And if I make it four hours every day?" "Well, in that case," answered the abbot, "more like 20 years." Meditation is only a means of waking up. Once awake, go for a walk. Enjoy what it is like to not sleep walk. Keep breathing, nothing more.

I have shown a few examples how to apply classical meditation techniques in a therapeutic way. Zen provides in this way several powerful cognitive-behavioral techniques. Having discovered that this is possible, other Zen Buddhist techniques come into focus. Proceeding this way, it is possible to construct a compendium of Zen inspired techniques and ultimately a complete system of tools to treat a wide variety of psychological problems. Let me briefly list these other techniques on which I cannot elaborate here due to space constrictions (LeShan, 1983).

(1) Awareness is a general factor for any thought, feeling, or action to be changed. Training in mindfulness of impermanence is to watch each thought as a bubble appearing, floating, and disappearing from each moment to the next.
(2) Sutra, a piece of ancient scripture usually recited several times a day in Zen; in therapy appropriate sutras (e.g. food aversion) can be read out loudly before a meal to help strengthen motivation to unlearn bad habits like overeating.

(3) Teisho, a lesson on the Buddhist teaching (Dharma), is a useful compo-nent in a group session to convey some Buddhist values like equanimity and compassion, but also to provide psycho-education on diagnosis and therapy. (4) Visualisation, like in Hakuin's Taoist practice to treat kundalini pathol-ogy. In this exercise one imagines a lump of butter on the top of the head and feeling it melting down through the body to the toes and thus healing strange sensations.

(5) Death contemplation as described by Thich Nhat Hanh and that forms a core practice for Buddhists of all denominations; this can be used to counter fear of death or practiced as bereavement therapy to overcome pathological grief.

(6) Derived from Naikan is the empathy contemplation that raises compas-sion and changes the rapport with someone by asking: What did I receive from others today? What did I give to others today? What trouble did I cause others today?

I hope these remarks will pave the way to a new use of ancient Buddhist methods in contemporary practices of therapy.

7

Emotion In Buddhist And Rational Emotive Behavior Practices

Paul Soons

Rational Emotive Behavior Therapy (REBT) aims at the elimination of negatively felt emotions in the personal realm, while Buddhist Psychology (BP) targets positively felt emotions in a "transpersonal" context. Kwee (1996) has proposed a list of basic emotions ranging from low to high levels of awareness and consciousness (i.e. from negative to positive experience): (1) depression, (2) anxiety, (3) anger, (4) sadness, (5) joy, (6) love, and (7) silence. The alleviation of emotional suffering is considered to be a prerequisite for working at having one's positive emotions and happiness come to fruition. Moreover, BP and REBT seem to complement each other: higher or positive emotions increased by meditation might work as a buffer preventing relapse, thus likely making therapy outcome more durable. How can REBT be complemented by techniques that develop higher emotions derived from BP? There a two kinds of techniques stemming from the Buddhist tradition: techniques that replace negative emotions by positive emotions based on the principle of incompatibility of opposite emotions and techniques that directly develop happiness through augmenting positive emotions, like particularly the social meditations known as the Brahmaviharas *(love, compassion, joy, and equanimity). These BP-techniques fit in a multimodal framework implying adherence to a cognitive-behavioral paradigm.*

This chapter explores the question whether the working of a specific mode of Cognitive-Behavior Therapy, Rational Emotive Behavior Therapy (REBT), can be enhanced by adding techniques derived from the Buddhist tradition. To provide an answer, firstly, a multilevel model of emotions will be presented, which discerns lower, intermediate, and higher levels of experience. Secondly, three kinds of techniques will be perused: (a) techniques derived from REBT that eliminate negative emotions in the personal realm, (b) techniques derived from Buddhist Psychology (BP) that replace negative emotions by positive emotions in the personal realm as well, and (c) BP techniques that aim to pursue higher emotions in a "transpersonal" context in a direct way. Thirdly, an effort will be made to formulate the BP-techniques that aim at developing positive and higher level emotions within a cognitive-behavioral framework.

A Multilevel Model of Basic Emotions

Kwee (1996) proposed a new taxonomy of basic emotions based on a thorough review of the psychological literature. He tentatively postulated seven basic emotions:

> (1) Depression: ranging from feeling blue to dejection, dysphoria, down-heartedness, despondency, low spirits, melancholia, and dysthymia.
> (2) Fear: ranging from worry to apprehension, anguish, anxiety, fright, horror, terror, and panic.
> (3) Anger: ranging from annoyance to contempt, hostility, animosity, fury, rage, amok, and resentment;
> (4) Sadness: ranging from pity to sorrow, distress, grief, affliction, agony, mourning, and pain.
> (5) Joy: ranging from feeling pleased to being glad, happy, in good humor, funny, euphoric, and maniacal.
> (6) Love: ranging from tenderness, to fondness, intimacy, compassion, infatuation, eroticism, passion, and ecstasy.
> (7) Silence: ranging from "Christ-consciousness" to Buddhahood, the Tao, no-mind, cosmic or oceanic feeling, enlightenment, Satori, and Nirvana.

The latter is also indicated as an absolute awareness or inner liberation, equifinality (end-stage), or "point Omega." Other terms used are: a state of pure consciousness, in which (while breathing) life and death are transcended into a silence that is neither objective nor subjective and just "is."

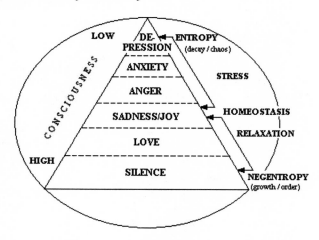

Figure 1. A hierarchically ordered model of basic emotions (Kwee, 1996, p. 259)

Each of these feelings and emotions do not occur separately. Like in the Buddhist teaching of the interdependence of all phenomena (*pratitya samutpada*), they appear and act in concert and in the context of multimodality that is here operationalized in thinking-feeling-acting The latter can be more specifically expressed as the "BASIC-I.D." (see Fig. 1): Behavior-Affect-Sensation-Imagery-Cognition-Interrelations-Drugs (the latter stand for Biology). Thus Affect (a generic term), feeling (relatively less intense emotions), and the basic (or primary) emotions originate, arise, and subside interdependently together with Behavior-Sensation-Cognition-and-Imagery. These movements are usually interpersonal but may also be biologically wired (implying that the BASIC-I is modifiable psychopharmacologically). The basic emotions are comparable to the basic musical notes or colors. Amalgamated with the other modalities basic emotional tones might become feelings that are relatively better characterized as an attitude or belief. Thus for instance: guilt is more of a belief (a relatively fixed cognitive pattern) combined with fear, while jealousy is more of an attitude toward somebody else, a negative image with an undertone of anger. All feelings can be analyzed using the BASIC-I.D. template, giving us an assessment and insight in the relative loading of each of the modalities (Kwee, 1998).

Three Kinds of Techniques for Changing Emotions

Here are the three kinds of psychological techniques to facilitate emotional change.
   1. *The elimination of negative (irrational) emotions by REBT techniques.* These negative emotions and feelings, called irrational in REBT, are experienced as inadequate and considered to be the result and concomitant of corresponding irrational ideation, which is to be detected in order to enable change of the thinking and the resulting unwanted basic affects of depression, anxiety, anger, or sadness. The goal of REBT is to eliminate these feelings by deconstructing the dysfunctional thoughts and constructing new rational ideas that are based on a relative stance. In REBT several kinds of techniques are used in the dialogue between client and therapist (Walen et al., 1992):

> (1) Cognitive disputation strategies are attempts to change the client's erroneous beliefs through philosophical persuasion, didactic presentation, Socratic dialogue, vicarious experience, and other modes of verbal expression. REBT's centerpiece is that it is not the Activating event (A) but our own Beliefs (B) that lead to the Consequence (C): what we feel and how we act. There are three kinds of questions that a therapist poses to dispute clients' irrational thoughts: *logical-causal* (Is it logical what you think? Is it "true" what you think? How do you know this?); *reality-testing*: (Where is the evidence for these beliefs? Why cannot you stand it? So what if it happens?); *pragmatic/goal-oriented* (Is it worth it? Does that thinking motivate

you to reach your emotional goals and help you in what you wish to do?). Other effective cognitive strategies of disputation are based on didactics (mini-lectures, analogies, or parables), exaggeration, humor, and vicarious learning or modeling.

(2) Imagery-based disputation strategies: subsequent to the verbal disputation, the therapist usually asks the client to vividly imagine being in the troublesome situation and visualize the problematic details. This may allow the therapist to see if the emotion has changed. If it has, the therapist questions the client about what he is now telling himself as a way to rehearse the newly learned rational beliefs. If the emotion has not changed, there might be other irrational beliefs maintaining the negative feelings, which need detection. In negative rational-emotive imagery clients visualize the problem situation while experiencing the negative emotion after which s/he is instructed to change this feeling through self constructed rational thoughts. More disputation might be required. If the emotion has changed fundamentally in the situation, positive rational-emotive imagery is applied to visualize the attended problem event during which the client feels and behaves differently.

(3) Behavioral disputation strategies: the client is encouraged to behave in a way opposite to what her/his irrational beliefs evoke to do. Behavioral change reflects the newly acquired rational outlook and the degree to which it has been internalized. Techniques that are aimed at behavioral change are: homework assignments, risk taking exercises, shame attacking exercises, exposure tactics to stay in the feared situation, role playing, and rational role reversal. REBT aims at eliminating negative feelings one suffers from by combating negative, irrational, dysfunctional thoughts and by behaving according to the newly acquired ideation. Performance based methods have definitely been proven to be indispensable to encourage new thinking and to eliminate unwanted affect.

As a cognitive-behavioral mode of treatment REBT postulates that emotional and psychological disorders are largely the result of thinking irrationally, dysfunctionally, negatively, absolutely, or illogically. Furthermore, REBT theorizes that rational and irrational thoughts are incompatible. Humans are able to get rid of most of their emotional and mental unhappiness, inefficacy, or disturbance if they learn to maximize rational and minimize irrational ideation (Ellis, 1994). REBT holds that sustained negative feelings, such as intense depression, anxiety, anger, and guilt, are almost always unnecessary to human living. They can be eradicated if people learn to consistently think straight and to follow up their straight thinking with effective action. REBT is a psychotherapeutic approach that views emotional change from a multimodal perspective of the BASIC-I.D. Changing feelings takes place by changing thought and action: individual behavior and interpersonal inter-actions. From a multimodal point of view emotions cannot be changed directly, they can only be changed through mediation by the other modalities like cogni-tion, imagery, behavior, interrelations, and psychopharmacology.

2. *Techniques derived from BP aiming at replacing negative (irrational) emo-tions by opposite-positive emotions.* These techniques are based on the BP's obser-vation of many people's experience for about 2500 years that opposite emotions are incompatible and thus do not occur simultaneously. Although this mechanism had also been applied in behavior therapy that began in the fifties — particularly in Wolpean systematic desensitization, whereby relaxation is alternately and gradu-ally infused to reciprocally inhibit anxiety responses — it was already known and practiced in the Buddha's time. Paraphrasing Humphreys (1968), the Buddhist view on this matter can be understood in terms of ignorance versus wisdom. Igno-rance has no autonomous existence and is only the absence of wisdom. The real ignorance comes from the human intellect and the beginning of it stems from man gifted with reason, who turns away from nature. Man is the origin of ignorance, and ignorance is the origin of passion, hate, delusion, and fear. It is important to discard ignorance and its resulting delusions. One of the methods to do this is to transform these passions by introducing something better, "Hate vanishes not by hate, but stops only by love" (p. 107).

Goleman (1988) has also noted that the Abhidhamma already described the use of mindfulness as an antagonistic response to counter human existential suf-fering and stress (*dukkha*) and thus unknowingly applied the learning principle of counterconditioning before the common era. Abhidhamma — the third of three canonical books of the Theravada (Early Buddhist Teaching of the Elders) — dis-tinguishes healthy versus unhealthy factors and calls for a strategy that strives at reaching healthy states of mind neither by pursuing them directly nor by fighting the unhealthy ones. The preferred way is equanimity by meditation, which might imply that confronting stress during mindfulness (i.e. being attentive and aware of the present moment without any judging) will likely reduce stressfulness. Every negative factor has a corresponding positive counterpart. When a positive/healthy state of mind is realized, the negative/unhealthy one has no chance to appear. Bennett-Goleman (2001) states the principle: one has to harness the negative emo-tions to positive ends by mindfully embracing them. Thus, the essence of mindful-ness meditation is to make use of all experiences, even of the negative ones, as aids that help to progress on the path. In such way all possible disturbances and antago-nistic forces will become our teachers.

This way of dealing falls in the broad range of Buddhist approaches to cope with disturbing emotions. Three main strategic stances can be discerned:

(1) Abandoning the disturbing emotions by arduous mindfulness practice aimed at ceasing the disturbing and unhealthy emotions entirely.

(2) Transforming the disturbing emotions into positive ones by opposing each negative state with a replacing antidote like loving-kindness.
(3) Including the disturbing emotion as part of one's path by utilizing negative experiences and turning these "enemies and foes" into friends.

The latter is a tough challenge, known as the "steep" path. One learns to regard detrimental emotions as an opportunity to gain wisdom and develop further toward awakening. The underlying idea is that negative emotions are not inherently bad or undesirable but as a fact of life that by frustrating us has to tell us something important.

Thus, in the Vajrayana Buddhist teaching of Tibet the instruction is not to suppress or oppose the energy fuelling the negative, unhealthy, destructive emotions but to transform these by redirecting the very same energy into fueling positive, healthy, and constructive emotions (Conze, 1959). A model and system to this end is known as the Five Buddha Families derived from the Mahayana cosmology — which is in a teaching of emptiness necessarily on the bottom line void — classifying all existing phenomena in five distinguishing categories. The system applies abstruse techniques that are passed on by a lama (guru) to a disciple as a secret and that are capable to positively transmute the detrimental emotions and their corresponding behavioral tendencies: hatred-clinging, greed-grasping, ignorance-craving, pride-downing, and jealousy-separating. Such techniques target the transformation of negative, illusory, and defiled affect into positive, illuminated, and luminous affect of an enlightened mode through various guided visualizations. This might include Tantric (sexual) visualizations of the idealized Buddha embracing his female counterpart in blissful states. The embodiment of such imagery is supposed to accrue positive affect as well as health. All negative affect with the quality of "neurotic" attachment are thus transformed into liberating ones and eventually wisdom is acquired.

3. *Techniques derived from BP aiming to pursue higher emotions in a direct way.* The *Brahmaviharas* derived from the Theravada contain contemplative meditations with a social content that stem from the dwelling place of Brahma (in the Buddhist context used as a metaphor for something great). Being akin to Brahma — the divine but transient ruler of the higher heavens (i.e. positive feeling/mind states) — they are incompatible with hating and other negative states of the mind. This contemplative practice seeks to embody the sublime states of loving kindness, empathic compassion, shared joy, and meditative equanimity. Therefore, the mind should be abundantly and thoroughly saturated by them. This should be done by aggrandizing these feelings "immeasurably" and by projecting them into the world in an "endless" and "beginningless" way. They are the alpha and omega of Buddhist practice, capable of preventing emptiness from sliding into a horror vacuum (depicted in Zen as a circle without beginning or end, called: *enzo*). Thera (1999) states that these four attitudes are said to be sublime because they excel as

the right and ideal manner of conduct towards all sentient beings. They are the great removers of social tension, the great peace-makers in conflict, and the great healers of wounds suffered in the struggle of life and the battle of existence. As they level social barriers, they build harmonious communities, awaken slumbering magnanimity long forgotten, revive joy and hope long abandoned, and promote human brotherhood against the forces of egotism.

These four qualities are also known as the boundless states because in their perfection and their true nature they should not be narrowed by any limitation as to the range of beings they are extended towards. They are advisably non-exclusive and impartial as well as unbound by selective preference or prejudice. A mind that has attained the boundlessness of the Brahmaviharas will not harbor any hatred based on national, racial, religious, or class differences. There are two simultaneous methods of developing the sublime states: by cultivating practical conduct that directs thinking appropriately, and by meditation that systematically targets equanimity through meditative absorption. The latter implies arduous practice of meditation that aims to gradually achieve higher states of mental concentration and absorption called *jhana*. The meditations on love, compassion, and joy may each produce the attainment of the first stages of absorptions, while meditation that directly targets equanimity will lead to the jhana of equanimity. A mind that has achieved concentration, absorption, and equanimity and that is pervaded by the sublime states of the Brahmaviharas will be pure, tranquil, firm, collected, and free of coarse selfishness. It will thus be well-prepared for the final work of deliverance which can be completed only by wisdom through insight into the acquired essential knowledge of the Buddhist teaching.

The Buddha allegedly has said that the mind will bend and incline toward what a person considers and reflects upon for a long time. The sublime states will be likely cultivated by repeated reflection upon their positive qualities, the benefits they bestow, and the dangers looming from their opposites. The qualities may be increased by four exercises a fragment of which exemplifies its practice:

> (1) Loving kindness: First, immerse yourself with love... then imagine a friend and do the same with this friend... Next, turn to someone to whom you are indifferent to, without feeling any attraction or aversion... Visualize this person vividly and send love to him/her... Subsequently, evoke an image of an enemy... see your enemy sharply in your mind's eye... and send your love to her/him... Then... turn to mankind... to all forms of life... and to the whole universe... Eventually you become the well and embodied spirit of love itself...
>
> (2) Empathic compassion: Start with raising empathy... and embody compassion... Then vividly radiate this compassion to people who are extremely unfortunate, who are poor and hungry and have no roof over their heads... visualize them clearly in your mind's eye and send your compassion to

them... Next, feel and radiate your compassion to people with other kinds of suffering... to people who live in zones of war.... who are chronically ill or have an incurable disease... Uphold a clear image of such people all over the world...

(3) Shared joy: Begin by feeling happy and joyful... then embodying somebody else's happiness... Feel happy because someone's fortunate day or event, it can be a neighbor or a colleague, or perhaps even someone you dislike... Share the joy of whoever appears in your mind's eye and be joyful... This is an antidote against selfishness and will transform egotism... Just imagine somebody who is very lucky and happy and full with joy, it can be a friend or a foe... Aggrandize your joy... feel joy for them and send it to them... and to all happy people...

(4) Meditative equanimity: be ever mindful of the present... from moment to moment... Whatever appears in the mind's eye, do not judge or evaluate it... it might be a thought, a concept or an image... or a feeling, a sensation or an emotion... Only watch... be detached and unmoved... stay calm and serene... Radiate this consciousness of equanimity to friend... and foe... and gradually to all forms of life... Go from love, compassion, joy... back to this imperturbable inner centeredness that cannot be disturbed by trivial externalities...

Note that these exercises are cognitive-behavioral interventions, as they are practiced in daily conduct with the ultimate aim to increase positive affect that corresponds with high levels of awareness. Reality is there where conscious attention is directed and focused.

Discussion and Conclusion

The quintessential question is whether it is possible to reframe Buddhist techniques in a cognitive-behavioral paradigm. Considering the above, the answer must be: yes. The working of REBT can be enhanced by cultivating higher levels of awareness through using techniques derived from BP that seek the sublime. REBT and BP-techniques can be scrutinized by a multimodal or BASIC-I.D. template and its components can be accordingly subsumed under the categories of action, thought, or feeling. These three kinds of techniques are springboards serving different goals: the changing of negative affect or emotions of lower levels of consciousness (depression, anxiety, anger, and sadness), the substitution of these feelings into positive emotions of higher levels of consciousness (joy and love), and the direct pursuit of these positive affects and feelings leading to serenity and silence (i.e. a halting of inner moving experience), which is known in Buddhist terminology as emptiness or not-self (Kwee & Ellis, 1998).

Clearly, if the person is struggling with intense negative and disordered emotions, the intervention's aim must be directed toward eliminating the psychopathology and its symptoms (medication might also be useful). For clients who suffer from existential neurosis or "normal" psychological problems of living that nobody can escape the suffering the Buddhist teaching usually targets] — replacing negative emotions by positive ones is the preferred strategy. The third way is to be pursued if the person is free from psychological disturbance, does not suffer too much from the slings and arrows of daily misfortune, and lives a relatively balanced life, socially and personally. Here meditation might enhance the desired goal of becoming a Buddha. Paraphrasing Wilber (1986), three phases are discernable: the strictly personal phase, the intermediate phase wherein a shift is worked at from the personal to the transpersonal, and the strictly transpersonal phase. Working in the third phase is only possible if the two previous phases have been passed successfully. The intermediate phase necessitates a successful passing through the first phase of emotional disorder. Thus, if one is for instance seriously depressed, it is strongly advised to first work on alleviation of this pathological suffering and on grounding one's personal balance before embarking on a transpersonal journey.

The choice of intervention can be guided by the type of emotion that defiles one. The model of basic emotions proposed by Kwee (1996) may prove to be useful for other clinicians in distinguishing the functions of various techniques and the level of consciousness each intervention works on. It helps to formulate indications and provide a provisional answer to the question of specificity: what works for whom under which condition? REBT can be enhanced with BP-techniques to encompass positive, higher, or healthy affect and emotions. It can be fruitfully combined with meditation, contemplation, and concentration to augment targeted effects and to pave the way for experiencing serenity, silence, and emptiness (Soons, 2004). Although practitioners might find the preceding guidelines useful, still much needs to be done to discover effective routes to emotional change and the shortest road to the sublime.

8

Buddhist Psychology
And Defensive Conditioning[1]

Adeline van Waning

In many western psychologies the emphasis has been on contents of the mind rather than on process, the workings or "behaviors" of the mind. Buddhist Psychology (BP) focuses on the latter. The author explores the cognitive distortions of defensiveness that lead people to avoid painful reality or to escape anxiety and confusion consciously, in a reflex, or through conditioned learning. These movements "away from what is" are detectable in selective perception and in preconceptions. These issues lead to this chapter's focus to compare three Buddhist views (the 3 roots of existential suffering, the 4 Maras or evils, and the 5 skandhas, heaps or aggregates) and views on defensiveness derived from psychodynamic psychology and classified by the Diagnostic Statistical Manual of Mental Disorders (DSM). The following questions are dealt with: (1) How to see and label defensive avoiding (2) How to evaluate its existence (3) How are we to understand the overall perspective and ultimate purpose of mental functioning, and (4) How to handle avoidance while realizing the aimed perspective and purpose? While the notion of undistorted perception is used in Buddhist and western psychologies, the descriptions and strategies to reach this state are less radical in western as compared to BP. In the West defenses are conceived in a developmental phase-model framework in connection to a rather linear view of personality development from childhood to adulthood. The Buddhist conception is described in the skandha cycle of personality functioning that emphasizes here-now spiraling processes of conditioning. There is a growing consensus that BP and psychotherapy complement each other in several ways.

One of the areas where the Buddha's message finds a remarkably warm welcome is in psychotherapy. Of the growing number of westerners who are students of Buddhist meditation — Zen, Vipassana, or Tibetan ways — are a relatively large number of psychotherapists. Three avenues through which Buddhist views find their way to psychotherapy are: (1) Buddhist practices such as meditation, mindfulness, non-judgmental awareness; (2) Buddhist understandings of the workings of the mind and ways of conditioning (as in the "Five Skandhas model"); and (3) Buddhist ethics and values that refer to the Three Empirical Marks of Existence (suffering-unease, impermanence, non-self) and the interdependency of all phenomena and all beings.

The core differences between BP and psychotherapy are found in the views on self, self-experience, and subjectivity. My reflections will focus on the workings of the mind.

Western psychology and psychotherapy emphasize contents of the mind rather than workings and behaviors of the mind. In cognitive approaches attention is paid to cognitive distortions but not particularly to cognitive defensive reactions that, stemming from psychodynamic therapy, are universally accepted in psychiatry (DSM). Here, I wish to explore and discuss perspectives on the conditioned ways people defensively avoid anxiety, confusion, and life's pains. By doing so, they avoid and distort daily reality. Defensive avoidance is observable in "movements away from what is." On this broad description most Buddhists and western colleagues might be willing to agree. This chapter focuses in more detail on three Buddhist psychological views (paragraph 2) — the "Three Roots of Suffering," "the Four Maras," "the Five Skandhas" — and on western views (paragraph 3). I will pursue the following questions:

1. *How to see and label these defenses and avoidances?*
2. *How to evaluate the existence of these defenses and avoidances?*
3. *What is the overall perspective and ultimate purpose in mental functioning?*
4. *How to handle these defenses and avoidances, while attempting to realize the aimed perspective and purpose?*

Let me first elucidate the terms "conditioning" and "defense" as these are used throughout this chapter. In modern learning theory three types of conditioning are hypothesized and largely verified: (1) classical conditioning, learning takes place as a result of the contiguity of environmental events (when events occur closely together in time, one will likely associate the two); (2) operant conditioning, learning results from the consequences of one's actions; and (3) vicarious conditioning, learning occurs through modeling or imitation. Social learning theory incorporates classical, operant, and vicarious learning and includes a determinism based on reciprocal interaction between the person, the behavior, and the environment (Kaplan & Sadock, 2003). BP tells us that our mentality is conditioned as well. However, it must be realized that the Buddhist use of the term "conditioning" is different from the above understanding: "conditioning" in BP has both a broader and simpler meaning. In a relative broad sense all things in the world arise in dependence upon causes and conditions, including our mental states. This notion incorporates the three types of conditioning. In a relative simple sense it means that for instance regularly going for a walk in nature or going to a place where one had very stressful experiences will have a different conditioning effect on one's preoccupations. Here the Buddhist and western meanings seem to concur.

The psychotherapeutic notion of defenses, defensive mechanisms (patterns or reactions) is derived from the psychodynamic approach that started with Freud's psychoanalysis. Defenses are taken to be automatic psychological processes that protect the individual personality against anxiety and any other internal or external dangers occurring in awareness. Individuals are often unaware of these processes as they operate. Defenses are conditioned phenomena and defensive conditioning is a particular form of conditioning. Defensive conditioning and conditioned defenses are metaphorical deep grooves in our minds that form behavioral patterns motivated by a need to preserve experiences of personal identity. Defensiveness in the psychotherapeutic context allocates a central place to personality. It is viewed as a coherent, separate, and independent mechanism.

Buddhist Psychology: Views on Defensive Conditioning

Let me now explore — with the bias of looking through a psychotherapist's lenses — three Buddhist psychological views on defensive conditioning. A basic aspect in BP is the absence of a separate core self or personality as an independent entity and the recognition of an elementary suffering (*dukkha*), that starts at birth, as an unavoidable part of human life. There is the suffering due to illness and loss as a consequence of the givens of impermanence and the ultimate fact that we have nothing really to stand on. What create the most suffering are exaggerated desires and attachments to satisfy the separate or independent personality, a construction that originates from ignorance. One could say that defenses, taking up the function of protecting this illusory personality, create a "surplus" or extra suffering, also called *dukkha-dukkha*. This surplus suffering can be ended by wisdom accrued by a right way of living and meditation as described in the Buddha's Eightfold Path. To emphasize this distinction: in western theories the attachment to the personality is generally accepted, while BP submits that there is no such separate or independent entity. We can experience and get to know our ever-changing impulses, feelings, sensations, thoughts, behaviours, abilities, skills, etc.

1. *How to see and label these defenses and avoidances?* BP describes the Three Roots of Suffering stating that all mental suffering can be traced back to three bitter poisons: greed (possessiveness, addiction), hatred (ill-will, anger), and delusion (ignorance, illusion). Preferences and dislikes as such are not mental afflictions. They become afflictions if conflated with attachment. This is the case with greed (*lobha*), hatred (*dosa*), and delusion (*moha*) as human inclinations and motivational driving forces. They lead to attraction or to aversion and are manifestations of an underlying ignorance. As they obscure the true nature of our being, they may be seen as "avoidances" that function to keep us away from seeing the ultimate reality that we have nothing to stand on. In our defensive handling of inner driving forces, the basic proclivities of greed/attraction, hatred/aversion and ignorance/delusion can be distinguished. For instance, if I cannot tolerate jealousy

in myself, I may tend to project that onto someone else and pretend that it is not me but the other person who is jealous (and feels the aversion). The three patterns defend against a reality that is unconsciously imagined (in an unaware fashion) as unbearable because it signals a danger to the existence of self or even might mean the end of personality. At the same time they are obstructing our potential to experience reality and liberation. Greed, hatred, and ignorance are the bitter roots of all emotional defilements (*kleshas*) that obscure the mind. On the other hand, wholesome states are linked to the sweet roots: generosity, loving-kindness, and wisdom.

Another view to the ways in which we try to escape the reality of the human condition of dukkha is through the Four Maras. The forces of Mara attacked Gautama on the night of his awakening. The story goes that they shot arrows and threw swords at him to no avail as these weapons turned into flowers. Explaining the Maras, Tibetan Buddhist teacher Chödrön (1997), infers them as ways in which we, just like the Buddha, are seemingly being attacked everyday. Being under attack we turn away and do not want to confront the obstacles that are right here-and-now. She discerns four styles in which we react defensively and avoid "being with what is":

(1) *Devaputra Mara* (approach-avoidance). Greed or attraction leads us to approaching or seeking pleasure and avoiding or escaping pain. As we cannot stand the anxiety, the heat of anger arising, the chilling despair, we grasp for something pleasant or distracting and become addicted to avoiding pain. Here is a connection with Freud's "Lust-Unlust" principle (that strives for pleasure and draws back from unpleasure).

(2) *Skandha Mara* (the old self). After feeling that "all is lost" (e.g. wealth or prestige), we seek ways to recreate ourselves and try to be who we think we are. We try to earn some ground back, to be our old self and to return to the "solid ground" of our self-concept as quickly as possible. However, it is a redressing in the emperor's cloths. Trungpa Rinpoche used to call this "nostalgia for samsara."

(3) *Klesha Mara* (emotional heat). We use our emotions to keep ourselves "asleep," un-conscious, and ignorant. Here, with strong emotions, for instance when angry, we begin to weave our thoughts into a story line, which gives rise to bigger emotions. We keep the narrative inflamed and hot by elaborating on the pain. By exaggerating and reproaching we take others into the heat. What begins as an open space may become a forest fire, a world war.

(4) *Yama Mara* (life/death-anxiety). All Maras arise from our fear of death and this variety is particularly rooted in such angst. It may be that we wish to perfection our lives and feel good about ourselves as we gradually find our way and think: "that's a perfect life." But from an awakened point of

view such perfect state of non-development equals death. Actually, Yama Mara is the anxiety to live in imperfection. It leads to controlling and closing off instead of turning the obstacles of powerlessness and uncertainties into our path.

The Five Skandhas (the Second Mara) point at a basic grasping, a falling back and fleeing back into our illusory old self. The skandhas show how defensive conditioning develops, shapes, and forms the conditioned self (Rahula, 1974). Driven by the roots and urged by the Maras, the conditioned self is continually being constructed, deconstructed, and reconstructed. Let me illustrate the working of the Five Skandhas by my recent encounter with a dog: (1) form, physical body, or input (*rupa*): "a dog, physically startling," (2) sense feeling — pleasant, unpleasant, or neutral (*vedana*): "unpleasant," (3) perception and re/cognition and the first automatic thoughts (*samjna*): "noticing the dog is big, I remember feeling threatened at other dog-meetings and messages as a child that big dogs bite," (4) conditioning, mental formation and habitual patterns leading to impulses and behavioral output (*samskara*): "I wanna get out!," (5) consciousness and mentality that is self-centred and dualistically connected with winning versus losing (*vijnana*): "I hate dogs." This dog may be the kindest, sweetest, and most non-violent pet of the world but I am not able to see the animal newly and freshly "as it is." This illustrates how earlier conditionings and defensive patterns do construct and cloud my perception and how distorted experiencing narrows consciousness, which blurs next experiences and hampers my problem solving repertoires, etc. Such is not a linear process but an associative-networking, cyclical, spiraling, self-reinforcing process that ingrains and deepens the grooves of ego-defenses.

2. *How to evaluate the existence of these defenses and avoidances?* The roots of one's prolems, the Maras, and skandhas, create and feed the illusion of personality's existence as a fixed person to identify with and which one needs to defend. Threats to this illusion have to be warded off. Thus, we suffer from irrational anxieties and become gradually unable to see things-as-they-really-are. Defenses are also used against constructive change and prevent us from realizing our interdependent nature. Separateness, our basic existential *dukkha*, starts from birth fortifies by increasing defenses as we grow older. The tragic paradox is that while trying to escape our existential suffering, we construct a personality that needs to be defended, a manoeuvre aggravating *dukkha* into *dukkha-dukkha*.

3. *What is the overall perspective and ultimate purpose in mental functioning?* Buddhist practice aims for a clear and clean state of mind in which one can learn to watch the world beyond preconception, selective perception, or other defensive distortions. BP enables us to experience our basic obstacle, existential suffering due to impermanence (and its consequences like non-self, illness, and death), without self-deception. Once awakened, we can accept and embrace it and eventually we will be able to utilize it, turn it into our path and include it in

our lives. In the end the practice aims at awakening/enlightenment that evaporates defensiveness.

4. *How to handle these defenses and avoidances, while attempting to realize the aimed perspective and purpose?* One needs not per se consider defenses as obstacles. BP rather sees in them opportunities to observe what we do when facing pain. As Chödrön (1997) states, we can look at the arrows and how we react to them. Instead of trying to get rid of something and moving into a dualistic sense of being attacked, we can learn to see how we close down when in pain. Thus, we open our hearts, awaken our intelligence, and connect with the enlightened Buddha-nature. We can do this in non-judgmental awareness and by being mindful of the here-and-now. By embracing the pain, not indulging in escaping, we go beyond the pain. While perceiving and experiencing the pain, we gradually and perhaps even miraculously discipline and transform the pain.

Psychotherapy: Views on Defensive Conditioning

A psychodynamic shorthand way of viewing personality helps to locate the defenses. This model distinguishes the id or drives, the super-ego or conscience, and the ego or reality principle that stands for negotiating with drives, conscience, and the outer world. Metaphorically, the ego is an active, adaptive, organizing function in us, which also encompasses the defenses. Defenses aim to avoid danger, anxiety, and "unpleasure" and to reduce or eliminate threats to the integrity and stability of the personality. Defenses begin in childhood and are conditioned by our lifetime experiences. Different defense types are presented below. Analogous to the previous paragraph, the same four questions are posed here.

1. *How to see and label defenses and avoidances?* Defenses can be categorized according to one's relative maturity in psychological development. Grossly, four groups can be distinguished:

> Narcissistic *defenses are the most primitive and appear in children and people who are psychotically disturbed.* Immature *defenses are seen in adolescents and some non-psychotic patients.* Neurotic *defenses are encountered in obsessive-compulsive and hysterical patients as well as in adults under stress... And there are the* mature *defenses for the healthy ones.* (Kaplan & Sadock, 2003, p. 207)

According to the "defensive functioning scale" of the DSM IV (2000) 31 forms of defense are elaborated on seven levels that run from high to low adaptation:

> (1) High adaptive level: resulting in optimal adaptation in the handling of stressors (e.g. anticipation, humor, self-assertion, or self-observation).
> (2) Mental inhibition or compromise formation level: defensive functioning keeps potentially threatening ideas, feelings, memories, wishes, or fears out

of awareness (e.g. intellectualization or isolation of affect; like telling about an emotional experience in an intellectual insensitive way).

(3) Minor image-distorting level: there are distortions in the image of the self, body, or others that may be employed to regulate self-esteem (e.g. devaluation or idealization, like boasting in insecure circumstances about successes).

(4) Disavowal level: unpleasant or unacceptable stressors, impulses, ideas, affects, or responsibility are kept out of awareness with or without misattributing these to external causes (e.g. denial or projection, like someone who does not recognize own jealousy but ascribes this to another).

(5) Major image-distorting level: there is gross distortion or misattribution of the image of self or others (e.g. splitting of self-image or image of others, splitting in good versus bad extremes, like putting the bad rage away by projection, "it's not my but her feeling," and by projective identification).

(6) Action level: the defensive functioning deals with internal or external stressors by action or withdrawal (e.g. acting out or passive aggression).

(7) Defensive dysregulation level: this is characterized by failure of defensive regulation to contain the individual's reaction to stressors leading to a pronounced break with objective reality (e.g. a psychotic distortion, a delusion or delusional projection disconnected to reality; usually recognized as being mad, insane, or crazy).

2. *How to evaluate the existence of defenses and avoidances?* According to the psychodynamic discourse, nobody is ever without defenses. Defensiveness is conceived of as unavoidable. We all use a characteristic repertoire of defensive reactions: psychological health and illness form a continuum. Someone's typical profile is a good barometer of psychological health (Gabbard, 1994). Character traits owe their existence to the success of the mother of all: repression. Here the defense achieves its aim of putting away threats and dangers to personality integrity an independent entity. Personality or character is here conceived as one's habitual or typical identification and conditioned pattern of adaptation to temperamental constitution, internal motivational forces, and external environmental circumstances.

3. *What is the overall perspective and ultimate purpose in mental functioning?* The overall goal of psychotherapy is to alleviate mental suffering to thus promote adjustment to normal" living in a social context. Primarily, its practice is to change neurotic and other mental suffering in "ordinary" daily and existential suffering, in which change and loss do play a large role. The person, as Freud said, is to regain the ability to love and work. If the need to distort reality diminishes and conditionings of habitual patterns become less fixed and limiting, then there is a healthy mental functioning. Therapy's purpose is to find compromises in defensive arrangements that are least (self) destructive, with a good share of high adaptives.

4. How to handle defensive conditionings while attempting to realize the aimed perspective and purpose? Psychotherapy might be defined as handling and structuring, in a methodical way, a relationship of client and therapist, with the help of certain interventions. It is imperative to recognize clients' defensive patterns in the therapy room. In so called transference reactions occurring in the client — therapist interactions, old unresolved issues and specific expectations are projected onto the therapist. Two different therapeutic approaches are applied. The first aims at opening, uncovering, and exploring the anxieties behind the resulting in the insight that one's are outdated. Having served their aim of avoiding anxiety and protecting the personality, they are now obstructing growth. Suffering is not so much due to some underlying condition but to s that have outlived their usefulness. Therapy then is to explore the defensive conditionings in their inter-subjective dynamics and in repetitive transference patterns in order to confront and challenge them, stop using them, turn them around, and eventually work through the underlying pain. The second approach works at covering and is merely focused on adaptation. Such approach aims not at deepening insight but at finding an improved balance for defending and to teach coping methods that support and strengthen the ego-personality.

Buddhist Psychology Versus Therapy: Comparing Views on Defensive Conditioning

Applying the same four questions, the following comparisons can be made:

1. How to see and label defenses and avoidances? Common ground is found in the Maras that classify mechanisms. Most of the 31 fit in its four categories. For instance, denial can be subsumed under "approach-avoidance" (*Devaputra Mara*) and acting out under "emotional heat" (*Klesha Mara*). Defenses can also be listed under the three roots; for instance denial under "aversion" and intellectualisation under "ignorance." Whereas the defenses are originally conceived in a linear and macro-model of the psychodynamic phase theory of personality development, BP emphasizes micro perceptual-cognitive-emotional-behavioral events from moment to moment as exemplified in the skandha cycle. Targeting change, it primarily addresses the here-and-now, self-reinforcing, and conditioning aspects thus bearing strong resemblance with cognitive-behavioral therapy.

2. How to evaluate the existence of defenses and avoidances? BP and therapy share common ground in T.S. Eliot's "Humankind cannot bear very much reality." Defensive reactions are the crutches we apply to avoid reality (Walsh, 1966, p. 397). By using fixed notions of personality and character, the psychodynamic approach emits a view that considers a person less apt for change. Moreover, s are considered as relatively irreversible, a pessimistic outlook, which is in stark contrast to the Buddhist optimistic view of working on strengthening abilities and skills. Such concurs with the basic reality of impermanence that opens possibilities to always have the opportunity to change, to construct, deconstruct, and reconstruct without bothering to defend an inherent personality. As to self and self-experience, maybe a "bridge" can be constructed by conceiving "self" as the representation of a function of coherence, continuity, agency, and relationships that makes possible for us to perceive ourselves as a single, integrated, subjective embodiment. Thus, "self" is seen as a shorthand help-construction, a developmental metaphor, while we know that, in fact, this coherence and continuity are an illusion (Van Waning, 2002).

3. *What is the overall perspective and ultimate purpose in mental functioning?* A common ground is that both BP and therapy strive at helping people gradually perceive with less defensive distortions, in a less impeded or even unimpeded way. This is a recipe to help toward happiness and liberation. The notion of undistorted perception and the strategies for reaching this are significantly less radical in psychotherapy than in BP. While Buddhist practice aims to lead to enlightenment that dissolves s, clients in therapy must suffice with less harmful and less destructive defensive formations in a dualistic context. An ultimate purpose of Buddhist practice is to gain wisdom that evaporates ignorance, whereas insight in the mechanisms of defenses in order to "know thy self" is a practical aim in psychotherapy.

4. *How to handle defensive conditionings while attempting to realize the aimed perspective and purpose?* Common ground is found in the view that defenses are evoked by suffering due to external circumstances (e.g. people frustrating us), as well as from internal fabrications (e.g. confusion). Similar to other conditionings there is no escape: s are likely to return if we do not attend them. It is a reminder telling us that there is some work to do. The mechanisms need to be unravelled and the pain residing behind the has to be embraced. Both approaches may emphasize not to identify with but to explore the pain. A noticeable difference between BP and therapy is the degree in which pain can be avoided. BP regards suffering as unavoidable and an essential part of the human condition to energize resilience and development. To compassionately embrace the pain is to let outdated defenses be deconstructed and equals the acceptance of being human. Mindfulness, being with what is in silence means confiding in one's self-healing quality. This basic attitude is supplemented by specific interventions.

Applying the Four Noble Truths as a template, BP and psychotherapy seem to share the premise that life is suffering and, partly, that the cause of suffering is clinging to greed, hatred, and ignorance. However, the insight that suffering can be ended via the Eightfold Path (which comprises among others morality, meditation, and wisdom), transcends therapy's view on the human predicament. As psychotherapy deems suffering's dissolving impossible, the Buddhist point of view regards therapy as limited to finding compromises and unlearning habitual patterns.

Buddhist Psychology and Defenses: A Case in Point

In the following case of my client Ann, the workings of attraction, aversion, ignorance, and resistance to insight are illustrated and explained in terms of the skandha
process. Ann came to consult a psychiatrist because she felt threatened whenever
her boyfriend looks at another woman. She is instantly very jealous and recognizes
that her reactions are heavily exaggerated. She suffers from this condition. It stimulates her to secretly scan his diary and look through his stuff regularly, about which
she feels very much ashamed. She nags and challenges him in ways that create an
interactional cycle that spirals down: her intrusiveness and controlling attitude backs
him off to seek pleasure elsewhere, which turns her to become more jealous and
controlling, etc. The skandha cycle, in simplified form, shows: (1) bodily reaction:
e.g. due to his being late, he may have been socializing with a woman in Ann's
mind's eye; (2) sensing unpleasantness: she feels aversion; (3) visualizing: seeing
him thus, Ann travels on "automatic pilot" and closes off her perceptual-cognitive
intelligence and abilities; (4) conditioning: mental formations of anxiety due to
thinking "being left out, abandoned, or cheated/not getting her share, seen, and
respected" lead her to act habitually; (5) consciousness: a mentality of being on
guard is present such that if there is the slightest sign the cycle is re-ignited.

In therapy we recognize this pattern. Ann sees the painful consequences of her
inadequacy. A mentality in the form of a cognitive scheme can be easily detected
when spelling out a specific event. Mentality shows in step 5, while the cycling
process can be found in the steps 1-4. Ann suffers from an old pain due to being
abandoned as a child. This experience is basic to the over-stimulation of patterns
in her memory or "storehouse" consciousness (*alaya vijnana*) that are thrown up
whenever in pain that resembles the old one. Due to therapy, Ann recognizes her
mentality and patterns of defensive reactions. She divides the world as being "either for or against me," a based on a mechanism known as splitting. She also projects
onto me. In her idea I am "against" her, while in fact she is the one who opposes
me and is angry at me, particularly if I suggest her to try to look from another
person's perspective or to think in somebody else's frame of reference. When she
splits and projects I advise her to be mindful of what is happening here-now between her and me (1). I ask her to take a step back, to watch and feel her cramps, to
disidentify from whatever she senses, and to realize that her personality is not
being threatened nor in danger. Ann is able to become aware of her conditioned
body reactions as they occur. Mostly she feels tension or a little sick (2). We seek
ways for her to gradually stop reacting automatically early in the chain. Therapy
focuses on her greediness to look into his agenda, the hate and anger toward him,
the addictive quality of her attraction and aversion, and the automatic pilot reaction to her phantasies and ruminations (3). She is able to become timely aware
when slipping into conditioned ways of behaving and talking and to its maintaining factors of her conduct and speech (4). She applies mindfulness and grounding

exercises to break the cycle of seeing in self-centered terms and works to disidentify from the young child Ann (5). Eventually, she is able, with compassion, to gain insight into the troublesome feelings of jealousy and see the unresolved emotional knots from long ago. Eventually, she is also able to disidentify the feelings that she experiences as not being "she," she is so much more. Growing stronger, Ann learns to "water the good seeds" in her "storehouse" in order to breaking through resistant behavioral patterns. By experimenting with her strengths she learns to emit positive action when interacting with her partner thus experiencing possibilities to turn around. In addition she learns to express her needs and wishes instead of reproaching herself for experiencing them.

Embracing the Pain and Beyond — Conclusion

To conclude, here is a glimpse in how to embrace pain and a reflection on BP and psychotherapy. In what other ways may BP and psychotherapy enrich each other and how does Upaya (Buddhist skillful means that translate and adapt BP to local whereabouts while keeping its core message intact) help?

1. *Why and how to embrace the pain.* Why? There are basically two ways of being in the world, two ways of responding to suffering due to impermanence and the fragility of our constructed selves. On the one hand, we can try to control and fixate the world at the price of amputating and misleading our senses and eventually ourselves. On the other hand, we can open ourselves up to the world with an acceptance of open-endedness and relax while realizing we have nothing to stand on. These are ways of being, either in fear (due to greed and hatred) or in ignorance-transcending love. The latter is to be preferred. How? As to defensive conditioning, both BP and some therapies teach to actively engage in uncertainty, confusion, and pain as opportunities for insight and liberation. Their advice is to stand and embrace the pain and to attend the tendency to avoid and flee. BP considers our obstacles of daily living as our friends teaching us how we block, trap, and stuck ourselves. By mindfully exploring and embracing our stumbling blocks, instead of escaping or indulging in them, we open our hearts, deal intelligently with what is presenting here-now in our lives, and find out what needs to be done. Although both psychotherapy and BP stimulate people to drop their impeding s and to perceive in a non-distorted way, therapy that restores personality integration has a limited agenda as compared to BP that aims to awaken and see the ultimate reality of non-self.

The Brahmaviharas of the Theravada, also known as the social meditations (on kindness, compassion, joy, and equanimity, and the Tibetan meditation of *Tonglen* are ways to radically embrace pain in a self-transcending way (not only for ourselves but also for others and the world at large). In Tonglen one breathes in the hurt and the pain of somebody one likes and then, breathing out, one sends her/him happiness, joy, or whatever can relieve the other's pain. It can be done for a person one dislikes but who is in pain. It can also be done for oneself; when I suffer for instance from doubt, I can practice Tonglen simultaneously for all those who are in kindred doubt. Technically, I texture the inhaling and exhaling by visualizing the in-breathed air as brown and sticky and the out-breathed air as a golden flow. I can apply it to all people in the world, to the ones in charge of chasing and bullying others, and to those who feel threatened and hurt. Embracing the pain — seeing as it is — has an urgent survival value for all of us, personally and collectively. As Chödrön (1997, p. 93) formulates: "Tonglen reverses the usual logic of avoiding suffering and seeking pleasure. In the process, we become liberated from very ancient patterns of selfishness. We begin to feel love for both ourselves and others... Tonglen awakens our compassion and introduces us to a far bigger view of reality."

2. *Buddhist psychology and psychotherapy: a reflection.* Buddhism can be seen as a religion or philosophy, a way of life, a blueprint for civilisation, and/or a path of personal salvation. It is all but also none of these. The emphasis here is on psychology and therapy. The domain of psychotherapy is limited to dealing with clients on the basis of a dualistic conceptualization of personality in order to solve emotional problems. In BP-terms, it deals with the daily "relative" dimension of life. Construction, deconstruction, and reconstruction combine in forming the dynamic personality and its vicissitudes. Within the domain of therapy there is no place for the "ultimate" dimension that is non-dualistic and non-conceptual to which the notion of non-self belongs. In this dimension, that transcends and includes the provisional dimension, we might experience and see things as they really are. The deconstruction of ego-personality is a first step in a transformational process prior to liberation of any construction in the emptiness of non-construction. On the level of the ultimate, suffering and pain are not solved through words but dissolved in silence. The talking cure of psychotherapy helps to transform neurotic suffering into existential suffering. BP aims at liberation of existential suffering by embracing its pains.

This chapter has mainly addressed what I have indicated as defensive conditioning from a westerner's perspective. Such is necessarily culturally bounded. As Walsh (1966, p. 399) elucidates: "Our addictions, aversions, and faulty beliefs filter and distort our perception, motivation and sense of identity in such powerful yet unrecognized ways as to constitute a form of delusion or psychosis, a form that is rarely appreciated because it is culturally shared." As the "dis-ease" of personality or self is not recognized in western cultures there is no "cure" for it available in the West. Psychotherapy is meant for neurotic problems as acknowledged by the culture and indicated in psychiatry handbooks. The latter fact makes the condition a diagnosed illness according to criteria pointing at severe mental suffering. In western terms BP addresses "normal" problems of people considered "mentally healthy" within the culture they live. For them BP stimulates to follow the "transcultural" Eightfold Path as a healing method for existential suffering. BP and psychotherapy complement each other when identification with symptoms and problems prevents one from being able to walk the Buddhist path. Such individuals are usually hampered by necessitating therapy that likely helps to make Buddhist practice possible. Likewise, mindfulness that sharpens self-reflection and heightens awareness to experience seems to be an adequate preparation for and a general factor facilitating a successful therapy of any denomination.

---

1. I like to thank Prof. Henk Barendregt, Ph.D. for his comments on an earlier draft of this chapter.

9

Body Awareness And Cognitive/Emotional Functioning

Noriko Kubota

The Buddha regarded "bodymind" to be an indivisible whole, accessible by mindful awareness that observes in a neutral way. This generally heals and lifts suffering if focused on the mind and its contents as well as on the body and its feelings. The author examines the role the body plays in psychotherapy by examining the process of Dosa Therapy, developed in Japan. Dosa means voluntary body movement to bring about relaxation and changes in stuck emotions and irrational thoughts. Dosa was first developed in a rehabilitation setting for people suffering from cerebral palsy and was also found effective in changing behaviors of children with autism and ADHD. Subsequently, it began to be used as a psychotherapeutic intervention for various problems, such as obsessive-compulsive and mood disorders, or stagnating interpersonal relations. A case report illustrates that learning to make specific movements slowly, intentionally, and smoothly by relaxing arising tensions leads to beneficial psychological effects. This makes it possible to shift toward a new perspective and to view issues rationally, based on known facts, resulting on its turn in experiencing feelings naturally. It seems that such healing effect is due to consciously uniting body with mind. Through creating spaciousness for sensations, the body might become one's center of experience ameliorating mental functioning. The body thus becomes a powerful tool in the process of regaining "biopsychosocial" health and well-being.

Recently, Buddhist teaching has been reevaluated from a psychological perspective. Buddhist scholars already contend that their teaching is about insights the Buddha penetrated on how to live well and exist as fully functioning human beings (Ando, 2003). Moreover, it is a system of practical knowledge, an applied psychology, to liberate from existential suffering (due to birth, illness, aging, and death). It is quite logical that researchers in psychology since its birth as a science at the end of the 19th century showed an interest in the Buddha's teaching and that psychotherapists utilized meditation. Although the prime interest of Buddhist meditation, which is based on mindful awareness of the present moment in a neutral way, is awakening/enlightenment, some of its varieties are apt as therapeutic intervention to remedy mental suffering. A wholistic view on the "bodymind" is one of the main tenets in the Buddhist perspective on human existence. In the West, body and mind have been viewed as two separate entities, particularly since Descartes' conceptualization in the seventeenth century. "I think, thus I exist" reflects a stance in which mind is given a superior position, while body is given a subordinate status. The body is seemingly controlled by the mind. Contrary to this view, in the East, particularly in the Buddhist teaching, mindbody is viewed as an indivisible whole. Bodymind is intricately connected and works simultaneousy in refined coordination to perform all human functions.

The interest in the Buddhist outlook seems to signify the limitations of industrialized society that highly values science, technology, and economical growth rather than the development of human potentials. This prime interest in the human inside nature has lead to value knowledge gained through concrete action and experience as more significant than knowledge obtained through abstractions that are isolated from actual experience. The best of both worlds can evolve into something new. From such a framework a body-psychotherapy — called Dosa Therapy (DT) — was developed in Japan. Through a case report this new type of psychotherapy that uses the body as a springboard to connect to mind will be explained. This chapter examines its effectiveness by exploring body-mind interactions and assessing the role the body plays in changing psychological functioning.

Body Focus in Psychotherapy

In order to access experiential levels of functioning, humanistic psychologists have incorporated techniques that address the client's bodily awareness (somatic sensations). For example, Gendlin (1986), an experiential therapist, developed "focusing" highlighting internal experience, and Kepner (1987), a Gestalt therapist, incorporated body-oriented techniques enhancing self-awareness. An emphasis on the body in psychotherapy can be traced back to Reich (1897-1957). He pioneered the use of the body as a tool to understand and solve psychological problems through body movements. As a student of Freud, he considered libido to be essential in human functioning and developed the concept of orgone energy (comparable to what we would call *Ki* in Japan). Reich thought orgone energy is actually body energy. Based on this notion, he conceptualized neurosis as the physical blockage of the flow of orgone energy in the body. He assumed a parallel between rigidities in the body and rigidities in the mind. The latter is reflected in disturbed thinking about one's self, one's world, and some other issues. Reich listened not just to what people say, but watched also how they say what they say and particularly observed what their bodies do when they talk. He inferred from one's body language defensive mind patterns, which he called body armor created through childhood experiences (Reich, 1972). In order to release such rigidities, Reich developed techniques to work with the body; he focused on posture, muscular tension, and breathwork (West, 1994). Reich's students developed their own form of body-oriented psychotherapy: Bioenergetics (Lowen, 1976), Core Energetics (Pierrakos, 1987), and Biosynthesis (Boadella, 1986).

The body has also been addressed in various forms of relaxation that facilitate self-control in Cognitive-Behavior Therapy. For example, autogenic training (Schultz & Luthe, 1959) progressive relaxation (Jacobson, 1974), biofeedback (Schwarts, 1973), and Zen (Shapiro, 1980) emphasize the utility of relaxation skills as an alternative that reduces anxiety reactions (Kazdin, 1984). Particularly, Wolpe (1976) who in the early days of Behavior Therapy developed systematic desensitization incorporated Jacobson's relaxation to reciprocally inhibit anxiety and other stress reactions. Goldfried (1971) further developed Wolpe's systematic desensitization by not just regulating the physiological arousal of anxiety, but by also applying relaxation as a cognitive self-control strategy in a coping skills framework. In the same vain Shapiro (1980) reformulated Zen Buddhist meditation as a cognitive-behavioral self-control application to be readily used whenever and wherever necessary. In these interventions, the working mechanism is explained mainly by the physiology of relaxation, which is assumed to countercondition unwanted emotional states. In this line of innovations, Kabat-Zinn (1990) developed a stress reduction program utilizing "mindfulness," a term used from the early twentieth century on to refer to Vipassana or insight meditation that stems from the Theravada (Early) Buddhist school. The difference between this Buddhist based approach and cognitive-behavioral tactics is that relaxation is not pursued, but rather the acceptance of whatever appears on the screens of body/mind. The focus is on awareness (observing thinking, feeling, and the nuances in sensations' texture) without a goal. Rather than targeting on relaxation to eliminate emotional disturbance, the emotional suffering is accepted and befriended. The contents of thinking and feeling are changed by how one relates to these inner phenomena, including painful bodily experiences.

In sum, the body has been addressed in various ways in psychological interventions. The degree of body focus, the theory on the body's role in etiology, the way to use the body to bring about change, and the conceptualization of underlying mechanisms vary depending on the therapist's theory. However, there is one common thread, which is the underlying assumption, that body-and-mind function in full synergy by closely interacting with each other. This is also the basic idea of DT (Naruse, 1973, 1992) that has been applied to help individuals cope with their problems in various clinical settings. Clinical studies have been conducted to examine its effectiveness with various client populations in Japan and the results are supportive (Fujioka, 1987; Hoshikawa, 1992; Kubota, 1991, 2000; Ogawa, 1992; Shimizu, 1992; Tsuru, 1982).

Historical background of Dosa Therapy

Dosa means motor action and DT utilizes voluntary movements as a means to bring about changes in cognitive, behavioral, and emotional functioning. This method was originally developed as a psychological rehabilitation program for cerebral palsy and was called Dosa training (Naruse, 1973, 1985, 1992; Ohno, 1978). Motor difficulties due to cerebral palsy are allegedly caused by damage in the brain's motor areas. Conventional rehabilitation programs are based on neurological understanding and aim to inhibit abnormal muscle tone and to facilitate normal movement patterns (Bellenir, 1997). A new approach was initiated by a group of Japanese psychologists who addressed problems in motor control due to cerebral palsy from a psychological point of view. They investigated the psychological factors that play a direct role in the motor control process. As a result, they developed and launched a rehabilitation program to remedy the motor problems of cerebral palsy.

Based on his understanding of the motoric problems in cerebral palsy, Naruse (1973) proposed the concept of Dosa as a process of human voluntary motor movement in general and depicted the motor control process on a behavioral level. The Dosa process is a psychological, self-regulatory process controlled by higher mental operations under which physiological systems are subsumed. This process consists of three components: intention, effort/striving, and physical movement (see Figure 1).

Figure 1: Diagram of the Dosa process

For instance, when we perform a voluntary movement, we first intend to perform a specific movement and make a plan to do so (Intention). Based on this plan, we exert efforts to move relevant parts of our body (Striving) to actualize the intended movement (Physical Movement). When the effort is adequate, the intended movement will be the result. During this process, a person operates his/her body based on sensory feedback. In this respect, the Dosa process is an active self-operational process rather than a merely automatic, physiological process. Naruse, thus, differentiated the Dosa process from physical movement; the former focuses on psychological operation during motor control, while the latter addresses neurological and musculoskeletal mechanisms, the hardware of voluntary movement. He also emphasized the Dosa process as a dynamic interplay between various control systems, which include mental activities of motor control, neurological circuits, and musculoskeletal systems.

Along with this conceptualization of the Dosa process, experiments expanding the application of Dosa training for individuals with problems other than cerebral palsy were conducted. Konno (1977) used Dosa training to treat a boy's behavioral problems due to Attention-Deficit Hyperactivity Disorder (ADHD). He aimed to facilitate the attention-focusing and behavior-regulation abilities through Dosa training. Besides characteristic behavioral problems such as impeded concentration and impulsivity, children with ADHD generally show problems in motor coordination. They tend to tense their entire body when moving a specific body part, which suggests a lack of differentiation of body parts. Konno hypothesized that if he could teach the boy how to relax, he might learn how to focus his attention to control disruptive behaviors. His studies show the effectiveness of Dosa training in changing the emotional and behavioral problems typical among children with ADHD. These and other studies suggest the possibility that the improvement of motor control ability influences one's psychological functioning. Based on this assumption, psychotherapists started to use the exercises to work with various other psychological problems and examined Dosa's effectiveness as a psychotherapeutic technique. Thus, DT was coined as term for this new psychotherapeutic intervention (Naruse, 1992).

The Client

The client (N) was a married woman of 28. When she consulted me in the beginning, she suffered from a phobia of traveling by train. Taking or anticipating taking a train alone, she would sweat excessively, her heart would beat wildly and her legs would tremble. If someone was with her, this distraction helped her to decrease her anxiety. Knowing in advance that she had to take a train, she would become so nervous the day before that she would not fall asleep at night. At night N feared death and dying. Such fear occasionally overwhelmed her all of a sudden, seemingly without any cause or trigger. She then became restless and broke out in a cold sweat, and her heart pounded accordingly. N was diagnosed as having a panic disorder with agoraphobia.

History of problem. The fear of death haunted N since her grandfather died when she was in the 6th grade. Whenever she saw or read about death-related news on TV or in the newspaper, she started to worry and her heart began to pound. One day when in the train on her way to work, her heart suddenly started to pound and she felt the urge to get off the train immediately. She was so frightened that her mind went blank. Although she could take a train after this incident, one night she woke up with a fear of death. She panicked and ran out of the house. After this incident she became afraid to travel by train. Her condition gradually generalized to other types of events. For example, she became afraid of meetings and other situations from which she could not escape easily. Around this time she started to see a psychiatrist who prescribed her medication that helped a bit. Despite taking pills, N felt anxious while waiting for a train on the platform, but if she did not need to wait long, her fear was less intense. After getting married, her condition improved for a while and her fear of traveling by train disappeared. However, one day, when sitting in a train feeling tired, fear took her by surprise. After this event, her condition deteriorated and there was a relapse to the level prior to her marriage. She became housebound, impatient, and angry at herself, throwing and kicking things. Unable to eat well, she disclosed her troubles to the husband.

Family structure and personality traits. N is the second of two daughters; she was born in a traditional three-generation Japanese family. Ten years younger than her sister, the latter took care of her as a child. It felt as if she has had two mothers. At school her friends were caring girls who provided her a lot of help when she needed it. She heavily relied on her sister and friends during childhood. There was no need for her to resolve things independently. She described herself as someone who is nervous and very timid. Tending to worry too much, she had a penchant to feel depressed. Unable to tolerate being alone, her overall proclivity might be called dependency.

Problem hypothesis. N's panic attacks seem to have developed as a condition beyond her control. Because N could not exert control over her uncomfortable physical reactions, she became more and more afraid of situations likely to induce anxiety. Therefore, she requested help. The therapy should aim at obtaining control over her panic and changing her attitude toward it. I offered her DT comprising exercises in motor control in order to pursue this goal. By slowly moving her body in a specific direction and relaxing the tension in various parts of her body (which arises while making an intended movement), I assume that N would gradually experience/accept her body as her own and would feel that she is capable to control her body movements. It was hypothesized that the experience of reunifying mindbody and owning/accepting her body as part of her self-control system would change the way she views and feels about the situation and that this would subsequently lead to a change in her physical reactions of fear.

Treatment Report

Dosa relaxation exercises of shoulders and torso were used as task movements. The first exercise was for her to pull her shoulders up toward her ears and gradually release the tension while in a sitting position. The torso exercise makes N bend her upper body backward. It has her to sit on the floor with crossed legs and to gently pull her upper body backward while holding the lower back stable. In another torso exercise, she twists the upper body while lying down on her side. While holding her lower back stable, I slowly push her upper shoulder toward the floor and helped N twists the upper body. The focus during these exercises was on having her pay attention to somatic sensations. Thus, while making the specified movement, she learns to become aware of subtle changes in various body parts. From this awareness she will naturally find a strategy or tactics to relax tension, which arises while pursuing the task movement.

The treatment process was spread during four months and contained 15 sessions. N and I met for one hour a week. The first half of the session was used for the talking cure, which includes counseling and discussing the self-monitoring homework notes, while the second half was devoted to Dosa. I explained DT as a type of relaxation. When relaxed, it is more likely that one will view problems from a different angle. The client was interested in DT, saying that as a high school student, she was told that she had developed scoliosis, a condition of a slightly bent spine. That is why she often felt an uncomfortable stiffness in her shoulders. When I asked N to stand in an upright position to observe her posture, her left shoulder was positioned slightly higher than the right one. Her shoulders stooped, her chin stuck out. During the shoulders exercise, although she was unable unable to release the tension easily, she reported feeling relaxed as if she was falling asleep. When I assisted her to stretch her stooped shoulder by gently pulling up the back of her neck, she did not resist this movement, relaxed the back of her neck, and felt comfortable. And when I helped her bend backward by gently pulling her jaw, her upper body moved back a little and the strong tension in her whole upper body disappeared. Able to release this tension on her own after a while, she became aware of the relaxation and reported that the back of her neck was stretched, a comfortable feeling. She also had a throbbing pain in the temples before the practice, but this disappeared during the exercise. In general, she felt refreshed. When the exercise was over, N stated that she felt her neck had become a little longer than before and that she could feel her blood circulating all the way to her fingertips. Moreover, she felt very comfortable and saw things more brightly than before.

In the following few Dosa sessions, N learned to relax tension in her body more smoothly and at the same time she also became aware of her body sensations more clearly. This combination of body awareness and increased relaxation made the way she feels about her body change. Her body felt calm and she had a much clearer awareness of her physical state. When she released tension from her shoulder, she noticed that her restlessness before the exercise subsided. In relaxing her body backward, strong tension appeared in her whole upper body when her lower back was lifted up from the floor. She felt tightness in her lower back without having a clue how to release this; she also felt uneasiness in letting go of the tension. When I gently pushed her lower back toward the floor, it helped her relax the tension in her lower back. Releasing the tension in that part, she felt more comfortable. In the third session, N reported that as she tried to relax her body, too much attention was focused on the specific area and as a result that hindered her from relaxing the tension as intended. In twisting the upper body, strong tension arose in the torso and the movement of her body stopped. She managed to relax the tension after a while and felt as if her body was moved by the therapist. In the fourth session, she became aware of subtle sensations in various parts of her body and reported changes therein as she relaxed. When standing up after the exercise, the left shoulder's elevation decreased substantially and when upright, she naturally put weight evenly on both legs instead of putting her weight on one leg as she used to do. Her stiff shoulders became more flexible. From this point on her condition improved gradually.

N's condition in daily life started to change. She did not have stiff shoulders for a whole week, went to a sale, and bought many things. Thinking that she had bought more items than necessary, N felt disgusted with herself. Her heart started to pound when getting on a train to go home. She told herself that it was a short ride and that she would get off before long. Surprisingly, the anxiety disappeared instantly. While on the train, she thought about her reaction prior to the disgust and came to the conclusion that not having known how to handle her feeling of disgust might have triggered the anxiety. She started to see herself objectively by analyzing the situation which caused her to experience negative feelings. N began a part-time job around this time. Every morning she worried whether she would be able to go to work, but her anxiety did not worsen. Thus, she was able to go to work every day. As her negative thinking became less obsessive and she was able to think that she did not necessarily have to go to work every day and if she did not feel like going, she could always take a day off and go back to work, refreshed, on the following day. Around this time, her mother was hospitalized and she had the task to take care of her father at her parents' house. This means that she was obliged to go to her parents' house frequently for a while. N turned into a busy woman. However, she could use her time efficiently by making a schedule. Thus, she was able to take care of things as planned. By reviewing these changes, she recounted feeling strange, not able to believe this was real. She commented that since childhood, she was neither able nor capable of coping with difficult situations and always blamed herself for that. Since the recent change, she is able to console herself about her situation by thinking that there are times things don't go well no matter how hard one tries. Things are as they are. N realized that accepting makes a situation less stressful and easier to take.

In the fifth session, N stated she could release the tension more easily than before and also anticipated the feelings of relaxation before she actually relaxed her body. During this period, more changes in her daily life occurred. Going on a new railway line, her heart started to pound, but after taking medication she was able to get on the train. N came to realize the futility of worrying about how others see her and of acting like someone who is liked by everybody. This theatre she played only for herself, exhausted her. In the sixth session, she managed to release the strong tension in her upper body after struggling for a while and stated that she could relax her body from the upper back to the lower back, which brought a refreshed sensation between her eyebrows. When her upper body returned to the upright position after relaxation, she felt as if her head is sitting squarely on top of her spine. After the practice, with contentment on her face she reported being satisfied having accomplished a difficult task. At this point in time, she took a vacation abroad. The night before taking the airplane, she was overwhelmed by the fear of dying. She took medication and started reading a guidebook, which distracted her. This changed her mood to a pleasant one, such that she could fall asleep. The next day when she took the plane, she was excited about the trip rather than being fearful. She enjoyed her holidays as never before. Change occurred at the worksite as well. At a previous job, when she thought her assignment was too difficult, she became pale and anxious, and left the office. However, now she was able to talk about it calmly with her coworkers. This lifted more weight from her shoulders. N came to realize that everyone might feel the same hassle as she does. She saw her current condition, which is going to work every day and taking things easy as strange and unlike her, but hoped this would last forever. The way of exerting is different and she is convinced that the new efforts will lead her to the right direction. In the eighth session, N could relax smoothly: she now knows how to release tension without too much effort. She felt comfortable and was able to conjure up this condition by herself.

During this time, her husband's relative died. While attending the funeral, she was calm throughout from the wake to the burial. Although feeling fear before going to bed that night, she fell asleep eventually without medication. When N got on a train with her husband they could not sit together because of the crowd, she was able to sit alone without having to distract herself. Her change was noticed by both husband and mother (who meanwhile recovered well), who commented that N looks happier than before. In the following few sessions, N's self-relaxation skills progressed. Even if she felt tension at the beginning, she could release it in various parts of her body by paying attention to the relevant parts. She could do so more easily and stated having control over her body. N thus dared to go to a movie with a colleague after work. When the preview started, she became fearful thinking about what she should do if she would become sick. Somewhat later, when the movie started, she realized that if sick, she could always get out. The fear subsided; N could enjoy the movie. She became aware of a shift in her experience. While she would force herself to calm down before in this kind of situation, simply accepting when it happens calms her down now. N reiterated that it felt strange to recall that she did worry about all these things so much in the past. In contrast, if she cannot perform a task at work, she allowed herself to say so assertively rather than acting against the grain. One day, N even fell asleep on the train. It was for the first time since her anxiety disorder started that she could feel that kind of relaxation. From that time on N started to take the train alone. Although she felt some fear about taking a long-distance train, she no longer experienced any physical reactions because of it. Not only was N able to independently schedule and plan activities in advance, she was able to start to feel control over her life. The overall decrease in anxiety has lead to an increase in confidence and contentment. She moved to another town due to her husband's job transfer and thus the DT was terminated. A follow-up session was held on the telephone about one year after the termination. N reported that she was continuously enjoying her life and that she became anxious when traveling with a long distance train, however, she was able to sit on the train without any uncomfortable physical reactions and was medication free.

Discussion

This discussion examines the process of the DT, the accompanying awareness, and modes of experiencing during the in-session exercises meant to bring about changes in the client's daily life. Juxtaposing this process and the client's changes in the course of treatment, parallel patterns of experiencing are noticeable.

Mode of experiences in Dose exercises. Overall it was observed that N learned to relax and move her body more smoothly and intentionally as the practice proceeded. In other words, N broke out of her old, dysfunctional movement pattern, re-encountered her body, and owned/accepted her body in a new, more cooperative manner. This also can be viewed as a process in which N became an active agent and that she came to generate autonomy in striving for self-relaxation. Specifically, when N relaxed the tension in her body in the first session, she became much more aware of positive changes in her body's sensations. N felt comfortable and her report suggests that she experienced relaxation as salubrious. There is openness for new experiences. In the second session, there was an awakening for bodily sensations. As she relaxesd her body, N came to sense feelings in her body more clearly and actually in the here-and-now. This suggests that she started to feel her body more fully and vividly through the experience of being able to relax her body by herself. But, the self-relaxation exercise did not progress smoothly and she continued to experienced difficulty relaxing her body. The same applies to the third session; although N intended to relax her body, she failed to do so. Struggling to relax her body, she focused too much attention on specific areas and as a result was hindered from completely relaxing tensions. This indicates that her strategy for self-relaxation did not yet work. Relaxing tension by herself, she felt as if the therapist had moved her body. This implies that self-relaxation was experienced in a passive mode. In other words, sensations of bodily tension and relaxation were not yet fully experienced as her own, not accepted and kept out of awareness.

In the fourth session, N specified the tense parts of her body and released the tension in the identified areas. This indicates that the self-relaxation had progressed. She was able to relax her body more intentionally in the right direction against previously unconscious intentions, strivings, and movements. It also indicates that she was becoming actively involved in the self-relaxation process. A change in her posture was observed around this time. It is assumed that through the exercise N learned to hold her body in a less tense and more coordinated way while seeking position in three-dimensional space. In the fifth session, she could release the tension more easily and reported having signs of relaxation in advance. This suggests that N became aware of subtle changes and that she was involved in the relaxation process from an early stage rather than noticing it after or while it happened. In the sixth session, relaxation of her upper body progressed. Although N experienced strong tension in her body and struggled to relax the tension, she eventually managed to do it and was satisfied. This experience suggests that N was actively learning a strategy for self-relaxation. In the eighth session, N relaxed her occurring tension with less effort in moving her body and was able to relax without forcefully trying to do so. In the twelfth session, while relaxing her body, N could relax it as intended, and in the fourteenth session, she could relax her body without paying too much attention. N's self-relaxation skills improved markedly; relaxation became more natural and with less striving, thus more "automatically." She came to own/accept her body and to incorporate it into her new self-control system. It is inferred that these experiences made N feel contented and confident.

Effects of Dosa experience on behavioral changes. In the second session, N started to observe herself more objectively by analyzing her reactions in anxious situations. By doing so, panic subsided quite quickly. It is assumed that paying attention to body sensations and movements in a neutral manner during the first Dosa exercise helped her view herself and the situation in real life from an objective perspective. *Here is a mindful awareness component that de-automatized her thinking and behaving not only the Buddhist way, but also the cognitive-behavioral way.* Such helped her distance herself from her reactions, thus preventing her from being swallowed automatically by anxiety. In the third session, N's decreased obsessive thinking is observed in her stating that she does not have to go to work every day and, if she does not feel like going, she could take a day off and go back to work on the following day, refreshed. In the fourth session, N also showed an attitude of accepting reality without blaming herself by expounding that there are times when things don't go well, no matter how hard we try. These comments illustrate that N came to view challenging situations from a very different point of view and to accept reality, including herself, as the way it is, without trying to pretend to be someone else. In the Dosa exercise, she started to learn how to release bodily tension and succeeded. It is assumed that the experiences of being able to overcome the obstacles in her body by simply being aware of it and to accomplish self-relaxation led to the changes in her cognition to accepting things as they are.

In the fifth session, N could take a train route she had never taken before. She proved thus to be able to cope with new anxiety-provoking situations. Along with this behavioral change, she recognized unconscious motives and consequent negativity when interacting with others. Previously she had tried too hard to adjust herself to others' expectations. In the Dosa exercise, when N noticed subtle changes in body sensations, the scoliosis moved to the background. This posture change illustrates that N learned to adjust her body against gravity by fine-tuning the delicate balance between tension and relaxation in various body parts. This awareness/

experience of body adjusting in three-dimensional space might have helped her to adjust in relationships. In the sixth session, N could enjoy an airplane trip and showed further improvement in her condition. She could also cope with her stress at work by complaining to her colleagues and described the current attitude as more productive than ever before. In the Dosa exercise, N came to learn relaxation strategies that felt more naturally and deepened the sense of being able to do it herself. It is assumed that this experience has led to a coping attitude in life (based on a sense of self-efficacy). In the seventh session, N could fall asleep even if anxious when thinking about death. In the following week, she could take a train without having to distract herself. In the ninth session, she went to a movie and enjoyed it. When N started to worry, she accepted rather than avoided whatever popped up in her mind.

These events illustrate the decrease in her anxiety level and how it might have come about. The changes in body condition appeared to have lead to a change in her attitude: from an attitude of avoidance for anxiety-provoking situations to an accepting, if not confrontational one. N dared to be different. In the tenth session, N reported acts of self-confidence and being contented with her life. She at last was living her own life and this new stance continued until treatment termination. Unfortunately no follow-up reports are available. In N's experience, it was through DT that she could regain her daily life in a satisfying way.

Conclusion

This report demonstrates that DT might well improve motor control ability (i.e. to incorporate body in one's self-control system), naturally affect how a client views herself/her world, and spontaneously modify the way she interacts. Specifically, as N learned to move her body smoothly and intentionally, and as she regained control over her body, the excessive emotional reactions to anxiety-provoking situations decreased. As a consequence, her life also changed toward adaptation and independence. Seemingly, this process of awareness and relaxation led her to expand her consciousness. By knowing herself better and bringing her potential into full play, wellbeing was the result.

On a more theoretical level, DT as foremost a body therapy that emphasizes relaxation parallels, other psychotherapies wherein talking is the cure. Both strive to change emotional disturbance and its concomitant behaviors and cognitions. Obviously, relaxing only the body is a different kind of springboard than only talking; DT, as a form of psychotherapy combines the two. In both cases, awareness of what one thinks, feels, and does is a prerequisite to changing them. In both approaches, mindful awareness of what needs to be changed is implicitly assumed. However, DT's neutral observation to have clients pay attention to body sensations and become aware of subtle changes in the various parts of the body, while doing task movements, is implicitly an awareness exercise. In contrast, most of the talking cures do not attend such training in awareness as a first step. Learning to discern between intention, striving, and physical movement is an implicit way to teach clients sensory awareness, the essence of mindfulness. In fact, in the concept of intention lies a world of ideas that is known in the Buddhist teaching as karma (intentional activity). In a way one might say that learning to be conscious of intentions and strivings to move or act is to change karma.

As DT is not per se a Buddhist exercise (no therapy is), there is no compelling need to disclose the rich source of Buddhist Psychology to clients. It suffices here to conclude that DT implicitly contains components of mindful awareness. One might even submit that analogous to Mindfulness-Based Cognitive Therapy (see elsewhere in this book), a new brand of therapy had been practiced that could be coined: Mindfulness-Based Dosa Therapy.

Part II

Horizons
Of Research

Introduction

Upaya or "skillful means" refers to the proficiency in method for bringing about change in well-being. Although this ability was already applied by the Buddha who adjusted what he taught to the audience he addressed, it became considerably important four centuries later in the Mahayana movement. Upaya belongs to the basic skills of the Buddhist teacher, pre-eminently represented by the Bodhisattva, who is dedicated to freeing others from the shackles of ignorance. The multiple arms in the symbol of compassion (the bodhisattva Avalokiteshvara) depict all possible means available in helping to liberate — from straightforward talk to conspicuous miracles. Several scriptures deal with the issue of skilful means, amongst others the Lotus Sutra, in which a rationale is given through parables as to how the upaya can be handled as a strategy, tactic, and technique. For instance, presented as a wise and kind father the Buddha modeled the skill of telling lies to his foolish children to lure them from a burning house. This educative narrative allows relative freedom to act out of compassion. To approach "different folks with different strokes" in a provisional world requires the teachers' capacity to adjust to the relativity of changing times, persons, and places.

This book aims to move beyond the well-trodden tracks previous upayas have taken, largely because we feel they cease to be viable either in speaking to large sectors of contemporary culture, or in contributing to conditions of global well-being. Rather, traditional upayas often rely on an esoteric metaphysics, and create a religious-like orientation that divides and separates the world's peoples. Although functional in speaking to illiterate people in cultures where magic is ubiquitous, such upayas are nowadays confusing and suspicious. They honor the converted while disparaging the less than worshipful. It is in this sense we strive to rejuvenate the Dharma as a transcultural (i.e. transparent) orientation to practice that converges with the cutting edge of social, clinical, and neuropsychological research. In effect, contemporary upaya may be better achieved by employing the skilful strategy of contemporary research, the results of which are open to all for examination and discussion. In attempting to realize a New Buddhist Psychology, or Neoyana, it is useful to operationalize the *Dharma* as a science and practice of psychology, a non-theistic and non-metaphysical orientation to practice. The systematic methods of the sciences employ narratives and metaphors that invite broad, non-partisan participation.

In this move toward research methodology we do not at all wish to abandon the upayas of the past. Many continue to speak in special ways to contemporary audiences throughout the world. However, our primary aim is to augment these traditions with forms of illumination that speak more effectively in the present. This is not to endorse the fruits of contemporary research as somehow closer to

Truth than earlier metaphysics and religious teachings. It is here that the Dharma joins social construction in cautioning against ultimate commitment to any specific discourse about the world or self. Rather, we do believe that empirical findings can generate useful predictions (e.g. gauging the efficacy of a particular practice), translate abstract and otherwise esoteric terms into concrete practices, and generate new and enriching understandings of our circumstances. Of special concern, contemporary research methods are also linked in significant ways with therapeutic practices. Evidence based therapy is now embraced in large sectors of western culture. To see empirical research as a means of being "guided by experience in exploring the world," strongly links the Dharma, social construction and upaya.

In Part II we extend the horizons of research in Buddhist Psychology with 10 exemplars. These inquiries employ a rich variety of methods, measures, and populations of study. The first studies are those of Fusako Koshikawa and her colleagues. In Chapter 10 she and Yasutomo Ishii consider several important issues in the Zen tradition, and particularly ways in which to empirically determine the beneficial effects of Zen practices. In Chapter 11 they are joined by Ayako Kuboki to explore the practice of Shikanho, a cognitive-behavioral method for achieving a state of non-self. As their research demonstrates, the Shikanho method is effective in alleviating feelings of negativity provoked by unpleasant events. In Chapter 12, Michael de Vibe describes a program of mindfulness training concerned with reducing stress and enhancing health. As his research shows, this program is quite effective, and its results continue from at least 3-6 months after the program is complete. In a similar vein, Fabio Giommi (Chapter 13) demonstrates the positive effects of a mindfulness-based stress reduction program in treating emotional disorders. The pivotal process seems to be the capacity of mindfulness to direct attention. Rounding out this concern with the efficacy of mindfulness, Yoshinori Ito, Rieko Katsukura and Kaneo Nedate describe research in which Zen meditation is effective in modifying metacognitive awareness, and thus reduce depression. The results were achieved in 10 sessions (20 minutes each) of sitting, in addition to homework on Buddhist wisdom and zazen rationale.

The remaining chapters in Part II focus on more specialized issues. In Chapter 15, Nedate, Katsukura and Ito present a Japanese measure of awareness and coping in autobiographical memory, a useful instrument in assessing the experience of negative thoughts and feelings as they arise. In the following chapter, Yoshinori Sugiura explores various personality correlates of mindfulness. He concludes that "refraining from catastrophic thinking" may be the most powerful working ingredient in mindfulness practice. In Chapter 17, Michael Tophoff presents the results of an empirical study demonstrating that managers participating in a sensory awareness seminar not only became increasingly aware of bodily signals, but more content with both their relationships and their functioning on the job. Miguel Quintana then demonstrates the efficacy of combining Tai Chi (moving meditation) with Zen meditation (sitting meditation), in reducing anxiety (Chapter 18). Finally, in

Jane Henry's contribution we find that in a survey of people from many different professions, various practices of "quietening the mind" are preferred over many other means of achieving a sense of well-being. As she concludes, talk therapy may be overemphasized as a tool for enhancing the lives of clients.

In our view, these contributions offer substantial reason for confidence in the efficacy of Buddhist practices for bringing about human change. Never in the history of therapeutic psychology has such a concerted effort been made to generate reliable evidence for a given orientation. To be sure, as innovations are spawned and the meaning of these practices becomes more fully disseminated, new research will be necessitated. There is a particularly important need for expanding the research focus beyond the effects on individual well-being, to the relationships in which people are engaged. In any case, the present offerings provide a solid grounding from which such research may proceed.

10

Zen Buddhism And Psychology: Some Experimental Findings[1]

Fusako Koshikawa & Yasutomo Ishii

It is surely true to say that the ancient tradition of Zen Buddhist thought and practice has been handed down in living form to the present day because of its positive effect on people's minds and behavior. We believe strongly in the need to determine how this discipline can be put to beneficial use today. In this chapter we discuss three topics. The first is related to our idea about how to comprehend the concept of "real self"/non-self in Zen thought from a psychological standpoint. The second is related to the technique for realising the non-self state of mind, and we provide some experimental data on it. The third is related to the application of Zen thought to areas of psychology such as health, clinical, and personality psychology. A definition of non-self (Sanskrit, anatman*), which is a most important concept in Zen, is given with an explanation in psychological terms. The applicability of non-self to personality theory as well as to health and clinical issues are discussed. A detailed description of* Shikanho, *a technique based on "just looking," is offered as a practical way to reduce mental problems.*

Zen as a meditational practice arose in India and Zen Buddhism in China. The seeds of Zen Buddhism were brought to China by the Indian monk Bodhidharma in 521 or 527 and the groundwork for the subsequent development of Zen thought in China was laid by Hui-neng (Eno, 638-713). In contrast to Indian Buddhism, which attaches particular importance to philosophical ideas, Zen emerged as a practical discipline dealing with questions concerning the conduct of everyday life. Later on, during the second half of the Japanese Kamakura Period, the monk Eisai (1141-1215) introduced the Rinzai school associated with Tai-hui (1089-1163) and Dogen (1200-53) introduced the Soto school associated with Huang-chih (1090-1157). These two schools reached their zenith between the 13th and 15th century (corresponding to the Kamakura and Muromachi periods). Soto and Rinzai as they exist today have their own distinctive features, but their underlying premise is the same, namely that awakening to reality is possible only when one attains a state of non-self and lives each moment for itself.

There are two principal characteristics of Zen, manifest in the concept of non-self and the unique training system known as *zazen*, or sitting in Zen meditation.

The aim of meditation in Zen is to realise the state of non-self by dropping all self-related concerns. The belief is that the "real self" takes over when the self is removed and the state of non-self is attained (Akizuki, 1990).

The Idea of Non-Self

Non-self is a concept unique to Buddhism and asserts that there is no substantive self (Sanskrit, *atman*). Why was there a need for a philosophy of non-self? It was because Buddhism teaches that the roots of human suffering lie in attachment to the self. Accordingly, the desire to be truly free from suffering can be realised only by ceasing to be preoccupied with the self. Buddhism also teaches that preoccupation with one's own self begins with discrimination between oneself and others. Discrimination results in a continuing preoccupation with targets of discrimination. For example, I'm sure you will notice that there's a difference on an emotional level between saying "I have 10 yuan and you have 1000 yuan" and "here are 10 yuan and there are 1000 yuan." Using the words "here" and "there" instead of the personally discriminatory "I" and "you" transmits different feelings because we all tend to feel happier when we have more money than others. There is discrimination here between "I" and "you." Zen Buddhism places absolute importance on one's state of mind before discrimination and it teaches us that we should resolve to keep ourselves in that state of mind. Because we often use language as a tool for making distinctions or for discrimination, Zen instructs us to experience situations directly as they are without resort to language. It is contrary to Buddhist thought to allow ourselves to use language as a tool for discrimination rather than using it as a tool in our lives.

A Psychological Approach to Non-Self

I (FK) became interested in Zen Buddhist philosophy when I was relatively young. At the time I was sceptical about whether it would be possible to approach Zen Buddhist thought from a psychological perspective. As the assertion of non-self is tantamount to saying that there are no verifiable objects, it was my belief that the idea of non-self did not lend itself to treatment as a subject for psychology, which methodology is based on scientific verification. However, it dawned on me that if non-self is taken to mean a unique type of belief supported or crystallised by a certain experience referred to as *satori* or enlightenment, then the non-self concept is directly related to the targets of Cognitive Therapy and Rational Emotive Behavior Therapy. This finding opened my eyes to the fact that a psychological approach to non-self is possible if the non-self belief or state is treated as a subject for study rather than if the non-self concept is handled directly as a subject of psychology. This was the starting point for my research.

I felt, however, that most people, unless knowledgeable about Zen, would not readily be able to accept the non-self theory. In fact, the studies I have conducted concerning the effects of self-instruction point out that people find it difficult to change their behavior or mental state if they follow a belief only outwardly and without true personal conviction (Koshikawa et al., 2001). I then went on to examine how it might be possible to describe non-self in psychological terms. Earlier I explained that Zen is a technique to induce the state of non-self, and that its underlying principle is to deny one's self or your self completely, to get rid of self and to realise the state of non-self. How can one understand from the point of view of psychology the idea of getting rid of one's self and acquiring a state of not-self or non-self?

I began by using my own experience of Zen meditation as the basis for my studies. I once had a very interesting experience. I was watching a particular scene when it suddenly transformed into something that I could describe only by saying that it was colorless and serene. It then returned to its former state. I was very surprised. The phrase that came to my mind at the time was *shiki soku ze ku, ku soku ze shiki* in Japanese (generally this phrase is translated into English as "matter is void, the very emptiness is form"), which is so often used in the world of Zen. From my own experience, the formless, colorless and serene scene overlapped with a situation in which my value judgments, discrimination, and language were completely gone. This experience made me realise that all occurrences are essentially the same, that although they are distinguishable physically, they cannot be discriminated one from the other, and that it is my own value judgments and discrimination that give them form. This led me to conclude that if my value judgments and discrimination are what is being described as form or matter in the phrase *shiki soku ze ku*, then my state of mind free from such value judgments and discrimination may accord with the ideas of non-self, emptiness, and void.

Zen attaches importance to a state of mind free from discrimination. Perhaps I might explain this state as follows. Let's assume that you are frightened of black shadows. If an acquaintance tells you that seeing a black shadow will bring you happiness, then what will happen if you take him at his word? Perhaps the black shadow will cease to frighten you and, on the contrary, will become something you aspire. The black shadow is thus not something to be discriminated against in its own right. Originally there is merely a distinction between black and white. Zen teaches that it is we who create discrimination and that this is the cause of our suffering. From a psychological perspective, discrimination is a belief and form of cognition that we have ourselves adopted. By freeing ourselves from this belief and form of cognition related to discrimination, we are able to free ourselves from suffering. This is the concept of Zen seen from a psychological perspective.

On the basis of my own experience as referred to earlier, I have decided to use the "mind state without discrimination" as a working hypothesis for understanding the idea of non-self from a psychological standpoint and for applying this idea to psychology. I have earlier presented papers on this topic in Japanese in 1994 and in English in 1998 (Koshikawa, 1994, 1998). How is it possible then to attain a state of mind without discrimination? I have examined this matter from various angles, taking a hint from Vipassana meditation and Dogen's *shikantaza*, which means "sitting in meditation without any superfluous thoughts." I directed my attention to the idea of seeing a phenomenon without any ulterior motive. I decided to adopt the idea of simply seeing without making judgments or discrimination as a method for attaining a state in which there is no sense of discrimination. I refer to the procedures that make such an approach possible as the *shikanho* that literally means just (*shi*) looking (*kan*) technique (*ho*), and I decided to examine its effects empirically.

Experimental Research Using Shikanho

Guidance in the shikanho technique is as follows. (1) Sit in a chair in a comfortable posture. Try to recall an unpleasant incident you may have experienced recently or in the past which may have hurt or angered you and which continues to concern you today. (2) Next, while recalling the unpleasant memory, try to remember exactly what happened and how you felt at the time as if the event were occurring right now. (3) While recalling the incident and the feeling you had at the time, try to imagine a situation in which your other self is watching the scene from a little way above. Positing your other self in this manner is a good way of shifting your attention from the standpoint of the self involved in the unpleasant incident to the standpoint of the other self, who is just watching the incident as it unfurls. The most important point is that the other self is just watching everything without exercising discrimination or judgment. Unpleasant feelings may of course arise in this case too. If they do, just watch them without making any judgement. The emotions aroused in a situation where you are a mere observer are always neutral. In most circumstances you will tend to make judgments, criticism, and discrimination, and you may get caught up in unpleasant emotions. All you have to do then is to observe yourself experiencing these unpleasant feelings and making judgments. You just watch yourself, as if you were watching a bird that comes to rest in a tree, chirps, and then flies away. (4) After hearing these explanations, you practise the technique. After the practice, you will be asked your impressions, things you were not sure of and things that you could not do well and you will receive help to understand fully the correct way of practising the technique.

I would like now to present an experiment using the shikanho technique and its results (Koshikawa et al., 2002, 2004). My reason for wishing to present experimental data is connected with the fact that it is because the concept and state of non-self have been practically effective in freeing people from suffering that they have been transmitted down the ages for more than 2500 years. Accordingly, I believe that psychological research on non-self needs not just to examine this concept from a psychological standpoint but also to corroborate psychologically how the state of non-self actually alleviates human suffering.

Experimental Effects of Shikanho on Accessibility of Positive Words

My purpose is to study whether the shikanho technique makes it possible to alleviate negative influence brought about by unpleasant experiences. In this experiment, alleviation of negative influences is measured in terms of increase in accessibility to positive words by means of the following method.

The participants were 62 undergraduate students. They were divided into three groups, a shikanho group, a breathing technique group, and a control group. The process of the experiment is shown in Figure 1. The former two groups were given the explanations of the respective techniques (shikanho/breathing) prior to the experiment. At the outset of the experiment, the participants were asked to recall certain unpleasant incidents they experienced in the past and to retain the images for five minutes for the purpose of inducing unpleasant moods. Then, the first selective recognition test (Sakairi, 1999) was conducted as a pre-test. This test employed two different sheets, a "stimulus-words sheet" and a "checklist sheet for recognition." In the former sheet, twenty words, ten positive and ten negative adjectives concerned with self-evaluation such as "big-hearted," "foolish" were randomly listed. In the latter sheet, these same twenty words and another ten interfering words (five positive and five negative) were located randomly.

At first the participants were exposed to the stimulus-words sheet for fifteen seconds. Then, with the sheet turned over, they were asked to count aloud backwards from 200 to 1 for one minute to prevent rehearsal. After that, they were asked to stare silently at the checklist sheet for fifteen seconds and to recognize a maximum of fifteen words, entering figures from 1 through 15, in the order of certainty of recognition, in the brackets beside each of the words.

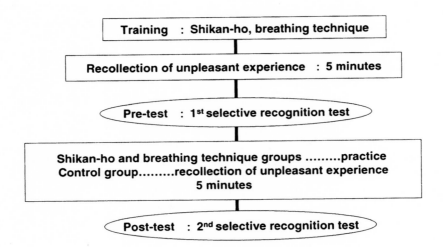

Figure 1: Process of the Experiment

After this pre-test, the shikanho group and the breathing technique group were asked to practice the respective techniques for five minutes. The control group was asked to recall unpleasant incidents for five minutes. This procedure was undertaken to examine whether the shikanho was more effective than exposure, to partial out the effects of shikanho's feature of exposure. Following this, the second selective recognition test was conducted as a post-test. In the selective recognition tests, two versions of the sheets were prepared. In the pre-test, version A was used for half of the subjects in each group, and version B was used for the rest. In the post-test every subject completed a different version of the sheet from that used in the pre-test.

Results and Discussion

For the purpose of comparing the three groups, an analysis of covariance was computed, with the type of group as the fixed factor, the number of positive words in the post-test as the dependent variable and the number of positive words in the pre-test as the covariate. Figure 2 shows the results. The analysis shows that the main effect of the groups was significant (F[2,58] 3.65, p<.05). The multiple comparison based on Bonferroni's test showed the number of recognized positive words in the post-test of the shikanho group was significantly greater than that in the control group (Mse 2.41, p<05). No significant difference was observed between the breathing technique group and the control group, or between the shikanho group and the breathing technique group.

These results show that being able to observe an unpleasant event from a neutral standpoint without discrimination or from the standpoint of non-self gives increased accessibility to positive words and lessens the negative effects an unpleasant event exerts on us. We have been looking at the short-term results of this method, but, independently of this, the method was applied for a fortnight to stressful situations. The results in this case showed that there were significant decreases in stress reactions measured by the six sub-scales of the Cornell Medical Index-Health Questionnaire and the subjective stress scale using a seven-point rating scale. The reasons for such effects can be explained from the standpoint of cognitive-behavioral pathology, but I have reported on this matter elsewhere and will therefore refrain from going into any further detail here (Koshikawa et al., 2002, 2004).

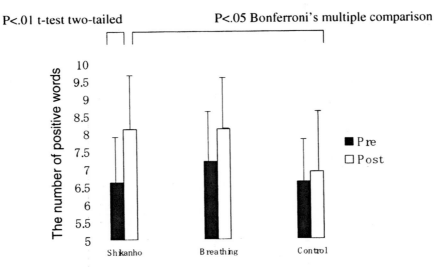

Figure 2: The number of positive words

Similarities and Differences between Shikanho (Themeless Meditation) and Mindfulness Meditation

Shikanho is similar to mindfulness meditation, which has recently drawn attention for its effectiveness in preventing the recurrence of mental depression (Segal et al., 2002). Mindfulness meditation requires that the subject be aware of each moment without being critical or judgmental. Mindfulness meditation and shikanho both stress the point of not making any evaluations or discriminations. The difference between the two methods is that shikanho deals with unpleasant experiences as targets of training. The reasons why shikanho adopts unpleasant events are discussed in the next chapter from the perspective of Zen and the application of this technique to everyday life. Another difference is that while mindfulness meditation stresses the point of awareness, shikanho stresses the point of just observing by setting intentionally the observing subject. It seems that shikanho helps you understand with the senses the fact that whether to become preoccupied with an experience or to let it go hinges on no one but yourself, by means of setting the observing subject who lets everything go (who never clings to everything) in its procedure.

Comparison between Shikanho and "Real Self" in Zen Buddhist Thought

We believe that shikanho is a technique that gives psychological expression to the features of non-self (i.e. its original aspect). One might feel tempted to question the consistency of reference to non-self while positing the existence of an observing subject (self). What is important here is that the subject is in a situation prior to one where things begin to take on colors because of discrimination. The subject concerned here is the same as what we think of as our selves physically in our daily lives. However, it is a subject without the act of making discriminations. In this sense the subject may be described as one that observes things in a situation prior to one where things are expressed in language or are given names. In other words, it is prior to a situation where I am distinguished from someone else. I tentatively define such a self in terms of the state of non-self from a psychological standpoint (Koshikawa, 1994, 1998, 2000ab).

In Zen Buddhism, as shown in the series of ten "Zen drawings of the bull," which express the process of Zen Buddhist's training, a person who experiences non-self does not live only in lofty realms, the profound/ultimate level that is a state prior to the ordinary state in which all values arise. S/he also lives fully in a conditional and value-laden world at the same time. In shikanho, similarly, a person who feels negative emotions lives in a realm of conditional values (as a self that lives in the ordinary world). However, s/he also lives at the same time in a realm without values as non-self by making no attempt to judge and merely continuing to watch and observe. The mental state shikanho thus brings about parallels the state expressed in the tenth drawing of the bull that symbolizes awakening/ enlightenment (emptiness) on the market place (form) and in contentment of the laughing Buddha also known as Hotei. Shikanho provides a way for someone to live in a world dominated by values as "ordinary self" and to exist at one and the same time (here-and-now) as the "real self," that is: non-self. Therefore, shikanho is a technique that enables its practitioners to access the ultimate state aimed at by Zen Buddhism, albeit in a concrete and concentrated form.

Our hypothesis is that shikanho expresses the non-self characteristic of the "real self" in Zen from a psychological standpoint. Other important characteristics of this "real self" are currently being discussed and may be considered to be the springboard of free and altruistic activities. This is the freedom of selection only possible when we put ourselves in a situation where no values are attached to things. The question of whether the freedom for such ideas and behavior can be cultivated by means of shikanho is a topic for future consideration. However, it has been reported that people are able to attain a higher level of creativity when free from evaluation (Silvia & Phillps, 2004) and these results suggest the possibility of enhancement of freedom and creativity by just observing events without judgments using the shikanho technique. In this connection, Suzuki (in Akizuki, 1990, p. 144) said: "One cannot expect to gain spiritual enlightenment without metaphysical understanding... Spiritual enlightenment necessarily requires psychological experiences backed by intellectual interpretations... psychological experiences alone might lead the wrong way." In other words, in observing an event using shikanho, it may be necessary for acquiring freedom and creativity to give a valid interpretation, such as "real forms can be distinguished from each other, but cannot be discriminated," in addition to the psychological experience through "just observing an event without making any discriminations."

Applications of Zen Buddhist Thought to Personality Psychology

As to the application of Zen Buddhist thought to personality psychology, we are currently in the process of analysing data provided by a questionnaire aimed at discovering the functions and structure of non-self. This questionnaire consists of items that express the beliefs and behavior occurring in the non-self frame of mind. These items were compiled with the kind cooperation of Prof. Nishimura, former President of Hanazono University, which is associated with the Rinzai Zen. The results of analysis show that "freedom for preoccupation with the self" is a personality trait of non-self.

Behavior derived from this personality trait might seem to be similar to behavior derived from ethics and altruism. However, there would appear to be some difference between these two types of behavior. The former type of behavior is not aimed at acceptance by other people or even by the subject himself, because it results from the state of mind or conviction that there is no discrimination between the subject and the other even though the subject is separated from others physically. It would be interesting to study from structural and functional perspectives how the properties of "release from obsession with the self," which is the result of freely selecting the conviction that there is no distinction between the self and the other, differs from the modern sense of self, in the case of which personal identity is established by means of discrimination between the self and the other.

Applications of Zen Buddhist Thought to Health/Clinical Psychology

The goal of Zen as well as of Buddhism as a whole is to free people from suffering. This coincides with the aims of clinical and health psychology. As regards application to health psychology, the results of our experiments on subjects in the normal healthy group showed that the shikanho method based on Zen Buddhist thought had long-term and short-term effects, more specifically reducing daily stress response and enhancing accessibility to positive words. In health psychology, it is important to reduce daily stress levels and thereby prevent mental illnesses such as depression.

As regards application to clinical psychology, we do not at present possess any data on shikanho targeting a clinical group. However, several reports on mindfulness meditation, the core of which is similar to that of shikanho and involves "watching without judgment," applied to a clinical group have shown that this method is effective for alleviating chronic pain and curbing mood disturbance ((Kabat-Zinn et al., 1985), relieving eating disorders (Kristeller & Hallet, 1999), and deterring recurrence of depression (Segal et al., 2002; Teasdale et al. 2000, Williams et al., 2000). These may be regarded as examples of applications of the idea of non-self to clinical psychology. In reference to the application of meditation techniques to clinical patients, Ando (2003) interprets these as uncovering techniques and maintains that uncovering is effective for patients with neuroses. On the other hand, for patients with borderline or narcissistic personality disorders and psychoses, it is important to use structure building techniques that strengthen the power of exerting the necessary repression and to build up firmly the structure of ego. Zen's teaching to "get rid of your ego" presupposes that there is an ego to get rid of in the first place. However, it has proven to be possible to effectively apply these techniques to personality disorders under appropriate treatment conditions. This is exemplified by Linehan's (1993) Dialectical Behavior Therapy that uses Zen as a component in borderline cases. For now, we think it would be safest to limit the scope of application of shikanho to the neuroses.

---

1. This study was supported by a Grant-in-Aid for Science Research (C) (2) (project number: 14510171) from the Japan Society for the Promotion of Science.

11

Shikanho: A Zen-Based Cognitive-Behavioral Approach[1]

Fusako Koshikawa, Ayako Kuboki & Yasutomo Ishii

This chapter examines a psychological approach to non-self (muga, *Japanese;* anatman, *Sanskrit), one of the central concepts of Zen Buddhism, and introduces* Shikanho *(meaning "just looking technique"), a cognitive-behavioral method related to the state of non-self. We also present an experimental study that was conducted to assess the effectiveness of the shikanho technique. The idea for shikanho was suggested by Zen meditation. The aims of this technique are to encourage de-centering and to alter the relation to an object by changing the viewpoint from which the object is seen, and to bring about a decrease in negative feelings provoked by an object by linking the object with neutral feelings. In the experiment we investigated how effective shikanho was in influencing negative moods caused by unpleasant events. Sixty university students took part in the experiment, 30 of whom were assigned randomly to the shikanho group, while the other 30 were assigned to a control group. The former group used shikanho when imagining or foreseeing an unpleasant occurrence, while the control group did not. The effects of shikanho were evaluated at two points in time (before and after using the technique) by means of POMS (Profile of Mood States), JIBT (Japanese Irrational Belief Test), and degree of positive or negative mood (assessed on the basis of 10 words that come to each participant's mind in line with a 7-point Likert scale). Each subject's pulse rate was also measured throughout the experiment. The measured scores were significantly lower in the shikanho group. This finding suggests that the state of non-self is effective in alleviating feelings of negativity provoked by unpleasant events.*

Non-self (Sanskrit, *anatman*; Japanese, *muga*) is an important Buddhist concept. Because of its close connection with the concepts of ego and self in psychology, it has in the past been subject to examination in Japan, albeit by a very small number of researchers (e.g. Sato, 1951; Okamoto, 1976; Kitamura, 1991). But if the concept of non-self can be subsumed entirely within the concepts of self and ego in psychology, there is no need for research on non-self, nor is there any need to use the concept itself. With regard to this point, in an explanation of the Freudian ego and the Jungian self, Suzuki (1990) writes:

There are those who would advance still further. The action of transcendence
continues in effect once the self has been transcended. Such people transcend
even the self's expanded and strengthened "lines." The manner of transcendence
is somewhat unusual. They transcend "lines" by becoming aware that there are
no "lines" present in the first place (pp. 252-253).

He thus suggests that there may indeed be a mode of being of the self that
transcends the concepts of self and ego. Kitamura (1991) points out, that in the
West Lersch and Maslow have raised the question of non-self, but that both writers
are still treating non-self in a restricted manner, with Lersch taking the term to
mean abandonment of self-centred volition to enable survival and Maslow stress-
ing self-effacement in the context of action. These studies suggest that the concept
of non-self includes aspects that cannot be adequately subsumed within the concepts of self and ego as envisaged by psychology and that it is a concept that merits
study.

In this chapter we will begin by examining the important Zen Buddhist concept of non-self from the standpoint of psychology and attempt to clarify the features of non-self and the way in which it differs from the concepts of self and ego
in psychology. We will then examine how the idea of non-self can be used as the
basis of a cognitive-behavioral psychology, introduce *shikanho*, a cognitive-behavioral technique inspired by the concept of non-self in Zen Buddhism that involves deliberate changes of perspective, and report on experimental studies conducted on the effectiveness of this technique.

The Psychological Features of Non-Self

Non-self is a term that implies denial and transcendence of attachment in general
but especially attachment to self. Attachment to self or self-centredness is a state
of egoism, which transcendence means a return to the state of "things as they
really are." Self-centredness means being enclosed within the framework of one's
own cognition and judging, whether something is good or bad on the basis of one's
own values and criteria, and acting on the basis of such discrimination. In contrast,
the state of things as they really are within the context of non-self means departing
from the framework of one's own cognition, in other words becoming decentralised
from oneself as a being who discriminates between things, and seeing phenomena
including oneself from a meta-perspective that stands above one's own personal
values and criteria (Koshikawa, 1994, 1998, 2000a, 2000b; Koshikawa et al., 1997).

Let us take an example to illustrate this point. Suppose you are looking at a
spherical object, which left and right hemispheres are black and white respectively. Someone looking at the sphere from the right will assume that it is white;
someone looking at the same sphere from the left will assume it is black; and
someone looking at the sphere from behind will say that the right hemisphere is

black and that the left hemisphere is white. From his particular standpoint each person is correct and the others are in error. But someone who realises that these opinions are in fact interpretations from different perspectives and who does not become attached to the reality immediately visible to her/him will be able to depart from a two-dimensional perspective and assume a three-dimensional perspective instead. S/he will thus realise that every opinion is correct from a particular perspective and that there is nothing contradictory about this. This is an example of decentring in non-self.

Theories of the Self/the Ego in the West and Non-Self in Zen Buddhism

Let us now examine the differences between theories of the self and the ego in the West and the features of non-self in Zen Buddhism. In functional terms, the main differences may be pointed out as follows. Most theories of the self and the ego in the West set mental faculties such as integration, thought and judgment at the core of self and ego functions. In contrast, the idea of non-self in Buddhist philosophy sets a transcendental vision at the centre of non-self functions, specifically in the form of the mental function known in Japanese as *kan* (S, *vicara*), which means minute contemplation of things as they really are. Perhaps one might describe this function as being knowledge-transcendent, in the sense that one thinks and reaches judgments on an intellectual basis but then observes these thoughts and judgments too as they really are.

On a theoretical level, theories of the self and the ego in the West set up a separate entity — a "subject" — that integrates multiple dimensions when reaching an understanding of the phenomena that surround her/him. On the other hand, non-self in Buddhist thought rejects the idea of this integrating subject. Accordingly, most therapies in the West have involved a strong emphasis on the subject in the form of the ego and the self, positioning the various experiences with which the subject is involved on an appropriate coordinate axis and integrating and controlling them. Setting of these coordinates comes within the framework of theory relating to the self and the ego and constitutes the structure of the ego in this theory. This is why the application of theory to the self and the ego is so advanced in the West. In contrast, in Buddhism, the perspective which is the generator of the various experiences (and the subject who possesses this perspective) is considered to be without substance and, rather than attempting to control or integrate the subject, one is expected to separate oneself from this perspective. If a subject is present, it will become the starting point and everything will be positioned along its system of coordinates or frame of reference. This then becomes the cause of the next mental anguish. Because of the awareness that there is no subject present, it becomes necessary to obtain a state in which the starting point is not fixed at any specific point. For this reason, rather than theorising the self and the ego, Buddhism developed a methodology for "emptying" the subject with its perspectives, that is to say a methodology that leads to enlightenment. Expressed differently, non-self is all about distancing oneself in an absolute sense from conflict through the realisation that there is no fixed coordinate axis, or attempting to solve conflict by examining things without being entrapped by a fixed coordinate axis, assuming that the coordination axis has been established hypothetically. In the case of Zen, when it comes to such peak experiences, the emphasis is placed not on the experience itself but on the experience followed by its abandonment (Koshikawa, 1994, 1998, 2000ab). Zen is in this sense a discipline that aspires to thoroughgoing decentring.

Non-Self in Zen Buddhism and Cognitive-Behavioral Approaches

Zen Buddhism and Cognitive-Behavior Therapy (CBT) are concerned with releasing people from mental suffering. CBT is the generic term for therapeutic approaches that are concerned not only with behavioral and emotional problems but also with problems of a cognitive nature; such therapy strives to make improvements by effectively combining behavioral techniques and cognitive techniques whose efficacy has previously been substantiated. Looking at the process of practical training in Zen in the light of this definition, one might say that Zen therapy targets all types of cognition, behavior and emotional affect caused by attachment to the ego, and that its approach involves freeing people from suffering by effectively combining the practice of *zazen* as a behavioral technique whose effectiveness has been empirically confirmed with cognitive restructuring based on a cognitive technique that involves moving away from attachment to the self towards a state of non-self.

The main difference between Zen and CBT lies in what is adopted as a functional scheme or as a rational belief. CBT deals with non-functional ways of thinking as evident in individual stress situations that the client is confronting, while Zen is concerned with the attachment to the self that lies at the basis of all forms of stress. The advantage of CBT lies in its efficacy in treating specific manifestations of stress, while the strength of Zen lies in its power of generalisation. CBT has hitherto been concerned primarily with specific non-functional ideation in response to specific symptoms. However, ever since the emergence of Mindfulness-Based Cognitive Therapy (Williams et al, 2000; Teasdale et al., 2000; Segal et al., 2002) using mindfulness meditation, it would seem that "attachment to the self" as a more basic form of non-functional ideation has been incorporated within the scope of therapy. This is because mindfulness meditation is a technique for getting away from the "self-judgment and self-evaluation" that lie at the core of attachment to self.

As a general therapeutic strategy, CBT does not target cognitive restructuring with the goal of helping clients move away from attachment to the self towards non-self. This is presumably because it is possible to lessen the client's anxiety without raising the question of non-self. Moreover, if we were to propose an approach based on the idea that the self does not possess any essence to which attachment is possible, it seems unlikely that people would be immediately convinced that this is an appropriate and functional approach on either the cognitive or the practical levels. The Buddha might have agreed with them earlier in his life since he was unaware of the concept of non-self prior to his enlightenment. This means that the Buddha did not set out on the spiritual path from the standpoint of non-self. He began with a sort of behavioral technique known as *dhyana* (in Japan known as Zen) and it was this practice that led him to the concept of non-self. Enlightenment is the term used to describe a mental state in which awareness of non-self is thoroughly embedded in one's consciousness and exists in one's mind as a self-evident truth. This means that if the concept of non-self is to be used to enable release from mental suffering, the most important thing is to develop a technique which will make the subject aware of the validity of non-self, after which there will be a need for cognitive restructuring in the form of the conviction that release from attachment to self will indeed bring about a decrease in mental suffering, a conviction reached through the experience gained by exercising this technique. The technique employed in Zen is sitting in meditation (*zazen*). Zazen has been shown to be effective in various ways, but this is unfortunately not a technique familiar to people in the modern world. We thus need to develop a technique that can be used in modern everyday life that retains the features of Zen and zazen. We are currently making use of the shikanho technique because it uses the mind set implicit in the non-judgmental approach adopted by mindfulness meditation to unpleasant events that we have experienced in the past. We are deliberately applying this particular mind set to unpleasant occurrences primarily for the two following reasons. The first is that the practice of Zen in a certain sense deliberately creates a situation in which the subject falls into self-denial as an environment for inspiring an awareness of non-self and the way things really are. The second is related to the standpoint of efficiency as regards acquiring the technique and applying it to everyday life.

The importance of the *koan* in the practice of the Rinzai school of Zen in Japan is well known. The student is given a *koan* riddle to solve, and s/he then has the experience of his answers to the riddle being negated over and over again by the master. In other words, traditionally speaking, the state of "self-denial" is used in order to encourage the pupil to experience the true nature of self. This denial of the self provides us with the ideal opportunity for us, as we live in a world of given values, to regain the true nature of things before values come into being. This implies that, when we transcend the state that negates the self, we are more easily able to experience how and why non-self is able to free us from suffering. In other words, the state of "self-denial" provides us with the ideal conditions for regaining the true nature of things before values come into being. On the other hand, living as we are in a world of values and suffering in consequence, we are constantly in a position that negates the self. Most of the unpleasant experiences we have on a daily basis are connected with denial of the self. For example, when we feel anger towards another person, what is actually happening is that the anger is felt by our self, since this self is not receiving respect from that other person, in other words by a self that has been denied by the other person. This is tantamount to saying that denial of self lies at the root of our unpleasant experiences. This is one of the reasons that we have deliberately used unpleasant experiences as the object of this technique. In the shikanho technique, this procedure is applied using unpleasant experiences that we have actually been through. It is the task of the instructor to check that the technique is being skilfully applied in a correct manner. Reduction of anguish is easily felt in the case of unpleasant experiences, and this makes it easy for users to confirm the effectiveness of the technique. Similarly, it is easy for the instructor to check on whether the method is being applied effectively. No matter what the technique involved may be, practice under the most necessary conditions will stimulate use under these conditions more readily. In other words, by concerning oneself with past unpleasant experiences, this technique can be more easily applied to unpleasant experiences that one may encounter in the future. These practical benefits are the reason that shikanho concerns itself with unpleasant experiences.

Movement of Perspective in the Shikanho Technique

We have recently incorporated procedures related to deliberate movements of perspective into the procedures involved in shikanho, to ensure the more appropriate use of this method and to encourage the "decentralisation," which is a feature of Zen.

As a result of experiments conducted hitherto (Koshikawa et al., 2000, 2002, 2004), we have discovered that there are people who find it relatively easy to see themselves in a state of turmoil without being judgmental and others who find this more difficult to do. We have also found that strong emotions tend to be aroused when we deal with occurrences that involve a strong sense of denial of the self, and that this makes it more difficult to remain focused on unpleasant memories. We decided therefore to incorporate procedures that involve changing the position from which we observe phenomena. In this procedure, participants are required to look at an unpleasant experience from a variety of angles without making value judgments. Since subjects are instructed to change their perspective after a short time, it becomes possible to look on phenomena without bringing evaluations and strong emotions into play. There are many participants who grasp the sense of observing without making judgments. Moreover, since strong emotions were not induced under these procedures, one can foresee the possibility of applying this new version of the shikanho technique to situations in which the self is subjected to strong repudiation, in other words to situations in which strong emotions are called into play.

The idea of incorporating this transfer of perspective or of coordinate axes into the shikanho technique was suggested by a feature of Zen, whereby coordinate axes for evaluation and judgment are set freely and are not allowed to remain fixed. In earlier versions of shikanho, which have not included this movement of perspective, the non-self aspect of the true nature of self as advocated by Zen would seem to have been realised on the psychological level, but there was only a flimsy connection with the free and open-minded approach that is so important in terms of expression of the true nature of self in the context of everyday life. We decided therefore to adopt a method whereby the subject unencumbered by conditional values (i.e. the subject viewing phenomena in a disinterested manner) is able to experience in a real sense his/her active nature by transferring one's perspective at one's own volition. (When practising this technique, the subject begins by changing perspective on the command of the instructor.) Incorporation of this change of perspective may well have resulted in a technique that further encourages the process of "decentralisation" on the psychological level.

Practical procedures involved in the application of this technique are described here. (1) Sit in a chair and assume a comfortable posture. Think of an unpleasant occurrence that still affects you strongly today (i.e. an occurrence that offended you, angered you, made you feel disconsolate, etc.), either recently or in the more distant past. (2) Next, while summoning forth the unpleasant memory, try to recall the occurrence and the feelings that it evoked in you as if you were actually present on that occasion. (3) Look at the situation as you imagine it without making any evaluations or judgments. Do the following to make it easier for you to look on without evaluating or judging. We'll use the word "front" to refer to the images in the worst of the scenes that you've imagined. Look at these images from an angle 90 degrees to the right; these images will be referred to as "right." Move on a further 90 degrees and the images seen from the back will be referred to as "rear." Moving on again by 90 degrees, the images seen from the left will be referred to as "left." In accordance with instructions to change the angle of vision given by the experimenter, gaze on the worst images from four difference directions. Signals are given once every two seconds, although a change is made once every second if the feelings experienced are particularly unpleasant. A single set lasts 30 seconds. Take a deep breath once the set has been completed. (4) The session will be over when the negative feelings have ceased and the feelings have become neutral.

A study of how these procedures have an effect on negative feelings is the subject of the psychological experiment described below. The reason for presenting corroborative data based on experiments is that we consider it important that psychological studies of non-self are concerned not merely with examining this concept from an experiential and qualitative standpoint but also with providing evidence that the state of non-self alleviates human suffering on a quantitative level.

The Effects of the Shikanho Incorporating Movements of Perspective

We conducted an experiment concerning the effects of the shikanho technique with the aim of studying whether shikanho incorporating movements of perspective is able to mitigate the negativity of events. The method was as follows.

1. *Participants.* Sixty university students were assigned at random to a shikanho group (n=30) and a control group (n=30).

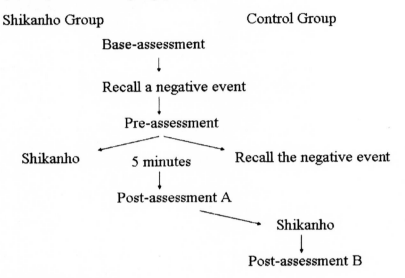

Figure 1. Procedure

2. *Instruments.* (1) Scale for measuring emotional values in respect to verbal associations: 7-point Likert scales. The degree of positivity or negativity in respect to 10 words associated in the mind of the participant with the negative event was assessed. (2) POMS (Profile of Mood States, Japanese version; Yokoyama & Araki, 1994).[2] (3) Scale for measuring the level of comfort or discomfort at the present moment: Assessment on a comfort-discomfort axis. A 9-point Likert scale was used, with three stages each for discomfort, neutral, and comfort. (4) Scale for measuring the extent of comfort-discomfort in respect to an unpleasant event: Assessment on a comfort-discomfort axis. A 9-point Likert scale was used, with three stages each for discomfort, neutral, and comfort. (5) JIBT (Japanese Irrational Belief Test-20; Mori et al., 1994).

3. *Procedures* (see Figure 1). Shikanho group: (a) Answering scales (baseline assessment). (b) An unpleasant event experienced in the past is recalled in as much detail as possible along with the feelings it evoked. Since this was not a therapy

session, the duration for implementation of the technique was only five minutes to avoid causing serious psychological distress. (c) Answering scales (pre-technique assessment). (d) The shikanho technique accompanied by movements of perspective as described above was carried out in eight sets lasting five minutes. (e) Answering scales (post-1 assessment). Control group: (a), (b), and (c) as above. (d) During the five minutes that the shikanho group are practising the technique, the control group recall an unpleasant experience once again without using shikanho. (e) Answering scales (post-1 assessment). (f) Shikanho is practised. (g) Answering scales (post-2 assessment).

Results

In order to examine the effects of the technique, a two-way analysis of variance, one within-subjects factor (time point; pre vs. post-1) and one between-subjects factor (shikanho group vs. control group), was conducted using the scores of the scales as the dependent variables. In this experiment, since the control group also practised shikanho after giving the data as the control group, a one-way analysis of variance (one within-subjects factor, post-1: after non-use of the shikanho vs. post-2: after use of the shikanho) was also performed using the scores of the two time points in the control group. The variables indicating the effectiveness of the technique were as follows.

(1) Emotional values with respect to verbal associations (positive-negative). The results show the state of changes in emotional values in respect to verbal associations. There was a significant interaction between 2 groups and 2 time points ($p < 0.01$). Simple main effect analyses indicated that negative emotional values were less in the shikanho group than in control group ($p < 0.01$) and negative emorional values decreased significantly ($p < 0.01$) only in the shikanho group. In the case of the control group, negative emotional values decreased significantly ($p < 0.01$) after use of the shikanho technique (at the post-2), in which case negativity lessened as far as to the neutral point.

(2) The POMS scores show changes on each scale involved in the profile of mood states (POMS). As regards variables for which differences between the two groups were significant at the pre-technique, we employed an analysis of covariance using the scores at this point as the covariate. There was a significant difference (T-A and C: $p < 0.01$) or a significant difference tendency (F: $p < 0.06$, D and A-H: $p < .0.09$) between the two groups at the post-1, in the case of which the scores were better in the shikanho group than in the control group. In the control group, there was a significant change in a desirable direction in each mood after use of the shikanho ($p < 0.01$).

(3) Extent of comfort and discomfort. The extent of comfort and discomfort show a significant interaction between the 2 groups at each point in time.

Simple main effect analyses revealed that the score for discomfort was less in the shikanho group than in the control group (p<0.01), and the score decreased significantly (p<0.01) only in the shikanho group. In the case of the control group, the score reduced significantly (p<0.01) after use of the shikanho technique (at the post-2).

(4) Extent of comfort and discomfort in respect of unpleasant events. With regards to the extent of comfort and discomfort in respect to recalled events, there was a significant interaction between 2 groups and 2 time points. Simple main effect analyses indicated that the score for discomfort was less in the shikanho group than in the control group (p<0.01) and the score decreased significantly (p<0.01) only in the shikanho group. In the case of the control group, the score decreased significantly (p<0.01) after use of the shikanho technique (at the post-2).

(5) JIBT20 (Japanese Irrational Belief Test 20). The results show changes in scores according to the criteria of powerlessness and self-expectation. In each factor, there was a significant interaction between 2 groups and 2 time points. Simple main effect analyses revealed that the scores were less in the shikanho group than in the control group (p<0.01) and they decreased significantly (p<0.01) only in the shikanho group. In the case of the control group, the scores decreased significantly (p<0.01) after use of the shikanho technique (at the post-2).

Discussion

As we have seen above, the results of our experiments indicate that the shikanho technique, accompanied by deliberate transfers of perspective, is able to alleviate negative emotional distress in stressful situations. Particularly interesting results were obtained as regards how feelings in respect to verbal associations changed from negative to neutral. In general, when we have an unpleasant experience, we attempt to discriminate on the comfort-discomfort dimension, either consciously or unconsciously, against things that are linked to this experience, as indicated through verbal association. The results obtained on this occasion show that the shikanho technique is able to alleviate such discrimination. The technique is particularly effective on the emotional level, but the results of JIBT may well be taken to suggest that irrational beliefs related to a sense of powerlessness and self-expectation brought about by a negative occurrence can be suppressed through use of a technique such as this.

It has been reported that the results obtained employing behavioral techniques can be maintained for longer due to the effects obtained through inclusion of cognitive restructuring (Durham & Turvey, 1987). It seems likely that, having experienced liberation from suffering through this practice of meditation, the beneficial results can be maintained for relatively longer periods. We propose that they can also be generalised through cognitive restructuring when they are clearly related to an interpretation that these results are due to release from attachment to self — that is to say from evaluations and judgements, although on this occasion our research did not include experiments extending as far as cognitive restructuring. In the future we plan to look into questions such as what effects come about as a result of including cognitive restructuring in the procedures and which functional thoughts are appropriate to use in this sort of cognitive restructuring.

Conclusion

In this chapter we have been considering how the idea of non-self in Zen Buddhism should be interpreted in psychological terms. We have discussed a technique intended to generate a state of non-self and have demonstrated the effectiveness of this technique. We believe that the effectiveness of Zen Buddhism, with its long history, and its powerful assortment of effective techniques explains why they have been handed down to the present day. But in spite of this, the discipline of psychology has in the past paid little attention to this philosophy and its practice. Perhaps the main reason for this is that Buddhism is first and foremost undertaken as a religion and thus has ignored the psychological significance of the concept of non-self in clinical research. As we are ourselves psychologists and not advocates of religion, we are in the fortunate position of not having to prove or believe in the proposition that "the essence of the self is non-self." The focus of our interest as psychologists is the functional aspect of non-self and in showing in practical terms what happens to our mental health when we assume a state of non-self, in other words when we lose attachment to the self. If it can be shown that detachment from the self and decentring are of use in mental health, we need to develop behavioral and cognitive techniques that are able to encourage this process, to examine the effectiveness of these techniques, and to continue developing more effective techniques along these lines. This is the task we are now undertaking.

---

1. This study was supported by a Grant-in-Aid for Science Research (C) (2) (project number: 14510171) from the Japan Society for the Promotion of Science.

2. The Profile of Mood States (POMS; McNair, Lorr, & Droppleman, 1992), is a 65-item questionnaire to measure mood. Items are summed to yield six emotion factor scores of Anxiety (-Tension, T-A), Depression, Anger (-Hostility, A-H), Vigor, Fatigue, and Confusion.

12

Mindfulness And Health Intervention

Michael de Vibe

Mindfulness based health interventions have developed over the last 25 years into a method for managing stress and health problems. The method has been tried out on 144 patients in general practice in a randomized study with waiting-list control group. The participants were patients troubled by stress and chronic illness. The effect on quality of life was measured using WHO's questionnaire. Subjective health was measured using the Subjective Health Complaint inventory and the Hopkins Symptom Checklist. 90% completed the 8-week course, and the participants rated its importance to 8.5 on a scale from 1 to 10. There was an increase in quality of life and subjective health (p<0.001) from start to finish of the courses, while the waiting-list control group remained unchanged. The changes in quality of life remained stable at 3 and 6 months follow-ups, while subjective health continued to improve in the follow-up period. The changes were independent of age, sex, education and marital-, work-, and health insurance status. The effect was positively correlated with the reported degree of mindfulness training. The method gives the patients a tool that they can use themselves to improve their health and quality of life through changing the way they view themselves and their life. This change in perspective is in line with Antonovsky's "Sense of Coherence" and improves understanding and manageability in patients' lives. The method could beneficially be taught in schools and universities and patient education centers.

I have really been enjoying my work as a general practitioner over the last 25 years, but at times I have felt frustrated at my inability to help many of my patients whose complaints are stress-related. Research has found that more than 50% of all patients consult their doctors with stress-related disorders (MacFarland, 1985) and that the majority of all medicines prescribed by doctors are for stress-related conditions such as anxiety and depression, insomnia, gastrointestinal disorders, hypertension and high cholesterol levels (Pharmacy Times, 2002). As a consequence of suffering stress and anxiety myself in my youth, I took up yoga and meditation, practiced these disciplines, and experienced great benefit over many years. It seems obvious to me as a general practitioner that patients could have similar benefits if I were to teach them these skills. Thus, I searched the literature for places where this approach had been systematically tried already and came across the work of

Jon Kabat-Zinn in USA at the Center for Mindfulness in Medicine, Health Care, and Society at the University of Massachusetts Medical School in Worcester, where mindfulness-based health interventions have been used since 1979.

The method for applying mindfulness to stress-related ailments is well described in international literature and extensive research has been carried out on chronic pain conditions, fibromyalgia, bulemia, anxiety, depression, and emotional disturbance in relation to chronic illness (see for example: Bishop, 2002). The last metastudy was published in 2003 and concluded that there is good evidence of its efficacy. However, better-designed clinical trials are needed (Baer, 2003). With support from the Norwegian Medical Association, I spent three months as an intern at the center in Worcester, Massachusetts in 2002, studying the approach and methods. I translated and adjusted its curriculum so as to be able to assess it in a randomized study with waiting-list control group in a Norwegian general practice.

Method

1. The participants. In 2003 I contacted the general practitioners in my area, along with the health insurance agencies and was interviewed by the local papers, inviting patients suffering from stress or chronic illnesses to come to an information meeting. Some 160 patients turned up — the majority because of the interviews in the papers — and ultimately 144 signed up for the study. The participants were randomised into 5 groups using a dice; 44 patients waited for 6 months before they attended the course and constituted a control group; I had only met 9 of the 144 patients earlier in consultations.

2. *The course.* The courses lasted for 8 weeks and consisted of 8 weekly sessions of 2-1/2 hours and a whole day session after 7 weeks; all run by me. The Regional Ethical Committee for Medical Research approved the protocol for the study. The essence of the courses was training in "here and now" full awareness in daily life activities such as taking a shower, drinking tea, communicating, or going for a walk, through the practice of meditation, body-scanning, yoga, and the awareness of breathing. The training in awareness of body and mind, along with an accepting, caring attitude, gave the patients a way of *accepting themselves as they were*. They could find a balance between "doing" and "being," and this gave them new ways of handling their stress and illness.

Each section of the course had corresponding exercises for the patients to do at home. The course elements consist of: (1) a course manual containing theoretical knowledge on mindfulness-training, stress, body-mind connection and communication; (2) experiential learning through exercises taking place both during the course and after by means of CDs at home; and (3) a group process in which small groups reflected on what they experienced in body and mind during the exercises.

3. *Evaluation protocol and instruments.* Participants filled out an evaluation protocol when they started and finished the courses and at a 3 and 6-month follow-up. The control group also completed the protocol 6 months prior to starting the course. Two reminders were sent for undelivered protocols. In addition to demographic data and health insurance status, participants were asked the reasons for attending the course. Other questions: How important do they rate it? Did they make any life-style changes as a result of the course? How many times did they exercise? In addition they were also encouraged to write stories about their course experiences.

I used the short version of WHO's quality of life inventory (WHOQOL-BREF) to measure *quality of life* and compiled the data. I chose this partly because it has been developed and validated in Norway in conjunction with many other countries (Skevington et al., 2004), and partly because it has been shown to reliably measure changes in quality of life in clinical trials (Taylor et al., 2004). The WHOQOL-BREF inventory has 24 questions grouped into four domains: physical function, psychological function, social relationships, and environmental factors. In addition it has one global question on the quality of life and one on health status. A high score indicates a high quality of life.

I measured *subjective health* using the Subjective Health Complaint (SHC) inventory, developed by Holger Ursin (University of Bergen, Norway); it is independent of diagnosis and includes normative values for the Norwegian population (Ihlebæk, 2002). In many studies in Norway and abroad SHC measurements have shown good reliability and validity. The SHC inventory contains 29 questions on common symptoms grouped into 5 domains: musculoskeletal, pseudoneurological, gastrointestinal, allergy and flu. A low score indicates few subjective health complaints.

To improve the measurement of *psychological health complaints*, I used a short version of the Hopkins Symptom Checklist (HSCL-25) (Derogatis et al., 1974), called SCL-5 (Tambs & Moum, 1993). The score range is 1-4, with increasing symptoms and a value of more than 2.0 is indicative of mental disorder. SCL-5 has good specificity (82%) and sensitivity (96%) for mental disorder compared with the HSCL-25 inventory, and correlates well with other self-rating scales on mental health (Strand et al., 2003).

4. *Hypothees.* The hypothesized effects of the course were: (1) An improved quality of life, mainly in the physical and psychological domain, with no improvement in the environmental domain; (2) A decreased in subjective health complaints, mostly in the musculoskeletal and pseudoneurological domain; (3) An improved mental health status; (4) The changes, assessed at follow-up, were stable; (5) No changes in the control group; (6) A lower number of patients receiving health insurance benefits; (7) That changes in quality of life and subjective health are dependent on the level of attendance, and how much the home-exercises were

practiced; (8) That changes are largest among those with musculoskeletal and mental problems, those who report to be ill at the start of the course and those who receive national health insurance benefits; (9) That changes are independent of age, sex, education, work, or marital status.

Results

I analysed the data with the statistical package SPSS (version 12), and the measured changes using the independent group t-test, paired t-test, chi-square test and covariance analysis. Effect size was calculated according to Cohen's d (Cohen, 1988), which states that an effect size of 0.2 is considered small, 0.5 medium, and 0.8 big.

1. *The participants.* 144 people, 127 women and 17 men, aged 17-69 (47, SD 9.5) started the courses. There were 11 drop outs, who gave the following reasons: private life events (4), anxiety because of large group size (2), hip-replacement surgery (1), hospital admittance for depression (1), pregnancy (1), and unknown (1). The dropouts did not differ significantly from the remainder at the start of the course with regard to their subjective health or quality of life. The participants were better educated than the general Norwegian population, with 46% working full-time and 26% part-time. The percentage of manual workers was lower, and a higher proportion (56%) was on health insurance benefit (Norwegian National Statistical agency; <www.ssb.no>). The participants gave the following reasons for taking the courses: musculoskeletal problems (29%), stress (18%), different chronic illnesses (15%), anxiety/depression (11%), musculoskeletal and anxiety/depression (10%), burnout syndrome and insomnia (9%), and self-development (8%). Quite a number (37%) reported that they were ill when they started the course.

Average attendance rate was 7.3 (SD 1.5). At the end, the importance of the course as a whole was rated at 8.5 (SD 1.6), on a scale from 1 (completely unimportant) to 10 (very important). At 6 months follow up, the average was 7.5 (SD 2.0). When asked if the course had given them anything of lasting value, 123 answered yes, and specified 144 answers that were categorized as shown in Table I. A total of 76 people, who listed 141 changes, reported life-style modifications as a result of the course. Of these, 66 were alterations in diet, physical activity, alcohol, smoking or television viewing. Other changes included taking better care of their own needs, setting new limits, slowing down and increased awareness on what activities they undertook.

Table 1. Lasting benefits as reported by participants at end of course (N=122)

More aware of my breath and using it in daily life	43
Lower tempo and being more relaxed	36
More accepting of myself and having less bad conscience	20
More aware of what stresses me and handling it better	17
More confidence in myself and life	17
More present here and now	17
More aware of my body and handling pain better	14
Exercises	8

2. *Quality of life and subjective health complaints.* Compared to the Danish female population (Noerholm et al., 2004), the quality of life among the course participants was significantly lower (p<0.001) on all domains using independent t-test.

For subjective health complaints the course participants reported significantly more health complaints than the Norwegian female population (p<0.001) in the musculoskeletal, pseudoneurological, gastrointestinal domains, and the total complaint score using the independent t-test. The mental health status based on the SCL-5 was also significantly worse (p<0.001) than the average female Norwegian population.

3. *Changes in quality of life and subjective health complaints.* Tables II and III show the total domain scores for all 101 participants with complete protocols at all measure points. The same analysis was run separately for each domain. The number of participants that could be compared varied from 124-132, but the only difference in results was that, from the start of the course to its finish, the change in the environmental domain of quality of life now reached significance (p<0.001).

4. *Demographic factors.* All changes in participants' quality of life and subjective health during the courses were controlled for: age, sex, marital status (married/cohabitants vs. single/widow/er), education, health insurance status (receiving benefit vs. no benefit), work-status (working vs. not working), reporting ill at the start of the course versus not reporting ill, and the reason for taking the course. Covariate analysis, where the above named factors were used as covariate, showed

no significant findings. The effects of the course were therefore not systematically different between the different demographic groups, illness status, or reason for taking the course.

5. *Change in health benefit status.* At the start of the course, 66 people were on different health insurance benefits; 26 were on sickness benefit; 16 on rehabilitation benefit, and 16 on disability benefit. The remaining 8 received maternity benefit and different pensions. The number that received benefits at the end of the course and at the 6-month follow-up was significantly lower than at the start of the course (chi square test $p<0.001$). The whole difference is due to a reduction in the number receiving sickness benefit from 26 to 14.

6. *Changes according to the amount of home-exercises.* At the end of the course and at the 3 and 6-month follow-ups, the participants reported how much of the home-exercise element they undertook at that time. A sum score for all exercises was made and the participants divided into 3 groups according to how much they exercised

Table 2. Quality of life by WHOQOL-BREF, domain-score 0-100 scale
Changes tested for significance with paired t-test for the change from inclusion to start of course (row 3), from start of course to finish (row 4), from finish to 3-month follow-up (row 5) and from 3-month follow-up to 6-months follow-up (row 7); * $p<0.01$, ** $p<0.001$.

Point of measure & groups compared	Global QOL	Global Health	Physical Function	Mental Function	Social Relations	Environmental Factors
1. Danish Women (n=578) (ref. 12)			75	76	70	74
2. Control Group Inclusion (n=42)	71	54	56	56	52	67
3. CG Start of course (n=42)	73	51	54	57	56	70
4. Start of course (n=101)	69	56	56	56	58	70
5. End of course (n=101)	77 **	66 **	65 **	64 **	65 **	73
6. 3-month follow-up (n=101)	77	68	65	64	65	72
7. 6-month follow-up (n=101)	78	68	65	65	65	75 *

At the end of the course there was no significant correlation between home-exercises and changes in quality of life or subjective health complaints compared to when they started the course (assessed by co-variate analysis), but most of them exercised daily at that point. However, at the 6-month follow-up there was a significantly ($p<0.001$ to 0.038) greater improvement in all domains of quality of life among those who exercised most. For total subjective health complaints there was the same tendency, but it did not reach significance.

7. *Change according to course participation.* I assessed the connection between participation and effect by grouping together the 15 people who attended 3, 4 or 5 times. Co-variate analysis showed that, from start to finish of the course, changes in the quality of life and subjective health complaints were weakly correlated with attendance. However, this did not reach significance (lowest p 0.12).

8. *Effect size.* The effect size (Cohen's d) for changes in the quality of life domains averaged 0.49 at the end of the courses and 0.50 at 6-month follow-up. The effect was greatest within the psychological function domain (0.54) and lowest in the environmental domain (0.36). The subjective health complaints had an average effect size of 0.36 at the end of the course and 0.55 at the 6-month follow-up. The effect size was biggest in the pseudoneurological domain (0.59) and least in the allergy domain (0.16). The effect size of the SCL-5 was 0.57 at both points of measurement.

Point of measure and groups compared	Musculo-skeletal	Pseudo-neuro-logical	Gastro-Intestinal	Allergy	Flue	Total health complaints	SCL-5 anxiety & depression
1. Norwegian (n=454) (ref. 6)	4.9	2.9	2.1	1.0	.7	12.1	1.4
2. CG Inclusion (n=42)	9.3	7.2	3.7	1.3	1.0	22.3	2.2
3. CG Start of course (n=42)	9.3	6.4	3.4	1.0	.6	200.4	2.1
4. Start of course (n=101)	8.3	6.4	3.0	1.0	.7	19.3	2.2
5. End of course (n=101)	7.0 **	4.7 **	2.3 **	1.4 *	.8	16.2 **	1.83 **
6. 3-month follow-up (n=101)	6.7	4.9	2.3 *	.9	.5	15.4	1.8
7. 6-month follow-up (n=101)	6.0 *	4.4 p=0.2	2.0	.9	.5 *	13.9	1.8

Table 3. Subjective health complaints (SHC) average domain score and average sum-score for SCL-5
Changes tested for significance with paired t-test for the change from inclusion to start of course (row 3), from start of course to finish (row 4), from finish to 3-month follow-up (row 5) and from 3-month follow-up to 6-months follow-up (row 7). CG: Control Group; * = p<0.01, ** = p<0.001.

The Stories of the Participants

The participants wrote fifty stories on how they experienced the course. Here is a small selection: (1) "The most concrete result I have experienced is increased awareness of my kids! Now I can really see the drawings that they show me. How often I've said: 'How nice!' while at the same time being occupied with something else and therefore not really seeing what they wanted to show me. It is really good to be fully present for them." (2) "First and foremost the course has taught me to have a more accepting attitude toward the thoughts and feelings that arise in me. I have always thought that one should try and turn all frustration, anger, sorrow etc and think positively. You know, I looked up to those who saw more joys than worries and always seemed happy but that made me hold myself responsible for my own misery, sadness and pain, if only I could manage to think other thoughts, feel differently etc! But now I think it is better to realize that my life is as it is, and that it is good enough!" (3) "I was very anxious and stressed out when I started on the course and was always running in front of myself. After starting, reflecting and becoming conscious of where my breath is, I have become very calm. I carry my breath with me at all times and am much more conscious of it now. I am better at thinking, 'Well, well. So what?' and try to learn from my experiences. After I had cancer and two of my siblings had cancer, I always had to be on the move and experience something. I had no time to wait. Something had to happen all the time; terribly exhausting. That's why it was so nice to hear my sister say: 'I have got my old sister back.' It was so heartening." (4) "Earlier I had learnt about the importance of trust and acceptance theoretically. But because of the course and through bodily experiences I have learnt what trust and acceptance really are. Learning is discovering. I am deeply grateful." (5) "I am kinder to myself, and don't demand so much from myself anymore. I needed the course to dare to lower my expectations. I am more relaxed. It is lovely and liberating. I take deep breaths and stay present, trying to accept things as they are just now." (6) "The course has been an important key in my search after my wholeness. I have worked on consciously focusing on the now and letting unwanted thoughts and feelings pass, and feel that I have succeeded. Everything feels easier in my daily life. I feel more 'alive,' and my relationship to nature, which has always been close, has become even closer and stronger. My self confidence is getting stronger every day, and my sexual life, which has been absent for many years, is again a part of me."

Discussion

The participants were a selected group with a very high proportion of women. My experience over 25 years is that women are more easily attracted to courses where the focus is on becoming conscious of one's own experiences. The course concept would probably have to be altered and promoted differently to appeal to men. Those that came accepted the course and 90% completed them. Participants reported a lower quality of life and more health complaints than the general population and, because women generally report lower quality of life (Skevington et al., 2004; Antonovsky, 1979) and more health complaints (Ihlebæk, 2002) than men, I have compared our figures to the figures for the general female population.

The effect of the course on the quality of life and subjective health complaints is in the same order as was found in the meta-study from 2003 (Skevington et al., 2004), where 15 independent studies showed an average effect size of 0.59 both at the end of the courses and at follow-up. Whether the effect seen in my study is actually due to the course could not be firmly established. One explanation might be a spontaneous "returning to the mean" quality of life and subjective health complaints in participants who had entered the study at a stressful point in their lives.

The control group showed a small improvement in subjective health complaints on all domains, except musculoskeletal, and in the social and environmental domains of quality of life and, additionally, to the global question on quality of life. If the group had been big enough this improvement might have reached significance. On the other hand, the quality of life, physical function domain and global health questions did show a worsening in the same period, and there was no change in anxiety or depression judged by the SCL-5.

Additionally, the control group showed the same improvement as the other participants from the start to the end of the course, and this strengthens the probability that the course did in fact contribute to the improvement seen. As hypothesized, quality of life increased the most in the physical and psychological domain, but also somewhat in the environmental domain. This could be explained by the assumption that our relationship to our environment is dependent on our relationship to ourselves, a view supported by the analyses of the seven questions within the environmental domain. In this, 36% of the change in the domain came from the question "How safe do you feel in your daily life?" while the other questions on economy, transport, health services, information, and leisure activities show little change. It is difficult to say for sure what change in quality of life is clinically relevant but if the change is accompanied by a similar change in subjective health complaints, as seen in this study, it could have an effect on daily function and work capacity and thus be relevant.

The effect of the course on mental symptoms is underpinned by the fact that the changes in SLC-5 show the largest effect size of 0.57. Within quality of life, the largest effect size is also within the psychological domain (0.54), and a separate analysis of the questions within this domain, shows that the biggest change is in the question: "How satisfied are you with yourself?" followed by the question: "How often do you experience negative feelings like being sad, worried, or depressed?" The results are in accordance with a recent study of awareness training where functional brain scanning showed changes in activity in the areas in the brain responsible for emotional balance (Davidson et al., 2003). The changes in quality of life seen in the present study arose during the course and remain stable in the follow-up period. The same is true for the changes in mental symptoms as judged by SCL-5, while the improvement in health complaints was less during the course but continued in the follow-up period.

One way of understanding this phenomenon is in describing the action of awareness training as changing the "perspective" of the participant. In other words, the participants change the way they view themselves and their world. Through increased acceptance and trust in themselves — their bodies, their minds and their world — there comes about a fundamental shift in attitude. When I can handle myself and the world as it is, it then all becomes more comprehensible and manageable. This perspective is in line with Antonovsky's term "sense of coherence" (SOC), which has been shown to correlate with stress management (Antonovsky, 1979) and is born out by the stories of the participants and in a study showing increase in SOC following awareness training (Weisbecker, 2002). From here it can be reasoned that when such changes in someone's perspective have occurred, the results will continue to influence that person's health, and health complaints. This is in accord with the theories that an increase in health complaints in our society is due to stress-related sensitization against "normal" health complaints (Eriksen, 2002). These complaints are normalized through the changes in perspective that awareness training brings about. This theory is also supported by the fact that the distribution of subjective health complaints among the course participants resembles the normal population, and that the total subjective health complaints at six months follow-up is coming close to that of the normal population (Table III).

The correlation between the effects of the course and the amount of awareness training participants undertook has been shown in some studies but not in others (Bishop, 2002; Baer, 2003). It may be that the amount of training needed to have an effect is an individual matter depending, among other things, on personality and the subject's natural awareness (trait mindfulness). Researchers at the The University of Kentucky are currently studying this. Because of the small numbers, the decrease in number on sickness benefit after the course is an uncertain finding. The study would have to be repeated with larger numbers on sickness benefit and with a longer follow-up period. The health insurance benefit status at the start of the course does not seem to have influenced the effect of the course. Nor did the reason for attending given by the participants or whether they rated themselves as ill when they started. This could be due to the fact that most of the participants had stress-related problems even though they gave different reasons for signing up for the course. In our group of participants we can conclude that the effects of taking the course were little influenced by demographic factors. We know that subjective health complaints are responsible for more than 50% for sickness benefits, a third of disability pensions and for more than half of all consultations with family doctors in Norway (Tellnes & Bjerkedal, 1989). Furthermore studies show that 50-70 % of consultations in primary health care are due to stress-related disorders (MacFarland, 1985). A simple method that patients themselves can use to improve these problems could be of great importance both for the patients and the society and could, for example, be readily taught in schools and universities and patient centres to good effect. Monash University in Australia has already integrated such an obligatory course for all first year medical students. The University College, Oslo, includes mindfulness as a central element in a postgraduate education program for health and social workers that trains teachers to run groups for chronically ill patients.

13

Mindfulness And Its Challenge To Cognitive-Behavioral Practice

Fabio Giommi

This chapter consists of two parts. The first provides some general considerations and introduces the second, a comparison study on mindfulness training as an effective component in treating emotional disorders. Part I. Mindfulness approaches challenge some basic tenets of clinical cognitivism. Firstly, the pivotal aspect in the therapeutic process seems to be "deautomatizing-disidentifying" rather than changing attitudes, schemas, etc. To escape automaticity, patients learn to relate to experiences as mental events within a field of awareness. Secondly, a question is posed by mindfulness approaches: is there a non-conceptual way of conscious knowing? Mindfulness is spoken of as "insight meditation" (i.e. "a non-conceptual and penetrating seeing into the nature of mind"; Kabat-Zinn (2003). Such non-conceptual "seeing" is a form of knowing not yet recognized in any cognitive model of mind, and results as the key factor in reducing dysfunctional automaticity. Part II. F. Giommi, H. Barendregt, L. Oliemeulen, J. van Hoof, J. Tinge, A. Coenen, and P. van Dongen conducted a randomized controlled trial. Mindfulness-Based Stress Reduction (MBSR) was compared to Psychoeducation (PE, a standard psychiatric intervention) in a sample of patients with emotional disorders. Assessments were made on symptoms reduction (5 scales of depression, anxiety, quality of life) and attentional functioning (6 neuropsychological tasks, EEG recordings). MBSR was found at least as efficacious as PE. Preliminary results suggest that MBSR exerts a positive effect on attention. To date no comparison with an established intervention has been performed: this was the first exploratory study on such issue, and the first to consider the specific effects of mindfulness on attentional processes. New confidence is gained in applying MBSR as an effective component in treating emotional disorders.

I

It becomes critically important that those persons coming to the field with professional interest and enthusiasm recognize the unique qualities and characteristics of mindfulness as a meditative practice, with all that implies, so that mindfulness is not simply seized upon as the next promising cognitive behavioral technique or exercise, decontextualized, and "plugged" into a behaviorist paradigm with the aim of driving desirable changes, or of fixing what is broken (Kabat-Zinn, 2003, p. 145).

Despite the fact that the use of mindfulness-based approaches is very recent, it is already possible to outline a map and pick out some of the trendlines. In the recent cognitivist community's fast growth of interest in mindfulness, two different approaches can be discerned. They are profoundly different and potentially divergent in perspective. There are those who view the expression mindfulness-based in a "radical" manner; in the actual sense of placing mindfulness at the very root and heart of therapeutic interventions. These researchers see the meaning and value of mindfulness in the opportunity it provides to explore new clinical directions, broadening the conceptual and epistemological categories of present-day cognitivism, and opening the way for a constructive exchange with meditative traditions that study the nature of the mind. I call them "radicals" and I reckon this list might include Segal, Williams, Teasdale, Linehan, and Schwartz. I believe that most radicals are generally recognizable, and characterized by the fact that they refer more or less directly to the fundamental experiences of Kabat-Zinn's Mindfulness-Based Stress Reduction (MBSR) program. This is based on mindfulness and on the knowledge that comes from the Buddhist tradition *and that's it*, without the addition of cognitive techniques and models, even though it does make precious use of research (e.g.on stress). Another characteristic is that they all have a non-superficial familiarity with the practice of meditation, particularly Vipassana — insight or mindfulness meditation — and its core ideas. For them it is perfectly clear that any talk about the development of mindfulness has no plausible meaning other than within direct, personal experience.

On the other hand, it seems that a second group of researchers, whom I shall refer to as "incorporationists," can be characterized by the fact that they seem to consider mindfulness as a concept or a procedure that might be usefully incorporated in existing clinical protocols *if* translated in cognitive-behavioral conceptualizations. These researchers tend to reformulate and accept mindfulness' perspective in as far as it fits into the already existing conceptual framework. For them, cognitive-behavioral theories come first and from this starting point it is possible to explore the clinical utility of mindfulness. Their attitude towards meditation seems, all things considered, somewhat perplexed; some of them actively seek alternative methods, using cognitive "technologies" other than meditation, to develop mindfulness. I believe that a list of incorporationists would include Wells, Roemer, and Orsillo, who work particularly with cognitive psychopathological models to treat anxiety.

It seems to me that the radicalists' approach is more fruitful: if we take mindfulness seriously (and indeed, mindfulness is just a consequence of "taking consciousness seriously"; Chalmers, 1996), this might open up innovative and promising horizons for the cognitive approach. The study presented in the second part of this chapter exemplifies a radicalist's stance. This is the first comparison study to date showing that a mindfulness-based program is at least as effective as a well-established psychiatric treatment in reducing symptoms in a mixed sample of patients with depression and anxiety disorders. This study corroborates the literature suggesting that a wide range of psychological disorders are positively affected by mindfulness. This indicates that mindfulness operates in processes at a basic/transversal level of various kinds of emotional disorders. Mindfulness seems to be a general factor that affects the mechanism of emotional change. Which are these processes and what might be the factor capable to affect them? In trying to outline an answer, it appears quite clear that mindfulness challenges some of clinical cognitivism's basic tenets. We shall here consider two of these challenges.

De-Automatizing Versus Changing Cognitions

Mindfulness operates by modifying not the contents of the mind but our relationship with them. Experience teaches that by means of an intuitive, immediate "seeing" — and accepting attitude — the coercive force of some cognitive-affective mental contents gradually becomes weaker and fades away. The central issue of cure then becomes that of *disindentification from our own thoughts-emotions through awareness*. In conjunction, the central theme of "neurotic" disorders appears to revolve around the *automatization* of cognitive and emotional processes and around the crystalization, at various levels, of thoughts, feelings, and body-reaction patterns, which automatize outside awareness and volition/intention. Segal et al. (2002) point out that *de facto* traditional Cognitive Therapy (CT) itself is probably effective especially as a result of this! This runs counter to the declared purpose of CT: to modify beliefs regarding the *content* of dysfunctional thoughts. However, this objective actually promotes an implicit process that first (and perhaps foremost) involves a change in the *relationship* with dysfunctional thoughts and emotions, leaving them to be perceived increasingly as events in the mind, and thus not as reality (Teasdale et al., 2002; Barber & DeRubeis, 1989).

Decentering, considered by classic CT as a means to change content, could be the factual therapeutic factor. There is a huge amount of experimental study showing the effects of automatic biases induced by anxiety and depression on the perceptive processes during the initial phases of information processing (Gotlib & MacLeod, 1997). Studies have also examined the creation of automaticity in higher cognitive processes and its consequences (Bargh & Ferguson, 2000). A study on CT revealed that the intensity levels of depressive thought in terms of content are not predictive for relapse, whereas their form (i.e. the *automaticity and rapidity* of depressive thoughts with respect to their deliberation and intentionality) is (Teasdale, 1999). Worrying and ruminating are unproductive, repetitive thinking styles that contribute to anxiety and depression. In another study it was hypothesized that *repetitive thought* itself is a general concomitant and a predictive factor of negative mood (Segerstrom et al., 2000).

The mindfulness perspective highlights that automaticity (cognitive, percep-tual, or mnemonic) leads to the biased characteristic of dysfunctional thoughts, depressive ruminations, anxious worries, and obsessional thinking. Mindfulness operates in the opposite direction to automaticity and is likely able to do so in low-level perceptual as well as in high-level cognitive-memory processes (Ramel et al., 2004). One might wonder: is it really that simple? Yes, it is, but this seeming sim-plicity conceals profound implications, which when viewed in perspective involve not only clinical aspects but also our conceptualization of the mind and its nature. The repeated dis-identification/detachment through non-discursive mindful aware-ness from what we *believe* is real, is the fundament of the therapy. This core aspect has been recognized and referred to by the Buddhist tradition. The *Anguttara Nikaya*, an Early Buddhist text attributed to the Buddha, states: "It is not through actions or words that one gains freedom from mental afflictions but through seeing and ac-knowledging them over and over again."

Non-Conceptual Conscious Knowing Versus Metacognitive Knowledge

Is it possible to conceive a kind of knowledge that goes beyond conceptual thought? The mindfulness perspective shows us that there may be a form of knowledge that only appears when the ongoing discursive activity of the mind calms down and a space is created that permits the spontaneous emergence of silent awareness, a *presence* beyond words, concepts, thinking, and meaning. This non-conceptual mode of comprehension and of conscious attention to what appears in the mind opens the way for dis-identification from the content of the mind: an act of im-mense therapeutic potential as was recently discovered by cognitive-behavior thera-pists. To refer to this kind of knowledge the notion of "metacognitive awareness" has been coined, derived from the concept of metacognition. This has been refor-mulated to show that a knowledge exists that encompasses different processes of thinking, and yet consists of an intuitive knowing and immediate *awareness*. Metacognitive insight implies experiencing thoughts as thoughts as they occur (Teasdale, 1999). Teasdale and others (2002, p. 227) pointed out that "It is impor-tant to distinguish *metacognitive awareness* from *metacognitive belief*, as the lat-ter has figured prominently in recent theorizing on emotional disorders and their psychological treatments. Metacognitive beliefs refer to how much individuals believe particular thoughts about cognition to be true... and is concerned with thoughts about thoughts or feelings ... By contrast, metacognitive awareness refers to the extent to which thoughts are experienced as thoughts (mental events) rather than as aspects of self or direct reflections of truth."

As Pensa (2002, pp. 50-51) has observed, we are totally captivated by the indiscriminate fascination of thinking: "It is a sort of blind faith, in which we abandon ourselves to the supposedly magical power of thought and of rethinking, of compulsive cogitation or mental proliferation... It is precisely our attachment to proliferation that makes us blind to fundamental capabilities of the mind other than thought — in particular *sati* (awareness/mindfulness) and *metta* (unconditional loving kindness) — in other words the ability to confer upon the objects an affectionate and accepting awareness that is equally silent and non-judging." What is obscured by the proliferation of the discursive thought is precisely awareness, the very factor that is able to show us that *thoughts are just thoughts* and the possibilities of the mind are not just confined to thinking. This faculty of intuition embarrasses contemporary cognitive psychology as it is hard to categorize it within standard models of the mind, even though it was early recognized in western tradition, at least until the beginning of Modern Age. In none of Plato's dialogues did Socrates, the quintessential symbol of discursive thought in modern philosophy, comprehensively define an Idea in purely logical-linguistic terms. Acute, discerning analysis was instead used to loosen up the intellectual "cramps" that prevent an aperture towards the experience of an intuitive insight of the Idea (Friedlander, 1969). One way of making use of discursive reasoning still applied today is the Zen *koan* that utilizes paradoxes to go beyond discursive thinking. In Tibetan monasteries monks spend years exercising meticulous logical analysis and dialectics in order to be able to see *beyond*. Will a deeper understanding of mindfulness help reacquire mental faculties that make us more fully human?

II

Mindfulness-Based Training and Emotional Disorders[1]

F. Giommi*, H. Barendregt*, L. Oliemeulen**, J. van Hoof*, J. Tinge***, A. Coenen****, & P. van Dongen**[2]

We adopted Kabat-Zinn's (1990) MBSR program that has been applied in a variety of health care settings by several researchers (Kabat-Zinn et al., 1992; Teasdale et al., 1995; Schwartz, 1997) in slightly different ways. A growing number of studies show significant reduction in medical and stress-related symptoms, including chronic pain, breast and prostate cancer, and psoriasis. Baer's (2003) review suggests that mindfulness is an effective component in treating a wide spectrum of emotional and psychiatric disorders. This includes decreasing Generalized Anxiety Disorder and Panic Disorder (Miller et al.,1995), anxiety in non-clinical populations exposed to stressful conditions (Astin, 1997; Shapiro et al., 1998), heterogeneous physical and psychological symptoms in a clinical population (Reibel et al., 2001), mood disturbances and stress symptoms in cancer diagnosed patients (Speca et al., 2000). In addition, several cognitive-behavioral programs that incorporate a substantial mindfulness component could reduce self-harm in Borderline Personality Disorder (Linehan et al., 1991), Obsessive-Compulsive Disorder (Schwartz, 1997, 1998), and Binge-Eating Disorder (Kristeller & Hallet, 1999).

Recently, Segal and others (2002) have developed Mindfulness-Based Cognitive Therapy (MBCT) that combines Kabat-Zinn's method with techniques drawn from CT, which has led to conceptual advances in the modeling of affective change in mood disorders (Teasdale, 1997; Sheppard & Teasdale, 2001). MBCT has turned out to be quite effective in the prevention of relapse in major depression (Teasdale et al., 2000; Ma & Teasdale, 2004). However, the claimed effectiveness of mindfulness training needs to be investigated further (Bishop, 2002). Baer (2003), in her recent review incorporating meta-analytic procedures, concluded that in spite of significant methodological flaws, the current literature suggests that mindfulness-based interventions do help in a variety of mental health problems and improve psychological functioning. But, she insists that additional research and more rigorous tests should compare mindfulness-based interventions with established treatments and that the effect of mindfulness needs to be investigated within a broader range of outcomes, such as quality of life, to further determine the mechanism through which mindfulness brings about clinical change.

To our knowledge, no randomized controlled studies have ever been conducted to compare MBSR with other interventions, nor have neuropsychological measurements been included in order to investigate the attentional processes that are supposed to be specifically involved in mindfulness. The purpose of our study was to explore these issues. MBSR is a highly structured, manualized program. During the 8-week course participants attended a weekly 2.5 hour group session, in which they were guided through the program, motivated, inspired and supported by an MBSR experienced trainer (J.T.) educated at Kabat-Zinn's Center. As a comparison, we offered Psychoeducation (PE), which as MBSR has a manualized group format and is widely used as a structured psychosocial intervention for in- and outpatient psychiatric populations. It consisted of 8 weekly group meetings of 2.5 hours. In each session a psychiatrist (T.v.B.) educated and discussed with participants about their individual disorder's characteristics (natural history, diagnosis, treatment, etc.) as well as early detection and problem-solving techniques. The goal of PE was to promote the patients' knowledge and understanding and to teach them how to improve their managing-capability of their symptoms. Outcome research supports PE's designation as a "probably efficacious" treatment and its use as an adjunct to pharmacotherapy for emotional disorders (Barton, 1999). In unipolar depression PE increased treatment adherence and significantly reduced symptomatology (Van Dam et al, 2003; Rush, 1999; for a review, see Cuijpers, 1998). A large multicentre, randomized, controlled trial with depressives in the community showed reduction in number of cases and significant improvement in subjective and social functioning (Dowrick et al., 2000). In bipolar disorders several studies showed PE to be an effective adjunct to pharmacological treatment that improves clinical outcome (Gonzales-Pinto et al., 2004; Parikh et al., 1997); a large randomized trial found a significant reduction of recurrence and a lasting effect that goes beyond mere compliance enhancement (Colom et al., 2003). Although PE's application in anxiety disorders was less studied, symptoms were significantly reduced following PE in elderly female depressives (Schimmel-Spreeuw et al., 2000); significant changes were found in youths with generalized social anxiety disorder (Chavira & Stein, 2002).

The present exploration aims at corroborating previous findings, suggesting that MBSR is an effective component in the treatment of emotional disorders, by comparing MBSR to PE, by investigating whether MBSR is able to improve attentional performance, and by collecting additional evidence to support mindfulness' broad-spectrum efficacy claim. The specific questions addressed are: (1) Is MBSR effective in a sample of emotionally disordered patients in terms of pre-post clinical measurements on depression and anxiety symptoms and on perceived quality of life as compared to PE, a standard treatment used in psychiatric settings? (2) Is MBSR able to enhance attentional performance on standard neuropsychological tests? (3) Are EEG pre-post changes in this sample comparable to those drawn from previous research on meditation in non-clinical populations?

Method

1. *Participants and Design.*

Sample. At the onset we selected a sample of 25 patients suffering from disturbances that met DSM-IV criteria for Anxiety or Mood Disorders. They were recruited at an institute for mental health care (GGZ, Oost-Brabant, Netherlands) and were either hospitalized during the research or within the five preceding years. During the study patients continued receiving medical Treatment As Usual (TAU). Exclusion criteria were any psychotic state related to a diagnosis of schizophrenia or mania. Patients gave their informed consent. No-one showed any signs of alcohol or drug abuse at the time of testing and none had severe neurological or physical illnesses that might influence the task performances.

Design. We adopted a randomized pre-post comparison design with two comparison groups. According to Dutch legislation and recommendations of its ethical committee it was mandatory to give each control group an extra treatment besides the usual (medication) therapy. Therefore, no TAU or placebo control group was allowed.

Assignment. Data were derived from a sample of 5 males and 20 females who met inclusion criteria and who attended the pre- and post- measurements. Participants were allotted to MBSR or PE through a matched random assignment. First, clients' names were coded by using numbers, subsequently, a number was extracted randomly and the data corresponding with that specific number was paired with another number. Each pair was matched on the following variables: Sex, Age, Education, Hamilton Depression Scale and Continuous Performance Test scores.

The average age was 41.00 (SD 11.42, range 22-69); the median of educational level was 4 (on a 7-point scale), which corresponds to a secondary education level. Of the 25, 14 were in-patients and 11 out-patients; 19 (76%) had a diagnosis related to Mood Disorders, and 6 (24%) to Anxiety Disorders. None of the Bipolar Mood Disorder patients were in a maniacal state at the time of the study. In the MBSR group (n=14), 10 subjects had been diagnosed with Mood Disorder (4 Unipolar Major Depressive Disorder, 3 with Dysthymic Disorder, 3 with Bipolar Disorder), and 4 with Anxiety Disorders (1 Anxiety Disorder NAO, 1 Post Traumatic Stress Disorder, 2 Panic Disorder with Agoraphobia). In the PE group (n=11), 9 had been diagnosed with Mood Disorder (7 Unipolar Major Depression, 2 Dysthymic Disorder) and 2 with Anxiety Disorder (1 Anxiety Disorder NAO, 1 Panic Disorder without Agoraphobia). To check the random assignment procedure, the two groups were compared by one-way ANOVA on the matched variables. No significant differences between groups were found on Sex, Age, Education, on the first session of Hamilton Depression Scale, and on the Continuous Performance Test.

2. Measurements. During two sessions, both pre- and post-, we measured 13 outcome variables: 5 derived from clinical symptoms rating-scales, 2 related to a quality of life questionnaire, and 6 variables derived from 5 different neuropsychological tests. In the present text the clinical variables are sometimes referred to as C1... C5; the quality of life as Q1, Q2; and the neuropsychological-attentional ones as N1... N6.

Clinical variables. To assess treatment effects, we administered five standard rating scales. C1: the Hamilton Rating Scale for Depression (17-items; score range: 0-52) (Hamilton, 1960; Williams, 1998). C2: the Hamilton Rating Scale for Anxiety (14-items; score range: 0-56) (Hamilton, 1959). Both are interviewer-scales and scored by a psychiatrist (M.R.). C3: the Zung Self-Rating Depression Scale is a self-administered rating scale (20 items; score range: 20-80) (Zung, 1965). C4 and C5: the Visual Analogue Scales for Depression and for Anxiety are self-rating analogue indicators: symptom intensity is rated along a 0 to 100 line (Aitken et al., 1969); they were administered by a psychiatrist (M.R.).

Quality of life assessment. To evaluate changes in perceived quality of life, we used the extended Dutch version of the Lancashire Quality of Life Profile (LQLP). This questionnaire consists of 156 items, covering 11 different domains related to various aspects of life (Van Nieuwenhuizen, 1998). Domains 1 to 6 are rated according to a 7-point satisfaction scale (they refer to the perception of the different socio-economic aspects of life) and domains 7 to 11 are rated on a 3-point scale (they refer to the perception of more "self-related" aspects of life). The psychometric properties of the extended Dutch version were found to be sound and in agreement with the original (Olivier et al., 1997). We derived from this version two outcome variables: LQLP-3 (expressing the mean of the scores of the self-related domains) and LQLP-7 (incorporating the means of the external-related aspects). Two trained clinical researchers (L.O. and M.P.) administered the questionnaire.

Neuropsychological variables. To assess treatment effect on attentional processes, we administered a test battery. It comprises five neuropsychological tests; from these we selected six variables — one task producing two different measurements. N1: the Stroop Color-Word Test is considered to measure selectivity of attention: a decrease in performance time means improvement. N2: Continuous Performance Test is designed to measure sustained attention and involves a rapid identification of a target while withholding response to distracting stimuli. The correct-positive (hit) and incorrect-positive (false alarm) are registered. Perceptual sensitivity (d') was the outcome variable: such index of overall signal/noise discrimination (Nuechterlein et al., 1988) is considered to be closely related to the level of attentional arousal: high scores indicate better performances. In addition to the previous tests, we also used three tasks linked to executive and psychomotor functioning. The term psychomotor characterizes a variety of actions involving both attentional and sensorimotor processes. These three tasks were administered on a digitizing tablet allowing the precise recording of the pen movements made during the tests. This technique has recently been applied in psychiatric research to increase precision (Sabbe et al., 1997). N3: the Trail Making Test B, from the Halstead-Reitan Battery, is widely employed to specify test flexibility of attention, set-switching, visuomotor speed and working memory. The outcome measure consists of the time required to complete the task: the lower the score, the better the performance. N4: WISC-Maze Test that is part of the Wechsler Adult Intelligence Scale-Dutch version (De Bruyn et al., 1986) measures planning ability. The time needed to complete the mazes is the outcome variable: the lower the time, the better the performance. N5 and N6: the Digit Symbol Substitution Test is another subset of the Wechsler Scale; subjects are requested to substitute symbols for digits as quick as possible according to a key, for 90 seconds. The measure of this performance is the number of correct responses obtained and is referred to as "raw score." The DST owes its clinical sensitivity to requiring selective attention, sustained attention, working memory, and visuomotor coordination; however, standard DST gives only the raw score, which make it impossible to identify the contributions of the different processes. By means of the digitizing tablet, we could differentiate between the motor component, (the time taken to write a symbol) and the cognitive component (sustained and selective attention, i.e. the time needed to match the current digit with the proper symbol). Thus, we have two outcome variables from DST. N5: Raw-score, the standard DST outcome: higher scores indicate better performance and N6: Matching-time, the specific attentional component: lower scores indicate improvement.

EEG Measurements. 21 patients' EEGs (16 with Mood Disorders and 5 with Anxiety Disorders) were recorded before and after the two treatments. Electrodes were placed according to the International 10-20 System on eleven locations (F3, F4, C3, C4, P3, T3, T4, P4, Fz, Cz, Pz); the right mastoid was used as reference. During recording the patients were quietly laying on a medical bed in a room isolated from the recording equipment. After placing the electrodes, a rest period of 15 minutes was used. Then the EEG was recorded during 5 minutes with eyes open and subsequently 5 minutes with eyes closed.

3. Procedure. Two cycles have been completed: the first including 14 patients, the second 19 patients. All subjects in the first cycle were inpatients; in the second were 3 in-patients and 16 out-patients. Interventions have been offered at the same hospital where all the patients had their health care. At the beginning of each cycle, patients were informed that they would be assigned randomly to one of the groups after the first general session of measurements had been completed. Each participant had four individual consultations within a seven days' span, prior to the first week of treatment: to complete the clinical ratings scales, to perform the neuropsychological tests and the LQLP, to get instruction from the MBSR or PE trainer, and to have the EEG measurements. This sequence was randomly alternated. Following the same procedure, the second set of measurements was completed within two weeks after the end of the trainings. To minimize biases related to expectancy of change, we calculated the neuropsychological results only after all the data had been collected. To avoid the experimenter effect as much as possible, neither the clinical researchers who administered the rating scales and the tests, nor the MBSR and PE trainers were involved in the research design or interpretation.

Results

1. Data. To summarize: thirteen outcome variables and EEG alpha-power have been determined in this study. Four variables (N1, N3, N4, N6) were checked as not being normally distributed and have been normalized by applying a natural-logarithmic transformation, indicated with Ln. Unfortunately, due to unintentional reasons, it was not possible to obtain a complete data set for eight of the patients who had been initially included in this study. Therefore, full pre-post data set were obtained in 17 out of 25 cases.

2. Analysis. Between-groups comparison. The main purpose of the analysis was to compare the outcome of MBSR and PE (grouping variable) on multiple variables. An alpha level of .05 was set. We considered that different subsets of the outcome variables were measuring, in a likely overlapping manner, the same constructs, such as depression and anxiety. Thus, we decided to adopt a multivariate approach. To compare the overall effect of MBSR with that of PE, MANOVA was run (SPSS10; GLM-Multivariate). For each outcome variable, the effect of the interventions was considered to be the difference of the measurement after the training minus those before the training. Therefore, the goal of this analysis was to look specifically at the Group X Time interaction to determine whether one group improved more than the other. The result, Wilks' Lambda = .006 (F 35,589; df [1,19]; p <.0067; eta-squared .994), shows a very significant difference in the sample means and a large effect size value, indicating that the effect may be considered as a clinically relevant one (Huberty & Petoskey, 2000, p. 197). How, then, can such a multivariate difference be analyzed?

(a) Consistent with our multivariate approach the 13 variables can be conceptually separated into different classes of partially overlapping measures, each class measuring a different construct; we defined four classes: depression (C1, C3, C4), anxiety (C2, C5); quality of life (Q1, Q2), and attentional processes (N1, N2, N3, N4, N5, N6). To examine whether the overall difference between treatments can be attributed to one or more of these four distinguished classes, we conducted a between-groups MANOVA on the pre-post mean differences, for each class. We set an alpha value of .0125 adjusting (Bonferroni) for multiple comparisons. Results: the effect did not attain statistical significance for any class (see Table 1). To further investigate between-group differences, additional (univariate) ANOVAs were conducted on each variable; none of the differences reached significance.

(b) We then assessed the multivariate distinct (within) effect of each intervention on the 13 pre-post mean differences by mean of an extension of the MANOVA procedure based on the homoscedasticity assumption that is already implicit in the MANOVA procedure for assessing the difference between trainings. The extension was needed because the sample sizes of the two trainings were too small to make inference on them separately. An adjusted alpha value of 0.025 (Bonferroni) was set. Using a modified form of Muirhead's (1982) theorem: both treatments showed a (very) significant effect. For MBSR: Hotelling's T Squared = 8175.22 (F 125,772; df [13,3]; p <.0010). For PE: Hotelling's T Squared = 22500.30; (F 346,158; df [13,3]; p <.0002). Differences were in the expected direction: both MBSR and PE resulted in a within-group significant positive effect, corroborating previous research suggesting their efficacy.

(c) In order to consider the clinical significance of the comparison of MBSR with PE, we analyzed the effect sizes of the between-group MANOVAs on each class (see Table 1). Notably, the between-groups eta-squared values — a multivariate effect size measure — evidenced that two classes exhibited a remarkable effect magnitude. The anxiety class showed a small but not trivial value of .295, while the attentional-processes class showed a small-to-medium value of .378.[3] Both effect sizes are evidence in support of a larger clinical efficacy of MBSR. Because in the attentional class MBSR showed pre-post mean differences larger than PE on five out of six variables. In the anxiety class a small difference unfavorable to MBSR on the variable C2 is balanced by a huge difference in favor to it on C5. Besides the between-group effect sizes, we considered the magnitude and the directions of the pre-post mean changes of each outcome variables: MBSR induced larger improvements than PE on three of the five clinical variables (C3, C4, C5); and on five of the six attentional variables (N1, N2, N4, N5, N6). Moreover, a close scrutiny evidenced that MBSR univocally induced a positive, systematic change in *all* the variables of *all* the four classes, whereas for PE such consistent improvement on all the variables of a given class is limited to depression and quality of life.

Table 1. MANOVAs between MBSR and PE groups

Class of variables	Wilks' Lambda	df	p-value	eta-squared
All 13 variables	.006	(1,19)	p = .0067*	.994
Depression var.	.850	(1,19)	p = .418**	.150
Anxiety var.	.705	(1,19)	p = .042**	.295
Quality of Life var.	.945	(1,22)	p = .551**	.055
Attentional var.	.622	(1,18)	p = .316**	.378

*Alpha = .05; * *Alpha = .0125 (Bonferroni);

Table 2. MBSR and PE pre-post within effect sizes (d)

Outcome variables	N (pairwise)	MBSR Cohen's d	PE N (pairwise)	Cohen's d
Hamilton Depression	12	.85 large	11	1.25 large
Hamilton Anxiety	12	1.00 large	11	1.00 large
Zung Depression	12	.67 medium	11	.64 medium
VAS Anxiety	10	.69 medium	11	.19 *
VAS Depression	10	.82 large	11	.44 small
Lqlp_7	14	.18 *	11	.64 medium
Lqlp_3	14	.64 medium	10	.61 medium
Stroop Test (Ln)	14	.64 medium	11	.15 *
CPT_d'	14	.59 medium	11	.72 medium
Trail-Making B (Ln)	14	.62 medium	9	.73 medium
WISC-Maze (Ln)	14	.29 small	10	.11 *
ST Raw-score)	12	.67 medium	10	.17 *
DST Matching-time(Ln)	11	.72 medium	10	.04 *

* Not relevant effect in Cohen's terms

MBSR's clinical significance. In addition to the between-group comparison, we are interested in the clinical and practical significance of MBSR. The effect sizes of the MBSR within-group differences assessed by mean of Cohen's d evidenced improvements of a substantial effect (i.e. >.20) on 12 of the 13 variables, while PE showed substantial effects on 8 variables (see Table 2). On the Hamilton Depression and Hamilton Anxiety Scales, the pre-post mean reductions were 23% and 36% respectively. This is in line with the 23% and 34% reductions on the Hamilton Depression and Hamilton Anxiety scales (observed in previous research on MBSR with patients suffering of anxiety disorders; Miller et al., 1995). The mean reductions on the Zung and VAS Depression/Anxiety were 11%, 24%, and 30%, respectively; these instruments were not used in previous research. The MBSR size effects were large for three variables and medium for two, whereas those of PE: large for two, medium for two others, and not meaningful for one (Table 4). As to the attentional variables, in MBSR five out of six showed within-group improvements with effect sizes of medium magnitude; in PE only two did.

EEG findings. The alpha power was calculated as the mean power of frequencies in the range 8-13 Hz. Data were log transformed for statistical analysis. To determine the experimental effects, repeated measures ANOVA with pre-post, conditions (eyes-open, eyes-closed), and electrode placement as within-subjects factors, and treatment (MBSR, PE) as between-subjects factor, was carried out. A significant increase in alpha power as a result of both treatments was found at all electrode locations for the whole sample (both groups): F = 6,060 (df [1,19]; p <.023).

Discussion

1. *Between-groups comparison.* It might seem odd that the overall significant variability, as revealed by the Group X Time MANOVA between treatments, has not been resolved to a significant degree in any of the distinguished classes of variables. However, such result seems to support the conclusion that the difference that results in comparing the two trainings are of a very multivariate nature crossing through all the classes of variables. In addition, it must be considered that on the one hand both treatments proved to be effective, therefore as a consequence driving most of the outcome variable means of both groups in a positive direction. On the other hand, due to the previously described practical and ethical constrains to our clinical trial, the sample size and the statistical power of our study were rather limited. These two conjoint factors are likely to reduce the probability obtaining statistically significant differences in the between-groups multivariate comparisons on the classes of variables, as well as in the univariate comparisons on single variables.

In order to provide a more reliable interpretation of our data we decided to consider both their clinical and practical significance. Referring to the size of the effects provides useful information that can be used in judgments of practical and scientific importance of an effect (Hallahan & Rosenthal, 2000, p. 136). Consequently the magnitude of an effect might provide some support to a scientific hypothesis even when statistical significance has not been obtained. Moreover, Kirk (1966) remarked that Cohen's meaning of small, medium, and large effect (Cohen, 1997) remains approximately the same across the several different measures of effect sizes. In the present study the between-groups effect sizes evidenced that MBSR exhibited remarkable magnitudes in the anxiety and attentional classes, and this result supports MBSR's large clinical efficacy.

2. *MBSR clinical significance.* The MBSR within-group effect sizes' changes evidence improvements of a substantial effect on 12 of the 13 variables, while PE shows substantial effects on 8 variables (Table 2). For the clinical variables such magnitudes are consistent with those found in the literature on mindfulness training with anxious and depressed patients (Baer, 2003). These findings confirmed MBSR's capacity to decrease levels of psychological symptoms. Furthermore, because our sample included patients with several diagnoses, this result brings new evidence in favor of the claimed wide-range efficacy that appears to be peculiar for mindfulness. To date, no study has specifically investigated the effect of the MBSR on attentional processes, neither in normal subjects, nor in clinical populations. One aim was to explore the hypothesis that low-level automatic attentional processes may also, as was already shown for memory and metacognitive higher processes (Teasdale, 1999; Williams, 1996), be modified by means of mindfulness. The between-group MANOVA on the attentional class did not reach statistical significance: this result did not support the hypothesis of a specific, differential effect of MBSR on attentional processes. However, once we considered the clinical meaning of the effect sizes observed in the MBSR group, it seems possible to collect some useful clues. Although between-groups comparison on the attention class was not statistically significant, it showed nonetheless a small-to-medium effect of .378 in favor of MBSR. Moreover, in the MBSR group, five of the six attention-related variables induced within-group improvements of medium magnitude, whereas in PE only two did (Table 2). All in all, these data seem to support the hypothesis that MBSR was able to specifically promote improvements in the low-level attentional processes involved in the neuropsychological tasks. However, this support is indirect, drawn from considerations based on the clinical significance of the observed effects sizes. Further study is needed.

3. *EEG.* In adults the power in alpha frequencies band is inversely related to cortical activation (Davidson, 1995). The alpha power increase in the sample is interpreted as enhancement of the amount of relaxation or a decrease in tension or distress (Coenen, 1995). Both treatments are to be regarded as effective. This is consistent with previous research on meditation, which repeatedly indicates an increase of alpha power waves in non-clinical populations while practicing different forms of meditation (Jevning et al., 1992). Although the alpha power

increased more in the MBSR group, no significant between-groups difference could be established.

4. *Limitations of this study.* Four main limitations need to be discussed: (1) To obtain a larger sample we included patients with different emotional disorders; this implies a mixed nature of our sample. In the outcome literature, it is usually accepted that the effectiveness of an intervention is studied only in relation to a specific clinical disorder because it is generally considered unlikely that any one intervention is equally effective for different disorders. By mixing different diagnoses it might be possible to conceal the effects of the intervention on one disorder in the lack of effectiveness on other disorders. However, because we are interested in the proclaimed characteristic of MBSR as a wide-ranging treatment, this limitation might even be useful to study. (2) It was not in the scope of this study to assess long-term effects; thus, it cannot be concluded that the short-term changes are lasting: this question should be answered by future longitudinal research. (3) The impossibility, due to ethical constrains, to set a TAU control group requires the necessary prudence with pre-post designs: other factors could have favored the positive changes. (4) The small sample size affected the statistical power and subsequently the chance to achieve statistical significance, particularly in the between-group comparisons.

5. *Conclusions.* A Group X Time MANOVA comparison between MBSR and PE revealed a significant difference. However, on the one hand, the between-groups MANOVA comparisons on the distinct classes of variables did not attain statistical significance; on the other hand, in the anxiety and attentional areas the effect sizes of such comparisons evidenced meaningful differences favorable to MBSR. This inconsistency might be explained by two facts: (1) both interventions produced distinct significant improvements within-groups and (2) the low statistical power (due to the small sample size) made it unlikely to detect significant but small differences (explaining the inconsistency). Such results, together with the comprehensive consideration of the mean differences of the single outcome variables discussed above, might represent a hint for interpreting the significant difference revealed by the between-group MANOVA as a larger effect of MBSR compared to PE. Nevertheless, in spite of these clues in favor of MBSR, our conclusion is prudential: the present comparison study shows that MBSR resulted in being *at least as efficacious as* PE in promoting improvements in a number of outcome variables in a sample of patients suffering from emotional disorders. It is the first time, to our knowledge, that a comparison study has been conducted to evaluate the effects of MBSR vis a vis a standard intervention established as "probably efficacious" (Baer, 2003). Such conclusion provides new confidence in addition to what has already been found in research on MBSR as an effective component in treating emotional disorders. Furthermore, this is as yet the first study that explored attention-related neuropsychological measures. Research on emotional disordered patients has evidenced neuropsychological attentional deficits on the same tasks we

have used in the present study (Schatzberg et al., 2000; MacLeod & Rutherford, 1998). Our study yields support, even if only indirectly, to the hypothesis that MBSR might exert a positive effect on attentional processes. Our results indicate that further research is needed to determine the clinical effectiveness of mindfulness in the context of our present knowledge of mind (Barendregt, 1998).

---

1. We thank T. van Bakel for directing the PE group, M. Kunicki, E. Wronka, A. Smit, and A. Sambeth for EEG recordings and data elaboration, M. Rijtema, M. van Gool, and I. Sturkeboom for recording clinical and neuro-psychological measurements, H. Oud for his support in working with SPSS, H. Hendriks for his careful advice on statistical methodology. J. Teasdale gave critical and useful comments on a draft of this paper. We express gratefulness to the Board of Directors of Radboud University Nijmegen, Netherlands, for funding this study

2. Faculty of Science, Mathematics & Computing Science, Radboud University Nijmegen, Netherlands; ** Institute for Mental Health, Oss, Netherlands; *** Tinge Training & Therapy, Rolde, Netherlands; **** Faculty of Social Sciences, Radboud University Nijmegen, Netherlands

3. Cohen described effect sizes larger than d = .20 as small, d = .50 as medium, and d = .80 as large

14

The Influence of Mindfulness/Zazen On Depression

Yoshinori Ito, Rieko Katsukura & Kaneo Nedate

The purpose of Buddhist meditation is to obtain the distinctive cognitive attitude which is "enlightenment" through de-automatization (Deikman, 1966) by a "watcher self" (Deatherage, 1975). Such process refers to mindfulness or metacognitive awareness in which one is fully conscious of thoughts and feelings in a wider context rather than responding automatically/habitually to thoughts and feelings as if they belong to self or identifications of reality. It has been claimed down the ages that meditative de-automatization nourishes physical and mental wellbeing. Although a range of benefits have been pointed out, there have been few studies to evaluate de-automatization's underlying cognitive attitude, which is metacognitive awareness or the practice of mindfulness. Metacognitive awareness can be measured by the Measure of Awareness and Coping in Autobiographical Memory (MACAM) (Moore et al., 1996) that evaluates the extent to which one objectively experiences thoughts as thoughts (mental events) in the moment they occur. This chapter reports how meditation in Zen — particularly in sitting only meditation or zazen — modifies the extent of metacognitive awareness and is able to impact depression. In order to compare the effects of zazen on metacognitive awareness and on depression, 22 depressed undergraduate students were randomly assigned to a meditation group and a control group. The first group practiced zazen 10 times (20 minutes a time) for 2 weeks as homework and received psycho-education on Buddhist wisdom and zazen's rationale. As a result, the MACAM showed that at post-test, three weeks after pre-test, metacognitive awareness significantly increased in the meditation group compared with a control group. Along with increased metacognitive awareness, zazen had an effect on bringing about a significant decrease in the scores of ruminative cognitive style and depression.

Cognitive-Behavior Therapy (CBT) is shifting to the third generation (Hayes, 2004). During the first generation, the emphasis was on describing the mechanism of efficacy for emotional and behavioral disorders by applying the conditioning theories and using the empirical method to evaluate and assess treatment effectiveness. Back then, the cause and context of behavior were not regarded as a subject for consideration; instead, understating and improving symptoms through the functional analysis of behavior and its environment was the target of concern. In the

60s, after the cognitive revolution, attention was paid to cognitive processes as the underlying factor of behavior (such as beliefs and memories). The empirical orientation was carried over to cognitive therapy, which interventions focus directly on modifying automatic thoughts and schemata. Second generation CBT includes Ellis' Rational Emotive Behavior Therapy (REBT), Beck's Cognitive Therapy (CT), and Meichenbaum's Self-Instructional Training (SIT). These interventions emphasize the replacement of dysfunctional/irrational thoughts by functional/rational cognitive contents. Third generation CBT considers this a bone of contention. Replacing cognitive contents is based on the idea that there is something problematic with the client's thoughts. Treatments thus conducted value clients' cognitions depending on the therapists' judgments. However, as thinking develops through one's unique living conditions, it is necessarily relative and cannot be labeled as good or bad by anyone. Minding behavioral-cognitive-emotive intricacies, the emphasis is on multiple functions related to context and a thorough understanding of the individual by her/himself. The treatment's aim thus shifts to transforming the client's relationship to what s/he thinks, feels, and does. It was Teasdale (1999) who theorized that CT's effectiveness is not due to alterations of cognitive content but rather to the alterations in clients' relationship with the act of thinking thoughts.

Third generation interventions include Mindfulness-Based Stress Reduction (MBSR; Kabat-Zinn, 1990), Mindfulness-Based Cognitive Therapy (MBCT; Segal et al., 2002), Acceptance and Commitment Therapy (ACT; Hayes et al., 1999), and Dialectical Behavior Therapy (DBT; Linehan, 1993). The common technique used in these various therapies is mindfulness meditation. This ancient oriental method, mostly practiced in the beginning while in a sitting position, is considered to be an important active ingredient in the abovementioned therapies. Mindful sitting is the best known meditation method that has been practiced by the Buddha some 2500 years ago; it is called zazen in Zen. Dogen (13th century), the founder of Zen's Soto school taught *shikantaza* (just sitting) and expounded that that is the only way to attain awakening (Ando, 2003). Shikantaza is usually taught by a Roshi (from Lao-Tzu, a Zen master) who begins with educating the novice by explaining Buddhist sutras (scriptures) prior to the sitting practice. The student's understanding of its rationale is likely to enhance effectiveness. Such psycho-education seems also necessary when applying zazen in the framework of therapy. The aim of applying zazen to therapy is not enlightenment, but to ameliorate stress in an efficient way. It contains elements essential to mindfulness: (1) a passive attitude (letting it happen) (Benson, 1975), (2) a non-analytical focused attention (Shapiro, 1982), and (3) receptivity (letting be) (Smith, 1991). During the 70s and 80s this practice had been studied in terms of relaxation and physiological reactivity; its outcome in curing specific disorders has yet to be demonstrated.

The interest in mindfulness has energized research in that direction. Mindfulness is defined by Kabat-Zinn (1994, p. 4) as "paying attention in a particular way: on purpose, in the present moment, and nonjudgmentally. This kind of attention nurtures greater awareness, clarity and acceptance of present-moment reality." If mindfulness meditation is effective when such a cognitive set is formed, it can be regarded as a cognitive strategy that is able to cope with various stressors (Bishop et al., 2004). The Buddhist definition of *sati*, the basis of mindfulness, is not surprisingly very similar to that of mindfulness; it is the awareness of one's feelings, experienced "objectively," at the present moment. Sati is the cognitive skill required to attain enlightenment that inheres in mental health and that is able to defeat existential suffering due to life's impermanence. This study focuses on suffering of undergraduate students, who had experienced repeated episodes of depression and who are not currently diagnosed with depression but still have a high depressive proclivity. A compelling reason to select such a group is to be able to compare our results with those of Teasdale and his colleagues. They conducted in-depth studies on the mechanism of the development, persistence, and treatment of depression.

According to Teasdale's model, vulnerability to relapse/recurrence of major depression arises from repeated associations between depressed mood and patterns of negative, self-critical, hopeless thinking during depressive episodes, leading to changes at the cognitive and neuronal levels. As a result, individuals who have recovered from major depression differ from individuals who have never experienced major depression in their patterns of thinking when activated by a future sad mood (Teasdale, 1988). Specifically, in recovered depressed patients, the thinking activated by dysphoria should be similar to the negative thinking patterns previously present in the episode. These patterns of thought, typically involving views of the self as worthless/inadequate and of the future as hopeless, are assumed to contribute to the maintenance of depressive symptoms. Reactivation of these patterns in recovered patients by dysphoria would act to maintain and intensify the dysphoric state through escalating and self-perpetuating cycles of ruminative cognitive-affective processing (Teasdale, 1988; 1997). In this way, in those with a history of major depression, states of mild dysphoria will be more likely to progress to more intense and persistent states, thus increasing risk of further onsets of episodes of major depression (Segal et al., 2004).

To end vicious cycles formed with thoughts and feelings, mindfulness may be effective in two ways. It can offer the chance to practice allocating the controlled processing resources that are often dominated by a depression-related process to different ones. Furthermore, in mindfulness people continue paying attention to various physical sensations. If in a state of an idle mind (intrusive thought or *zatsunen*) or when loosing concentration, they are to repeat this process. The relation between the subject (the one allocating attention) and thoughts/feeling can thus be changed and viewed from a new perspective. Teasdale calls this new perspective metacognitive awareness that he defines as the process of experiencing thought and feeling from a decentered perspective. Decentering means: to relate to negative experiences as mental events in a wider context or field of awareness, rather than simply being these emotions or identifying personally with negative thoughts and feelings. In other words, developing metacognitive awareness as a cognitive skill means that the idea of "what I think or feel is who I am (feeling = myself)" is changed to the idea of "what I think or feel is just one of something I experienced." In fact, they have shown that CT in reducing relapse/recurrence in recovered depressed patients increased accessibility of metacognitive sets (Teasdale et al., 2002).

In this study, metacognitive awareness was measured to investigate whether mindfulness is effective for decreasing depression through acquiring metacognitive skills. As automatic allocation of controlled processing resources is excessively biased toward the depression process, mindfulness might not be effective for people with acute depression. The present study was conducted with undergraduates not currently diagnosed as depressed, but who have high depressive tendencies. Those who didn't experience repeated depressive episodes were excluded from this study in order to have a group Teasdale's theory was designed for.

Method

Participants. Twenty-two undergraduates (age 19-25) were screened according to two criteria: (1) a score above 16 on the Beck Depression Inventory (BDI) and (2) having experienced a depressive episode at least twice. They were randomly allocated to a meditation (MT) group and a waiting list control (WLC) group according to baseline scores. 5 Males and 6 females were included in each group (MT: M age 20.45, SD1.81; WLC: M age 20.41, SD1.62). Nobody dropped out during the experiment.

Measures. (1) *Screening measures.* The BDI (Beck et al., 1961; Hayashi, 1988) is a 21-item self-report measure of depression. Here it is used for screening purposes and evaluating the efficacy of zazen. The Frequency of Depressive Episode Experience (FDE) is a one item measure made for this study to estimate the frequency of previous depressive episodes. Participants are asked to rate their past experiences such as persistent depressive and low energetic episode on a 4-point scale ranging from 1-"not at all" to 4-"extremely." Clinical interviews were also conducted to exclude those affected with a mental or physical disorder including major depressive disorder at the pre-test. (2) *Assessment measures.* These measures were completed during four different periods: (1) pre-assessment period, (2) post-assessment period, (3) 1-month follow-up period, and (4) 6-months follow-up period. We used three categories of measures: cognitive skills measures, cognitive styles measures, and other measures.

(1) *Cognitive skills measures.* The Measure of Awareness and Coping in Autobiographical Memory (MACAM; Moore et al., 1996; see Katsukura et al., this volume) is a measure that includes a semi-structured interview and ratings. Metacognitive awareness is referred to as the cognitive set in which negative

thoughts and feelings are seen as passing mental events rather than as aspects of self or reality in one's autobiographical memory that is accessed by vignettes containing depression-related cues. As the only Measure of Awareness in Autobiographical Memory (Japanese version: J-MAWARE), a subscale of MACAM, reflects the extent of metacognitive awareness, this is used at the pre-assessment and the 1-month follow-up periods. A second measure in this category is the Body Awareness Questionnaire (BAQ; Shields & Simon, 1991; Shibahara, 2000), which is an 18-item self-report list of body awareness comprising four subscales: awareness of bodily function, awareness of sleep rhythm, awareness of food taking, and awareness of fatigue. A third measure in this category is the Unconditional Self-Acceptance Scale (SAS, Takai, 2002), a one item self-report measure of unconditional self-acceptance.

(2) *Cognitive styles measures*. Firstly, the Response Styles Questionnaire (Nolen-Hoeksema & Morrow, 1991; Nagura & Hashimoto, 1999) is a 52-item self-report measure of response styles on depression. It consists of four subscales: negative rumination, analytic rumination, distraction, and interpersonal relationship seeking. Secondly, the Scale of Meditation-Related Cognitive Styles (SMCS, Sakairi, 2001), a 21-item self-report measure of cognitive style related to enlightenment with three subscales: flexibility, receptiveness, and happy-go-lucky-attribution.

(3) *Other measures*. To evaluate the degree of MT group participants' familiarity with Buddhist ideas, zazen, and psycho-education, some questions were prepared for this study (e.g. "Do you understand that the universe came into existence as the result of various causes and interdependent relationships?"). Participants rate on a 7-point scale (ranging from 1-"not at all" to 7-"completely"). After the post-assessment, a simple interview was conducted with the participants about the experiment.

Pre/post-session measures. Before and after the training sessions, participants filled in: the Depression and Anxiety Mood Scale (DAMS, Fukui, 2002), a 9-item self-report measure of mood with three subscales: anxious mood, depressive mood, and positive mood. For MT participants, some questions were prepared in this study to evaluate the achievement of practice (e.g. "I could concentrate on my breathing").

Procedure

Assessments. All participants came to the laboratory five times in total. At the 1st visit, both groups received the pre-assessment J-MAWARE, after informed consent. At the 2nd visit, the following week, each group came to the laboratory to complete questionnaires and to receive psycho-education plus instructions for homework. The MT group practiced zazen with the experimenter. At the 3rd visit, in the third week, both groups gathered and had their homework checked. In addition, the MT group practiced and discussed zazen. At the 4th visit, in the fourth week, the experimenter checked homework and participants were asked to complete the post-assessment questionnaires. At the 5th visit, the 1-month follow-up, we conducted the J-MAWARE assessment and again requested the participants to fill in questionnaires. For the 6-month follow-up, the questionnaires were sent to and returned by the participants after completion by mail.

Psycho-education. Psycho-education was provided by audiotape, lasting approximately ten minutes, and recorded by the experimenter. Topics include: (1) what is depression; it is a condition that can affect anyone "like a mild cold of the mind," (2) Buddhist teachings; life history of the Buddha, law of karma, attachment, non-self, and *shogyou-mujyou* (all things are in a state of incessant change), (3) relation between improvement of the depression and Buddhist teachings, (4) relation between improvement of depression and zazen. These treatment principles are designed with references of the treatment principles of Segal and others (2002), Hayes (2002), and Buddhist scriptures, and supervised by the head of the Soto school at Sojiji Temple.

Zazen. The MT group was instructed by audiotape recording on how to practice sitting meditation: the body in an upright posture and held still. The breath is to be used as a focus of alert attention. In order to concentrate on breathing, participants counted their own breathing cycles; one in- and out-breathing is one cycle. When the cycle reaches ten, the counting starts again from one, etc. Whenever one notices his/her mind wandering and not counting breathing cycles, s/he is to acknowledge the condition in a nonjudgmental manner and bring the mind back to the breathing.

Homework. The MT group was asked to practice 8 sessions of zazen (each lasting 20 minutes) during a period of two weeks, to complete the DAMS before and after a session, and to answer some questions that evaluate the achievement of their practice. The WLC group only completed the DAMS, 10 times during the same period.

Results

As the data from the 6-month follow-up were being analyzed, the following reports the results based on data of the MT and WLC group (the pre-/post and 1-month follow-up assessment. A 2 (MT vs. WLC) x3 (pre- vs. post- vs. 1month follow-up) repeated measures ANOVA was calculated using the score of each questionnaire as the dependent variable.

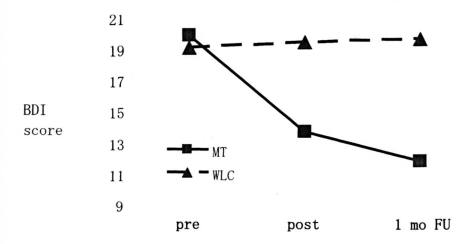

Figure 1. BDI score in each group

As predicted, Figure 1 indicates that depression significantly improved in the MT group, while there was no improvement in the WLC group (see Figure 1).

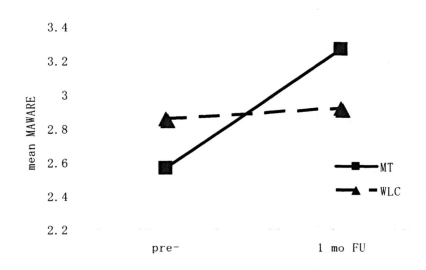

Figure 2. MAWARE score in each group

Figure 2 shows mean J-MAWARE scores at pre-assessment and at 1-month follow-up. A 2 (MT vs. WLC) x 2 (pre- vs. 1-month follow-up) repeated measures ANOVA with the J-MAWARE as the dependent variable, revealed no significant effects or interaction. To answer J-MAWARE's questions according to the standard procedure, participants must retrieve the most negative memory they have experienced. Because this study compares the results right before the intervention versus one month after the intervention, recalled memories may be redundant. To avoid redundancy, we use experiences happening right before each intervention. Coincidentally, some of the recent experiences have been the most negative ones for the participants. Therefore, the experiences of a middle level of unpleasantness (50% or >) were selected and analyzed. As predicted, the results on J-MAWARE (recent 50) suggest that the MT group shows signs of having developed metacognitive awareness, while no change was shown by the WLC group. The scales on Self-Acceptance and Body Awareness detect neither significant effects nor interactions.

Among RSQ's four subscales, only the negative rumination style shows a significant decrease. This suggests that zazen practice improves negative ruminating. Finally, SMCS's total score increases significantly, implying that zazen is able to help acquire a cognitive style toward enlightenment.

Discussion

The aim of this study was to investigate whether two weeks of zazen can result in reducing depressive tendency and acquiring metacognitive skills by depressed undergraduates. The results reveal that zazen was effective for depressive participants with ruminative cognitive styles related to depression as compared to a waiting list control group. This finding supports earlier claims that mindfulness impacts depression positively (McQuaid & Carmona, 2004). Our participants developed not only a flexible and objective cognitive style, but also cultivated a metacognitive awareness. However, no effect was found on self-acceptance and body awareness. Also, no change was confirmed among the participants of the WLC groups. Our results suggest that mindfulness can be effective to curb depressive proclivity and improve mild depressive symptoms. Zazen could induce current depressive tendency. This is in line with what Segal and others (2004) presume namely that MBCT is not effective for acute depression. We conjecture with them that in order to practice mindfulness, participants require the abilities of executive functions such as being able to pay attention to their breathing and posture instead of focusing on their negative thoughts or feelings, and to maintain this condition for a while. When depressive symptoms occur, the executive functions may be disrupted, however if the subject's symptoms are mild enough, at a level high enough to attend college, it is inferred that although disrupted, the level of executive ability is also high enough for practicing mindfulness. This study was based on group work and the participants were assigned homework, which made the treatment very cost-effective. With further investigation to identify the level of executive function required for effective mindfulness practice, the training can be made even more effective and cost-beneficial for clients in the range of mild to moderate depression.

We also have examined the hypothesis that depression decreases due to one's acquiring metacognitive awareness and our results confirm this significantly. This consistent finding plus the fact that no changes were found among the subjects in the WLC group, is an indication for the clinical validity of J-MAWARE (see Katsukura et al., this volume). This and other previous studies by Teasdale and others indicate that the mean scores of non-depressed subjects are generally a little higher than three. When a score of three or more is obtained on the MAWARE/J-MAWARE, it is assumed that at the time of potential relapse, one is able to experience and interpret thoughts and feelings through a decentered perspective with a beneficial relapse/recurrence preventive effect. The fact that in our study the mean score of the MT group increased from 2.58 to 3.27 leads us to infer that the change is quite considerable. Our participants have acquired the (Buddhist) wisdom that thoughts and feelings are not "I"/"myself" or "truth/reality." One will likely execute such a decentered/disidentified perspective at times of potential relapse and negative thoughts/feelings reactivated by dysphoria are consequently less likely to lead to the escalation of a depressive spiral. However, contrary to our predictions, there were no significant differences on the body awareness between the two groups. There is one exception: the score on the degree of felt proprioception during each session was significantly increased at the latter half of the practice period. These are conflicting findings attributable to the fact that an increase of body awareness requires a much longer practice before it can be applied in everyday life. The validity of the self-acceptance scale is uncertain and needs further investigation.

There was no attrition during the training period. This may be explained by the psycho-education offered. The content of the psycho-education was designed with the aim to show the relation between the Buddhist teachings and depression, and to cultivate motivation for zazen. If minimum psycho-education can improve the dropout rate, a serious problem in therapy as well as in meditation, it may provide the key to solve this problem. We surmise that this psycho-education may be particularly effective when the participants have a Buddhist background. However, this could not be studied, because none of the participants had advance knowledge about the information given during the psycho-education. In addition, none of them had an interest in any belief system. This is in line with recent data; more than 80% of Japanese undergraduates disbelieve or are not interested in Buddhist teachings (Kawano, 2005). Such information reveals that young Japanese of today are less attached to the Buddha than in prior times. Therefore the Buddhist psycho-education might be perceived and received as novel ideas to the participants. In fact, the interview after the post-assessment, which measures the understanding of the psycho-education, corroborates the speculation that the participants received information as novel and interesting thoughts. We assume that similar reactions would be observed when Buddhist psycho-education is given to clients with another cultural or religious background. As we consider the Buddhist teaching as a psychology, it might be combined with any religion. It should therefore not to be concealed as is often the case (e.g. in MBSR, Kabat-Zinn, 1990). The Buddhist teaching as a psychology of health and contentment is a psycho-education that emphasizes practice and enhances self-inquiry and self-knowledge.

In conclusion, the purpose of this study was to investigate the possibility of mindfulness influencing metacognitive awareness plus other cognitive styles. Most of the results support our predictions. At the same time, we could not identify which ingredient influenced which specific effect. To find the active ingredients it is necessary to further examine the effect of each component of zazen/mindfulness during the training. Secondly, it was not certain whether the MT participants performed exactly as instructed since the zazen was for a great deal homework and we do not have the appropriate tools to assess the extent they follow the instructions. In this study we had to rely on a questionnaire to assess their performance. However, self-reports indicate that they had properly followed our instructions. Thirdly, our participants were all Japanese undergraduates who although with a penchant for depression never had experienced a major depressive episode. Therefore, it is difficult to generalize our results to the major depressive disorders. Further investigation is needed, which includes severe clinical samples. Fourthly, since the current study relied mostly on self-report questionnaires, except the J-MAWARE, other kinds of assessments are required to empirically demonstrate the effectiveness of mindfulness/zazen training.

15

Awareness In Autobiographical Memory: A Japanese Measure

Rieko Katsukura, Yoshinori Ito & Kaneo Nedate

In practicing mindfulness meditation, one sees negative thoughts and feelings as passing events (rather than as self or truth/reality). Teasdale and others (2002) called this disidentified or decentered cognitive attitude "metacognitive awareness" and developed the Measure of Awareness and Coping in Autobiographical Memory to assess it. They suggested that metacognitive awareness reduces the risk of a mild dysphoria escalating to major depression or a relapse. The purpose of this study is to develop the Japanese version of the Measure of Awareness in Autobiographical Memory (J-MAWARE). We confirmed satisfactory internal reliability and validity of the J-MAWARE. Inter-rater agreement was in the acceptable range. The resulting J-MAWARE confirmed that it is a useful instrument to measure the process in which negative thoughts and feelings are experienced as they arise.

The Buddha, having accepted life's reality, experienced pain but did not suffer from it. He could end suffering by "seeing things as they are," accepting them nonjudgmentally, and thus letting go of craving. The identification of the "self" as a separate autonomous being, which is an illusion, is the root cause of human existential problems. Such identification and attachments to contents of the mind that go against impermanence and lead to grasping things in egocentric ways will result in existential suffering (De Wit, 2000). A central notion in the Buddha's way of seeing is called mindfulness, written about extensively in the Buddhist literature. According to Kabat-Zinn (1994, p. 4) mindfulness is "paying attention in a particular way: on purpose, in the present moment, and nonjudgmentally." Mindfulness might be a useful cognitive skill to alleviate psychological problems; theories to that account have been proposed (Teasdale et al., 1995; Marlatt & Kristeller, 1999). Teasdale and others (2002) conceptualized mindfulness as one of many cognitive modes incompatible with relapse engendering and suggested enhance mindfulness training as a route to relapse prevention for depression. Thus Mindfulness-Based Cognitive Therapy (MBCT) was developed. Recently, MBCT has proven to be effective in preventing relapse/recurrence in patients with major depressive disorders who had been previously relapsing three or more times (Segal et al., 2002; Ma & Teasdale, 2004). In examining the effect of MBCT on recurrent major depression, the cognitive mode was assessed by an instrument called the Measure of Awareness and Coping in Autobiographical Memory (MACAM; Moore et al., 1996). This chapter aims to develop the Japanese version of MACAM. After a brief further introduction, two studies on the development of the Japanese version of the Measure of Awareness in Autobiographical Memory (J-MAWARE) will be presented.

1. *Mindfulness and meditation.* Mindfulness is a form of meditation that disidentifies with whatever appears in the mind. In the awareness of daily living, thought seems to predominate over feelings (sensations and emotions). It continually evaluates, judges, interprets, classifies, blames, criticizes, rationalizes, and identifies with an ungraspable abstraction: the self. However, during mindfulness, sensation, emotion, or cognition appearing in consciousness is observed nonjudgmentally and given up unconditionally. It is a "simply" letting go without identifying with it or reacting to its content. Thus, the essence is noticing whatever arises in consciousness while refraining from elaborating. Mindfulness does not erase feelings and thoughts that continuously keep coming into consciousness. By letting go without attaching to or identifying with them, suffering is eventually alleviated. An important realization through mindfulness is that sensing, emoting, and cognizing fluctuate; these are transient processes that pass by "like waves in the sea" (Linehan, 1993b, p. 87). By practicing mindfulness one eventually learns to understand the dual separation of the observer and the observed contents of mind.

2. *Mindfulness in clinical settings.* Recent efforts across a wide range of clinical disorders have begun to focus on mindfulness-based interventions, both as standalone treatments (Kabat-Zinn, 1990) and as a component of integrative treatment approaches (Hayes et al., 1999; Linehan, 1993a; Marlatt & Gordon, 1985). Kabat-Zinn (1982) has brought mindfulness into clinical settings and performed several studies on stress reduction. His Mindfulness-Based Stress Reduction (MBSR) program could not only reduce stress, but seems also to be a relevant contributing factor in curing psoriasis, fatigue, hypertension, chronic pain, anxiety-panic disorder, and eating disorder. The essence of clinical mindfulness is to increase patients' awareness of present, moment-to-moment, experience and of the fact that things are in a state of flux and thus constantly changing. Teasdale and others (1999, 2002) became interested in the effect of Kabat-Zinn's mindfulness training on autobiographical memory in the case of depression for two main reasons. Firstly, MBSR includes homework tasks that train patients to notice the specific aspects of their environment, thus potentially reducing overgeneric encoding, which is characteristic in depression. Hierarchical search models of memory assume that encoding and retrieval share common processes; making encoding more specific will also make retrieval more specific (Goddard et al., 1996; Kuyken & Brewin, 1995; Moore et al., 1988). Secondly, MBSR explicitly focuses on allowing mental contents to occur without judging them or trying to suppress or avoid

them, thus potentially reducing the tendency to truncate the memory retrieval process as a means of regulating affect.

MBCT was developed by combining MBSR with some techniques drawn from Cognitive Therapy (CT). MBCT was specifically tailored to train patients in skills relevant to the prevention of depression relapse. MBCT-clients learn mindfulness in an eight-week class during which they also do exercises and listen to tapes at home. It includes breathing meditation, yoga stretching, basic education about depression, and several CT exercises showing the links between thinking and feeling and instructing how to look after oneself when depression threatens to be overwhelming. MBCT helps to see the patterns of the mind and to learn how to recognize the signs of decreased mood. It helps break the links between negative mood and the negative thinking that would otherwise have been triggered. Clients develop the capacity to allow distressing mood, thoughts, and sensations to come and go, without combating them. They develop the ability to stay in touch with the present moment, without having to ruminate about the past or worry about the future. These structured exercises reflect Buddhist Vipassana (insight meditation) that has been taught for more than 2500 years (Goldstein & Kornfield, 1987).

3. *Relapse/recurrence in major depressive disorders and the mechanisms of CT.* The World Health Organization projected that, by 2020, unipolar major depression will be the second greatest burden of ill-health (behind ischaemic heart disease). Judd (1997, p. 990) contends: "It has been established that unipolar major depressive disorder is a chronic, lifelong illness, whose risk for repeated episodes exceeds 80%, and patients will experience an average of 4 lifetime major depressive episodes of 20 weeks duration each." Despite the growing evidence in favor of CT, the processes underlying significant reduction in the incidence of relapse/recurrence in major depression are not well understood (Teasdale, 2002). CT suggests that vulnerability to major depression depends on persistent underlying dysfunctional attitudes, particularly those involving a dependence of self-worth on others or on the success of activities (Beck et al., 1983). From this stance, relapse/recurrence reductions following MBCT would be seen as the result of CT reducing dysfunctional assumptions. However, this hypothesis has received little support (Barber & DeRubeis, 1989); even when CT has produced significantly better long-term outcomes than pharmacotherapy, the two treatments often do not differ on posttreatment measures of dysfunctional attitudes such as the Dysfunctional Attitude Scale (DAS; Weissman & Beck, 1978; Simons et al., 1984). Based on a certain view of cognitive vulnerability to depression, Teasdale and others (1997a, 1997b; Teasdale & Barnard, 1993; Teasdale et al., 1995) formulated an alternative account of the way that CT might reduce depressive relapse/recurrence. They claim that CT leads to changes in the cognitive sets patients use to relate to and interpret depressive symptoms, thoughts, and feelings at times of potential relapse. This creates a store of representations in the memory, where new relationships to depressive experience are encoded. Consistent with this suggestion, Segal

and others (1999) reported that, when the DAS was administered following a dysphoric mood induction, posttreatment DAS scores were significantly lower after CT than after pharmacotherapy. Particular importance has been attached (Moore et al., 1996; Teasdale, 1997b; Teasdale et al., 1995; Teasdale et al, 2002) to the shift in cognitive set known as "decentering" or "disidentification," in which rather than simply having emotions or identifying with negative thoughts and feelings, clients relate to negative experiences as mental events in a wider field of awareness.

It is suggested that as a result of repeatedly identifying negative thoughts as they arise and standing back from them to evaluate the accuracy of their contents, clients shift to a decentered perspective on negative thoughts and feelings. Experienced and interpreted through such a decentered cognitive set at times of potential relapse, negative thoughts and feelings will have different cognitive, emotional, and behavioral consequences than if they are interpreted and experienced as "that's reality" or "that's me." Traditional CT typically focuses on changing the content of (irrational) cognitions. On the other hand, this account suggests CT focuses on changing one's relationship to one's thoughts and feelings, encouraging the viewing of thoughts as thoughts rather than as reality (Teasdale et al., 2002; Segal et al., 2002). Earlier, a similar account was presented by Barber and DeRubeis (1989) who claim that CT works by teaching patients to reappraise or have "second thoughts" in relation to depressive cognition. Although the importance of decentering had previously been recognized, it served as a means to the end of changing content, rather than being an end in itself. Teasdale and others (2002) refer to the process of experiencing negative thoughts and feelings within a decentered-disidentified perspective as metacognitive awareness and suggest that CT creates a store of memories in which depressive phenomena have been experienced within a metacognitive perspective. Metacognitive awareness refers to processes of the mind that selects and constructs contents and that focuses on and provides awareness of the contents.

4. *Distinction between metacognitive awareness and metacognitive belief.* For further clarification of the metacognitive awareness concept, Teasdale and others (2002) distinguished metacognitive awareness from metacognitive belief. The latter has figured prominently in recent theories on emotional disorders and their psychological treatment (Wells, 1999). Metacognitive belief refers to how much individuals think particular thoughts about cognition are true and is concerned with thoughts about thoughts of feelings. What matters is the thoughts' content. The extent of believing the contents of thoughts to be true can be rated using appropriate questionnaires. Metacognitive awareness refers to the way negative thoughts and feelings are experienced as they arise. Particularly, it refers to the extent to which thoughts are experienced as thoughts (mental events) rather than as "self" or "the truth." This distinction is congruent with Mikulas' (2000) contents and behaviors of the mind. He explained that contents of the mind include the

various objects that arise in consciousness and that behaviors of the mind refer to those processes of the mind that select and construct the contents, and that focus on and provide awareness of the contents. Behaviors of the mind occur prior to, during, and in response to any particular content. Behaviors of the mind can be worked with directly, independent of its contents, by the same general principles of behavior and behavior change that affect all behaviors. This implies a new and important domain for Cognitive-Behavior Therapy. Thus, metacognitive awareness and behaviors of the mind refer to how the mind behaves or relate to its contents.

5. *Assessment of metacognitive awareness.* Metacognitive awareness is less easily measured by questionnaires. As no satisfactory measure exists, Teasdale and others (2002) developed an instrument called the Measure of Awareness and Coping in Autobiographical Memory (MACAM; Moore et al, 1996) based on models of autobiographical memory research. They assume the way individuals' thoughts and feelings are experienced is determined by the cognitive sets accessed in memory. By accessing a metacognitive set, it becomes likely that feelings and thoughts are consciously experienced as mental events. For an individual at a given time, the accessibility of metacognitive sets in response to negative thoughts and feelings is a function of the availability of such sets in memory and the prevailing context. From the point of view of understanding recurrence/relapse of depression and their prevention, the accessibility of metacognitive sets in the context of dysphoria is of central importance. To measure this, they created appropriate contexts using emotive vignettes, asked for recall of autobiographical memories cued by the dysphoric feelings, evoked by the vignettes, and thus obtaining for each memory detailed descriptions of how the individual had related to negative thoughts and feelings in that memory. From those descriptions, we could infer the cognitive set that prevailed in relation to negative thoughts and feelings at the time of the remembered event. We assume that the extent to which the inferred cognitive sets demonstrate metacognitive awareness in the memories most readily accessed by depressing vignettes reflect the accessibility of metacognitive sets to negative thoughts and feelings in the context.

6. *Effects of metacognitive awareness on depressive relapse.* Teasdale and others (2002) developed the MACAM and used it to have a rater code the participants' relationships to their own thoughts and feelings after listening to them recount autobiographical vignettes. They examined the effectiveness of CT/MBCT on metacognitive awareness by using the MACAM and found that both CT/MBCT increased metacognitive awareness. Williams and others (2000) explored the impact of MBCT on overgeneral autobiographical memory deficits and found that individuals who received MBCT recounted more specific autobiographical memories than the treatment-as-usual control group. They conclude that MBCT can alter the trait-like avoidant style of cognitive processing that typically characterizes individuals with recurrent depression. On the basis of several studies (e.g. Williams

et al., 1997), it is concluded that overgeneral memory is a cognitive style, a long-term trait-like phenomenon. Although this conclusion was based on the finding that overgeneral memory was not mood-state dependent, Teasdale's conclusion suggests that rigid cognitive patterns may be altered by mindfulness.

A special device that measures metacognitive awareness is lacking in Japan. Two studies are here presented, which aim is to develop the (J-MAWARE) — a subscale of the MACAM — that assesses the extent of metacognitive awareness. In Study 1, we prepare all the materials which were used to assess meta-awareness. In Study 2, we examine the reliability and validity of the J-MAWARE developed in the first study.

Assessing Metacognitive Awareness

Previous studies confirmed the hypotheses that reduced metacognitive awareness is associated with vulnerability to further major depression and that CT/MBCT reduce depressive relapse by increasing metacognitive awareness. In order to be able to examine the role of metacognitive awareness in reducing depressive relapse in Japan, a special device such as the MACAM to measure metacognitive awareness is developed. Based on Moore and others' (1996) original material, we prepared a Japanese version of all the materials used to assess metacognitive awareness. Particularly, appropriate dysphoric vignettes to recall the participants' memory were prepared by investigating the types of dysphoric vignettes, that would satisfy the instrument's purpose.

1. *Method.* The MACAM measures metacognitive awareness (the cognitive set in which negative thoughts and feelings are seen as passing events rather than as aspects of self) in the autobiographical memories accessed by depression-related cues (Teasdale et al., 2002). It is assumed that these cognitive sets are most easily accessed by vignettes of mildly depressing situations that reflect the cognitive sets most likely accessible in real world situations (preceding the onset of major depression). Thus, dysphoric vignettes are necessary to assess metacognitive awareness. However, translating the original mildly depressing vignettes into Japanese may not be the most appropriate solution because the events in which Japanese activate depressive mood are not the same due to cultural differences. The vignettes therefore need to be ones to which Japanese subjects will respond. The original version contains 16 mildly depressing vignettes, divided into two sets so that each participant is assessed by either Set 1 or 2. Each set thus consists of 8 vignettes and each participant can for example be posttest assessed with a set different from the one used for the pretest assessment. In analogy, we also prepared 16 mildly depressing vignettes in this study able to accessing the participants' meta-awareness. Also, vignettes should contain a variety of situations so that as many people as possible can respond to as many vignettes as possible.

2. *Procedure.* The following procedure was used to meet these requirements: (a) translating the original 16 vignettes; (b) thematizing each vignette; (c) examining references (Sakamoto, 2000; Sakamoto et al., 2002) written about Japanese depressive disorder and extracting the most typical depressive situations for Japanese people; (d) thematizing each of the extracted depressing situations; (e) choosing and deciding the following eight subjects from those obtained from the original vignettes and from those generated from the extracted depressing situations: (1) gossip; (2) falseness; (3) guilt; (4) spending time with a person with whom you feel uncomfortable to be; (5) failure/incompetence; (6) loss; (7) embarrassment; (8) procrastination; (f) preparing four vignettes for each subject (32 vignettes in total); (g) creating a questionnaire whose purpose is to have the participants answer questions in order for us to select two of the most applicable mildly depressive vignettes from the four vignettes prepared per category; (h) dividing the resulting 16 vignettes into two sets such that both sets included all eight subjects and, simultaneously, were similar in quality. All these procedures were administered by one master's-, three doctoral-, and one assistant teacher's -level psychologists. Participants were asked to answer a questionnaire which includes "yes"-"no" questions for Item 1 and a set of 5-point Likert questions for Item 2 and 3, and which consisted of 32 vignettes with three questions each: if you have ever had an experience similar to the described situation (Item 1); the extent to which you can imagine a described situation (Item 2); and the extent to which you feel depressive mood (Item 3). The questionnaire was administered group-wise, in class rooms.

3. *Translating the original materials.* For the assessment of metacognitive awareness, we translated the following materials in addition to the 16 mildly depressive vignettes: (a) a coding manual; (b) a coding sheet for the assessor; and (c) a self-report coding questionnaire for the respondent.

4. *Participants.* The participants consisted of 125 volunteered undergraduate university students and 30 technical college students in Tokyo, Japan (M age 20; SD 2; Female 53%).

5. *Results.* Two of the most applicable vignettes per subject were chosen. Table 1 exemplifies depressing vignettes contained in Set 1.

Table 1. Subjects and short descriptions of depressing vignettes in Set 1

---

(1) Gossip: "You overhear your co-workers gossiping about you. You start to feel weak and miserable"

(2) Falseness: "The friend cancels just before the time you arranged. As you think that you might not be cherished by the friend, you start to feel gloomy"

(3) Guilt: "You have to cancel an arrangement to meet a friend as you have another appointment. You blame yourself for carelessly having two arrangements on the same day and you feel disappointed in yourself for letting the friend down"

(4) Spending time with a person with whom you feel uncomfortable: "You happen to meet one of classmates in a bus with whom you feel uncomfortable to talk to. You start feeling depressed at the prospect of spending time with him/her for the next several minutes"

(5) Failure/Incompetence: "When you help a friend move some furniture around, you make a small but noticeable scratch on the furniture. You think how careless you have been and your stomach sinks"

(6) Loss: "You are shocked to learn from your friends that a person you are dating is going out with another wo/man. You begin to feel low and miserable"

(7) Embarrassment: "Everybody, except you, in a group looks excellent while doing exercises. Afterwards as you dwell on the embarrassment of it, you start to feel low"

(8) Procrastination: "You have only one week left before the submission of an assignment. When you start to think about how it may take ages to complete it, your body feels like lead and you just can't face it again, which makes your mood sink"

We used the unpaired t-test to compare the two sets: items 1 (if you have ever had an experience similar to the described situation), 2 (the extent to which you can imagine a described situation), and 3 (the extent to which you feel depressive mood) are similar as the t-statistics did not approach statistical significance.

6. *Discussion.* Successfully, this qualitative study developed two similar sets of mildly depressing vignettes suitable for Japanese subjects. We elicited their accounts of depressive experiences from which meta-awareness was assessed. Each set consisted of eight subjects and both sets yielded similar results as the questionnaire data. Meta-awareness assessed with these two sets is examined in Study 2. (Both sets are supposed to have equivalent ability to assess metacognitive awareness.)

Establishing Reliability and Validity

This second study aims to calculate the reliability and validity of the J-MAWARE developed in the preceding study. We targeted an analogue sample, non-clinical undergraduate university students, while Teasdale and others' (2002) study employed clinical depressive patients. Although ours is an analogue study on the prevention of depressive relapse, it is warranted on theoretical grounds, which assume that metacognitive awareness can also be assessed in non-clinical populations, because the cultivation of (dis)identified or (de)centered perspectives applies to anyone who suffers from "not seeing things as they are."

1. *Method.* The method to determine J-MAWARE's reliability and validity is reported below.

2. *Participants.* 44 Undergraduate university students (M age 20; SD 2; Female 52%) with no history of mental disorders, of consulting a psychiatrist or therapist, and without physical disorders were randomly chosen from 620 students (M age 20; SD1.5); Female 49%) who volunteered in the preliminary screening so that the number of participants, their gender ratio, age distribution and Frequency of Depressive Episodes (FDE) scores were similar to the distribution of each quartile of the Beck Depression Inventory (BDI) score among the 620 students. Table 2 shows the characteristics of the participants by each quartile of mean BDI scores. As part of the J-MAWARE, the participants were randomly presented with either Set 1 or Set 2 of the vignettes.

Table 2: Participants' characteristics in terms of BDI scores

| | BDI score | | | |
	score 0-5 (n = 11)	score 6-9 (n = 11)	score 10-16 (n = 9)	score 17-42 (n = 13)
Age	20.3	21.3	19.7	20.3
Mean BDI (SD)	2.9 (1.5)	8.0 (1.0)	14.0 (1.6)	21.5 (3.1)
Female %	45	55	56	38

3. *Measures.* Measures included the following:

(1) BDI: a 21-item self-report measure of depressive symptoms with good psychometric properties (Rabkin & Klein, 1987). It measures the severity of affective, cognitive, behavioral, and somatic symptoms of depression; scores range from 0 to 63.

(2) FDE: a self-report measure consisting of one item specially developed for this study. Participants are asked to rate their past experiences such as persistent depressive and low energetic episodes on a four-point scale, rated from 1 "never" to 4 "frequently"

(3) J-MAWARE. The following procedures of assessing the meta-awareness are based on existing manuals (Moore et al., 1996; Teasdale et al., 2002). Descriptions of 8 mildly depressing situations, recorded in a flat, depressing tone of voice, are presented by tape recorder (see Table 1). Respondents are asked to put themselves into the situations and experience the feelings described. After each description, they are asked to recall and briefly describe a specific occasion brought to mind by the feeling elicited by the vignette. After all vignettes are presented, the interviewer uses semi-structured interviewing to elicit detailed descriptions of occasions (and when they occurred) and asks the participants to rate the bad feelings at the worst point of each occasion, using a 0-100 scale anchored at 0 "not at all bad" and 100 "as bad as you can imagine." Thus, the interviewer gets detailed

descriptions of the participants' responses to those feelings at the time of the original event.

The interviewer rates, through a coding manual, the meta-awareness shown at the time of the original event using the following scale: 1 "minimal discrimination of different negative thoughts and feelings, being immersed in undifferentiated bad feelings." This may be reflected in the use of global descriptions of thoughts and feelings (e.g. "bad," "awful," "crap" or of less global terms being used interchangeably. The participant may report being "swamped" by the thoughts and feelings, which they may attribute directly to an event or circumstance. They report no wider perspective. Rating 2 means "discrimination of different negative thoughts and feelings." The participant is able to report different strands of negative feelings and the different thoughts associated with them. A single but precisely described feeling may be taken as evidence of such discrimination (i.e. the participant is aware of feeling more x than y). Precision of description is more important than is the presence of two or more different feelings. Rating 3 means "some discrimination of self and own reactions from the situation." The participants have a sense of their thoughts and feelings as being distinct from the external situation. They would thus be potentially able to question or consider the appropriateness of their feelings or their perspective (e.g. "I'm too upset to think straight"). This may be reflected in some acknowledgement of internal generation of feelings (e.g. "I felt that I was being lazy"). The participants may report knowing that their views might be different once the mood changes or that other people might have a different view. They may arrive at this new perspective by talking to someone else. Rating 4 means "discrimination of self from thoughts and feelings." At some point, the participants can stand back and see their thoughts and feelings from a wider perspective. They may report being able to "stand back from the depression," to "catch it," or to "see what was going on." They may report being able to link their thoughts and feelings to personal characteristics (e.g. "I'm being self-critical") or may intentionally adopt an attitude toward those thoughts and feelings (e.g. "I'll see if that's right" or "I'll try to let go of this"). Rating 5 means "persistent or extensive distancing from thoughts and feelings."

The level of awareness obtained at Score 4 may be reached more quickly, more clearly, or may persist continuously once it has been reached. After the interviewer assesses the J-MAWARE scores, the participants rate their own J-MAWARE on each memory on a self-report measure (translated from Moore and others' original measure). An independent rater also rates the tape recorded descriptions. Both raters received extensive prior training in the use of this scale. If the interviewer's and independent rater's ratings of a memory are within 1 scale point, the interviewer's rating is used as the final rating. For larger differences, a final rating is established by review and consensus.

4. *Results (interrater and internal reliability).* The assessor served as the interviewer and the independent rater assessed metacognitive awareness from the

participants' descriptions, which were tape recorded. The interrater agreement was in the acceptable range (r .56, p < .001). Cronbach's α, the conventional measure of internal validity, is not readily applicable for J-MAWARE measures as too many participants failed to retrieve a memory to one or more cues. Instead, for the sample of 44 participants, we calculated the odd-even split-half reliability for mean meta-awareness measures. This yielded a satisfactory correlation for Set 1 (r .53, p < .008) and for Set 2 (r .69, p < .001).

(1) *Comparison of the two sets of vignettes.* J-MAWARE scores assessed by each set were compared by two-tailed t test to see if there were differences between the two sets. Results showed no significant differences between J-MAWARE scores assessed with each set. The results revealed that both sets can be used interchangeably as both sets showed little differences on the J-MAWARE scores.

(2) *Correlations between J-MAWARE and severity of depressed mood at the time of the remembered events.* To determine if metacognitive awareness ratings were artefactual of the severity of depressed mood originally experienced at the time of the remembered events, we examined the relationships with the negative mood during the remembered events measured on a 0-100 scale and J-MAWARE, using Spearman's rank correlation coefficient. Mean negative mood was significantly correlated with mean J-MAWARE scores (r [44] = -.42, p < .005). This result showed mean J-MAWARE scores are moderately dependent on levels of negative mood during the remembered events, which was against the hypothesis. J-MAWARE scores are assessed from the participants' detailed descriptions of how they had related to negative thoughts and feelings in recalled memories cued by the mild dysphoric feelings evoked by the vignettes. It seems that J-MAWARE measures might not be able to reflect the studied relationship in a measurable degree in terms of negative thoughts and feelings. The non-clinical university students may have recalled relatively weaker negative thoughts and feelings in retrieved memories cued by the mild dysphoric feelings as compared to the levels of negativity among patients in Teasdale's studies. To investigate this, we examined the relationship between the scores of negative mood during the remembered events, which was > 70, and the mean J-MAWARE scores. Results shows that the mean negative mood was not significantly correlated with the mean J-MAWARE scores.

(3) *Relationship between J-MAWARE and BDI.* Furthermore, it was hypothesized that there are significant correlations between BDI and J-MAWARE score as metacognitive awareness was not dependent on the state of depressive mood. To test this hypothesis, we used the two-tailed t test to compare mean J-MAWARE scores of the group with higher BDI scores (> 17) that were a half SD (= 3.74) bigger than the mean BDI (11.93) versus the group with lower BDI scores (< 8) that were a half SD smaller than the mean BDI. As predicted, the mean J-MAWARE scores between two groups were not significantly different. This result confirms the constructive validity of one of the aspects.

(4) *Relationship between J-MAWARE and FDE.* In Teasdale and others' study (2002), MAWARE predicted the risk of a relapse by having low metacognitive awareness predict early relapse. Similarly, the current study hypothesized that subjects with a higher frequency of depressive episodes shows higher mean J-MAWARE scores. Furthermore, according to Ma and Teasdale's (2004) replicated findings, MBCT helps those who had three or more previous episodes. It had no effect on those who had two episodes in the past. It substantially reduced the risk of relapse among those who had three or more previous episodes of depression from 66 to 37%. The participants reported being able to develop a decentered-disidentified relationship to their experience. They could view their depression-inducing thoughts from a wider perspective as they occur. These results support a model of cognitive vulnerability to depressive relapse (Segal et al., 1996; Teasdale, et al., 1995), which assumes that individuals who had previous episodes of major depression differ from those who had not. They differ in the patterns of negative thinking that become activated in mildly depressed mood. This supports the assumption that in recovered depressed patients, dysphoria is more likely to activate patterns of self-devaluative/depressogenic thinking (similar to thinking that prevailed in preceding episodes).

To assess this hypothesis, we firstly compare the mean J-MAWARE scores of the FDE score 3 group with those with FDE score 2 group, using the two tailed t test. Although criteria of subjects in Ma and Teasdale"s (2004) study were different from ours, results show no significant difference between the two groups (t [35] = 0.30, p >.1). Secondly, we compare the mean J-MAWARE scores of the high FDE scores ($\leq$ 2) group and low FDE scores (< 2) group. The mean J-MAWARE scores between the two groups were significantly different (t [42] = 2.10, p < .05). Thirdly, we compare the mean J-MAWARE scores of the FDE score 3 group versus the FDE score 0 & 1 group. The two groups differ at marginal significance (t [19] = 1.81, p < .10).

(5) *Correlations between the assessors' and participants' J-MAWARE measures.* We calculated Spearman's rank correlation coefficient between J-MAWARE scores of the assessors and those of the respondents for confirming criterion-related validity. The result was significant (r .43, p < .01).

5. *Discussion.* The aim of Study 2 was to examine the reliability and validity of the J-MAWARE. We confirm satisfactory internal reliability obtained from the relationship between the two sets of vignettes, and some validity. The interrater agreement was in the acceptable range, but one relationship between the severity of depressive mood and mean J-MAWARE measures disconfirmed prediction. Teasdale and others examined interrater agreements on three separate measures derived from all memories (MAWARE) — from the five months preceding the MACAM assessment at posttest (MAWARE $\leq$ 5) and from before then (MAWARE > 5) — so that they could examine the predicted effects of CT and MBCT on the MACAM measure of metacognitive awareness. They hypothesized that the effects

of the interventions on encoding occur only after the start of CT and MBCT, which was five months before the post-treatment MACAM assessment. Their resulting interrater agreements were: r .77, p < .01 (MAWARE); r .64, p < .01 (MAWARE ≤ 5); r .83, p < .01 (MAWARE > 5), all of which were higher than our results (r .55, p < .001). The different sample from their study might account for modest interrater reliability. They used the MACAM measure of metacognitive awareness to assess the accessibility in the context of depressing experiences and the MACAM measure of metacognitive sets to assess negative thoughts and feelings in a sample of clinically depressed patients. However, we examined a group of undergraduate university students with no history of clinical depression. As stated earlier, overgeneral autobiographical memory is a characteristic of depression. It is estimated that more patients described their experiences in such a way that the assessor could easily decide to assess score 1 (minimal description of different negative thoughts and feelings) or score 2 (discrimination of different negative thoughts and feelings) on MAWARE, while our group reported in such a way that the assessor could choose from wider score selections.

There is another reason why the interrater agreements are in the acceptable range. The interviewer coded the J-MAWARE scores directly from the subjects' report face to face while the independent rater rated from the participants' responses to the upsetting situations recorded on a tape recorder and elicited by the interviewer. The independent rater didn't experience the process of interviewing, questioning the respondents, and eliciting sufficient information for the other rater to be able to give ratings, while, in Teasdale and others' (2002) study, both raters experienced the role of the interviewer as the primary assessor and as the independent rater. This account might have affected the result of our interrater agreement. Further improvements in interrater agreements are obviously desirable. As noted, we obtained a significant correlation between the severity of depressive mood of remembered events and mean J-MAWARE measures, while Teasdale and others (2002) found no evidence that prediction of relapse from MAWARE ≤ 5 depended on the correlation of both with levels of negative mood during the remembered events. When the score for the severity of negative mood evoked by the vignettes in our study was limited to one that is > 70, the correlation of the levels of negative mood with mean J-MAWARE scores was not correlated, which was in accordance with hypothesis. The current results suggest that the J-MAWARE scores obtained here might have been the results of assessing the relationship to relatively milder negative thoughts and feelings in recalled memories cued by the lesser dysphoric mood evoked by the vignettes than the dysphoric mood what clients had evoked in previous studies.

Another account might be suggested. Metacognitive awareness should reflect how people respond to or experience the contents of the mind, independent of the nature of the content. However, it is also natural to think that the nature of the content affects how people respond to the contents of the mind or vice versa;

subjects with lower metacognitive awareness report higher severity of negative mood by interpreting their remembered events from less decentered or disidentified perspectives. Since changes in the relationship to contents may result in content changes and vice versa, further study should test these two aspects. Can they be assessed without affecting each other (by including a clinical depressive relapse group)? We conclude that metacognitive awareness is not dependent on the state of depressive mood as for instance measured by the BDI, but it might be dependent on reported negative mood during remembered events.

Closing Remarks

The importance of awareness and metacognitive awareness for psychotherapy in general has been recognized by several authors for several decades ago. Hendricks (1975) stated that "since nearly everyone has a number of neurotic thoughts, mental health is dependent upon the ability to recognize that they are "just thoughts" (p. 145). Rice and Greenberg (1984) noted that the development of meta-awareness of an internal experience has been seen as a core task in many forms of psychotherapy. There can be little doubt that the cognitive-behavioral approach that provides a paradigm that is compatible with Buddhist mindfulness tactics. It is no coincidence that cognitive and behavioral therapists and researchers are now providing evidence that supports this assertion. Indeed, the following quote sounds like it has been drawn from a Buddhist textbook: "…metacognitive knowledge involves thinking about thoughts as 'other than facts' or knowing, intellectually, that the content of thoughts does not always correspond to the state of the world" (Teasdale, 1999, p. 147). Metacognitive awareness refers to actually experiencing thoughts as thoughts in the moment they occur in an impermanent world. It includes the meditative observation of behaviors (including the behaviors of mind), cognitions, and emotions.

The aim of our studies was to develop the J-MAWARE. During the process, we confirmed satisfactory reliability and some validity except with regards to interrater agreement and to the construct validity (correlation of the levels of negative episodes and mean ratings of metacognitive awareness). However, we have to limit the present positive findings, until we re-examine them on clinical subjects with criteria similar to those defined in Teasdale and others' research. Nevertheless, most of our findings are consistent with the hypothesis and with the results of their study. If metacognitive awareness is a cognitive set (in which negative thoughts and feelings are seen as passing events in the mind rather than as reflections of an abiding self or as truth) to be developed through mindfulness, then metacognitive awareness as assessed in our sample of students should have a similar cognitive set as found in Teasdale's clinical sample. In addition, there were not enough participants to be able to standardize the J-MAWARE. The results warrant a useful instrument, but flaws in the present study limit its scientific status: J-MAWARE is at a preliminary stage of development. There are several factors and analyses obtained in this study that are not included in this chapter, such as the relationship between the response latencies and BDI and FDE scores, as well as analysis of mean J-MAWARE scores by memory age. These findings will be reported separately.

Metacognitive awareness that is currently mainly examined in cognitive-behavioral circles is a disidentifying and decentering perspective, which involves the suspension of habitual cognitive construing. This suspension creates stillness, silent nothingness, and empty spaces, into which fresh ideas can flow; after all, emptiness is the source of fullness. In Lao Tzu's Tao Te Ching (6th c BCE), a series of images show the potency of that-which-is-not. For example (Chapter 11),

> *The thirty spokes unite in the one center,*
> *but it is on the empty space for the axle that the use of the wheel depends.*
> *Clay is fashioned into vessels,*
> *but it is on their empty hollowness that their use depends.*
> *The door and windows are cut out from the walls to form an apartment,*
> *but it is on the empty space that its use depends.*
> *Therefore, whatever has existence serves for profitable adaptation,*
> *and what does not have existence for actual usefulness.*

Metacognitive awareness seems to create spaciousness where one's own nature begins to take care of itself through suspending logic, dwelling in uncertainties, simply watching, and letting be without trying to change or judging thinking's content. Further studies are underway to learn better understand the role of metacognitive awareness and mindfulness in psychotherapy. With plans to further develop the J-MAWARE, we will continue examining metacognitive awareness to advance health.

16

Personality Correlates Of Mindfulness

Yoshinori Sugiura

Mindfulness is closely tied to meditation, yet it can also be perceived as a naturally occurring psychological experience, independent of specific interventions (Brown & Ryan, 2003). Valid measures are necessary to investigate the nature of voluntary mindfulness. A joint factor analysis of the measures related to mindfulness extracted five factors: Refraining from Catastrophic Thinking, Logical Objectivity, Self Observation, Acceptance, and Detached Coping. The relations of these factors with the Big Five and a self-report measure of attention control were then examined. Regression analyses indicated that these variables are important correlates of mindfulness. The Big Five link as follows, (a) Openness to experiences was related to all mindfulness dimensions; (b) Neuroticism was positively related to Self-Observation and negatively related to the remaining dimensions; (c) Extraversion was positively related to Acceptance and negatively to Logical Objectivity; (d) Agreeableness was related to Detached Coping; and (e) Conscientiousness was positively related to Logical Objectivity. Among the attention control factors, Sustained Attention was related to all mindfulness dimensions except Self Observation, while Divided Attention was related to Refraining from Catastrophic Thinking and Detached Coping. Overall, the results indicate both overlapping and distinct features of mindfulness dimensions. The common superfactor may be Openness. Refraining from Catastrophic Thinking revealed the strongest symptom-reducing effects and thus can be considered as the most powerful working ingredient of mindfulness. The negative relation with Neuroticism underscores this interpretation. In addition, its relation with Divided Attention is indicative of an attentional underpinning. Finally, the positive relationship between Neuroticism and Self Observation is indicative of the maladaptive nature of self-focus.

Recent Cognitive-Behavior Therapy (CBT) witnessed new types of intervention philosophy and techniques, referred to as the third wave. Examples are Acceptance and Commitment Therapy (ACT; Hayes et al., 1999), Dialectical Behavior Therapy (DBT; Linehan, 1993), and Mindfulness-Based Cognitive Therapy (MBCT; Segal et al., 2002). These are in contrast with traditional CBT that actively changes behavior and cognition. The third wave emphasizes acceptance and mindful awareness and shares the following characteristics: (a) Decentering: maintaining distance from problems or negative thoughts and not becoming overly involved with them and (b) Acceptance: not avoiding problems or negative thoughts, but rather observing and acknowledging them for what they are. In addition, third wave CBT is influenced by Buddhist meditation. Despite the oriental influence, the emphasis on scientific background is what distinguishes third wave CBT from similar interventions (e.g. Morita Therapy). For example, Teasdale et al. (2000) conducted a randomized controlled trial of MBCT and found a reduced relapse rate among recurrently depressed patients (who had experienced three or more relapses). Some researchers have attempted to explain the mechanism of mindfulness using cognitive models (e.g. Wells, 2002; Teasdale, 1999). There is now evidence supporting the efficacy of mindfulness intervention for a variety of problems, including anxiety, depression, and somatic disorders (Baer, 2003). However, there has been no satisfactory progress in elucidating the mechanism of mindfulness. The foremost difficulty is the relative lack of operational definition and measurements.

1. *The need for operational definition.* The heterogeneity of mindfulness-based interventions underscores the need for measurement. Mindfulness is not a single technique, but involves multiple and diverse skills. For example, Mindfulness-Based Stress Reduction (MBSR; Kabat-Zinn, 1994), the original application of mindfulness meditation for health problems, involves breathing awareness, body scan visualizing, and Hatha Yoga. Wells (1990) developed an intervention called Attention Training (ATT) for depression and anxiety, intended to increase attentional flexibility by exercising selective attention, attention switching, and divided attention using non-threatening external sounds as stimuli. Wells (2002) regards ATT as mindfulness; however, it is very different from MBSR both in form and underlying model. Therefore, the working mechanism of mindfulness may not be monolithical. Baer (2003) listed the potential mediators: (a) exposure to distressing stimuli; (b) cognitive change; (c) increased self-management, based on self-observation; (d) relaxation; and (e) acceptance. Bishop et al. (2004) recently attempted to operationalize mindfulness and specified two components: self-regulation of attention and orientation to experience. The former is related to focusing attention on present moment experiences, while the latter includes acceptance of feelings. The two dimensions seem to substantiate the core feature of Kabat-Zinn's (1994, p. 4) brief definition: "paying attention in a particular way: on purpose, in the present moment, and nonjudgmentally."

Discussions on the multifaceted nature of mindfulness point to the need for multidimensional measurements; the other requirement is applicability to a wide population (Baer et al., 2004). Although mindfulness was originally tied to meditation, it can also be examined outside that context. For example, Teasdale et al. (1995) predicted that even traditional CBT techniques with emphasis on a logical analysis would enhance a mindful attitude, and supported this claim (Teasdale et al., 2002). Those studies suggest the need to define mindfulness in the context of interventions other than meditation as well as outside the context of any intervention (i.e. as a voluntary psychological mode; Bishop et al., 2004). This approach contrasts with measurements intended for use with meditators, such as the Freiburg Mindfulness Inventory (Buchheld et al., 2001) or the Toronto Mindfulness Scale (Bishop et al., 2003).

2. *Existing measures of mindfulness.* A few measurements existed and others were published after this study was proposed. Brown and Ryan (2003) developed the Mindful Attention Awareness Scale (MAAS) to measure mindfulness as an individual difference variable. The MAAS approach captures the proposed core dimension of mindfulness. It measures awareness of the present moment and attention to ongoing activities. MAAS has a single-factor structure; studies with students, Zen practitioners, and breast or prostate cancer patients support its validity. The issue in question with MAAS is exclusive reliance on reversed (mindless) items. A comparison of mindful and mindless items indicated better psychometric properties for mindless items. The reason remains to be clarified.

Baer et al. (2004) developed the Kentucky Inventory of Mindfulness Skills (KIMS), a multi-dimensional scale of mindfulness for the general population. KIMS draws on DBT; it has conceptually derived and factorially confirmed four subscales: Observing, Describing, Acting with Awareness, and Accepting without Judgment. The Describing subscale was most consistently associated with measures of wellbeing. All subscales except for Observing were negatively related to Neuroticism and psychopathology and distinguished borderline personality disorder patients from normal students. Heavy reliance on reversed (less mindful) items were again observed for Acting with Awareness and Accepting without Judgment. The most striking feature of KIMS is its multidimensionality. However, it is not exhaustive, partly because of its theoretical emphasis on DBT. Baer and others suggested that future measures should include interest and curiosity about inner experiences, which are included in MBCT (Segal et al., 2002). Furthermore, KIMS' attention focus is chiefly on inner experiences, while people can also be mindful of external stimuli.

Hayes and others (2004) presented the Acceptance and Action Questionnaire (AAQ). While it is named "acceptance," the construct AAQ intends to examine is experiential avoidance. AAQ is a unidimensional measure. However, AAQ is intended to measure a broad range of experiential avoidance, unlike MAAS, which measures narrowly delineated core mindfulness. It was designed to overcome the limitations of more specific measures of avoidance (e.g. the White Bear Suppression Inventory for thought suppression; Wegner & Zanakos, 1994).

Moore and others (1996) developed the Measure of Awareness and Coping in Autobiographical Memory (MACAM), a semi-structured interview to assess metacognitive awareness. Teasdale et al. (2002) defined metacognitive awareness as "a cognitive set in which negative thoughts and feelings are seen as passing mental events rather than as aspects of self" (p. 275). MACAM measures a cognitive set achieved by mindfulness skills. MACAM mediated the relapse prevention effects of both the standard CBT and MBCT (Teasdale et al., 2002).

The Structure of Mindfulness

The scientific study of mindfulness is in its infancy, thus diverse approaches are required to clarify the constructs of mindfulness. The present study is a joint factor analysis of existing measurements related to mindfulness. It has two central themes: (1) Skills are not confined to mindfulness, therefore scales are included from focusing, Transcendental Meditation, classical CBT, and stress coping, as well as from a social psychological study on self-focus. Although CBT-like skills are not central to mindfulness, I included these skills to reinterpret the effects of CBT in terms of mindfulness (cf. Teasdale et al., 2002). Mindfulness as a naturally occurring individual difference is also a central topic. Therefore, a self-report format was chosen for use with our participants. (2) Both internal and external attention focus were included. Mindfulness techniques such as breathing and body scan emphasize focus on inner experiences. Bishop et al. (2004) confined their discussion to the internal focus in part to distinguish their concept from Langer's (1989) definition of mindfulness, which is about creative and flexible problem-solving. However, attention to aspects of the environment is also relevant (Kabat-Zinn, 1994); for example, we can wash dishes mindfully (Borkoven & Sharpless, 2004). Thus, this study includes the currently available measurements related to mindfulness with less emphasis on the strict boundaries of mindfulness. Five measures were used in the factor analysis are:

(1) *Scale of Meditation-related Cognitive Styles (SMCS; Sakairi, 2004)*. SMCS is composed of 24 items to measure the cognitive styles achieved during Transcendental Meditation. It has three subscales: Receptiveness, Happy-go-lucky attribution, and Flexibility. For purposes of clarity, Sugiura (2004) renamed the Receptiveness "Detached Objectivity," and the Happy-go-lucky attribution "Trust in Good Luck." Items were rated on a 5-point scale, 1 (*not at all true*) to 5 (*very true*). All the items in the Flexibility scale were reverse-scored, and the contents reflected worry-proneness or obsessiveness. Therefore, it was not used in this study to avoid confusion with symptoms. Only Detached Objectivity and Trust in Good Luck were used here. Detached Objectivity has 8 items (e.g. "I see things as they are" and "I can think objectively when I am in trouble") and Trust in Good Luck has 5 items (e.g."Good things happen to me" and "Things always fall into place for me").

(2) *Cognitive Self-Regulation Skills Scale (CSRS; Sugiura & Umaoka, 2003)*. CSRS was developed to measure the voluntary use of CBT-like skills in daily life. CSRS is a valid measurement that uses items based on the cognitive techniques used in CBT (Freeman, 1989; Freeman et al., 1990). Participants were asked the extent to which they thought they could perform the tasks described in each item when they were anxious. They responded on a 4-point scale, 1 (*absolutely, I cannot*) to 4 (*surely, I can*). CSRS has two factorially derived subscales: Logical Analysis and Refraining from Catastrophic Thinking. The former reflects active and

objective problem-solving skills, while the latter measures the ability to be detached from negative thinking to alleviate catastrophic cognitions. Logical Analysis has 6 items, such as "I can think of several alternatives for how to think or act." Refraining from Catastrophic Thinking has 5 items, such as "I don't develop a bad scenario from the situation." This two-factor structure was validated by a confirmatory factor analysis. Both subscales of CSRS revealed good to acceptable internal consistency ($\alpha > .72$; Sugiura et al., 2003; Sugiura & Umaoka, 2003). Furthermore, Logical Analysis was related to trait self-efficacy and problem-focused coping style (Amari & Umaoka, 2002; Sugiura et al., 2003), which suggests that Logical Analysis reflects active orientation towards problems. In contrast, Refraining from Catastrophic Thinking was positively related to optimism and negatively related to negative beliefs about intrusive thoughts (Cartwright-Hatton & Wells, 1997), which suggests that Refraining from Catastrophic Thinking can alleviate negative thinking.

(3) *Focusing Manner Scale (FMS; Fukumori & Morikawa, 2003)*. FMS was developed to measure Focusing-like attitudes in daily life. FMS has 23 items in total, rated on a 5-point scale, 1 (*not at all true*) to 5 (*very true*). It has three subscales: Trusting One's Experience (e.g. "I trust my inner feelings"); Connecting to One's Experience (e.g. "I tend to pay gentle attention to inner experiences); and Clearing a Space (e.g. "When faced with daily problems, I refrain from ruminating on them"). The FMS total score and two of the subscales (Trusting One's Experience and Clearing a Space) were negatively correlated with psychological symptoms, as measured by the General Health Questionnaire (Goldberg, 1978).

(4) *Rumination-Reflection Questionnaire (RRQ; Trapnell & Campbell, 1999)*. Trapnell and Campbell (1999) tried to distinguish adaptive and maladaptive self-focus in relation to the Five-Factor Model of personality. Their study resulted in the Rumination-Reflection Questionnaire, which has two factors: Reflection and Rumination. Reflection is adaptive and related to Openness to experiences (e.g. "I love exploring my 'inner' self" and "I'm very self-inquisitive by nature"). In contrast, Rumination is maladaptive and related to Neuroticism (e.g. "I always seem to be rehashing in my mind recent things I've said or done" and "Long after an argument or disagreement is over with, my thoughts keep going back to what happened"). Mindfulness is related to Openness (Baer et al., 2004; Bishop et al., 2004), and breathing meditation includes a curious attitude towards oneself. Thus, Reflection is expected to be a key component of mindfulness. Conversely, Rumination is clearly a symptomatic dimension, and thus was not included in the current factor analysis. We used the Japanese version by Takizaki and Koshikawa (2000). The Reflection subscale has six items (the items were reduced based on a factor analysis in the Japanese version), rated on a 5-point scale, 1 (*not at all true*) to 5 (*very true*).

(5) *Coping Styles Questionnaire (CSQ; Roger et al., 1993)*. CSQ is a coping scale with four factors: Rational Coping, Avoidance Coping, Emotional Coping,

and Detached Coping. Three of these correspond to repeatedly found coping dimensions, Task-oriented, Emotion-oriented, and Avoidance-oriented (Endler & Parker, 1990). Detached Coping is a new construct. Sample items are "See the situation for what it actually is and nothing more," "Feel independent of the circumstances," and "Respond neutrally to the problem." Only 10 items of the Detached Coping subscales were used. Items were rated on a 4-point scale, 1 (*never*) to 4 (*always*).

Correlates of Mindfulness

Relationships to various constructs were examined to clarify the nature of mindfulness factors.

1. *The Big Five.* The Big Five traits are the repeatedly found broader level factors of personality. The Big Five factors have been shown to be stable and robust (John & Srivastava, 1999). Thus researchers have attempted to classify items tapping various constructs in relation to the Big Five. John and Srivastava (1999) defined each dimension of the Big Five as follows. (1) Extraversion is an energetic approach to the world. (2) Agreeableness is a pro-social and communal orientation. (3) Conscientiousness is socially prescribed impulse control. (4) Neuroticism is negative emotionality. (5) Openness represents the breadth, depth, originality, and complexity of mental and experiential life. Sugiura et al. (2003) examined the relation between the CSRS subscales and the Big Five. A partial correlation analysis controlling for each CSRS subscale revealed that both CSRS subscales were correlated with Openness to experience. In addition, Logical Analysis was correlated with Agreeableness, while Refraining from Catastrophic Thinking was negatively correlated with Neuroticism.

2. *Attention control.* The core characteristic of mindfulness is attention control. Bishop (2002) argued that mindfulness involves sustained attention, attention switching, controlling attention to terminate thinking about inner experiences, and paying attention to all available information. The mindfulness skill of focusing attention on breathing or parts of the body will enhance attention control. Attention training (ATT) by Wells (1990) has exclusive focus on attention control. ATT has patients exercise selective attention, attention switching, and divided attention, using external sounds instead of bodily sensation. These discussions suggest that it would be useful to examine the correlation between attention control and mindfulness dimensions. Several measures of attention control exist, examples of which are Stroop color naming and Wilkins' Counting Test (Wilkins et al., 1987). We used a self-report measure of the daily experience of attention control (Shinohara et al., 2002).

3. *Problem-solving.* Mindfulness is often contrasted with traditional CBT, which emphasizes active problem-solving. However, Teasdale and others (2002) found that even standard cognitive therapy enhanced metacognitive awareness. CSRS contains Logical Analysis based on this notion. DBT emphasizes the synthesis of

change and acceptance. In addition, Sugiura and Sugiura (2004) found that a change-oriented process enhanced an acceptance/mindful process. These findings indicate that examining the relation between mindfulness and problem-solving skills would be informative.

4. *Symptoms.* Depression and worry-proneness were included to examine the effects on symptoms. Both are very common psychological symptoms among clinical and general populations and mindfulness has been applied to each (Segal et al., 2002; Roemer & Orsillo, 2002).

Method

Participants. Japanese college students (*N*=226) attending an introductory psychology course, completed questionnaires during the class. This was part of a large survey project. The total sample consisted of 104 men and 122 women with an average age of 19.74 years (SD 1.14). Some received partial course credit for their participation. The remaining students participated voluntarily, since the course evaluation system in the class they attended was different. All students were free to omit the questionnaire, however, no student refused to complete the questionnaire.

Questionnaires. In addition to SMCS, CSRS, FMS, RRQ, and CSQ, the Big Five, attention control, problem-solving, worry, and depression were measured. These latter are numbered in addition to the foregoing four instruments.

5. *The Big Five Scale (BFS; Wada, 1996).* The BFS was developed to measure the Big Five personality traits, whose items are based on the Adjective Check List (ACL; Gough & Heilbrun, 1983). A series of factor analyses of 198 theoretically selected ACL items resulted in the 60-item BFS. Each of the five factors contains 12 trait adjectives. Items were rated on a 7-point scale, 1 (*not at all true*) to 7 (*very true*). The trait adjective approach has been known to be factorially robust (Wada, 1996). Kashiwagi (1997) suggested that the ACL items (Japanese version), on which the BFS is based, could be theoretically classified under each of the five domains of the NEO PI-R (Costa & McCrae, 1992), the most widely used measure of the Big Five.

6. *Daily Experience of Attention Control Questionnaire (DEACQ; Shinohara et al., 2002).* DEACQ measures the attention control in daily life with five factorially derived subscales (item numbers in parentheses): Dual Task (4), Lack of Awareness (2), Sustained Attention (5), Attention Dysregulation (9), and Divided Attention (8). Attention Dysregulation represents nonspecific attention problems. Lack of Awareness is the failure to notice objects. Sustained Attention is the ability to focus and sustain attention to tasks. Divided Attention represents the ability to do things in parallel. Dual Task is similar to Divided Attention, but places more emphasis on concrete situations (e.g. working while listening to music).

7. *Problem-Solving Inventory (PSI; Heppner & Peterson, 1982).* PSI measures the individual's problem solving style. Items are rated on a 6-point scale, 1

(*strongly agree*) to 6 (*strongly disagree*). PSI has three subscales (item numbers in parentheses): Approach-Avoidance Style (16), Problem-Solving Confidence (11), and Personal Control (5). A high score indicated a maladaptive problem-solving style in the original version. However, the subscale scores were calculated in this study so that a high score indicated more active and confident problem-solving and perceived control. (The Japanese version was provided by Dr. Heppner, May 2003.)

8. *Penn State Worry Questionnaire (PSWQ; Meyer et al., 1990)*. PSWQ is a 16-item questionnaire measuring the frequency and intensity of worry (worry-proneness). Items are rated on a 5-point scale, 1 (*not at all true*) to 5 (*very true*). PSWQ has excellent psychometric properties (Molina & Borkovec, 1994). The Japanese version by Sugiura and Tanno (2000) used in this study has psychometric properties compatible with the original version.

9. *Center for Epidemiological Studies Depression Scale (CES-D; Radloff, 1977)*. CES-D is one of the most widely used depression scales, particularly in nonclinical populations. The Japanese version was developed by Yatomi and others (1993). It has 20 items. The Japanese version exhibits good psychometric properties. CES-D was originally rated on a 4-point scale; however, the Japanese version requires respondents to rate each item in terms of how frequent they experienced such feelings on a 3-point scale, 1 (*seldom*) to 3 (*frequent*). It is unlikely that this change significantly alters the construct or degrades the psychometric properties. In fact, CES-D revealed good internal consistency in this study ($\alpha = .88$).

Results

Simple statistics. Means, standard deviations, and α reliability coefficients of all scales are given in Table 1.

Table 1. Simple statistics and internal consistencies of all variables

	M	SD	α
Mindfulness			
Logical Objectivity	31.86	4.73	.81
Self-Observation	26.09	6.59	.84
Refraining from Catastrophic Thinking	37.41	7.71	.88
Acceptance	29.51	5.33	.78
Detached Coping	17.10	3.80	.75
Big Five			
Neuroticism	53.13	13.32	.92
Extraversion	56.07	11.92	.92
Openness	51.20	9.76	.84
Agreeableness	53.61	9.10	.83
Conscientiousness	48.53	9.09	.83

Attention Control			
Dual Task	11.89	3.46	.68
Lack of Awareness	5.78	1.65	.44
Sustained Attention	12.06	2.96	.69
Attention Dysregulation	28.84	4.94	.71
Divided Attention	20.49	4.98	.82
Problem-Solving			
Approach-Avoidance Style	58.64	9.22	.81
Problem-Solving Confidence	40.37	7.17	.81
Personal Control	16.96	3.90	.60
Symptoms			
Center for Epidemiological Studies			
Depression Scale	32.26	7.56	.88
Penn State Worry Questionnaire	50.78	11.53	.93

All scales except a few subscales of attention control and Personal Control of PSI demonstrated acceptable to good reliability (α = .71-.93). The lowest alpha was observed for Lack of Awareness, which contains only two items. The second-lowest alpha was found for Personal Control of PSI. Although the original PSI demonstrated a reliable three-factor structure, the factorial coherence of Personal Control appears to be problematic in the Japanese version.

The factor structure of mindfulness. A joint factor analysis was conducted for measurements related to mindfulness. A principal component analysis with equamax rotation was performed. Equamax was chosen to facilitate even distribution of items among the factors. A varimax rotation tends to yield an overly heavy first factor when the items increase. Cattell's Scree Test suggested three to seven factors. Five factors were extracted based on interpretability, accounting for 39% of the total variance.

Factor 1 was made up of items from Refraining from Catastrophic Thinking of CSRS and from Clearing a Space items of FMS. This factor was named Refraining from Catastrophic Thinking, representing skills of being detached from stressful thinking and the ability to think flexibly. *Factor 2* was mainly composed of the items of Reflection items from RRQ. These items involve observations of inner experiences with curiosity or interest, and thus Factor 2 was named Self Observation. *Factor 3* contained items from Logical Analysis of CSRS and Detached Objectivity of SMCS. This factor was interpreted as Logical Objectivity. An interesting note is that typical CBT skills (Logical Analysis) merged with meditation derived objectivity (Detached Objectivity). *Factor 4* was composed of items from Trusting One's Experience of FMS and Trust in Good Luck of SMCS. The former items are related to inner experiences, and the latter are related to the external environment. Nonetheless, both share acceptance of or trust in experiences. *Factor 5* represented the Detached Coping items of CSQ and was referred to as

Detached Coping. Detachment is also a feature of Factor 1 (Refraining from Catastrophic Thinking). However, the emphasis of Factor 5 was on detachment from problematic situations, as opposed to detachment from one's thinking.

Simple statistics of mindfulness dimensions. Subscales were constructed by choosing items that loaded heavily on each factor. Items loading .40 or higher on appropriate factors and less than .35 on other factors were retained. However, a few violations of this rule were allowed, considering the item contents.

Table 2. Intercorrelation among mindfulness dimensions

	Self Observation	Refraining from Catastrophic Thinking	Acceptance	Detached Coping
Logical Objectivity	.39 ***	.55 ***	.36 ***	.50 ***
Self-Observation	1.0	.15	.27 ***	.28 ***
Refraining from Catastrophic Thinking		1.00	.48 ***	.45 ***
Acceptance			1.00	.33 ***
Detached Coping				1.00

*p<.05; *** p<.001

The means, standard deviations, and alpha reliability coefficients of all scales are provided in Table 1. All mindfulness subscales demonstrated acceptable to good reliability (α = .75-.88). Intercorrelations among the five dimensions are listed in Table 2. All correlations were significant and in the small to moderate range (.15-.55). Thus, these dimensions can be subsumed under the rubric of mindfulness and still be distinguishable.

The Big Five and mindfulness. Table 3 lists the correlations between the Big Five and mindfulness dimensions. Table 4 presents the results of a series of stepwise multiple regression analyses that predict mindfulness by the Big Five dimensions. The *p* value for entry or removal of predictors was set for .01, considering the relatively large sample size.

Table 3. Correlations between mindfulness and other variables

	Logical Objectivity	Self Observation	Refraining from Catastrophic Thinking	Acceptance	Detached Coping
Big Five					
Neuroticism	-.31 ***	.11	-.66 ***	-.37 ***	-.35 ***
Extraversion	.08	-.02	.39 ***	.37 ***	.08
Openness	.55 ***	.37 ***	.49 ***	.48 ***	.35 ***
Agreeableness	.20 **	.01	.30 ***	.17 *	.26 ***
Conscientiousness	.22 ***	.03	.00	.16 *	.04
Attention Control					
Dual Task	.20 **	.00	.27 ***	.14 +	.26 ***
Lack of Awareness	-.05	-.07	-.12	-.04	.03
Sustained Attention	.31 ***	.14 +	.25 ***	.27 ***	.25 ***
Attention Dysregulation	-.14 +	.20 *	-.23 **	-.05	-.14
Divided Attention	.23 **	.04	.27 ***	.11	.30 ***
Problem-Solving					
Approach-Avoidance Style	.38 ***	.31 ***	-.04	.16 *	.17 *
Problem-Solving Confidence	.35 ***	.15 +	.47 ***	.46 ***	.46 ***
Personal Control	.24 ***	-.03	.26 ***	.2 +	.21 **
Symptoms					
Center for Epidemiological Studies Depression Scale	-.22 **	.16 *	-.43 ***	-.24 ***	-.22 **
Penn State Worry Questionnaire	.30.***	.04	-.69 ***	-.31 ***	-.41 ***

+ $p<.10$; * $p<.05$; ** $p<.01$; *** $p<.001$

These regressions revealed the following relations. (a) Openness was positively related to all mindfulness dimensions. (b) Neuroticism was negatively related to all mindfulness dimensions except Self Observation, to which it exhibited a positive relation. (c) Extraversion was positively related to Acceptance and negatively related to Logical Objectivity. (d) Agreeableness was positively related to Detached Coping. (e) Conscientiousness was positively related to Logical Objectivity.

Attention control and mindfulness. Table 3 presents the correlations between attention control and the mindfulness dimensions. Table 4 provides the results of a series of multiple regression analyses that predict mindfulness by attention control. The analytic procedure used for the Big Five was followed. These regressions revealed that (a) Sustained Attention is related to all mindfulness dimensions except for Self Observation and (b) Divided Attention is positively related to Refraining from Catastrophic Thinking and Detached Coping.

Problem-solving and mindfulness. Table3 shows the correlations between problem-solving skills and the mindfulness dimensions, Table 4 the results of a series of multiple regression analyses that predict mindfulness by the problem-solving skills. The analytic procedure used for the Big Five was followed. These regressions revealed that (a) Problem-Solving confidence was related to all mindfulness dimensions except for Self Observation and (b) an active problem-solving style (high Approach-Avoidance Style) was related to Logical Objectivity and Self Observation.

Table 4. Regression anallysis predicting mindfulness

	Logical Objectivity	Self Observation	Refraining from Catastrophic Thinking	Acceptance	Detached Coping
Big Five					
Neuroticism	-.20	.24	-.57	-.20	-.22
Extraversion	-.20			.17	
Openness	.53	.44	.32	.36	.26
Agreeableness					.17
Conscientiousness	.16				
R^2	.36	.18	.52	.30	.20
Attention Control					
Dual Task					
Lack of Awareness					
Sustained Attention	.31		.21	.27	.20
Attention Dysregulation					
Divided Attention			.24		.26
R^2	.09		.11	.07	.12
Problem-Solving					
Approach-Avoidance Style	.32	.31			
Problem-Solving Confidence	.28		.47	.46	.46
Personal Control					
R^2	.21	.09	.21	.20	.21

Note. Standardized regression coefficients (p <.01) are shown.

Predicting symptoms by mindfulness. The relations with the symptoms were examined to confirm the adaptive effects of mindfulness (Table 5). Table 3 indicates that all mindfulness dimensions except for Self Observation were negatively related to both symptoms. Stepwise regression analyses were conducted to clarify the specific relationships. The p value for entry or removal of predictors was set for .01, considering the relatively large sample size. Two mindfulness dimensions emerged as significant predictors for depression (CES-D). Self Observation enhanced depression, and Refraining from Catastrophic Thinking reduced depression. Detached Coping was also significant when predicting worry-proneness (PSWQ) in addition to the same two predictors of depression. Again, Self Observation enhanced worrying and Refraining from Catastrophic Thinking reduced worrying. Detached Coping also reduced worrying.

Table 5. Regression analysis predicting symptoms by mindfulness

	CES-D	PSWQ
Logical Objectivity		
Self Observation	.24	.21
Refraining from Catastrophic Thinking	-.46	-.65
Acceptance		
Detached Coping		-.19
R^2	.22	.53

Note. CES-D = Center for Epidemiological Studies Depression Scale
PSWQ = Penn State Worry Questionnaire
Standardized regression coefficients (p <.01) are shown

Discussion

This study conducted a joint factor analysis of related measurements in an attempt to clarify the construct of mindfulness. In addition, the relations of mindfulness dimensions to other variables were examined. The results are considered in turn below.

The structure of mindfulness. Factor analysis revealed five interpretable factors: Logical Objectivity, Self Observation, Refraining from Catastrophic Thinking, Acceptance, and Detached Coping. These dimensions are meaningful in terms of mindfulness, even though each original measure is based on divers e clinical theories. What is striking is the trans-theoretical nature of the resultant factors. For example, Refraining from Catastrophic Thinking includes items from CBT,

Focusing and meditation. Logical Analysis combines items from CBT and meditation. People can be mindful of internal and external stimuli, but existing measurements of mindfulness focus mainly on attention to internal experiences. In contrast, the mindfulness dimensions obtained here involve both internal and external focus. Logical Objectivity and Detached Coping are primarily related to external problems. Refraining from Catastrophic Thinking and Self Observation are chiefly related to internal experiences. Acceptance contains attitudes toward internal and external environments.

Refraining from Catastrophic Thinking resembles metacognitive awareness, which is: perceiving negative thoughts as just thoughts, not as self or reality (Teasdale et al., 2002). Self Observation is curious and interested self-focus. Many mindfulness techniques involve this type of attention. Logical Objectivity resembles orthodox CBT skills, although it also contains items from Transcendental Meditation. Logical Objectivity may not be central to mindfulness meditation, but it is of theoretical interest considering the relation between CBT and mindfulness (Teasdale et al., 2002). Furthermore, Langer's (1989) concept of mindfulness taps awareness and flexibility in problem-solving. Acceptance deals with both internal and external objects. Acceptance items are relatively passive (Sakairi, 2004) despite its positive tone, unlike well-known positive thinking measures such as self-efficacy. Detached Coping is similar to Refraining from Catastrophic Thinking in its emphasis on detachment and distancing, but different in its external focus.

Positive intercorrelations among the five dimensions suggest that these dimensions can be subsumed under the rubric of mindfulness, while still remaining distinguishable (Table 2). Close inspection revealed that correlations involving Self Observation tended to be low (mean $r = .27$) compared to other correlations (mean $r = .44$). This is consistent with the result of Baer and others (2004); the correlation involving the Observing subscale was relatively low. In addition, their Observing subscale was negatively correlated with the Acceptance subscale. They interpreted this result as a demonstration that self observation tends to be judgmental in non-meditating populations. However, they found that the more experience a person has with meditation, the higher the Observing score becomes. It is thought that Self Observation is an important mindfulness dimension. However, we must be cautious of the negative effects of self-focus, considering the symptom-enhancing effects of Self Observation.

Mindfulness and symptoms. The relation of mindfulness to depression and worry was examined to clarify its adaptive effects. Refraining from Catastrophic Thinking was the most powerful reducing factor for both depression and worry. Detached Coping also had a reducing effect for worry-proneness; however, the magnitude was relatively small ($\beta = -.19$, compared to $\beta = -.65$ for Refraining from Catastrophic Thinking). Thus, Refraining from Catastrophic Thinking is the most powerful active ingredient of mindfulness. This is consistent with the discussion by Teasdale and others (2002), which suggested that metacognitive awareness is the mediator of the effects of mindfulness. This notion indicates the possibility that the effects of other mindfulness dimensions are mediated by Refraining from Catastrophic Thinking. Table 2 indicates that all mindfulness dimensions were positively correlated to Refraining from Catastrophic Thinking. When regression analysis predicting Refraining from Catastrophic Thinking was conducted, Logical Objectivity, Acceptance, and Detached Coping had a positive effect on Refraining from Catastrophic Thinking, while Self Observation reduced it. Thus, Refraining from Catastrophic Thinking might mediate the effects of three of the remaining mindfulness dimensions.

Self Observation enhanced the symptoms. However, Self Observation may also have an adaptive effect since it had weak but positive correlations with other mindfulness dimensions. Nonetheless, the correlation with depression was positive (Table 3). This ironic effect of Self Observation is consistent with the well documented negative effect of self-focus (e.g. Wells & Matthews, 1994). However, it is surprising that Self Observation is made up of items that tap the adaptive side of self-focus, distinct from rumination (Trapnell & Campbell, 1999). This maladaptive effect of Self Observation may be due to its analytic and conceptual nature (e.g., I love analyzing why I do things). Recently Watkins (2004) contrasted conceptual-evaluative and experiential modes of self focus, then found the former is maladaptive. Including items tapping feelings and present-moment experiences will reverse the maladaptive effects of Self Observation.

Personality, attention, and problem-solving. The relationship between mindfulness and other variables exhibits both overlapping and distinct features of the mindfulness dimensions.

(a) *Commonality among mindfulness dimensions.* The common correlate of mindfulness was Openness. Miller (1991) suggested that Openness facilitated responsiveness to psychotherapy. In addition, three individual difference variables were related to four of the five mindfulness dimensions, excluding Self Observation: Neuroticism, Sustained Attention, and Problem-Solving Confidence. Neuroticism was negatively related to the four mindfulness dimensions but positively related to Self Observation. This is consistent with the finding by Baer and others (2004) that the subscales of KIMS, except for Observing, were negatively related to Neuroticism. These results support the clinical utility of mindfulness. However, caution is required in the use of self-focus skills. This notion is further underscored by the positive relation between Problem-Solving Confidence and mindfulness dimensions, excluding Self Observation. Problem-Solving Confidence is similar to self-efficacy and thus is considered to be one of the well-being indexes. Sustained Attention was also common to the mindfulness dimensions excluding Self Observation. The essence of mindfulness may be attention skills: paying purposeful attention to breathing, bodily sensations, external sounds, and so on. Furthermore, it is understandable that logical and objective problem-solving require substantial attention. Considerable attention resources are necessary for appropriate objectivity, since so many human behaviors are automatic and prone to biases (Segal et al, 2002). However, Self Observation, which can be considered as deliberate attention to inner experiences, was not supported by Sustained Attention.

(b) *Distinct features of mindfulness dimensions.* The correlates of mindfulness also revealed the distinct features of each mindfulness dimension. For attention control, Divided Attention was related to Refraining from Catastrophic Thinking and Detached Coping. This is understandable since both of those mindfulness skills involve detachment from stimulus. Detachment indicates being not preoccupied with an object while acknowledging it. It is also consistent with ATT (Wells, 1990). ATT aims to increase flexible attention control and involves divided attention exercises. ATT was found to reduce negative beliefs about worry (Papageorgiou & Wells, 2000). The Approach-Avoidance Style was positively related to Logical Objectivity and Self Observation. This suggests that both mindfulness skills are related to an effortful and active style. Logical Objectivity and Self Observation both involved deliberate attention. However, it should be remembered that Self Observation was not related to Sustained Attention. Some of the Big Five dimensions evidenced a weak relation to mindfulness. Extraversion was negatively related to Logical Objectivity and positively related to Acceptance. Extraversion is thought to underlie positive emotions. It is understandable that the trust and appreciation involved in Acceptance is related to positive affect. On the other hand, its relation to Logical Objectivity is difficult to interpret. Agreeableness was related to Detached Coping. Agreeableness is related to pro-social and communal orientation. Good interpersonal relationships may enhance detachment from difficult stressors, a significant portion of which may be interpersonal. Finally, Conscientiousness was related to Logical Objectivity. This indicates that Logical Objectivity reflects a sincere and effortful process.

Summary

Each mindfulness dimension can be described as follows, based on the above discussion. Logical Objectivity is an effortful and attentive process aimed at rational problem-solving. Although it resembles orthodox CBT skills, it also enhances metacognitive awareness. Self Observation is also an effortful process. Although it is supported by curiosity, it has negative effects, possibly due to its conceptual or analytic nature. The refinement of items contents will change the results. Refraining from Catastrophic Thinking may be the most proximal mediator of the adaptive effects of mindfulness. It resembles metacognitive awareness (Teasdale et al., 2002) and is supported by the cognitive ability to divide attention. Detached Coping is similar to Refraining from Catastrophic Thinking in that both reflect a detached attitude, although the objects of detachment differ. Acceptance involves both internal and external stimuli. Although it has a nuance of positive thinking, it is a relatively passive attitude, unlike self-efficacy or self-esteem.

17

Chan-Based Sensory Awareness And Managerial Functioning

Michael Tophoff

An empirical study explored whether managers participating in a Sensory Awareness seminar became (1) more aware of their bodily signals and (2) felt better as to their bodily functioning. It was expected that (1) they would become more content about their relationships and (2) feel better functioning in their job. Using psychometrically reliable and valid measuring instruments, results showed significant changes; there was improvement in all of the above-mentioned categories. The factor of seminar duration is of significance for the effectiveness of this method, while factors such as sex, age, or the manager's type of company are not.

The concept of mindfulness, the most essential feature in Buddhist practice, is based on the Sanskrit *smriti*, which may be translated as mindfulness or as remembrance. Thich (1998, p. 59) interprets mindfulness as "remembering to come back to the present moment." According to Mikulas (1990, p. 151) mindfulness refers to "the subjective conscious experience of noticing." In the definition of Harvey (2000, p. 38) mindfulness is "a state of keen awareness of mental and physical phenomena as they arise within and around one." Kabat-Zinn (in Segal et al., 2003, p. viii) describes mindfulness as a way of seeing that involves "coming back to one's senses" in every meaning of that phrase. Mindfulness may be defined as "a meditative state, *continued into the action itself*, characterized by awareness and an attentive openness towards the present moment" (Tophoff, 2003, p. 123).

Mindfulness, which is one of the key elements of the Buddhist Noble Eightfold Path, has been made applicable to day to day human behavior in the Chinese tradition of Buddhism (i.e. Chan Buddhism) (Tophoff, 2003). This tradition, other than its Indian ancestor, squarely emphasizes the pragmatics of behavior. In fact, the practice of mindfulness can be conceived as meditation-in-action or as meditation-in-the marketplace. Both meditation and mindfulness have to be trained. The beneficial effects of meditation have been extensively demonstrated in the literature (e.g. Murphy & Donovan, 1999; Carrington, 1984; DelMonte, 1984; Kwee, 1990a, Kwee & Holdstock, 1996). Likewise, the positive effects of mindfulness-training have been shown by a number of studies. In these studies, however, Kabat-Zinn's method of Mindfulness-Based Stress Reduction has been used (Kabat-Zinn,

1982, 1987, 1993, 1996; Kabat-Zinn et al., 1985; Teasdale, 1999, 2000; Teasdale et al., 2000). Though there are similarities between Sensory Awareness and Kabat-Zinn's method. there are a number of important differences. In Kabat-Zinn's method, activities are exercised and rehearsed, such as the Body Scan, sitting meditation and Hatha Yoga. In the Body Scan, attention is systematically focused on separate body parts and regions. In Sensory Awareness there are no exercises, but an open-ended exploration of whatever is present in awareness. Attention is rather of a "free floating" type, where letting happens and permitting of what presents itself is central. Since the work in Sensory Awareness consists of everyone's daily and ordinary activities, generalization of the learning experiences is facilitated.

The present empirical study is directed to explore the effects of the method of Sensory Awareness as training in mindfulness in a normal sample.

Method

Sensory Awareness. Sensory Awareness was originally developed by Selver (1974); an extensive description of this method is offered in Tophoff (2000, 2003). It is about the mindful exploration of what one experiences in what Buddhists call "The four Dignities of Man," namely in sitting, walking, laying and standing; in other words in our ordinary day-to-day activities. The focus is on how mindful the immediacy of one's personal experience can become and on how we construct this experience from moment to moment. The practice of this method does not consist of exercises (which are prescribed and are to be executed), but of experiments (where the person mindfully explores his/her sensations). In such an experiment, for example, the participants may be asked to spread their arms. First, they let their arms "drop," something which they may already be acquainted with from relaxation-exercises (in Cognitive-Behavior Therapy). Then, again with the arms spread wide, they are asked to "accompany" their arms ever so slowly downwards, attentive to the influence of gravity. Participants explore the difference between relaxation and liveliness. They discover how they may hinder their liveliness (e.g. by blocking their breathing or by treating their arms as an object that one can "drop"). While mindfully accompanying their arms downwards, participants can experience how standing indeed is a proper dignity. They come to understand that "letting go" is not the same as "dropping." In an atmosphere of acceptance, one may verbalize the awareness of sensations, emotions, remembrances, etc. These are not, however, therapeutically worked through.

Implementation. In this study, Sensory Awareness is presented in the form of a residential seminar of varying duration. In order to study the effect of duration on outcome, the seminars differed in duration from 1.5, 2, 3, and 5 days. Each day two sessions of three hours were offered. The format of each session, which was identical in all seminars, consisted of a 70-minute period of non-verbal experiments, followed by a 20-minute period of verbal sharing.

Participants. The sample (N = 68) consists of managers from three different populations: Managers from different companies (Management Mix, N = 41). A retail company in Belgium (In company-B, N = 18). A retail company in the Netherlands (In company-NL, N = 9). Every participant attended one seminar during the period from 2000 to 2002. The duration of the seminars varied (see Table I). The Management Mix group consists of managers from different fields such as information technology, consultancy, accounting, and engineering. The seminars for the retail managers in Belgium (In company-B) and in the Netherlands (In company-NL) have the format of an in-company training solely for managers from the same company. Participants in all three groups usually did not know one another beforehand.

Measures. Two questionnaires for measurement have been used: the Somatic Awareness Questionnaire (SAQ) and the Outcome Questionnaire (OQ®-45.2). The original American version of the OQ®-45.2 is presented in Appendix IV. The SAQ was developed by Gijsbers van Wijk and Kolk (1996; Kolk et al., 2003) to assess "selective attention to the body." This is the tendency to be aware of, or sensitive to, internal bodily processes, and global bodily states not typically associated with disease, illness, or emotion. The questionnaire consists of 25 statements that refer to attentiveness to common and frequently occurring physiological processes (e.g. hunger contractions in the stomach, or global bodily states such as energy level). Items are rated on a 5-point Likert scale (from "not at all applicable to me" to "very much applicable to me") with a high score indicating a high selective attention to the body. Gijsbers van Wijk & Kolk (1996) constructed the SAQ on the basis of a pool of 29 items, which they translated into Dutch, deriving from three scales, measuring virtually the same concepts. These scales were: the Body Awareness Questionnaire (BAQ) (Shields et al., 1989), the Amplification Questionnaire (AQ) (Barsky & Goodson, 1988) and the Private Body Consciousness Scale (PBCS) (Miller et al., 1981).

Gijsbers van Wijk and Kolk (1996), in a first study with 490 psychology students, eliminated 4 of the 29 items because of item-remainder correlations below 0.20, so that the current SAQ, used in this study, contains 17 BAQ-items, 4 AQ-items, and 4 PBCS-items. The authors mention means and standard deviations, as mean item scores, for a student sample (N = 88) of men and women respectively as 2.8 (0.13) and 2.8 (0.11). The reliability of the SAQ is to be considered as high. Cronbach *a* is above 0.70, which had been fixed as an acceptance threshold for internal consistency. Homogeneity and stability likewise are acceptable. Discriminant validity was assessed by correlating the SAQ with other reliable and valid measures, such as the Spielberger State-Trait Anxiety Inventory, the State-Trait Anger Scale, the Amsterdam Biographical Questionnaire (i.e. its two subscales Neurotic Lability and Neurotic Lability as manifested in the expression of Neurotic-Somatic Complaints) the SCL-90 (a measure of clinical symptomatology) and the Health Associations Rating Scale. SAQ scores were unrelated to all personality measures, including somatic neuroticism.

The Outcome Questionnaire (OQ®-45.2) (Lambert et al., 2001, 1998) was developed as a screening and outcome assessment scale that measures progress in therapy along three dimensions: Subjective Discomfort (SD) or "How does the person feel inside?," Interpersonal Relations (IR) or "How does the person get along with significant others?," and Social Role Performance (SR) or "How is the person doing in important life tasks (e.g. work)?" Items are rated on a 5-point Likert scale, ranging from "never" to "always," according to the applicability to the person. The OQ yields a Total Score and scores on SD, IR, and SR respectively. In line with common practice in this study only the total scores will be used. The higher the score, the more pathology in the individual can be inferred. Lambert and coworkers present means and standard deviations of the total score of 45.19 and 18.57 in a normal sample (N = 815) (Lambert et al., 1996, 2001). These authors present high test-retest reliability scores and highly acceptable Cronbach's α's with regards to internal consistency in the total score as well as in the three individual domain scores. They show concurrent validity for the OQ and its individual domains with different criterion measures as being significant beyond the 0.01 level of confidence. As a research version of the OQ®-45.2, De Jong (2000) devised a Dutch translation, used in this study and available at the American Professional Credentialing Services. In a normal population (N = 90) the mean and standard deviation of the total scores were 39.07 (SD 14.94). As to internal consistency, Cronbach's α's were satisfactory in a pilot study with students as subjects.

Procedure. The SAQ as well as the OQ were sent by mail to the future participants of the seminar Sensory Awareness after they had registered with the request to complete both forms two days before the beginning of the course. After the seminar had ended, they were requested to complete these forms again two days later and to return them by mail to the trainer.

Results

In this study data from six different seminars have been used. Each participant attended once. For calculations, the four different durations have been summed up in three different groups. Group 1 (1.5 and 2 days), Group 2 (3 days), Group 3 (5 days). Table I shows both groups are of about the same age.

Table 1. Participants: Age and sex distribution

Subjects	N	Range	Mean	SD
Women	20	25-56	40.5	9.70
Men	48	25-57	41	7.15
Total	68	25-57	41	7.74

Table 2. SAQ-scores and seminar duration

Duration	SAQ-1 (Means, SD)	SAQ-II(Means, SD)	N
1	3.23 (.43)	3.18 (.46)	15
2	3.17 (.44)	3.42 (.42)	30
3	3.14 (.45)	3.28 (.56)	17
Total sample	3.19 (.45)	3.32 (.47)	62

Table 2 shows SAQ results before and after seminar participation for three different duration groups. The scores are rendered as mean-item scores to make comparison possible with the earlier-mentioned data of the student sample of Gijsbers van Wijk and Kolk (1996). In our sample, the SAQ-I scores start much higher. ANOVA with repeated measures showed that there were no significant differences on SAQ-scores between the three duration groups (F [2,59] = - .29, p = .75). Overall post SAQ-scores were significantly higher than the pre-scores (F [1,59] = 9.26, p = .003. Inspection of the interaction showed a difference between Group-1 and Groups 2 and 3. The differences between pre- and post-scores for Group-2 were significantly larger than for Group-1 (t [43] = 3.53, p <.001). Groups 2 and 3 did not result significantly in differences between pre- and post-scores.

Table 3. OQ ®-45.2 scores and seminar duration

Duration	OQ-I (Means, SD)	OQ-II (Means, SD)	N
1	43.70 (15.63)	42.32 (16.08)	16
2	55.28 (20.47)	46.23 (18.23)	31
3	45.13 (16.57)	43.08 (21.48)	17
Total sample	49.69 (18.91)	44.42 (18.45)	64

Table 3 shows the results of OQ®-45.2 before and after the seminar. The overall tendency of these results is the same as the outcomes of the SAQ. The results are rendered in total-scores to make comparison possible with the data of the normal population presented by De Jong (2000). Our sample's base rate is considerably higher. The data from Lambert et al. (1999) of a much larger, normal, community sample are more in agreement with our results. Again an ANOVA was conducted, showing no significant difference through time between the three groups (F [2,61] = 1.37, p = .26). Overall post OQ-scores were significantly lower than pre OQ-scores (F [1,61] = 6.16, p = .016). The difference between pre- and post-scores for Group-2 looks much larger than the difference in both other groups.

Due to the amount of variance in the OQ-scores within the groups, these differences are just marginally significant.

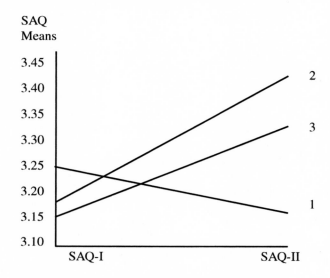

Figure 1. SAQ: Duration and rate of change

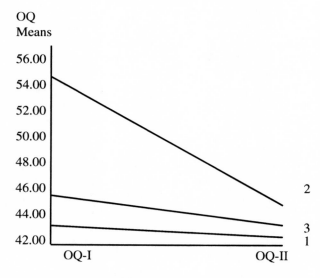

Figure 2. OQ®-45.2: Duration and Rate of Change

Comparing the difference within Group-2 versus the difference in Group-1 accrues ditto results (t [47] = 1.96, p = .055). The same applies to analog Group-2 versus Group-3 (t [46] = 1.82, p = .07).

The graphs in Figures 1 and 2 illustrate the aforementioned data. They show the interaction effect between the three groups as to their SAQ and OQ scores. A high SAQ-score indicates a high selective attention to the body. The lower the OQ-score, the less pathology, the better the person feels inside as to his interpersonal relations and his social role performance. The difference between Group-1 and Groups 2 and 3 is obvious for the SAQ-scores. For the OQ-score the pattern is not very clear.

Finally, we posed the question whether it was the age of the participants or the seminar duration, which could account for the changes. In considering the spread of age in relation to duration of the seminar and to the results of SAQ and OQ-scores, the hypothesis was formed that the differences between pre- and post-seminar SAQ measurements in the total sample were not based on seminar duration but rather on age of the participants. In order to test this hypothesis, an ANOVA was conducted with age as a second between factors. As to age, participants were split into two groups: Age-1 ≤ 40; Age-2 > 40 per each of the three durations. The hypothesis that age should have an influence on the change in SAQ-scores was rejected. There was no influence of age at all, while all previously mentioned results could be maintained. OQ-scores show similar results. The hypothesis that age should have an influence on the change in OQ-scores has to be rejected, while all previously mentioned results could be maintained.

Discussion

In selecting the measurement instruments for this study, the Somatic Awareness Questionnaire has been chosen, because it seemed relatively close to measuring the crux of mindfulness (i.e. the manager's awareness of what is happening within his body) and because of its psychometrical qualities of reliability and validity, in a Dutch-speaking sample. The Outcome Questionnaire likewise measures how a person feels inside, as well as his relationships and social role. This questionnaire has also been selected as to the question of whether it would support the SAQ findings. As the results of the present empirical study clearly show, managers change significantly. They improve after participation at a Sensory Awareness seminar of longer duration on the dimension of awareness of bodily processes and wellbeing, as well as on positive feelings about interpersonal relations and social role. Both instruments, on every occasion, point to the same direction.

The present sample shows a higher SAQ base rate scores than SAQ scores in a normal population reported in the literature. The fact that participants in this study display a greater degree of awareness of bodily processes may have contributed to their motivation to attend the seminar. As to the OQ-results, the picture is different and dependent on which population is used for comparison. Compared to the normal sample of De Jong (2000), participants in the present study had higher total-score base rates. Compared, however, to the large normal sample of Lambert et al. (1999) these results match with their sample. Within this perspective, it is worthwhile to note, that the present sample still improves on both measures, even with higher base-rates.

In this study, no differences were found between the *three groups of managers*: Incompany-B, Incompany-NL, and Managers-Mix. There were, however, important differences as to the seminar's duration. Seminars of short duration (1.5 or 2 days) do not lead to significant changes. The changes occur in seminars lasting 3 to 5 days. This finding corresponds with my trainer's impression that participants, who are not used to this type of seminar, need time not only to get acquainted with the approach but also to grasp and internalize the experiences and to "see" and recognize its applicability to their professional lives. The question as to if and how these experiences are translated into measurable changes in managerial behavior over a longer period of time after the seminar is the focus of a future experimental study.

The notion that female participants might be more aware of their bodily functioning, or that they might change differently over time compared to their male counterparts, was not confirmed in our results. As to the measures, no significant *sex differences* have been found. As to the factor of *age*, it could be hypothesized that the older managers, based on personal experience with aging or a beginning decrease of physical functioning, would be more aware of their bodily states than the younger ones. In that case, higher base rate SAQ scores would have to be expected in the older participants. In this study, however, age had no influence on change in any of the applied instruments. Younger and older managers profit equally from participation in the seminar.

Based on these results, it is worthwhile to consider participation of managers in a Sensory Awareness seminar of longer duration, be it as part of a training process for trainees and starting managers or for senior managers in a process of continuing education. In a future experimental study that is underway, longitudinal effects must first be measured, and than a comparison made between experimental and control groups.

18

Inner Paths In Outer Settings: A Wellbeing Tourist Program1

Miguel Quintana

Vacation is a suitable period to implement a program that aims to reduce stress and increase psychological wellbeing. Studies in daily life suggest that medita-tion/exercise-based programs need to last at least 9 weeks in order to decrease trait anxiety. The present study explores the outcome of a 6-day residential Wellbeing Tourist Program specifically based on Tai Chi (moving meditation) and Zen meditation (sitting meditation). Results indicate that trait anxiety — con-sidered relatively stable — decreased significantly after the program as well as state anxiety (already during the program). Participants reported benefits on measures of wellbeing and stress due to single session bouts of Tai Chi and Zen.

A person seeking for a sense of "feeling better" and release from daily stress, finds there are plenty choices available. Fitness centres' and sports clubs' activities, worksite wellness programs, and health holidays provide promising options. Health, fitness, wellbeing, or wellness is usually achieved by training that might range from arduous exercises, to enjoyable activities, to relaxation-meditation practices. Which of these interventions works for whom, and in what specific domains of health? Which one would fit personal objectives best? What is the influence of situational factors on the outcome? For example, how effective are worksite wellness programs compared to those offered in the neighbourhood or during a holidays trip? Rather than assuming that each offering is equally effective, these questions require a thorough study. Subjective wellbeing is made up of various factors that include both negative and positive affect, pleasure, life satisfaction, and a sense of happiness (Diener, 2000). Physical exercise changes mood and affect (Landers & Arent, 2001) and habitual physical activity seems to benefit individuals' sense of wellbeing (e.g. Berger & Motl, 2001). It is generally accepted that different types of exercise elicit different psychological effects. For instance, stress levels decrease after non-competitive, rhythmical physical activities that promote abdominal breath-ing, such as jogging, swimming, or Hatha Yoga (Abele & Brehm, 1993). Psycho-logical benefits attained through exercise may range from hours to weeks. Short-term effects on state levels of mood, stress, anxiety, and depression, are linked to a single exercise session and its benefits have a time course of 4 to 6 hours after one's single bout participation (Landers & Petruzzelo, 1994). In order to acquire significant long-term benefits (e.g. on trait anxiety), non-residential exercise programs need to exceed 9 weeks and are preferably 15 weeks long (Petruzzello et. al., 1991). It has also been reported that social environment factors such as instructor characteristics and the involvement of other participants, modulate the outcome (Turner & Rejeski, 1997).

Relaxation and/or meditation techniques accrue comparable effects to physical exercise on reducing state and trait anxiety, modulating mood state, and enhancing psychological wellbeing. Various studies conclude that all above and kindred interventions elicit psychological benefits on enhancing mood and decreasing anxiety related states (Bahrke & Morgan, 1978; Berger et al., 1988ab; Jin, 1992). Although it has been argued that some meditation effects might be gained through sitting quietly and resting (Holmes, 1987), it is presently generally accepted that various types of meditation, as well as various kinds of relaxation, have positive short-term effects in reducing stress and tension (Sheppard, 1992). There may also be longer-lasting benefits due to long-term meditation training in terms of stable changes in mood, anxiety, depression, and cognitive styles (e.g. Sakairi, 1998). Similar to exercising, different types of meditation practice seem to produce different effects. For instance, a meta-analysis examining the effects of relaxations/meditations showed that Transcendental Meditation (TM) is the most effective technique in reducing trait anxiety (Eppley et al., 1989). Despite the salubrious effects of relaxation, it might paradoxically evoke anxiety through a phenomenon called Relaxation Induced Anxiety that occurs in rare cases in clients who fear loss of control (Heide & Borkovec, 1983).

Programs that include physical exercise and relaxation/meditation techniques claim to preserve health and promote wellbeing in the physical, psychological, social, and spiritual domains (Greenberg & Pargman, 1989). Exercise/meditation-based programs are able to balance and facilitate improvements in those different domains, although the extent and the type of benefits may be diverse and depending on situational context. For instance, stress reduction programs in the workplace are effective in reducing psychophysiological indicators of stress, specifically due to meditation, exercise, and biofeedback (McLeroy et al., 1984). Another study focused on the order and combination of activities within a program consisting of managerial skills training, meditation, and exercises, and concluded that different combinations and orders of these components lead to similar beneficial effects (Bruning & Frew, 1987). The influence of expectation and regularity of practicing has also been studied. For example, in a TM-based worksite program to reduce anxiety of businessmen, the degree of expectation on TM and practice frequency was examined. It was concluded that regular and non-regular meditators attained similar benefits and that expectations did affect state anxiety negatively, but did not impact trait anxiety (Sakairi, 1992).

As yet, no empirical study has explored the anxiety reduction effects of a wellbeing program in the context of holidays and whether motivation and expectations influence the outcome. The Wellbeing Tourist Program (WTP) comprises a journey to a residence with a specialized accommodation, which offers a comprehensive package of services that meet the participants' prime motivational needs. The purpose of the present study is to explore the outcomes of WTP.

It is assumed that one's first motivation to embark on this program is to preserve health and promote wellbeing. Thus, the program includes a package of services: exercise/meditation activities, educational workshops, and other wellness offerings. Other reasons to take part might be: venue surroundings, social atmosphere, or additional services, which may not all be controlled. However, in general the setting and fixed period seem to be able to offer a standard condition of a "naturalistic laboratory" that wards off disturbing factors (Gilbert & Abdullah, 2004). Results found just at the start and the end of the program will give a clear indication of the immediate effects of the interventions per se. A within-subjects quasi-experimental design serves to minimize the influence of individuals' differences on psychological traits, baseline states, expectations and motivations, experience and skills levels.

Method

Participants. Sixty people took part in the WTP. They had the option to not participate in the activities scheduled in the program. Thus, only those who engaged in the activities, which included all of the sessions under study, and filled in all the required assessments, were included in the data analysis. The final sample comprised Spanish adults in their fifties (8 males, 22 females), the majority of which was non-medicated (n: 23, 82.1%).

The following participants' data emerge from a general survey. They are mainly university graduates, who are most active (75%) during daily chores and stressed by job factors (77%). Regular physical exercises (83%) are part of their daily lives 1 to 4 times a week for 30-60 minutes each time; they are currently active (92%) for one year or more (83 %). Also, they have been practicing meditation, Zen (52%) or other methods (30%); mostly they practice meditation with a specific purpose (89%), such as to calm down. Meditation was practiced regularly (80%) from 1 to 4 times per week for 20-45 minutes each time. They are currently active meditators (91%), but fewer have been active for one year or more (67%).

Design. As a form of applied research this exploration employs a quasi-experimental design — a within-subjects design — apt to the practical objective of studying the external validity of WTP's naturalistic setting. Two single sessions of meditation, two sessions of exercise, and the total WTP are specified as the independent variables. WTP consists of a 6-days hotel stay in the Pyrenees (Lérida,

Spain) at an altitude of 1630 metres above sea level. Zen meditation practice, physical exercise sessions, and hiking excursions were conducted each day. Other activities include workshops (on health behavior, psychology, and philosophy), meals, and spare time during which alternative activities were not provided. The time schedule was as follows: at 7.00: waking up, 7.30-8.00: exercising, 8.00-8.40: Zen, 8.40-9.30: breakfast, 10.00-18.00: hiking, 19.30-20.00: Zen, 20.00: dinner and spare time. Participants were instructed not to have any verbal interaction during the experimental sessions and to keep socializing to a minimum during the whole period of six days.

The meditation practice was based on Zen and was lead by a Zen master (Mr. Celso Navarro, contemplation master and Catholic priest). This ancient Japanese meditation method consists of sitting in a specified posture while focusing attention on a particular object and keeping a passive attitude toward distracting thoughts and feelings — a "letting be" attitude (Nakamura, 1992). Participants adopt either a sitting posture on a chair or a *seiza* bench (seated on a low platform, legs folded under the bench, and knees firmly on a *zabuton* cushion on the floor). The back is kept straight upright and the hands held in the lap in a cosmic *mudra* (position). Thus, participants sit down quietly during 25 minutes with the eyes slightly open, while attention is focussed on either one's own abdominal breathing pattern or on an individual mantra (a word or sentence subverbally repeated). The physical sessions called "Exercise" consist of 10 minutes warming-up exercises followed by 20 minutes Tai Chi. Tai Chi is an ancient art originated in China and practiced worldwide. Its basic components are slow body movements, body awareness, inward attention, and breathing regulation (Shou-Yu & Wen-Ching, 1996). Sessions were instructed by the experimenter. The participants performed slow and smooth bodily motions and body movements; body weight was shifted and balanced from one foot to another while monitoring postural alignment, and maintaining abdominal breath awareness.

Measurements. Psychological wellbeing, distress, fatigue, and anxiety levels were the main targets of scrutiny. Spielberger's State Trait Anxiety Inventory, (STAI) provides reliable self-report measures of state and trait anxiety. Subjects are instructed to report how they feel "right now, at this moment" (20 items) and "generally" (20 items) by ratings on a 4-point scale, ranging in the Spanish version from 0 to 3. This version's coefficients are for A-State between 0.90 and 0.93 and for A-Trait between 0.84 and 0.87 (Seisdedos, 2002). The Subjective Exercise Experiences Scale (SEES) was developed to indicate the positive and negative aspects of exercising (McAuley & Courneya, 1994). SEES is a 12-item inventory, set to a 7-point Likert scale ranging from 1 ("not at all") to 7 ("very much so"), which consists of three subscales. The Positive WellBeing and Psychological Distress subscales represent the positive and negative aspects of psychological health. The Perceived Fatigue subscale detects that the occurrence of any feeling state is accompanied by a feeling of physical exhaustion. The reported internal reliability of SEES' three subscales is 0.86, 0.85, and 0.88 respectively. The Spanish version showed high internal reliability scores of the three subscales analogous to the original version (De Gracia & Marcó, 1997). The Borg RPE Scale measures perceived exertion and effort in physical work and focuses on the subjective aspects of stimulus intensity and the sensory experience of exercise. "Perceived exertion is the feeling of how heavy and strenuous a physical task is" (Borg, 1998). RPE is 15-grade scale ranging from 6 ("no exertion at all") to 20 ("maximal exertion"). The reliability coefficients are at least .90. The Spanish version used was translated by the back translation method; psychometrical data are underway (Geisinger, 2003). As indirect dependent variables, perceived exertion, and attention-concentration process and its difficulty were rated only post-session.

In addition to these instruments, a general survey and self-elaborated scales were used. Attention-concentration processes and the difficulty paying attention to the relevant cues, while performing the physical exercise or meditation practice, might play an important role in the results. Assessing how intensively an individual is working on a particular activity is done by asking to estimate or comparatively judge the mental workload experience at a given moment (Reid & Nygren, 1988). A brief questionnaire assesses whether one has kept their mental effort in performing the activities' requirements and how difficult it was. The self-elaborated scales consist of six questions rated on a 6-point Likert-type scale ranging from 0-"not at all" to 5-"very much so." Statements were adapted from the Test of Attentional and Interpersonal Style (TAIS) (Nideffer, 1976). The general survey is a pre- and post-program participation list that includes questions related to individuals' general data (gender, age, nationality, etc.), work and daily chores characteristics, health status, medication taken, exercise and meditation habits, lifestyle and motivation for taking part in the programmed activities. The post- or program-completion survey asks three questions: a question on retrospective recall of pre-program expectations ("At the beginning of this study to what extent did you expect that the different activities will provide you a 'feeling better" sensation afterwards?"), a question on activities satisfaction, and a question on whether they become annoyed or "automatic" in responding to the repeated testing. Expectation, satisfaction, motivation, general feeling of health and wellbeing were also rated on a Likert-type scale from 0-"low" to 5-"high."

Procedure. Six experimental sessions were conducted during the 6-day WTP. An opening-study session on the 1st day, two study sessions on the 2nd day (on Exercise and Zen), two study sessions on the 5th day (on Exercise and Zen) and a closing-study session on the 6th day. To explain the purpose of this study, an orientation-screening session was conducted at the opening-study session; the research was introduced during 30 minutes. The participants were informed about requirements and exclusion factors. These are among others: (severe) depression, serious or recent disorder affecting bones, ligaments, or muscles; if individuals had been advised by a physician to not undertake relaxation-meditation activities or moderate physical activity (as walking in a comfortable pace), they were excluded too. A requirement was not to take any alcoholic beverages or non-prescription drugs that might alter their state of consciousness. The researcher asked and answered the participants if they have any question related to the study. Participants read and signed an informed consent, filled in the pre-program survey, and rated the A-Trait Scale.

During the 2nd and 5th day, the scheduled-activities of Exercise in the morning and Zen in the evening represented the treatment conditions of the experimental sessions. The first and third experimental sessions of Exercise took place outdoor (days' temperature 7.5° C / 6.5°C, humidity 70% / 75%) at a grass ground meadow beside the hotel during the morning (from 7.30 to 8.00). The second and fourth experimental sessions of Zen took place indoor (temperature 20°C, humidity 40%) in a 200 m2 hall in the basement of the hotel during the evening (from 19.30 to 20.00). Prior to experimental condition sessions participation (during the 2nd and 5th day), a checklist to control adequate participation was administered. The list included: intake of alcoholic beverages, caffeine, other drugs, or any recent or serious disorder affecting bones, ligaments or muscles, any life-event that affects mood or emotions during the past weeks). Then, participants were asked to fill in the A-State Scale and the SEES. Next, participants engaged in the treatment conditions. Finally, post-treatment condition assignments were distributed. Participants were asked to successively rate the prepared Six-Question Scale, RPE Scale, A-State Scale, and SEES.

At the closing-study-session on the 6th day (at 19.00), the post-program survey and the A-Trait Scale were distributed and completed by the participants.

Results

Statistically, the WTP as a whole yields beneficial results on trait anxiety. A-trait decreased significantly after completion of the 6-days ($t = 2.07$, df 29, $p < .05$). A-State decreased significantly ($t = 4.89$, df 29, $p < .001$) during the program. However, it did not decrease within the program (between the 2nd and 5th day measurements) (see Figure1).

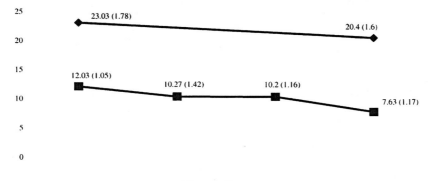

◆   **Trait Anxiety. 1ˢᵗ and 6ᵗʰ day measurements**

■   **State Anxiety. 2ⁿᵈ and 5ᵗʰ day measurements**

Figure 1. Trait and State Anxiety: measurements during the program — Means and (Standard Deviations)

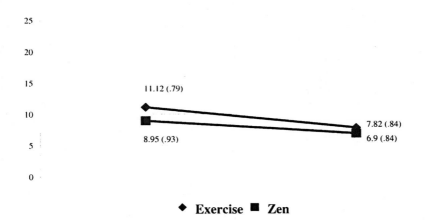

◆ **Exercise** ■ **Zen**

Figure 2. State Anxiety — pre-post sessions' measurements of Exercise and Zen, Means and (Standard Deviations)

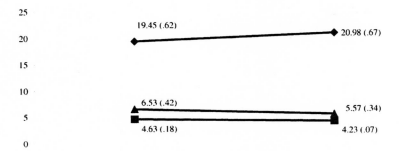

◆ **Positive WellBeing** ■ **Psychological Distress** ▲ **Perceived Fatigue**

Figure 3. SEES — pre-to-post sessions' measurements of Exercise, Means and (Standard Deviations)

Significant differences on A-State were found between the 1st and 3rd measurements (t = 2.19, df 29, p< .05), 2nd and 4th (t = 2.34, df 29, p< .05), and 3rd and 4th (t = 3.02, df 29, p< .01). Marginal statistical differences were found between the 1st and 2nd (t = 1.48, df: 29, n.s.) and the 2nd and 3rd (t = .052, df: 29, n.s.) measurements. Positive WellBeing was increased irregularly through the program. Significant WellBeing differences were found between pre-participation measurements on treatment conditions of first Exercise session (2nd day) and second Zen session (5th day) (t = 2.15, df 29, p< .05). No significant differences were found between the in-between measurements of WellBeing.

Single bouts of Exercise and Zen sessions were found to be effective. Zen and Exercise sessions were both effective in reducing A-State. Figure 2 shows pre-to-post A-State decrements of the two sessions' means of both Exercise and Zen. Exercise sessions yielded positive psychological results: A-State decreased (t = 5.60, df 59, p< .001), Positive WellBeing increased (t = 4.29, df 59, p< .001), while Psychological Distress (t = 2.65, df 59, p< .01) and Perceived Fatigue (t = 2.44, df 59, p< .05) decreased as well. These results of SEES' mean scores on pre-to-post measurements of the two Exercise sessions are shown in Figure 3.

The Zen sessions yielded significant differences pre-to-post intervention. A-State was decreased (t = 4.46, df 59, p< .001), Positive WellBeing improved (t = 2.74, df 59, p< .01), and Psychological Distress decreased (t = 2.32, df 59, p< .05). However, Perceived Fatigue only showed a marginal difference (t = 0.71, df: 59, n.s.). Figure 4 shows SEES' pre-to-post mean scores of the two Zen sessions (see Figure 4).

During the Zen and Exercise sessions, factors assumed to influence the results were considered as indirect dependent variables and were taken into account. To which extent participants focus on the activities' requirements (Cognitive Intensity: CI), how difficult it was to focus attention on the requirements during the sessions (Cognitive Difficulty: CD), and how much they felt physical exertion (PE) were measured only after participation. The Exercise sessions means are for CI: 9.12 (SD 3.11), for CD: 11.00 (SD 3.18), and for PE: 9.87 (SD 2). The Zen sessions means are for CI: 8.80 (SD 2.76), for CD 8.42 (SD 2.39), and for PE: 9.93 (SD 2.64). Regression analysis showed that these factors did not affect the sessions' outcomes.

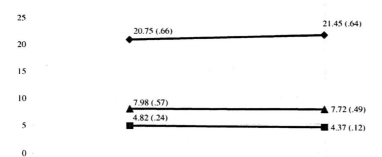

◆ **Positive WellBeing** ■ **Psychological Distress** ▲ **Perceived Fatigue**

Figure 4. SEES — pre-to-post sessions' measurements of Zen, Means and (Standard Deviations)

WTP participants' motives and their pre-sessions' motivational levels were rated on a scale from 0-"low" to 5-"high." The practice of Zen (M 4.57, SD 0.69) was the first motivational element to engage in the program followed by the environmental and socio-cultural elements of the tourist destination (M 3.25, SD 0.90). The motivation levels prior to each of the four treatment sessions were generally rated as quite high and as follows, 1st session: M 4.17 (SD 0.87), 2nd session M 4.20 (SD 0.96), 3rd session M 3.97 (SD 1.10) and 4th session M 4.37 (SD 0.93). General feeling of health and wellbeing, expectations, and satisfaction were also rated on a 6-point scale. Participants rated their health status as: M 3.64 (SD 0.80) and their general feeling of wellbeing as: M 3.70 (SD 0.95) at the beginning of the program. At the completion of the program, they were asked in retrospect to which extent they expected (before participation) that the different activities would provide them a "feeling better" sensation as an effect of their participation. The results were as follows, sport activities: M 3.45 (SD 1.38), relaxation/meditation activities: M 3.66 (SD 1.54), visit of environmental and socio-cultural resources M 3.79 (SD 1.45), and staying in the hotel: M 3.17 (SD 1.67). No correlation (rs -.089) existed between the level of expectations and the extent of benefits on the A-Trait Scale. The satisfaction level of the WTP as a whole was rated high (4.79, SD .41). Four participants reported (14%) having responded automatically

Discussion

The levels found on baseline measurements of participants' trait anxiety were high prior to the WTP. The decrement of trait anxiety after the completion of the WTP could be attributed to the specific characteristics of the 6 days. Caution is due before concluding that the effectiveness of this program on trait anxiety was solely caused by the Exercise and Zen sessions. Its program's other components, especially the hiking tours and workshops on health behavior, psychology, and philosophy could also have added to the beneficial change in trait anxiety. Less probable, but still possible, is that some optimized non-specific features (like social desirability, staying in a hotel, its natural and social environment) have contributed to the decrease in trait anxiety. It is unclear to exactly which extent WTP's situational context within a holiday period modulated the beneficial outcome. On the bottom line however, considering the fact that on top of the holidays significant differences were found on a relatively stable trait, the inference is warranted that the specific interventions for which the participants came and paid for have made the difference in this motivated group of responders. Previous studies suggest that significant results on trait anxiety scores can only be attained if a program would last at least 9 weeks on an ambulatory basis (9 sessions). This study's findings demonstrate that a succinct 6-day WTP (15 sessions) is able to reap an equivalent result in trait anxiety. However, its sample size, design, and exploratory-nature permit limited generalizability of the results.

Because it was rather convincingly reported in previous studies that combination of components and order of activities within a program do not lead to significant differences in outcome, this study did not scrutinized these as independent variables. A point of discussion, however, is that the Exercise component contained aspects of meditation as well, although from a different tradition. Tai Chi is a form of Taoist meditation in action as opposed to "just sitting in Zen. Both Tai Chi and Zen are inner paths and it is worth mentioning that Zen originated in China and is in fact an amalgamation of Buddhist and Taoist practices (the latter aims at energizing by increasing Chi or vital energy). Zen always had Taoist tenets incorporated from its inception. The present study suggests that Tai Chi (a "behavioral" meditation) accrued a specific result on one's fatigue as compared to Zen (a "cognitive" meditation).

Unfortunately, 30 participants did not participate in some of the study sessions or did not fill in the measurements so were not included in the data analysis. A larger study population would have provided more external validity. Possible interferences in the study might relate to participants' background characteristics (motivation and expectation, health status, meditation experience, etc.) and to program participation (physical and mental effort invested in the interventions); however no correlation was found that linked this factor to the overall outcome. Motivation levels prior to the four intervention sessions were significantly high. However, this "necessary but insufficient" condition alone seems unlikely to account for the significant results. With regard to expectation and benefit, the present finding confirms that there is no correlation between expectation and benefits on the relatively stable level of A-Trait. Furthermore, the health domains and the general feelings of wellbeing in this sample seem to be discernable in three dimensions: physical, psycho-emotional, and social health. These can be bound together with spiritual health to the general feeling of wellbeing. This validates our understanding of humans as Bio-Psycho-Social/Spiritual beings.

How long the psychological benefits of the WTP last remains unknown. A follow up of the WTP's outcomes would have afforded us the opportunity to assess for how long the effects remain and to study the direct implications for holistic wellbeing in everyday life. The inclusion of a no-treatment control group might have provided much clearer empirical support. As the literature suggests that one's sense of wellbeing increases prior to holidays and non-specific factors were optimized in the present trial, it is necessary to further investigate the specific influences of situational context on WTP. Thus in future studies, it is necessary to compare programs that promote wellbeing in different settings as work-site, daily life leisure time, clinical context, or during a vacation period.

---

1. We thank the clients for their participation and the organization managers for their support. Special thanks are due to the Zen Master Celso Navarro. We are also grateful to the committee of the Prof. Yutaka Haruki Award 2005 to award this study. This field research is a part of the Master's degree requirements under the guidance of Prof. Dr. Yosuke Sakairi (University of Tsukuba, Japan).

19

Long-term Benefits Of Spiritual And Therapeutic Strategies

Jane Henry

This chapter outlines some key results from a series of studies aimed at determining strategies perceived to be effective in engendering long-term improvement in wellbeing by experiments from a non-clinical population. The information was gathered in a series of workshops and by questionnaire from adult psychologists, managers, and educators. The findings show a surprisingly high proportion favored strategies based around quieting the mind, more reminiscent of "spiritual" approaches to development such as meditation and mindfulness than the more usual forms of talking therapy and counseling. Other approaches cited by participants include social support, physical involvement, and discussion. The chapter argues that though caring professionals tend to place far more emphasis on talking therapy as a route to the resolution of life's difficulties, a significant proportion of the population, including those naive to spiritual discourse, appear to have found approaches centered around quietening the mind more effective.

When younger I used to ask practitioners from different professions what they would advocate for depression. Therapists normally advocated some form of talking therapy, but Buddhists were more likely to say something like wait for it to pass or try keeping your eyes above the horizon. Their contrasting responses enhanced my interest in the effectiveness of different strategies for different people.

Most of the other research chapters in this book concern investigations of particular Buddhist practices, especially mindfulness. This chapter takes a rather different tack and concerns a series of inductive investigations, which deal with the topic from the other way round: aiming to see which approaches and practices a non-clinical population of adults have found efficacious in changing themselves or their attitudes to themselves in a direction they find helpful and improving their sense of personal wellbeing. Only a small part of the population ever receive professional counsel to help deal with personal problems, so most people have to find their own way to solve issues. This applies to both the worried well, who need ways of dealing with the vicissitudes of life, and the majority of people with clinical symptoms. One UK study found that less than a fifth of those with clinical symptoms reported these to the doctor (Hannay, 1979). The popularity of TV shows such as Dr Phil and Oprah and the size of the mind/body section in your local bookstore attests to the wide interest in ways of developing the self.

Many caring professionals whether clinical psychologists, social workers, psychotherapists, counselors, coaches, or teachers engaged in personal, social, and health education tend to adopt goal oriented cognitive-behavioral type approaches to development. These encourage clients to become more self-aware, set goals, and break down actions into achievable steps, essentially to control, cope, or cure the problem often by focusing first on what is wrong. Many encourage clients to challenge what they see as faulty thinking, and undertake homework, often some form of journaling. Parallels have been noted between certain cognitive-behavioral and Buddhist approaches to development (e.g. Crook & Fontana, 1990). In addition, an increasing number of therapists are including some form of mindfulness alongside a cognitive approach to therapy (Williams & Duggan, this volume; Teasdale, Segal, & Williams, 1995). In contrast, many self-help approaches seem to place considerably less emphasis on understanding the problem and working out a rational plan of how to get to a desired end and rather invest more time on less cognitive approaches, such as visualizing a desired end, concentrating on more positive aspects of life, for example through affirmations, and sometimes attending to the body, or approaching the mind through the body. Buddhist practices, along with those in many other spiritual traditions, have tended to emphasize the importance of quietening the mind, and detaching from ego and emotions to perceive experiences of self in a more encompassing, accepting, and compassionate perspective.

Many of the participants in my studies seem to favor strategies that tend to have more in common with the emphasis found in Buddhist practice and self-help than that found in mainstream approaches to psychotherapy.

Studies

The studies described here aim to find out what strategies adults found helpful in improving their wellbeing over the long-term. Fourteen studies have been carried out over the last ten years. The sample size of these studies varied from 4 to 36, totaling over 300 participants mostly aged 18 to 50; about two-fifths female, around three-fifths were from the UK, about a third from Continental Europe, and a tenth from elsewhere in the world. The participants were mainly managers, educators, and psychologist who were attending courses or conferences that gave the author the opportunity to conduct this research. In the course of the studies the participants were asked a series of questions about their personal development, including what they would like to change about themselves, what they had tried to help change or improve themselves, which of these strategies and practices they had found produced lasting benefit over the long-term (i.e. 5 to 10 years), and which failed to help. In most cases questionnaires and discussion were used to glean this information. The questionnaire was filled in privately before any group discussion.

Nearly all the samples report positive changes of one kind or another. The things that this normal population wanted to change in themselves varied but often concerned a desire to be more in control of themselves and know more about others, for example to be more confident, to accept themselves, be more aware of others, less bothered about things, less irritable, more responsible, and on time more often. Some of these qualities tend to improve over time as a consequence of experience and maturation, for example many people become more confident, and more balanced as they get older. However, for others these are clearly ongoing problems whether due to temperament, socialization, lack of understanding, unhelpful habits of thought and/or other factors. There were also some sex differences, for example women are more likely to report becoming more assertive over time.

There appears to be a fairly strong relationship between certain aspects of personality the participants wanted changed and their personality type. The tender- minded, those with a strong Feeling preference on the Myers-Briggs Type Indicator (MBTI, a high Agreeableness score on the Big Five; see Sugiura in this volume) appeared more troubled by negative emotions and more likely to be overwhelmed by feelings. They seemed to benefit from dissociation strategies as a way of dealing with engulfing feelings. The more tough-minded — those with Thinking preference on the MBTI (low Agreeable score on the Big Five) and those with an angry temperament — often seemed to have problems stemming from not giving others enough attention Many of these people felt they had benefited from strategies that got them to listen to others' views.

Effective Strategies

Over the course of these studies, many strategies have been volunteered as effective means of changing unwanted behaviors in a more desirable direction or developing behaviors and attitudes seen as more desirable. They include a wider range of strategies than would normally be considered by personal and career development professionals. For example, an eastern orthodox female explained to how she was fundamentally changed for the better through the practice of gilding, a process where gold leaf is carefully applied to detailed work. Gilding is apparently commended by the eastern-orthodox church as a spiritual practice. It is a practice that entails absorption in the present and concentration on the action of gilding, which leaves little time for negative rumination.

The interesting outcome of these studies in the context of this book is that so far quietening the mind is the most common activity to be judged as helpful in achieving long-term improvement in the participants' own personal development. The form that the quietening the mind takes varies; for many people it is formal meditation, mindfulness, or contemplation. For others (many without the benefit of a spiritual discourse to guide them), it takes other forms, such as learning to listen to their intuition, for example going to bed and expecting a clearer way forward to come to them in the morning or not bothering to analyze a problem but to focus instead on following their bliss as Joseph Campbell puts it. For others, it is more a question of relaxing; in some cases this included fishing. Angling is the most popular sport in the UK though anglers catch fish relatively rarely. However, they generally stay still and silent for a number of hours while fishing; it is an activity that encourages a quiet absorption in the present. Other quietening strategies reported centre round self-acceptance, for example being kind and gentle with yourself, caring less about what others think, forgetting yourself and letting go.

One third of participants volunteered some form of quieting the mind as helpful to their endeavors to transform themselves. Of course this is not a random sample, so the percentage may not be typical. But equally the conferences and courses the participants were attending were not focused on spirituality and the majority of subjects were naive to spiritual discourse; so, the author was surprised by the high proportion of people citing a quietening the mind strategy. The next two most popular strategies also eschew cognitive analysis of the issue.

Many participants argued that physical involvement has helped them deal with mental problems. This physical involvement can be walking, exercise, dancing, running, some form of yoga, bodywork, e.g. aromatherapy, bio-energetics, or being outside in nature. Aerobic activity such as running tends to increase endorphins, which is known to enhance mood. Being outside or involved in some kind of physical activity may well absorb the body and mind sufficiently to avoid unhelpful preoccupying thoughts. Being outside can encourage people to direct attention out to what is around them rather than inside to the machinations of their own thoughts. As described by the participants, the benefits claimed for these various forms of physical activity is more than a case of dissociation helping to break a negative mood and leaving people freer to deal with troubling issues more rationally; rather the involvement in walking/dancing/being in nature is seen as helping make people happier in and of itself. Previously troubling issues seem to dissolve as people turn their attention to other things. Possibly taking up activities of this kind helps people lead a more balanced life. It probably also makes it easier for a non-conceptual form of knowing to surface, as many people claimed that running or being outside enabled them to see things in perspective and gave them clarity about what to do.

Others judged social support to have been critical in helping them change and seeing them through hard times. The support of a close friend or sympathetic other seems to be enough to make people feel reassured and cared for. This is not surprising given the extensive literature on the benefits of being socially embedded, for example in terms of elevated happiness ratings and quicker recovery from illness, and longer life (Argyle 1987; Myers 2000.). Other interpersonal strategies the participants cited as beneficial include the familiar talking about the problem, for example in therapy, self-help groups, talking to others with similar issues or different perspectives, and reframing the problem. The ways individuals found it helpful to express feelings were very variable, for some this involved music, art or poetry, for others it was more about being concrete about feelings (i.e. recognizing specific feelings explicitly). Some, perhaps especially those inclined to negative rumination found it helpful to make a point of remembering when they had done things well or being happy and a few others found affirming a positive future was helpful.

Developing a sense of mastery was also significant for some. For example: managing something not previously under control, learning to say no, taking on less, and being present-centered in a practical sense. Also various forms of daring and assertiveness, essentially daring to do something that is scary, whether standing up to someone; for those scared of heights flying; for procrastinators and perfectionists, making a decision quickly, committing to something; for others delegating or being self-reliant. In these cases the participants were approaching and accepting rather than avoiding an issue that had been previously troubling.

Other participants found drugs, laughter, remembering their positive qualities, or expressing their feelings helpful. The drugs referred to were both prescription and non-prescription drugs. A few claimed to have been transformed for the better after taking Ecstasy. One person claimed a similarly beneficial change after they made a point of watching funny films and TV programs to make sure they had a good laugh often. A few claimed to have had instant improvement in wellbeing after interaction with a guru. Given that caring professional discourse has, until very recently, concentrated heavily on analytical routes to self-development, it is striking that so many of my participants value non-analytical routes to self-improvement such as quietening the mind, accepting and letting go, physical exercise, being in nature, laughing and social support.

Participants were also invited to volunteer strategies that they had tried but had not been helpful in helping them change personally. The strategies cited include exhortation, analysis of problems, talking about problems, planning, advice, insight, and reliving emotions. It is intriguing that these tactics are central to many caring professionals in dealing with problems their clients present. Judging by my participants a significant proportion of people do not find this approach helpful. It seems for some people turning their attention away from the problem is more productive. It is perhaps significant in this context that quite a large number of people fail to complete the course of therapy they are offered (Turvey, 1997). In post-traumatic counseling talking about the problem can be counter-productive for many people. Randomized controlled trails of psychological debriefing for victims of acute trauma show post-traumatic counseling makes the situation worse for a large proportion of recipients (Bisson, 1997). It seems that talking therapies are not for everyone.

Buddhist teaching pictures the discursive mind's ego attached ruminations as central to their existential problems. It seems many of my participants have found that further planning, analysis and rumination about their goals and needs has not been a fruitful route to ameliorating their problems or enhancing their sense of wellbeing. Various experiments support the idea that rumination is counterproductive for those who are already depressed. Lyubomirsky and Nolen-Hoeksema (1995) have shown that rumination makes people, who are already somewhat depressed or in sad mood, feel worse whereas a distraction task lifts their mood. Those mood of those not initially sad is unaffected by rumination (Lyubomirsk, Caldwell, & Nolen-Hoeksema, 1998). In some cases verbalization seems to interfere with complex unconscious reasoning. Schooler has demonstrated how verbalization can interfere with long-term decision satisfaction <www.gallup.hu/pps/henry_long.htm> For example, when asked to justify a decision between two possible courses of action either verbally or merely make the decision intuitively, more of those who followed their hunch were happier with the decision six months on.

Buddhism differs from mainstream cognitive approaches in placing less emphasis on analyzing the contents of consciousness and working towards goals and more emphasis on changing the way information is processed, redirecting attention, and refining the instrument of perception so there is a greater chance of seeing things from a more encompassing perspective. My participants' route to personal development often seems to have been absorption in something else other than in themselves, sitting quietly, dancing, looking outside at trees rather than focusing on conjectures inside their head. The effect of this absorption seems to have been to dissociate somewhat from emotions and the sense of self. Rather than reaching for a goal and a solution to achieve this and acting on it, a number of my participants seems closer to dissolving the problem in a non-cognitive way. The improvement often comes from an acceptance and reframing of an issue rather than a tactic for dealing with it. The effect seems to be that people put more attention on the world and rather less on themselves. This seems to have more in common with Buddhist ideas of surrendering, releasing expectations, detaching from emotion, accepting reality, and living in the present, than striving after goals and explicitly outlining the steps needed to achieve them in painstaking detail often found in the therapies of the West. This route also avoids the danger of fanning the flames of pointless rumination by giving it more attention.

Conclusion

My studies on what approaches ordinary people cite as helpful in changing things about themselves and improving their wellbeing over the long-term suggest that non-conceptual approaches such as quietening the mind, accepting the self, letting go, daring, receiving social support, being outside in nature, engaging in physical activity, and absorbing pleasurable tasks are perceived as helpful. The approaches many of my participants value echo certain Buddhist and other spiritual approaches to development in that they have the effect of redirecting attention to a wider perspective. In this normal population absorption for a period of time in something external seems often to be sufficient for troubling issues to dissolve. In contrast with traditional talk-based therapeutic approaches, the strategies my participants have valued feature quietening the mind and getting absorbed in activities unconnected with the problem more commonly, than analyzing conceptually what to do about issues. The former also seem to have the effect of decreasing rather than increasing rumination about ego and emotions. Nearly half of people who begin psychotherapy quit, dissatisfied, against the recommendation of their therapist (Harvard Mental Health Letter, August 2005). Judging by this high proportion of people who drop out of talking therapy, a greater emphasis on other strategies like quieting the mind, physical absorption, and social support may prove more productive and appealing for those not currently attracted to talking therapy.

Part III

Expanding Theoretical Horizons

Introduction

Duhkha is a central notion in the Dharma that has given rise to much scholarly theorizing. Mostly translated as suffering, its alleviation is the *raison d'être* of all Buddhist teaching. Literally, the term refers to a stuck or wobbling wheel that makes smooth turning impossible. The opposite of duhkha is *sukha* that denotes an internal condition of pervasive happiness, cultivated through seeing reality in its interdependent, non-singular/non-dual, nature. Consequently one might view duhkha as suffering due to erroneously attributing misery to external factors and thus adopting constructions that lead to delusional craving, clinging to I/me-mine-self possessions, and grasping personal identifications that stand in the way of realizing our "inter-being." Existential suffering, or the agony of human existence from which there is no escape, is another candidate for duhkha that appeals to many therapists. Another word that approaches this meaning but excludes the pathological flavor is "dis-ease" (the inability to achieve peace), that for Zennists gives birth to practices for bringing about the "man-at-ease." For many Buddhists, finding the path to ease depends on finding the answer to humanity's great puzzle: what is this life all about? In any case, a significant key to exiting the prisons of daily life, of finding liberation, is the eradication of primeval ignorance and imbibing instead Buddhist wisdom.

It is to the articulating and disseminating of wisdom that many of the sutras over the millennia have been devoted. And it is out of this concern that we include in the next section, contemporary contributions to the continuing conversation. As both Buddhists and social constructionists concur, we should not rely on theory for a picture or map of what is true, real, or right. Yet, there are significant functions for theoretical deliberation save those of truth telling. It is largely through dialogue that we are able to traverse the boundaries of traditional understanding and co-construct new meaning and new forms of action. In the dialogic process discursive regimes begin to crumble and new formulations emerge. These new formulations may carry with them traces of multiple traditions, thus bringing humankind into increasingly viable coordination. With effective dialogue we approach inter-being.

It is in this spirit that we include in Part III eight theoretical contributions to the expansion of horizons in theoretical understanding. In the first offering, Gergen and Hosking (Chapter 20) elaborate on the relationship between the Buddhist tradition and contemporary theorizing in social construction. This affinity has been central to the formulation of the present work, and will be especially illuminating for readers whose primary background is in Buddhist or cognitive therapeutics. In Chapter 21, Belinda Khong focuses on the relationship between Buddhist psychology and cognitive-behavior therapy. She points out important ways in which they augment each other, and in which the relationship can be strengthened. In the following chapter Henk Barendregt gives a careful reading of the Abhidhamma texts from the Theravada tradition, and applies their concepts to contemporary concepts of neurosis and psychosis. Through this lens he also addresses the implications of mindfulness for psychotherapy. In Chapter 23, Rika Kawano and Masao Suzuki focus more fully on the contemporary implications of the Eight Sacred Paths. As they see it, an invigoration of the paths and their implications of unconditional acceptance of the present could be useful in anger management in Japanese youth. Then, in Chapter 24, Mark Williams and Danielle Duggan examine the theoretical underpinnings of their practice of mindfulness-based cognitive therapy. Their chapter places special importance on the Buddhist emphasis on embodying cognition.

The relationship of social construction to Buddhist thought is again taken up by Genji Sugamura and Scott Warren in Chapter 25. In this case they also treat constructivist psychology, and drawing from certain convergences among the three orientations, lay out the rationale for a dissolution oriented approach to psychotherapy. Their concept of dissolution is resonant with Michael DelMonte's concept of adaptive de-construction, the focus of Chapter 26. They also take up the important issue of whether letting go of attachments may sometimes increase social isolation. In the final offering, Paul van der Velde takes up the problem of viewing Buddhist teaching as dogma versus non-dogma, or pure as opposed to culture-bound. This chapter is important to the development of a New Buddhist Psychology, in its support of a continuous modification of Buddhist teachings and their attendant forms of practice. This chapter also serves as an excellent précis to the integrative work of Maurits Kwee and Marja Taams that follows in Part IV.

20

If You Meet Social Construction Along The Road: A Dialogue With Buddhism

Kenneth Gergen & Dian Marie Hosking

The origins of Buddhist teachings are over 2,500 years old; social constructionist thought comes into intelligibility only within the recent decades. Buddhist teachings were grounded within an ancient cultural milieu, often identified as traditional; social construction gains impetus in a rapidly globalizing, or postmodern world in which we become increasingly conscious of multiple representations of the real, the rational and the good. And yet, we find remarkable affinities in major assumptions and implications. We explore, in particular, both intersections and tensions in the accounts of suspended or contingent realities, a constructed or non-substantial self, and an ultimate but unutterable condition of relatedness. Further, both orientations are deeply concerned with fostering practices that may contribute not only to individual but to societal and global well-being. In the end, it is not the particular array of words or theoretical formulations that are important, but the forms of practice that they encourage or invite.

The two of us have been long and deeply immersed in social constructionist inquiry. At the same time, we have both been absorbed — both theoretically and personally — in the Buddhist tradition. Neither of these investments were derived from each other. They emerged in quite different contexts. However, their co-existence was scarcely fraught with conflict; on the contrary they seemed to play in scarcely conscious but harmonious parallel. The time has now arrived for meeting along the road, for exploring the possibility of kinship. Through this exploration we hope to locate the basis for this sense of harmony. We anticipate that its dimensions will be conceptual, practical, and personal. It is our hope that we shall not only locate mutually supportive relationships, but scaffolding for new developments, and an appreciation for neighboring endeavors in research and therapy.

As the reader will note, we write here of anticipation and hopes, of insights not yet formed. And this is indeed the case. We do not begin here with answers already in place, but with questions and curiosity. For this exploration we also choose the medium of the dialogue. In fact, this choice serves as the first signal of affinity between these traditions. Within the constructionist domain dialogue plays a pivotal role as the progenitor of all meaning. And, within the Buddhist tradition it is within dialogue with the wise that the neophyte achieves illumination. Meaning and illumination walk hand in hand. It is in this spirit that our conversation begins:

Encountering Social Construction

Ken: Especially for the readers of this book, I think it would be useful to begin with a brief account of social constructionist deliberations. This will prepare the way for exploring connections with Buddhist traditions. There are many variants of the constructionist story but one that I have tried to articulate in previous writings (Gergen, 1994, 1999) involves a particular orientation to knowledge. This orientation assumes that all we take to exist, to be real, to be the subject of scientific or spiritual consciousness is constructed in relations with others. This contrasts with the more usual assumption that accounts of the world are reality driven. In this sense constructionism stands in striking contrast to several hundred years of Western thought that views knowledge as built up from the individual's observations and rational thought. On this traditional account, careful observation can inform the individual of "what there is," and one's thoughts about the world can be tested against reality. In this way we move progressively toward objective truth. For constructionists, however, whatever there is becomes meaningful to us primarily as a result of our relationships with others. Not only will different communities of scientists each have their own particular language of description and explanation, but so will various religions, professions, ethnic traditions, and so on. The constructions of the world will be tied closely to the shared values of these groups, whether it be in sending a rocket to the moon, spiritual illumination, relieving mental anguish, or making chicken soup. Any observational test of a proposition must rely on a set of communal agreements about what exists and how it is manifest. There are no foundations for such agreements. Thus, all empirical truth is communally based.

Dian Marie: Indeed there is considerable diversity within what we could broadly refer to as the dialogues on social construction. My own orientation emerged from my involvement in social psychology in general, social processes in particular, and a concern for what social psychology could offer to studies of organizational life. This meant exploring what is distinctive about a social-psychological view of personhood, drawing upon approaches such as symbolic interactionism and phenomenology and exploring the "how" of reality construction processes as ontology rather than knowledge.

Ken: Both of us have found that once you have entered the dialogues on constructionism, it is difficult to return to the traditional view of knowledge as a mirror of reality. We are indeed speaking of communally constructed ontologies. For me, the focus is on the ways in which realities and values are created within relationships. This focus has fostered two dramatic revelations. First, we recognize that *all claims to knowledge are culturally and historically situated*. In spite of the claims of many communities to universal and trans-historical Truth, there is no means of justifying such claims save through a community's limited premises. This recognition invites critique and humility — essential both to prevent totalitarian expansion and to soften the boundaries of separation and difference. The second important realization is that we are *free to create together* new realities and related ways of life. We need not be bound by any conception, tradition, or vaunted claim that degrades or destroys the processes by which meanings come into being. In effect, we have an enormous canvas available for painting new futures.

Dian Marie: I think it might be a good idea to sound a cautionary note at this point. As we both have seen, social constructionism can easily be misunderstood as some liberal, individualistic and naïve story that we are free to create anything we like, in other words "anything goes." Indeed, social constructionist lines of argument are often misunderstood because people relate to them on the basis outworn assumptions. I have found that it can be useful to invite people to explore the potentials of social constructionism by assuming that they *don't know* what "it" is. So, for example, the critique that "anything goes" suggests that social constructionism has foolishly rejected "external reality" as a real-world source of constraints. But, in my view, the social constructionist orientation "emphasizes the historical-cultural rather than the natural-scientific" (Hosking, 2005). This means a focus on processes of social construction and the ways these simultaneously resource and constrain action within whatever it is we are calling reality. Central to these processes of social construction is language — now viewed as a vehicle for reality construction rather than reality mapping.

Ken: It is true that language has played a central role in most constructionist scholarship to date. In part this is because much of what we take to be knowledge is constituted in language. We use lectures and assign books to "impart knowledge"; we view our libraries as repositories of knowledge, and the endpoint of most of scholarly and scientific research is contained in publications. At the same time, the unquestioned trust of western scholars and scientists in the capacity of language to mirror or map the world has left the knowledge making disciplines in a very vulnerable position. As philosophers (see for example, Quine, 1960), linguists (see for example, Saussure, 1983), and sociologists (see for example, Garfinkel, 1967), have shown, whatever relationship our words have to the world depends on highly malleable social conventions. The world does not dictate a particular account of its nature. Which is to say, the world makes no ultimate demands on what we take to be true. In this context, constructionists also draw heavily from Wittgenstein's *Philosophical Investigations*. In his account of the language game, Wittgenstein generates a replacement for the traditional mapping and mirror metaphors of language. Wittgenstein compellingly develops a view of language as a pragmatic medium through which we do things with each other. In effect, language becomes a relational medium.

It is largely for these reasons that many constructionist scholars focus on the way in which linguistic devices such as metaphor and narrative function in our constructions of reality. For example, many cognitive psychologists rely on the metaphor of the brain as a computer (see for example, Leary,1990). Once a mechanistic metaphor like the computer is in place it will largely determine what we can say about the nature of thought (e.g. the "truth about the mind"). Similarly, many constructionists focus on narrative constructions of reality (see for example, Sarbin, 1984, M. Gergen, 2001). Narrative structure is essentially viewed as a property of language, and once we begin to describe the world in narrative or story form, it is the demands made by traditions of narration that will determine what we take to be true. Thus, for example, the constructionist will question the "truth of evolutionary theory," or the capacity of historians to give a true account of history. Rather, they will be drawn to the uses made of these accounts in cultural life.

Dian Marie: Perhaps this is a good point to note that the constructionist view of language can be narrow or broad. Wittgenstein can again be helpful here — in his expansion from talk of "language games" to talking about "forms of life." This in turn connects with the constructionist move that treats language as a form of communicative action. In this sense, "language" can also be taken to include other formal systems such as music, mathematics and statistics (e.g., Iverson, 2003). In addition, non-verbal actions, and co-ordinations of bodies, things, and events may also be included as ways of "doing" particular "forms of life" (see e.g., Hodge & Kress, 1988; Latour, 1987).

This broadening in the conception of language also sensitizes us to historical-cultural shifts in the ways cultures communicate. Particularly important in this regard is the shifting dominance of vision relative to audition and how this relates to constructions of nature, what it is to be a person, constructions of sacred and secular, knowledge, and so on (e.g., Berman, 1983, 1990). So, for example, in aural/oral cultures sound dominates and word and sound are strongly related. Language is a matter of vocalization — a here and now happening — a live event and the past is present in what people say and do i.e., in live action. In contrast, cultures of the alphabet and print communicate more by visual means. In so doing they give a more permanent sense of existence to words, freeze words in space and time, and make it possible to "look up" the past. These cultural shifts increasingly link language with visual perception and with dead words and ideas. Thinking becomes a silent mind operation — stripped from its connection with communication in live action. So, whilst constructionism centers on language, it is clear that this can mean a lot more than just spoken and written forms of action.

Suspending Realities

Ken: For me, it is this emphasis on the constructed world that forms an initial bridge to much Buddhist thought. I recall my initial excitement with Buddhist ideas when I encountered its deep suspicion of the taken for granted concepts through which we understood the realities of the world and self. The work of Suzuki (1973) and Watts (1957) was most inspirational to me, and in significant ways these ideas launched me toward a constructionist conception of psychology (Gergen, 1983). In fact, a 12th century koan of Tai-hui could serve as a constructionist centerpiece: "If you call this a stick, you affirm; if you call it not a stick, you negate. Beyond affirmation and negation what would you call it?"

Dian Marie: This suspicion of the conventional forms of understanding "the real" also furnishes one of the chief grounds for meditation practices. One might say that such practices help us to pay attention to our discursive mind and the ways it gets tricked into believing in the representation of things. Studying Buddhist texts is said to be not so much a matter of "acquiring new information" but more a matter of learning a view that helps us to attend to what we are doing (Jamgon Mipham 2000, p. 14). In effect meditation practices help us to avoid being captured by the taken for granted, by thoughts, concepts and conditionality.

Ken: There is a parallel theme in social constructionism. For the constructionist there are two major moments in practical work, the first being *deconstructive* and the second *reconstructive*. It is the deconstructive turn that is most similar in its effects to meditation. That is, one comes to break the spell of language as a map or picture of the real, and to understand it as situated culturally and historically. One comes to see the possibility that one's understandings are not demanded by "what there is," but are means of constructing it for some human purpose. Such realization may often come by learning that there are multiple ways to construct the existing state of affairs, that one's characterizations of the real are dominated by traditional literary forms (e.g. narrative structure, metaphor), or that one's understanding of the real and the good are specific to a particular tradition. Most of these realizations are accomplished in language and not meditative action, but the immediate ends are similar. In a broad sense one might view the result as *liberation* in both cases.

Yet, for many constructionists the liberatory move is insufficient. In particular, for practitioners the primary goal is reconstructive. That is, they seek to locate or co-create alternative realities more serviceable within the life of the person in his or her relationships. Narrative therapy is a good example here (see for example, Angus and McLeod, 2004). As narrative therapists generally agree, the goal of therapy is to re-story. Rather than living in misery resulting from understanding one's life as failure, for example, is it possible to work with the client and others in his or her life, to comprehend this same life as one of heroic survival? As the constructionist would understand it, one cannot step out of history and culture. All intelligible actions are lodged within a history of relationship. If all intelligibilities were abandoned, there would be a void. And this would not be the void of "no mind," for even the meditative state of Buddhism is what it is by virtue of the Buddhist tradition of intelligibility.

Dian Marie: Yes, but for many Buddhists there is a strong sense that we should somehow suspend stories and live in the real world. As Sakyong Mipham Rinpoche observed, "The point of meditation is to have a genuine experience... as close to reality as possible" (Jamgon Mipham 2000, p. 59). And the "absolute truth" of reality cannot be expressed in words. Perhaps this is one reason why novice practitioners are constantly storied as being socked on the nose by their master or given an absurd answer when they try to discover the truth about the Buddha outside themselves and in language.

Ken: Let us put aside the issue of whether one can experience reality for what it is, and focus on the more profound implication that both Buddhism and social construction share: in using language we are unable to "tell the truth" about either Buddha or social construction! For constructionists it is consciousness of the constructed character of constructionism itself. Because our words are not maps of the world, but born out of communal convention, there is no final or accurate or foundational account of the process of construction. And herein lies the choice of our title for this dialogue, The Buddhist saying asks us to avoid externalizing, solidifying and deifying the Buddha by "killing him" at the moment we think we have met him. In the same way constructionists warn against any final fixing of constructionism itself. There is a certain humility here that I find an attractive alternative to the attempt of so many theorists (along with religious teachers) to treat their accounts as final truths. Speaking of deconstructing the taken for granted, I think it would be useful to now illustrate some of these ideas by turning to the status of the self in social construction and Buddhism.

The Self as Construction

Dian Marie: To appreciate the Buddhist orientation to the Self, I think it would be useful to say something about the three major occasions on which the Buddha taught — usually referred to as the three turnings of the wheel of Dharma. In the first turning (The Hinayana teachings), the Buddha talked about the Four Noble Truths. The first truth is the truth of suffering which the Buddha said was part of the human condition. Second, is the truth of the origins of suffering — said to result from attempts to create and hold on to a solid and stable concept of Self, from seeing Self as a source of pleasure and from actions oriented towards making

Self bigger, better and more special relative to others. Third is the truth of the cessation of suffering i.e., the possibility of giving up the struggle "to be me." And fourth is the truth of The Path. Broadly speaking, this involves learning to let go of ego (the fixed and solid sense of self) and ego-centered constructions of reality with the help of practices such as meditation.

Ken: This echoes our previous conversation about the suspicion of language and the ability to remove oneself, either through meditation in the Buddhist case or by deconstructing and reconstructing in the constructionist orientation. If we think of therapy, it seems that all these practices are similar in their outcome. Here I begin to think more eclectically. What are all the available means at our disposal for problem dissolving and for opening ourselves to new futures?

Dian Marie: Let me elaborate on this issue of "dissolving" a little further from a Buddhist perspective. I think it is helpful here to have a look at the conceptual framework or "View" that is both central to the earlier Hinayana teachings, but also to the later Mahayana refinements. The View provides an all-important context for the methods (the Path) by which the practitioner can experience "cessation" (the 4th Noble Truth). Many aspects of The View, particularly the Mahayana version, seem to resonate with social constructionism. Key amongst these is how Buddhism breaks down the seeming solidity of what is conventionally experienced as a very solid body (person) and a solid and stable Self. To understand this we have to know something about the Abhidharma — the basic conceptual framework of Tibetan Buddhism. The central concept is *dharma*. This is conceptualized as the smallest unit of experience of which humans are capable. The concept refers to a momentary appearance that "is what it is" and has nothing "behind it." When consciousness, also storied as a dharma, connects with other dharmas the result is *an experience*. Dharmas are organized in a variety of different conceptual frameworks each of which helps our understanding of non-self. Most relevant to our present purposes is the framework of The Five Skandas.

The Five Skandas were introduced by the Buddha in response to people's questions about his teachings on non-self (Jamgon Mipham Rinpoche, 1999, p. 82). Apparently he received questions along the lines of "oh yeh, so what is this body and mind then, huh?" (rather like the stone kicker or table thumper out to refute the supposed claims of constructionist relativists!). So the Buddha answered by speaking of the 5 Skandas as different types or aggregates of *momentary experiences* that together make up our experience of our (apparently solid) Self. The Skandas can be summarized as follows. (1) Form "... refers to those momentary events that we experience as physical" (Ray, 2000, p. 373). It includes physical elements, sense organs and their corresponding sense objects. (2) Feeling refers to the more or less fleeting sensation of positive or negative affect or of indifference. (3) Perception refers to the categorization of something as unfamiliar or as a member of some known conceptual category. (4) Karmic formations refers to all the extra discursive fragments and narratives that we attach to the experiences of the first three skandas. And finally (5) consciousness (*vijnana* in this context) involves relating to the first four skandas in terms of how they affect "me." The key point of all this is that it is possible to explain experience without resort to the assumption of a solid, stable Self. In following The Path, practitioners find that when they examine their experience they cannot find a solid, permanent Self or "I." The Fruition then is that they can give up their struggle to sustain that which doesn't exist! For the Hinayana practitioner who seeks individual liberation this is "cessation" i.e., the fruition or realization of the 4th Noble Truth.

Ken: Social constructionists would fully support the notion of a non-foundational self, and the significance of being able to suspend this particular construction. Yet, there are interesting differences to consider, as well. You point out that the basic unit of the skandas is the momentary experience, and that the experiencing agent ultimately finds that one may engage in experiences without resort to a conception of the Self. The constructionist would fully concur in the notion of an artificial, or let us say non-foundational, sense of the self. However, to bring up an earlier point, the question of experience remains to be illuminated. The danger for the constructionist is that the concept of experience will ultimately reinstate the individual as a primary source or ontological foundation of being. Most constructionists would wish to avoid this conclusion. Rather, we might view the very activity of experience as ultimately an outcome or expression of fundamental relatedness. Could constructionists and Buddhist converge, then, on an understanding of experience as in itself relational?

The second issue has to do with whether the liberation achieved by deconstructing the self is a sufficient end in itself. As we recognized, many constructionists are critical of the ideology of the self-contained individual, and for many of the same reasons that Buddhists find this conception problematic. However, there is a common understanding among constructionists that to abandon a tradition of understanding is also to suppress traditions of living, to silence voices. This would be to eradicate forms of relationship. Thus, the process of deconstruction is considered non-lethal. That is, while we are liberated from the presumptions of the individualist tradition, we may continue on a contingent basis to live within its forms of life. We may, for example, wish to sustain the traditions of democracy, public education, and trial by jury for the time being, because these are more comfortable than the alternatives currently available.

I think these remarks will be clarified if we take up the central issue of relatedness.

The Primacy of the Relational

Dian Marie: Yes, both constructionism and Buddhism are invested in the periodic suspension or dissolving of the self. But in the same way that their approaches are lodged in different traditions so too are their approaches to relationship. I think the most important thing, however, is the resulting affinity. And, because these affinities are put in different terms both orientations stand to gain; we see new ways to understand and appreciate, and to expand our sensitivities.

Ken: We have found that for both constructionists and Buddhists the Self ceases to occupy the center stage of society. And in the constructionist case, it was proposed that all intelligibility, reason, standards of right and wrong, and the like, emerge from the process of relationship. In this sense, relationships are not the result of individuals coming together, but rather it is out of relationship that the very concept of the individual arises. Or, to put it another way, the individual, rational agent is a social construction.

Dian Marie: The way constructionists place the idea of a bounded self in brackets is similar to the distinction in Buddhist writings between conventional mind and the mind of a meditator. Conventional mind is said to assume that the world is composed of individual, bounded, and relatively stable entities, each possessing its own defining characteristics. This goes together with a *view of relationships* as either *inter*-personal or *intra*-personal. A related development is the view of knowledge as "in the head" and communicated in words.

The term *"Subject-Object"* (S-O) has been used to speak of this (conventional mind) construction of relations. Briefly, the S-O construction makes a dualist opposition between the rational and responsible agent (Subject) and Other who is acted upon in causal fashion. The Subject is storied as active in building their own individual knowledge (as a private possession) useful for achieving their own goals in the world. At least one of these goals is to avoid letting others gain power over one's actions (e.g. freedom), and by implication, to secure one's autonomy by ensuring that others are not free to act upon one's Self in any way they wish. Relationships are reduced to largely instrumental means for enhancing one's own well-being. One asks, "what about me?" and "what can Other do for me or against me?" The centering of Self leaves little space for asking "what about you" or for the appreciation of Other in ways that are untainted by one's own Self-oriented interests and constructions. This S-O construction of relations seems very much connected with our earlier (and necessarily) brief discussion of language and with the emergence of individualism in cultures increasingly dominated by vision.

Ken: I am glad you brought up the issue of instrumentalism. Whereas Hinayana Buddhism focuses on the shortcomings for the person when the self is "made real," constructionists and Mahayana Buddhism emphasize the societal repercussions when we construct ourselves as autonomous and self-contained individuals. Thus, to construct oneself as independent, generates a fundamental sense of distance between us; "care of self" becomes a primary goal in life; we begin to see a world of competition, of "all against all," in a Hobbesian sense. As Edward Sampson (1993) has called it, the West is dominated by an ideology of self-contained individualism.

Dian Marie: As I see it both social constructionism and Buddhism offer a radical re-storying of "conventional mind" and its view of relations. In this re-storying, relational processes become the constantly moving "construction site" in which Self, Other and relations are always in the making. The conventional view of stable and solid entities in S-O relations is replaced by a view of ongoing processes in which entities and relations are always becoming. For constructionists "thingness" and indeed no-thingness are a byproduct of language-based relational processes. Further, we could say that relational constructionism views Self and Other as a relational unity in ongoing construction in relational processes.

Ken: One of the ways I have tried to articulate this concept of relational unity takes as its metaphor the way meaning is created in language. Single words standing alone typically lack significance. The words, "tree," "river," or "grew" are virtually meaningless in themselves. They begin to come into meaning when they are supplemented by other words as in "the tree grew by the river." It is the same for our words and actions. Alone they are virtually meaningless. It is when others supplement them with other words and actions — affirmations, questions, elaborations, associations, and so on — that they begin to take shape as meaning this and not that. One may say that the voices in a conversation, like the moves of two tango dancers, are co-constituting. In this sense we see that we have a world of fundamental relatedness from which all meaning is derived. This is a world of ultimate fusion, as opposed to separation.

Dian Marie: Yes, another way to put it is that the Self is no longer viewed as necessarily fixed in Subject-Object relation, independent of Other. Instead, we see that the sense of a fixed, solid and closed Self is an achievement that requires ongoing maintenance through the active (re)construction of closure from Other and Otherness. But now of course it is clear that experience could be otherwise. In other words — and as Buddhism emphasizes — it is possible (and from certain points of view desirable) to construct relations in ways that are other than Subject-Object.

Ken: As I have tried to set this out in various lectures, we can view the person as the common intersection among a multiplicity of relations. That is, I carry with me residues of an enormous array of relationships. Every word I write, every action in which I engage, is issuing from this array of relations. It is not that I am produced or determined by these relations. One cannot separate out the participants from relationship, so there is nothing extraneous to me that has determined or caused my potentials in the moment. There is a quote in Herrigel's early book, *Zen in the Art of Archery*, that speaks to me in this case. The author has learned the art of archery from a Zen master. At the close of the book, the teacher says to him, "You have now reached a stage where teacher and pupil are no longer two persons, but one. You can separate from me at any time you wish. Even if the broad seas lie between us, I shall always be with you when you practice what you have learned." In effect, we are at this moment, cemented to all those with whom we have related in the past. And the moment we communicate we bring together worlds of relationship, creating yet a new form that will follow us into the future.

Dian Marie: I think this is the point to explore relations with another important framework in Buddhism, namely The Twelve Nidanas. Like the Five Skandas, it addresses issues that arise when the solidity and permanence of Self is questioned. But this framework provides a way of talking about what constructionists refer to as relational processes. So, rather than experiencing a separately existing Self, the practiced meditator will experience a stream of momentary and constantly changing dharmas (now viewed as Nidanas rather than Skandas). The particular contribution of this framework is that it provides a way of talking about relations between past, present and future and what goes from lifetime to lifetime — given that there is no Self. In this aspect, it provides a way of storying ongoing processes as they construct seemingly solid "things" — or not.

In the Hinayana tradition the Nidanas are links in a chain of "conditioned co-production." But there is an important shift in the (later) Mahayana view of the Nidanas and their relations. This change comes in Nagarjuna's reinterpretation of the Hinayana view of "conditioned co-production." Nagarjuna critiqued the interpretation of the 12 Nidanas in the Abhidarma, asserting that it failed to appreciate their "critical *relational* dimension" (Ray, 2000, p. 395, emphasis added). So the more highly developed relational interpretation emphasizes that every Nidana (indeed, every dharma) has existence and meaning in relation to the web of relationships in which it appears, viewed as a totality that could never be put into words. The re-interpretation of conditioned co-production emphasizes simultaneity and the mutual co-construction of interrelated dharmas. *All dharmas* now are viewed as empty of self-nature — not just the Self — but also Other.

Ken: It is this metaphor of the web of relations that I find most congenial with constructionism. As I pointed out earlier, from a constructionist perspective the person is never an independent being. Not even the body is independent of all else. Most importantly, the person is inherently the manifestation of an infinitely extended process of relationship. In this sense, in my constructionist orientation I am drawn to the early metaphor of Indra's net, a net that stretches infinitely in all directions, and at every node we find a jewel that reflects the surface of all other jewels in the net. I also like one of Shunryo Suzuki's (1973) contributions, to the effect, "When you become Zen... you have become one with our surroundings." As I understand it this is the Tibetan view of *dependent origination* in which *all things* come into being only by virtue of other things, with no starting or ending point. I have also been quite taken with Thich Nhat Hanh's (1999) articulation of *interbeing*, which essentially means that "everything is in everything else." Constructionist ideas indeed grow richer through these insights. As I mentioned earlier most constructionist work centers on human relations alone. Buddhism invites an expansion of the notion of relation to include all that there is. Meaning emerges from the matrix of all, and "the all" cannot be captured by any particular assemblage of words to which it has given birth.

Dian Marie: We seem to have reached the domain of the unspeakable. Perhaps this is a good point to turn from words to various life practices invited by social constructionism and Buddhism. Will you start by saying something about social constructionism, Ken, and then I will say something about meditation. And if we each continue to articulate these two voices then we can both finish by saying something of how each shifts to talk of society and the kind of societal practices that might break out of "self contained individualism and its ethics of individual freedom and success.

Life Practices

Ken: One of the affinities between constructionist and Buddhist orientations that I especially appreciate is their mutual concern with everyday practices. For both orientations there is a substantial theoretical foundation. Each draws from a rich theoretical tradition, and in the Buddhist case the literature is enormous and the tradition longstanding. However, unlike most world views, neither is content to issue wisdom unattached to specific forms of action. Rather, both are ultimately concerned with how we live our lives from day to day. In constructionism this concern with action follows congenially from the theory itself. As we have discussed, for constructionists language does not function as a mirror or map of the world, but is itself *action within relationship*. The function of theory, then, is not to tell us how the world really is, so that we may know how to act. Rather, by engaging in theory we are already participating in a relationship of a certain kind. The question, then, becomes one of the limits and potentials of differing forms of relationship.

Very much like the Mahayana Buddhist tradition, for many constructionists there is profound concern with enhancing the human condition — from issues of local suffering to those of societal and even global concern. For constructionists there are certain domains in which there has been a flowering of practices. I have already mentioned some of the work taking place in the therapeutic community. However, there are also notable developments in organizational change practices, conflict reduction, education, mediation, and research methodology. I should point out that in most of these cases the emphasis is placed on collaboration among people as opposed to changes within the single individual.

Dian Marie: It is true that most practices in the Buddhist tradition are focused on the individual practitioner. However, as we saw in our discussion of ultimate relatedness, "the individual" is not the "self-contained" entity of western individualism. Furthermore, Mahayana Buddhism extends its interests well beyond the individual practitioner. Let's return to this issue later. First I think we need to explore meditation and related practices a little further since they are key to letting go of the overly solid and permanent sense of Self ("ego") and Self-related constructions (the fourth "noble truth"). Strictly speaking, we should be speaking more generally of The Path — which includes meditation. Further, we must be careful not to entify "meditation" as some-thing; as the practitioner continues to practice the distinction between meditation and "post meditation' becomes more and more blurred.

With these caveats in mind, and using the language of relational constructionism, we could say that meditation provides a practical methodology for dissolving the differentiation of self and other — by seeing both self and other as "empty" of independent existence. This implies that the ground of any and all "life practices" must come from the first hand experience of meditation and openness to Other, to relatedness, to multiplicity, simultaneity and ongoingness. In this context, meditation is *not* about learning to concentrate, *not* about connecting with some higher being or state, and *not* about trying to escape from some external world (Chogyam Trungpa, 1996, p. 60). Rather, it is for example, "concerned with trying to see what is here and now," including becoming aware of and developing an up-close familiarity with the patterns we continually re-create and of which we are a part. Meditation is a process of: softening and dissolving of Self; becoming more and more open to Buddha nature (we could say, basic goodness), and; feeling a growing compassion for (and desire to do something about) the suffering of others.

Ken: But I think that a common view of meditation (held by non-Buddhists) is that it is about stopping thinking — about "getting outside" of discursive mind so to speak.

Dian Marie: Yes. But, at least in the Tibetan Buddhist tradition with which I am familiar, the idea is *not* to suppress thought — but rather to see the mind as a mind stream of multiple and constantly changing moments of experience. The idea is *not* to try to change or to reject thoughts or to blame one's Self or other(s). Rather the idea is *not* to get involved — by applying concepts to label some thoughts as "positive" and others as "negative" — with the intention of grasping more of the former and rejecting the latter. "So… concepts are very good, like wonderful manure" (Chogyam Trungpa, 1996, p. 22). "The whole point is to cultivate the acceptance of everything, so one should not discriminate or become involved in any kind of struggle" (Chogyam Trungpa, 1996, p. 78). The practitioner learns to observe, accept and respect; *it is an appreciative orientation.*

Ken: This emphasis so much resembles one of the pivotal ideas in constructionism. In that context we talk a lot about the power of affirmation or appreciation in constructing worlds together. It is that moment in which your words bring forth an affirming embrace by another that you sense exciting potential. As you are quite aware, one of the most widely used constructionist practices, developed by our Taos Institute associate, David Cooperrider and his associates, is called Appreciative Inquiry (Cooperrider and Whitney, 1999; Barrett and Fry, 2005). This practice is often used to create organizational change or reduce conflict in organizations. It begins by having people speak in pairs to each other, telling stories about times in the organization that have given them joy or life. These stories are shared with others, until the point that the larger group can begin to locate major themes. The group then inquires into the implications of these positive themes for building the future of the organization. Plans are then developed with future meetings established to discuss progress. The future of the organization thus represents not the vision of a select few at the top, but by the bulk of its participants. It is an enormously inspirational practice, and is now used around the world.

Dian Marie: Along these lines Chogyam Trungpa Rinpoche described meditation in many ways, one of which was a "widening and expanding outward" (Chogyam Trungpa, 1996, p. 63) and developing *openness.* As we noted earlier, this involves collapsing the self-other distinction. It includes learning ways of relating that could be called *not knowing.* Here I think we can see important connections with constructionism and with related "life practices" that try to avoid (re)constructing Subject-Object relations where e.g., the therapist or change-worker knows better than the client and attempts to achieve influence over the client (see e.g., Anderson, 1997; Hosking, 2005). So, for example, the Madhyamaka (part of the Mahayana) speaks of letting go of fixed reference points (Ray, 2000, p. 417). And knowing that you don't know (Ray, 2000, pp. 413-414) is linked with the experience of "emptiness" and with freedom from discursive thinking — which gives room for spontaneous compassion and creativity.

Ken: I want to focus for a moment on this subject of compassion. Many Buddhist writings speak about the ways in which meditation or mindfulness practice brings forth a sense of compassion for others. I have sometimes heard people voice suspicion of this view as such practices seem almost exclusively to emphasize well-being of the self. Yet, when we put together the Mahayana view of conditioned co-production (inter-being or dependent origination) with what you say about "not knowing" it is easier to see how these practices are linked with compassion. It is through these practices that we realize the insufficiency of Self, and our profound connection with others.

This also reminds me of the focus of many constructionist practices in education and research. The term "compassion" would not be so appropriate, but the emphasis on ultimate connection is wonderfully congenial with Buddhism. For example, in education, there are significant movements toward "collaborative classrooms," educational contexts where teachers facilitate students working together to achieve educational goals. In many cases students may even write essays or reports together, each contributing from their own resources and informed by the knowledge of others. In a similar manner, many researchers in the social sciences now turn from doing research *about* other people, to carrying out research *with* them. Many of the more recent developments in "participatory action research" are based on just such a premise (see Reason and Bradbury, 2006).

Dian Marie: This brings me to what perhaps should be a final point about meditation and the purpose of meditation practice. I think you are right in pointing to the frequent misunderstanding that these practices (and Buddhism more generally) are quite compatible with the assumptions of self-contained individualism. This turns meditation into an individual practice aimed at individual liberation — in the sense of freedom from suffering. But such a construction would fail to understand the significance of the Mahayana teachings and, as I said earlier, would be to construct meditation as a bounded "thing" or set of techniques that one is either doing or not doing. As one progresses along the Path, the distinction between meditation and post-meditation becomes more and more blurred. Furthermore, the "techniques" are but scaffolding — just temporary structures that at some point become unnecessary. As someone remarked somewhere, Tibetan Buddhism offers a very "earthy spirituality" which, whilst collapsing Self-Other dualism, also collapses the sacred and the secular or mundane. Now everything is sacred: the words we use, the ways we dress and occupy space, our home, the natural world… everything is alive, we are part of the living world, and we are responsible. This means that Buddhism is not so much an individual life practice as a matter of "developing an enlightened society."

Ken: I like this expanded view very much. One of the companion concepts in social construction is that of *relational responsibility* (McNamee and Gergen, 1998). The idea here is to set aside our traditional tendency to view the world as made up of self-contained agents of responsibility. This is a world in which we blame individuals for evil acts, and make heroes of those who champion our values. However, if each of us is altogether related with others, this tradition is severely limited. Rather, we should think in terms of our collective responsibility to the process of relationship itself. For, it is to the relational process that we owe any sense of the good.

Dian Marie: The Mahayana path in Buddhism especially emphasizes liberating all sentient beings through a commitment to put others before oneself, to becoming more open and responsive to the wider world, to the liberation of all sentient beings — without expecting anything in return. And it is a commitment grounded in knowing that one *doesn't know* — doesn't know what to think — and cannot know what others might need. The experience of *emptiness* disables conceptual or discursive activity and provides the basis for being-in-the-moment (nowness), open to what the situation might call for and open to Buddha nature and compassion. According to the Mahayana, it is "ineffable reality, the very nature of emptiness that... alone provides a sound basis for ethical conduct" (Ray, 2000, p. 413). And "ethical conduct" is key to producing a better society. "Like any other ideas, like science, economics and politics, Madhyamaka philosophy is trying to create a better society, very simply speaking. In fact, if possible, the Madhyamaka aims to create an enlightened society" (Dzongsar Khyentse Rinpoche, 1996, ch. 6, pp. 70-71).

Ken: Of course, we may well want to press forward past society to thinking globally. Isn't the implication of both Buddhism and social constructionism that global harmony and well-being is the ultimate goal? But perhaps what is called for at this juncture is a deep breath of humility.

21

Augmenting Cognitive-Behavior Therapy With Buddhist Psychology

Belinda Khong

Today, it is common to hear of accessing ancient eastern wisdom through psychotherapy and vice versa. While Buddhism and psychotherapy can provide valuable insights for each other, the interchange should not be undertaken in a way that romanticizes or devalue one tradition at the expense of the other. Of the modern psychotherapies, Cognitive-Behavior Therapy (CBT) is increasingly employed as a paradigm through which to apply Buddhist practices and ideas in counseling. Although both CBT and Buddhist Psychology (BP) are concerned with helping people to overcome mental and emotional suffering, their philosophical frameworks and methodologies differ. What are some of the parallels and divergences? How can CBT and BP contribute to each other? The exploration of these questions grounds this chapter. I explore such ideas as (1) how CBT focuses more on the contents of thinking, while BP focuses more on the processes of the mind, (2) the use of Buddhist concepts as acceptance and letting go in promoting attitudinal change, (3) the importance of experiencing the self as a process, (4) coping with change, and (5) understanding the interdependence between mind and body. Clinical vignettes and anecdotes illustrate how the Buddha's teachings can augment CBT. The larger question of how the relationship between BP and psychotherapy can be enhanced is also addressed.

When I first discussed the title of this chapter with colleagues in therapeutic and Buddhist circles, their responses were interesting and varied, ranging from disbelief "How can you, they are so different" to genuine curiosity "We could all learn something new; what do they have in common?" These responses are typical of the range of reactions that one encounters when attempting to examine critically two well-accepted schools of thinking: CBT and Buddhism. In the present context the latter term is used to refer to the philosophy and psychology underlying the Buddha's teachings rather than the "religion" of Buddhism. Today, it is common to hear of accessing ancient eastern wisdom, especially the Buddha's teachings (*Dhamma*)[1] through the sciences, particularly human sciences. The word dhamma, literally meaning carrying or holding, is a central concept and employed in a variety of ways (Fisher-Schreiber et al., 1991). Gombrich (1996) explains that when used as a singular noun (and with a capital D), the term refers to the Buddha's teachings. From this perspective, the term precedes the historical Buddha, and the Buddha's teachings are intended to draw our attention to the cosmic or universal laws underlying our world (Ling, 1981).

In his foreword to the book Destructive Emotions (2003), the 14th Dalai Lama sees the dialogue between science and Buddhism as a two way conversation and elaborates on the usefulness of this association:

> *When it comes to the workings of the mind, Buddhism has a centuries-old inner science that has been of practical interest to researchers in the cognitive and neurosciences, and in the study of emotions, offering significant contributions to their understanding... On the other hand, Buddhism can learn from science as well... If science proves facts that conflict with Buddhist understanding, Buddhism must change accordingly.* (pp. xiii-xiv)

Many Buddhist ideas and practices are commonly employed in conjunction with psychotherapy. This is a welcome development as the "religious" aspects of the Dhamma often obscure the psychological import of the Buddha's teachings. Psychotherapy provides a modern discourse for highlighting the relevance of the Buddha's teachings to the concerns of contemporary society and there are significant parallels between the two systems. As the Dalai Lama pointed out however, it is a two-way dialogue. While Buddhism and psychotherapy can provide valuable insights for each other, it is important that the exchange does not romanticize or devalue one tradition at the expense of the other. For example, romanticizing Buddhism by not having a proper understanding of its philosophical and psychological ground runs the risk of turning Buddhist Psychology (BP) into a new age psychology that diminishes the relevance of the Buddha's teachings to human suffering.

CBT is at the forefront of the psychotherapies currently engaged with Buddhist ideas and practices. Examples of this lively exchange can be found in research, writing, and at conferences. Although both CBT and BP are concerned with helping people to overcome mental and emotional suffering, their philosophical frameworks and methodologies differ. What are some of the similarities and differences? How can CBT and BP contribute to each other? The exploration of these questions grounds this analysis. I discuss (1) how CBT focuses more on modifying the contents of thinking while BP focuses more on understanding the workings of the mind, (2) the use of such Buddhist concepts as acceptance and letting go in promoting attitudinal change, (3) the importance of experiencing the self as a process, (4) coping with change, and (5) understanding the interdependence between mind and body.

Within the scope of this chapter, it is not possible to engage in an exhaustive discussion of all the concepts in CBT and BP. Thus, I will limit my focus on the major concepts and methodologies that each discipline employs to help people reduce their emotional suffering and develop good mental health.

Basis for Comparison: The Ontological Difference

A basic question that I encounter when comparing CBT with BP is "Is there a basis for comparing the two schools of thoughts?" This question is pertinent given that CBT and BP developed from radically different cultural, historical, and geographical origins. CBT is a contemporary form of psychotherapy, developed by Aaron T. Beck in the USA in the early 1960s to deal with depression and subsequently with other types of psychological anomalies such as obsessive-compulsive disorder, posttraumatic stress disorder, and personality disorders (Beck, 1995). The Buddha on the other hand promulgated his Dhamma in India more than 2,500 years ago as a soteriology.

The concept of the ontological difference as enunciated by the German philosopher Martin Heidegger (1927/1962) provides a constructive basis for making the comparison between the two apparently disparate schools of thought. Briefly, the notion of the ontological difference highlights the difference between the Being of beings (ontological) and particular beings (ontic). For Heidegger (1988), the ontological refers to the fundamental nature of beings, things, and phenomena, while the ontic points to those characteristics of Being which are manifested in the ordinary everyday world of beings. According to Heidegger, the ontological and the ontic are indivisible, as the former provides the conditions for the possibility of the latter. For example, sight and perception are ontological characteristics of human beings, as everyone possesses these capacities. What each person sees or perceives is ontic, determined by his/her emotions, culture, environment, and personality. Many of the Buddha's teachings incorporate this integrated ontological-ontic dimension (that largely parallels the levels of the ultimate and the conventional or provisional discerned in the Dhamma). One of the Buddha's aims was to help people to understand how the ontological nature of human existence being one of impermanence, can give rise to a feeling of dissatisfaction, when things come to pass. At the same time, the Buddha had a more pragmatic objective of helping individuals to recognize that the way they have lived their lives ontically, as if permanence is the norm, can give rise to suffering. In short, the Buddha was concerned with helping the individual relate the ontological situation (that everything is impermanent) to his/her own personal situation (that I am impermanent). While BP addresses both the ontological (the ultimate) and ontic (the provisional) spheres of human suffering, CBT focuses more on the ontic or conventional dimension like helping people to modify their irrational thoughts and beliefs into rational ones and hence bring about a change in their behavior. The concept of the ontological difference can help to demonstrate the shared and differing aspects of CBT and BP.

Framework for Comparison

Both BP and CBT recognize that people's perceptions and thoughts play a major role in influencing their responses and actions. As Beck (1995) explains, "cognitive therapy is based on the cognitive model which hypothesizes that people's emotions and behaviors are influenced by their perception of events" (p. 14). Similarly, the Buddha allegedly made the observation that "in this one-fathom long body along with its perceptions and thoughts, do I proclaim the world, the origin of the world... and the path leading to the cessation of the world" (Samyutta Nikaya I. 62), which defines the Dharma as a psychology. Using the Buddha's teachings contained in the Four Noble Truths as a framework for comparing the CBT and Buddhist approaches in dealing with human suffering, I discuss some of their major similarities and differences and suggest how each discipline can contribute to the other. This will enable us to address the larger question of enhancing the relationship between BP and psychotherapy.

According to the Buddha, the three ultimate or ontological characteristics of all existence are impermanence (*anicca*), insubstantiality or non-self (*anatta*), and pervasive unsatisfactoriness (*dukkha*). The Buddha's teachings related to these concepts and his exposition on how they apply at the ontical or conventional level are contained in his discourse on the Four Noble Truths, which set out that there is (1) suffering (*dukkha*), (2) a cause (*samudaya*) of suffering, (3) an end to suffering (*nirodha*), and (4) a path (*magga*) out of suffering (Thich, 1998; Sumedho, 1992).

The First Noble Truth

In the First Noble Truth, the term dukkha is commonly translated as suffering. However, this translation does not adequately capture what is intended to be conveyed by the idea of dukkha, which incorporates not only the idea of overt suffering associated with daily living but also the more profound notions of impermanence, imperfection, emptiness, and insubstantiality (Dhamma, 1997). Hence, a more adequate translation of dukkha would be pervasive unsatisfactoriness. In the First Noble Truth, the Buddha explicated three types of suffering or unsatisfactoriness: (1) the "suffering of suffering," (2) the "suffering of change," and (3) the "suffering of conditioning" (Gyatso, 1997, p. 50). The first type of suffering is associated with change derived from ordinary living such as death, old age, pain, and sickness. The second type of suffering refers to the individual's experience with the transitory nature of experiences, feelings and thoughts; even happy and pleasurable states are liable to change, as they are relative. These two types of suffering reflect the individual's experiences and are therefore easier to comprehend and to accept. The third type of suffering, of conditioning, refers to the impermanence or transient nature of "composite states" (Thich, 1998, p.18). This type of change points to the idea that everything in the universe, whether physical or mental, which comes together (conditioned), eventually passes away (Dhamma, 1997). Since this type of transformation often takes place naturally and at an imperceptible rate (e.g. the decay of mountains and rivers or the transformation of the body), it is more difficult to comprehend and to accept (Khong, 2003a). In short, the Buddha's theory of suffering (dukkha) is grounded on the idea of impermanence (anicca), the changeability of things. The concept of anicca encapsulates the idea that everything in this empirical world is in a constant state of flux and transformation. As Dhammananda (1987) explains, "change is the very constituent of reality" (p. 86). The message the Buddha wished to communicate in the First Noble Truth is that anything (including human existence) that is inherently impermanent is not capable of bringing about lasting happiness and could cause suffering when it eventually dissipates.

The Buddha also taught that the self that is conventionally experienced shares with all phenomena the quality of transitoriness; it is devoid of independent existence and is causally produced. This is the essence of the idea of non-self (*anatta*). According to the Buddha, the human being is a "psycho-physical complex" (*nama-rupa*) (Nyanatiloka, 1970, p.103) made up of five groups of aggregates comprising body-mind, sensation-perception, ideation-conception, motivation-action, and consciousness (see also, Silva, 1979; Rahula, 1978). From the Buddhist perspective the self is not a static entity but is constantly evolving. As Dhammananda (1995) notes, the self is a process "never being, but always becoming" (p. 16). The Buddhist understanding of the self as a process has significant implications for therapy. A main goal of therapy is to help the individual develop a healthy sense of self in order to function more effectively in the world. One of the techniques promoted in CBT to bring about this kind of change is to encourage clients to undertake a self-comparison (i.e. to look at how they presently are as compared to how they were before the onset of the disorder) and to acknowledge positive self-statements in contrast to the negative self-statements they held of themselves previously (Beck, 1995). While this technique is helpful to effect cognitive change at the ontic individual level, the Buddha's teachings of understanding impermanence at the ontological level of existence and in particular that of the self can bring about deeper psychological and emotional changes.

Claxton (1992) points out that people are accustomed to thinking that the most important role of the self is to instigate, plan, and deliberate. It is something that we feel we need in order to function in the everyday world. The terms we use such as "I" and "me" distract people from actually seeing the "ecological systematic nature of the organism" (Claxton, 1994, p. 88). While psychotherapy encourages the person to perceive her/himself as a process in terms of responding differently to various situations and contexts, BP takes the deconstruction of the self to a deeper level and sees each aggregate within the person as constantly changing and evolving. From the Buddhist perspective the idea of process is perceived not only in terms of individual actions and reactions, but also as taking place organically within the individual. This understanding of the self at the onto-logical level appears to be absent from the CBT framework. As Welwood (1983) points out, a key task of therapy is to assist individuals in integrating various aspects of them and to expand their sense of self. In contrast, he notes, instead of shoring up or expanding the self, Buddhist meditation practice is a way of "inquiring what this 'I' consists of" (p.46). The Buddha's teachings relating to impermanence and the deconstruction of the self into aggregates can contribute to CBT and to psychology by assisting people in understanding the self at the ontological level as opposed to their experience of self in the conventional, ontic sense.

How does an appreciation of the ideas of impermanence and non-self help the individual psychologically? Many of my clients who have experienced depression and anxiety explained that they found these to be psychologically freeing, as these notions suggest that there is room for growth and change. This was the case with Diana, who came to counseling to learn to cope with her clinical depression and panic attacks.[2] I encouraged her to get in touch with her feelings through mindfulness. Briefly, mindfulness, or insight meditation (*vipassana*) as it is usually referred in BP, is a way of helping individuals to maintain "bare attention" (Nyanaponika, 1992) of the workings and contents of the mind. Bare attention involves cultivating constant awareness to what is "actually happening to us and in us" (p.30). By learning to register what is taking place moment by moment, the individual is better able to experience the transitory nature of the mind and to make space for their feelings, emotions, thoughts, without judging, repressing, or wishing to change them and to let them be. Using this practice, Diana found that she was able to make space for her feelings of depression and anxiety, and to manage them:[3]

> *I am better at dealing with my feelings than I used to be. I used to wallow a lot and feel sorry for myself. Now I just pay bare attention to them and see if I can see what the problem might be "why do I feel like that" or "what has happened to me feel like this?" Now I don't allow myself to wallow anymore and ruminate. I kind of accept my feelings. I go with them, knowing that they will be over. It is a matter of time. I have learned that no matter how bad I feel, it will be over, and it won't last forever. I find being mindful of my feelings very helpful. I don't feel stuck... It encompasses the whole Buddhist thing about acknowledging feelings, and moving on. It seems to work with every emotion that I have.*

The Second Noble Truth

In the Second Noble Truth, the Buddha explained that the primary cause or origin of suffering is craving or desire (*tanha*). Thich Nhat Hanh (1998) notes, that because craving is listed as the first of a number of mental afflictions, it is often mistakenly regarded as representing the entire list. In fact the Buddha described fourteen unwholesome mental states including craving, ignorance, delusion, greed, and worry, which can all contribute to emotional suffering. However, as craving is perceived to be the most palpable and pervading cause, it is often considered to be the root cause of suffering (Rahula, 1978). Craving is usually translated as "thirst" and signifies "attachment to" (Rahula, 1978, p. 30) or a "wish for satisfaction" (Epstein, 1995, p. 84). The Buddha emphasized three aspects: craving for sense pleasure, for existence and becoming, and for non-existence or self-annihilation (Bodhi, 1993). Sumedho (1992) notes, that these are not different forms but different aspects of craving. In the context of the Second Noble Truth, there are important parallels and divergences between CBT and BP. In this area each discipline can contribute significantly to the other. Here, my discussion will focus on the craving for sense pleasure and in particular on the concepts of attachment and letting go.

One of the parallels between BP and CBT relates to their elucidation of the influence of cognition, beliefs, and perceptions on human behavior. The aim of the CB therapist is to help clients identify their dysfunctional thoughts and beliefs and to assist them in changing their ideation into rational ones (Burns, 1980; Yapko, 1997). As an illustration Beck (1995) discusses a client's cognitive self-downing process. Sally's core belief "I am inadequate," impacts on her intermediate belief and attitude: "It's terrible to be inadequate." This in turn triggers off automatic thought such as "I can't do this" and results in her feelings of inadequacy and depression. The explanation of the relationship between cognition and behavior in CBT has parallels in the Buddha's teaching on "dependent origination." Also known as the Buddha's "teaching of cause and effect" (Thich, 1998, p. 206), the doctrine of dependent origination proffers the notion that all phenomena are built on a network of relations that are conditionally related with each other (Dhammananda, 1987). In the psychological sphere, the doctrine is used to explicate the interdependence of a series of twelve interconnected factors that link the aggregates during an emotional episode (Jacobson, 1983). For example, it explains how contact with an object via the senses gives rise to consciousness, which then gives rise to feelings, craving, attachment, and finally to the (re)birth of emotional suffering (see also Bodhi, 1994; Varela et al. (1993).

The idea of causation contained in dependent origination should not mislead us into thinking that this sequence operates in a linear fashion. The Buddha does not postulate a first cause. Since everything is interconnected, a first cause is inconceivable as the cause becomes the effect and the next moment the effect becomes the cause to produce another effect (Dhammananda, 1987). This is particularly the idea contained in the concept of karma: every action causes and produces a reaction. Any of the twelve links, for example consciousness, feeling, or attachment, can contribute to the cycle at any point in the episode. The psychological factors highlighted as contributing in dependent origination to the perpetuation of suffering are attachment to (over) desire, aversion, ignorance, whereas "letting go" leads to its reduction. According to the Buddha, we hanker after pleasant experiences, material things and even eternal life. We desire something more or something different. We become attached to beliefs, ideas, and opinions. Abe (1985) notes that when the Buddha pointed to attachment as one of the causes of suffering, he was not merely referring to the attachment to pleasure but to a "deeper and more fundamental attachment that is rooted in human existence, that of loving pleasure and avoiding suffering..." (p. 206). On a similar note, Batchelor (1997) explains that feelings of attachment and aversion underpin this type of craving, "If something makes me feel good, I want it (at all costs). If it makes me feel bad, I will avoid it" (p. 73). Craving is also linked to ignorance or delusion, which refer to a lack of insight or awareness. As Brazier (1995) points out, traditionally, Dhamma does not talk about evil but rather about ignorance. If we are mindful of the negative impact that our actions have on ourselves and on others, we could elect to adopt a way of life that reduces this negative impact.

As an antidote to reducing attachment, aversion, and ignorance, the Buddha encouraged people to learn to let go by comprehending and accepting the true nature of things and of life as impermanent and changeable. Towards this end, he promoted the use of meditation and mindfulness as a way of helping people to experience the phenomenon of change for themselves. As Puriso (1999) notes, intellectually we can understand and even acknowledge that things are impermanent. However, understanding impermanence intellectually is far removed from coming to terms with it. In fact, most of us live our lives as if permanence was the norm. Take the example of our thoughts: we often perceive our thoughts as continuous when in reality they are a quick succession of changing phases, continually rising and falling away. During meditation, when we experience within ourselves how no single phenomenon, whether mental or physical, remains the same for two moments, we gain insight into impermanence and insubstantiality. This encounter with impermanence can help us to experientially realize that change is natural and inevitable, and to learn to let go of things when they come to pass (Khong, 1999, 2003b).

The Buddhist practice of learning to be mindful of our attachments and to let go is relatively absent in CBT and can significantly contribute to the latter's goal of promoting cognitive and behavioral modification. To facilitate this kind of modification, CBT encourages the practice of decentering, distancing, and reality testing. Some of the methods employed in CBT to bring about cognitive-behavioral change involve engaging the clients in behavioral experiments and role-playing in the therapy room to help them evaluate and test out the beliefs after having these decentered and looking at them from a distance (Beck, 1995). This bears some resemblance with a meditative stance. Combined with an experiential strategy CBT can thus modify a person's beliefs more powerfully than with merely verbal persuasion. Like CBT, Buddhism also promotes reality testing by training the mind, as illustrated by the following quotations of the Dhammapada, allegedly spoken by the Buddha:

The trained mind gives one the best:
What neither mother, nor father,
Nor any relative can do,
A well trained mind does; it elevates one.

However, there is a significant difference between the approaches adopted by the two schools. According to Beck (1995), the CB therapist employs various methods to produce cognitive change in order to bring about emotional and behavioral change. Towards this end, CBT encourages the individual to work through the issues with the help of the therapist. In contrast, the Buddhist training involves the individual learning primarily through personal effort to let go of his/her negative thoughts and feelings during the practice of meditation. In order to encourage individuals to understand change and to learn to let go experientially, the Buddha fostered the use of the breath as a focus of attention during meditation. The rationale behind using the breath is to train the person to be mindful and accepting of the present and to learn to relinquish things when they come to pass. By focusing on the present breath, a person learns not to be immobilized by the past, which s/he cannot alter, or to be too preoccupied with the future, which has not arisen. The psychological effect of learning to let go is a reduction in ruminative thinking enabling a person to calm down and respond to emotions, feelings, and thoughts in an open way. This sense of inner relinquishment, absent in CBT, would be invaluable in motivating clients to let go of irrational beliefs.

One of my clients, Zita[4], found this meditative way of approaching her emotions and beliefs helpful. By learning to accept her feelings and thoughts and allowing them to be, she was able to let them go. Her explanation illustrates the usefulness of the Buddhist approach in dealing with emotional suffering:

I didn't do anything. I just let it happen. I am feeling much better. I don't have depression anymore. And when I have something, it goes very quickly, because I know that it is temporary. I am learning to accept whatever is happening... I am not even trying. It is happening. That is the difference! *Even though I was working at the level of the relationship between the breath and the body, the mind came in too. I could see how the thought made the breath agitated. And when the breath is agitated, the body is contracted. I realize that this is what they are talking about, realizing the non-self (italics added). One conditions the other. There is no "I" there... Previously I was looking for that big enlightenment and because I was clinging to that, I couldn't experience the good moments. It is more than what happened in my childhood. Maybe that was forming the patterns. But it is also my own impatient nature. Wanting things done and not wanting to work*

things through. It is the same with my attitude. Wanting a perfect marriage, per-
fect body and a perfect life. I realize that it is about learning to enjoy the moment,
every moment, and not just the achievement.

This vignette highlights another contribution that BP can make to CBT. The Buddhist approach towards understanding the nature of the mind and learning to let
things be can assist clients in relating to their feelings, emotions, thoughts, and
beliefs differently, that is in a more open way rather than trying to avoid or change
them. Thus, they will find that the thoughts and feelings are likely to dissolve in a
relatively effortless way.

The comparative analysis also shows how CBT can augment BP. The Buddha
offers no techniques for dealing with psychological disorders as specific as in CBT.
Since the Dhamma is not another school of psychotherapy, it was not intended for
this purpose. The Buddha was more concerned with helping people come to terms
with existential issues such as coping with change, impermanence, living and dying. However, as many psychotherapists (Kornfield, 1993; Welwood, 1983) con-
versant with meditation noted, there are many personal concerns that meditation
alone cannot exorcise. In such instances therapy can help people connect with
these larger questions by attending to personal problems first. In this respect, the
specific techniques and practices developed in CBT can contribute to BP by helping people to identify and modify their dysfunctional thoughts and beliefs. For
example, using the strategies employed in CBT, individuals can identify how their
core belief (desiring things to remain permanent) influences their intermediate
beliefs (fear of aging and attachment to youthfulness), attitude (I need to stay young
to be attractive for others), emotions (anxiety and resentment) and subsequent
thoughts (like, How can I prevent aging?), resulting in frantic actions to stave off
the process of aging and to remain young. In helping people to unravel personal
problems and to modify the contents and products of their mind, CBT can help to
free the mind and enable individuals to live in a less emotionally constricted way.

The Third Noble Truth

In the Third Noble Truth, the Buddha explained that suffering could be extinguished
through insight, awakening or enlightenment: the experiencing of *Nirvana*. Nirvana is a state related to the continual reduction of craving and embodying peace
of mind, rather seeking to be in the hereafter or reaching a certain goal. Although
both CBT and BP promote the attainment of peace of mind, the purpose and "end
result" of achieving this state differs in the two disciplines. One of the major goals
of CBT is to bring about symptom relief and a reduction in the client's level of
distress. Hence, CBT is goal oriented and problem-focused. In BP the idea of
peace of mind encompasses more than symptom and distress relief. It is primarily
focused on gaining insight and wisdom.

In the various Buddhist traditions, there are differing views pertaining to Nirvana such as it being a state of release from the unwholesome mental states of greed, hate, and delusion (Fisher-Schreiber et al, 1991), freedom from the cycle of birth and death (Johansson, 1969) and a state moving beyond duality (Abe, 1983). A prevailing view of Nirvana amongst Buddhist scholars is that it involves realizing a state of mental calmness, quietude, and harmony (Punnaji, 1978; De Silva, 1979). This view suggests that Nirvana has more to with our states of mind. In "The Psychology of Nirvana" (1969), Johansson discusses how Nirvana operates in various spheres, the most important psychological state taking place in the "transformative sphere" (p. 131). He explains that this transformation involves a cessation of speculative views and of ignorance through the attainment of insight and wisdom.

To overcome ignorance, the Buddha encouraged people to see the nature of reality (the macro) and the nature of the mind (the micro) as analogous. Both are impermanent, devoid of independent existence (non-self), multi-causally produced by conditioning and interconnectedness. If people can experience and accept the changes taking place within their own minds, it is easier for them to accept change universally and vice versa. This insight can reduce the tendency for people to cling to their emotions, experiences, and to life itself. Wisdom refers to the ability to apply this insight to the way individuals live our lives and to take responsibility for their actions in the light of the frailty of existence. From a Buddhist perspective, a person who develops this attitude is able to enjoy things without self-projection, to live fully in the present moment, and to appraise realistically the relativity of the situation (Bodhi, 1994, Rahula, 1978). According to the Buddha, Nirvana entails learning to "see things as they really are" (Jayasuriya, 1963, p. 8), detachment, and letting be.

Boss (1982), the Swiss Daseinsanalyst describes *Gelassenheit*, a German word meaning releasement or a meditative state in terms comparable to the Buddha's teaching on Nirvana:

> *This state of mind (releasement)... allows for the individual to catch up with himself and become aware of his fundamental condition. However, the summons back to himself in the released state of mind is not one forced upon him as in the state of anxiety, but rather one that he chooses freely... People who are able to enter into a deep meditative state will know all about that. It constitutes an indispensable openness to the world...* (pp. 55-56)

From this analysis, it can be seen that the peace of mind promoted in CBT is primarily at the ontic level and aimed at reducing symptoms, solving personal problems, and developing a functional sense of self. The type of peace of mind countenanced in BP goes beyond this functional self and is oriented towards assisting the person to get in touch with the larger fabric of existence and to engage with the world in a more inter-connected way. A transformative element is absent in CBT. It highlights another area whereby BP can add a different dimension to the goals of CBT. Welwood (1983) notes,

> *Eastern psychologies have helped many Western psychologists realize that there is another dimension of growth beyond merely finding fulfillment in achieving personal goals... Important as personal fulfillment is, it does not prepare us for dealing with impermanence, death, aloneness...* (p. 51).

The Fourth Noble Truth
In the Fourth Noble Truth, also known as the Eightfold Path, the Buddha enunciated a set of practices that the individual can adopt to overcome his/her own suffering. The Eightfold Path deals with the aspects of basic moral conduct, mental cultivation and self-discipline, and knowledge-wisdom. It comprises the following factors (Dhammananda, 1987, p. 90; Dhamma, 1997, p. 33):

Morality	Mental Culture & Discipline	Wisdom
1. Right speech	5. Right mindfulness	7. Right understanding
2. Right action	6. Right concentration	8. Right thought
3. Right livelihood		
4. Right effort		

The word "right" used to qualify each factor of the path does not imply moral judgments concerning sin and guilt or arbitrary standards imposed externally. The Buddha did not dictate what is right or wrong. Instead he spoke of skillful (wholesome) or unskillful (unwholesome) actions and explained that the path merely serves as a guideline or a "raft" for helping people to take personal responsibility (Majjhima Nikaya, 1.260). Through our own awareness and understanding we ascertain what is right (beneficial) or wrong (non-beneficial) (Thich, 1998). The word "right" is synonymous with harmonious, that is being in harmony from within and from without (Punnaji, 1978, p. 46). From this perspective, it can be said that the Eightfold Path balances or grounds our mental attitude. Adopting the right attitude frees the individual's mind from remorse and helps him/her to acquire peace of mind (Khong, 2003c).

In this chapter, I focus on the factor of right mindfulness, as it is a practice that can contribute to the goals of CBT significantly. According to Nyanaponika (1992), mindfulness schools people in the art of letting go, weans them from the busy-ness and the tendency of the mind to ruminate and to judge, and is indispensable to right thinking and right living. Right mindfulness involves "the bare and exact registering of the object (of attention)" (p. 32). The normal tendency of the mind is to wander and also to infuse what is perceived with preconceptions and subjective elements. Right mindfulness helps people to reduce this internal dialogue and to see things for what they are, that is "bare of labels" (p. 32). Mindfulness practice is not advocated as a solution to clients' problems. Rather, it provides an efficacious mechanism for clients to be become aware of and to deconstruct what I refer to as the workings or conditionings of the mind. Employing the practice of mindfulness as an adjunct to counseling and therapy where appropriate, I encourage clients to be mindful of their feelings and thoughts moment by moment while recognizing the tendency to avoid painful or negative experiences and to hang on to pleasant ones. The idea of adopting a neutral stance towards our experiences incorporates a letting be. Additionally, by being mindful of their bodily sensations, emotions, images, and internal dialogues, clients learn to distinguish between these elements, and to separate their responses to a situation from the situation itself. The point of letting go allows clients to make space for but not to identify with experiences (Khong, 2004).

The experience of my client, Andrew illustrates the usefulness of mindfulness practice in helping the individual gain increased self-awareness and insight:[5]

> The idea of labeling feelings and not being so close to them does a couple of things. One is that obviously it gives you distance to think about what is actually happening. The other thing is that it reinforces my total sense of well-being, my total being at one, being whole, and being worthy... Makes it very clear there is a juxtaposition of there being an essential me that is worthwhile and valued, and then there are those feelings. But when I get them all crowded together, it is like dirty water, and I start to think, "Oh, I am not a worthy person. Look how I feel." But the feelings are not me and I am a worthwhile person. So the experience provides an immediate reinforcement of this feeling. It also helps me to respond to my wife Mary and to other things differently... The turning point was after our session, Mary was angry, and instead of running away from that I sort of label it, "you are really angry"... I wasn't actually taking the blame for everything but presented the facts as, "This is what happened." It gave her a chance to let go of stuff and she is resorting to humor now, rather than to anger.

Andrew's experience with mindfulness demonstrates that maintaining constant bare attention of the processes of the mind increases the individual's awareness of the circuitous nature of the mind as enunciated by the Buddha in his teachings of dependent origination and karma. How does mindfulness help the individual to break the circuit of negativity? In understanding the processes of he mind and the perpetuation of this cyclical process, individuals can take the responsibility to disrupt it so that things can be otherwise either by letting go or working through the emotion and associative feelings. According to Kabat-Zinn (2005), when unattended, our thoughts tend to run our lives, whereas with mindful awareness we gain self-understanding and are able see what is on our minds and relate to our thoughts differently so that they no longer govern our lives. He contends "we can taste some very real moments of freedom that do not depend entirely on inner or outer conditions of calmness, or the limited stories we tell ourselves..." (p. 406). Andrew's experiences are a positive testimony to the possibility of getting in touch with these moments of freedom by being mindful.

In the discussion on the Second Noble Truth, I have demonstrated how the techniques and practices in CBT and BP complement each other in helping individuals to identify and modify dysfunctional thoughts and feelings. However, there are significant differences in the two approaches. CBT is more concerned with helping the individual to modify the contents and products (the what) of the mind. Towards this end some of the techniques employed include thought monitoring, challenging, cognitive rehearsal, generating alternative options, and activity scheduling (Segal et al., 2002, p. 23). BP is primarily concerned with helping people to gain an increased awareness of the nature and processes (the how) of the mind. Meditation is promoted as a means of helping individuals to be aware of the tendency of the mind to ruminate, attach, or avoid. Mindfulness assists with the development of skills to make space for whatever arises in the mind and to learn to let go by experiencing change as a natural, ontological phenomenon. As Goleman (1988) notes, generally psychotherapies seek to break the hold of past conditioning on present behavior and personality, whereas meditation and mindfulness practices aim to alter "the process of conditioning per se so that it will no longer be a prime determinant of future acts" (p. 171).

The Buddha's teachings in the Fourth Noble Truth understood in conjunction with the Buddha's dependent origination highlight another area where BP could augment CBT. As I noted earlier, the CB therapist works with the client to try and modify the dysfunctional belief by formulating a functional alternative; for example, changing the belief from one of "If I don't do as well as others, I'm a failure," to "If I don't do as well as others, I'm not a failure, just human" (Beck, 1995, p. 151). Similarly, the Buddha encouraged people to change their negative thoughts and behavior into positive ones. There are two main differences between the approach that CBT and BP takes towards change. The first difference is that CBT focuses on understanding and producing changes at the ontic or conventional level, notably of daily thoughts and behaviors. The Buddhist approach incorporates understanding and accepting change at both the ontological and ontic levels. Basically, the Buddha encouraged individuals to understand and accept change as an ultimate or ontological phenomenon (that includes the ontic), which is the sublime idea that impermanence is the nature of reality.

The second difference is that at the ontic level, the Buddha encouraged us to make positive change not only to our thoughts, beliefs, behaviors, and attitudes but also to every aspect of our life. Hence in the Fourth Noble Truth, he promoted a path that embraces many aspects of living: morality, discipline, and wisdom. According to Brazier (1995), the Buddhist stance implies "a radical change... of *heart and mind*: the experiential realization that there is an altogether better way to be" (p. 126, italics added). In short, this stance encourages people to reduce their own suffering by adopting a change in attitude that engages different dimensions of their lives. Although both BP and CBT share the aim of effectuating change in the ontic sphere, the Buddhist approach of promoting personal change through an understanding of change at the ontological level appears to be absent in the CBT context. This difference suggests that BP can help CBT to advance its therapeutic goals from a more encompassing perspective.

In Conclusion

In this chapter, I have shown that in many instances, CBT and BP can co-exist on philosophical grounds and complement each other in practice. This would also apply to the relationship between BP and psychotherapy in general. Additionally, I have discussed how each discipline can contribute to and augment the other. While meditation and mindfulness practice can enhance the effectiveness of therapy, in some instances, the early reduction of cognitive and behavioral dysfunctions based on the CBT approach could help individuals to overcome personal concerns and enable them to deepen their spiritual practices.

Given their respective strengths and limitations, BP and psychotherapy in general, and BP and CBT in particular can complement rather than substitute each other. The Zen Buddhist teaching of mountains and rivers provides a metaphor how this co-existence can take place. According to this Zen analogy (D.T. Suzuki, cited in Fontana, 1990), before enlightenment, mountains are perceived as mountains, and rivers are perceived as rivers. When one gains a certain level of understanding and insight mountains are no longer perceived as mountains, and rivers are no longer perceived as rivers. However, when after much self-reflection and soul searching, one attains awakening, mountains are again perceived as mountains, and rivers are again perceived as rivers. I see the relevance of this teaching to the relationship between BP and psychotherapy/CBT as follows. At the first level, the tendency to dichotomize and discriminate is prevalent (i.e. when seeing mountains and rivers as distinct entities). One would tend to see BP and psychotherapy as two distinct schools that are separate from each other. At the second stage there is a reduction of the tendency to view the world in terms of "I" versus "them," when mountains and rivers are considered in broader terms (both being part of nature). However, while people may see the bigger picture, they may not necessarily appreciate the uniqueness of and interconnectedness between the parts that make up the whole landscape. Hence, at this stage, BP and therapy tend to be regarded as part of a compendium for helping individuals but less regard is given to their distinctive qualities. The third level of understanding signifies a profound recognition of the interrelatedness of the two helping disciplines: mountains and rivers are appreciated for their distinctive qualities as well as for their being inter-connected parts, where one element is less meaningful without the other.

A harmonious way for BP and CBT to co-exist is at this third level of the Zen teaching. Here, both are viewed as complementary approaches for helping people to alleviate their suffering and improve their sense of wellbeing. At the same time, each disciple is appreciated for its unique qualities and strengths. In this way, in-stead of imposing an arbitrary distinction between the disciplines and asking our-selves whether BP or CBT or any other type of therapy is best suited to help indi-viduals, we could learn to ask which approach is better suited to serve which indi-vidual needs, and in which kind of situations, and respond appropriately.

---

1. The Buddhist terms used in this paper are derived from the Pali language except where the Sanskrit equivalents are more familiar, for example using *nirvana* and *karma* (San-skrit) instead of *nibbana* and *kamma* (Pali). For simplicity, I have kept accents and diacriticals of Buddhist terms to a minimum.

2. All names and personal identification of clients mentioned in this paper have been changed.

3. For a more extensive discussion of the use and benefits of mindfulness practice in therapy, see Khong (2003b).

4. For a more detailed discussion of this clinical vignette, see Khong (2003a)

5. For a more comprehensive discussion of this clinical vignette, see Khong (2003a).

22

The Abhidhamma Model Of Consciousness And Its Consequences[1]

Henk Barendregt

An important compilation of canonical Theravada Buddhist texts consists of the Abhidhamma collection, one of three sets of volumes known collectively as the Tipitaka ("Three Baskets"). The texts in Pali, an ancient language related to Sanskrit, are compiled in the approximate period 500 BC to 250 BC. They cover about 5000 pages and deal with phenomeno-logical psychology, obtained as side effect of meditation used as trained introspection. The Abhidhamma describes in a cryptic way an intricate model of consciousness on three levels. The first level consists of a discrete, serial stream of "atoms of awareness" called cetas. *Secondly, a linear sequence of cetas may form a "molecule," called* vithi, *being a cognitive-emotional conscious unit. Finally, each ceta has a substructure of conscious mental factors ("elementary particles"), called* cetasikas, *acting in parallel. An important part of the Abhidhamma is the* Patthana, *covering about 2600 pages, that describes the mechanism of conditioning (*kamma) *between these cetasikas and cetas. A short sketch of the Abhidhamma model will be given. This is done by giving an interpretation of the theory, thereby reflecting the author's present understanding and non-understanding. Through the model an interpretation will be given of notions like neurosis, psychosis, and also various coping mechanisms. Thereafter, the model is used to describe the process of mental purification by the practice of mindfulness towards insight. The effects of mindfulness in psychotherapy fit in this explanation. Finally, some methodological considerations and views on the compatibility with neurophysiology are presented.*

The Abhidhamma Model of Consciousness

The Abhidhamma, sometimes rendered as "deeper teaching," but also as "analytic insights regarding phenomena of existential importance," deals with consciousness in an analytic and synthetic way. A classification is made of several types of consciousness and of the various objects it is directed to. For example, the sight of a woman or the memory of the sound of a frog jumping in water is such an object; these are types of consciousness perceiving these objects with calm joy or with restless desire. The topic of investigation is phenomenological: it is about consciousness as it appears, like (perceived) sight, sound, and memory, and not about women, frogs, or water.

During the course of the last two millennia several commentaries and subcommentaries (and commentaries upon commentaries) have been written on the Abhidhamma. Good modern commentaries are Nyanaponika (1998) (an introduction) and Bodhi (2000) (a summary). Next to this there is an oral tradition, notably flourishing in Myanmar, explaining the field. Not all volumes of the original Abhidhamma are translated in English (5 volumes of the *Patthana* are missing). Parts of those volumes that have been translated are considered by U Nandamalabhivamsa to be based on a poor understanding of the subject and therefore not suitable for study. This shows the importance of the study of Pali and the oral tradition. Because of the complex nature of the topic, the text is rather technical and comparable to what is in science the periodic system of elements, tables of compound materials and their melting and evaporating temperatures. At the same time issues as compassion, shared joy and other ethical values are deeply interwoven in the theory. This paper is intended as a systematic interpretation of the Abhidhamma, version AM_0.

1. *Nama-Rupa: mind and body.* The Abhidhamma states that consciousness performs a task of "selfless" data processing — there is action without an actor — and speaks mainly about conscious cognition, the dynamics of input and output. The Abhidhamma is not solving the body-mind problem, not even addressing it, but speaks from the conscious phenomenological side. On the other hand the "qualia" of consciousness are addressed in an axiomatic fashion. One speaks about pure consciousness and nibbana (nirvana in Sanskrit and English). These two concepts are not analyzed any further, but play a definite role. Later Mahayana[2] Buddhists, outside the tradition of the Abhidhamma, have equated pure consciousness and nibbana.

The input data, the objects of consciousness, come partly from the physical senses: sight, sound, smell, taste, and touch. This type of input is called *rupa*, often translated as body or matter.[3] Other input to consciousness comes from consciousness itself, outside the part coming from the physical senses. Hence consciousness is also busy with itself next to the part coming from the physical senses. Consciousness as input is called *nama*, translated as mind (see Fig. 1). Below we see that consciousness with rupa as object is immediately "copied" to consciousness with a corresponding nama as input. It is emphasized that part of rupa does not come from the physical senses, but from mind. Examples are the "mental glue" that puts clouds of colors together to form "visible objects." Also there are immediate judgments that some of these visible objects are edible or not and that other ones possess sexual quality. This is an understandable faculty of the human nature, as eating and mating are important survival factors. These parts of mental input are also classified as rupa. In Figure 1 the five physical senses and their physical organs are displayed explicitly. "Eye," "ear," "nose," "tongue," and "body" stand for what is called "the sensitive (part of the) eye, of the ear, nose, tongue, and body." In the Abhidhamma also the mind is considered as a sense.

The physical organ corresponding to mind is called the "heart base"; the tradition was unfamiliar with the brain. Since one can observe relatively easily that emotions have an effect on the heartbeat, one can understand this choice.

On the other side of the data processing by consciousness there is output. Next to the already mentioned output towards consciousness itself, the output also consists of initiation of body movements and speech. How this output is determined depends on what is called "causes and conditions." Next to rupa as object for nama and nama as object for nama there are two other kinds of mental objects: concepts and nibbana, to be discussed below.

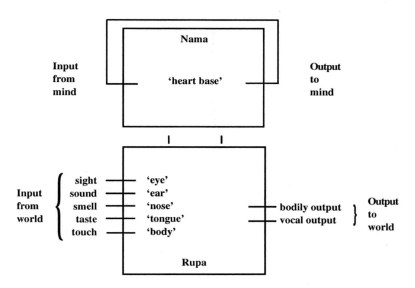

Figure 1. Nama-Rupa

2. *Cetas: mental "atoms."* The main thesis in the Abhidhamma model is that consciousness is not continuous, but comes in discrete packages of consciousness flashes. Each flash is called a *ceta*. As commentators hold, a ceta has the three phases of arising, existing, and disappearing. The duration of a ceta is short. What we call thoughts consists of streams of many cetas, discussed later. The main task of a ceta is to be concerned with some object. A ceta is said to be directed towards it. Furthermore a ceta contributes to the determination of future cetas. We call this the kammic effect of the ceta, which depends partly on the object captured by the present ceta. But there are also different *types* of cetas. For example, a certain visual object can be the data of a ceta with desire and attachment, with disgust and hatred or with loving kindness and compassion. Both the type and the object of the

future cetas depend on those of the past ones. This leads to the *accumulated kamma*, transferred and augmented from ceta to ceta. This kamma, in Sanskrit and English called *karma*, may activate something in the next ceta or in a near or distant future ceta. The kamma is determined by the trace of the types of past cetas. It has the objects of the present ceta as side condition. Some types of ceta may have a direct effect on the following cetas (producing kamma), some have to collaborate with others (supporting kamma). Also the kamma force of some cetas can work against the effect of other cetas (obstructing kamma), and it is even possible that the potential action of a ceta is forever prevented by a later one (destructive kamma). The Abhidhamma distinguishes 89 types of cetas, see Figure 2. These types are divided into two major subgroups: those ceta types with strong kamma that has a direct effect without the need of supporting kamma, and those with only indirect (supporting) effect. The ceta types with producing kamma can be subdivided into unwholesome and wholesome. Unwholesome cetas lead to attachment and increased suffering. Wholesome cetas lead to freedom and decreased suffering.

Kind Plane	Direct effect		Indirect effect	#
	Unwholesome	Wholesome		
Sensual	12	8	34	54
Sublime		9	18	27
Supramundane		4	4	8
#	12	21	56	89

Figure 2. Classes of types of consciousnesses *(cetas)* and the number of their elements

Perpendicular to this there is a subdivision in spheres. There are the sensual, sublime, and supramundane spheres. The sensual sphere consists of those ceta types directed to pleasant feeling coming from the physical senses, e.g. caused by input from good food, beautiful sights or erotic pleasures. The expression "being directed to" means that a sensual ceta causes behavioral action that tries to prolong or repeat these pleasures. Cetas in the sublime sphere are directed to mental pleasures like being in love or in a mystical state. In these, there is a high mental concentration often accompanied by bliss and rapture. It is emphasized in the practice of Vipassana (insight) meditation (stemming from the same tradition as the Abhidhamma) that mystical consciousness may be pleasant, but does not lead to purification or greater freedom. One needs the rare or supramundane (not the supernatural) types of cetas for this purification. These are directed to nibbana or pure consciousness. See Bodhi (2000) for a detailed description of the 89 types of consciousness.

Here are examples of the 7 displayed classes of ceta types. Unwholesome are cetas based on greed, hatred, or ignorance. For instance, 3 of these 12 cetas are: (1) greed combined with pleasure, prompted with wrong view (occurring when one someone is prompted to steal something, without having insight that this is wrong). (2) Hatred with indifference, unprompted without wrong view (this is when someone wants to kill a person, knowing it is wrong, not in a rage but based on one's own cold considerations). (3) Ignorance with restlessness (e.g. occurring after being criticized, desperately trying to defend a position with little success, without realizing it.). Wholesome cetas have mindfulness and thereby non-greed and non-hatred as a base. For example, a ceta with pleasure and knowledge is in this sub-class of 8 sensual ones. Of the class with 34 ceta types 15 types are concerned with physical input, some as a result of unwholesome or of wholesome cetas. In daily life only 45 cetas play a role, a subset of those in the sensual sphere (the other 9 are only for Arahats, fully enlightened persons that no longer use unwholesome cetas). Among the 9 sublime wholesome ceta types one distinguishes the initiation of various kinds of mystical states (*jhanas*). The other 18 cetas in the sublime sphere are the blissful effects of these states (9 for Arahats and 9 for others).

The 4 wholesome supramundane cetas are called *maggaceta* (path consciousness) and have nibbana as object. One can have these cetas only once during one's existence. These 4 occur as transition from the worldly state to the supramundane state (enlightenment, purified mind). They have a strong kammic effect. The consequence of their occurrence is that some of the unwholesome consciousness types will no longer be available. These 4 types of cetas are immediately followed by a corresponding ceta among the 4 types listed under "indirect effect," also having nibbana as object. These may occur several times, even for a long period. After the occurrence of the 4 maggacetas one is an Arahat, who does no longer have any cetas with productive kamma, but still can be affected by kamma from such previous cetas. The sensual and sublime cetas together are called the "mundane" cetas.

3. *Cetasikas: mental factors.* The cetas may be compared to atoms of consciousness that, unlike the material atoms, do not occur in space but in time. Each mundane ceta may be considered as being composed of mental "elementary particles," the *cetasikas*. Literary, cetasika means "born together with a ceta" and they are officially not part of the ceta. But as the term "ceta" is most frequently used for the combination of ceta with associated cetasikas, a *pars pro toto*, one can consider the cetasikas as part of the associated "extended" ceta[4], see Figure 4. Not only do the cetasikas appear simultaneous with their ceta, they also have the same object. The cetasikas may be compared to coloring the otherwise clear pure ceta. Most ceta types are fully determined by their cetasikas. There are three main groups of cetasikas: unwholesome, neutral, and beautiful[5] ones. Perpendicularly, there is another main division: universal and occasional, see Figure 3.

	unwholesome	neutral	beautiful	#
universal	4	7	19	30
occasional	10	6	6	22
#	14	13	25	52

Figure 3. Classes of mental factors *(cetasikas)* **and the number of their elements**

Below are examples of cetasikas for each of the 6 resulting classes; also an important feature of the way the cetasikas do associate will be explained. The 7 universal neutral cetasikas are present in all mundane cetas. Typical ones are "contact" (input), "feeling" (a value judgment, being either pleasant, or unpleasant, or neutral) and "volition" (being the driving force of kamma). The class of 6 occasional neutral cetasikas contains for example "energy," "concentration," and "bliss." They may be added to the previous 7 and if nothing more is added one obtains factors necessary for the already mentioned mystical states. Next to the 7 universal neutral states one may (going over to the left in Fig. 4) include the 4 universal unwholesome cetasikas. These include ignorance and restlessness. Making consciousness worse, one may go downwards and add some of the occasional unwholesome mental factors, like greed or hatred. The Abhidhamma states that these two cannot occur together, so there are several possibilities, resulting in the 12 unwholesome cetas. Having a ceta with the factors of ignorance and hatred, things really become dangerous if one adds to the mixture concentration and energy from the occasional neutral group. Equally dangerous and perhaps more explosive is the combination of ignorance, greed, energy, and bliss. As soon as consciousness cannot obtain what it wants (object of the greed), then it may suddenly flip to hatred and react in unexpected ways.

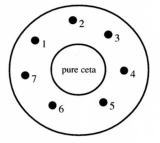

1. Contact (obtaining input)
2. Feeling (value judgment)
3. Volition (motivation)
4. Perception (rudimentary distinctions)
5. Attention (choosing input)
6. Cooperation (synchronization)
7. One-pointedness (focus)

Figure 4. The minimal (extendeed) *ceta* **consisting of pure ceta with the universal neutral** *cetasikas*

Let us go over to the right, towards universal beautiful cetasikas. The main mental factor here is "mindfulness." It freezes the kammic effects of consciousness by reflecting on it and by going to another level. For this reason mindfulness is called meta-awareness by Teasdale (1999). See Nyanaponika Thera (1998), Thich (1976), and Barendregt (2005b) for descriptions of the power of mindfulness (the latter in terms of the foundations of mathematics and computer science). The power of mindfulness is so strong that 18 other factors arise automatically, including non-hatred, non-greed, and malleability of body and mind. Then one may go down in the table and add items from the list of occasional beautiful cetasikas, like "compassion" (staying close to another if that person suffers) and "shared joy" (enjoying without jealousy the joy of others). The combination of the occasional neutral cetasikas with the beautiful ones gives a particularly effective wholesome kamma. As will be explained, there is an important difference whether this is done together with all the 25 universal and occasional beautiful cetasikas or only with a subclass of these (that must contain at least the 19 universal ones).

4. *Vithis: cognitive-emotional processing.* Now we come to the "molecular" level of consciousness, consisting in a serial collaboration of cetas. The entering of physical input (*rupa*) is modeled in the Abhidhamma as a sequence of 17 cetas, forming a so-called vithi, a ceta *street*. Most cetas in a vithi have the same object. The first 8 cetas in a vithi serve to start the process and to receive input. Then follow 7 cetas (so-called *javanas*) of the same type containing strong kamma. Finally, two cetas are used to terminate the vithi. Such a cognitive-emotional unit is placed in what may be called *baseline* consciousness (*bhavanga*). This is a series of cetas of the same type and having the same object that for each individual remains constant during life. In particular one's birth and death consciousness (cetas) have the same type and object as the ones in baseline consciousness. Although there is no productive or destructive kamma in the baseline, its supporting or obstructing kamma has a strong influence on one's life. The initial and final phase of a vithi starts from and returns to bhavanga. Next to vithis based on rupa, there are vithis for nama. These have a shorter length, namely 12. There is more "work to do" going from baseline consciousness to physical input and back, then to mental input and back.

A vithi for physical input is always followed by three vithis for mental input, copying the object mentally and giving it a name and meaning. So, the cognitive-emotional process consists of four vithis, where each time one has to rise from and go back to baseline consciousness. In some sense this is a bit cumbersome. During mystical experiences, the so called *mental absorptions* or *jh_nas*, the cognitive processing is different. In this consciousness process the vithis may be prolonged indefinitely. There is no need for departing and going back to baseline consciousness. One of the vithis that can be reached through mental development contains *maggaceta*, path consciousness, leading to enlightenment. The effect is that fewer cetas with strong unwholesome kamma are available for use as consciousness.

Therefore, less accumulation of kamma occurs. As stated before, an Arahat is a fully enlightened person, in whom none of the cetas with strong kamma are used. For the wholesome cetas a "clone" is available for them having the same effect, but no addition to the (in this case wholesome) accumulated kamma.

5. *Classification of objects.* The meaning of the term "object" in the Abhidhamma is different from that in daily life and science. Matter forms an object for consciousness. But, as we saw, consciousness also can have (previous) consciousness as object. Next to rupa and nama there are exactly two other kind of objects: concepts and nibbana. Concepts can be thought to emerge from in the vithis. One can compare the first two kinds of objects to black letters on white paper, while concepts correspond to the words printed by these letters. The cognitive-emotional process corresponds to forming a sentence. In this simile nibbana may be compared to the white between the letters. This whiteness can be an object of observation, try it while you read on. The elements of the class rupa and nama and also nibbana are all called absolute objects (*paramattha*). Ideas are called conceptual objects (*paññatti*). The reason for this classification seems to be that nama, rupa, and nibbana fit in one ceta, while concepts need vithis in order to be perceived.

Next to the classification between absolute and conventional objects, there is the division between conditioned and unconditioned ones. Traditionally, only nibbana is considered as unconditioned object. Slightly extending the analysis in the Abhidhamma one can put mathematical ideas also among the unconditioned ones. In this way one obtains a classification as in Figure 5. A concept like "dress" is called conditioned, as it depends on fashion what kind of arrangements of cloth are thus called. Nevertheless, it is a concept that has reality value. A concept like "dragon" is also conditioned, as it depends on the myths of a certain culture how such an animal is imagined. We know that there are no dragons. Therefore, one calls a dress an existing conceptual object and a dragon a non-existing one. A third class of ideas is unconditioned: mathematical concepts, like prime number. Nibbana is an object that is both absolute and unconditioned. One may wonder why one needs the concept of pure ceta (i.e. ceta as the awareness part of the ceta and cetasikas combination). The cetas have as a task to direct themselves to objects, but the cetasikas are already doing this. So there seems to be no need for pure ceta

	conditioned (*sankhata*)	unconditioned (*asankhata*)
absolute (*paramattha*)	matter, mind	nibbana
conceptual (*pannatti*)	'existing' concepts, 'non-existing' concepts	mathematical concepts

Figure 5. Classification of objects

to do this as well. Another role for pure ceta is to give consciousness its "qualia" aspect. Now consciousness without cetasikas (i.e. the pure ceta) is said to have nibbana as object. So this pure ceta has an active description, while nibbana is passive. But in its passivity nibbana becomes active, notably if it is seen in the metaphor of the white page on which the black letters come "to life." Therefore it seems that one may eliminate one of the two primitive notions "pure ceta" and "nibbana." This thought does not occur in Theravada. It has been stated by the Mahayana philosopher Nagarjuna that "nirvana is samsara,"[6] thereby equating it in fact with pure consciousness.[7] This is an attractive approach and fits with the use of Ockham's razor.

Nibbana plays an important role in the Abhidhamma model. If it is used as object of consciousness (*maggaceta*), then part or all of the unwholesome cetas are "rooted out" (i.e. forever removed). Why is this? The following seems to be the case. At first the discontinuity of consciousness (discreteness of the cetas) seems dangerous and frightening. It is related to egolessness (i.e. uncontrollability of what happens). Together these aspects of existence are metaphorically called "the void" or "emptiness." But a clear view on nibbana, the essence of being aware, gives the insight that the void is not dangerous at all. This insight makes the kammic force (nausea) of the experience of emptiness disappear and thereby causes the purification of consciousness.

Psychological Consequences

In this section several phenomena, known in clinical psychology, will be interpreted on the basis of the Abhidhamma model. That several symptoms or syndromes can be described does not imply that there is an obvious way to treat them. Nevertheless, the modeling of the symptoms may lead to a theoretical explanation why some methods of mindfulness-based therapy are successful.

1. *Neuroses.* As stated before, all cetas contain the cetasika of feeling. In a vithi this is enlarged by the seven occurrences of javanas. On the other hand, several vithis together, as a long train of cetas, constitute the cognitive-emotional process. The feeling present in the single cetas may prefer things different from the thoughts in the vithis. In this way an inner conflict can result. This is an interpretation of Freud's description of neuroses as the conflict between the super-ego, at the level of cognition, and the *id* that directs our drives. Freud made a good point when he noticed the unscrupulous power of the *id* doing things that morality does not allow. This is an example of producing kamma that cannot be avoided. The organization of consciousness, as described in the Abhidhamma model, shows that we have a basic neurotic core in our mind. Some forms of psychotherapy are directed to address the cognitive level of our mind by trying to modify one's thinking (i.e. one's vithis). One may learn that one should not desire some things that do not belong to us. But this does not help if there is inside us a ceta with strong cetasika

that desires that very object. Working directly with the cetas and cetasikas may be a powerful addition to psychotherapy.

2. *Psychoses.* Later psychoanalysts, for example Eigen (1986) and Suler (1993), speak about the basic *psychotic core* of the mind. This can be explained in a natural way from the Abhidhamma model as well. Falling apart from the apparent continuous consciousness to its true scattered form of ceta-based vithis can be seen as the underlying mechanism. This also explains why psychotic episodes tend to reoccur. If one has seen things as they are, then that insight remains. Psychosis can be linked to phenomena of dissociation. In a light and innocent form a dissociation occurs in children (and older humans as well) doing the "repeated word game." Taking a word like "yellow," they speak it out repeatedly. After a while they notice that the word loses its meaning. In psychology one speaks about a "semantic fatigue" or a "*jamais vu*." Usually there is a close connection between a word as sound and the meaning of a word. These two come in consecutive vithis. After repeating the word many times, the sound function gets emphasized and may occur without an immediately following meaning, which may be absent for a short moment. The child has succeeded in separating the sound and the meaning that are both associated to a concept.

In stronger forms of dissociation cognitive formations may be not functioning as usual, by being temporarily dysfunctioning or even being completely absent. From the Abhidhamma model this is quite understandable: cognition has to be formed by an active process and this may temporarily not be the case. For the common sense intuition the phenomenon may be quite startling. One loses grip as the usual model of the world and of oneself slides away. As a reaction mental alarms may start to ring. It is the presence of these alarms that makes the dissociation be felt as an extremely painful experience. Indeed, the alteration of perception of our body, our person, or our world (desomatization, depersonalization, or derealization) may be utterly shocking. During a neurosis the observer can feel that it is his/her view that is in conflict. During a psychosis it feels as if the actual world, our actual mind or body is no longer there.

The presence of these powerful secondary reactions is one of the reasons that the phenomenon of psychosis is a serious one. The other reason is that the phenomenon is based on actual experience: that of the dancing cetas making up the vithis. If it were the case that the underlying phenomena were a rarity, like seeing a disgusting sight, then one would be able to overcome the traumatic experience more easily. But in case of the psychosis, based on the experience of an omnipresent actual internal phenomenon, more is needed to comfort the traumatized person. On the other hand, the possibility of purification described in the Abhidhamma model seems to imply that one can be cured from reoccurring psychoses. This view on mental illnesses (often seen as incurable) has been stated by Podvoll (1991). Menninger and others (1963) even described that some schizophrenics get "weller than well." This may also be related to the process of purification. The present author does not have a view on whether reoccurring psychoses may be cured, but likes to emphasize, on the basis of own experience with the purification path and of the Abhidhamma model, that it is worthwhile to seriously investigate this possibility.

3. *Cover-up of emptiness.* The experience of fragmented personality and cognition as a stream of cetas is known to meditators. According to the above discussion it may cause in a person (familiar or not to meditation) an acute psychosis. This "existentialist" experience is so horrendous that if one wrongly would see someone else as its cause, one could kill that person. For this reason I called this experience the "very cause of war" (Barendregt, 1996) in order to emphasize its power. As is well-known Buddhism often speaks about suffering (*dukkha*). Here, one may think of negative aspects of life, including transiency, as its cause. But, as explained by Buddhagosa (ca. 450/1999), the principal meaning of this Pali word comes from its two roots *du* and *kha*, the first standing for "disgust" and the second for "emptiness." In this respect the existentialist "nausea" related to "nothingness," found in the work of Sartre, comes very close.

To the person experiencing the void, whether meditator or psychotic, it comes as a shock. In many cases some emergency mechanisms automatically start to work to avoid the emptiness. My father J.T. Barendregt, during his life a professor of clinical psychology, specialized in working with patients suffering from phobias. His clinical observation was that all these patients had previously experienced a form of depersona-lization in which they became aware of an inner "chaos" and experience of "being without control." He coined the hypothesis that phobias are a way of repersonalization based on fear, avoiding the feeling of uncontrollability (Barendregt, 1982). Indeed, the state of fear may be unpleasant, but gives a psychological hold. Therefore, by the sufferer it is "preferred" over the state of the void. But it should be emphasized that the person in question does not make a conscious choice. The phenomena just happen. In my own work (Barendregt, 1996) this hypothesis about the role of fear is extended to other strong effects, like hatred and desire. This is based on experience reported in that paper and in Barendregt (1988). Also depression may be seen as a cover-up of emptiness. The emergency exit from emptiness does not need to be a "negative" affect. For example, falling in love is viewed by J.T. Barendregt (1982) as a "pleasant" form of avoiding the emptiness.

There is a third way of avoiding the emptiness: using drugs, either medically prescribed ones or street-drugs. In fact, the pharmaceutical market for antipsychotics is 20 billion US$ yearly. That of street-drugs is unknown, but it is claimed that the number of deaths from overdoses of prescribed drugs exceeds that of street-drugs by far. Be that as it may, it is clear that the fragmentation of consciousness as a chain of cetas has far reaching consequences by the claimed nauseating feeling it causes. Another "neutral" way to cover-up the ceta process may be the clinging to ideas. This can be seen as the reason behind religious wars.

Finally, the most elevated way to cover-up the void is developing "mystical experiences," the so-called states of "mental absorption."

The three ways of cover-up can be seen as hatred, greed, and ignorance, the main symptoms of continued suffering. All forms of cover-up of the void or emptiness caused by the deterministically flowing stream of cetas are seen in Barendregt (1996) as a symptomatic medicine. They act as glue and make consciousness apparently continuous. But it does not change the fundamental fact that we do not have an absolute control over our mental life. The negative and positive affects as well as the hiding by drugs and ignorance are all seen in the Abhidhamma model as unwholesome. The Pali word for unwholesome is *akusala* being the opposite of *kusala*, which literary means taking out (*sala*) the nausea (*ku*, being a synonym of *du*). The discrete essence of consciousness and its resulting counter-reactions can be seen as its main cause. From the ceta model it seems to follow that one either suffers from psychosis or is involved in a symptomatic cover-up. Cultivating the middle way using mindfulness provides a way out of either form of suffering. This and its therapeutic consequences will be discussed.

Development of Mindfulness and Compassion

The Abhidhamma model coming from the Buddhist tradition has been obtained as a side effect of completing the path of purification. Having the description of that model, the path itself can be stated in a relatively simple way. It should be emphasized that the path is a practical course, similar to learning how to sail on the ocean. Therefore, the explanations below, not to be found in the Abhidhamma itself but in the Suttas, do miss something: the actual experience that cannot be conveyed in words.

1. *Mental development.* The goal of the path of purification is to prevent that unwholesome cetas are being used. In this way no new negative kamma is accumulated and one obtains a larger degree of freedom. Lower insects are programmed in such a way that they fly towards a source of light, including a dangerous candle. Higher insects can avoid this. The path of purification may be compared to the transformation from a lower to a higher insect. In order to avoid unwholesome cetas one needs the intuitive insight that the apparent need to use them is unjustified. Our system seems to be based on the need for desire, hatred, or ignorance in order to glue the fragmented cetas to a whole. But this is not the case. This fundamental insight, however, cannot be forced; it has to come "by itself." But it can only develop if the mind is relatively calm and concentrated. Concentration cannot be forced either. It has to be developed following a certain plan. It is like a plant that grows from a seed, provided that one gives it soil, water, and light. This simile shows that in its turn concentration needs another mental factor: discipline. At first will power can be used to obtain discipline that is needed. Using this initial discipline one can build an initial degree of concentration. Then using this

concentration a higher degree of discipline can be obtained. At the same time one's view of what has to be done can be sharpened. In this way one obtains the right conditions on which insight can grow.

2. *Mindfulness*. The main tool in this process of mental development is mind-ful-ness. It is the capacity to be close to mental input, cetas and cetasikas, without being sucked away by them. For example, one can be close to a desirable or fearful object without losing control of what happens next. Mindfulness in its first approximation consists of naming what is happening. "Oh, there is desire" or "Oh, there is fear." Later, one can improve mindfulness to *noting*. This is like naming, but without making use of natural language. Indeed, "there is fear" is a weak and inaccurate substrate of the real fear. The right mindfulness (*samma sati*), is directly present as cetasika in the cetas. The aim is to develop mindfulness in such a way that it addresses the cetas "one at the time, on time and all the time," as a good meditation teacher will instruct. In this way all the hidden corners of the mind can be reached and purified. The first milestone to be reached is the purification of the "course defilements" such as doubt, sleepiness, greed, hatred, and restlessness. This can be accomplished by developing confidence, effort, mindfulness, concentration, and analysis. It is important that these five faculties are developed in a balanced way.

3. *The Three Characteristics*. After that, sharper mindfulness will reveal to the meditator a clear vision of the the ceta process. One is able to observe the *three characteristics of existence*: chaos, nausea, and uncontrollability. This is the meaning of the Pali terms *anicca*, *dukkha*, and *anatta* that usually are rendered as impermanence, suffering, and egolessness. It is the penetrative function of mindfulness that brings the meditator to this experience. The experience is overwhelming. The reason is that for the first time one observes the self-less phenomenon of consciousness. Because the meditator is not ready for this, s/he will go through phases of anxiety, disgust, or depression. This state of mind can be compared to a psychotic dissociation with its known effects. In the context of the path of purification it is considered as a *disidentification*.

4. *Purification*. At this point the protective function of mindfulness needs to be developed. With proper effort this can be done relatively quickly as the necessary prerequisites are already present. The meditator has to observe, while continuing the practice, the occurring of short moments of a calm mind. Podvoll (1991) calls these "islands of calm," from which, if developed, a calm and blissful state can be obtained. Arrived at this stage in mental development, there is nothing more to do than to keep performing the act of mindfulness. At some point one considers making mindfulness a burden. With the right intention and surrendering one may stop having to make mindfulness. When the meditation practice has grown to a mature level, then mindfulness may flow by itself and one obtains a purely observing stream of consciousness. If this happens, the fundamental purifying insight that sets one free arises.

Purification happens in four consecutive stages. Each time the meditator is brought closer to full enlightenment. In the first stage, the meditator becomes a *stream-winner*, who has eliminated the cetasikas of wrong view (of the existence of ego as a solid object) and doubt (needing to defend this ego). At the second stage of a *once-returner* the sharp force of greed and hatred is attenuated. At the third stage, one has eliminated the use of greed and hatred and becomes a *non-returner*. At the last stage one becomes an *arahat*, having no more pride, restlessness, sleepiness, desire for mystical states or existence and ignorance.

The need for purification due to the flashing cetas before meaning is caused by ego's existential need to be in charge. Perceiving that one is not, causes fierce fear. The path of purification domesticates this fear. The existential fear may be compared to our feelings of dizziness and nausea while falling. These can be domesticated: an experienced parachutist or astronaut, also subject to the same lack of gravity, enjoys the wide view from above.

5. *Modeling the Purification.* Even if ordinary consciousness consists of the discrete cetas, it seems to be flowing continuously. One can imagine that the object of consciousness is determined by a gradient (i.e. a direction that metaphorically is an indication of the character of the object). Then ordinary consciousness may be depicted stylistically as follows.

$$\backslash\backslash\backslash\backslash\backslash\text{-----}/\!/\!/\!/\!/\text{IIIII}\backslash\backslash\backslash\backslash\text{-----}\_\_\_\_/\!/\!/\!/ \qquad (1)$$

This means that the object and type of the cetas do vary, but not too fast and in a smooth way. Now imagine that the chaotic consciousness of the three characteristics starts for a moment as follows, including unwholesome kamma denoted by __. This is the phase in which one sees the fluctuating three characteristics for the first time.

$$\backslash\text{I}\_\_/\text{-}/\_\text{---}\text{-}./\backslash\text{--}\_\backslash\backslash\text{-}\text{----}/\text{II}\text{-}\backslash\text{-}\text{---}\text{-}/\text{-}/\!/\text{---}\_\text{-}\text{I} \qquad (2)$$

Then the movie gets saturated or "covered-up" (Barendregt, 1996) with strong feelings that reinforce themselves. This develops into an overwhelming kammic experience that causes strong mechanisms of fear, disgust, or depression, a relatively stable state.

$$\left. \begin{array}{l} \backslash\_\_\text{I}\_\_/\_\_\text{-}/\_\_\_\text{-}\_\text{---}\_\text{---}/\_\_\backslash\_\text{-}\_\text{-} \\ \_\_\backslash\_\_\backslash\_\_\_\text{-}\_\_\text{-}_____/\_\_\text{II}\_\_\text{-}\_\_\backslash \end{array} \right\} \qquad (3)$$

If one uses psychopharmacological or some other drugs one may obtain a similar but even more rigid state of mind.

$$\left. \begin{array}{l} \backslash\_\_\text{I}\_\_/\_\_\text{-}/\_\_\_\text{-}\_\text{---}\_\text{---}/\_\_\backslash\_\text{-}\_\text{-} \\ \_\_\backslash\_\_\backslash\_\_\_\text{-}\_\_\text{-}_____/\_\_\text{II}\_\_\text{-}\_\_\backslash \end{array} \right\} \qquad (4)$$

If, as alternative possibility, one continues to practice meditation, then it may happen that one obtains the ability to look with equanimity at consciousness described in (2) and (4). Then maggaceta removes the poison of kamma from this type of consciousness:

$$\text{\textbackslash I/-/\_-\_/\textbackslash--\textbackslash\textbackslash\_-\_-/II-\textbackslash} \tag{5}$$

This is still chaotic, but quite bearable because the painful experience is taken out. Pretty soon consciousness turns back to normal as in (1) by the natural tendency to concentrate. The natural order in which these types of consciousness streams occur is as follows: (1), (2) for a short while, (3) glued, (2) but now possible for a longer period, maggaceta, (5) and then (1). This is when one is lucky enough to be in the great monastic places, the laboratory of the mind. If one is not protected by the right knowledge (Dhamma), but finds oneself in ignorant modern society where panic gets replaced by drugs or compulsory behavior, then the sequence may be: (1), (2), (3), (4), (3), (4),... During the meditation practice one learns that it is better to first use mindfulness in order to *cope* with the situation. After that, insight can *cure* the mental state.

6. *Ethics.* The practice of mental development through mindfulness meditation has ethical value for an interesting reason. The claim is that what is fundamentally good for a person is good for everyone. As long as there are still active cetas with greed or hatred, the person in whom this is the case will encounter situations that cannot be manipulated and hence suffering arises. Only if these two types of cetas are eliminated, and those with ignorance as well, the practitioner becomes really free. Thus it happens to be the case that ethical behavior is a necessary condition for the obtainment of the mentioned purification. This has been emphasized in the so-called Noble Eightfold Path in which the right speech, action, and livelihood are being emphasized. One behaves correctly, first out of duty and later, after purification, out of virtue.

7. *Mahayana Buddhism: Compassion and Koans.* In the Mahayana tradition it is not mindfulness, but compassion that is the principal cetasika being developed. As compassion is an occasional beautiful cetasika, this has the advantage that one develops mindfulness and all the other universal beautiful cetasikas as well. An important point is that in the presence of compassion, maggaceta leading to purification cannot occur. This is because compassion has human beings as the object, while maggaceta has nibbana as the object. This fits exactly with the Mahayanists' Bodhisattva vow of not wanting to become enlightened before all other beings are. Thus the Mahayana practice of compassion has a double goal of developing more beautiful cetasikas and postponing maggaceta. Another particular aspect of Mahayana Buddhism, notably in the Rinzai Zen tradition, is the "koan" practice. In this lineage the meditator is asked to work on a problem that does not have a logical solution. The purpose is to work hard on it so that the vithis of

rational thought get tired and stops working. In this way one may eventually enter the three characteristics of broken consciousness and obtain purification.

Methodology and Initial Evidence

We will discuss the methodology on which the Abhidhamma model was constructed and speculate how it could fit within neurophysiology.

1. *Methodology.* One may wonder whether the Abhidhamma model has anything to do with reality as it is obtained through meditative experience, which is a form of trained introspection. We claim it does. The first argument is that mathematics, rightly considered as one of the most exact sciences, is also based on trained phenomenology. True, in this discipline results are based on calculations and proofs. But in its turn, one needs a mental judgment whether a calculation does apply and whether a proof is correct. Therefore mathematics, as emphasized by Husserl, Gödel, Bernays, and others, can be seen as a phenomenological enterprise. The second argument comes from the so-called Newton-Goethe dispute about colors. These two gentlemen did not live at the same time; they represent the position of the physicist and of the phenomenologist in a controversy about the nature of colors. Newton held that colors are a 1D (one dimensional) phenomenon. Indeed, light comes with a wavelength and different wavelengths correspond to different colors. Goethe on the other hand held that colors form a 3D phenomenon. He took a bag of 125 cubes each with a different color and wanted to order them in the "Montessori way" (such that if their colors are similar, then they have to be placed near each other). Goethe could not do this putting the cubes in a linear array, nor in a plane, but with the cubes placed in a 3D fashion (in a 5x5x5 cube) this was possible. Therefore, Goethe held that colors are a 3D phenomenon. For a while the two positions seemed to be irreconcilable, but then a solution came from the physician Young and later the physicist Helmholtz in the 19th century. They independently stated the hypothesis that the sensitive eye has three different kinds of receptors for color vision, each with its own sensitivity for the light spectrum. Then *one* wavelength λ gives rise to a *triplet* of reactions in the three different kinds of receptors. Hence, light has both a 1D and a 3D aspect, depending on whether one considers its production or its perception. Later the hypothesis of the three kinds of receptors turned out to be correct. Not only was the controversy settled, the obtained insight in the functioning in color perception also gave raise to the multi-billion US$ industry of color monitors, flatscreens, and projectors. The moral is that both science and (trained) phenomenology are important, and can reinforce each other.

2. *Parallel and serial processing.* The presence of the cetas in the Abhidhamma model emphasizes that consciousness has a strong serial component. The collaborating cetasikas point at a parallel processing. It is well-known from neuropsychological experiments that consciousness has parallel and serial aspects. Spotting a

red letter on a page with further black letters is instantaneous and therefore the mind works here in parallel. On the other hand, if the task is to find a red T on a page with black T's and F's and further only red F's, one has to scan the possible candidates one by one (i.e. in a serial fashion). A possible implementation in the brain of the serial discrete series of cetas is the firing of one group of neurons. Indeed, this firing is happening in discrete units. Also the action potential of each neuron has clearly an arising, existing, and disappearing phase, which comes close to the described life cycle of a ceta. Some empirical evidence for the discreteness of consciousness is found by Lehmann et al. (1998). In this paper multichannel EEGs are studied by making a map of iso-potential lines. It was observed that the "landscape" makes a sudden change about every 100 ms. The 1981 "synchronicity hypothesis" (Von der Malsburg, 1994) states that in order to represent an object in the brain, a population of neurons fire simultaneously. This then happens in a serial way: objects being formed one after the other. The similarity with Abhidhamma's model of the cetasikas and cetas is close. The four types of kamma (producing, supporting, obstructing, and destructing) fit very well with the well-known collaborating excitatory and inhibitory types of neurons. Finally, the notion of accumulated kamma may be implemented by the development of new synapses between neurons.

   3. Cover-up. If consciousness consists of a discrete stream of mental atoms, it is likely that there is a mechanism that regulates and smoothens the transitions between the cetas. The idea of "volume transmission" (Nieuwenhuys, 2000), first formulated under a different name (Nieuwenhuys, 1985), states that next to synaptic transmission in the brain from neuron to neuron, there is also a non-synaptic transmission, in which the chemical messenger is diffused over the extracellular space (volume) within the brain.[8] Indeed, the idea implies the possibility that the diffusing neurotransmitter of a particular kind may act as a neuromodulator. This may set the mind in a particular mood, so that there is not a high degree of variability. Stress hormones and opioids may play a role in the implementation of the unpleasant or pleasant cover-up as coping mechanism.

   4. Purification. Given the Abhidhamma model and the possible way it is implemented in the brain along the lines sketched above, there is an inherent danger for humans. The cover-up may fail, causing dissociation with a panic effect that often may be a psychosis or a cover-up as emergency exit. The claim is that mindfulness can be developed as cure for some forms of distress, as it takes out the poison of kamma from the impersonal potentially chaotic process of consciousness. Evidence comes from *Mindfulness Based Stress Reduction* (MBSR) developed by Kabat-Zinn (2003) and later from *Mindfulness Based Cognitive Therapy* (MBCT; Segal et al., 2002). It is emphasized that therapists using MBSR and MBCT should have a pretty good experience with mindfulness meditation. This is an important remark for at least two reasons. Firstly, the practice of mindfulness cannot be taught in an intellectual level, but needs a living example. The second reason is that it is important for the therapist to have experience with the three characteristics. Another point to be made is that psychotherapy and mindfulness meditation are different methods going in the same direction. Undergoing psychotherapy may be compared to learning to swim, while practicing mindfulness corresponds to learning to dive. It is helpful to know that coming up after a dive swimming is within one's range of capacities. Psychotherapy works towards building some form of stable ego. Meditation on the other hand leads to the ability to detach from this ego, depending on the occasion. First things first; the simile also shows that there is a difference in scope. Therapy is good for acting in the world, for life, while meditation is good for one's total being, including the fact that we are mortal.

How mindfulness can be implemented in the brain may be speculated as follows. The phenomenon could be related to reflection, familiar from Gödel's self-referential statement or from the universal Turing machine (Hofstadter, 1979; Barendregt, 2005b). The important point is that reflection is a mechanism that is relatively simple and can easily be implemented by a network of firing neurons within one ceta.

Postscript

The Abhidhamma model of consciousness comes from a millennia long tradition of trained introspection and has been verified by meditators that have taken the effort to do the investigating work. This does not imply that science should believe that the model is "correct": the role of science is to be sceptical. What we hopefully have shown, is that the model is of enough interest that it and its consequences deserve closer investigation. This not so much for a neurophysiological underpinning of the effects of meditation, but more for a top-down and bottom-up inspiration for neurophysiology, coming from a serious phenomenological study of consciousness. The Abhidhamma model implies that neuroses, psychoses, and an armored personality are natural phenomena, and that there is also a systematic training to go beyond these modes of living.

---

1. This paper is based on inspiring lectures of venerable Sayadaw U. Nandamalabhivamsa (Mahasubodhayon, Sagaing Hills, Myanmar) as well as on the Bodhi (2000) and Nyanaponika (1998). It could not have been written without experience with intensive Vipassana under the skillful guidance of the most venerable Phra Mettavihari (Buddhavihara, Amsterdam, The Netherlands). I thank H. Blezer, F. Giommi, S. Hermans-van Strien, O. Meijer, and A. van Waning for useful discussions.

2. Mahayana stands for the large vehicle. This form of Buddhism developed in China, Korea, Japan, and some other countries. The emphasis is not on becoming enlightened but on starting the process of purification so that equipped with extra possibilities one may care for the world. Theravada Buddhism is often called *Hinayana* (small vehicle) by the Mahayana Buddhists, with an intended pejorative taste.

3. The intended meaning is *perceived* matter, not the thing in itself.

4. The isolated ceta, not the total of ceta and cetasikas, is called *pure consciousness (ceta).*

5. The beautiful cetasikas are not called "wholesome" as they have too little kammic force to have such an effect. Only in combination with some other cetasikas, related to energy and concentration, wholesome cetas are formed.

6. *Samsara* is the circle of birth and death, to be avoided.

7. It is unknown what pure consciousness is. In Vipassana retreats one is not allowed to think about it, as it distracting. Opinions about this notion vary. Some authors propose to extend contemporary physics in order to accommodate pure consciousness (Chalmers, 1996); others claim it already fits within quantum physics (Stapp, 1993; Schwartz & Begley, 2002); then there is the proposal to treat pure consciousness as a primitive term (Hut & Shepard, 1996); others contend, it is a superfluous concept (Dennett, 1991).

8. This idea has been specialized to the "liquor hypothesis," which states that the cerebrospinal fluid plays the role of mediating volume. One of the reasons for this hypothesis is that if opioids are placed in the liquor, then a peculiar anesthesia results: the pain remains but is no longer perceived as unpleasant. Exactly this phenomenon can be observed during concentration meditation. Calle et al. (2005) have observed that in the periventricular parts of the brain there are many liquor contacting cells containing opioids and stress hormones.

23

The Eight Sacred Paths And Anger Management In Japanese Youth

Rika Kawano & Masao Suzuki

This chapter describes the need to re-introduce to Japanese youth the Buddhist teaching of the Eight Sacred Paths, also called the 8-Fold Path: the cultivation of right mindfulness, concentration, understanding, intention, effort, action, speech, and livelihood. A recent survey showed that the young people's interest in the Buddhist way of living has declined significantly, whereas emotional disturbance like kireru *(sudden outburst of enragement destroying others and/or oneself by otherwise normal youngsters) is growing rampant. The authors argue that Mindfulness-Based Stress Reduction — that has become popular in the West and which is mainly based on the Theravada technique of fully attending and unconditionally accepting the present — presented as* kata *(personalized form and shape of exercising) may re-invigorate Japanese youths' interest in the Buddhist values that once inhered in Japanese society.*

Our own research — conducted amongst 400 Japanese college students living in the Tokyo area (ages ranging from 18-23) — shows that their level of understanding and impressions of Buddhism are poor. Through surveys we found that about 80% of these students are not interested in Buddhist Dharma (teachings) in general and that largely there is no interest whatsoever in Zen. Their ideas of what Buddhism in itself might entail were reflected in direct associative expressions that represent their thinking: a "funeral ceremony," "priests," "Buddha statues," "strict rules (religious precepts) and training," as well as "historical constructions in Kyoto and Nara." It can thus be inferred that for the present younger generations in Japan urban society Japanese Buddhism and its concomitant culture are crumbling and has gradually been turned into "just a ceremony" or nothing but "philosophical relics."

On the other hand observers noticed an increasing trend among Japanese youth in the number of collective suicides through morbid "how-to-die" websites and other anomalies like *hikikomori* and *kireru*. These are two opposite phenomena that belong to our area of expertise. In this chapter we will restrict our focus on the latter subject. While hikikomori — social withdrawal of mostly boys, who probably cannot cope with the demands to excel, by locking themselves up in a room and refusing to exit while being cared for by the parents who hope the behavioral disorder will disappear one day — manifests itself in for about one million school-children. Kireru or "snapping" is a sudden outburst of violent rage in run-of-the-mill youngsters with frequently a fatal consequence qualified by experts as criminal. Decrying an increase in kireru the news media for instance reported an extreme incidence: "several middle-class high school boys murdered a mutual friend after a minor disagreement. There seemed to be little real hate in the act — the boys even stopped to share refreshment with their friend before dealing him the killing blows" (Washington Post; August 24, 2003). How many youngsters are afflicted by kireru is unknown, but a recent study found that in general as many as 30% of junior and senior high school students have experienced sudden acts of rage at least once a month (Obayashi, 2005).

Kireru and Mukatsuku

Japan seems to be experiencing a tsunami of snapping amongst high school students who are seemingly ordinary but who unaccountably become violent for quite a while (Miyashita & Ohno, 2003). Questionnaires completed by 5138 junior and senior high school students from the metropolitan area (Tokyo, Kanagawa, and Saitama) revealed that kireru-prone students had much stress in their interpersonal relationships with family and peers at school and in society. They feel oppressed and depressed. It was found that kireru is associated with having meals alone, lack of conversation, lack of sleep, feeling too burdened and irritated in daily life, and being bullied. Kireru sufferers are often depicted as criminal and delinquent if judged by the consequences of their acts. However, in our assessment of their psychological condition they cannot by definition be called juvenile delinquents. They are mostly ordinary Japanese students who unexpectedly exhibit an extreme loss of control because they cannot take abnormal stress anymore. In a way it is a "normal" reaction to "abnormal" environmental demands they could not any longer cope with, which give rise to breaking through their mental defences of repression. They were never diagnosed as psychopathological before and did not meet any DSM criteria for Conduct Behavior, Attention Deficit/Hyperactivity Disorder, Asperger's Syndrome, or Oppositional Deficit Disorder.

Why does kireru prevail in the Japanese younger generation? Why do basically normal students suddenly blow up and commit violent acts toward others and themselves? Japanese psychologists, educators, teachers, therapists, and social workers who face the puzzling problem in the community have been trying to explain this phenomenon, but have thus far failed to develop a satisfying conceptual framework. There seems to be neither apparent nor significant differences that distinguish normal students from kireru "delinquents" making the phenomenon hard to predict. The basis for the outrage seems to be rooted in normal frustration and anger (*mukatsuku*) that belong to the daily hassle of living, a suffering from which nobody can escape as already averred by the Buddha. Mukatsuku usually refers to feelings of irritation-anger and frustration, but can also signify a feeling of being dissatisfied or offended; it also might mean a repressed state from which one cannot find release and thus reflecting a being on the verge of emotional explosion. Youngsters tend to use mukatsuku when expressing an attitude of rejection or dislike toward somebody in an aggressive way (lower grade students) or when s/he feels inner turmoil and dissatisfaction (higher grade students). In other words the semantics might vary depending on context and the term might refer to various states of mind with one common denominator: the basic emotion of anger. In the Buddhist tradition such collection of angry affect is called the poison of hatred that might vary in intensity ranging from animosity, annoyance, contempt, fury, hostility, rage, resentment, to *amok* (Kwee, 1998). The latter might be the South-East Asian equivalent of kireru as they both carry the meaning of a prolonged repression of anger that eventually turns into a blind fury with devastating aggression and often a fatal outcome.

Thus, mukatsuku if left unattended might eventually lead to kireru. This hunch has found some corroboration in a survey, conducted by the Benesse Educational Research Foundation, among 1235 students in the 7th to the 9th grades at four junior high schools in Tokyo. This survey revealed that 17% of those who experienced mukatsuku everyday succumbed to kireru everyday and that 91% of the daily kireru sufferers also felt mukatsuku everyday (Fukaya, 1998). As mentioned earlier most if not all kireru students who snap and become enraged report malaise, mentally and physically. They feel discomfort in their daily lives at home and at school. An overwhelming majority of students who are enraged on a daily basis tend to not have one single friend to share experiences with or that might be willing to listen when they feel despondent. Only 10% of the students reported rarely feeling angry. While half of the students try to control their anger, others act out violently toward people or objects. There seems to be a tendency to act out the anger in physical activities like vigorously engaging in hazardous or risky behaviors. Kireru."s extreme loss of control might explain the variance perceived in the violent youth crime in Japan. This increasing frequency of juvenile delinquency points at these misbehaving youngsters with their uncontrollable emotions and impulsive way of conduct that has been labeled "criminal" with detrimental consequences for their future (Miyashita et al., 2001).

Buddhist Values in Japan

Peculiar emotional disturbances as described above exist seemingly as a sign of the times in contemporary Japan, which is in an industrialized society. During six decades since World War II western values have been overwhelming Japanese culture to such a degree that our traditional ways of living is crumbling if not collapsing. The present cosmopolitan and globalist values of postmodernity even influenced the educational system, resulting in the emergence of individualism, (over)assertiveness, and/or lack of discipline, once considered to be non-Japanese. As a result, youngsters show tendencies implying disrespect for traditional values, which have been rooted for centuries in culture, such as being calm, tranquil, and thoughtful toward others, or showing respect toward older persons. Even their eating and drinking habits turned out to be problematic leading to overweight and other life-style related diseases. We are not expounding here that western, cosmopolitan/global, values are evil, but without having the genuine historical and cultural background of social interconnectedness as a sound basis the application of individualistic and in traditional eastern eyes "selfish" ways of thinking and behaving will likely lead to alienation and emotional derailments as earlier prognosticated by social critics. We hypothesize that the ultimate consequence of our westernized culture might partly explain the phenomenon of kireru and that Buddhist meditation practice might be able to counter its growing upsurge just like the present frenzy in the Dharma in the West seem to be able to successfully tackle stressful ways of living in Europe and in the US.

If eastern and western are taken not as geographical locations but as mentalities, Japan surely has transformed into a western country with all the ailments of industrialized societies in need for healing. Buddhist values have been an important part of Japanese culture and turned out to be the most relevant in the past out of a few other values (derived from Shintoism, Confucianism, and Taoism). Particularly Zen as a Buddhist variety had been imbued in many areas of life after having been cultivated in the past centuries. (Zen) Buddhist practices aim to nurture inner balance through equanimity and self-control, loving kindness, compassion, and contentment (*ware tada taruo siru*), eventually unveiling human innate suchness (Buddhanature). The method to embody these basic values is contained in the Eight Sacred Paths designed by the Buddha in order to release humanity from suffering due to existence itself. By thinking through kireru along traditional Buddhist lines, we surmise that there exists a way that might be helpful to prevent and "cure" the affliction by emotionally (re-)educating young people by means of daily meditation. Our hope is that we are likely able to motivate youngsters by teaching them first of all a historical sense of the ingrainedness of Buddhist values in Japanese culture that goes back to Prince Shotoku Taishi (574-622) who unified the nation < http://theosophy.org/tlodocs/teachers/PrinceShotoku.htm > and is considered the founder of Japanese Buddhism.

Buddhist teachings (Mahayana) reached Japan about 1000 years after the Buddha's death in 538 when a delegate from the Korean kingdom of Paekche offered the court of emperor Kimmei several Buddhist scriptures and a gilt bronze, solemn gleaming Buddha statue (which was a revelation, since in Japan until then the sacred never took a human form). After some disputes between clans Buddhist teachings were adopted by Empress Suiko, who reigned in the early 7th century after succeeding her brother Yomei. It was the latter's son Shotoku (a nick name meaning "holy and virtuous") who as his aunt's regent was factual ruler and whose first deed of regency at age 19 was to proclaim the Buddhist Dharma as a state religion. In 604 he spelled out a 17-Article Constitution that was based on Buddhist and Confucian ideas. This *kempo* (Jushichijo kenpo) was not a set of laws but rather a statement on the moral basis of sound government and Japanese society based on harmony (*wa*) through the practice of compassion emphasized in the second article promulgating the "worship of Buddhism" giving the state a unique Buddhist quality. The idea of the Buddha as a redeemer implies the supreme value of each individual, since anybody can be one with the Buddha in consciousness. Analogously, the singular status of the monarch as *Tenno* (heavenly ruler) implies the equality of all people suggesting the need for a single emperor. Under Shotoku the Dharma flourished in Japan reminding us of another great Buddhist Emperor, Asoka (299-237 BCE), who was ancient India's greatest ruler (Kitagawa, 1984). As the spiritual leader of his people Shotoku was a proponent of the Nagarjuna's heritage (*Sanron*/Three-Treatise School) he also lectured about. Furthermore, he wrote commentaries on the Lotus, Vimalakirti, and Lion's Roar Sutras that contain parables representing his intentions at best.

After Prince Shotoku and Zen's great impact the Buddhist influence in almost every aspect of Japanese culture is undeniable. Mentioning Japanese culture without Buddhism is untenable (Watanabe, 1958). The present revival of the Buddhist Dharma in the West, is a source of inspiration to re-think our heritage and re-invigorate our own Buddhist traditional values for the sake of mental health, preventing and healing conditions like kireru.

The Eight Sacred Paths

Re-introducing the Buddhist teachings to youngsters, it is not only imperative to motivate them but also to present the principles of the Dharma as simply as possible. The 4-Noble Truths and the 8-Fold Sacred Path are to date the Buddha's most clear exposition to cultivate a virtuous way of life. The 4-Noble Truths state that (1) life inheres in suffering due to ignorance on impermanence, (2) it is caused by greedy clinging or hateful rejecting, (3) it can be terminated by choice and awareness, and (4) the end of suffering can be achieved through the Dharma, also called the Middle Way that is operationalized in the 8-Fold Path. These Eight Sacred Paths comprise (Fischer-Schreiber et al., 1994):

(1) Right view
(2) Right intention
(3) Right speech
(4) Right conduct
(5) Right livelihood
(6) Right effort

(7) Right mindfulness

(8) Right concentration

The numbers seven and eight on the path — mindfulness and concentration — form the general factor accompanying all Buddhist practice and meditation and are extensively described in the *Nikayas* (discourses of the Buddha; *Mahasatipatthana Sutta, Digha Nikaya* 22) preserved in the Hinayana (Theravada) tradition. Being mindful means to bear in mind and implies being regardful, attentive, heedful, and observant, which requires concentration and being in the here-and-now. A succinct definition of mindfulness meditation is to pay attention in a particular way: on purpose, in the present moment and non-judgmentally (Kabat-Zinn, 1994). Other authors emphasize acceptance (whatever is as is) and commitment to gently stay in the present while also willfully acting on the moment's demands (without being compulsory) (e.g. Linehan, 2003). In such practice, attention if distracted is brought back gently and friendly to the present. The effect of training is comparable to find the remote control of one's TV set. Mindfulness is a highly refined, systematic, intentional strategy to develop a calmness of mind-and-body as well as a deep insight into an array of mental and physical conditions that inhibit an individual's capacity to respond effectively and proactively in everyday life. To manage problematic behaviors (and its concomitant cognitions) the paying of attention to the mind and its contents is significant to come to grips with impulsivity. To master mindfulness leading to a decrease in mukatsuku and kireru for youngsters is an arduous task that, if successfully acquired, might be an invitation to walking the rest of the path.

Mindfulness is a mental skill that can be learned like learning to ride a bicycle or to play the piano and there is therefore nothing mysterious about it. Like learning any other skill one starts with the basics and easy practice to progress into harder practice. Mostly someone who is a few steps ahead and more experienced teaches the practice in a class or a group of mind-likes that can be supportive to encourage each other. Without doubt the exercise is something that one does all alone and improvement depends on practice, practice, and practice. Progress results in the "birth" of an "observing or wise mind" (Buddhanature, true self, or the mind's eye) that prevent the mind from being hijacked and synergizes thought-feeling-action so that wisdom and skilful action prevails even in life's hard circumstances. The practice will not prevent rain or pain from entering one's life but will help in surfing on the waves of one's inner stormy weather and endure life's troubles. Instructions for mindfulness sound deceptively plain. However, to be aware of the world without judging and to take life as it is, oneself as one is, others as they are, in the here-now, via direct and immediate experience may turn out in the beginning to be difficult. At a certain point mindfulness suddenly is and one discovers to be awake to whatever is on its terms and to be fully alive to each moment as it arrives, is, and goes. Before one applies mindfulness while in action, walking, lying, or standing, one sits comfortably with the spine upright and, if on a chair, with the soles of the feet flat on the floor.

A two-tiered working definition presented by the Transcultural Society for Clinical Meditation and which has also been used as an effective instruction goes as follows (also described in Chapter 28):

> (a) Cultivating a neutral presence by remembering to attend in a watchful, focused and compassionate~tolerant way to the stimuli entering consciousness via the senses and any thinking-feeling passing in the space of BodyMind.
>
> (b) Noticing receptively (no purpose or interference) the internal stimuli attended to in a choiceless awareness (no expecting, desiring, or evaluating) while surfing from-now-to-now without clinging or grasping, like a mirror.

Mindfulnes-Based Stress Reduction

The frenzy or hype in the West on Buddhist meditation has been partly fed by a stress reduction program called Mindfulness-Based Stress Reduction (MBSR) that has been developed since 1979 at the University of Massachusetts Medical Center in Worcester, Massachusetts, USA by Jon Kabat-Zinn (1990, 1996). The central focus is training in mindfulness and its integration into the challenges of everyday life. Since its inception in 1979 more than 16.000 people have completed the 8-week program have been taught to make use of innate resources and abilities to respond more effectively to stress and stress-related conditions. Over 4000 physicians referred patients in the past 25 years. Acknowledged as the most effective and widely researched stress inoculation programs, MBSR is now offered at over 200 hospitals, clinics, and university facilities in the USA. As a complementary treatment (not a substitute medical/psychological treatments) it has been gaining ground for managing various ailments and is of use to people not only to cope with stress (job, family, relationships, financial, grief, type A behavior), but also with chronic mental conditions (pain, sleep disturbances, hypertension, headaches, fatigue, depression, anxiety, panic, GI-distress) as well as with debilitating physical ailments (psoriasis, cancer, side effects of cancer treatment, heart disease, HIV infection, AIDS). Other applications are in elementary schools, prisons, companies, and with athletes, judges, attorneys, and health professionals. Studies are underway on eating disorders, addictions, immune function, prostate cancer, fibromyalgia, and irritable bowel syndrome. Mindfulness' root as a meditation practice stemming from the Buddhist (Theravada) tradition was at first being hidden not to back off potential clients and MDs, but this omission has now largely been restored.

The generic training program (mixed groups with different diagnoses) is offered in classes up to 40 people and consists of 8-weekly sessions, each lasting 150-180 minutes. The group provides support for participants in fostering a daily practice and discussions about how to integrate mindfulness into various aspects of everyday life. There is a one day silent retreat in the sixth week to help participants deepen their practice that consists of the following components: (1) *Body Scan Meditation*, a slow inner scan of the entire body (greyhound bus tour with the mind's eye in lying position), (2) *Gentle Hatha Yoga*, a technique applied with mindful awareness of the body, (3) *Sitting Meditation*, a training in mindfulness of the breath, body, feelings, thoughts, and emotions, and (4) *Walking Meditation*, a standing and moving whereby one enjoys every step in the present moment without any intention to arrive somewhere. The program is completed by homework: 6-daily assignments of 45 minutes sitting meditation (guided by instructions on CDs) and 15 minutes of informal practice (e.g. in routine activities and relationships) and daily awareness exercises in workbook. The aimed for result is the opposite of mindlessness (living on autopilot and mechanically) simply by cultivating moment to moment non-judgemental awareness by paying attention and listening to the heart. This is in fact a re-awakening of our "Buddhanature or true nature" (what one already is) and of a universal innate capacity that was waiting to be ignited, released and flourish. Being anchored in the bedrock of applied science, the time seems ripe to integrate mindfulness meditation into the larger cloth of society as this is what the world might have been longing for (Kabat-Zinn, 2005).

Although the MBSR program was introduced to Japan in 1993 (through the translation of Kabat-Zinn's book *Full Catastrophe Living* under the editorship of Y.Haruki), it has not become so popular among Japanese readers as in the West. This is rather puzzling because the teaching method of MBSR is very well known through the Japanese Buddhist term — *shugyo* — that might be translated as learning and mastering something by doing. Perhaps some 15 years ago it was awkward for Japanese psychologists to have a Buddhist training re-imported from the West with resistance as a result. We do not have a straight-forward explanation why MBSR remained on the fringe of mainstream science in Japan. However, since the MBSR program has proven to be effective as a therapeutic tool and is enjoying a growing popularity among professionals in western countries, we reason that it might be suitable to teach it to westernized Japanese youngsters especially to teach them to cope with mukatsuku and kireru. But, there is a "but": we advise that it should be offered as *kata*.

MBSR and Kata

In the Jataka stories a classic story is narrated about Prince Gautama, also known as Shakyamuni or the Buddha. When he was struggling in his meditaton training in one of his previous lives, he decided to stop and to descend from the mountain. While descending, he saw a squirrel by a lake. He observed the squirrel putting his tail in the lake and pulling it back on the ground shaking it to dry. He was doing that over and over again. When the Prince asked him what he was doing, he said "I am trying to dry out the water of this lake; you can't understand me because you gave up your training so easily." Hearing this, the Prince made up his mind and climbed up the mountain again. He sat for a long time with new resolve and determined to carry on with perseverance. He understood that a resolute heart that will never turn tail is a prerequisite for the effective use of kata like breathing and sitting that characterize MBSR.

Another Japanese value at risk these days is the assumption that "body control is mind control." This idea has gradually been supplanted by the assumption that "language controls the mind." Kata is the Japanese word for shape or form that precedes, determines, and contains content. The character for kata 型 is composed of three simpler ones. The one in the upper left means shape, the one in the upper right means cut, and the bottom character means ground. A kata is a shape that cuts the ground. Thus, for instance, the form the body takes signifies one's state of mind and reflects its mental content. It functions as a catch word (that Japanese children learn) for the way to master a skill, which is through formal practice, and is derived from the martial arts. The image associated with kata is that of a karate practitioner performing a series of punches and kicks in the air in public demonstrations. This method of teaching goes back to around the year 500 when the Indian monk Bodhidarma (Tamo, Chinese; Daruma, Japanese) the founder of Chan/Zen who allegedly also developed Kungfu in the Buddhist Shaolin monastery in the Hunan province, China. In the Zen tradition, there are three stages of learning: "shu" (becoming familiar with the technique), "li" (leaving what one has imitated as it is), and "po" (breaking away from the learned pattern to infest the technique with one's personal "chi," "ki," or vital energy). These stages point at the student's need to first mimic the master before developing independent ideas. This method emphasizes the specific before the generic, thus first the bodily form then the skill that involves body-and-mind. Kata is a platform on which skills are developed.

Thus not only the martial arts, but anything requiring skills in Japan is preceded by kata that goes beyond mere ceremony, for instance having tea or a meal, flower arranging, kabuki dancing, aikido training, etc. Among the samurai the kata of not showing any emotion in one's facial expression when confronting difficult situations was considered a valuable discipline serving the purpose of survival. Because it is derived from Zen, kata is very apt as analogy to teach MBSR and meditation from which the analogy was derived in the first place. In fact sitting, taking any posture of sitting with the intention to meditate or practice Zen, is manifesting kata. This also applies to walking with the intention to meditate. One performs the same moves again and again with such full awareness that one is only focused on the walking, which becomes an antecedent to forget oneself; by forgetting oneself, one likely stops worrying or building up troubling emotions. The body control of kata has something esthetic and personal and is derived not only from experience due to endlessly repeating the form practice but also from the memorizing how something has been done. To start sitting or walking may thus become an antecedent event or conditioned stimulus to find rest and mindfulness. Thus youngsters might learn to master MBSR as a personal kata to cope with their daily frustration, anger, mukatsuku and kireru.

Kata might function as a catch word depicting a new found savvy mental pattern for youngsters, in particular a personalized judicious way of applying MBSR that might likely break the mental condition of kireru, which is a self-destructive habit resulting from mukatsuku patterns of uncontrollable thinking-feeling-behaving. The fact that MBSR has proven quite effective for various conditions supports our confidence that it might well be successfully applied to westernized Japanese youngsters who experience the daily stress of anger. MBSR may thus become a spring board for youngsters to re-invigorate and remember their forgotten Buddhist heritage and raise their interest to cultivate not only right mindfulness and concentration, but also right view, intention, speech, conduct, livelihood, and effort completing the Eight Sacred Paths.

Closing Remarks

In the past decade many Japanese parents have been shocked by a series of murders, knifings, assault, arson, and other horrendous incidents attributable to kireru of ordinary children who act out outrageous aggression. These kids seemed to be normal in the classroom and/or at home until they snap. This implies that all young people are capable of such deeds. Several causes have been pointed out, such as: lacking a network of supportive relationships, regression to earlier developmental stages, no skills to express frustration and channel stress, inability to express in a socially acceptable manner, and/or maladjustment due to being forced to grow up too quickly (Fukaya, 1998). Although diverse models fail to account for the exact causes of kireru, identifying habitual and reactive ways of handling stress and developing mindful alternatives, like for instance living each moment of life as fully as possible, improved communication, and empathic compassion might well be of help to prevent and overcome the aberration.

While other forms of meditation involve a sound or phrase to reduce distracting thoughts, mindfulness does the opposite. In MBSR one does not ignore distracting thoughts or physical discomfort, but one rather focuses on them. An integral part of its practice is to look at, accept and actually welcome the disturbing experiences that surface to acknowledge present moment reality as it is in order to change one's relationship to it. The empirical benefits of mindfulness are possibly engendered by: (1) exposure and desensitization (experiencing distress without excessive emotional reactivity that makes symptoms worse), (2) cognitive change (non-judgemental observation leads to insight that thoughts and feelings do not necessitate escape or avoidance), and (3) self-management (improved self-observation promotes use of a range of coping skills and activating events are noted not acted upon) (Baer, 2003)

Considering the fact that meditation is something that people in general, particularly youngsters, keep distance from in Japanese society while it may accrue salubrious results, we submit that its use should be re-imported into Japanese society thus restoring 1400 years of traditional Buddhist values. Re-introducing Buddhist meditation might be done via MBSR suitable to modify typical Japanese emotional anomalies like kireru. We predict that if successfully implemented the increasing statistics of juvenile delinquency will be contained and therefore consider setting up a research project to study MBSR's outcome with such sample. MBSR, not a miracle cure, seems suited for youngsters afflicted by kireru because of various reasons. It is a life-affirming program in conscious living that is highly participatory and practical in enhancing everyday awareness. Furthermore, it is not a therapy but a short educational training that contains individually tailored instruction, group dialogue, and daily home assignments that invite participants to learn more. However, its educational orientation will require a strong and determined commitment to gentle but rigorous daily discipline throughout the entire eight weeks of the program and beyond. To implement such an approach to troubled youngsters would undoubtedly require considerable professional coaching.

Living in Japan, although we sit on a wealth of Buddhist treasuries, we must start anew as we are yet incapable of re-inventing our Buddhist assets. While adopting "western" values we have not cared enough about the possibilities the Dharma has to offer us to attenuate the stress of industrialized society. While the West is discovering Buddhist meditation as a beacon of psychological balance longed for by a growing number of people hungry to cultivate inner peace, we have yet to rediscover mindfulness' benefits. In the Zen spirit of *shoshinsha* (beginner's heart) we close with a phrase of T.S. Elliot's poem (Four Quartets) often used in MBSR to contemplate on:

And the end of all our exploring
will be to arrive where we started
and to know the place for the first time.

24

Mindfulness-Based Cognitive Therapy And Embodied Cognition

Mark Williams & Danielle Duggan

Mindfulness-Based Cognitive Therapy (MBCT) is an approach that was developed to reduce the risk of future episodes of major depression. MBCT is based on the Stress Reduction program at the University of Massachusetts Medical Centre, and also includes basic education about depression as well as several exercises from cognitive therapy that show the links between thinking and feeling and how best participants can look after themselves when depression threatens to return. This chapter examines current research on the patterns of information processing that maintain depression and make people vulnerable to future episodes. The processes include the way in which mood activates negative and dysfunctional thought patterns and ruminative processes in previously depressed patients. Many of these risk factors arise from an attempt to use verbal-analytic processing to help solve problems of "self" and "mood." The chapter discusses how mindfulness allows people to learn to pay attention in ways that enable them to recognize and to shift these patterns of processing, with special reference to theories of embodied cognition, theories that emphasize the way that cognitive processes are influenced in fundamental ways by the quality of sensorimotor interactions with the external world.

Depression is often a reaction to an intolerable situation — it occurs in the face of uncontrollable stress from the outside world, but even when it seems to come out of the blue, it is often then maintained by a sense of helplessness arising from an inability to control the inner turmoil of the mind. Core features of clinical depression are low mood and lack of interest in daily activities, but these are not enough to justify a diagnosis of major depression, for which at least four other categories of physical and psychological changes are required out of: changes in appetite and weight, changes in sleep patterns, increased feelings of guilt, inability to concentrate, agitation or retardation, increase in levels of fatigue or the presence of suicidal ideas. Clinical depression is on the increase: epidemiological surveys show that first episodes of depression are occurring at younger ages. It is becoming a major public health problem, with about 20% of the population at risk of clinical depression at some point in their lives (Kessler et al., 1994).

Although a first episode of depression may be precipitated by a major life-changing event, further episodes are more easily triggered (Kendler et al., 2000). The result is that 50% of people who recover from a first episode of depression experience a second within one to two years. Once a person has been depressed more than twice, the risk of further episodes increases to over 80%. Some clinicians now view depression as a chronic, lifelong illness. One review has concluded that those who suffer from one depressive episode will go on to experience an average of four major depressive episodes of 20 weeks duration each over their lifetime (Judd, 1997).

The aim of our research is to understand the nature of this accumulating risk for depressive recurrence and to examine if and how a mindfulness approach may help. The first question is: what is it that keeps people vulnerable to further depression, even after they have recovered?

What Keeps People at Risk?

According to Beck's original cognitive model of depression, people remain vulnerable to further episodes of depression because of the continued presence of dysfunctional attitudes (assessed using the Dysfunctional Attitude Scale; Weissman & Beck, 1978). These general, long-lasting assumptions about the world represent the way in which a person organizes his or her past and current experience. Here are some examples:

> *"I cannot find happiness without being loved by another person"*
> *"People who have the marks of success/ good looks/fame/wealth are bound to be happier than people who do not"*
> *"My worth as a person depends entirely on what others think of me"*
> *"Turning to someone else for advice or help is an admission of weakness"*

According to the theory, dysfunctional attitudes develop over many years and can be activated by any stressful experience that matches the theme of the attitude. In themselves, the attitudes are not depressive; anyone may believe them without being made to feel sad. However, they are like the premises of a syllogistic argument. Just as an argument may follow the form: "All sheep have wool: this is a sheep; *therefore*, it must have wool" so a dysfunctional attitude can provide a premise for a negative self-belief. For example: "Turning to someone else for help is an admission of weakness: I have just asked for help: *therefore*, I am weak." Or, "People who show their emotions by crying are pitiful: I have just cried in front of a friend; *therefore*, I am pitiful." We can see how particular events may combine with such attitudes to trigger depression. Someone who has come to believe that "to be happy, I must succeed in everything I do" may fare perfectly well until they fail an exam at school or college. The failure activates the underlying attitude and they conclude "I cannot be happy" or "I cannot live with this failure."

This cognitive account of relapse in depression makes sense. Cognitive Behavior Therapy (CBT) reduces risk of recurrence (Hollon, 2003), and the theory would assert that this follows from helping people to change their underlying dysfunctional attitudes. By contrast, antidepressants reduce relapse and recurrence *while people are taking them,* but have no long-lasting effect once medication is withdrawn. It was thought that this was because antidepressants reduce acute mood symptoms, but do not modify long-held dysfunctional assumptions. But study after study found that things were not so simple. Ingram and others (1998) reviewed the extensive literature on this topic and found that, so long as a patient is completely recovered, dysfunctional attitudes return to normal, even if they have only received antidepressants. It seems that patients who recover following antidepressant treatment cannot be distinguished in their level of dysfunctional attitudes from people who have had cognitive therapy, nor even from people who have never been depressed before in their lives. Despite being unable to distinguish them, we know that such patients remain more vulnerable for future depression. What is it that makes them vulnerable?

1. *Differential activation.* To cut a long story short, further research has shown that *vulnerability consists of the ease with which dysfunctional attitudes, and other negative self-referent patterns of thinking, are activated by small disturbances in mood.* The typical experiment takes two matched groups of participants, testing them individually in the clinical laboratory. The first group has never been depressed; the second (matched for age, sex, and educational level) are currently non-depressed, but have been depressed in the past. The participants in the two groups are matched for level of current depression and pre-tested for dysfunctional attitudes. In the non-depressed state, both groups show normal scores on this measure. Participants are then given a Mood Induction Procedure for 5-10 minutes (listening to sad music and either reading negative statements such as "all in all, my life is not going too well at the moment" or retrieving sad memories). Both groups become a little sadder, more depressed, a mood change that lasts for five to ten minutes. But whereas participants who have never been depressed express sadness, they do not show an increase in dysfunctional attitudes. They simply feel a little sad. By contrast, the previously depressed participants start to endorse the dysfunctional beliefs. Members of this group are now more likely to feel like their worth as a person depends on what others think of them, and to believe that to be happy they must succeed in everything they do. These studies suggest that risk of depression consists of "over-recruitment" of negative, self-critical thought patterns in response to relatively small changes in mood. Negative thoughts and images then become self-perpetuating. They are more and more easily triggered, making further episodes of depression more likely to occur, even in the absence of negative life events (Post, 1992; Segal et al., 1996; Lau et al., 2004).

The key finding that confirmed to us that this "differential activation" theory was correct was published by Segal and others in 1999. They took patients who were recovered from their depression following treatment with either antidepressants or CBT. If the theory was right, then three things should follow. First, antidepressants should have been as successful as CBT in lowering levels of dysfunctional attitudes. This was true: there were no group differences in dysfunctional attitudes at the end of treatment. Second, because antidepressants reduce such attitudes by bringing about an improvement in mood, the reverse might happen if negative mood was increased: the attitudes might reveal themselves again. By contrast, patients who received CBT would have learned to notice the connection between mood and attitudes, and so would not react to low mood with increased dysfunctional beliefs. Following CBT, mood could deteriorate without escalating into dysfunctional beliefs. This was also found to be the case: the mood challenge (sad music and sad memories) increased DAS scores in the antidepressant group but not in the CBT group. Third, risk of future relapse and recurrence should be predictable from the extent to which mood challenge increased dysfunctional attitudes. This was also shown. Segal and colleagues have now replicated this important result (Segal et al., 2003). It is clear that a critical aspect of the vulnerability of people who have recovered from depression once is that although dysfunctional attitudes are not apparent when they are feeling well, they are reactivated when mood begins to slide.

2. *Global negative self-descriptions.* Other studies find similar differences in the cognitive patterns that come to mind when mood deteriorates between previously depressed and never depressed groups. For example, in their self-descriptions, mood challenge causes people to be more likely to refer to themselves as "worthless" etc. One method of assessing people's tendency to react to mood with such global, negative self-descriptions is to ask what feelings they have experienced at a time when they were feeling depressed over the past month. Of course, in the extent to which people have felt down, or low, over this period varies, but for each unit increase in disturbed mood, those who have been depressed before experience a larger increase in self-denigration (Teasdale & Cox, 2001).

Further research by Willem van der Does and colleagues at Leiden University has shown that people are able to report on their own level of differential reactivity. When asked to imagine themselves becoming a little sad, participants differ, one from another, in how they say they react. This suggests that the assessment of differential reactivation in individuals who have recovered from depression may not need a mood induction procedure (Van der Does, 2002). In a study of 198 participants, the Leiden Index of Depression Sensitivity (LEIDS) was found to distinguish those who had, from those who had not, experienced depression in the past. In a further study (N = 48) the LEIDS was found to correlate with the change in Dysfunctional Attitude Scale following an experimental mood prime. In the original LEIDS, participants are asked to imagine themselves feeling moderately depressed (3 to 4 on a 10 point scale where 0 is "not at all sad" and 10 is "extremely sad"). Using a modification of the LEIDS to bring it closer to Teasdale and Cox's method, we have been collaborating with Van der Does to investigate changes in reactivity over time in suicidal patients.

3. *Rumination.* Finally, risk of recurrence in depression is heightened if people tend to react to their negative mood by ruminating about themselves and their problems, for example; *"Why do I feel this way?" "Why can't I handle things better?"* or *"What am I doing to deserve this?"* (Treynor et al., 2003). When asked about such rumination, patients say that asking "Why?" questions will help them understand themselves better. They believe that if they can answer these questions they will be able to put an end to their suffering or solve their problems.

Research shows that just the opposite happens: rumination produces more severe and persistent depression, and impairs problem solving, rather than enhancing it. Why does this happen? Because: the rumination holds in mind — as its priority — all the negative thoughts and feelings in order to try and "problem solve" them. This means they are constantly available to bias memories of the past and anticipation of the future. Note how the "ruminative mind" attempts to solve problems of mood, using techniques that work well to solve problems in the world generally. In trying to solve a day-to-day problem in normal life — like driving from Oxford to Cambridge — we ask ourselves how far we are from our desired destination, a question that does not itself change how many miles there are to go. But if the problem is "me and my worthlessness," focusing on the gap between how I feel and how I'd *like* to feel actually widens the gap. We feel worse and worse just by considering the question. In driving, if we have got lost, it is legitimate to ask, *"Where did I go wrong?"* By considering such a question, we may recall the road junction where we took a wrong turn, and this helps us get back on track. It seems obvious to use the same technique on problems of ourselves and our mood. But if we consider our own lives, the same question *"Where did I go wrong?"* simply reinforces the conclusion *"My life has gone wrong."* Mood worsens, and that in itself provides further evidence of our inadequacy. No wonder that, when rumination fails, people try to suppress their negative thinking. Yet such suppression and avoidance only serves to make the thinking more likely to return (Wegner, 1994; Wenzlaff et al., 2001). We can become completely entangled.

In summary, risk of further depression is high if small amounts of negative mood have the power to reactivate (a) thought patterns with particular content (global, negative, and self-referent) and (b) maladaptive cognitive processes (cycles of rumination and suppression). Small mood shifts can rapidly bring about a state of mind in which the whole conceptual apparatus of the mind is hijacked by self-denigration and despair.

Self-Reflection and Direct Sensation

Notice that self-reflection is the predominant feature of all the cognitive vulner-abilities we have described (activation of dysfunctional attitudes, negative self-description, rumination). How is self-reflection so easily "taken over" in this way? The answer seems to be that because such conceptual, language-based processing is so clearly useful in other contexts, we carry on using it long after its usefulness has passed (Williams et al., in press a). In fact, because we do not realize that the way we are trying to solve our problems is actually making things worse, the mind falls into the trap of trying to use it, even redoubling its efforts. The problem is not the use of self-reflection per se, but rather its being used to try to solve problems that it was not designed to solve.

It is useful to divide mental functions into conceptual (language-based) pro-cessing and sensory-perceptual processing. In every waking moment we are re-ceiving *sense data* (Latin for *"what is given"*) — sights, sounds, tastes, smells, touch. We usually operate in conceptual mode, with our attention and memory processes taking little account of sensory input except to confirm our conceptual understanding. From time to time, something new or unexpected occurs in the environment and attention shifts automatically to take in more data about it. Take the example of seeing a milk carton in the refrigerator. If you expect to see a carton there, when the sense data comes to the eyes, we need very little sensory process-ing for our mind to label it as "milk." If we are visiting a friend in another country, however, we may look for a while in their fridge for the milk, because the carton is a different shape or color. We intentionally shift attention "downwards" to take in more sensory information. We may make the same shifts with sensations from inside our bodies. If we feel intense sensations, we may label it rapidly as "pain" without checking to feel what actual sensations are giving rise to the intensity. If we feel heaviness in the arms or legs, we may label it as "sleepiness" without further direct processing of the sensations.

The conceptual system gives an abstract, semantic map of the world (not an analogue map). Its "currency" is concepts, thoughts, words, abstraction. It is rule-governed (see Hayes et al., 1999). It is less sensitive to environmental changes than the sensory-perceptual system, and this ability to abstract is immensely use-ful: a table seen from different angles remains a table. It allows self-reflection and a sense of being able to call up" and "inspect" past events and future possible events. It allows us to compare ideas and concepts with other ideas and concepts, to judge the match or mismatch, and to plan how to close the gap between them. It is indirect, using conceptual structures (*about*-ness), rather than direct sensation of the world. It allows elaboration along conceptual links. So I may hear the word "doctor" and think "nurse" and "hospital" — then… ambulance — accident — my car accident in 1983 — my family at that time — my convalescence — my getting behind with work — my current workload — my stress — my poor memory —

last night's conversation about memory - last night's conversation about our plans for the house — our bank balance (how did I end up here?).

The sensory-perceptual system gives an analogue map of the environment and our interaction with it, including limits of our embodiment (i.e. the limits placed on us by the physical body form that we inhabit). It is specialized for learning environmental contingencies, and remaining responsive to changes in those contingencies. It is "data-driven," so within this system, attention can be drawn to objects involuntarily and memory retrieval is direct, situationally driven. It does not rely on concepts, but is sensitive to repetition (priming). Learning within the system is implicit. The sensory-perceptual system can automatically pick up and react to stimuli in the environment that might be important for survival. Sensitivity to patterns and contingencies over long periods means that such stimuli can act as guides to action. These reactions of the body to environmental contingencies are the "somatic markers" that need to be processed to assist us in making wise decisions (Damasio, 1995).

1. *The development of self-reflection in the young child.* Very young infants, with little "conceptual" apparatus, are limited to taking in sensory information, and responding to it mainly in terms of innate reactions of approach (liking) and avoidance (disgust, fear, sadness, and anger) With the development of language and the rapid increase in brain size and cognitive complexity, a fundamental change happens. Between the ages of 3 to 4, children start to self-reflect. With it comes the development of autobiographical memory, the ability to retrieve, at will, events that occurred in the past. Before this age, children may recall events they have experienced, but during this period their recollection is often non-specific. *"Memory of what has happened before 'now' is simply general knowledge without specific reference to a point in the past. The specific past, and the specific future, involve an ordering in time of things that happened before now, and things that will happen after now. Talking about experienced events with parents who incorporate the child's fragments into narratives of the past not only provides a way of organizing memory for future recall but also provides the scaffold for understanding the order and specific locations of personal time, the essential basis for autobiographical memory"* (Nelson & Fivush, 2004, p. 500).

This development of self-reflection continues well after the point at which children can clearly understand and narrate an event in the past, with the learning of how to use *relative* time markers such as *yesterday* and *tomorrow* occurring at the relatively late stage towards the end of the fifth year (Harner, 1982; Habermas & Bluck, 2000). Nelson and Fivush (2004) review a large amount of evidence suggesting, that the greater the extent to which parents (usually the mother) provide an elaborative framework for recollection with their children, the earlier and more elaborative the recollections of their children are. Such recollection by adult caregivers assists, and is assisted by, other developmental changes such as the acquisition of linguistic skills and meta-representation abilities (e.g. in a theory of mind and the growing sense of the distinction between the self and another person). The advantage for the child in having conscious recollection of particular episodes (and knowing that they know — *autonoetic* consiousness or *extended* consciousness (Damasio, 1999) is that they become more proficient at solving novel problems (engaging in "mental time travel" to help them (Tulving, 1983) and can participate in shared conversations that help social meshing (Reese, 2002). A system that allows recollection of specific events allows also the construction of a sense of self in relation to others and construction of a shared narrative.

2. *Problems with self-reflection as its own problem-solver.* Such self-reflection is an amazing capacity of the mind, but it tends to lose touch with the sensory and perceptual systems out of which it emerges. This is the mode in which most of us usually operate for much, if not most of the time. It is not surprising, then, that if we become depressed we try to *think* ourselves out of our problems. If this fails, we try to *suppress* the negative images or thoughts that come into our minds. We try to avoid or escape from our own mental states. There are two problems with this. First of all, although our evolutionary inheritance has given us the skills to escape or avoid an *external* threat, such as a predator, the aversive mental states that are themselves *created* by the self-reflecting mind cannot be evaded. The second problem is that some of our mental states (e.g. emotional memories) are not encoded or stored conceptually, so that self-reflective tactics to suppress them cannot work. Fragments of sensory perceptual input will produce involuntary memories and flashbacks from the past. If a person is able to allow these to occur, then they will gradually diminish in frequency and intensity. But if, when they occur, they are seen by the self-reflective mind as evidence of "my own weakness," then the verbal conceptual system will start to try and do what it does best: problem solve. This is experienced by us as worrying, brooding and ruminating. The mood will deteriorate and the frequency and intensity of these interruptions will become worse rather than better.

We end up taking a "military" approach to our own mind, trying to *control*, *eradicate*, or *defeat* our own mental states, when they are already part of us. Might we instead adopt an ecological metaphor? Ecology is concerned with the *patterns of relationships* of living organisms within their surroundings, habits and modes of life. It may be possible to change from an approach in which we attempt to "overcome," "eradicate," or "defeat" our depression, to a stance that begins to see all aspects of our mind and body as part of an ever changing landscape with its own unique ecology (Williams et al., in press a). How might this be done? Can a mindfulness approach help, and if so, why?

Mindfulness-Based Cognitive Therapy

MBCT was developed as a way of training patients who had recovered from depression in techniques they could use to help them stay well (Segal et al., 2002). It is based on Mindfulness Based Stress Reduction as developed at the University of Massachusetts Medical Centre (Kabat-Zinn, 1990). MBCT combines intensive training in mindfulness meditation with key elements of cognitive therapy, held over eight weekly based class sessions. Each class is two to two and a half hours in length with approximately 12 participants in each class. It has now been shown that *in people who have suffered three or more previous episodes of depression* MBCT can reduce the likelihood of relapse by about 50% (Teasdale et al., 2000; Ma & Teasdale 2004).

Elements of cognitive therapy involved in MBCT include education about the symptoms and the warning signs of depression in order to help participants develop crisis plans that can help to deter potential relapse. Participants are also taught how negative thinking may be exacerbated by our usual coping strategies e.g. by ruminating and/or avoiding. This demonstrates the importance of being able to identify patterns of emotional response that participants may slip into when in a low mood, in order to prevent potential relapse. The main component in MBCT is the mindfulness practice. Mindfulness has been described as "a particular way of paying attention: on purpose, moment-by-moment, and without judgment" (Kabat-Zinn, 1994). Participants in MBCT develop this particular way of paying attention through both formal (prescribed periods of) and informal (incorporating into everyday life) meditative practices (see Table I). The mindfulness component of MBCT is important because of its emphasis on acceptance rather than change. This means that training in mindfulness will encourage the development of a non-ruminative way of processing information. It also means that rather than changing the content of any negative thoughts the classes encourage awareness and acceptance of the thoughts so that a different attitude towards the thoughts may develop (development of meta-awareness; the ability to see thoughts as mental events that can be held in awareness without automatically reacting to them as "true"). Within the classes participants are taught to focus attention on specific aspects of experience such as body sensations or the breath before moving on to learn how to bring mindfulness to a broader range of internal and external experiences. In between classes participants are given tapes or CDs to help them practice both formal and informal meditative practices for one hour per day, six days per week for the duration of the course.

Table 1. Main practices within MBCT: Description of formal and informal practices within MBCT (see also Williams et al., in press b)

Body Scan Paying attention to different parts of the body in turn.

Mindfulness of Routine Activities Paying attention to everyday objects and actions(e.g. eating) that would usually be ignored or taken for granted.

Mindfulness of Breathing Using the breath as a focus of attention.

Mindfulness of Pleasant/Unpleasant Activities Using daily activities as a focus of attention.

3-Minute Breathing Space Using mindfulness of breathing for short periods at set times and when required.

Mindfulness of Body Using the body as a wider focus of attention.

Mindful Stretching/Yoga/Walking Bring attention to the body as it moves.

Mindfulness of Sounds, Thoughts, and Feelings Bring attention to sounds, thoughts and feelings.

In mindfulness meditation we focus on the body in order to be more even-handed about all aspects of mind. The body is the focus of awareness in both in the Body Scan and in the Breath Meditation. In the Hatha Yoga, the *body in movement* is the object of awareness. In later sittings the wider awareness of the body becomes important to detect the *feel of things*, to become intimate with the tendencies of the mind-body to react with aversion (pull away from) anything that is judged to be unpleasant. In a brief meditation practice called the Breathing Space, the first step is recognizing what is arising in the mind and body; the second step is focusing on the breath; the third step is the wider awareness of the body. What emerges is an approach to prevention of depression that is different from cognitive therapy in several respects. It does not attempt to change the degree of belief in negative thoughts, but instead teaches people to see thoughts and feelings as mental events, passing mind-states. Teaching such a decentred perspective on mental states was always implicit in cognitive therapy. The mindfulness approach makes this explicit, and does so by using direct sensations of the body a central vehicle for teaching. In doing so, it shifts from a theory of cognitive processing, to a theory that includes the body: it uses embodied cognition.

Embodied Cognition

Embodied Cognition refers to a family of theories within psychology that share the view that a necessary condition for cognition is the way our sensori-motor capacities enable us to interact with our environment. It attempts to capture the way in which mind, body, and world mutually interact and influence one another to promote adaptive success. In doing so, it provides a counterpoint to cognitivist theories that view the mind as a passive organ that receives input and builds up a map of the world in our heads, and in which cognition is seen primarily in terms of internal cognitive processes (i.e. those involving computation using rule-based symbolic processing and representation). By contrast, embodied cognition theory focuses on the way our bodies place limits on our interaction with the world and determine the type of minds we have. It sees the body as fundamental to how the mind operates. Let us consider three different ways in which the body is known to affect the mind, as examples of this approach.

1. *Antonio Damasio and Descartes' Error.* Damasio's work with neurological patients has found that the mind needs the body for successful engagement with the world, and cannot be separated from the body, as Descartes proposed. Damasio (1995) starts with a description of Phineas Gage who, in 1848, had a responsible job supervising workers building a new railroad. He was tamping explosives into a hole in a rock with an iron rod when it exploded prematurely and the rod went through his head. All the onlookers expected this to have killed him, but he did not die. The rod had gone right through his brain taking out a part of the front of the brain, the ventromedial pre-frontal cortex. Although his performance on intelligence testing was normal after his accident, his life deteriorated rapidly. His social life began to include gambling, financial incompetence, and very bad inter-personal decisions. He died penniless at the age of 32 after spending time as an itinerant worker.

Damasio has examined a number of patients who have brain damage in the same part of the brain. He finds that they have lost the ability to use subtle sensory cues from the body to inform complex decision making. They become locked in interminable doubt, which alternates with impulsive decisions that take no account of the long-term costs. To get a feel for this phenomenon in everyday life, imagine the feeling you get when you are house hunting. You might like the place on paper, but when you visit to get the feel of it you decide it is not for you. You cannot quite articulate what it is about it that you do not like, but you have a very strong feeling that this is not the place for you. Imagine if you had lost the ability to gauge the feel of things in this way. First of all you would be in a complete quandary as to how to process the information about the house, with a lot of competing information that, without the gut feelings, would seem to be unable to tell you decisively whether you should go ahead with the purchase or not. In the end, you may make what appears to be an impulsive decision based on dubious or un-compelling evidence, a decision that takes no account of long-term costs. Patients who have lost this ability to use bodily sensory cues take high risk gambles, they show no signs of bodily anxiety when they are about to take a risk — bodily signs that would alert most people to the fact that they might be about to make a bad decision or lose a lot of money.

What is particularly interesting is that this part of the brain lies very near the point that is known to underlie our ability to intuit other people's beliefs and feelings, critical for smooth social interaction and attentiveness to other people's points of view, an ability that was greatly diminished for Phineas Gage. The implications of this work are that *if we cannot attend to our body we are cutting ourselves off from a great deal of information about our own needs and those of others.* Body sensations help us to know important social and emotional information about ourselves and others. Other related research that suggests the mind needs the body for successful engagement with the world includes the work of Hohmann (1966). He studied veterans who had spinal cord lesions. His work suggests that decreases in the veterans own perception of their general emotional feeling, especially with regard to certain emotions such as fear and anger, was related to the degree of disruption that their autonomic nervous system had experienced. Those veterans with higher levels of disruption were unable to experience emotions in the same way as they had been able to before their spinal cord injuries. More recent work suggests that those who have higher levels of visceral perception (perception of the internal body systems) experience more intense emotions than those with lower levels of visceral perception (Wiens et al., 2000).

2. *The effect of the body on judgement.* Focusing on the body can tell us about the consequences of bodily changes on our feelings and emotions. A number of studies have shown that movements of the body make a difference to judgements that are normally thought to be "in the mind." For example, if people are asked to rate how humorous cartoons are and are asked to hold a pencil between their teeth then, because this activates the same muscles that are involved in smiling, people rate the cartoon as being funnier than if they are asked to hold a pencil in their pursed lips (Strack et al., 1988). If people adjust the face in a way that uses the muscles involved in frowning, people rate cartoons as less funny (Laird, 1974). In another striking demonstration of a similar effect, Wells and Petty (1980) showed that ratings of the quality of headphones could be affected by whether people were asked to keep their head still or to shake or nod their head "to simulate the effects of wearing headphones while jogging." If people *nodded* their heads (a movement usually associated with saying "yes"), then they thought the headphones were of better quality. However if they were asked to *shake* their heads (usually associated with a "no") they judged that the headphones were of lesser quality.

More strikingly still, the participants were also asked to rate speech quality. The speakers on the tape to which the participants were listening were discussing whether tuition fees should be raised in the next semester of this particular university. Afterwards, apparently as part of another experiment, the students that had taken part were asked what they thought the fees should be at that university. Those who had kept their heads still came out with an average of $582, those who shook their heads came out with an average of $467 and those who had nodded their heads when listening to the speech about tuition fees rising came up with an average of $646. The judgements about tuition fees were affected by the movements of their heads they were making as they were listening to the speech. All this happened without the awareness of the participants. These findings illustrate how input from bodily states may serve as a source of information for decision-making (as suggested by Damasio's somatic marker hypothesis). With regard to the reoccurrence of individual patterns of responding it is conceivable that bodily information may not only serve as an intuitive input for cognition, but, through repeated associations with cognitive responses, may itself become part of a constellation of bodily and cognitive responses, stored as a schema or response stereotype. We suggest that such constellations are re-instantiated, once aspects of it, bodily or cognitive, are primed or activated, an idea that is consistent with the findings showing that induction of mild negative mood in previously depressed patients leads to the reoccurrence of negative self-judgments and dysfunctional attitudes.

3. *Ruminative self-focus versus perceptual self-focus.* We have seen that focusing on the body may give us an early warning system, informing us of what is going on with our emotions and also telling us more about our emotions and those of others. We have also seen that feedback from the body can affect our judgments unbeknownst to us. Is there anything we can do to deal skillfully with the mind-body connections that cause difficulty? Recent research suggests that there is. We are helped by knowing that a characteristic of focusing on the body is that it gives us this information in a different way: in a way that is non-conceptual. A useful index of the extent to which people are inclined to be locked into conceptual thinking is the degree of difficulty they have in coming up with specific memories (Williams, 2004). When locked in conceptual thought and given a word to act as a cue for recollection, people tend to retrieve an abstract memory, such as "the times I have got angry with my family," that does not hone in on a single event. Instead such memories summarize a number of events; they give a *category* of events rather than a single episode. People who are depressed or suicidal, or suffering from post-traumatic stress disorder tend to get stuck in such a conceptual mode. Even after depression has remitted, people find it difficult to access specific event memories. This phenomenon is important because it impairs problem solving, makes people vague about the future, and allows the escalation of negative mood-thought spirals (Williams et al., in press c). We can use such memory responses to tell us the extent to which people are getting stuck in the conceptual, thinking mode of mind and are not able to allow the sensory and perceptual mode of mind to help them in their memory. What keeps people in such a mode?

In a series of elegant experiments, Watkins and Teasdale have found that rumination is one of the things that will keep a person locked into a conceptual mode of mind. As we have observed earlier, people find their minds whirring round and round, asking "What am I doing to deserve this?," "Why do I have problems other people don't have?," "Why can't I handle things better?" (Treynor et al., 2003). If this sort of thinking continues, it can be shown to maintain an over-general style of memory. If you distract people from this mode of thinking, memory becomes more specific (Watkins et al., 2000). But there is a further twist to the story. If people are encouraged to focus on the experience of feelings in their *body*, then the very act of bringing awareness to the bodily sensations is effective at switching off the conceptual mode of mind and allowing the memory to be more specific (Watkins & Teasdale, 2001, 2004). In depression, it is not self-focus which is the problem, but the mode of mind we are using. If we are self-focused in a *conceptual* way, this will perpetuate rumination. If we are focused on the direct sensation of our bodies, we activate a mode of mind which is non-conceptual and is intentionally focused on the present moment. It is interesting to note that the MBCT approach has been found to increase the specificity of memory (Williams et al., 2000).

Focusing on the Body in Mindfulness Practice

Figure 1 represents a way of understanding what we practice during mindfulness meditation. Points (C) and (D) on the left hand side of the Figure (placed closest to the environmental input) represents attentional shifts that occur automatically in reaction to stimuli in the environment. Points (A) and (B) on the right hand side represent shifts in attention that are made deliberately, intentionally, voluntarily. Notice that shifts upwards or downwards result in changes in the proportion of the

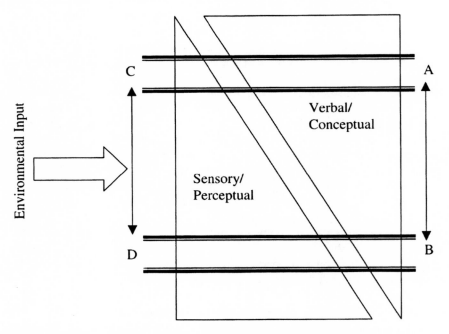

Figure 1. A schematic representation of the division of the mind and the way that mindful attention to the body shifts the focus away from conceptual thought.

conscious mind that is processing either (a) sensory/perceptual information *from* the external world or *from* the body, or (b) conceptual information (e.g., thoughts *about* the world or the body).

It is not surprising that mindfulness instructors have evolved ways of enquiring about people's experience by asking questions that direct attention away from thinking about things, and instead practicing shifting attention to direct sensations; "What do you notice about that?" "Where do you feel this in your body?" "What sensations are here right now?" It is now more possible to see why such focus on the body is so skillful: (1) The body is part of the loop that maintains emotion; direct focusing on the body can provide an early warning system of change in mood. (2) Bringing awareness to the body itself weakens habits and slows down one part of the system that normally maintains depressed mood (the body loop). (3) It results in direct sensory experience and so can provide an alternative to rumination (conceptual thought) or suppression. The issue that is bothering the person is still there but seen from a new perspective. It shifts away from dealing in the currency of ideas. (4) It is present moment focused, encouraging the person to see more clearly when they are "living in" the past or the future. (5) It is curiosity-based, providing a counterpoint to the tendency to avoid or escape, by switching instead to an "approach" mode of mind

Concluding Remarks

MBCT has been developed from MBSR as a way of preventing relapse and recurrence in depression. It does so by focusing not on changing the content of thought, but encouraging people to relate differently to their thoughts. It does not attempt to change rumination, but by focusing on "acceptance" rather than "change," it gradually undermines the discrepancy-based processing mode that motivates rumination. In this way we move from trying to overcome, defeat, or even control emotion; away from a military metaphor to an ecological metaphor. Coming to know the mind requires awareness of and openness to the way in which our cognition is embodied: the way in which the mind is expressed in the body, and the body in the mind. In mindfulness approaches, we have the opportunity to understand the ecology of the embodied mind. We are able, through continuing research and practice in this approach, to help deal more skillfully with the tendency for moods to overwhelm us.

25

Conjoining Paradigms: A Dissolution-Oriented Approach To Psychotherapy

Genji Sugamura & Scott Warren

Inspired by Zen Buddhism, this chapter proposes a Dissolution-Oriented Approach (DOA) for psychotherapy integration. While the term "solution" may refer to finding, explaining, and answering a problem, "dissolution" signifies destruction and disappearance of the problem. While greatly informed by constructivist and social constructionist ideas, Buddhist and Taoist philosophy form the core of the theoretical integration of this approach. These philosophies are often understood as radical in their attempt to dissolve the concept of the self and even logic itself. A contrast of mindfulness/body-fulness is introduced to clarify aspects of the dissolution-oriented meditative approach. Also, applications of humor and laughter in the therapeutic setting are classified and discussed in terms of Taoism and Zen Buddhism. Throughout these discussions, the framework of the DOA is developed.

The correct approach to philosophical problems is not to attempt to solve them but rather to reach a point where the problems dissolve of their own accord.
— Ludwig Wittgenstein (1889-1951)

Since its inception in the late 1800's, the "talking cure" of psychotherapy has a history of just over one hundred years. However, despite such a relatively short period, a number of unique approaches have subsequently emerged with current estimates of more than 400 different systems of psychotherapy (Corsini, 2000). While this approximation does include the multiple schools arising from a single theory — for instance, Freud's psychoanalysis giving rise to self-psychology and object-relations approaches — still, the typical mainstream approaches used by counselors and psychotherapists number over at least 10 (Corsini & Wedding, 2000; Sharf, 2000). Each of these approaches has different characteristics in terms of historical background as well as distinct views of personality, assessment, and treatment, with many of the elements mutually exclusive with one another. According to Arkowitz (1997), there are currently two directions for psychotherapy integration other than technical eclecticism: Theoretical integration and the common factors approach. Proponents of the former have expressed dissent about the assumptions of the single-school approach and attempt to present new ideas for theory and practice by integrating the various underlying theories. The latter, on the other hand, presumes that there are deeper common factors among different psychotherapies that are masked by surface differences. This approach attempts to develop a more refined approach by focusing on common characteristics.

In this chapter, a Dissolution-Oriented Approach (DOA) is proposed, emphasizing that the concept of "dissolution" could be cited as a unique common factor and that the Buddhist/Taoist philosophy from which it is adopted might be a promising meta-theory for integration. Thus, the DOA is not an additional approach to psychotherapy, but an attempt to reveal and reorganize the unfocused aspects of the multiple theories and practices of psychotherapy. Although there may be more psychotherapy systems that resonate, either explicitly or implicitly, with the dissolution concept, this chapter will focus on (1) social constructionist therapies, (2) constructivist therapies, and (3) Buddhist and Taoist practices. Each of the three frameworks will be examined from the viewpoint of the DOA.

Contrasting *Solution* and *Dissolution*

Before investigating the relationship among the systems of psychotherapy cited above, it would be helpful to define the meaning of "dissolution." The concept of *problem dissolution* appears to merely be in opposition to the concepts of *problem creation* or *generation*, but this is not exactly true. The relationship between these terms is rather complicated and will be further elaborated in the section discussing Buddhist and Taoist perspectives. Here, the definition of *dissolution* will be described in contrast to the term *solution* with which it is frequently confused

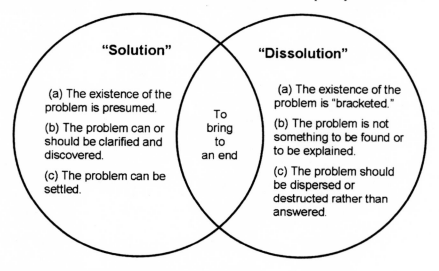

Figure 1. *Solution* and *Dissolution* by Contrast

According to the *Merriam-Webster Online Dictionary* (2005-2006), both *solution* and *dissolution* have a meaning of "to bring to an end" in common. The word *solution* means "an action or process of solving a problem" and to *solve* is "to find a solution, explanation, or answer." On the other hand, the term *dissolution* is explained as "termination or destruction by breaking down, disrupting, or dispersing" and to *dissolve* means "to cause to disperse or disappear" and "to destroy." *Collins Cobuild Dictionary* (Sinclair, 2004) also reads: "Dissolution is a process in which something becomes weaker and then disappears." That is, both terms have a similar meaning in that they indicate ending something, but the ways of ending are different. The term *solution* refers to a process of finding explanation and answer to the problem, whereas *dissolution* signifies "destruction and disappearance of the problem." More specifically, in the word *solution* (a) the existence of the problem is presumed, (b) the problem can or should be clarified and discovered, and (c) the problem can be settled. In the term *dissolution*, on the other hand, (a) the existence of the problem is not necessarily presumed or is sometimes "bracketed," (b) the problem is not something to be found or to be explained, and (c) the problem should be dispersed or "de-structed" rather than answered. Figure 1 (Venn diagram) illustrates the similarities and differences between solution and dissolution.

Some therapies tend toward using the term *solution* in constructs such as "problem-solution" or "solution-focused" (e.g., D'Zurilla, 1986; Lipchik, 1999). At the outset, it is important to recognize that the DOA is not antithetical to these approaches. What the DOA intends, however, is to additionally reveal some *dissolution*-oriented aspects of existing psychotherapy systems, despite the fact that they are often labeled as *solutions* as well as to further explicate these theories and practices in the light of this contrast.

The Social Constructionist Perspective

Social constructionists challenge traditional psychology in many aspects. Epistemologically, they resist empiricism, rationalism, and objectivism. Although social constructionism is frequently confused with constructivism, because these thoughts are quite complex and opaque at times, their theoretical orientations are distinguishable (Franklin, 1998; Gergen, 1994; Glasersfeld, 1995). Approaching these ideas from the framework of a DOA, it is particularly important to note their different views of the process of meaning construction. A leading figure of social constructionism, Gergen (1999), stated that it is possible to explain and describe a phenomenon in an infinite number of ways:

> *First, we must suppose that everything we have learned about our world and ourselves that gravity holds us to the earth, people cannot fly like birds, cancer kills, or that punishment deters bad behavior could be otherwise. There is nothing*

about "what there is" that demands these particular accounts; we could use our language to construct alternative worlds in which there is no gravity or cancer, or which persons and birds are equivalent, and punishment adored, (p. 47)

Following this statement, he articulated that the modes of explanation and description originate in our relationship:

On this account, language and all other forms of representation gain their meaning from the way in which they are used within relationships.... Meanings are born of coordinations among persons, agreements, negotiations, affirmations. From this standpoint, relationships stand prior to all that is intelligible. (p. 48)

Thus, for social constructionists, language and relationship are the two most important notions in creating our reality

Narrative Therapy

White and Epston (1990) have clinically applied the insights of social constructionism, developing the approach known as Narrative Therapy. The externalizing technique used in Narrative Therapy is considered one of the most interesting innovations in the practices of constructionism (Gergen, 1999). This technique attempts to separate the client from "problems" and, instead, locates them in a social context. "In contrast to the common cultural and professional practice of identifying the person as the problem or the problem as within the person, this work depicts the problem as external to the person" (Roth & Epston, 1996, p. 5). If clients presume that the problem is an integral part of them, it would be more difficult for them to change. By resituating the problem within the cultural discourse, this technique attempts to empower the client.

Gremillion (2003) conducted ethnographic and interview research on anorexia nervosa in an inpatient unit of a major hospital in the US. She asserted that the current mainstream treatment is centrally structured to reinforce anorexia and encouraged Narrative Therapy as an alternative approach. According to Gremillion, the objective measurement of clients' progress in body weight tended to exacerbate their problems, not only by reinforcing the belief that they must gain control over their bodies, but also by fostering their skills to lose weight. On one hand, the social and cultural ideals of gender and individualism have an influence on the dramatic increase in the incidence of anorexia nervosa since the 1970s; while on the other hand, anorexia intensifies dominant discourses of femininity in contemporary society. Through this vicious circle, anorexia has been socially constructed. Although Gremillion recognizes the difficulties in the treatment of anorexia, she suggests the use of Narrative Therapy to dissolve the problematic assumptions underlying mainstream treatment strategies. The externalizing technique might be used to de-pathologize and externalize anorexia to the socio-cultural context by asking a client specific questions. For example, "How do you think anorexia formed the idea that women and girls should be a certain size?" etc. This approach can be interpreted as an attempt to *dissolve* the problem inside of the client by the linguistic practice of externalization.

Like in Behavior Therapy, problems are dissolved by *externalizing* them to the physical environment, but narrative therapists extend further by *externalizing* them to a social, cultural, and political context. Thus, the practices of social constructionism may be construed as dissolution-oriented in a deeper and more radical level.

The Constructivist Perspective

While most constructivists recognize the significant roles and functions of the sociocultural dimension in the creation of reality, they differ from social constructionists in their tendency to make more of the personal dimension in the process of meaning construction and reconstruction.

Personal Construct Psychology

A constructivist view of human nature is well expressed by the idea of individuals as practicing scientists. Kelly (1955) argued that the scientific attitude could be seen in everyone, including clients. Prediction and control is not specific to scientists, but rather all people are motivated to infer, hypothesize, predict and control the situations surrounding them. Individuals perceive the world through the patterns and categories they have constructed. Kelly referred to these patterns as "personal constructs."

> *"[Constructs] are ways of construing the world. They are what enables man, and lower animals too, to chart a course of behavior, explicitly formulated or implicitly acted out, verbally expressed or utterly inarticulate, consistent with other courses of behavior or inconsistent with them, intellectually reasoned or vegetatively sensed." (p. 9)*

Unlike objectivists, constructivists hold that the individual tests constructs not by verifying the patterns with external realities but in terms of "viability" (Mahoney, 1991, 2003). As Von Glasersfeld (1995) stated, "in the constructivist way of thinking, the concept of viability in the domain of experience, takes the place of the traditional philosopher's concept of Truth, that was to indicate a "correct" representation of reality" (p. 14). From such primitive constructs as "that is dangerous" and "this is edible" to higher ones such as "democracy is a government by the people," the individual lives by pragmatically testing the usefulness of constructs moment-to-moment. Because an individual's constructs are closely related to how they behave, think, and feel, "[t]he classical threefold division of psychology into cognition, affection, and conation has been completely abandoned in the psychology of personal constructs" (Kelly, 1955, p. 130). Instead, the concept of the personal constructs makes it possible to understand human experiences and actions in a holistic manner. Thus, constructivist therapists attempt to deal with how clients construct their worlds, themselves, and their relations with others. Each client is understood as a person who is in a process of testing, elaborating, and revising their constructs rather than a person controlled by past traumatic experiences or whose behaviors are determined by contingencies of reinforcement (Neimeyer, 1987). Constructivist therapists encourage the client to elaborate his or her own constructs, looking upon the client not as a reactive or passive being but as an anticipatory active being.

From this assumption, there appear two dissolution-oriented approaches within constructivist therapies. Both have to do with the constructivist understanding of problems as process of meaning creation and of the clients as proactive scientists. This view enables the therapists to see clients' problems not as something static and constant but rather dynamic and changeable. In addition, clients are not seen as people *with* problems but as ones testing and revising their narrative *about* problems. Thus, some constructivist therapists attempt not to fix the problems but, instead, to help the clients better organize meanings, allowing problems to be dissolved through the process. Others attempt to intervene more directly with the process of meaning creation and change the client's semantic framework.

Constructive psychotherapy techniques: Encouraging more diverse and complex meaning creation

Mahoney (1983) has proposed the "stream of consciousness" technique to promote the client's constructs of reality. This term originates in James' (1890) idea that experience is a manifestation of an ongoing stream of consciousness. Mahoney (1991) defines this technique as "an exercise in which the client is invited to attend to and, as best one can, report ongoing thoughts, sensations, images, memories, and feelings" (p. 295). There is some similarity to Freud's free association technique, but unlike in psychoanalysis, constructive therapists do not interpret the client's report, believing that there is no single or accurate interpretation. When the client asks the therapist the meaning of his or her constructs, the therapist may encourage him or her to explore the meaning by asking questions such as: "What do you think?" "How do you interpret it?" "Is there anything you remember?" "How do you feel?" The individual's statements are best understood from the client's own viewpoint because it is here where one's meanings and order are fundamentally formed

Neimeyer (2000b) pointed out that constructivist psychotherapy for the experience of loss "prompts the articulation and elaboration of the client's narrative of loss in a way that promotes a new sense of coherence, continuity, and consensual validation of an enlarged identity" (p. 290). Also, he articulated how constructivist therapists regard the client's constructs in terms of life story:

> *Because of the frequently competing discourse we take up in our daily lives, no "text of identity" is truly coherent and unambivalent. Instead, it may be more useful to construe the self-narrative as fraught with internal tensions and contradictions, encompassing "fragmented" subsystems of meaning that may or may not be inferentially compatible (Kelly, 1955). However, in contrast to conventional humanistic models of personality, the present constructivist position would not view this internal complexity as inherently problematic, as something to be ultimately resolved or "integrated" (Neimeyer, 2000a [a added]). Indeed, it may be precisely the features of our experience that fail to fit within the master narrative of our lives that deconstruct its apparent authority (Derrida, 1978) and open our story to new and more complex telling.* (p. 266)

Such a constructivist position is resonant with the clinical practices of social constructionism. While Anderson and Goolishian (1992, p. 27-28) criticize the traditional systemic or cognitive constructivism and make much of linguistic practice, they presume that (a) "A therapeutic system is a system for which the communication has a relevance specific to its dialogical exchange," (b) "The therapeutic conversation is a mutual search and exploration through dialogue... in which new meanings are continually evolving toward the "dis-solving" of problems, and thus, the dissolving of the therapy system," (c) "The therapist is a participant-observer and a participant-facilitator of the therapeutic conversation," and (d) "We live in and through the narrative identities that we develop in conversation with one another" [italics deleted]. These assumptions are quite similar to those of contemporary constructivism. Although these ideas are highly abstract, a number of empirical studies have shown that narrating or writing human experiences, including past traumatic experiences, could improve both mental and physical health (Esterling et al., 1999; Pennebaker, 1995). This implies that the process of ordering our experiences itself might assist in dissolving problems.

Constructive psychotherapy techniques: Changing the semantic framework
Some therapists have also proposed techniques to promote change of constructs in a direct manner. A well-known technique used to change the client's semantic world is *reframing*, developed at the Mental Research Institute in Palo Alto. Here the role of therapy is to re-construct the reality that the client constructed (Watzlawick, 1984). For example: A couple seeking marital therapy described themselves as "hopeless." The therapist said, "You have a wonderful relationship. You stopped by my clinic because you wanted to improve the relationship better than ever and you are striving together for an ideal relationship" (Hasegawa, 1987). In this way the reframing technique can be understood as an

attempt to dissolve rather than to solve the problem by changing the entire semantic system. There is a similar approach in the social constructionist therapy of Epston, White, and Murray (1992) known as "re-authoring therapy." They defined a story as "a unit of meaning that provides a frame for lived experience" (p. 97) and argued that these stories determine our lives and relationships. Because stories are indeterminate in nature and have some degree of uncertainty, ambiguity, and inconsistencies, they attempt to make the most of these characteristics to create an alternative story or "revision of one's life."

Both techniques appear to change the client's semantic framework, but constructivist brief therapists tend to focus on a core, underlying semantic basis, while social constructionist therapists attempt expand the focus over a relatively longer life history. Some constructivists/constructionists prefer to use humor or jokes in order to shed new light upon or dissolve the problem. Humor can be a very effective reframing tool, but it seems possible that the function of humor could go beyond the current theoretical framework of constructivism. Hence, this chapter will further discuss and deepen the use of therapeutic humor and laughter in terms of eastern philosophies in the next section.

Buddhist and Taoist Perspectives

While Buddhist and Taoist philosophies have not systematically been discussed in the field of psychology they are most conducive to a dissolution-oriented approach. This is not only because the concept of dissolution is central to them but also because they are both the most radical in their use of the concept and their ideas provide a scaffold to connect the other conventional perspectives discussed earlier.

Taoism is often interpreted as a radical system in its aims to deconstruct the fundamental value of the self. While Western traditions employ ideas such as enhancing self-esteem and self-empowerment, many Asian cultures endorse self-humiliation both as a personal and interpersonal value. This orientation is strongly influenced by Taoist and Confucian traditions. The Tao, or way, is an attention to the dynamic wholeness of things in which the individual ego or self-sense is discouraged. Buddhism, especially as it manifests in the school of Chan or Zen Buddhism, endorses the Doctrine of the Buddha-Heart (*buddhahridaya*), which could be understood as the most radical in its attempt to deconstruct all logical and representational systems, including the concept of the self.

Although arguably traced to the historical Buddha Shakyamuni, it is commonly accepted that the originator of Zen Buddhism is Bodhidharma, an Indian monk who allegedly traveled to China in the 6th century to introduce a type of Buddhism that became Chan. The practice of Zen, or *dhyana* (meditation), originates in ancient India and is not sole property of Zen Buddhism. However, Zen alone emphasizes the importance of meditation alone for the attainment of direct intuitive discernment of Buddhahood (*furyumonji*). Further, Zen emphasizes the non-symbolic nature of this insight in the relevance of nonverbal transmission to a disciple of the central tenets of Buddhism (*ishindenshin*). Neither of these ideas is common in the earlier Indian traditions (Mori, 1969). These two theses developed further through the influence of Taoist ideas upon Buddhism as it made its way East. Kanaya (1993) argues that Buddhism has largely prevailed through the medium of Taoist ideas of Tao and "nothingness" and thus has evolved into more of a distinctly Chinese philosophy. After the 11th century Chinese philosophers of the Chuan-chen (Complete Reality school) further situated Taoism as a central philosophy and integrating it with Zen Buddhism and Confucianism (Wong, 1997). Thus, Buddhist and Taoist philosophies discussed in this chapter include Chinese philosophy as an integration of these thoughts as well as an early Indian version of Buddhism.

Relations to other perspectives

Buddhist and Taoist perspectives can offer a great deal in regard to alternative understandings of the constructivist, and social constructivist approaches. These ideas can contribute to a larger theoretical integration of these approaches, but distinctive differences among them should also be noted. Most generally, there are fundamental epistemological contradictions that limit the ability to fully integrate the ideas.

However, Chinese philosophy does posses unique characteristics that enable one to hold completely antithetical ideas simultaneously via the logic of "*sive.*" This is what the Japanese philosopher Kitaro Nishida (1939/1989) referred to as the "absolute-contradictory self-identity," a concept without any clear correlate in the western traditions of philosophy. Unlike Hegel's dialectics, Nishida denied the synthesis of opposites. One of the descriptions expressing this idea is that an individual maintains its identity independent of and, at the same time, dependent on other individuals, and thus, an identity holds itself in an absolute contradiction (Nishida, 1934/1994). In Haruki's (1997) straightforward expression, this indicates the idea that "while black and white are mutually exclusive concepts, they are fundamentally identical" (p. 11). When attempting to examine different psychological theories through the lens of eastern philosophy, it is important to recognize this unique characteristic (Sugamura, 2003).

Relation to social constructionism

Buddhism and social constructionism share an interesting similarity with regard to their views of the self, but they possess a vital difference in their approach to language. For example, Gergen and Kaye (1992) noted from a social constructionist standpoint:

> *... the relationship takes priority over the individual self. That is, selves are only realized as a byproduct of relatedness. It is not independent selves who come*

*together to form a relationship, but particular forms of relationship that engen-
der what we take to be the individual's identity.* (p. 180)

This idea bears a considerable resemblance to the Buddhist concept of not independent origination (*pratityasamutpada*). Nagarjuna, a 2nd century Indian Buddhist philosopher who reorganized the notion of emptiness, held that everything
exists only in relation to all other things and fundamentally denied any form of
independent self-existence of and, as a consequence, the concept of self. Nagarjuna
further develops the concept of non-self, which will be described later as another
component of the dissolution-oriented approach.

In contrast to social constructionism, which asserts that meaning and reality,
as such, emerges solely by means of linguistic inter-subjective relationships, Taoism and Zen Buddhism both bracket the relevance of language in constructing the
world. A Taoist classic book the *Chuang-Tzu* says:

*What people treasure are books. But what they really treasure are words written
in the books. However, words themselves are not treasurable but the meanings
within the words are more important. Yet, the meanings are not ultimate things.
The facts to which the meanings are directed are the most important. Nevertheless, these facts are not delivered by languages. What languages can convey are
only the names and voices. Can the names and voices really deliver the actual
state of the facts?* (Mori, 1969, p. 148)

The reason why the Chuang-Tzu appears skeptical of language is because he be-
lieves that any attempt to name or label reality somehow diminishes its true nature.
A kindred view of language can be seen in Zen Buddhism. Suzuki (1914/1964)
stated that personal experience is everything and simple and unsophisticated experience is the foundation of every concept. Thus, he cautioned: "The letter must
never be followed, only the spirit is to be grasped" (p. 72). While Zen has a number
of sayings that may be interesting or useful, fundamentally the words are thought
to only be a kind of scaffold to access innermost reality (Suzuki, 1914/1964). To
develop this point, it would serve one to contrast Buddhist/Taoist philosophy with
constructivism.

Relation to constructivism

Constructivism inclines to emphasize differentiation and contrast in the construction of reality. For radical constructivists (Glasersfeld, 1984, 1995), cognition
is basically an operation of distinction: The identification of "A" is based on a
distinction of "A" and "not-A." This binary coding, also known as the Aristotelian
law of the excluded middle, signifies a type of logical classification in which two
logical partitions are mutually exclusive (Kawamoto, 2000). When we perceive
object X, X is either A or not-A and there is no in-between. For example, X is

either a "cat" or "not-cat" and, logically, it cannot be neither "cat" nor "not-cat." Frequently used examples are truth/falsehood and existence/nothingness. Such binary coding can be applied to every phenomenon using this form of A/not-A. Fundamentally, it does not require one to use a pair of antonyms, but may include coding such as existence/not-existence or truth/not-truth.

Critical constructivists, on the other hand, emphasize the ordering and organizing of experience by means of contrast rather than of binary coding. Some of them prefer to use binary codes, but they typically do not hold that drawing a distinction between "A" and "not-A" is the basis of the constructivist theory of the meaning creation. The term *contrast* is relatively fuzzy in logical classification (i.e., it induces many-valued logic) whereas binary coding is based on two-valued logic. Contrary to two-valued logic in which a proposition could either be true=1 or false=not-true=0, many-valued logic allows more than two truth-values. For example, between "true" and "false" may lie "possible," and moreover, it may involve an infinite number of truth-values, albeit theoretically. Complex linguistic or symbolic understandings could better be viewed in terms of this logic. The concept of *change*, for instance, is understood in such contrasts between as "old-new," "known-unknown," and "static-dynamic" (Mahoney, 1985, 1991).

In contrast, when the Chuang-Tzu states that language may ruin nature as it is, it implies that language destroys a fact as an inseparable single entity. Because language limits the unlimited, the unlimited that language depicts is thus only a limited fact. Language cannot tell the truth, nor can silence. The single path remaining in Taoism is within "non-language and non-silence." Mori (1969) interpreted this as an attitude to use language not following language itself. In Taoism language is something to be used to somatically comprehend reality; once comprehended, language ceases to be necessary and may be done away with.

Zen Buddhists also prefer to cite examples of the Chuang-Tzu as Zen riddles. Zen, too, aims to go beyond language and logic and strives to deny all kinds of conceptualization. Suzuki (1914/1964) powerfully articulated this point:

We generally think that "A is A" is absolute, and that the proposition "A is not-A" or "A is B" is unthinkable. We have never been able to break through these conditions of the understanding; they have been too imposing. But now Zen declares that words are words and no more... Ever since the awakening of consciousness we have endeavored to solve the mysteries of being and to quench our thirst for logic through the dualism of "A" and "not-A."... For we now realize that "A is not-A" after all, that logic is one sided, that illogicality so-called is not in the last analysis necessarily illogical; what is superficially irrational has after all its own logic... The meaning of the proposition "A is A" is realized only when "A is not-A." To be itself is not to be itself - this is the logic of Zen. [For example,] birth and death no longer torment it; for there are no such dualities anywhere; we live even through death. (pp. 59-60)

Thus, Buddhist and Taoist philosophies of language seem to be opposed to both constructivism and constructionism. What about *critical constructivism*? In this version of constructivism, importance is not placed on rigorous binary coding but, instead, upon the dynamic balance of contrast. This balancing is not something that divides phenomena in a dualistic way. For example, imagine a child playing on a seesaw. There are an infinite number of balancing points on it. However, it is infinite in a given dimension and other seesaws would be necessary to fill in other dimensions. Similarly, although there are an infinite number of points in a given contrast, the contrast itself is an abstraction of reality because the language employed inevitably limits the phenomena in some way. Indeed, the "semantic differential method" (Osgood, 1952) makes it possible to abstract a part of reality by pairs of adjectives. But it then logically requires an infinite number of pairs of adjectives to describe facts as they are. Isn't this practically impossible?

Several years ago, Sugamura asked this question of Michael Mahoney whose response was unexpected. Mahoney slowly answered after a little pause: "There are two kinds... hmm. Genji, this is a kind of Koan." And he continued, "There are two kinds of people in the world: Those who believe that there are two kinds of people in the world, and those who don't." This is the very type of exchange that provides a vivid account of critical constructivists' view that we cannot know the world as it is via language or any logical system. Specifically, Mahoney taught the limitedness of contrasting by showing a contrast. The koan above is stimulating in the point that it uses *self-referential* logic in which a part of the proposition denies the whole. As long as one understands the statements and follows the logic, this proposition would never be comprehended. It is going beyond the limitations of language and logic. In a similar way, this alludes to what Paul Valery noted, "To see is to forget the name of the things one sees" (cited in *Constructivism in the Human Sciences,* 5, p. 88).

With regard the relationship of constructivism to Buddhism, Mahoney (1991) cited the Buddha's statement: "We are what we think. All that we are arises with our thoughts. With our thoughts we make the world," and thus, recognized the Buddha as one of forerunners of constructivism. From this angle, it is true that constructivism possesses some aspects of subjectivism, but it is actually neither subjective nor objective. While it treats this philosophical *aporia*, some clarification may be found in Vaihinger's philosophy of "as if" (1911/1924). For instance, Vaihinger argued that subjects operate as if the external world existed. That is to say, while one cannot know objective reality directly, one instead assumes to live *as if* one does. With this assumption we can pragmatically function within the world. This world of *as if,* or world of fiction, is as important as the "real" or "actual" world suggested by everyday language (Vaihinger, 1911/1924). The introduction of Vaihinger's philosophy allows constructivists to be hypothetical realists and oscillate between realism and non-realism in a monistic way. This

ontologically free nature of constructivism is similar to the Buddhist/Taoist sublimation of realism and idealism.

Toward Effective Psychotherapy Practices

As illustrated above, Buddhist and Taoist philosophies share important ideas with
social constructionism and constructivism. In this last subsection, therapeutic techniques or developmental exercises applying the philosophies of Buddhist and Taoism will be introduced and discussed in terms of the concept of *dissolution*.

Meditation: from self to non-self

There seem to be two kinds of meditation in the world; self-oriented meditation and non-self-oriented meditation. To be precise, these are actually two aspects
of meditation, and a single meditation technique may display both aspects in regards to different stages or even at the same stage. However, drawing this tentative
distinction allows one to better illustrate both the dissolution-oriented aspects of
meditation and also to organize the ideas of meditation in a more Zen fashion.

The *self-oriented meditation* is a kind of meditation in which the goal is to
gain insight into oneself through self-attention. A classic example would be *mindfulness* meditation that has become increasingly popular in psychotherapy (see
Baer, 2003 for a review) and everyday life (Kabat-Zinn, 1994). According to Kabat-
Zinn (1994), mindfulness implies "*paying attention* [italics added] in a particular
way: on purpose, in the present moment, and nonjudgmentally" (p. 4). Kristeller's
(2003) also defined it as "a means for promoting *self-awareness* and general self-
regulation, for decreasing emotional reactivity, and for *enhancing insight* [italics
added] and the integration of perceptual, cognitive, and behavioral aspects of human functioning" (p. 108). From this perspective, meditation is construed as "a
consciousness discipline" (Kabat-Zinn, 1996, p. 161) or "inherently a cognitive
process" (Kristeller, 2003, p. 114).

In terms of the DOA, the nonjudgmental nature and the moment-to-moment-
based experience of mindfulness cultivate an attitude that transforms "problems"
into "not-problems." As a matter of fact, Segal, Williams, and Teasdale (2002)
clinically demonstrated that a mindfulness-based approach, referred to as Mindfulness-Based Cognitive Therapy (MBCT), is an effective treatment to prevent
relapse/recurrence in depressed patients with three or more previous depressive
episode. The core skills learned in MBCT are letting go and becoming mindful.
Letting go signifies relinquishing involvement in the patterns of negative thinking
and becoming mindful implies being aware of thoughts, feelings, and bodily sensations as they occur. Both aspects are considered important because "we can't
intentionally let go of unhelpful patterns unless we are aware of them" (Segal et
al., 2002, p. 93).

This approach appears quite reasonable and there is no doubt that mindfulness meditation seems practical and beneficial in dissolving problems. However, from the viewpoint of the DOA, this kind of self-oriented meditation could be understood as a first step toward a more radical dissolution. Becoming conscious, aware, or mindful is not always necessary and is to be done away with once the individual has acquired the skill. This is essentially because it is likely that enhancing insight into the self could mislead the individual to discover "problems" that had never been "problems" before becoming aware. For example, a meditator who considered as quite peaceful, eventually *discovered* irritation in her mindful process and could not let it go, with the negative feeling intensifying over time. Even though the intention of mindfulness practices is to facilitate *letting go*, such a process inevitably involves a risk that one cannot let something go after becoming mindful of it.

In contrast, the *non-self-oriented meditation* represents a more subtle stage of Zen/Taoist practices. Here, as opposed to mindfulness, the essence of the non-self-oriented meditation is *"bodyfulness."* In spite of the fact that mindfulness meditation originates in Buddhism, there is no correspondent Japanese word for mindfulness. A leading Buddhist psychologist, Yutaka Haruki, often questions as follows: "What's "mindfulness"? Does it mean a state full of mind? Attention, awareness, consciousness, or what?" Despite understanding the operational definitions proposed by a number researchers and practitioners, the fundamental concept remains elusive. One day Sugamura asked him, "what if one said that meditation was a bodyful process?" He answered, "I would instantly and completely get the meaning of it" (Y. Haruki, pers. comm., 2006).

It seems that these two contrasting expressions derive from the differences between the Indian and the Chinese versions of Buddhist meditation. The former could be conceptualized as becoming artifice and being oneself (*uishizen*), whereas the latter as abandoning artifice and being oneself (*muishizen*), considered to be the highest state in Taoism. More precisely, the common term *shizen* refers to nature or as it is, *ui* means doing (committing or performing) something, and *mui* signifies doing nothing. Original Buddhism is thought to be *uishizen* in nature because becoming conscious is essentially an artificial process due to its purposiveness and intentionality. In contrast, Taoism denies *uishizen* and adopts *muishizen*. Buddhism emphasizes the "enlightenment" by one's own exertion, whereas Taoism encourages enlightenment through the benevolence of others. Thus, mindfulness meditation tends to be uishizen and bodyfulness meditation muishizen. However, these two states are not incompatible. According to Mori (1969), in Zen Buddhism one's practice is artificial at the beginning, but the state that Zen ultimately aims to attain is no different from abandoning artifice. In this sense, bodyfulness meditation has the same goal as mindfulness meditation, but the way of meditating tends to be more Taoist in nature. Zen meditation has both aspects of meditation.

Here is an episode that exemplifies the bodyful nature of Zen Buddhism, presented as a contrast to Kabat-Zinn's (1990) popular "raisin exercise" in which meditators are encouraged to eat a raisin as mindfully as they can.

> *Gensha Shibi (834-908) of Fukushu was one of the chief disciples of Seppo. One day he took up a turnip and asked a monk: "This is a turnip, and any remarks to make?" There were over one hundred monks, and many responded to the master's challenge, but none pleased him. Later Gensho appeared and said, "I'll eat, master." "What will you eat?" asked Gensha. "I'll eat the turnip," said Gensho. This satisfied Gensha very much, who said, "You know it, you know it."* (Suzuki, 1950/ 1972, pp. 43-44)

There is no mindful process in this, just eating. In Zen, the goal is to cut off the conscious self from the body. Herein lies the state of non-self. Non-self means "denial and transcendence of attachment in general but especially attachment to self" (Koshikawa, Kuboki, & Ishii, Chapter 11). However, indeed, the assertion of non-self as the goal of Zen has historically brought about many a slap in the face, as teachers scolded their students for harboring such an attachment. For example, Nagarjuna argued that attachment to no-self was more treacherous than attachment to self. However, one should note that this kind of argument emerges originally from an Indian, *uishizen*-based understanding of meditation. Although these cautions are very important to remember, an alternative would be exploring Taoist, bodyfulness or *muishizen*-based approaches. What would be the difference here from simple lack of consciousness, i.e. deep sleep or death? Haruki stated that there would be no subtantial difference. For Haruki, meditation is a practice to become like an "empty-headed idiot" (Y. Haruki, pers. comm., 2003). Becoming an empty-headed *body* might be a point where all things dissolve of their own accord. Here, not only is the mind abandoned but, in that there is no reflective awareness, the body is no longer required. There is semblance here with Dogen's admonition of *shinjin datsuraku* (the dropping off of both body and mind).

It may appear that the non-self-oriented meditation is somewhat of a shortcut to dissolve any and all problems. Perhaps it may be. However, as one can recognize that as the raisin exercise is used as a first step in mindfulness meditation, in a similar fashion, becoming mindful may be a crucial step to becoming bodyful. As Dogen (1233/1994) said, "To learn ourselves is to forget ourselves" (p. 34). In this sense, both self and non-self may be non-discriminative in nature and these two kinds of meditation could be understood as complementary rather than contrasting.

Therapeutic laughter: from logicality to super-logicality and to objectless
Attaining such a state of non-self can be conceptualized as the most radical version of a DOA, but it generally lacks practicality unless one has taken up the monastic life. In contrast, there is another way to presumably dissolve problems in daily lives, namely through the therapeutic application of humor or laughter.

In clinical settings, some therapists, especially constructive therapists, have used humor as a reframing tool in order to give clients a new perspective regarding their concerns. In fact, the use of jokes and humor could be understood in terms of constructivism to some extent. However, some kinds of nonsense humor cannot be specifically explained through the use of Western logic or dialectics. This is essentially because laughter does not require one to be logical. Moreover, it has been quite difficult to determine what kinds of conditions cause people to laugh in spite of numerous explanations by philosophers and psychologists. In this section, the following three kinds of *problem-dissolutive laughter* will be addressed: (a) Laughter caused by a sudden change of meanings; (b) laughter at foolishness, (c) laughter at nonsense, and (d) objectless laughter.

People often laugh due to a sudden change of meanings. Most have had the experience in which a mild joke has aroused laughter and diminished tensions. For instance, a therapist asked, "What's your boss like?" The client responded, "He treats everyone of us like trash." "Well at least he's always fair," replies the therapist. Using humor, the therapist may have intended to show another side of the boss to the client. On the other hand, the client may think that the therapist does not understand her complaint. But if the client elects to burst into laughter, she would have *dissolved* at least a part of her problems at that point. It would be very helpful to be able to laugh even in a difficult situation. The humor itself can be explained by constructivist terminology. For example, constructivists may argue that the client has incorporated another's perspective and thus has become more adaptive. However, changing meanings does not necessarily cause laughter. Sometimes it facilitates insight, relief, or even anger. The relationship between humor and laughter appears to be shrouded in mystery. A Japanese philosopher, Tsuchiya (1997) articulated that the more serious the situation is, the more difficult making a joke would be. This is even more so for the person immersed in the problem at the very moment. For this very reason, the ability to joke when in a difficult situation is to be even more admired. Tsuchiya's example is: When Germany enforced a naval blockade against Britain during the Second World War, the headline of a British newspaper read, "Eurasian Continent Isolated." Another example by Freud (1905) is as follows: A man, mounting the gallows on Monday, looked up into the sky and said, "This week has a good beginning."

People also tend to laugh at other's foolishness. As a matter of fact, there are many jokes that merely depict foolish conversations. For example, at an electronics store, a clerk recommended the latest computer, "This will cut your work in half." "Good. I'll take two of them," said the customer (Satonaka, 2004). It is often easy to laugh at others' foolish behaviors or failure, however it is much more difficult to admit and to laugh at the fact that we too are often foolish, silly, weak, and funny (Tsuchiya, 1997). Although most of western therapies place great emphasis on enhancing the self-confidence of the client, another way to dissolve problems could be by encouraging clients to become aware of their foolishness and choosing to laugh at themselves. For example, Tsuchiya (1998) introduced himself: "I, as a person, am confident in saying that I don't have any special faults to mention except my appearance, personality, and intelligence." Humorous self-mocking may paradoxically enable us to empower ourselves by devaluing ourselves. This form of humor can be a powerful and wide-range life skill rather than merely a means of situation-specific coping.

People sometimes laugh, not because they were surprised by an unexpected perspective or were tickled at someone's foolishness, but because they simply cannot make sense of the situation. One day Sugamura told Mahoney that his 2000 car did not pass the emission test and it cost almost $700 for repairs. Mahoney said, "How come? It's very frustrating, isn't it?" "Yeah..., oh, speaking of tests, I met Karina yesterday and she showed me the brand-new iPod. She said she bought it because she had passed the comprehensive exam. Perhaps I should buy one after I pass the emission test," Sugamura replied. This is humorous because he did nothing beyond spending $700 in contrast to the efforts of passing the comprehensive test. However, through the joke, Sugamura was attempting to detach himself from his frustration. This is foolish but not nonsense. Nonsense was Mahoney's reply that followed: "Baby (his dog) says that you should buy yourself an iPod because she is cute." Sugamura burst into laughter. Mahoney taught him with smile that it is called dog logic (Mahoney, pers. comm., 2004). Indeed, it is plausible that Mahoney facilitated Sugamura's awareness that buying an iPod did not need a reason and this relief induced laughter. Yet, relief itself does not always cause laughter. A better explanation seems to be that Sugamura laughed at the illogicality per se. Constructivism does offer a useful meaning-making framework, but jokes that lean toward meaning-*deconstruction* cannot be well explained. Some forms of humor simply go beyond logic and one laughs as a result of the nonsense. One's sense of humor or laughter seems to be inherently free from logic. The illogicality of jokes approximates the spontaneity or play of Zen and Taoism. In a similar manner, Zen's inclination to rise above logic is well illustrated in a number of koans. For example,

> *A monk asked Joshu, "What would you say when I come to you with nothing?"*
> *Joshu said, "Fling it down to the ground." Protested the monk, "I said that I had*
> *nothing; what shall I let go?" "If so, carry it away," was the retort of Joshu.*
> (Suzuki, 1964, p. 54)

What does this koan tell us? Of course, we can try hard to make sense of it, but we can also simply laugh it off. In fact, the koan is a method that teaches us to stop struggling so much to make sense of it and, instead, drop off one's meaning-making *obsession*. Koans are paradoxical exercises designed to *dissolve* the fundamental problem itself. One of the effective ways to accomplish this would be to *simply laugh it off* from a meta-standpoint. Wittgenstein (1953/1978) stated that all philosophical problems are grammatical jokes. Koans may function in a similar way.

The final possibility is to laugh at nothing. In other words, it suggests object-less laughter. The thesis here is that *laughing is not always laughing-at*. Tsuchiya (1997) discussed an ultimate way to *dissolve* suffering, citing an episode of Chuang-Tzu:

> *When Chuang-Tzu's wife died, he sang songs, beating a platter. Definitely, this is not because Chuang-Tzu was glad to be single once again. It seems that Chuang-Tzu himself intended to teach his disciples the non-discriminative nature of life and death. However, we can interpret this as a narrative that tells us we can laugh in any situations or at least we don't need to suffer. Once we attain such a state of consciousness, we would never suffer from unhappiness whenever it would happen. At this point, people can gain the upper hand over undeniable facts... It is necessary to understand that an ideal person would be a one who has grown mature enough to have it forgotten as a laughing matter unless it could be taken measures against.* (p. 119)

Tsuchiya (1997) cited Chuang-Tzu's episode, suggesting that laughing at one's self is a sophisticated way to cope with stressful situations. However, it can also be interpreted that this level of laughter is objectless. The situation that his wife died could never cause laughter. Also, it does not seem that Chuang-Tzu intended to laugh at his wife's death. Instead, at a certain state of consciousness people may be able to laugh regardless of external conditions. At this level, a change of meanings, foolishness, or illogicality is no longer necessary. There is just laughing; no longer laughing-at.

If this is the state called *muishizen* (abandoning artifice and being oneself), it bears significant resemblance to the highest developmental stage in Zen Buddhism. These stages are illustrated in the *Jugyu-zu* (Ten Pictures of the Ox) drawn by the monk Guo-an, in efforts to convey the process of *satori* (enlightenment), of which self-regulation may serve as a more psychological term (Haruki, 2004). This series of pictures depicts an oxherd who found and then tamed a lost ox, a metaphor for one's true nature. Through his trials, he eventually forgets the ox and ultimately himself, reflective of the early stages of enlightenment or insight. However, he chooses not to simply abide in this state of formless absorption, but, instead, he joyfully returns to the marketplace, as conveyed in the 10th picture. It is character-istic that the oxherd looks totally different from what he used to in the first picture. In the final picture, "entering the market-place with bliss-bestowing hands" (*nittensuishu*), he is simply laughing at nothing. Entering the market-place signi-fies that he returned to human society, and bliss-bestowing hands imply abandon-ing artifice (Ueda, 2002). Thus, in the final stage of development, one adapts to social life, relaxing, and laughing through whatever happens. "In Japan we refer to the person in this picture as "Hotei-san" who is believed to bring happiness. Hotei-san is always smiling" (Haruki, 2004, p. 104).

Arguably, to attain this state would be too difficult for most people. However, even if the final stage of enlightenment is impossible, the practice of making jokes, making fun of ourselves, and simply laughing would help in the development of problem-dissolution skills. Of course, it makes complete sense to try every possible way to *solve* problems. However, if one remains at a loss despite all efforts, it would behoove him or her to simply laugh and to *dissolve* them. Interestingly, a Japanese word *warahu* (laugh) originally meant grown flowers in blossom (Ishitani, 1995), that is, a reference to achieving a mature, well-developed stage of life. Problem-*solution* may be a logical and rational process, but problem-*dissolution* need not be. The use of humor may provide a *dissolving* framework that subsumes the existing self-narrative beneath a meta-narrative, in effect, transcending the duality of problem and solution. The ultimate goal of the dissolution-oriented approach may rest in transcending all duality.

In Conclusion

In this chapter a dissolution-oriented approach was defined and its implications elaborated. A number of psychotherapy systems share similarities with the idea of problem-dissolution to varying degrees. In this sense, a DOA is not truly novel but, rather, a re-conceptualization of conventional approaches. Nevertheless, these concepts have not previously been articulated in light of traditional psychotherapy. The DOA appears to be an integrative method through which one can connect various perspectives, particularly constructivist, social constructionist, Buddhist, Taoist. Although this is a preliminary investigation, we hope that the basic ideas of the DOA would increase the potency of psychotherapy integration toward a new and better theory along with refined practices of psychotherapy, self-help, and, ultimately, *non-self* help.

26

Lose Thy Mind And Come To Thy Senses: Adaptive De-construction

Michael DelMonte

Psychotherapy practice — from Freud's talking cure to cognitive therapy's dialogues and prescriptions — has been characterized by confidence in the ability of the rational mind to resolve psychological distress. However, there may be times when a much older approach to resolving difficulties is useful; for example, reflective silence as in meditation practice with its emphasis on no-thought, mindfulness, and the power of the embodied mind in the here-now. Ancient wisdom traditions, Buddhism in particular, with its various meditation exercises, use of koans, and promotion of compassion may even see the discursive, polarizing, and grasping mind itself as the main obstacle to be overcome if we are to leave suffering behind. The discursive mind can only build up knowledge and establish facts on the basis of objective evidence, whereas the intuitive mind is fostered during silence and meditation. Most of us form emotional attachments to people, objects, and ideas. We may also over-identify with them, especially in the context of idealization. Self-reflection as fostered by therapy and meditation may enhance awareness. This in turn may enable us to dis-identify from dysfunctional ideas, habits, norms, and attitudes and to let go of attachments which no longer serve beneficial purposes. However, detachment may be fostered defensively by some people and increase social isolation. Moreover, defensive introspection may lead to self-engrossment rather than to genuine self-awareness with its concomitant healthy relational engagement.

We live in an age of hyper-communication in terms of both sheer quantity and speed. If one takes a complete break from the office for a couple of weeks the emails, text messages, letters, faxes, phone messages, etc., pile up and await us in intimidating bulk, all demanding instant attention upon one's return. Then we have the ever-present radios, TVs, newspapers, magazines, videos, DVDs, and the like competing for our mental space. If this were not enough, bill-boards try to out-perform each other for our special attention as do the demands of our work, colleagues, and last but hopefully not least, the demands of our families and friends. Then there is the endless chatter at work, social gatherings, and conferences. The chattering species — or "homo chatteraticus" — would punningly describe our manifest nature, especially that subspecies that dwells in our modern expanding urban sprawls. Is it any wonder that we compulsively prattle so much? Our minds are probably over-stimulated, with a constant barrage of hyper-communication on a level to which our so-called primitive ancestors were relatively unaccustomed.

Our over-talkative mouths reflect our unstoppable minds, which find it increasingly difficult to switch off. Even when we go on holidays we take these over-stimulated, hyperactive minds with us on frenetic attempts to "enjoy ourselves" via novel forms of stimulation (De Botton, 2003). Not quite always, if we know how. Never has quiet meditation been more appropriate as an antidote to this volume of mental overdrive. A real mental vacation means just that: a vacant mind. Meditation, whether by means of concentration on only just one stimulus at a time or temporarily trying to remain mindful (i.e. practicing to be a neutral non-judgmental observer) aims at minimizing the thinking-analytical mind and fostering pure sensory awareness instead. Paradoxically, mindfulness meditation, if practiced competently, can eventually lead to peaceful "mindlessness" — characterized by a state of no-thought — even if it is only for brief moments initially.

What can we do with the chronically over-aroused mind? One option is to offer them the talking therapies with a talking cure in mind. We have Freud's free association monologues, cognitive therapy's restructuring dialogues, and many other variants all using verbalization as their modus operandi. No doubt, these are often very useful approaches, usually in the earlier or "repair" stages of therapy, but I am less convinced that this always remains the case with those among us with obsessive thinking patterns. Can problems of the pained and over-active mind exclusively be solved by the thinking mind? Hopefully some clarity on this shall emerge as we proceed.

Internality Versus Externality, Mindfulness, and Dis-Identification

One may object that I am right now engaging in communicative chatter. Yes as this has to do with externality. Talking and writing are useful means of communication between people as "objects." Internality, must not, however, be neglected. We are not just objects to each other, we are also subjects. Our internal space, our subjectivities, should not be overlooked. This is where meditation is also valuable. When we attend to our inner space, we often notice how our incessant thinking is like a compulsion, well-nigh impossible to stop, even when we claim that these thoughts are unwanted. This repetitive thinking has typically been dealt with by cognitive therapy via "thought stopping," but evidence suggests that a gentler approach based on acceptance of unwanted cognitions via mindful "witnessing" may be more effective (Tolle, 1999; Thich, 2003; Barnes-Holmes et al., 2004). Awakening our inner observer capacity is what mindfulness promotes. Much of our private thinking is comprised of unproductive monologues at best, but also by destructive imaginary internal disputes and conflicts. Many people suffer from minds that are ceaselessly engaged in anxious or depressive self-statements with little in the way of creative outcome. What can be done about this? For a start, one can raise awareness levels via mindfulness training.

It may be easier to start mindfulness by merely observing our physical bodies in action; for instance, by simply watching ourselves walking. We can do likewise for various other daily activities, while washing our hands or eating. Paradoxically, when we apply our inner observer to our own thinking minds in mindfulness, it is not with the intention of refining our thinking, but rather to dis-identify from it (Assagioli, 1965; Holmes, 1997; Tolle, 1999; DelMonte, 2000, 2003). Observing our thoughts, like clouds passing through the sky without clinging onto them, is what dis-identification is basically about. Thereby one learns to let go temporarily of unsolicited and invasive thoughts so as to have a less "muddied" consciousness and eventually to let go momentarily of all thoughts, leaving just moments of neutral perception, or better still, the "just being of clear consciousness." Although consciousness without thought is a possibility, its opposite, thought without consciousness is not. Consciousness is primary, and from it emerges thought as a secondary phenomenon, an epiphenomenon, which can become parasitic in the sense that consciousness can play the role of a reluctant host to our unbidded thinking.

Awareness

It is possibly clear that mindfulness practice can also be seen as a form of awareness training. We have several objects of choice on which to focus our attention, as on our breathing, walking, or hearing. In this way we learn to sensitize and train our senses, which is best done non-analytically and in the *hic et nunc*/here-now mode. We also observe our cravings, our clutching, and needy minds in action and via just letting-be, learn to side-step them. Identification with and attachment to the desired contents of mind lead to fear of their loss and consequently to emotional distress, pessimistic thinking, and compensatory behavior. These cravings can be simply observed, neither judged nor acted upon. We can also become attached to and identified with our pain, losses, and suffering as in a felt sense of prolonged victimhood.

Developing an awareness of our varied attachments is another aspect of mindfulness training, contradictory as some of them may seem to be. Craving for sensory gratification, for continued existence, and for annihilation, corresponding to the Freudian constructs of libido, ego, and *Thanatos*, can be problematic (De Silva, 1990). Dependence on sensory gratification implies dependence on externality. Craving for continued existence is a denial of impermanence, and craving for annihilation is surrender to the death instinct. This can be seen in impulsive aggression turned outwards on others (sadism) or inwards on self (masochism) as with substance abuse, self-mutilation, and suicide. Behind the death wish is often a desire to return to a non-suffering peaceful state free of longing and frustration.

This peace can be attained constructively via mindfulness and is referred to as "nirvana" when achieved.

Many approaches to mental health see the development of self-awareness as beneficial. The insight gained through psychoanalysis is purportedly transmutative in terms of neurotic symptoms (Freud, 1900). Likewise, the self-awareness fostered in Gestalt therapy (Perls et al., 1973) is seen as therapeutic. Schwartz (1983) saw self-attention per se as playing an important homeostatic and thus integrative role. It has also been argued, with some empirical support that meditation in general and mindfulness in particular are conducive to well-being (Shafii, 1973b; Carrington & Ephron, 1975; Deatherage, 1975; Brown & Engler 1980; DelMonte, 1984a, 1985, 1990; DelMonte & Kenny, 1985). Moreover, it was suggested that increased non-neurotic self-awareness, with its attendant clarity of vision, should allow one to make more informed choices thus enabling to discard old habits, attitudes, and attachments that no longer serve evolving needs. These claims are addressed below in the context of our attachments to people, objects, and ideas, as well as in the context of our attempts to foster self-awareness via self-attention strategies. Is there a link between self-attention and health?

Self Attention, Awareness, and Self-Regulation

Schwartz's (1983) disregulation theory can be catch-phrased as: repression and disease versus mindfulness and health. He postulated that awareness is linked to health and repression to "dis-ease" and produced considerable empirical evidence that repressors show elevated levels of psychophysiological distress, in brain-waves, musculature, and especially in cardiovascular arousal. The latter findings are consistent with some work of my own also showing a significant relationship between defensiveness and haemodynamic arousal in general and cardiovascular arousal in particular (DelMonte, 1984a, 1985). Repressors also report significantly more physical illness than low anxious subjects. Schwartz agrees with Galin (1974) when he proposed that repression is produced by a functional cerebral disconnection syndrome in which the left hemisphere (usually associated with verbal and analytic functioning) becomes functionally isolated to varying degrees from the right hemisphere with its relative non-verbal, emotional, and spatial function. He produced evidence that repressive subjects appear to show more (right hemisphere) cerebral lateralization with regard to negative emotions and in situations which are potentially threatening. He also quotes other evidence indicating a relative attenuation of information transfer from the right to the left hemisphere in repressive compared with low anxious subjects. Moreover, traumatic memories tend to be stored in the right parietal lobes (Van der Kolk & Fisher, 1995). Warrenburg et al. (1981) reported a significantly high proportion of hypertensive subjects being repressors. The more relaxed they said they were during the speech-task, the higher their blood pressure. This observation is supported by other evidence that high blood pressure (internal arousal or noise) can be used to dampen cognitive awareness of distress (Dworkin et al., 1979; DelMonte, 1984a).

Schwartz (1983) argues that self-attention, as practiced in mindfulness "seems to have specific autonomic, self-regulatory, and stabilizing effects on physiological functioning" (p. 114). He contends that self-attention can promote localized healing, "especially if the self-attention is guided by relevant imagery that is targeted to the appropriate part(s) of the body" (p. 114). This suggestion is interesting in terms of the work done by Simonton and Simonton (1974) and by Meares (1978) in which they used meditation and visualization with cancer patients. In a similar fashion the insight gained in psychotherapy may be beneficial. There is some evidence that those receiving therapy are less likely to subsequently report physical illness (Rosen & Wiens, 1979). Psychotherapy typically aims to enhance insight and awareness as well as provide corrective attachment experiences. Do we need to distinguish between such positive attachment experiences and our tendency to clutch indiscriminately in many directions?

Attachments

Much has been said elsewhere (DelMonte, 2003, 2004) about our clutching minds attaching to opinions, possessions, success, power, status, prestige, wealth, or pride. Less has been stated about our minds' equal capacity to identify and stay with suffering by either living in the past (and holding onto bygone insults, losses, hurts, defeats) or by anticipating the future (in pessimistic, paranoid, or hypochondriacal ways). Victimhood can become a fixed identity, even a way of life (Bruckner, 2000). The pain-body and the pain-mind (Tolle, 1999) are often characterized by an exaggerated need to wallow in and talk about suffering compulsively and self-righteously, usually blaming others for our misery. Then there is the compulsion to compare and judge others from a "knowing" position. Such non-compassionate sitting in judgment and forming opinions about others only isolates us. Psychic pain is inevitable if one is identified with an egotistic mind that seeks a constant array of gratifications, including the need to always right. Ego identifications lead us to cling to past gains, regret past losses, and worry about future snags, snares, pitfalls, and more losses. They take us away from living fully in the present which can have so much to offer. Life inevitably involves a series of gains and losses. Griffin (2001) saw adjustment to loss as a lifelong regenerative learning process.

Then, there is the social domain. We are popularly described as social animals. Attachment has bio-psycho-social components. Developing a theory of mind in childhood facilitates them (Fonagy et al., 1994). People often remark on the proclivity of human beings to form strong emotional bonds. However, there is considerable variation in this tendency to seek out others and maintain contact. Social stickiness does not appear to be spread out evenly in the population. Some individuals deliberately enhance their out-reaching skills, whilst others use various strategies to distance themselves from people or to withdraw into themselves. Much has been written about the manner in which children socialize as they grow up. Establishing healthy social links is seen as a prerequisite to mental health. Those of us who are unable to form and sustain intimate affiliations are likely to have serious emotional problems, but so are those whose emotional bonds are overly dependent. Extremes in emotional distance, being too closely enmeshed in a dependent way, or at the other end of the scale, being excessively self-reliant, are considered maladaptive (Birtchnell, 1997).

We not only become attached to people, we also form strong attachments to a range of objects and experiences, such as the taste of certain food and drinks, the sound of particular forms of music, our possessions such as childhood toys, paintings, ornaments, land, houses, or money. Moreover, we also become attached to the non-material realm in terms of our languages, religions, theories, ideologies, power, and achievements. We may identify with such attachments to the point of describing ourselves in terms of their labels. Thus, we may characterize ourselves as communist, nationalist, feminist, protestant, orthodox, liberal, left-wing, Afrikaans-speaking, humanist, etc. We also characterize these attachments in egotistical terms: my religion, my flock, my people, my career, my territory, my opinion, etc. Is our real identity the sum of such divisive and personal attachments or is this just our mask? We may cling as arduously onto non-material as onto material attachments (e.g. when trying to persuade an opinionated person to change his mind). Attachments do not always make much rational sense. We can become attached to or enmeshed with other peoples' difficulties, our own personal problems, or abusive relationships. Attachments can limit, hold, and constrain consciousness to particular viewpoints, attitudes, and perspectives. They can imprison us and impeach our further evolution.

Attachment, Loss, and Defensive Detachment

Attachment and loss are two sides of the same coin. Nothing is permanent. All is flux. Much is delusion. Investments are potential losses, if not during our current lifetimes, then certainly upon their physical ends. We all live in the shadow of death: the ultimate narcissistic loss. This knowledge, colored by our personal history of previous losses (emotional and material) has as a consequence that we can feel varying degrees of insecurity about our desired attachments. Paradoxically, the various objects and people on whom we have become dependent for our emotional identity and security may also become the very source of our deepest anxiety as observed in the separation anxiety linked to their feared loss. Although with emotional attachment comes varying degrees of social support, often at a price, namely that of burdensome counter demands and responsibilities! Caring for others can be emotionally draining, not just rewarding.

Some of us try to avoid this anxiety by means of a schizoid defense. It is likely to be found in those who are fearful of the risks involved in emotional interdependence (mostly due to past failures and hurts in this area). This defense is characterized by a largely unconscious, contrived emotional detachment based on an exaggerated attitude of personal self-sufficiency, especially when childhood bonding with care-givers was painfully inadequate or insensitive. In the absence of adequate parental attunement and nurturing behavior, emotional self-dependence may be sought via varying degrees of emotionally insulating and autonomous behavior. An extreme version of this defense could be the affective non-attachment and non-attunement found in borderline personality disorder, where long-term intimacy is too uncomfortable to be sustained (Holmes, 1997). However, several variants of defensive isolation or extreme egoism exist. Solipsism, for example, is an intellectual rationalization for this cut off stance in life. Is mere withdrawal adequate? How can one enjoy such false escapism when surrounded by others who may be in pain? This issue of defensive detachment shall be expanded on below when discussing detachment and disidentification. I shall go on to explore the way eastern techniques can be used to alter these apparently opposite inclinations to either connect with others or to retreat from them.

Adaptive Disidentification

Not all detachment is a maladaptive defense. Some therapists deliberately encourage a form of non-attachment as a way of coping with potential loss. For example, Assagioli (1965) and Holmes (1997) refer to the strategy of dis-identification when dealing with psychic pain. Assagioli's viewpoint was similar to that of Buddhists who perceive tendencies to identify in a clinging way with objects of desire as ultimately leading to the pain of actual or imagined loss. He described cognitive exercises to encourage the development of a mental set of dis-identification as a counterforce in coping with this tendency to over-invest and to over-identify with our physical bodies, emotions or thoughts, and with attachments in general. The objective of disidentification exercises is to be less at the mercy of longings, wishes, and desires. One finds an echo here of the Buddhist dictum: craving is the source of suffering. Mindfulness can raise awareness of our acquisatorial nature and help liberate us from the slavery of endless grasping of which contemporary materialism and consumerism are obvious hedonistic examples. For Freud (1900, 1912, 1930) the pull of the pleasure principle is not freedom. The other side of the dualism is displeasure that inevitably follows in the heels of pleasure seeking. Freedom comes from letting go of defensive and reactionary views and from moving above polarized construing as in "them versus us" attitudes.

For a non-clinical example of disidentification, the exile is an interesting case, especially if s/he comes from a poorly understood cultural background or ethnic group. Being an exile in a foreign land often means that one's former cultural identity has to be suspended while a new one is being constructed. Todorov (1996) refers to the latter process as acculturization. Here we should also speak of deconstructing one's former persona (by deculturization) and developing a new identity (or mask?). This can be a painful process characterized by considerable nostalgia for lost familiarities and by obsessional reminiscing about the lost world in an attempt to keep it mentally alive while constructing a new one. This process can rarely be fully complete so that one is left as a transcultural hybrid betwixt two worlds. Rather than view this new state of affairs as a failure, it could on the contrary be seen as an adaptive dynamic in which one's identity is elastic. Fixity gives way to resilience and flexibility in which gains by identifications are constantly being balanced by losses of dis-identification to produce a freshly evolving self.

Non-Attachment Techniques of the East

In the Orient there is a long tradition, going back thousands of years linked to Hinduism, Taoism, Shintoism, and Buddhism, of using various techniques such as meditation, Yoga, Tai-chi, Qi-gong, etc. to achieve altered mental states characterized by equanimity and non-grasping by moving beyond and transcending the issues onto which our thoughts can stick (Mascaro, 1962; DelMonte, 1995a, 2000). Buddhist meditation, Yoga, Tai-chi, and Qi-gong can be used to focus on bodily posture, breathing, and the contents of mind. Like in Zen koans, they play down the value of intellectualization, rationalization, and other aspects of what is known as *shi-shen* in Qi-gong. Shi-shen or conceptual knowledge must be balanced by *yuan shen* that lies beyond conceptual consciousness yet permeates all aspects of life being its very source. Yuan-shen is seen as the dynamic force inherent in Qi. This could be referred to as vital energy in the West. Its conceptual counterpart in Yoga appears to be *prana* and in ancient Greece probably *pneuma*. Yuan-shen, being essentially ineffable, is difficult to symbolize or put into words. During meditation and koan contemplation one tries to side-step the discursive mind with its focus on conceptual knowledge or shi-shen. The periods of meditative no-thought characterized by stillness, silence, and openness may present opportunities to experience the ineffable yuan shen. Moreover, yuan shen may be phenomenologically similar to Jung's (1958) collective unconscious, namely a vast, loose, preverbal, pre-conscious, and inchoate transpersonal resource of a vast potential. This can be tapped into more readily by the use of techniques such as mindfulness in which the chattering conceptual mind is temporarily silenced, hence lose thy mind and come to thy senses. Dorcas (1966) argues that meditation and Qi-gong are similar insofar as they both use attention, concentration, and mindfulness to tune the mind to "an advanced level of consciousness, in which the divisions between subject and object cease to exist, the division between me and not me melts away and in which one feels at one with the entire universe" (p. 13). This advanced state of consciousness is also hallmarked by "choiceless awareness" (Krishnamurti, 1991) in so far as such awareness implies a non-seeking and non-clutching approach to the contents of perception.

Bearing the above train of thought in mind, a distinction can usefully be made between detachment, which implies detaching, withdrawing interest, or giving up something previously valued, on the one hand, and non-attachment on the other, which implies a neutral or non-grasping stance whilst accepting, in a non-possessive manner, all of that which momentarily forms part of our experiential world. Whereas detachment can seem anti-social, non-attachment does not imply a lack of compassion, nor indifference to the world or to others. Detachment can also be seen as harboring strong defensive undertones and may have little to do with maturing through life's experiences related to love and work.

Mindfulness Meditation Practice

Advanced practitioners of meditation focus their attention on the phenomenology of consciousness by means of introspective mindfulness (DelMonte, 1995a). With mindfulness one is encouraged to maintain a quiet awareness, without comment of whatever happens to be here-now (Watts, 1957). The objective of mindfulness is "to come to know one's own mental processes, to thus begin to have the power to shape or control the mental processes, and finally to gain freedom from the condition where the mental processes are unknown and uncontrolled, with the individual at the mercy of his own unbridled mind" (Deatherage, 1975, p. 134). Hendricks (1975) sees such introspection as a form of discrimination training, which helps to observe thoughts in a detached way and speculates: "since nearly everyone has a certain number of neurotic thoughts mental health is dependent upon the ability to recognize that they are 'just thoughts' " (p. 145). This approach can be applied to depressive, anxious, and obsessive thoughts. Several authors have done just that (Kabat-Zinn, 1996; Teasdale, 2000).

A variant of mindfulness (analytic meditation) can also be used to observe the psychic nature of felt attachments with their complex interwoven webs of emotional, cognitive, attitudinal, and behavioral subcomponents. In observing the very construction of consciousness in this non-attached, non-grasping, and non-identifying manner practitioners hope, at least temporarily, to move beyond the pull of their unbridled yearnings. Being mindful of the impermanence of material and psychic attachments facilitates awareness of the ephemeral nature of our personal consciousness, laden as it is with regular eruption of instinctive craving. Freedom is where craving is converted into mindful choosing. If cravings are invariably suppressed then we are no freer than if we always yield to them. Mindfulness encourages an opening to higher consciousness. In this way it is similar to some forms of prayer. One can say that such meditation favors an opening of our intuitive self. It fosters this intuitive self over our more driven and reactive instinctive self as well as over our split-off cerebral self. The insights gained from meditation are not to be limited to personal gain, but should be transformed into relational acts of kindness, compassion, respect, and tolerance of others.

The Silence of Meditation

Mindfulness can become very simple. For instance, we can learn to observe the silence about as well as within us, if we progress that far. Moments of timelessness may emerge as may a sense of formlessness. Our personal experience of timelessness is just a small chip off the eternity block just as our experience of formlessness yields a sense of infinity. These moments of dwelling in timelessness and formlessness, however brief, nevertheless yield a sense of unity where the dualistic thinking mind has suspended its "me/other" construing. By letting go of dualistic sense-making and just letting be, one approaches whatever emerges with increasing equanimity. Deeply silent meditation characterized by no-thought and a sense of unity brings us face-to-face with the "unmanifest" or pure yet-to-be expressed potential, a break from repetitive and predictable thinking.

This dichotomy between the discursive mind and no-thought does not imply an inherent conflict. Thinking undoubtedly has its value and place, especially when we use thought and speech to facilitate informative, creative, humorous, or playful communication. Silence, on the contrary, facilitates communion (i.e. a meeting of hearts, non-verbally through intuition, feeling, empathy, and sensation; Shafii, 1973a). As Jung (1958) pointed out there are four ways of knowing: thinking, sensing, feeling, and intuiting, with thinking being increasingly favored in contemporary western culture. The silence of meditation uses focused sensory attention to foster the silence of the intuitive mind. The practice of silence leading to no-thought can be described as the *via negativa* (the empty way) as opposed to the *via positiva*, which is the more habitual mode as seen daily in our discursive minds. They represent opposite ways of sense making. The path of silence should not seek to negate the thinking mind, but rather to assist in the liberation of one's self from blind allegiance to our impulses, obsessions, and compulsions (Freud's id) and from the impoverishment resulting from our maladaptive defenses (harsh super-ego). Mindful silence thus facilitate the emergence of creative emptiness in which "benevolent depersonalization" (Moncayo, 2003) is fostered: the discarding of unhelpful id and super-ego impulses and control.

Silence in Psychodynamic Psychotherapy

Psychotherapy, compared with Buddhist meditation, is a neophyte on the world stage. Most forms of therapy use verbalization as their modus operandi. A common view held by psychoanalysts is that those who do not learn to think through (or symbolize verbally) are bound to act out and to go on suffering, as with the hysterically inclined who tend to feel too much. Hence we have the pain-body

(Tolle, 1999), impoverished in terms of capacity for reflective thinking. Whilst one would not dispute that there is great merit in the talking cure, there is nevertheless a growing corpus of opinion on the value of some fecund silence in therapy. For example, obsessionals, by thinking and often talking too much, block out feelings and demonstrate that one cannot always think one's way of out of problems. In therapy they typically have difficulty in being in touch with feelings — their own and those of others — and are usually very uncomfortable with silence. Hence the endless chatter, which is often split off from feeling. This is sometimes pejoratively referred to as "free dissociation" (Perls et al, 1973) or split-off intellect. These people may need to learn that speech, just like music, is given deeper meaning by being punctuated by fertile silence so that something more profound than words may emerge. According to O'Donoghue (1977) "if you are outside of yourself, always reaching beyond yourself, you avoid the call of your own mystery. When you acknowledge the integrity of your solitude and settle into its mystery, your relationships with others take on a new warmth, adventure, and wonder." Silence can foster a sense of compassionate communion.

However, Freud (1912) saw patients' silence as resistance. But Balint (1958) argued that if we can change our own approach from considering silence as a symptom of resistance to studying it as a source of information, we may learn something about this area of mind. Later authors saw silence as indicative of shyness, shame, sorrow, anger, hostility, psychic absence, and fear. Silence has also been construed, at times, as adaptive regression to pre-verbal sense-making (as opposed to malign or psychotic regression; Shafii, 1973a). Coltart (1992) goes as far as saying that her preference is for a silent patient. This may be because the silent patient allows the analyst ample time to work with the visceral felt-sense of the countertransference. It should come as no surprise that she also described herself as a practitioner of Buddhist meditation. This is a long way from Freud (1930) who did not work with the countertransference at all and who saw religious experience, meditation, and mysticism as regressive, irrational, and maladaptive phenomena, forms of "oceanic" fusion and oneness with mother and the wish to re-experience intra-uterine life. To facilitate the patient in adaptive regression the therapist must also be capable of silence like by avoiding premature, aggressive, and excessive interpretations, instructions, or comments. In this way pre-verbal traumata can be re-experienced and mastered again in silence (Shafii, 1973a).

Dreams also tend to be silent. It is well known that Freud (1900) described dreams as the royal road to the unconscious. Perhaps less well known is that Jung (1958) similarly described meditation as a "sort of a royal road to the unconscious" (p. 508). He, however, also saw meditation as a surrender to the collective unconscious as its practice leads primarily to an indefinite experience of oneness and timelessness, which he viewed as hallmarks of the collective unconscious. Kretschmer (1962) saw meditation in a similar light: "Dreams are similar to meditation except meditation gains the reaction of the unconscious by a technique which is faster than depending on dreams" (p. 76). However, it may take several years of practice to arrive at the adeptness of an advanced meditator. By now it should be obvious that it is not just meditators who strive to clear the mind of its sticky attachments. Psychoanalysts like Bion, Shafii, and Coltart also see value in analysts themselves temporarily creating an empty or fallow state of mind during sessions so as to be more receptive to the patient's transferences (DelMonte, 1995b). Bion (1970) advised therapists to forsake memory, desire, and understanding during clinical practice. He quoted from a letter written by the poet John Keats in 1817 referring to capability as "when a man is capable of being in uncertainties, mysteries, doubts, without any irritable reaching after fact and reason" (p. 125). Here we see a psychoanalyst advising his colleagues not to hold too tightly onto one's professional opinions and theories when dealing with patients. This is also a variant of non-attachment. Other forms of therapy, in particular Gestalt therapy, also question the value of too much focus on verbalization.

Gestalt Therapy Perspective

Perls was influenced by Tao philosophy as well as by Freud, Reich, Moreno, Gestalt psychology, and existentialism. He emphasized personal responsibility in the resolution of problems. Gestalt therapy and meditation focus on the *hic et nunc* of experience and play down the value of verbalization. In fact, Perls et al. (1973) stated that verbalization, as in free-association, could become an escapist free-dissociation from feelings and emotions. Together with obsessional verbalization, he also saw excessive rationalization as a defense against subjective feelings. Instead, Perls stressed the importance of contact and sensing, hence his admonition to lose your mind and come to your senses.

He described specific techniques, involving sensation, used to foster awareness. In this regard it is worth noting that he defined himself as an existentialist who applied the phenomenological approach. Many existentialists use this method of subjective inquiry originally developed by Husserl and later applied by Heidegger to examine immediate experience. It has to do with a critical and scrupulous inspection of one's mental processes and one's consciousness. It involves an attempt to exclude all assumptions about external causes of internal phenomena (DelMonte, 1989). As existentialist phenomenology concerns subjective awareness without prejudice or prejudgment, it could be argued that it closely resembles mindfulness in that the latter is purportedly characterized by a deautomatization of experience (i.e. the dropping or suspension of perceptual and cognitive habits). With both the mindfulness and phenomenological methods one strives for a permeable or open stance to the flux of consciousness without trying to punctuate any experience. In this way both methods are typified by what Perls calls "confluence," the absence of figure-background contrasts.

In meditation and Gestalt therapy the observer role is valued. For example, Perls encouraged patients to observe tension and anxiety and not to engage in premature relaxation. In other words, he promoted approach rather than avoidance techniques. In the same way in mindfulness meditation one is encouraged to observe steadfastly one's moods, feelings, or thoughts in a non-attached and non-judgmental way. Perls and many practitioners of meditation saw awareness per se as being therapeutic. This includes awareness of simply "being" for which he used his internal silence and "make a void" techniques, acknowledging an influence from Tao philosophy. The similarity between the internal silence technique and the no-thought strategy of concentrative meditation is striking (DelMonte, 1990). Perls also used breathing exercises similar to those in mindful breathing. Both involve paying attention to one's breath.

In Gestalt therapy there are also exercises for focusing on anxiety, panic, depression, fatigue, psychosomatic symptoms, and behavioral problems, all in order to integrate and resolve them, thus leading to Gestalt closure. Likewise, mindfulness is increasingly being used with a similar range of psychological disorders (Kabat-Zinn, 1996; Teasdale, 2000). Finally, it has been argued (McGee et al., 1984) that those experiences which are too threatening to one's core psychological functioning may be suspended as unexperienced experiences (i.e. without being fully processed or integrated at a conscious level). Such experiences remain akin to unfinished business, unfulfilled needs, or incomplete Gestalten. The latter tend to be at low levels of awareness and acted out behaviorally or hysterically in order to be communicated or when trying to achieve closure. In this sense the symptoms of hysteria are seen to be functional and symbolic (Szasz, 1972). It may be that the weakening of one's cognitive defenses during Gestalt exercises, free association, and meditation facilitates the abreactive emergence of incomplete Gestalten or repressed material.

Following abreaction, patients can check on any emotions that they have just experienced. Such enquiry should enable the client to put some verbal structure onto these preverbal feelings. By learning to put verbal form on feeling the client is in a better position to discuss his/her experiences with others — including the therapist. Verbalizing feelings, labeling them, is an aspect of constructivist psychotherapy.

Personal Construct Theory Approach

Kelly (1955) saw man as living in two realities, firstly, the primary reality beyond human perception and secondly, the interpretations or constructions of the first. Man is like a scientist developing bipolar constructs in order to make sense of the world by looking for repetitive patterns of similarity and difference among a series of events occurring through time. Even as infants, before we acquire language, we construe events dichotomously via bi-polar discriminations such as milk versus not milk, mother versus other, thick versus thin, hot versus cold, etc. Initially, these discriminations or constructs are preverbal (i.e. not yet verbally labeled). Although a growing child learns to attach verbal labels to such discriminations, much of adult construing remains non-verbal and somatic. As each person moves along the dimension of time, s/he develops his/her own personal construct system to be used in the anticipation of events. The construct systems of normal individuals are constantly being updated in the light of newly assimilated evidence. Such accommodation and revision of construct systems allow for a better fit with primary reality.

As McWilliams (1984) contends, both Buddhist Psychology and personal construct theory acknowledge that normal human understanding of the universe involves the use of dualistic dimensions to make sense of a unitary universe. Buddhist approaches emphasize the need to see through this illusion of duality via practices such as mindfulness. On the other hand, constructivist psychologists focus on the reality of a more sophisticated and effective personal construct system in order to be able to accurately predict events. Buddhists see suffering as stemming from our desire to force the universe to conform to dualistic and egocentric cravings, beliefs, and values. A fundamental concern about dualistic construing is that it creates divisions and boundaries in a universe that Buddhists postulate to be inherently holistic and unitary. To the extent that we attend to conventional, dichotomous, ideas about the universe, we are taken away from direct, immediate experience of the universe. The Buddhist viewpoint is that it is possible to transcend the delusion of our self-invented dualistic world and to see the transparency of our construct system in order to experience a sense of unity with greater reality. Such an experience comes from an awareness of how we personally construct our view of this reality. This awareness may be unfolded through arduous mindfulness practice.

Kelly was adamant on the notion of bipolarity of constructs. One always abstracts on the basis of similarity and contrast. Dichotomy is seen as an essential feature and limitation of thinking itself. Whilst one can transcend one's biography and not become a victim of circumstance, one can only do this through developing alternative constructs. One never escapes from one's construct system, but always assimilates the world through it. Thus, when transcending a particular bipolarity, one tends to climb to a higher and more abstract level, but to a level which, nonetheless, is structured in bipolar terms. It may be that meditation approaches are directly or indirectly attempting to elaborate the non-verbal construing of the person so that it supersedes the verbally labeled constructions. This is descendence from the psyche to the soma, rather than transcendence or ascendence. Descendence implies moving down from cognitive to preverbal or somatic construing. In psychodynamic terms this is known as adaptive as opposed to psychotic regression. Here there may be a gradual decrease in the level of cognition right down to the unconscious level. Ascendence describes a movement up to a higher and more abstract bi-polar construct, to superordinate construing within a personal construct system. Such superordinate construing may be seen as the supra-conscious (Assagioli, 1965) and may also be difficult to verbalize. Transcendence as in no-thought is the feeling of unity or bliss when the meditator has the experience that s/he has transcended the bipolarity of all construing, but nonetheless is still construing at a very basic somatic level in terms of balance, posture, respiration, osmo-regulation, blood pressure, and other vital aspects of metabolism. Transcendence is, therefore, where the person recovers his/her non-verbal sense of oneness or individuality by not confusing the duality of bipolar construing with the essential unity of greater reality.

Problems with Detachment and Dis-Identification

There are individuals whose attachments are problematic: being too intense and overly dependent or, in the other direction, being practically non-existent. Does meditation ever encourage an exaggerated introverted stance to the external world, at times bordering on pathological dissociation and fostering social isolation?

Epstein (1990) thought that meditation could lead to narcissistic emptiness as ego-strivings aimed at the external world are negated. Castillo (1990), in a similar vein, could see excessive meditation practice as leading to pathological derealiza-tion and depersonalization as both the external world and the self are eschewed. What is it about eastern techniques that may lead to these concerns? Are there any parallels with western techniques such as hypnosis? Wang (1998) described simi-larities between internal Qi-gong and self-hypnosis. Both can be used to raise fin-ger temperature, an indicator of relaxation (Song, 1998). It can also be argued that adaptive dissociative processes may be operative, to varying degrees, in medita-tion, hypnosis, and Qi-gong. All require a capacity for relaxed absorbed attention in the practitioner, which is directed inwards and away from external stimuli. Those meditations that employ a relaxed posture, closed eyes, and the rhythmical and monotonous repetition of a mantra, encourage a shift away from one's habitual construing of external reality towards a trance-like state in which suggestibility may be enhanced (DelMonte, 1981, 1984b). Thus, mantra meditation like hyp-notic induction can weaken one's ability to marshal ego defenses, thereby encour-aging partial dissociation between external reality and one's inner world domi-nated by memories, fantasies, wishes, or desires. It has also been argued that turn-ing attention away from the external world facilitates an exploration of the internal realm including the unconscious and archetypal imagery in the Jungian sense (DelMonte 1995a, 1995b). Such an exploration would usually be seen as adaptive regression that operates in the service of the ego (Shafii, 1973b). It purportedly leads to a fuller familiarity with one's internal world.

Pathological Regression

Adaptive regression can be contrasted by pathological regression. The practice of meditation is typically associated with the first, but it can also lead to regressing back to primitive psychic functioning with those who are emotionally vulnerable and probably in need of psychotherapy prior to taking up meditation. The practice of meditation can, especially with novices, increase suggestibility (DelMonte, 1981). The monotonous repetition of a mantra, the relaxed posture, and the reduced sensory input, all tend to increase regressive mentation and facilitate cognitive or intellectual defenses.

This regression becomes pathological when it no longer serves healthy ego functions of *Eros* (love, life-force, or Qi), but instead becomes fixated on the id, or worse, on *Thanatos* (the death-drive or wish to return to an undemanding preincarnate state). It is thus not surprising that several decades ago Alexander (1931) described meditation as "a sort of artificial schizophrenia with complete withdrawal of libidinal interest from the outside world" (p. 30). He is referring to the meditators' attempted non-attachment to desires and drives and to their avoidance of ego-gratification. Here people can be split off emotionally from others, from meaningful relationships and escape from troublesome aspects of social life into isolated self-absorption. This fostered dissociation between the self and one's surroundings can for those at risk lead to derealization as one becomes estranged from once-familiar aspects of the external world. It can also lead to defensive depersonalization as the excessive meditator may dis-identify from his/her peripheral social constructs (and even to some degree from one's personal constructs) and thus increasingly withdraw into a minimalist core, dissociated from the external trappings of selfhood and devoid of the necessary motivation to deal with outside demands. The twin effects of such avoiditive derealization and depersonalization can amount to a premature disengagement from life in which relationships of love and work are neglected in favor of an obsession with the complexity of one's internal space. Here, meditation may lead more to detrimental self-absorption than to self-awareness. Such self-absorption has little to do with either creative depersonalization or with adaptive transcendence. It lacks compassion for others and negates the relational aspect of growth.

The Vulnerable

Those who take up meditation in the West tend to be more anxious and neurotic and to report more problems than the population at large (DelMonte, 1990). The dissociated-identity disordered as well as psychotic, narcissistic, schizoid, paranoid, socially phobic, extreme shy individuals, and all those who are already having difficulties in the social domain (and whose ability to adequately read other people's emotions and to empathize is impaired) may inadvertently come to use meditation as a defense to escape even further from others and end up feeling even less connected and thus more isolated. Furthermore, immature or traumatized people with poorly integrated personalities may use meditation to escape into a split off sub-personality that is less adapted to the world. When meditation practice induces profoundly escapist dissociation, weakened alter-egos may emerge in those whose personalities only hold together rather loosely.

It thus is argued that the deliberate fostering of non-attachment to the external world may lead to a pathological detachment or indifference in those who are already emotionally and socially frail. Likewise, deliberate dis-identification from the contents of consciousness can also be used as a maladaptive defense by those whose self-identity never blossomed and remained underdeveloped. When they foster non-attachment and dis-identification, this might have varying degrees of pathological dissociation as its outcome. This is not to argue against the obvious benefits of adaptive non-attachment, dis-identification, and mindfulness as practiced by the majority of meditators. However, it does suggest that with more vulnerable individuals, particularly those with poor ego-strength, psychotherapy is indicated to help build up their ego-strengths before they embark upon prolonged meditation practice, which is about learning to sidestep, temporarily, our over-reactionary egos. It should be easier to meditate successfully with a reasonably well-integrated ego.

Conclusion

Buddhist meditation, Tai-chi, Yoga, Qi-gong, Gestalt therapy, and some forms of insight-orientated therapy, by encouraging quiet adaptive introspection, circumspection, and mindfulness can serve psychological growth (Eros) by encouraging the development of a more reflective self through exploring the furtive and dynamic aspects of consciousness and the clutching nature of attachments and obsessional thinking. The resultant self-awareness helps to clarify one's desires and choices.

However, mindfulness can be used inappropriately by the vulnerable. Thus, it can encourage disengagement and de-motivation with respect to the external world and lead to escaping into an inner-self, to the detriment of normal relationships, attachments, and cathexes. Here, neither love nor work satisfaction can be properly experienced, as the individual in the premature grasp of Thanatos forgoes compassion and the interactional aspect of living. Life does involve taking risks, both with attachments and with the building up of a sense of self-identity, even if death shall finally transform all physical and mental attachments into naught. The fear that nothing of the body and of the mind (like castles in the sand) can survive in their present forms prompts many of us to try to transcend these passing aspects of experience in a quest for something durable beyond the dance of earthly impressions. However, the defensive pursuit of escapist transcendence can itself become a form of ego-striving.

The challenge facing us as self-conscious and reflective beings is: how to build up and forge an internal sense of self, how to sustain this fragile sense of self and attain a continuity of identity, while living in the shadow of impermanence and discontinuity? The ancient practices of meditation and mindfulness as well as the contemporary practices of constructivism and psychotherapy offer us a choice of several possible approaches in dealing with this paradox, but no approach is without its own limits and risks. Balance is required. Our quest for knowledge and fulfillment has two principal orientations, namely those typified by introversion and those by extraversion. Both are valuable and neither should be neglected. It is a question of equilibrium. Introversion naturally implies introspection and elaboration of our subjectivity, whereas extraversion involves circumspection and adaptation to objective reality. With introspection one is connected inwardly with the mystery of the self. However, circumspection is the sine qua non of enhancing our sense of relatedness. Inwardness (subjectivity) and outwardness (objectivity) are complementary (Nino, 1997). In psychodynamic terms, self-psychology should be balanced by object relations. It may be tempting to escape from harsh external reality by taking refuge inwardly. Likewise, one can remain in exile from one's true core self by being overly adapted to and concerned with external reality. Bridging the chasm between our inner and outer worlds allows for a two-way flow that enriches both in the process. This is the nature of our connection with the social and physical worlds of which we form a part.

A final point is that the western obsessive focus on individualism with the forging of a strong individual identity can create a neurosis around the loss of this over-valued persona or mask. The traditional eastern emphasis on developing a social sense of collective identity, which does not overly depend on individualism for its survival, may facilitate attempts to dis-identify from over-invested ego grasping. The aim of Buddhist meditation and other eastern techniques and many forms of psychotherapy is not to become atomized emotional islands, but rather to be more in touch with the personal, social, and spiritual aspects of living. Some individuals also use meditation to foster a personal relationship with the Divine and as a preparation for an after-life. However, this quest is enhanced by wholeheartedly including the relational aspect of spirituality in our daily living by practicing compassion and loving kindness. We shall thereby evolve our capacity to perceive as well as to relate to the spiritual in others.

27

Navayâna and Upâya: The Buddhist Dharma As A "New" Medicine

Paul van der Velde

*This chapter deals with considerations on dogma versus non-dogma, pure versus culture-bound Buddhist teaching (*Dharma*) and the shifting emphasis of central notions in a developing new Buddhism. Since the 20th century the Dharma has proliferated in the West. The new spread over the globe justifies a new term for a fourth great current of Buddhist thinking, called* Navayana *(new vehicle). It is characterized as the Dharma that has developed in or under influence of the West while remaining firmly connected to its major schools: Theravada, Mahayana, and Vajrayana. Some of these ideas projected backwards on Asia might result in cultural confusion. Attention is given to some special traits of Navayana related to Asian traditions. Western ideas can generally be described as constructive. Although positive and affirmative, the Dharma does meet prejudices to its advantage or disadvantage of the same. The interest in the West seems to have resulted in a quest for a "pure" Dharma. This purity seeking is short-hand labeled as a process of "imagining Buddhism." Frequently, this has lead to an orientation on the Dharma's past, especially its early history, ending up in frustration. Despite research and attempts to reconstruct, little is known about its pristine developments. The search for purity is also sought through teachers from early traditions. Having made a choice for a teacher, one will yet meet hurdles. After all, a living tradition is part of a living culture with its own peculiarities requiring adjustment to a westerner. Whatever the quest, the Dharma has an ancient concept at hand which, with help, the message of the Buddha can be adjusted over time. Necessarily taking into account the particular time, prevailing culture, and characteristics of the individual teacher, it has been modified continuously. Teaching inheres in modifications effectuated by what is called in Sanskrit* Upâya: *skillful means. Its use is justified by the existence of past reconstructions and demonstrated by various schools. From biographies of the Buddha many instances are known in which the reader finds him as a skillful teacher who adjusted his wording to his audience. It is difficult to tell whether he was applying Upâya in a broad sense. Various traditions might have* made *him apply Upâya. Navayana's issues and opinions have much to say on people's needs when seeking fulfillment for which Upâya is prescribed to meet today's requirements.*

And he who sees the peaceful, auspicious passionless Dharma that is completely freed of old age and leads to the ultimate aim, he also sees the instructor of it, the choicest amongst nobles, he sees the Buddha, because he has developed the eye for this. Due to the fortunate teaching it is like when someone who is no longer ill, because he has been cured of the disease, is grateful to the physician and considers him full of respect because of his intelligence, his friendliness and his knowledge of medical sciences.   Saundarananda (XVII pp. 32 & 33)

This contribution focuses on the ancient traditional connection between the Buddha, physical and mental healing, and to his Dharma that is by tradition considered to be the ultimate medicine. Particularly, I will reflect on the concept of Upâya, the so-called skilful means, the implications and various interpretations of this concept, and on attitudes in various Buddhist teachings towards mental and physical disease. To cure or not to cure can be part of Upâya. The chapter closes with some reflections on implications the traditional attitudes in Buddhist thinking may have for the Dharma as it is spreading over the globe. For this recent development I use the word Navayâna, the "new vehicle," to designate the fourth main current of the Dharma, especially to indicate the Dharma as it is developing within western culture in recent times. Navayâna is a name for various currents of thinking. It is a term only rarely used by Buddhists themselves. There is hardly any new Buddhist who calls him/herself as a Navayânin. This sets it quite apart from the names of the other three great currents — Theravâda, Mahâyana, and Vajrayâna — that are widely used by traditional Buddhists themselves. Often we find that the new Buddhists in the West designate themselves as belonging to the schools of their teachers, whereas within these teachings characteristics can be found that are typical for the new vehicle.

The Buddha as Healer, the Dharma as Medicine

Early in the Dharma's history the person of the Buddha was connected with great healing powers. He came to be considered as the ultimate physician (*Bhisaj*) and his noble teachings came to be regarded as the *Bhaisajyarâja*, the king amongst all medicines or the "royal medicine." This connection may be related to the thought that the Buddha is the healer of the ultimate disease with which each living being is infected: Dukkha, often translated as suffering but actually it reflects a much larger concept: everything existing is permeated with an unbearable unsatisfactoriness, impermanence, and imperfection. Nothing seems to have anything that lasts longer than a mere moment. For this reason and instigated by the sensory impressions, beings constantly run after one experience to the next only to encounter more Dukkha in every new sensation. This ailment can be healed through the Dharma that indicates the path leading to Nirvâna, the place or state where Dukkha no longer exist and where impermanence and the fact that no phenomenon has anything of an essential self or soul become irrelevant. The Buddha analysed the cyclical world of suffering (Samsâra) in his Four Noble Truths, which was derived from the medical sciences of his day. There is the disease, Dukkha; there is its cause, Samudaya (the thirst of craving for experiences or Tanhâ/Trsnâ is its cause); the disease can be cured, Nirodhana; and this can be done by the medicine called Magga/Mârga, the path that consists of eight healing ingredients. Traditionally, it is stated that the Buddha on many occasions uttered that "anyone who suffers of craving for experiences is seriously ill." Given the fact that "present day beings" are in their intentional behaviors instigated by Karma (produced in "prior existences" as an attempt to satisfy desires) everyone is bound to this world of Dukkha and is for this reason ill. A being that is not ill is not born just like trees do not grow out of seeds that did not sprout. The hope for cure can only be found in the Dharma.

In the Saundarananda[1] the Buddha defines his analysis in the four steps of the noble teachings to his half brother Nanda. Once he has come to understand that ultimate healing lies in the path his elder brother developed, Nanda gave up his primary reluctance to follow the path (Saundaranda XVI.41 & 42):

> Therefore think about the truth of Dukkha as if it were a disease, in the vices (dosha) lies the cause of disease, in the truth about putting it to rest lies the ultimate health and in the path lies the medicine. Therefore you should understand that activities bring with them Dukkha and you should also understand that the vices (dosha) come forth out of the same activities, know that avoidance of activities is the antidote and know also that avoidance is the path.

Upâya and Upâyakaushalya

The healing to which the Buddha connects his disciples (clients or patients) therefore resembles that of a physician or therapist who first analyses the ailment and subsequently plans the individually tailored way to treat. This analysis and treatment adjustment to the disciple's character and inclinations are indicated by the concept Upâya. This concept is often found and heavily elaborated upon in Mahâyâna teachings that constructed and emphasized skillful means as a specific meaning of Upâya. The Buddha is often said to be especially skillful in dealing with his disciples because of his unique handling of *Upâyakaushalya*: abilities in the application and development of skilful means. Here as well a clear parallel with medicine can be distinguished as Upâya's translation comes close to treatment after the diagnosis. In a broader sense Upâya may also imply that the Dharma needs to be adjusted not only to a particular disciple but also to a particular society, culture, and time. Here we find an opening that is traditional in the Dharma when adjustment of the original teachings is required to new circumstances. In all cases however the remedy is the Dharma. Accordingly, many forms of the medicine were developed over time to serve particular cultures, societies, and individuals.

In the Saundarananda (XIII 3-8) the Buddha's handling of Upâya is described as follows:

> *The hero guided some with a subtle word, others in aloud voice, and yet others in both ways. Just like gold comes forward out of dirt and it is pure, free of filth and is shining, even if it lies in dirt, it does not get stained by filthiness. Just as a lotus leaf that originates from the water remains in the waters, and whether it is above the water or underneath it, it does not get stained by it. Just so a saint is born in the world and he does what is pleasing to the world for the reason of his status and purity he does not get stained by the figurations (dharmas) of the world. On moments when he gives his advice he does so the one moment binding, with abandon, friendly, in a harsh way, with stories or with concentration, but for the reason of the treatment, not just because he feels that way then. And he took on a body out of that great compassion: "May I in whatever way deliver the creatures of suffering!," because he experiences that much compassion with them.*

Adjusting his treatment to his disciples the Buddha does not instruct them for instance harshly because he is then in a bad mood but because s/he requires it.

Upâya and Upâyakaushalya also explain that some of the Buddha's teachings seem to be contradictory at first sight. Contradictions can be explained by the Buddha's adjustment to the moment on which he addresses his message and to the individual personality or to the group's spirit. Similar to medical treatment the pains arising out of the treatment might at first be worse than those caused by the disease itself. For example, Nanda, who was addicted to sensual passions, was led by the Buddha to passionless-ness by at first intensifying his passions. The similarity between the Buddha's actions and those of a skilled physician is phrased as follows (X p. 42):

> *Just like a man cleans a dirty piece of clothing by at first making it even dirtier by applying soda, just so the Wise One dragged him into even worse passions, but with the target of putting an end to this impurity, not out of the idea of causing more impurity to arise. Just like a doctor intent on banishing diseases from a body will at first exert himself to cause the patient to suffer more, exactly, in that very way the Wise One connected him with heavier passions, for the very reason of putting his passions to an end.*

Summing up, Upâya has at least four meanings: (1) the adjustment of the treatment to the suffering person after the particular diagnosis; (2) the adjustment of the Dharma to a particular society and period; (3) the explanatory principle for apparent contradictions in the Buddhadharma; (4) the explanatory principle for apparent contradictions in the teachings of the historical Buddha and Buddhas of the past and the future, as other times need other Dharmas. Here is my addition that might sound challenging: (5) Upâya is the principle of an innovative energy always present in the grand Buddhist tradition itself by means of which local traditions, rites, or beliefs can be integrated into the whole teaching.

Popular Tradition on the Buddha's Healing Powers and some Upâya Examples

In Asia we may nowadays encounter many groups, subgroups, and currents of thinking or practicing that at first sight seem to be far removed from any original message, whatever this may imply. There is Buddhist feminism or feminist Dharma, there is environmental Buddhism, there is Buddhist socialism, etc. Here are examples on supposed mental and physical healing capacities from mainland South East Asia and Tibet. My focus is on healing to increase awareness that present developments (e.g. the inclusion of the Dharma and Buddhist techniques find their ways into therapies) may actually boast of an ancient tradition in Asia and therefore do fit in within the tradition at large. Wherever the Dharma went in Asia it included in the spirit of Upâya local habits and traditions it encounters.

The healing powers of the Buddha (and the Buddhas of the past or even of the future) can be found above all in popular Dharma. These powers concern both mental and physical diseases and disorders as both arise from Dukkha, the elementary imperfection that characterizes anything that exists. Sometimes the two are discerned and for each type of complaints separate physicians may be required. On some occasions in the Theravâda space monks are invited to pronounce Parittâ wishes (Perera, 2000). These are usually composed in Pâli, a language that is thought to have healing (even "magical") powers from its very origin. The historical Buddha is thought to have delivered his sermons in Pâli — but it was in fact in a kindred language (Magadhi) — and therefore Pâli words are the closest one can get to the Buddha's healing powers. Thus, it is inferred that monks reciting Pâli embody one of the strongest forces thinkable, particularly to alleviate mental suffering. Often monks are requested to come to one's home to recite Pâli in order to cure mental disorders. Pâli recitation is supposed to be a strong remedy against demonic forces that may possess a person and reciting monks are exorcists (Mulder, 1996).

In Thailand amulets of the Buddha or of powerful monks inhering in a force called Sing Sakshit may as well protect the person who wears these against evil spirits attacking mental and physical health. Sing Sakshit, however, proves to be an ambivalent power. It will protect if the object or person embodying the force is treated well; if Sing Sakshit is provoked and insulted it will take revenge and cause illnesses or disasters. Anyone who lives on the fringe of generally accepted Thai society is in danger. If s/he ends up in isolation, chaos will prevail and only powerful monks are able to do anything at all. In Northern Thailand wooden stakes painted in red support branches of Bo-trees. By thus supporting the Buddhist faith mental ailments will vanish. Family members of mentally afflicted persons will especially do so. The temple of the Wat Pra Keo Don Tao in the Kokha district near Lampang is famous for this ritual.

In other cases special rituals can bring the various spirits living in the individual's separate body parts back to their original dwelling places. Spirits may leave the body due to various powers of others and rituals that make the spirits return to the bodies where they belong. A particular cord is bound at the wrist as a protection to prevent the spirits from leaving the body once more. In Laos the ritual is called Baci, in Thailand Bai Siim. There is no better form to reinforce the powers of these rituals than the Pâli reciting monks. The same applies to particular tattoos in sacred patterns providing particular abilities like a stable physical and mental health. Likewise, monks' old robes may have particular powers and are often considered to be a medicine's essential ingredient. Robes inhere in the monks' power and form an auspicious part of Sing Sakshit. Given the fact that many of these practices are widespread and concerned with conveying powers rather than with awakening and putting an end to suffering through the Dharma these phenomena have been classified as "Buddhist animism" (Terwiel, 1977).

Om mani padme hum is a famous and one of the most important mantras of Mahâyâna. There are various translations of this mantra and many commentaries have been written on its meanings and implications. Nowadays, one may hear in the bazaars of Kathmandu and Lhasa that the five syllables explained as "God gives long life" or "God gives good health." This seems to be quite remote from its original meaning(s) but it is too easy to simply explain such popular translation as just a trick to sell a bracelet or a ring with this mantra to a tourist. The mantra is dedicated to Avalokiteshvara, the Bodhisattva of compassion. If Avalokiteshvara provides one with good health and with a long life, healing is present already in this very promise. That is not the end to the story yet. If one has a very long life one may meet the future Buddha Maitreya and if one meets and hears him preaching this will immediately result in enlightenment and the experience of Nirvâna, hence an immediate end to all suffering. Hearing the Dharma directly from the mouth of an enlightened being will lead one instantly to enlightenment. Kaundinya — the seer who was present when the Buddha's birthmarks were identified in his father's palace and predicted that he will become a king of the Dharma — left to wait in the forest for Siddhârtha Gautama to start preaching. And when Kaundinya heard the Buddha's sermon in the deer park Sarnath, he was instantly enlightened. This example forms the paradigm that puts forward a quick path to enlightenment, which avoids the long path of meditation.

Tibetan Buddhism has a long tradition of healing and medical practices. Not all practitioners of Tibetan medicine are monks but amongst the Tibetan doctors there are many monks. Anything that can even remotely be connected with a Buddha is thought to possess healing powers here as well. Medication touched by living Buddhas has extra powers. It is even stated that medicines can be made out of the burnt excrements of high lamas. Moreover, the cult of Bhaisajyaguru (the

Buddha of medicines) is widespread in Asia. In Tibet Bhaisajyaguru is though to have a blue color of lapis lazuli and is often portrayed with a medicine bowl in his hands while giving a "magic bullet" or a flower to humankind. In Cambodia it was Jayavarman VII (1181-1220 BCE) who spread the Bhaisajyaguru cult. He founded many hospitals all over his kingdom. Unlike the hospital buildings made of wood, the hospitals' temples have lasted the ravages of time. These temples mostly show an image of Bhaisajyaguru on the doorway's lintels or pediments. Many Buddhas and Bodhisattvas are depicted with bottles of water to give life eternal (the Kamandalu or Amrtakalasha), thus saving from suffering and death.

A Paradox: The Attitude towards the Body and the Mind

1. *The body is impure, the mind is fickle...* If there is one space in which Dukkha and impurity can be experienced, it is the embodied person. Embodiment consists of fickle, ever changing configurations, phenomena of thought and feeling (dhammas). This implies impurity, and fluctuations; one can never rely on the construction of body and mind as both are ever changing. Changing moment after moment, the body will grow older and so will the mind. These are the spaces par excellence to experience suffering and imperfection.

The body is extremely impure. It is a sack of thin leather filled with entrails, worms, and excrements; it stinks, it falls to pieces moment after moment. Traditionally in Asia monks and nuns are advised to visit autopsies to convince themselves that the body is only covered with a skin as thick as the wing of a fly. Visualisation of one's own death and the process of how the body slowly decays can be part of one's spiritual path. Theravâda monasteries often have a human skeleton in one of their premises for meditating monks and nuns to convince them of the transience of all existence. Similar statements are made on the mind: it runs after each and every impression. It is as difficult to master as is the wind. Each and every sensory impression may lead to experiencing various identifications. It even creates an entire personality, poisoned as it is by the vices of illusion expressing itself in the form of greed and hatred. The senses drag the mind to all kinds of sensations. Therefore one can never rely on it. It changes as quickly as the body but mind's changes are even faster. In the Saundarananda human existence is explained to Nanda in the following words (IX pp. 6-16):

> Don't you know then that the body is a storehouse of diseases, it is subject to old age, its existence is unsure, it is like a tree on the bench of a river. Don't you know then that the body is vulnerable as a bulb of foam on water; do you really think that the force that resides in you will always remain firm? How can you have trust in your power, the body is always connected with disasters, it is always busy with things as "too much, too little," things like eating, drinking, sitting, walking. How can you be proud of your forces while you are always on your way to the end, it is

just like the rays of the sun that dry up the waters in the hot months. The world is fixed by cold, heat, diseases, old age, hunger etc. How can you even think of it that you are strong, while your body consists of skin, bones, flesh and blood and always is in need of food, always is subject to pain and always needs medicine? A man who deems himself to be strong and relies on his forces, and trusts on this accumulation (i.e. the five khandhas that make up a human being) that has no essence at all, and is entirely directed towards the senses, he is as a man who desires to cross a wild ocean, and for this takes his refuge to a pot of unfired mud. Frankly, I think this body has even less essence than a pot of unfired clay, because if this pot is well stored, it will remain for a long time. This accumulation, however, will fall to pieces anyhow, even if you take care of it to the utmost. If you see that the elements water, earth, wind and fire that have taken their refuge to this body, only oppose each other as if they were enraged snakes, how can you think then that you have got any force at all, while disease pervades you. Snakes can be put to rest by magical charms, but the elements cannot be brought to peace at all. Snakes may bite someone at times, but the elements always strike on everything. Even if this body is well taken care of over a long period, with helpful acts such as reclining, sitting, drinking, and eating, The body will not forgive it if only one wrong act is performed, it can easily be provoked as if it were a great poisonous snake were you to step on it. And given the fact that someone who feels cold looks for fire, and who is feeling hot seeks the cold, and who is hungry will look for food, the one thirsty for water, what then is the role of force, what is it? How does it work and to whom does it belong? Now that you know that the body is completely full of disease, how can you rely on force? The world has no essence, it is unhealthy and unsure; forces in a world that is so temporary will perish.

The female body is seen as the foremost example of impermanence and transience. In the Saundarananda we can find statements that the body of Nanda's beloved wife Sundarî is only that beautiful and attractive because it is well taken care of. If it were left in its original natural state it would merely be repulsive, so it is said. The male loses intelligence and force if he gets older but he is usually not said to become more impure. Kloppenborg (1995) pointed out that the male body rarely serves as an example for impurity. The decaying male body can serve as a meditation object but descriptions of impurity of the body mainly refer to the female body.

2. ... *yet it is the only place to reach enlightenment*... All the while as long as one has not yet reached the experience of Nirvâna life as a human is considered to be the most fortunate. It offers a unique chance to experience those aspects of life that are foremost appropriate for the attainment of awakening. It is stated that one can hear the Buddha preach in all realms in which a being can be reborn, for instance the six realms of humans, fighting demons, hungry demons, gods, hell, both hot-and-cold, and the animal world. Yet human living implies that one is gifted with a large intelligence and a proper memory. Thus, one is provided with excellent means to experience contrasts. It is exactly here that one may realize the

transience of all experiences and forms of existence, even of having an individual personality. Although the human condition may be impure and unreliable, it is at the same time an opportunity to reach the ultimate aim. The human mind is intelligent enough to be aware of one's own mortality. It is doubtful whether animals do have this ability. The Buddha was often born as a human but very often as an animal as well. Amongst the Jâtakas, the stories on his previous births, there are many in which he is born as an animal or even as the spirit of a plant or a tree. There it is proclaimed how he developed all of his perfections entitling him to experience final Nirvâna.

Meanwhile, one might meet a living Buddha. If one hears her/him preaching enlightenment will follow quickly, if not now then in a later birth. If one is born as a human, it will lead to a quick result. Siddhârtha Gautama is supposed to have met the previous Buddha Dîpankara three lives prior to be the son of Shuddhodana. He met Dîpankara when he lived as a recluse named Sumedha; subsequently he was born as prince Vessantara who excelled in the perfection of donations. After this he lived for many aeons as Setaketu, a heavenly creature until he was invited to be born in the perfected kingdom of Shuddhodana. He reached enlightenment, centuries after he met Dîpankara but only a few lives after this important event. The Buddha advises his brother Nanda to make use of the opportunity given to him. To be a human being is a rare occasion to reach enlightenment. Nanda's chances are exquisite as there is a Buddha living who happened to be his brother. In the Saundarananda the Buddha tells his younger brother that life as a human being may not be wasted in vanity. Though the body is impure and foul, human embodiment provides a rare chance to reach the almost impossible, Nirvâna: the extinguishing of the passions' fires that continuously bind one to this world's Dukkha. It is even because of Dukkha that one may experience enlightenment. From this angle we might say: luckily body and mind are fickle and always changing, otherwise it would be impossible to reach for awakening.

3. ... *it can even be perfected.* The human body can be perfected. It is often asserted that the Buddha is beyond humanity. Enlightenment implies that the body passes through a tremendous transformation in order to move beyond Dukkha. Various texts (e.g. the Lakkhana Sutta and the Ambattha Sutta in the Dîgha Nikâya) state that a Buddha can be recognized by body marks as a Mahâpurusha, a great person or a superhuman. The body of enlightened beings displays 32 main characteristics (Lakshanas) and 80 secondary characteristics (Upalakshanas). According to tradition a Buddha's body may look like a human body but is in fact quite different from it. Not only Buddhas show peculiar body characteristics, any Mahâpurusha has them. Universal monarchs in the Buddha's days were also supposed to have an outstanding body. The Jîna, the founder of Jainism, is thought to have had these characteristics as well. That the Buddha's body still looks like a human body can be seen depicted in art. Peculiarities can easily be recognized. For instance the Ushnisha, a protuberance on the head that looks like a turban; and the Urna, the

curl of white hair turning to the right between the eyebrows. The cult of the superior body has some tradition in India. In certain medical texts a procedure is narrated in which first the nails and teeth drop, then the body shrinks to a bag of thin leather filled with ashes, after which the body is restored to life and will last for thousands of years.

Concluding, it can be said that the human body is a space of Dukkha, a space of reaching awakening, and a space of perfection

The Attitude towards Treatments and Medicines

As diseases are considered to be of two kinds, physical and mental, two different types of doctors and treatments are discerned. An ascetic addresses Nanda as follows (Saundarananda VIII pp. 3-6):

> *Pain exists in two kinds, as we know, in mind and in body. Therefore, there are two kinds of physicians for these, skillful in the means dealing with holy words, and skillful in medication. Therefore, if your pain concerns your body, this must quickly and extensively be told to a doctor, because a sick person who hides his illness will soon come to worse things. But if this suffering concerns your mind, please then tell me so! I will here and now utter a treatment. Physicians for the minds that live in passion or darkness are those who carefully concentrate and know the human mind. Dear friend, the truth must be told extensively, if you deem it suited that you speak it out to me. The ways of the mind are manifold, and many things are hidden or full of delusion.*

However, physical and mental diseases or sufferings are generally considered to originate from a common source: Dukkha

In the Pâli Canon physical and psychological wellbeing are mentioned as a prerequisite for spiritual progress. Many monks and nuns live as ascetics and may fall ill easily (Birnbaum, 1979). Not eating after midday, the practice of most monks and nuns is supposed to improve physical wellbeing. Eating too little and suffering of pains will disturb mindfulness and the ascetic practices. Buddha spoke of various dishes that improve health. For instance, congee or rice and milk with honey give long life, beauty, ease, power, work against hunger, thirst, flagrancy, purify the bladder, and stimulate digestion[2]. The Pâli Canon, especially the Mahâvagga of the Vinaya Pitaka (on monastic life), is full of writings on medicines.

Yet, in the Dîgha Nikâya (11-24) many forbidden acts for monks are mentioned amongst which many medical treatments, such as: Administering emetics and purgatives; Purging people to relive the head (by giving drugs to make people sneeze); Oiling people's ears (to make them grow or to heal sores on them); Satisfying people's eyes (soothing them by dropping medicinal oils into them); Administering drugs through the nose; Applying collyrium to the eyes; Practicing as an oculist; Practicing as a surgeon; Practicing as a doctor for children; Administering roots and drugs; Administering drugs in rotation[3]. The forbidden acts may have to do with preventing alms relationship between the monk and the layperson he is treating. Monks should be monks, striving after Nirvâna or Arhatship. They may feel compassion for the sufferers and help them but would they change into doctors they would forget the original aim: awakening (Birnbaum, 1979). An interdependent relationship between ascetics and laymen is never to be developed. The tradition claims this to be the original instruction. Healing may be motivated by compassion and it may be part of Upâya but it may not become monks' livelihood. Nevertheless, shortly after the Buddha's death monks did become doctors. The monk Pârapariyâ complained about this (Birnbaum, 1979).

Other sciences and art forms are eventually utilized to help realize Nirvâna; for instance poetry. In the Anguttara Nikâya (III)[4] the following is said:

> *Furthermore, there will be Bhikkhus in the time that has not come yet with undeveloped bodies, with undeveloped virtues, with undeveloped wisdom who when the teachings of the Tathâgata are discussed that are deep, of profound meaning, supermundane and connected with emptiness, are not ready to listen to these teachings, they do not want to hear these, they do not want to put their minds to these, do not want to study these teachings nor do they want to learn these by heart. Meanwhile there will be poetical works made by poets who are outsiders (in other words: non Buddhists), with beautiful vowels, with beautiful consonants that are spoken to the disciples and when these are discussed they will be ready to listen to these teachings, they want to hear these, they want to put their minds to these, they want to study these teachings and they want to learn these by heart. Bhikkhus, this implies damage for the discipline and because there is damage to the discipline there will be damage to the teachings. This, oh Bhikkhus, is the fourth future danger[5] that now does not exist yet, but might exist in the future.*

Law (1946) points out that these words do not directly imply that the Buddha condemned poetry[6]. These were rather intended as a warning that disciples should be careful not to be carried away by poetry's emotional intentions. They should be careful not to sacrifice the truths for the sentiments. One might be tempted to get in touch with wrong teachings due to the beauty of sounds and words.

Ashvaghosha defends himself at the end of his Saundarananda where he explains that he has composed his works in the Kâvya court poetry style that is far removed from the monasteries and forests of the ascetics. Once more we find a medical comparison when Ashvaghosha explains that a bitter medicine can thus be applied more easily to a suffering patient. Yet, the contents of the message are of importance, not its attractive form. However, poetry may invite an audience (Saundarananda XVIII p. 63):

> *This poetical work focuses on the facts concerning enlightenment; it must lead to*
> *peacefulness and not just to pleasure. It is made in the style of the Kâvya works in*
> *order to fascinate the poetical imagination of the audience. Therefore I have also*
> *described things other than enlightenment, but in accordance with the rules of*
> *that same Kâvyapoetry, just like when you put something sweet to a bitter medi-*
> *cine so that one can drink it. Because I saw that the world usually has the lusts of*
> *the senses as its highest and is averse towards Moksha, for that very reason have*
> *I composed the truth here in the form of a Kâvya work: Liberation is the highest.*
> *Therefore if you understand this, you must take out of this that what leads to*
> *peace and not what is just charming, as a golden shape always emerges out of the*
> *dust from the gold ore.*

Thus, Ashvaghosha created a treatment out of his audience's "lust for sensual pleasures." Their minds will thus be fascinated. They will reach enlightenment or at
least will be connected to the Buddhist path through their addiction. This can be
called a proper application of Upâyakaushalya. Poetry serves here as Upâya, the
honey that is mixed with the medicine. So medical treatments could be part of
Metta, which should be "dispassionate compassion" and of Upâya, but monks may
not become doctors.

Dukkha and Upâya

The world that suffers from craving is ill and needs to be treated; it needs Dharma
medication administered by the prime physician, the Buddha. Yet we may question the meaning and position of suffering in the universe. It is due to Dukkha that
one realizes Nirvâna at the end. This may sound paradoxical because given these
facts we may question why the world exists at all.

Vulnerability for and causes of physical and mental diseases is the present
consequence of past intentional activity/Karma (Birnbaum, 1979). This implies
that the root cause for the disease is ignorance that leads to craving. Deliverance
from suffering is sought by the senses in the various sense fields. If the senses do
not experience rest, the mind will not experience any rest. In some cases it is better
to end the disease and in other cases it is better to have the old Karma burn. Once
it is burnt completely it will eventually accrue enlightenment. When questioned
about the reason why the world exists at all the Buddha refused to explain. Perhaps
the Buddha did not tell about any cause for the world to exist to prevent his disciples' digging in a remote past to account for the present. They might accuse
others in the past for their personal suffering, whereas Buddhist development is to
take place here-now. There are thousands of reasons why the things are the way
they are but if it comes to awakening none of these are of any importance now. The
task is to escape from Samsâra here. Some monks did allegedly develop a sense
for seeing past and future lives like the Buddha. This ability's application was only
allowed as part of Upâya and for someone's spiritual benefit. Otherwise it would

be a trick of magic to be frowned upon from a Buddhist viewpoint. The past is only interesting if one can learn from it. For instance, Buddhist sages' life histories teach how they reached their ultimate aim.

A prime way of Dukkha manifesting in the world is in the form of disease that hinders progress on the way. Birnbaum (1979) points to the monk Assaji who could not breathe properly and thus not enter the first Jhâna. The Buddha advised him to contemplate on thoughts of impermanence and not-self. Here the disease is utilized and becomes part of the "spiritual treatment," an integration in the framework of Upâya. As stated earlier, at all times the treatment must be adjusted to the patient and the disease, whether physical or mental. It is important to emphasize the patient, not the disease. Thus, in some instances the disease must be treated to enable the person to reach out for Nirvâna, in other instances it is the disease that assists the patient like in the case of Assaji. Through the disease the patient becomes aware that Dukkha pervades the world and cannot be avoided. Treatment may imply that the disease at first worsens, increasing suffering. At the end the suffering will disappear or at least become bearable. True healing entails the eradication of craving. Any person who suffers is craving, the root cause of the illness of Dukkha. To cure a disease one needs a doctor, likewise: to end craving one needs the most perfected doctor, the Buddha.

In the Majjhima Nikâya the Buddha is compared to a physician who pulls out a poison arrow from a wounded person. The patient at first experiences a worsening of suffering but subsequently the healing process can begin. The Buddha explained this analogy as follows: the wound refers to the six sense fields, the poison of the arrow to ignorance, the arrow itself to craving; the surgeon's knife is pure insight, the skilfulness of the surgeon is mindfulness, and the surgeon is the Buddha (Birnbaum 1979). Furthermore, the Dharma points at a strict interaction between body and mind. The three main vices (dosha) have a connection to the three vices of the Ayurveda: too much lust gives wind, anger gives bile, and illusion results in phlegm. Everybody suffering of craving is ill; therefore illness is much bigger than having a disease: we are born and therefore we are ill. Given the fact of impermanence we die each moment that is why there is actually no real difference between a lethal disease and a curable disease.

Thus, the Buddha is said to have cured in two ways or variations of Upâya: firstly by preaching the Dharma and secondly by performing miracles (but he rarely did so). If he resorted to a miracle or magic or even a small lie, these were allowed as Upâya.

Does Enlightenment Deliver from Suffering?

The Buddha himself got very sick the last period of his life before he died and entered the final Nirvâna. He almost even forgot that there is just suffering and no sufferer as formulated in the Mahâparinibbâna Sutta. At the end, however, his suffering did not affect him mentally. Suffering ends as well for the Arhat, an enlightened being, once s/he reaches final Nirvâna. However, it is questioned what would happen when a living Arhat for instance treads on a thorn. Does s/he feel pain or not? This issue was raised whenever the position of the living enlightened being was queried. It was amongst one of the so-called statements of Mahâdeva (allegedly lived in the 4th or 3rd c BCE) concerning the enlightened being and his/her relation to embodiment (Harvey, 1990). If it comes to what an Arhat supposes to feel if s/he treads on the malignant thorn it is said that s/he may feel the pain but does not identify him/herself with what is felt. There is a feeling but no subject that feels. S/he may feel the pain but does not identify him/herself with this pain psychologically. The same applies to a Bodhisattva who chooses to become incarnate on earth. S/he may get ill, very ill even, due to his grace. This sounds strange at first instance because the fact that one is a Bodhisattva implies that one is liberated from physical and mental suffering. Yet, the Bodhisattva suffers like other human beings on the conventional level but not ultimately. A Bodhisattva should not preach on the greatness of Nirvâna but on the greatness of becoming a Bodhisattva. It is noble to be a guide, to have people share the experience, and then to make them come back to the earth so that they on their turn will inspire others to reach for Nirvâna (Birnbaum, 1979).

Incarnated Lamas in Tibet can also be very ill due to birth as a human being and they carry their burden in worthy manner. Once Nirvâna is experienced there is no longer an ill person; there is only the disease in relation to a carrier that is actually empty of a person. Birnbaum (1979) quotes Vimalakîrti on the subject of the illness of Bodhisattvas. His quotations are from the Chinese translation of the Vimalakirti Nirdesha Sutra, in Chinese the *Wei-mo chieh so shuo ching*. The Bodhisattva chooses to be ill identifying him/herself with the suffering of the creatures in the world:

I am ill because all sentient beings are ill. If the illness of all sentient beings were to come to an end, then my illness would be ended. Why is this so? Because when the Bodhisattva enters into the realm of birth and death for the sake of all beings, he becomes subject to the laws of the realm and thereupon becomes ill. If all sentient beings were to be cured of their diseases, then the Bodhisattva would never again be ill. It is like a rich man who only has one son. When this son becomes ill, his parents also become ill. If the son is cured of the disease, so also are the parents. It is the same for the Bodhisattva: he loves all beings as if each of them were his only son. When all beings are cured, then the Bodhisattva will be cured... Because of his own illness he should take pity on all others who are sick. He should know of the sufferings of countless aeons of past lives, and because of this he should think of the welfare of all beings. He should be mindful of the pure life. Instead of generating grief and vexation he should constantly give rise to striving energy. He should become a king of healing and cure all ills.

Navayâna and Upâya: Implication for Psychotherapy

Wherever the Dharma arrived in Asia there always was a mixture with religious or philosophical thoughts and traditions already present in the area. Due to the concept of Upâya an opening can always be found towards the specific demands of an individual, a culture, or a time. Buddhist teachers were always ready to engage into this process. From this perspective there is no such thing as a pure Dharma.

However, traditional Buddhist thinking might take a conservative stance against recent developments. Buddhist traditions in Asia will mostly emphasize that there must be in whatever way thinkable a connection between the present-day teachings as proliferated in the West and the teachings of the historical Buddha. New Buddhist schools have thus always sought for ways to legitimize their teachings in order to defend themselves to opponents' attacks. The connections between Cognitive-Behavior Therapy and the Dharma are based on scientific study that combats ignorance, which is even from a traditional point of view absolutely legitimate. Upâya makes this possible, whatever conservative Asian tradition might say. Finally, in Navayâna teachings of the West one may often find ideas that the Dharma neither is a religion, nor led by dogma. For 21st century humanity appreciating freedom and democracy this seems to be of great importance. I assert that given the concept of Upâya it really is no problem at all to develop a non-dogmatic, non-religious, psychotherapeutic Dharma if time, culture, society, and individuals make that demand. This questions what one exactly considers to be a religion and a dogma rather than queries what the Dharma essentially is in its many currents as it developed in a period of about 2500 years.

---

1. This is a poetical biography of Nanda, the half brother of the Buddha, a text composed in Sanskrit by Ashvaghosha (2nd century BCE) describing the conversion of Nanda to his brother's Dharma. The translations quoted here are my own (cf. Johnston, 1928).

2. Birnbaum's (1979) study on the healing Buddha gives many examples of what Buddhist ascetics should or should not eat and of medical care amongst the ascetics and attitudes towards laymen.

3. Translation of T.W. Rhys Davids.

4. Cited by Law (1946). My translation is based on the Pâli text as given by Law.

5. In this text a number of dangers are discussed that threaten the teachings of the Buddha.

6. Bhattacharya (1976) calls the command of the Buddha an "express interdiction."

Part IV

The Horizon
Of Integration

28

A New Buddhist Psychology: Moving Beyond Theravada And Mahayana

Maurits Kwee & Marja Taams

New Buddhist Psychology (NBP) is a cutting-edge discipline meant for seekers of inner liberation from normal human suffering. The adjective Buddhist refers to the teachings (Dharma) as originally espoused by Siddharta (one-who-had-all-his-wishes-fulfilled), and that aim to cultivate positive emotional states (sukha). Human flourishing has been described in the Buddha's discourses of the Theravada tradition (Nikayas) and re-invented — as reflected in particular scriptures — in the Mahayana denominations called Madhyamaka ("Emptiness-only," 2nd century), Yogacara ("Mind-only," 4th century), and Hua-yen (Interpenetration, 6th century). If humans are taken as Bio/Psycho/Social systems bridges can be built across these seemingly different conceptualisations of being, thus going beyond Theravada-Mahayana views. In effect a new paradigm is warranted for the Dharma, allied with social constructionist theory, a metapsychology able to conjoin the practices of social, clinical, and neuropsychology. Such a paradigm is a 21st century "upaya," suitably called Neoyana: a new vehicle resulting from the "skilful strategy" to operationalize the Dharma as a science and practice of psychology that is necessarily non-theistic, non-metaphysical, and transcultural. As an applied psychology NBP provides practitioners a helicopter-view on the human predicament and offers helping tactics that are full of affect but empty of self.

The New Buddhist Psychology (NBP) envisioned in this chapter enables psychotherapists of any school as well as coaches of well-being and other change agents to improve themselves as well as their clients. The proposed NBP reduces philosophy to a minimum in favor of applications that remain grounded in pan-Buddhist Theravada-Mahayana tenets. It includes the Buddha's psychopathology (ignorance, greed, hatred), the Three Empirical Marks of Existence, (impermanence, suffering, non-self), the Inter-Dependent-Origination-Arising-Subsiding (IDOAS) of the psychological modalities (BodyMind aggregates and karma), the Four Immeasurables (kindness, compassion, joy, equanimity), and the widely known Four Noble Facts, emphasizing meditation and social action. NBP's centerpiece is the given that human beings function as Bio/Psycho/Social systems. This view invites a paradigm shift, moving from doctrines of metaphysics and semi-theistic deifying practices to an evidence-based practical orientation. It is in the integration of contemporary scientifically grounded psychology and the intrinsic psychology of the BuddhaDharma (Sankrit, refers to Mahayana) and the BuddhaDhamma (Pali, refers to Theravada) that we may find promise of a new and powerful movement. We shall explore these potentials in some detail.

The use of the adjective Buddhist does not refer to theism but to its founder who expounded a down-to-earth discipline. The moniker Buddha is derived from the root *bodhi*, meaning awakening or being awakened, thus the Buddha is "the awakened one." After introducing the background of NBP in both Theravada and Mahayana teachings, we venture various ways in which Buddhist and western psychological orientations may be bridged, enriching both, and opening new vistas of inquiry and application. Our hope is to integrate the earlier chapters in this book into an innovative reconstruction of Buddhist teachings that is transcultural and empirical. NBP is the result of the interchange between Buddhist ideas and the science of psychology since its inception until today. This new approach aims — in line of the tradition — to free human beings from suffering nobody can escape or avoid by a rejuvenated quest of the human predicament, the frustrations of everyday life, disease, decay, and death. The traditional spirit of *upaya* (skillful means and resources to adjust the teaching to changing circumstances) (see Van der Velde, Ch. 27) is the guiding principle of the present regeneration of the Buddhist teachings.

Thus, it embraces firstly the subjective phenomena observed in the inner world accessible only by the mind's eye that is able to watch consciousness' content from a 1st person angle. Secondly, it incorporates a 2nd person intersubjective stance that allows comparisons of individual experiences with those of others. Thirdly, it includes an objective 3rd person evidence-based viewpoint that is characteristic of an empirically validated (cognitive-behavioral) approach. Encompassing these three standpoints in differentiating NBP and an empirical position, the two disciplines are bridged by a new definition of empirical that discards metaphysics. Such includes observations of the behaviors in and of the mind (*dhammas* or *dharmas*) — that we call perceivables, imaginables, knowables, memorables, dreams/illusions, or in short "social constructs" — through the pivotal 6th sense, a metaperceptual capacity. This mind's eye is to be awakened and developed by enlightening the darkness of ignorance, greed, and hatred. Awakening forms a natural part of human beings' adult development for which embodying the Buddha's insights is pivotal. The result will be the discovery of what Mahayanists call: one's own Buddhanature. If developed collectively NBP might ignite a quantum leap in humanity's 350 generations' evolution from animalism via humanity to Buddhahood.

We submit the thesis that the traditional manner in which the Buddhist teachings are conveyed to this generation of interested people has outlived its usefulness. Taking into consideration the new facts which have emerged since these ideas came in touch with western civilization, there is a need for reanimation. Although the teachings have been reproduced numerous times in various cultural appearances, revitalizing on a content level has not taken place since the Yogacara or "Mind-only" school of the 4th century. The quintessence of the present innovation is the transcultural, non-metaphysical, and non-theistic view that brackets psychological concerns with the existence and the non-existence of a soul (and consequently its transmigration and reincarnation). We take a psychological stance — characteristic of the past century's developments — that we here apply to construct NBP. We have high hopes that the subculture of scientific psychology may provide a much needed transcultural language for the Buddhist discipline in the global village we inhabit. Our endeavor concurs with Gergen's (1999) social constructionism as a metapsychology that invites multiple perspectives into productive dialogue.

The remainder of this chapter is divided into three parts. In the first we take up fundamental elements contributing to a new vehicle: Neoyana. In the second we explore historical and theoretical backgrounds that help to flesh out this emerging development. Finally, in part three, we review the various ways in which eastern and western views are already integrating to form NBP.

I

Elements of a New Buddhist Psychology

To appreciate the scope of NBP, it is helpful to review its earliest roots in Theravada and Mahayana schools, and the 4 Turnings of the Wheel. The fourth turning brings Buddhist insights together with western psychology. We then explore several means of bridging Buddhist and western psychology, opening up new forms of inquiry and practice.

The Beginnings: Theravada

Dhamma's known oldest sources and extant until the present are those of the Theravada (teaching of the Elders), which is one of more than thirty once existing schools (e.g. Sautantrika and Vaibashika) all claiming to be pristine (Conze, 1987). Centerpiece is the *Nikayas*, a collection of 84,000 discourses (a symbolic number) ascribed to the Buddha, each strung together like a thread of flowers called *suttas*. These were written for the first time in Pali on palm leaves in the Sri Lanka of 94 BCE after having been orally transmitted during four centuries. It was brought there via an oral tradition from the western part of India, where Pali was spoken, by Emperor Asoka's son, Mahinda, in the 3rd century BCE. These discourses (11,854 suttas plus 18 books) are contained in one of the three volumes of the Pali canon (*Tipitaka*), which size exceeds the Bible by ten times. Its latest complete version stems from the 5th century. The other two books deal with the communal way of life (*sangha*) and with the ostensible higher teachings in a seven tome work, the *Abhidhamma*, that is not directly attributed to the Buddha. The latter is a *philosophical* psychology and is known due to Caroline Rhys Davids' (1900) work. She described its content full of tabulations and enumerations as a "valley of dry bones." We call the Abhidhamma the old Buddhist psychology. It is not yet completely available in English.

Of the Abhidhamma, allegedly once begun by Sariputta — a direct student of the Buddha — only four versions are extant (two in Pali, in Chinese, and in Tibetan). Proponents claim authenticity for their version while each version gives the impression of being unfinished. Experts clarify its significance in an equation: the Nikayas relates to the Abhidhamma as medicine to the drug's chemical analysis. Included in the canon in the 3rd century BCE, it was continually worked on by anonymous adepts up until the 4th century. Another Theravada standard work, from the 5th century, was produced by Buddhagosha (Buddha's voice) under the title *Visuddhi Magga* (The Path of Purification) (Nanamoli, 1975). This tome contains commentaries on the Nikayas over ten centuries. By that time a movement reacting dialectically to and criticizing the pristine teachings, the Mahayana, already co-existed for about six centuries (Buddhadasa, 1992).

Evolution: Mahayana

The first conflict amongst adherents occurred a century after the Buddha's death and concerned foremost the devotional stature of *arahants* (awakened individuals who in those days could only be friars or monks). In fact this clash, supposedly caused by a brotherhood led by Mahadeva, was a democratic upsurge sustained by the laity that questioned the behavior of those ostensibly awakened, monks who did not seem free from attachments, had nocturnal seminal emissions, and showed themselves to be in need of guidance. These "paradigm shifters" had a Council in Kushan (1st c BCE) at which point (the same time as the *Tipitaka* was written) new scriptures — written by anonymous monk brotherhoods — started to appear in Sanskrit. These sutras — produced during the next five centuries and exceeding the size of the Tipitaka by five times — gave birth to the new wave of Mahayana that gradually became systematized by individual authors (Conze, 1987). Mahayana and Theravada as well as 17 other elderly schools extant at the time, co-existed peacefully in the same monasteries and educational centers until 1193 when Buddhist civilization suddenly vanished in India after its university at Nalanda (with over 2,000 scholars, 10,000 students and 9 million books) was destroyed by Muslim invaders.

To derogate the early schools Mahayanists used the term *Hinayana*, or inferior vehicle, a term that nowadays is only meant to indicate the group of pristine teachings of which Theravada is the only one remaining. Although in India Hinayanists were in the majority until the 8th century, the rising tide of Mahayana resulted in their gradual decline. Meanwhile Mahayana, as well as Theravada, was successfully exported to neighboring countries. These schools were also split into several denominations of which more than twelve continue to exist today. Two of Mahayana's outstanding cultural varieties are Tibetan Vajrayana Tantra and Sino-Japanese Chan or Zen. These have now traveled around the world and their dialogues with western psychology are exemplified in this book (see Gyatso & Beck, Ch. 1, and Kief, Ch. 6). Here we hope to realize a paradigm shift from Mahayana — with the metaphysics and quasi theistic twists of some of its denominations — to a Neoyana, a new 3rd transcultural vehicle of applied Buddhist psychology that includes selected tenets of Theravada and Mahayana. To appreciate this possibility, we must consider the four turnings of the wheel.

Four Turnings of the Wheel: Neoyana

As elucidated in the *Sandhinirmocana Sutra* (2nd c), a scripture belonging to the "Buddha Womb Sutras" (on which Yogacara is based) Mahayana was intended to further the teachings. Its evolution is compared to the turnings of the Wheel of Dharma, which explain a dialectical development (Powers, 1994). This sutra elucidates upaya as a psychology of education: specific individuals and audiences with their specific capacities and levels of understanding in specific time periods require specific teachings. The text reveals that the first turning, the Buddha's original teaching, the Nikayas and its Abhidhamma extract, deals with provisional reality, a middle way between finity and infinity; emptiness is taken as not-self, a "hollowness" that hides a pervasive emptiness of ultimate reality. The second turning, Madhyamaka (a middle way between the Abhidhamma and Mahayana's "Buddha Womb Sutras"), comprises the philosophical systematization of the "Perfection of Wisdom Sutras" through the teachings of Nagarjuna (2nd c). He viewed the emptiness of self (*not*-self) as insufficient and alluded to the ultimate wisdom of total emptiness of all dharmas (*non*-self) by means of a complete negation (a *via negativa*), an "emptiness of emptiness."

The third turning, Yogacara, the teachings of Asanga and Vasubandhu (4th c), regarded Nagarjuna's emptiness as still a somethingness and proposed to eradicate this root problem by dissolving the "last" of the binaries, the subject-object binary, altogether. This is to be done through *being constantly aware of awareness or consciousness as dharmas, phenomena, things, or data (mind's representations that we infer to be social constructs)*. The key is the practice of an "epistemological" meditation — that emphasizes nondual awareness and unveils "suchness" without intruding thoughts, which in essence is a deconstruction of social constructs into emptiness — and the Buddha's four quintessential social practices: loving kindness, empathic compassion, shared joy, grounded in meditative equanimity. Yogacara is the systematization of the so-called "Buddha Womb Sutras," a *via positiva* that inheres in Nagarjuna's work. It fills pervasive emptiness with provisional concepts like the Buddhanature-principle, three transcendent-like Buddha bodies, five cosmic-like Buddhas, etc., all emanating from an empty "womb." Although the Tibetan schools may think differently, Zennists contend that Yogacara is an integrative teaching.

At this juncture in history a movement based on psychological insights and research sets in, which can infuse the Dharma with the strength of a tsunami. We envision this as a fourth turning of the Wheel, one that replaces metaphysical and other-wordly stories and analogies by narratives and metaphors derived from scientific psychology. We view this fourth turning, Neoyana, as the next dialectical step balancing the extremes of the past going forward. It is the chief thesis of Neoyana that in the 21st century the Dharma is most fully realized as a psychology. Why and how the Dharma is most adequately viewed as an evidence-based, applied neuro-clinical-and-social-psychology will be articulated in what immediately follows.

Bridging Psychologies I: Expanding the Empirical Horizon

Since Brentano's Psychologie vom Empirischen Standpunkte (1874) a third person view of objectivity in psychology is the dominant trend (so much embraced that the term "empirical" threatens to become metaphysics). We use the term empirical in a pragmatic sense as viewing a photo: frozen data in an impermanent watershed, flux, or film of consciousness. In trying to fathom the mind the meaning of empirical became restricted to studying what can be observed from the outside at the expense of the observational study of inner experiences assumed to be subjective, unreliable, and invalid. Introductory textbooks in psychology contain empirical information on human mind and behavior, principles found by studying subjects from "without."

In contrast, consider the most popular of the Buddha's discourses, the *Dhammapada* (sayings of the Buddha), a booklet that belongs to the gems of world literature. There we read (in Byrom's translation) the opening verses: "We are what we *think*. All that we are arises with our *thoughts*. With our *thoughts* we make the world. *Speak* or *act* with an impure mind, and trouble will follow you; as the wheel follows the ox that draws the cart. We are what we *think*. All that we are arises with our *thoughts*. With our *thoughts* we make the world. *Speak* or *act* with a pure mind. And happiness will follow you; as your shadow, unshakable." The Buddha gained his luminous insights through deeply looking inside and claimed that what he had observed in his private inner world has a universal value. He thereby remained this-worldly by delineating the consciousness he attended to within the limits of the sensorium (Hamilton, 2000).

While looking inside, the Buddha discovered the mind's eye — a sixth sense (*lokukan*, J) — that is often wrongly understood as the mind and usually results in nonsensical paradoxical deadlocks like: the mind observes the mind. To us, the sixth sense is like the other senses a biological organ capable to receive data from the brain (possibly the right hemisphere capable of projecting and perceiving its own projections at almost the same time). Thus, the brain's projecting function constructs internal objects on the screen of the mind and the brain's perceiving function is subsequently able to experience the projected constructs. These projections or internal dhammas, also known as "objects" or "existants," are always fresh and new. Constituting the data base and contents of our inner lives dhammas are indispensable to get to know our "selves." Attaching, grasping, or clinging to dhammas is the root cause of suffering that can be eradicated by meditation.

The concept of the sixth sense broadens the meaning of empirical to include a mental empiricism in which mental sense data and experiencing personal dhammas is recognized. On an empirical basis, we seemingly know disproportionally much about the external world (as perceived by the five known senses) at the expense of scrutinizing our own internal worlds. Although introspection has been discarded as subjective, it is the only method to observe and study the mind directly, which is from within. This can be done adequately by systematic training that enables to accurately and neutrally or "objectively" observe the empirical phenomena that we experience in our inner spaces of BodyMind. The Buddha gave us an example and offered a method to learn to know "self" by training to open our mind's eye (i.e. to willfully look inside from now-to-now and neutrally). This is a practice of merely looking at internal dhammas, the phenomena of and in the mind. During such observation dhammas are only watched, not judged or suppressed. Thus, we will be able to discover as he did that all sense data are not independently originated and are not permanent by nature.

These inner sensed interdependent and impermanent dhammas can only be introspected in the privacy of mind by the mind's eye and can be any apperceived datum stemming from the outside or inside world. They are formed by what has ever been perceived or can be possibly perceived via the six sense doors (perceivables), ever been or can be phantasized (imaginables), ever been or can be cognized (knowables), memorized (memorables), or dreamed about. Evidently, these dhammas, mind's representations and projections, are abstractions, which existence is necessarily construed through language and social consensus, hence are aptly called social constructs. Even facts are man-made. Literally "no-thing" that we perceive is real, unless people agree that it is (Gergen & Gergen, 2004). This little step to view the allegedly private dhammas as socially constructed is a "quantum leap" that warrants the predicate paradigm shift.

Contemporary psychology approaches this possibility in its inquiry into *metacognition*, an inquiry that originally stemmed from cognitive theory and educational psychology but has recently become en vogue in the literature. One description of this "fuzzy" concept is "knowledge and cognition about cognitive phenomena" (Flavell, 1979, p. 906). Cognizing might also mean: knowing that one thinks, feels, and behaves. Metacognition literally means (the capacity to) think about thinking and refers to knowledge about one's own thinking. It implies an *overseeing* of one's own cognitive behaviors (e.g. whether a cognitive goal has been met) and involves the reflective awareness of the processes of knowing, planning, and languaging. Metacognition refers not only to the monitoring of thinking but also to the regulation and orchestration of thinking, including learning to learn, and memory. For instance, one might declare to have monitored the "tip of the tongue" phenomenon during thinking. Teasdale (1999) infers mindfulness as a metacognitive process implying the perceptual monitoring of the stream of consciousness that makes the control of cognitive processes possible. He distinguishes between metacognitive *knowledge* (thoughts do not always factually match the state of the world), metacognitive *insight* (thoughts are momentary mental phenomena attended in awareness), metacognitive *awareness* (thoughts are mental experiences, not one's "self" or the "truth"), and metacognitive *beliefs* (thoughts reflect the truth).

The common denominator of what these metacognitive aspects seem to represent is the *perceptual overview of the mind's eye*. Cognitive therapy techniques linked to mindfulness reflect this meaning; "distancing" and "decentering" denote a viewing from a different perspective that refers to the perceptual act of looking differently at cognitions rather than thinking differently. To perceive and relate to thoughts as thoughts — as mind's automatic processes to be de-automatized — instead of delving in the content of those thoughts, immediately unveil illusory beliefs. This disengagement is the essence of the shift that is made from cognitive restructuring to the complementary mindfulness-based interventions. Thus, in NBP we prefer to use metaperception rather than metacognition also to indicate that mindfulness meditation helps us to come to our *six* senses (see Katsukura, Ito, & Nedate, Ch. 15; Ito, Katsukura, & Nedate, Ch. 14).

There is support for this view of metaperception in brain studies. The specific function to perceive brain's projections and the capacity to perceive and be aware of each of the six senses' separate and interrelated perceiving — an awareness of awareness/consciousness as socially constructed dharmas — implies cortical integration. It might well be that these circuits constitute the specific neurophysiological correlates of metaperception by the mind's eye. The Buddha's discovery might well be made tangible in what we hypothesize would likely be the right hemisphere's general overviewing function combined with differentiated functional patterns of momentary neuronal cell circuitries involving the whole brain. Thus, the mind's eye, although a metaphorical label, may not be a mere metaphor but may refer to the brain as a metaperceptual organ that is capable to be aware of awareness or consciousness as a sensation, a thought, or a feeling. Such implies that being mindfully aware is the awareness of apperception: the postperceptual but preconceptual act of attending and noting, which is closely connected to the processes of retention, recognition, and memory storage.

Bridging Psychologies II: Integrating Paradigms

The Buddha's psychology is not easily integrated with major psychological paradigms of the West. However, there are useful parallels in conceptualization, and these open the gate to useful interpenetration. On the one side we may take as our paradigmatic case in the West the Cognitive-Behavior Therapy paradigm. This CBT paradigm accepts a vision of (1) the world as it is (the "material" or "stimulus" world), (2) cognitive processes that both respond to and construe this world (the "organism"), and (3) resulting behavior (the "response").

As a variant on this traditional paradigm, and as practitioners of Lazarus' multimodal therapy (Kwee & Lazarus, 1987), we have found it useful to take into account the dynamic flux of intertwined modalities: Behavior-Affect-Sensation-Imagery-Cognition-Interrelations-and-Drives (the latter referring body). This is summarized in the acronym BASIC-I.D. In terms of common textbook usage in psychology, this model corresponds to coverages of individual conduct (B), motivation/emotion (A), perceptual processes (S), visual thought/memory (I), language/cognition (C), social interactions (I.), neurogenetic drives (D., drugs/medication). These merging modalities bring western psychology closer to the emphasis on non-independence or interdependence, a topic to be treated shortly (see Kubota, Ch. 9).

Turning to Buddhist psychology, it is first important to realize that Buddha was not essentially concerned with metaphysics. As he contended: "The eyes and forms, the ears and sounds, the nose and smells, the tongue and tastes, the body and tangible things, the mind and mental objects... If someone should set this 'All' aside and proclaim another 'All,' it would be just talk... Because this would be beyond the limits of his abilities" (SN 28). To appreciate the parallels with western psychology, it is insightful to relate the following story in the Jataka:

Once, a sleeping hare heard a hullabaloo. Believing it is the end of the world, he began to run. Thinking the same, one species after the other joined him in the flight and started running until all were in a frantic sprint that would eventually have lead to their demise. When the Buddha saw them in panic, he asked them why they ran: "Because the world ends," they said. The Buddha replied "That can't be true, let's find out why you think so." Questioning them in succession, he finally arrived at the hare starting the run: "Where and what were you doing when you thought of the end?" The hare: "I was sleeping under a mango tree." The Buddha completed "then you probably heard a mango fall, startling you. Thus, the Buddha saved the animal kingdom.

In effect the mango served as an impinging Stimulus: Sensation/Activating Event. "You thought this is the end of the world" emphasizes the Organism: Imagery-Cognition/Beliefs, irrational or dysfunctional, "took fright and ran" is equivalent to the Response: Affect-Behavior-Interpersonal/Consequences, emotional and behavioral. In Ellis' (1994) terms: not the Activating events in the world out there but the false Beliefs (musts, shoulds, oughts) lead to unwanted Consequences in the Affect and Behavior modalities (see Soons, Ch. 7). An awesome pile of empirical evidence has been gathered for the thinking-feeling-behaving interdependent connections as well as for the subjective construction of "self-efficacy" based on positive intentions and expectations as a relevant change agent.

At the same time there are differences in emphasis. For Buddhists the external world is only relevant as far as it is experienced in thought-feeling-action and has an intentional or karmic impact on Body/Speech/Mind. Not matter per se or its non-selfness but cognitive appropriation, attribution, and evaluation (craving-grasping-clinging) determine whether one is free or "attached." Yet, with the difference in emphasis there are parallels in practice. *On the level of action* the Buddha advises changing the intention of activities (karma) so as to avert rebirth of unwanted "BASIC-I.D. episodes" by assigning homework (e.g. having a grieving woman search for a mustard seed from somebody who does not know a deceased one) (see De Silva, 1996; Ch. 2). Ellis applies the whole gamut of behavior modification techniques from Wolpean desensitization and Skinnerian reinforcement to Marks' exposure, interventions that have an allegiance to Buddhist tactics. *On the thinking level*, both approaches have also gone through various forms of "dissolving" that are all in a way an antidote against mindlessness: de-automatizing (Beck), de-musturbating (Ellis), de-fusing (Hayes), and de-literalization/de-constructing (NBP). *On the feeling level*, to unlearn unwanted emotion implies applying the conditioning principle of extinction. Curiously *nirvana* also means extinction. To date it proves inadequate to "unimodally" draw on conditioning principles like on only counterconditioning, generalization, habituation, aversion, stimulus control, or modeling to implement change. A multimodal intervention that covers the whole range of the BASIC-I.D. will likely accrue longer lasting results.

It is interesting to note that the conditioning view in the Buddhist literature strongly resembles the behavioral three factor functional model of learning, wherein items in each of the BASIC-I.D. modalities are a function of antecedent, mediating, and consequent factors that obey classical, vicarious, and operant conditioning principles. The paradigms are parallelled in Table 1.

Table 1. The S-O-R paradigm and its multimodal variety in parallel with the Buddha's karma sequence

Cognitive-Behavioral Model	Multimodal Assessment	Buddhist Sequence (Karma)
Stimulus Discriminative Generalized	Sensation	Awareness/Consciousness 6 Senses + 0 - felt

Organism	Imagery	Ignorance
Cognitive	Cognition	Projections
Somatic		Illusion
		Delusion

Response	Affect	Craving: due to not/musts
Emotional	Behavior	Greed — Grasping
Behavioral		Hate — Clinging

Consequences	Inter-relations	Speech
Reinforcement	Drives — body &	BodyMind
Punishment	neurogenetics	

Beyond Linear Causal Sequence

The strong tradition in western psychology is one of linear causality. Impinging stimuli spark change in cognition (and vice versa), cognition evokes emotion, and emotion motivates behavior. Buddhist teachings invite an expansion of this narrow cause-effect reasoning. Here it may be said that things in this world do not exist in isolation or independently, nor do they exist in permanence. All phenomena as represented through the mind's eye exist in Inter-Dependent-Origination-Arising-and-Subsiding (IDOAS), also called the Buddha's non independent origination. The Buddha pointed out that liberation from suffering is advanced by insight in the *Interdependence* of causality (IDOAS) and the *Deconstruction* of BodyMind self (the BASIC *ID*, italicized to pronounce as id instead of idea or identity: I.D.) to arrive at Interbeing — a term coined by Thich Nhat Hanh that refers to an interpersonal, relational, or social self — via the social practices.

To render this view functional, we might say that Buddhist psychology invites us to consider a causality hypothesis that is not a unimodal one way street but a circular, functional, and multicausal process wherein "cause = effect and effect = cause." Such interdependent multicausality hypothesizes strong correlations between antecedent and consequent factors. Instead of a narrow view that only looks at one mode of being, an interrelated BioPsychSocial system (the Buddha's BodySpeechMind) acknowledging three levels of existence (dhamma realms) is emphasized. Unicausal linear chunks of conditioned relationships make more sense if embedded in a circular type of multicausality or rather interdependent multifunctionality with feedback and feedforward loops. Such NBP model is able to explain how experience originates as BASIC-I.D. — a complex matrix of inter-relatedness — that functions in a flux of IDOAS.

Bridging Psychologies III: Meditation Practices

Both the Dharma and western psychology are concerned with furnishing an account of human action. As we have seen, many parallels in these accounts can be discerned. However, there is also a sense in which NBP invites an additional path of exploration. Traditional psychological research is content to describe what the case is; that is, charting causal relationships among phenomena rather exhaust the research program. However, we invite the field to move beyond what is the case to what we may become. By emphasizing a sixth sense we confront the realization that in the ways we focus our attention, we can design and bring about change. NBP is centrally concerned, then, with developing and enriching practices that contribute to a better life. A useful bridge is provided by Mahoney (2003), who was part of the cognitive revolution in behavior therapy during the 1970s, but took our field one step further by introducing the paradigm of constructivism, thus adding a humanistic voice in a mechanistic cognitive-behavioral model. Constructivism engenders a paradigm shift: explaining (*erklaeren*) is to be complemented by understanding (*verstehen*), which implies the recognition that people are the architects and constructors of their own realities and their future actions.

It may be said the Dharma's centerpiece is the state and practice of awareness. The Buddha's heuristic scheme of karma serves to heighten operative skills, not theory per se. In the Nikayas (MN 1-2) we read about a man struck by a poison arrow (ignorance, greed, hate). The family provides him a surgeon, but he would not have the arrow removed until he knows the attacker's class and name, whether he is tall, short, dark, light, what the bow, string, shaft, arrow, feather, and quiver are made of, etc. These questions are irrelevant to solving the problem; he will die while searching for answers. He should therefore allow the helpers to leave these speculative questions unanswered and address instead the pressing problem of removing the arrow. In the case of daily life, we have poison arrows of greed, hate, the abuse of others, and so on. The need, then, is for practices that remove the mind's dis-ease, the root of which is: I-me-mine/self.

To solve this problem, The Buddha's remedy is mindful awareness: to be aware of awareness/consciousness as dharmas and social constructs as a silent witness. To be mindful of this is a *conditio sine qua non* for psychological change. It is a *G* (*general*) factor in all Buddhist meditations. The word is derived from the Latin: *meditare* or *stare in medio* meaning to stay in the middle, which emphasizes balance. Another Latin root is *mederi* that refers to curing or measuring. Here the emphasis is on using awareness as the measure of mind or to settle patterns of thinking-feeling-doing. As a psychological condition meditation might refer to a relatively passing *state*, a relatively stable *trait*, a technique and procedure, or a way of life. Depending on context we use each of these meanings. The Buddha offered the practice of mindfulness meditation to be aware in bare attention of IDOAS, the non-independence of all experience, to thus See-Things-As-They-

Really-Are (STATRA, as Zennists call it), namely as interdependent and impermanent mind's representations and projections. A continuing practice of mindful awareness deconstructs self toward *nibbana*, a state of experiencing liberty of self overflowing heart and head. The seminal *Satipatthana Sutta* (DN 22, MN 10) — a discourse on establishing mindfulness or heedfulness (*sati*) of conditioned relations (*patthana*/IDOAS) — depicts mindfulness as not only a means to an end but as an end in itself. In the Dhammapada the Buddha instructed as follows:

> *O Bahiya, whenever you see a form, let there be just the seeing; whenever you hear a sound, let there be just the hearing; when you smell an odor, let there be just the smelling, when you taste a flavor, let there be just the tasting; when you experience a physical sensation, let it merely be sensation; and when a thought or feeling arises, let it be just a natural phenomenon arising in the mind. When it is like this, there will be no self, no I. When there is no self, there will be no moving about here and there and no stopping anywhere. That is the end of Dukkha (existential suffering). That is Nibbana (contentment in life). Whenever it is like that, then it is Nibbana. If it is lasting, then it is lasting Nibbana; if it is temporary, then it is temporary Nibbana.*

Mindfulness: Its Four Frames of Reference

Modeled by the Buddha at the bo-tree at the moment of his awakening, the gate to nibbana is attained by being continuously mindful of changes in/of body-and-mind using mindfulness of breathing as an anchor to return to whenever the mind wanders (Anapanasati Sutta, MN 68). Thus, through mindfulness the Buddha attained calm concentration, smiling contentment, serene absorption, and equanimous stability, which are known as the fruit of *jhana* (P), *dhyana* (S), Chan (C), or Zen (J). By being mindful of the BodyMind and its contents, defiled mind and afflicted body can be overcome. There are four frames of reference or foundations of mindful awareness, instructing the student to direct attention to (1) the body in the body, (2) the external and internal behaviors of the body, (3) the mind in the mind, and (4) the behavior of the mind in exchange with the external world as sensed or phantasied, In more specific terms mindfulness rests on the sixth sense perception of Sensation, Affect, Imagery and Cognition. All of these can be viewed as behaviors of the BodyMind (and includes self-talk), every single one of which is to be disidentified from I-me-mine/self. Here is our working definition of mindful awareness based on Yogacara's "direct knowing" (*jnana*):

> *(a) Cultivating a neutral presence by remembering to attend in a watchful, focused and compassionate~tolerant way to the stimuli entering consciousness via the senses and any thinking-feeling passing in the space of BodyMind.*
> *(b) Noticing receptively (no purpose or interference) the internal stimuli attended to in a choiceless awareness (no expecting, desiring, or evaluating) while surfing from-now-to-now without clinging or grasping, like a mirror.*

The essence of Yogacara Buddhahood is to be continually aware of awareness/consciousness as the projecting/representing-and-perceiving brain. As a term mindfulness was used early in the literature (e.g. Rhys Davids, 1900) and is presently almost a household word. In the Buddhist meaning and Asian languages mindfulness not only denotes heedfulness via reason but through the heart as well. For instance, for Channists the Chinese character *nian* denotes "mind-heart now"; the Japanese term *kokoro* "heart or true nature" is meant in the same vain (Nakajima, 2000). The recent frenzy amongst mental health workers has resulted in new attempts to define mindfulness (e.g. Kabat-Zinn, 1996, Baer et al., 2004, Bishop et al., 2004; Germer et al., 2005). Each emphasizes different and overlapping aspects, including: an intentional attention (openness, acceptance), nonconception (nonverbal, nonjudgmental), curiosity (observing, exploring), present centeredness (unfolding, liberating). Austin (1998) reveals the necessary conditions of attention: arousal, receptiveness, and a reaching out to the object. Brown and Ryan (2004) point at a Gestalt view that attention relates to awareness as figure to ground. Our two-tiered definition sees consciousness (from Latin *con* "with" and *scio* "to know") as mind's mechanism that dualistically splits and functionally represents (a knowing together with perception rather than direct) to be aware of. Awareness can be nondual (choiceless) or dual, in which case it is equivalent to consciousness.

Elements and Intricacies of Meditation

It is useful at this juncture to consider more fully the practice of mindfulness. We first consider the Buddha's 12 meditations and the place of the body, followed by a discussion of the place of the mind and the Four Noble Facts. This will set the stage for considering Buddhagosha's extensions of some 1000 years after the Buddha. In the case of Buddha's 12 meditations, the core application of heartfelt-mindfulness (G-factor) is the participant observation of 12 specific kinds of BodyMind dhammas (MN 22; DN 10). Mindfulness of the body involves attending to (1) *breathing*, (2) *behavior*, (3) *repulsiveness*, (4) *elements*, (5) *decomposition*, and (6) *feelings*.

Sitting with an upright back one starts sensing the breath and uses the breath as an anchor whenever attention becomes distracted. The exercise is on the steady and effortless observation of abdominal *breaths*, how these naturally pass the nostrils in and out, as a gatekeeper not following the air in or outside. Awareness is on the type of each breath by covertly saying: "long," "short," "calm," etc., which tranquilizes the body when concentration, clarity, and balance are gained. Emotional disruption is to be desensitized (attended little by little with a smile) until it wanes. Delight, dispassion, relinquishment, and release also go along with a smile. The focus is on the unfolding "herenow," in this breath, in abiding calm concentration until, in absorption, self is forgotten and equanimity, contentment, luminousness, and serenity are felt.

Next, the focus is on the body's *behavior*: the Buddha gave up ascetism and propagated a middle way using the metaphor of tuning the strings of a sitar. The practice is to note in bare attention the four dignities and all other behaviors, like "talking," "drinking," "savoring," "toileting," etc. Then, the body's *repulsiveness* is attended to: the body is a bag with two openings full of grain, wheat, rice, beans, and seeds, etc. Enveloped by the skin it is made of hair, nails, teeth, flesh, nerves, bones, gorge, marrow, kidneys, heart, liver, midriff, spleen, lungs, intestines, feces, bile, phlegm, pus, blood, sweat, fat, tears, grease, saliva, mucus, urine, and other fluids. All of this will *decompose* to the *elements* earth, water, fire, and wind. As death is the sole certainty, contemplation focuses on refraining from clinging to the body through exposure to its decay by visualizing one's corpse, cut-up, bleeding, or gnawed. How its flesh swells, darkens, and cast in the ground, stinks, rots, dissolves, and eaten by vermin. How it reduces to a skeleton and scattered bones of the hands, feet, shin, thigh, back, hip, chest, rib, shoulder, neck, jaw, tooth, and skull. How the bleached bones of a shell color, more than one year old, lie on a heap, rot, and turn into dust. Mindfulness of *feeling* refers to skin deep Sensation and Affect, including deep-seated emotions. Note covertly the type of feeling: pleasant, painful, or neither-pleasant-nor-painful feeling. By applying a scaling technique the Buddha shows to be a psychologist "avant la lettre." The end result is to experience STATRA: emptiness of not-self and of non-self.

We now turn to the place of the mind in the Buddha's 12 meditations. Generally, mindfulness of the mind refers to what we call the Buddha's psychopathology comprising the three poisons: the varieties of (1) ignorance or stupidity (illusions, delusions [that self or soul exists], cravings, symbolized by a swine), (2) greed or cupidity (grasping, approach, "musts," symbolized by a rooster), and (3) hate or aggression (clinging, avoidance, "must not," symbolized by a snake). Meditation in this case is about the mindful observation that attends to (7) *hindrances*, (8) *modalities*, (9) *Six sense-bases*, (10) *awakening*, (11) *Four Noble Facts*, and (12) an *Eight Fold Path*, and the mindful attempt to discern their presence or absence and to what degree. Hindrances are obstacles of mood (to be turned into one's path): the sweetness of sensory pleasure, the bitterness of ill-will, the imprisonment of apathy (sloth, torpor), the swings of restlessness (agitation, worry), and the nervousness of doubt. The BASIC-I.D. modalities of clinging are to be destroyed by penetrating the insight of interdependence (in the flux of IDOAS) and by deconstructing the illusion of self. Next, the modality of Sensation requires attention. The internal-external sense bases: feeling pleasant, painful, or neutral, depending on contact between the six organs (eye, ear, nose, tongue, skin, brain) and the six external objects (of sight, sound, odor, taste, touch, thoughts), being always fully aware of all combinations without clinging to any of them. To further uncrave, ungrasp, and uncling, the awakening factors requires observation comprising an investigation of the internal dhammas of persistence (to improve), enthusiasm (to increase), serenity (to deepen), concentration (to sharpen), and equanimity (to balance).

The list ends with the Buddha's discourse on the Four Noble Facts and the Eight Fold Path to which we now turn. The most widespread entrance to the Dharma is the Four Noble Facts. As its essence is to cure psychological disturbance, we present it here as the Buddha's illness metaphor of an "auto-immune dis-ease." While no one escapes life's inherent conditions and individuals' responses to these are mostly detrimental to one's own well-being, the disturbance might as well be denoted as existential suffering or "neurosis," a chronic and self-inflicted malady of psychological uneasiness about life itself. This uneasiness starts inevitably soon after birth and becomes manifest in our dealings with physical disease, decay, and death. The resulting sense of *dukkha*, a term that defies literal translation, is usually indicated as suffering, unsatisfactoriness, or being stuck. It is a negative experience for which the Buddha prescribed a remedy that leads to attaining a salutary state of release/redemption/liberation that may be viewed as optimal functioning. The term "stress" seems not quite adequate because it is an ambiguous term that might be either unwholesome (contributing to disease) or wholesome "eustress" (contributing to wellness). "Dis-ease" (Kwee & Holdstock, 1996) reflects a more accurate meaning than stress since it resonates with the "man-at-ease" as often depicted in Zen.

In an illness metaphor the first step is *diagnosis* of dukkha: impermanence/imperfection of existence is the root of self-caused misery, dis-ease. Secondly, dis-ease has a *cause* (*samudaya*): the three poisons, which occur in interaction with the environment and result in yearning for permanence and perfection of I-me-mine/self. This is to be abandoned. Thirdly, the *prognosis* (*nirodha*): dis-ease can be contained, eradicated, and prevented by inoculating against the poisons. While aging and its ramifications are inevitable, self-caused mental suffering can be cured; to be realized. Fourthly, the way to cure dis-ease is to confide in the doctor and his *therapy* (*magga*), which is: right concentration and mindfulness (meditation), right understanding and intention (wisdom), right effort and action (discipline), right speech and livelihood (virtue), the Eight Fold Path; to be cultivated (see Khong, Ch. 21). Awakening can be attained by the arahant: someone who has defeated his "enemies." The enemy is *us*: our unwholesome intentions or negative karma we are able to immediately transform by refraining from the negative and starting to see the glass half full rather than half empty. We have to be courageous (noble) not to flee from existential suffering into neurosis.

Buddhagosha's Visuddhi Magga

Understanding the potentials of meditation also gains by a consideration of the *Visuddhi Magga*, a comprehensive manual by Buddhagosha who compiled existing Sinhalese commentaries (plus his own) on the Pali Canon in the Sri Lanka of the 5th century (Nanamoli, 1975). This work reflects the Dhamma's handing down in ten centuries and summarizes the relevancies of insight meditation, wisdom, discipline, and virtue. Its quintessence reads: "Suffering exists, but not the sufferer... Doing is, but where is the doer? Nibbana is, but not its seeker. The way is seen, not the traveler" (p. 587). The road map to purifying the mind toward not-self points at mindfulness of inevitable existential realities that are summarized in the Buddha's core teaching on the Three Empirical Marks of Existence from which no one is excluded. The prerequisite for Buddhahood is an in-dwelling insight into: (1) life is an incessantly IDOAS, and the dhammas are in impermanent flux (*anicca*): the mind and all dhammas change, they do not last nor remain the same, (2) dis-ease and suffering (dukkha) are the result of a craving for and reaching out (grasping and clinging) to an alleged permanence-perfection that does not exist, and (3) a Buddha is born as not-self (*anatta*), to be found in the pernetrating insight that I-me-mine/self lacks self-nature, impossible to attach to.

The Buddha's 12 meditations consist of 40 themes to concentrate and contemplate on. Buddhagosha discerned techniques of: (a) *absorption*: mindfulness to concentrate, calm, enjoy in playful tranquility, and equanimity (30), and (b) *insight*: mindfulness to contemplate on (10), like the Three Empirical Marks of Existence. Interestingly, Buddhagosha raised the issue of different meditation themes' suitability to the individual's temperament, we nowadays call personality. It was advised that a wise good friend suggests a starting theme according to the novice's temperament. In today's terms, it may be fruitful to match client and technique. Let us examine this possibility in Buddhist terms.

Matching Temperaments and Meditative Themes

Buddhagosha's archaic psychology classifies six basic personality types in three pairs: greedy and/or faithful, hating and/or intelligent, and deluded and/or speculative. Evidently, this taxonomy is an elaboration of the Buddha's psychopathology that discerns three root proclivities: greed, hatred, and ignorance (also indicated as illusion and delusion that refer to non-psychotic erroneous thinking like believing in a permanent self, soul, or god). Each of these six types and their combinations are the result of accumulated karma or what could also be called (in Wolpe & Lazarus', 1966, terms) habitual patterns of *mindless* and automatic responding due to conditioning.

A temperament is known through observation (Nanamoli, 1975, p. 106): "By the posture, by the action, by eating, seeing, and so on, by the kind of states occurring, may temperament be recognized." This statement reflects a cognitive-behavioral stance. The BASIC-I.D. is represented in the various temperaments. "In one of *greedy temperament* there is frequent occurrence of deceit, fraud, pride, evilness of wishes, greatness of wishes, discontent, foppery and personal vanity. In one of *hating temperament* we find anger, enmity, disparaging, domineering, envy and avarice. In one of *deluded temperament* we discern stiffness, torpor, agitation, worry, uncertainty, and holding tenaciously with refusal to relinquish. In one of *faithful temperament* we find free generosity, desire to see Noble Ones and to hear the Good Dhamma, great gladness, ingenuousness, honesty, and trust in things that inspire trust. In one of *intelligent temperament* there is readiness to be spoken to, possession of good friends, knowledge of the right amount in eating, mindfulness and full awareness, devotion to wakefulness, a sense of urgency about things, and wisely directed endeavour. In one of *speculative temperament* we confront talkativeness, sociability, boredom with devotion to the profitable, failure to finish undertakings, smoking by night (planning) and flaming by day (executing), and mental running hither and thither" (Nanamoli , 1975, pp. 108-109, italics added).

Although Nanamoli outlines a way of thinking about matching temperament to meditative themes, we have found our own clinical practice helpful in providing directions. Assessing individuals' proclivities for BASIC-I.D. modalities reveals useful clues (Kwee, Ishii, & Sakairi, 2001). Whether one has a penchant for behaving (B, I), thinking (I, C), or feeling (A, S) does matter in selecting the most effective technique. Basically, a doer, thinker, or feeler might generally profit from a respective corresponding kind of meditation. In order to gauge structural tendencies, the novice rates questions on a scale from 6 (high) to 0 (low) centered around each of the following items: B — How much of a doer am I? A — How deeply emotional am I? S — How much tuned in to senses (pleasures and pains) am I? I — How much do I think in vivid pictures? C — How much of an analytic thinker or planner am I? I.— How much do I engage in social activities? D.— How often am I ill? Despite its subjective nature, these ratings accrue relative pointers and avoid haphazard choices. Thus, for instance a doer (high on B & I) would profit relatively more from sitting, a feeler (high on S & A) from equanimity, and a thinker (high on I & C) from a mantra. Similarly, someone low on doing would benefit from walking meditation, if low on feeling from genuine smiling, and if low on thinking from a *koan* (a paradox sounding like a riddle that cannot be solved by reason).

The purpose is to adhere to the canon of scientific specificity and to find pointers for: which technique or meditation theme works for whom, under what conditions, when, and why?

II

Unfolding the Mahayana Tradition

We have now scanned some of the central ingredients for a fourth turn in the wheel, a Neoyana, bringing together major Buddhist ideas and practices with contemporary psychological science. In this second part we wish to take a closer look at a select but relevant range of Mahayana teachings and their implications for a full flowering of Neoyana.

From Ultimate Realities to Emptiness

The Theravada Nikayas already view two kinds of reality or selves that exist side by side: provisional (functional self) and ultimate (empty not-self) (elaborated later in the "Perfection of Wisdom Sutras" and systematized by Nagarjuna to become a pervasive non-self). Ultimate reality refers to the "absolute" empty world that goes beyond the ordinary reality of forms as can be seen by the awakened mind. Provisional reality refers to the commonly accepted "relative" world of forms as it appears to the unawakened mind of a householder and the awakened mind of a Buddha. While Mahayana views the provisional or conventional as abstract, internal representations that name things but are not the things, Theravada declares the external things themselves as "non existent." If torn apart these things' integrity disappears. Where is the thingness of a table if cut into pieces or where is the dog Fido if chopped by a butcher? The same applies to human beings. It is the constituent parts' combination that makes up a thing or a person.

A chronicle of the Greek-Indian King Milinda and the arahant Nagasena (2nd c BCE; written down in the 1st c) illustrates this point (Rhys Davids, 1890). The King: "By what name shall I know you, sir?" Nagasena: "My companions call me Nagasena, but the name and the person to whom the name refers do not really exist." The King: "If Nagasena and the person do not exist, who do people offer alms to and who receives these offerings? Since you receive them, you really exist. Why do you tell a lie in spite of your high nobility?" Nagasena: "Your majesty, did you come to this monastery on foot or by chariot?" The King: "By chariot." Nagasena: "Please show me your chariot. Is the horse the chariot? Is the wheel the chariot? Is the axle the chariot? Is the carriage the chariot?" The King: "No" to all these questions. Nagasena: "Your majesty, you came here by chariot; yet you could not show me the chariot! Why did you tell a lie in spite of your high honour?" The King consented. Nagasena: "Your majesty, Nagasena is to be understood like the chariot."

Abhidhamma's understanding of ultimate reality is: something that cannot be changed into another thing or divided up into other things. It is not created nor destroyed by man, is formless and shapeless, and holds on its characteristics till it perishes. In the Abhidhamma the apparent reality of a person is ostensibly made up of four ultimate realities: (1) body (corporeality or matter-energy: *rupa*) and mind (awareness or consciousness: *nama*), specifically (2) flash of conscious awareness: citta (e.g. seeing) (3) consciousness' concomitants: cetasikas (e.g. worry), and (4) nibbana (the extinction of inner fires) (see Barendregt, Ch. 22). Through mindfulness it can be experienced that Body/Mind works together (like the good eye-sight of a lame man sitting on the shoulder of the blind man with good legs), that the sensory aware mind (citta and cetasikas) cannot exist without the body's (i.e. brain's) support, and that there is absolute lasting peace in the state of nibbana. Unfortunately, the Abhidhamma account set forth an elementalistic ontology, one that seemed to violate the Buddhist vision of ultimate emptiness by imposing self-nature upon the four ultimate realities.

In the 1st century BCE not only the Tipitaka was written down (on palm leaves in Sri Lanka) but also the Mahayana sutras began to appear in Sanskrit writings (Gombrich, 1990). It is assumed that the Abhidhamma was the catalyst for Mahayana's criticism reflected in the colossal number of sutras that exceeds the Bible by fifty times. This might have blocked Theravada's further development and helped Mahayana to rise. These "heretical" texts were attributed to the Buddha himself, but are without any doubt man-made (by anonymous brotherhoods). Among these are the 100,000, 25,000, 18,000, 10,000, and 8,000 stanzas versions of the foundational *Prajnaparamita Sutra* (written in the 1st c BCE), also known as the "Perfection of Wisdom" (Conze, 1975), that alludes to the six characteristics of the Mahayana prototype of an awakened being (*bodhisattva*). S/he postpones Buddhahood for the sake of liberating others and through embodying: generosity, righteousness, forbearance, endeavour, meditation, and wisdom (*prajna*). The latter implies a deep understanding of Nagarjuna's view on the emptiness of all dharmas (*sunyata*): impermanence has no lasting self-nature and inheres in paradoxes like "emptiness = form and form = emptiness." Wisdom embodies both stances. Nagarjuna extensively scrutinized the Buddha's two levels of reality, not only to expose an innovative explanation but also to ferociously correct Hinayana's ultimate realities that seemingly inhere in self-nature. Hinayana alleged that provisional reality is composed of "atomic" dhammas (they had no idea that an atom contains interchanging waves and particles) that do exist impermanently. Such implies inherent existence (*svabhava*) and a regression to a permanent self or eternal soul. A plethora of terms are used in the literature to indicate self-nature or inherent existence: essence, substance, own-being, self-existence, essential nature, intrinsic reality, and god.

What Hinayana considers ultimate and absolute — possessing inherent existence — is considered functional, relative, conventional, and provisional by Mahayana. Prajnaparamita teaches that all dharmas do not ultimately exist, they are empty of any inherent existence, thus claiming to endorse the Buddha's pristine not-selfness of all dharmas. Not quite content to emphasize only the absence of self in persons (by viewing a person as a conglomerate of impermanent dharmic events), Mahayana argues that in order to get a full understanding of emptiness, one has to see those presumed ultimate realities (*nama-rupa, citta, cetasikas*, and *nirvana*) as empty as well. In other words, emptiness is not a mere hollowness of dhammas or a personal *not*-self, but is a *non*-selfness that pervades all dharmas of the universe in their entire totality (J, *muga/not-self, mushin/non-self*). Thus, abhidhammic ontological elementalism was rejected.

From Nagarjuna to Yogacara

One of the mind-boggling theses submitted by Nagarjuna (ca.150-250) is the paradox that the recurrent cycle of existential suffering and unsatisfactoriness of form (*samsara*) and the emptiness of nirvana — the lasting freedom of craving, grasping, and clinging (a deeply embodied contentment attained through skilfully handling ignorance, greed and hate) (SN 38) — are the same (Stcherbatsky, 1923). The sunyata (empty of inherent existence) of the "Perfection of Wisdom" was formulated into a Middle Way teaching (*Madhyamaka*). It was thus called because Nagarjuna wished to avoid the extremes of Abhidhamma's slipping in self-nature through the back door and "Buddha Womb Sutras' " Buddhanature, jeopardizing emptiness. He emphasized relativizing as a road toward emptiness, acknowledging a life in both worlds of convention and ultimacy. Nagarjuna's view on these two levels of reality is that the functional and the ultimate exist side by side. Under the provisional level all dharmas are subsumed. This is the apparent world of forms, wherein the dharmas are perceived and conceived through ignorance, illusion, delusion (based on dualistic/binary notions and on I-me-mine/self identifications and reifications). At the ultimate level that same world of dharmas' perceptions and conceptions are erased and experienced wisely through a profound insight that all dharmas are in IDOAS, momentary, do not have inherent existence, and are thus pervasively empty. Such emptiness is not the absence of something that once was, but an emptiness that is devoid of self-nature.

Nagarjuna applied a dialectic method — *a deconstructio ad absurdum* — by means of which he came to a logically proven emptiness. The tetralemna, a quadruple negation, is a case in point in which he explained emptiness as neither object nor non-object and neither subject nor non-subject. If dharmas are empty in the first place, they do not subside as they did not arise, they do not annihilate as they did not materialize, they do not unite as they did not diversify, and they do not disappear as they did not appear. For Nagarjuna polarities cannot ultimately exist each by themselves because each pole's existence always depends on its opposite. For each of one to originate and arise, the other is an inherent necessity. This also applies to the differentiation between functional and ultimate itself. The experience of samsara versus nirvana exists in relative interdependence and complementarity, each existence depends on one's momentary viewpoint. Thus, ultimately, both are illusory, empty, and in that sense identical. This reasoning boils down to the ultimate emptiness of all conditioned BASIC-I.D. dharmas in IDOAS. The revelation of nirvana amidst craving conditionings as an ultimate "emptiness of emptiness and of itself" is an experience of "thundering silence" during which all intellectual insights on emptiness are left behind. Those who persist are pronounced "incurable." Pointing at such emotional insight, Nagarjuna was eventually concerned with psychology.

In the 4th century, Yogacara — a second major Indian school of Mahayana — came to fruition (Chatterjee, 1999), which might be regarded as an extension of and a down to earth response to the highly abstract "Emptiness-only" musings of Nagarjuna. Its innovations were precursed by the "Buddha Womb Sutras" — written alongside the Abhidhamma and the "Perfection of Wisdom," during the 1st century BCE to the 4th century — scriptures that Nagarjuna in his time did not critisize but did not embrace either. As the name implies — yoga refers to meditation — yogacarins are keen not to philosophize but rather to prioritize embodied experience. This foundation has led their teachings to become permeated with the psychology of self-discovery in the best Buddhist tradition. Nagarjuna's "emptiness of emptiness and of itself" remains difficult to practice. It feels like a blind man's looking for a black cat in a dark cellar that does not exist. No specific instructions are given other than reifications will disappear on its own by "training in the view that all lacks entity" (Shantideva, as cited by the Dalai Lama, 2005, p. 59). In order to break from the captivity of philosophical binaries, a leap to the realm of practice is required and prescribed by the yogacarin.

The means and end lies in "choiceless awareness" (a term coined by J. Krishnamurti; 1895-1986). This unique capacity of the mind's eye to be meditatively aware of awareness amidst daily activity bypasses the use of a meditation object as in formal training (its practice is known in Chan as *wuwei*, elaborated later). One only monitors or "surfes" the dharmas, during whatever activity, in bare attention and focuses non-judgmentally on whatever arises in the flow of consciousness, thus excluding the duality of inner chatter. The slightest judgement, belief, criticism, or praise dualizes. Any ripple in the mind is noticed; any thought, any affect, any volition to act, and any restlessness or calmness as it arises, "is only mind." Choiceless means not dwelling on a single stimulus, a memory, or a goal, but floating: letting sensory input flow from all directions without manipulating. In such a state of alert passivity binaries are blocked from emerging and non-duality becomes immanent. There is *no transcendence* in this state, as all experiences are within the six senses and not beyond sensory awareness. Inner freedom is discovered as an epiphenomenon of a tranquil and complete acceptance that things are as they are. There is no becoming (tomorrow or yesterday can't be found), only the love for the moment [*jisso*, J]): from now to now. Thus, there is atonement ("at-one-moment" redemption) and a yoking with existence that Yogacara calls "suchness." Nondual awareness (BASIC *ID*) is realized: the observing subject and the observed object coincide in direct knowing through surrender (jnana).

The Yogacara Route to Awakening

The works of the brothers Asanga (*Cittamatra*) and Vasubandhu (*Vijnanavada*) are extant in Chinese and in Tibetan translations (with sometimes different views; e.g. Liu, 1985). Asanga convinced Vasubandhu to refute Abhidharmic substantialist's ideas and to adopt the bodhisattva ideal to help liberate others before self-redemption. The term "Mind-only" (*Cittamatra*) is a derogation used by opponents, notably Shantideva (7th c). Ironically but understandably, yogacarins were themselves later accused of substantialism for using terms like Buddhanature that they merely applied as an empty provisional teaching device.

The brothers' teachings include: the Turnings of the Wheel, the Three Self-Natures (as in the example of the rope), the Three Buddha Bodies, and the Eight Conciousnesses (the 7th is I-me-mine/self consciousness and the 8th is the alleged origin of all consciousness' content, a 4th century hypothesis on memory and retention). Similar to 21st century social constructionism (Gergen, 1999) and radical constructivist epistemology (von Glasersfeld, 1984), they hold that the world, as we know it, exists only in our representations, our construals or constructions, like pictures that we paint (see Sugamura & Warren, Ch. 25). Both expound — as cognitive therapists also do — that the subject cannot truly know the object itself, only its perception and its mental representation. The prime interest to change karma lies not in the reality of matter "out there," but rather in our maps of the world "in here." Matter in itself cannot be known. For the yogacarin a piece of filament in the dark can be perceived as a snake (projected reality), a rope (provisional reality), or as empty of self-nature (ultimate reality). Meditation should lead to the deconstruction of the projected and the provisional into the empty.

The question remains: what is Nagarjuna's emptiness and how can the subject ever experience it? Besides formulating an epistemology, Vasubandhu reinterpreted and expanded the scope and depth of Abhidharma. The quintessence of his endeavor was to expedite liberation by new insights and methods of neutralizing afflicted karma, the intentional activity of Body/Speech/Mind. No doubt, intention belongs to the category of cognition, thus what is non-cognitive cannot be karmic and what is cognitive can be karmic wholesome or unwholesome. Change is required if one is conditioned by unwholesome karma and the aim is to overcome existential suffering through eliminating its karmic conditioning. The commonality of this bacic tenet with CBT à la Beck, Ellis, or Lazarus (Kwee & Ellis, 1997) is striking. Both Yogacara and CBT point at our failure to distinguish the world "without" from the world "within." We do not recognize our own karma causing interpretations, constructions, and projections while perceiving dharmas (mind's representations). The later yogacarins, who walked along the epistemological rather than the cosmogonic path, not only differentiated perception from inference, but also discerned cognitions that are "unvalid" (a 7th c term used by Dharmakirti) or unwholesome versus "valid"/wholesome ones (that we define as rational, functional, and harmony-enhancing), by disengaging with one's relation to self-talk rather than modifying self-talk's content.

Unlike CBT's treatment of psychopathology, Yogacara serves as a guide in life's quest for liberation. In this quest Nagarjuna's philosophical musings on whether or which non-cognitive ultimate realities inheres in self-nature are useless. To end cycles of daily karmic rebirths, Yogacara's remedy is to deconstruct all self and non-self constructs. This starts with the insight that life's actual impermanent condition versus expectational demands result in dissonance and eventually in chronic existential neurotic suffering. Karmic self-obsession — a demand for permanence, a longing for self-nature, and a fear of the non-existence of self — is diagnosed as the cause. Yogacara advises awareness of cognitive mediation and the overturning of the subject-object duality in favor of a direct knowing that prevents karma to evolve. Such is done by obliterating duality via a movement from choiceless awareness to a total non-dual awareness. The grasper/subject-object/grasped duality is eradicated through jnana (direct knowing) of perceptibles, imaginables, knowables, memorables, and dreams/illusions by paying bare attention to what appears in the "mirror of awareness." Such awareness lifts greed, hate, and ignorance on impermanence, suffering, and non-selfness. This is not theory but an embodied deconstruction during meditation. It comes to dis-engaging, dis-owning, and dis-solving by un-craving, un-grasping, and un-clinging.

Yogacara's awakening process starts with an aspiring attitude to acquire the traits of a bodhisattva in order to apply these for the benefit of all, called *bodhicitta* (a mind, committed to awaken). Operation "enduring freedom" is successful if Buddhanature is revealed by paying full attention to this moment in time and to this place in space. This results in fascination of the now as the only time to be alive. Wherever one walks, there one is, wherever one falls, there one lies: always "herenow" and nowhere else. There is arrival before a start. An "I think, feel, or do"-consciousness is replaced by a nondual brainwave "it thinks, feels or does." At that moment the thinker has vanished, the feeler is not at home; there is watching but no watcher: craving, grasping, or clinging vanishes. If such is experienced in equanimity, a natural benevolence, contentment, and empathic compassion may arise (see Bankart, Ch. 3). It is then time to further cultivate and assist others in loving kindness, and shared joy. Thus, the Zen circle (*enso*, J) is in "full emptiness" round.

The seemingly quite easy way to attain Buddhahood by an intrinsically luminous mind traversing the Yogacara roadmap indicates that the mere practice *is* the attainment itself. This is called a metonym. To sit is to be awakened, as Buddhahood is already inherently present in us. If the right psychological method is applied, Buddhahood can easily be engendered. Apt for those days, the image appeared of an unborn Buddhanature residing in a Buddha womb (*tathagatagarbha*), in which is an embryo to be delivered. This is an extension of a storehouse seed analogy (karma in memory) and of a womb as a metaphor of emptiness. The innate potential that one is already a Buddha has been dealt with in as much as 10 sutras. With a substantialist-like Buddhanature residing in every sentient being, emptiness also became eclipsed by "a real and eternally existing essence that is primordially replete with all the qualities of a Buddha" (Keown, 2003, p. 296).

As the Dharma progressed further down the ages, the historical Budddha figure bleached to an extent that he eventually was replaced by cosmological figures. And as well, the voluminous works of Asanga and Vasubandhu also include the influential innovation of the Three Buddha Bodies. Once "born" the universal principle of

Buddhahood manifests itself in three bodies. (1) Teaching-body (*Dharmakaya*): the ultimate principle of the Buddha's timeless wisdom that is already present in everybody's nature (formless compassion, nonduality, suchness, and emptiness) and is beyond conception, (2) Bliss-body (*Sambhogakaya*): the principle of splendor and delight in a Buddhaland paradise where it is glorified by up to 50 celestial bodhisattvas, and (3) Phantom-body (*Nirmana-kaya*): the principle of infinite Buddhahood that appears in the dual world of space-time as an earthly manifestation to help all sentient beings end the cycles of suffering.

What started as an innovative idea to fill the emptiness by an empty/nondual Buddhanature as an educational tool not only came to inhabit three transcendent bodies and five cosmic Buddhas (*Vairocana* [Centre], *Akshobhya* [East], *Ratnasambhava* [South], *Amitabha* [West], and *Amoghasiddhi* [North]). These ideas became a craze, went berserk, and emanated a phantasmagoric cosmology of five bodhisattvas, elements, colors, sights, sounds, etc. These developments might have been exploited in the beginning as upaya to attract the superstitious, pious, and devout people at large with the appealing smell of "opium," but the airy notions eventually blurred the differences between Buddhadharma and Brahmanism (that considers the Buddha as a manifestation of the preserver god Vishnu). In trying to reach and serve humanity in need, the religious-devotional aspect flourished wildly, from the 4th century on, to such extent that a subsequent Mahayana wave known as Vajrayana Tantra (diamond vehicle based on magical methods called *tantra*) became a (sub)vehicle of Mahayana. Thus, the Indian Mahayanists succeeded in regenerating the Dharma and even exporting it, wrapped as a religion, to neighboring cultures and countries.

Mahayana's heuristic flirtation with religion and metaphysics and the promise of a transitional karma-reward paradise of divine enjoyment not only lured many but also led to the return of a soul via a back door, which in our assessment contributed to the decline of the Dharma in India that started in the 6th century until it vanished in the 12th century.

From Celestial Beings to Chan

Before extinguishing in India, roughly three periods in the history of Buddhadharma can be discerned: Hinayana (500 BCE-0), Mahayana of "Emptiness-only" and "Mind-only" (0-500), and Vajrayana or Diamond Vehicle (500-1200). According to Conze (1987), the Dharma has not had a new idea in 1000 years (a view that we wish to correct by launching Neoyana). The phantasmagoric and exotic character of Mahayana attracts spiritual seekers in the West. This is more so for Vajrayana that radiates mysticism and esoterism. A lifetime would be too short to fathom all its writings (*Tantrayana*) and occult practices.

This vehicle's teaching is alive and kicking especially in Tibet and surrounding areas where it is imbibed in the indigenous culture and daily life. To a very less degree it had been practiced in China (*Chen-yen*; in the 8th-9th c) and is still practiced in Japan (*Shingon*) since it was brought there by Kukai (774-835). The many complicated ceremonies and services did not fit the Chinese mind. Diamond Vehicle's tantras are texts that deal with secret techniques of visualization, and other means like sounds (*mantras*), gestures (*mudras*), and diagrams (*mandalas*). This approach was popular for the laiety as an accelerated way to attain bliss of a *siddha* (a wandering magician that replaced the arahant and the bodhisattva). Before embarking on this mysterious vehicle of ecstasy the student has to master many sutras and *shastras* (treatises). One could ask whether in that case tantras are necessary. The answer lies in the technical instructions that they provide to expedite nirvana, through mastering white (and black) magic like in the Kalachakra ritual that is about the wheel of time, sex, aggression, and destruction. Its basic idea is congenial with Brahmanistic practices that refer to the sexual unity of Shiva and Shakti that depicts the root metaphor of nonduality (mother and father in oneness; *yabyum*). The sexual connotative visualization technique has a definite Buddhist aim to extinguish or canalize the firy passions that attaches and leads to suffering. No doubt, sexuality is a strong neurogenetic drive that makes detaching from erotic appetite troublesome. The path pointed by the celestial Buddhas is to sublimate the poisons (extended to 5): ignorance, greed, hate, pride, and envy.

To enter the cosmic Buddhas' paradises one is obligatory guided by a guru, called *lama* in Tibet. To become initiated in one of the many tantras an absolute faith in a lama is demanded as well as many prostrations in the dust. The student ultimately confronts the limits of I-me-mine/self identifications by visualizing the tantras. There is a mother, father, parental tantra, the tantras of transcendental bodhisattvas, and female deities like Tara. As one progresses through the various purification stages (infatuation, love making, and orgasmic bliss) death is imminent. After quenching one's thirst by drinking all this nectar, either one has completely lost the way or an inflated bubble could be successfully lanced and a Buddhaland entered. For outsiders, much of Vajrayana is secretive. One must be initiated into understanding the Buddhist meaning hidden in the thicket of symbolic images. For instance, in the metaphor of the vehicle itself: the *vajra* (male) and the bell (female). A vajra stands for the indestructible diamond, thunderbolt, or scepter of Indra (king of the Brahma heaven) that cuts through all obstacles of awakening. A peaceful vajra has spokes that meet at the tip (a wrathful vajra is splayed). Five spokes symbolize five wisdoms or consciousnesses. The bell's hollowness represents emptiness, while the clapper stands for "the sound of emptiness." It is impossible to describe the numerous symbols that are systematized in this cosmology. Yet, the occult and esoteric language hides a clear teaching, and once the veil is lifted the inside is Mahayana as outlined above (consisting of Abhidharma, Madhyamaka, and Yogacara).

In 792-794 a debate was allegedly held in Samye, Tibet, between adherents of Kamalashila who was a tantric Mahayanist and the Chinese Chan monk Hwashang. The latter was said to have lost. The putative issue was gradual versus sudden awakening, but despite its refutation the subitist position was never abandoned and became incorporated in the teachings of the Nyingmapa lineage. This controversy boils down to the question of accumulating wholesome karma versus the redundancy of earning merit to become what one already is (Buddhanature), called in Dzogchen the primordial state (*ati*) of the individual who is already perfect. Dzogchen is a complete path in itself, traditionally taught in the final stages of a series of courses, which explains the nature of the mind and enables one to discover one's true nature and potentiality in a non-intellectual way. It is imperative to note that in Namkhai Norbu Rinpoche's book (1984) *Dzog Chen and Zen*, such kinship is explicitly stated. Dzogchen, the crown jewel of Tantra (*atiyoga*), unveils a naked pervasive awareness of an immediate luminosity (*rigpa*). The mind and its content are observed in all circumstances: it looks not but nothing escapes its attention. An intrinsic immovable tranquility appears whenever there is a direct knowledge of the moment's perfection (Dalai Lama, 2000). Another resemblance with Chan is its "anarchy" or free style of teaching. There are no rules of good or bad (on sitting, dressing, behaving, etc.) and there is nothing to learn. It all depends on oneself, but requires direct transmission.

Once as a Tibetan monk and translator of Shantideva's 7th century's, *Guide to the Boddhisattva's Way of Life* (the prime handbook in Tibet), Batchelor (1990) found out that a Tibetan version of the Satipatthana Sutta did not exist and lamented that it was impossible for him to receive Dzogchen teaching after he contracted a particular guru. Encapsulated in the atavistic tradition, he concluded that it is only possible to fathom Tibetan Buddhist teachings if one has a thorough knowledge of the language, which would require a Herculean effort. Frustrated by the hermetically closed system (where belief and magic overthrow reason) and cultural hurdles (where there is no room for doubt) he sought and found refuge in *Son* (Korean Zen) that is underpinned by a Chinese down to earth mentality.

Exploring the Wisdom of Chan

Before going into Zen, it is essential to explore the Chan school, one of the chief outcomes of Yogacara and the "Buddha Womb Sutras." It is important to note that the Tibetan and Chan/Zen traditions (only two of more then a dozen traditional Mahayana denominations extant in the Far East) are cultural applications of the sutras, which NBP as a transcultural and applied science — based on the same scriptures — is rivaling and competing with. Yet, NBP shares Chan/Zen's down-to-earthness and explicit non-philosophical, non-metaphysical and non-deifying stance that it has pioneered. We agree with Lin-chi (9th c) that there is not much in the Dharma after all. The below overview evidences that there is much wisdom and humor in Chan/Zen, but it unfortunately contains not much psychology.

Chan's anachronistic history begins with a legendary mission via the sea of the monk Bodhidharma (*Ta-mo*, C; *Daruma*, J; about 460-534) and was one of many Indian teachers who went to China. He was presumably a bluish-eyed Indian prince who personifies the historical *trait d'union* with the Buddha as the alleged 28th successor in Chan's lineage. His arrival at a harbor in the Guang-zhou province around 500 marks the start of an unorthodox teaching that aims at "direct awakening" through a "direct pointing" and a "direct knowing" of the mind (bespeaking a Yogacara background). Instructive is the vignette on his meeting with the emperor Wu, who asked: "What merit have I earned by building temples and feeding monks?" Bodhidharma: "None whatsoever"... "they are like shadows following the forms that inhere in no reality of themselves." Emperor: "What is the supreme meaning of the sacred truth?" Bodhidharma: "Vast emptiness, nothing sacred." Emperor: "Then, who stands in front of me?" Bodhidharma: "No idea" (*not-self, no identity*) (Vos & Zuercher, 1964).

The anecdote refutes the notion of accumulating good karma for awakening (good or evil deeds are empty) and renders the uselessness of worship or pious devotion. Legend tells that he subsequently went to the North — surfing on a reed on the waves of the Yang-tse River — to spend nine years sitting in forbearance while facing a wall (*zuo chan*; *zazen*, J) to contemplate on the Buddha-mind at the Shao-lin monastery. This legend illustrates that channists examine their inner space rather than the outer world. Bodhidharma landed on fertile soil considering the fact that the Lankavatara Sutra was available in Chinese since 433, and in 514 Northern China 2,000,000 adepts in 30,000 monasteries were counted (Zuercher, 1984). He probably was not the sole originator of Chan but the symbol of a warm embracing of the Dharma by the indigenous Taoists. There was a special enchantment with Chan because of (1) the directness in the method that points at the mind-heart now, (2) the attainment of Buddhahood by mindful observing of one's inner nature, and (3) the experiential transmission outside the scriptures.

Bodhidharma also laid the foundation for testing a student's level of awakening as in the following: Tao-fu said: "Truth is beyond affirmation and negation, for this is the way it moves." Bodhidharma replied: "You have my skin." Tsung-chi said: "It is like Ananda's sight of the Buddhaland, seen once it is forever." Bodhidharma: "You have my flesh." Tao-yuh said: "The four elements of fire, water, fluidity, and solidity are empty and the modalities are no-things. Void is reality." Bodhidharma: "You have my bones." Finally, Hui-ko bowed and remained silent. Bodhidharma: "You have my marrow!"

Indian Mahayana did not include Chan, but Chan includes Mahayana and the Tao. Chinese originality kicked in since Hui-neng (Yeno, J; 638-713), the illiterate sixth patriarch, who took over the torch from the Indian subcontinent (where Vajrayana Tantra rose). A developmental line can be traced from the Buddha's Nikayas via Nagarjuna (emptiness of emptiness) and Vasubandhu (awareness of consciousness as dualistic representation) to Hui-neng, who by radically eschewing the written and spoken word eradicated religion, philosophy, and metaphysical speculation altogether in favor of the mind's eye's direct experience. A totally new method emerged. The symbolic value of being simple is to emphasize everybody's potential to see the "wondrous Tao by carrying water and chopping wood." As a firewood seller Hui-neng once by accident heard somebody reciting the Diamond Sutra "*let your consciousness flow freely without clinging to anything*" upon which he immediately awakened. Chan does not require scholarship only an inquisitive mind that through inner observation discovers the private inner space wherein dharmas are directly pointed at. Such lifts the subject-object duality (symbolized as seeing the Tao, depicted in the *taichi* figure of YinYang) and is by definition non-conceptual or "speechless."

It is said that the Buddha kept completely silent when asked to deliver a talk in a gathering and passed on a golden flower that he held in his hand, saying: "I possess the *True Dharma Eye*, the Marvelous Mind of Nirvana, the True Form of the Formless, the Subtle Dharma Gate that *does not rest on words or letters* but is a special transmission *outside of the scriptures*. This I entrust to Mahakasyapa" (Dumoulin, 1988, p. 9, italics added). The Buddha's first Chan patriarch smiled when the Buddha was quiet. It was the wedge of the Tao of silence and Mahayana that brought forth Chan, with its matter-of-fact mentality free from dogma and creed. From the first encounters on, Taoists saw many commonalities endorsed by the translation of the Buddhist concepts into Taoist terms. Because of this kinship, its practicality and clarity, Chan could survive in China until today.

The Chanists' proclivity was to live the Taoist Arcadian poverty in reclusive contemplation, far from the city and infused with the eccentric image of a master as a "crazy" drunk who transmits a message beyond words. This craze can still be tasted in many iconoclastic-anarchistic Chan expressions like "the Buddha is a piece of manure," "kill the Buddha," and "clean your ass with *sutras*." Chan also possesses a Confucian outlook as in the saying, "One day without work is one day without food." Chan is Chinese by its realism, content, form, tactics, and transmission based on a love for irony, humor, and paradox (Chan, 1963).

Chan Reform: The Platform Sutra of Hui-neng

Everything we know about Chan's reformer, Hui-neng, stems from the "Platform Sutra" (780) that is named after a specially constructed podium for an audience of 10,000 people. The authenticity of this classic is questionable as the earliest extant copy dates from the end of the 8th century, long after his death. Curiously it is the originally Chinese text with the status of a sutra, which suggests a newly taken course and a substitute for the Lankavatra. The Chan sutra is replete with Sanskrit terminology and a contradiction to its revered simplicity. It includes autobiographical notes, teachings on the foolishness of mere reciting, sudden awakening, and direct knowing. Not yet ordained as a monk, Hui-neng received the insignia of succession from the fifth patriarch after winning a contest (Wong, 1969). The favorite candidate "the rational" Shen-hsiu wrote on a wall: "The body is a bo-tree, the mind is like a mirror stand, time and again brush it clean, so dust will not take hold." This hymn that expresses concern about future dust was rebutted by "the intuitive" Hui-neng: "Original bodhi has no tree, the bright mirror has no stand, since everything is already empty, where can dust hold on to?" After this event Hui-neng remained in hiding for 16 years, waiting for the right time to step forward.

When he reappeared, one of the issues he took up was the controversy between gradual versus sudden awakening, defended by Chan's Northern and Southern schools. Hui-neng belonged to the latter camp like his student Shen-hui (670-762), who probably fabricated the sutra and Chan's authoritative patriarchy. By promoting Hui-neng as the 6th patriarch he could secure the 7th position for himself and have his account as the standard history of the "subitists" triumph over the "gradualists." The Northern position, symbolizing sitting-only, was caricatured as the practitioners of tranquility by dhyana absorption. The Southern position, a Taoist-quietist stance, promulgates that since Buddhanature is an intrinsic quality (like fertility) awakening needs no practice just an opening of the mind's eye that directly sees and knows (jnana). Its "Mind-only" allegiance is illustrated in an anecdote of two venerables: "Does the flag move or the wind?" Overhearing this Hui-neng said: "neither the flag nor the wind, but the mind moves." This is called STATRA that occurs *suddenly* merely by pointing the finger to the moon (directly seeing the dharmas within). However this does not mean that existential hassles and suffering will also disappear at once. An arduous study of the sutras, implying a comprehending *gradually*, is necessary as well to acquire the art of living in harmony with nature the Chan way that disparages mind in favor of "no-mind."

Chan's Golden Age

Ferguson (2000) counted 167 classical masters and discerns three historical periods: (1) the legendary period (480-755) with heroic pioneers like Bodhidharma and Hui-neng; (2) the classical period (755-950) with giant exponents like Ma-tsu (died 788), Huang-po (d. 850), Lin-chi (d. 867), and (3) the literary period (950-1260) that includes the *koan* master Wu-men. To expedite awakening post Hui-neng, Chan uses peculiar, witty, mad devices to shock, including: shouting, slapping, striking, interjecting, tearing a sutra, pinching noses, urinating in the temple, vomiting, and even burning a Buddha statue. Nowadays one still can see devices for such activities displayed and used in a Zen session (e.g. a staff, brush of long hair, mirror, rosary, cup, pitcher, flag, moon, sickle, plough, ball, bell, drum, cat, dog, duck, earthworm, bow and arrow). These didactics beyond rationality are expressions of a wordless transmission and an iconoclastic anarchy. For instance, the mirror and tile: Ma-tsu (Baso) was practicing dhyana. Asked what he hopes to attain from sitting by his master, he answered: "Buddhahood." The master picked up a tile and rubbed it; Ma-tsu asked why he is doing that. The master: "I am polishing the tile into a mirror." Ma-tsu: "How can polishing make a mirror out of a tile?" The master: "How can sitting make you a Buddha? In another case Lin-chi

(Rinzai) tells his student about a meeting with Huang-po (Obaku). "What is the basic idea of the Dharma?" Before he could finish the question Huang-po hit him. This was repeated three times. When a monk explained that Huang-po had been kind and earnest, Lin-chi suddenly awakened and exclaimed: "There is not much in the Dharma after all!"

Lin-chi is known for a powerful school (founded in the 9th c), which is one of the five schools descending from Hui-neng. Lin-chi's famous admonition: "kill the Buddhas, kill the patriarchs, kill the arhats," might have helped to survive the political climate of this time of the Tang persecution (843-845) during which time some 200,000 of the clergy were forced into public labor, 5,000 monasteries were destroyed, and 40,000 objects vanquished (Chen, 1964). Lin-chi applied the whole gamut of "lightning" techniques to hit students in a clear blue sky, especially with paradoxes. His teaching was influential and vital such that it still remains very much alive (Briggs, 1961; Chan, 1963; Chen, 1964; Hoover, 1980; Faure, 1993; Kraft, 1988; Nan, 1995; Cleary, 2001; Wu, 2003; Kwee & Taams, 2002).

From Chan to Zen

The sudden awakening proposition probably coming via the Silk Route had already been put forward by Tao-sheng (355-434), who rejected the idea of a promised rebirth in Buddha's pure land paradise. Instead he promulgated the ineffable experience of awakening; only the immediate awakening counts, the rest is fluff. The thesis is that also non-Buddhists can attain Buddhahood. Such mentality moved away from theism, the tenet of karmic deeds, and a better reincarnation or a seat in heaven. This is to the detriment of the bodhisattva ideal but in favor of a swift personal awakening.

An expediting device is the *kung-an* (*koan*), originally meaning a legal document decisive for determining truth or falsehood beyond a private opinion. Typically, the koan is a little story beyond logic containing a poignant question and a baffling, enigmatic answer that elicits a sudden illumination. It might take the format of a Q & A between master and student (*wen-ta*; *mondo*, J) with a punch line (*hua-tou*) going beyond logic (e.g. "The wise seek not the Buddha, or the Buddha is dried dung," a statement used to dis-identify, not disgrace). Quintessential is the paradox to stop self-talk, foster intuitive wisdom, and transform rational thinking by a quantum leap into the silence of "no-mind" (*wu-shin*; *mushin*, J) — another word for Yogacara's nonduality, Nagarjuna's emptiness, or the Buddha's not-self — a key to attain *wu* (or STATRA). Through "sitting in the mind," the koan is to be dissolved. The first imperative barrier for the novice is the koan Wu or Mu, the mother of all koans. A monk asked Chao-chou (Joshu): "Does a dog have Buddhanature or not?" Chao-chou said: "Wu." If this koan is understood a gate is passed through. There is a sound that resembles a dog's barking but obviously that is not what is meant. If startled by the bark, part of the message comes through because when in shock, self-talk is absent. For the insider the simple sounding riddle contains a paradox (literally: beyond thinking). If the student would say "yes" he would be relying on text (sentient beings have Buddhanature) not on insight. If the answer is "no" he would deny the sutras. To break through this perplexing captivity it is necessary to break down thought and to come up with a non-conceptual response. Chao-chou's response "Wu" is the question's mirror reflection, which results in a move from a binary yes-no limit of the provisional to an ultimate post-perceptual and preconceptual awareness that ousts the usual subject-object dualism. Such understanding cannot be reached within rational confines and needs an intuitive approach of the mind's eye that views the question itself as just another dharma passing by in the space of mind. It is said that there are 1,700 koans and about 600 in use. The Pi-yen lu (Hekiganroku, J, the Blue Cliff Records, 1125) with 100 koans, and the Wu-men kuan (Mumonkan, J, the Gateless Gate, 1228) with 48 koans, are the most well known.

In the literary period the kung-an became the centerpiece of Chan's training. The indubitable Tao can only be found in contentment (*ware tada taruo siru*, J) through artistry and lightheartedness, jest, humor. A classic adage is "If there is no laughter, there is no Zen." Kensho (C, *jien-hsing*; an initial awakening to be deepened) and satori (to know one's Buddhanature) are recognized by the simultaneous utterance of "aha" (cognitive form, reason) + "haha" (conceptual emptiness, emotion). This awakening may happen at any moment, even when cleaning the toilet. It is not essential to sit like a mummy to achieve samadhic absorption. In fact since Lin-chi, Chan advocates meditation in a form of action known as wuwei (going with the flow of "herenow," an effortless effort that leaves nothing undone). However, sitting remains relevant as a start in basic introspection training. It is like learning to focus a telescope on the big dipper lying on one's back while tossing on the wild seas. The sitting or gradual awakening discipline was propagated by a 9th century contemporary and rival of the Lin-chi school called the Tsao Tung (Soto, J) school. Its founders, Tung-shan (Tozan, J) and Tsao-shan (Sozan, J), proposed five stages of awakening: (1) the ultimate (*li*) hidden in the provisional (*shih*) (emptiness hidden in the dharmas), (2) the provisional pointing at the ultimate (the dharmas contain traces of emptiness), (3) the ultimate entering consciously in the provisional (mindfulness unfolds the ultimacy of "herenows"), (4) the two arriving in harmony (a nondual lifting of the seer and the seen), and (5) reaching the heart of the harmony (the Taoist pervasive harmony with the "wherewithal"). The awakening itself is compared to waking from sleep.

Ironically during its decline, Chan was superseded by the worship of Amitabha (a cosmic Buddha of the Western Paradise), with whose practices of prayer it became amalgamated. Yet, while its unique artistry faded into obscurity, Chan's spirit had a rebirth in Japan as Zen.

The Opening to Zen

Although Chan had been imported into Japan in the 7th century, it was Eisai (1141-1215) who successfully introduced Zen in 1191. Having received a Lin-chi transmission seal, he is credited as the founder of Zen in Japan. He was also Dogen's teacher who later founded the Soto school. Studying with Eisai, Dogen (1200-1253) was puzzled by the question: "If Buddhanature is already possessed, why do Buddhas seek bodhi?" He went to China where he met Tien-tung Jung-ching, a Tsao Tung master, who facilitated Dogen's satori when hearing him scolding another student for sleeping: "The practice of Chan sitting is the dropping away of body and mind! What do you think that dozing will accomplish?" Dogen suddenly had a breakthrough and understood that zazen is not just sitting until a notional emptiness enters, but a direct opening of the mind's eye to its Buddhanature. On the moment of simply watching dharmas, all thinking is abandoned. The following dialogue ensued, Ju-ching: "Why do you light a stick (of insence)?" Dogen: "I have experienced the dropping off of body and mind." Ju-ching: "Body and mind have indeed dropped!" Dogen: "Don't give me your sanction so readily. Ju-ching: "I am not." Dogen: "Show me that you are not." Ju-chin (demonstrating): "This is body and mind dropped." Dogen bowed in gratitude; Ju-ching added: "That is dropping dropped" (Fischer-Schreiber et al., 1989).

At the age of 28 Dogen returned to Japan as Ju-ching's successor and stated that he came back empty-handed: "I have realized only that the eyes are horizontal and the nose is vertical." From this empty clarity came his teaching of silent illumination by *shikantaza* (nothing but sitting) that seems to be a reinvention of Bodhidharma's wall gazing. It is characterized by the hallmark of jnana and choiceless awareness wherein means-ends are fused in nonduality. If this is understood, the act of sitting itself is the actualization of Buddhanature (meaning impermanence to Dogen). One does not crave for satori but keeps faith that awakening will come through sitting itself, during which one does not think of good, bad, right, or wrong. Besides of staying non-judgmentally, he advised to sit in a quiet room and live a moderate life, free from relational bondage. Based on his Chan education Dogen *Zenji* (Zen master) could create a Soto Zen that is a unique blending that fuses koan study and jnana sitting. He wrote *Shobo Genzo* (Treasury of the True Dharma *Eye*) (italics added) from which we infer that he refers to the silent illumination of the mind's eye.

While Confucianism overshadowed a deteriorating Chan and the interchange with China diminished in the 14th century, Zen followed a bright course in Japan. Endorsed by the patronage of the *shogun* rulers, up until the second world war, Zen's impact gradually infused Japanese culture. As the *samurai* embraced Zen's concentration and martial techniques to improve their *bushido* (combat arts and readiness to die) temples like the prestigeous Daitoku-ji in Kyoto arose, radiating their close ties. Among the most influential Zennists was the eccentric *Ikkyu* (1394-1481) who gave unconventional praise as a poet, painter, and calligrapher to such unconventional topics as wine and sex. Although he tore his Zen master's diploma and lived like a Taoist madman, he was ultimately appointed by the imperial house to become the abbot of Daitoku-ji.

Another noteworthy figure was Bankei (1622-1693), a precocious child with a fear of death (Haskel, 1984). Seeking for the meaning of "bright virtue" he practiced zazen in such a fierce way that he contracted tbc and faced death. When spitting a gob of blood against the wall, he suddenly awakened. In an instant he penetrated the insight that all things are perfectly resolved in the Unborn Buddhamind. He recovered and from his 25th year spread Zen's iconoclastic views. In contrast to propping up classical texts on dead sheets of paper, he insisted on the relevance of daily spontaneity. He expounded a "Zen of the Unborn" by a direct teaching through spoken language. Hence he did not leave any writings. Koans are worn tools and zazen is nothing more than the Unborn sitting peacefully. Buddhanature is not something to achieve by hardship for it is already perfectly "there right where you are." It is impossible to become something that one already is. To contact the Unborn, the advice is to get rid of deluding habits of thinking-feeling-doing and negative emotions through dialogue, a non-judgmental attitude, and pure sensing (thoughtless smelling the cherry blossom or listening to the sounds of running water). By applying verbal means to change emotions, Bankei began to approximate a modern-day psychotherapist.

Zen would not be Zen without Hakuin (1689-1768), a maverick who revived Zen, denounced Bankei as lazy, and endorsed wuwei that he called "Zen Amidst Action" through effortless effort (Waddell, 2001). Hakuin's Zen was also centered in dissolving koans. Like his 12th century idol Ta-hui (Daie, J), he advocated that the true Zen adept keeps on training (also post satori) and focusing. It is as if seeking for the broken necklace's pearls on the ground in a rushing crowd, one remembers to concentrate. Hakuin invented a 500 koan curriculum, which includes the famous "what is the sound of one hand clapping?" His practice was to chew, swallow, and spit koans, thus infusing Great Doubt in one's 360 bones and 84,000 pores. Such doubt evokes Great Death, Awakening, Rebirth, and Joy. Among his students were many samurai whom he, in the best Buddhist tradition, assigned to contemplate on death. In his dead-or-alive "Bushido Zen" Hakuin must have been an unrelenting task master. At least 70 students died during torturous training. Famous is his zazen song of praise ending with: "Nirvana is before your eyes; this very place, the Lotus Land, this very body, the Buddha."

The Japanese guardians succeeded in having Chan/Zen survive and in bringing it to the West (Miura & Fuller Sasaki, 1965; see Koshikawa & Ishii, Ch. 10, and Koshikawa, Kuboki & Ishii, Ch. 11). For more on NBP's Zen, log on to: http://www.inst.at/trans/16Nr/09_2/kwee_taams16.htm.

III

Conjoining Buddhist and Western Traditions

Buddhist theory and practice has slowly but expansively entered the dialogues of scientific psychology and clinical practice. "Buddhology," the scientific study of the Dharma, is a term coined in the 1840s by E. Burnouf who translated *the Lotus Sutra* in French. This scripture, also the first available in English, has religious overtones. It is about Buddhas' cosmic transcendent character and includes a prayer for compassion. In 1893 western sympathy gained momentum when Soyen Shaku from Japan gave a talk on Zen and Dharmapala from Sri Lanka on Theravada at the World Parliament of Religions in Chicago.

The first encounter with psychology was through Dharmapala (like J. Krishnamurti an associate of the theosophist Madame Blavatsky) who gave a lecture at Harvard in 1904 by invitation of William James. Content with the performance, James told the audience that Dharmapala is better equipped to lecture on psychology than he is and spoke the historical words: "This is the psychology everybody will be studying twenty-five years from now" (DeLoach, 2000, p. 4). James (1902) not only predicted that the Dharma would be influential in the future; he agreed with the principle of karma — what goes around comes around — and borrowed the stream of consciousness metaphor. James' pure sensory experience, wherein subject and object are undivided, bears an undeniable kinship with Yogacara's nonduality. His radical empirical psychology can be denoted as the "Experience-only" school parallelling the Buddhist "Emptiness-only" and "Mind-only" schools. Unfortunately, in those days psychology was in its infancy.

In that Zeitgeist the Dharma was primarily understood in the West as a religion. Systematic study was advanced in England by T.W. Rhys Davids' *Pali Text Society* (1881) and C. Humphreys' *Buddhist Society* (1924). The latter was heavily influenced by D.T. Suzuki (1870-1966), once a Waseda student and one of Soyen's three pupils gone westward. Suzuki (1963) conveyed Zen not as a religion, philosophy, mysticism, or psychology but as "absolute realism." He left 30 books in English plus numerous articles. His work raised the interest of Jung and Fromm and his pioneering efforts influenced many of his contemporaries, including Dumoulin, Conze, and Watts. The latter explicitly connected applied psychology and the Dharma in his 1961 book *Psychotherapy: East and West*. This appeared in conjunction with the rise of Humanistic Psychology in the late 1950s, a third force after behaviorism and psychoanalysis, wherein Buddhist tenets were adopted and which was even more so in Transpersonal Psychology. These traditions have earned respectable credit and included proponents like Maslow, Rogers, Boss and more recently Ram Dass, Walsh, and Wilber.

Particularly, the inclusion of a chapter on Eastern Psychology in Hall and Lindzey's 3rd edition of *Theories of Personality* (1978) almost 30 years ago impresses as a turning point. Generally regarded as a transcendental teaching, the Dharma was subsumed as a philosophical and experiential psychological approach. To have a seat as a newcomer in psychology was a significant step, but in recent decades there have been enormous strides in the conjoining of Buddhist and western psychologies. In what follows we touch on a number of the most important developments, relevant for NBP.

The Neurological Correlates of Meditation

The first brain research reports stem from the 1950s and were conducted on Zen by among others Kasamatsu, Hirai, and Akishige (Murphy & Donovan, 1999). They studied the psychophysiological correlates of zazen through EEG, EMG, GSR, and other devices. The results suggested that the effects of zazen were not very much better than those of relaxation, rest, or a placebo effect (Holmes, 1985). Despite this outcome, the next 50 years accrued many more studies summarized by Austin (1998), a neurologist who reviewed the content of 113 pages of references in his encyclopedic *Zen and the Brain*.

Trained at Daitoku-ji, Austin's question boils down to: is there neuropsychological evidence for the sudden flash of kensho that cuts off I-me-mine/self? How do the molecules of a 10,000 years civilized cro-magnon-era three pound lump of tissue with at least one billion neurons under the skull allow us to achieve Buddhanature? He submits that nirvana is a brain condition characterized by extensively reorganized associative nerve cells circuits spread over subcortical and cortical levels. For the self to dissolve, substantial changes and enduring shifts in subcortical systems are suggested with a pivotal role of thalamo-cortical interactions in the front and the back of the brain. The thalamic reticular nucleus is a thin shield of neurotransmitters (GABA-cells) supposedly selecting information transmitted to the cortex and capable of blocking its excitation. To delete fear, its associated pathways have to be interrupted. This involves deeper structures like the amygdala, limbic, and brainstem circuitries. Other circuits also require major interruption, especially those regulating orientation in space and differentiating the self and the world (parietal lobe) and circuits engaging orientation in time and generating awareness of self (frontal and temporal lobe). The way neuroscience tries to illuminate satori resembles a climatologist's weather forecast. During Zen one is probably quieting the firing of nerve cells in the medulla and the region above it. "Probably" is emphasized for there is nothing so difficult to predict as "inner weather." This reflects the state of the art: we still know little about the neuropsychology of Zen.

Although a half century of research has not led to final answers on the *finesses* of how our brain works in a (sixth sense) state of conscious awareness, neuropsychological studies do suggest that most brain functions involve variable circuitries arising and subsiding, and dispersed across the whole brain. Probably connected to the sixth sense is Damasio's (2000) "feeling of feelings" that parallels our awareness of awareness. Inspired by Spinoza's BodyMind monism, he refers to "feeling" as the brain's perceiving act, and to "feelings" as the bodily perceived sense data, somatic markers that help to decide and guide actions (via direct and swift sensory-thalamic-amygdala links that bypass the cortex). Subliminal automatic emotional and bodily processes evaluate incoming stimuli even before cognitions take a hold. Having this body-based sense (affect/gut-feeling/intuition) one is driven to action by earlier formed neuronal patterns of mental configurations. Somatic markers are formed by a continuing representation of the body in the brain via brainmaps. Mapping takes place through discrete pulses lasting a fraction of a second that send body information to the brain. We depict these like photographic snapshots glued in a sequence constructing an illusion of continuity that resembles a film. Consciousness of thinking-feeling thus may be a synchronous process of swift flickering neurons. In these terms, a self comes about — is "born" or "reborn" — on a nonverbal level. Damasio's *proto self*, is a moment to moment neuronal pattern that automatically produces a map one is not aware of. If a certain object is perceived, a map of the event becomes fused with the automatically made body map. Out of the fusion of the two maps comes forth a second order map; a transformation takes place from an "unborn" *proto self* to a *core self*. A self is born one might say when a new neuronal and mental pattern is (re)cognized as for instance "my" fear. Subsequently an *autobiographical self* enters into the process that retrieves and stores kindred experiences involving imagery/self-talk on I-me-mine/self.

In line with Damasio's hypothetically pointing at the primacy of body and brain over mind, is the classical experiment conducted by Libet (2004) in 1983, who found through EEG measurement that a subject's moving a hand (action) is preceded (100 ms) by the consciousness of intention to move the hand, which on its turn is preceded (350 ms) by a brain wave. The latter parameter is known as the brain's Readiness Potential that prepares the body for the actual hand moving. This finding runs counter to what one would expect and suggests that we have no free will. However, we have a free "won't" — a veto — as we are well able to refrain from acting in a fraction of a second. It seems that the human predicament lies beyond free will and boils down to the neurogenetic drives for greed/attraction/grasping (e.g. overconsumption) and hatred/aversion/clinging (e.g. warfare). Unwholesome karma, negative intentional activities, leads to our detriment unless we do abstain from it, which requires training in mindfulness, discipline, virtue, and wisdom, in short the Eight Fold Path. The impact of Libet's results for the Dharma is profound and worth a separate article.

More recently, a controlled EEG study (Davidson et al., 2003) seems to support the hunch that the left prefrontal cortex is activated significantly as a result of "mindfulness." An MRI study (Lazar et al., 2005) also suggests insight meditation practice may produce long lasting changes in brain activity and changes in the brain's physical structure. In 20 experienced meditators, brain regions associated with focused attention to internal experiences, interoception, and sensory processing were thicker than in matched controls. Differences in prefrontal cortical thickness were most pronounced in older participants, suggesting that meditation is capable of offsetting age-related cortical thinning. The precise implication of Buddhist meditation on brain activity still remains a research question.

It is tempting to think that the results of meditation may be a substantial change in brain functioning, one that would generate a life-long tendency to care for relationships. Interestingly, Tibetan monks who permeated themselves with loving kindness and compassion for more then 10,000 hours, altered the structure and functioning of their brain (Lutz et al., 2004). They showed high amplitude gamma wave synchrony, high frequency oscillations (40Hz), indicating that the brain integrates ongoing processes by transient varieties of widely distributed parallel processes of neuronal networks into highly ordered cognitive-affective functions (perception, attention, learning, memory). This induces synaptic changes across the whole brain and suggests neuroplasticity (like sports sculpting muscles) in the form of lasting neural repatterning in the temporal area caused by loving-kindness/compassion.

The Therapeutic Fusion

The first encounters between the Dharma and psychotherapy were with the psychodynamicists (see DelMonte, Ch. 26). However, genotypical differences outweigh phenotypical similarities (wodka and water look the same until you taste them). The main motivating factors in psychoanalytic theory, namely libido and aggression, starkly resemble the Dharma's greed and hate that we consider are neurogenetic drives procreating interdependent origination and processes of arisings and subsidings in non-abiding cycles. However, the underlying paradigms seem irreconcilable. For psychoanalysts after the cure of neurosis, there remains the normal run of the mill misery (*dukkha*) for which there is no redemption. While the Dharma teaches to uncling from I-me-mine/self, the psychoanalytic emphasis is to develop a healthy ego, which is diametrically opposed to non-self. Jung associated not-self with a regression to earlier phases of ego development as well. Based on Christian mysticism and alchemical symbolism his system of archetypes is centered on an abiding self that is fully individualized. From the above it is obvious that a psychodynamic paradigm does not fit Buddhist views. There is an exception, in as far psychodynamic concepts are testable and thus came to belong to the field of experimental psychology there is some shared common ground. The defensive reactions that repress inner conflicts but truncate awareness and distort perception are a case in point (Shevrin & Dickman, 1980). We are referring to the self-beguiling tactics of repression (denial, undoing, sublimation, rationalization, projection, and identification) blurring the perceptual-cognitive process (see Van Waning, Ch. 8; Safran, 2004; Young-Eisendrath & Muramoto, 2002).

More successful is the Theravada inspired Mindfulness-Based Stress Reduction, pioneered by Kabat-Zinn in 1979, who in the beginning never mentioned its Buddhist origin so as not to scare people away. We object to the use of Buddhist meditation techniques without instructing its basic tenets. Kabat-Zinn's MBSR, has been researched to such an extent that the American Psychological Association's predicate "probably efficacious" applies. Mindfulness-based practices are presently on the way to becoming an accepted intervention, a valuable component or adjunct in the treatment of chronic pain, anxiety disorders, binge eating, fibromyalgia, psoriasis, cancer, coronary artery disease, depression, obesity, prisoners, and non-clinical stress (Baer, 2003, Grossman et al., 2004). There is also the more recent combination of Buddhist practices in combination with cognitive therapy Mindfulness-Based Cognitive Therapy is effective in reducing relapse in ex-patients afflicted by three or more previous depressive periods (Teasdale, 2000; Segal et al., 2002; Ma & Teasdale, 2004). These findings have contributed significantly to the acceptance of mindfulness practices amongst cognitive-behavior therapists (see Kristeller & Jones, Ch. 4; Tirch & Amodio, Ch. 5; De Vibe, Ch. 12; Giommi, Ch. 13; Kawano & Suzuki, Ch. 23; and Williams & Duggan, Ch. 24). Mindfulness is also used in Linehan's, *Dialectic Behavior Therapy*, and Hayes', *Acceptance and Commitment Therapy* (see Sugiura, Ch. 16).

While these ventures are notable, our view on Buddhist meditation as an intervention for relatively severe mental disorders is that it cannot replace evidence-based psychotherapy and medication. At best they can be: (1) a pretherapy to enhance consciousness of what needs to be changed, (2) an adjunct or component of clinical treatment, and (3) a relapse prevention and prophylaxis. A striking example is that in psoriasis, the addition of mindfulness to the usual treatment of ultraviolet light, produced a quicker recovery by a factor four (Kabat-Zinn, 2003).

The Buddha and Positive Psychology

In the 1980s we started to enhance positive emotions in our treatments of anxiety and depressive disorders in an inpatient setting. Particularly, we began to use Zen's laughing meditation in our clinical practice. The salubrious effects of laughter, joy and happiness were reported in Kwee (1990), "Up until now, psychological interventions and psychotherapy were mainly directed at eliminating negative conditions rather than promoting positive experiences, let alone spirituality. If psychology wishes to prevent and treat disease effectively, it will be necessary to develop new methods and instruments." (pp. 14-15). In effect, by moving away from the traditional therapeutic emphasis on repairing damage to enhancing positive emotional experience, this work prefigured the later movement now recognized as positive psychology (Kwee & Taams, 2006).

Christening "positive psychology" in 1998, Seligman and his colleagues attempted to steer psychology toward exploring the elements of a good and fulfilling life (Seligman & Csikszentmihalyi, 2000). Such includes the pursuit of a talent, lasting friendship, community spirit, and qualities like kindness, compassion, humor, and flow. There is a striking congruence between the optimal experience of Csikszentmihalyi's (1999) flow and Zen's wuwei of everyday living. Especially, the description of flow as an experience of being carried away by a current and everything moving smoothly without effort in an "extended now," is not discernably different from the jnana art and skill of wuwei (effortless effort): the absorption in choiceless awareness when meeting daily life challenges. To go with the flow is to shift into a natural, spontaneous, and positive state of experiencing, a nondual fusion of action-and-awareness, focused attention, rapture, playfulness, self-forgetfulness, non-concern for outcome, time sense distortion, wonderment, ecstasy, and effortless performance (see Quintana, Ch. 18, Henry, Ch. 19).

As "mindfulness-in-action," flow is the bridge that connects NBP and positive psychology. Awareness not only advances high performances like managerial functioning (see Tophoff, Ch. 17), it is Zen's way *par excellence* to travel to the zone of bliss in ordinary life. The empirical approach to flow provides wuwei a substantial scientific basis, and represents a western confirmation of practices mulled over for centuries by Buddhist advocates.

The Flower Adornment of Social Construction

There is one school among more than eight denominations in China called Huayen or Flower Garland, founded in the 6th century (Kegon, J), that excells because of its impact and strong allegiance with the social constructionist approach (Gergen & Gergen, 2004). Social constructionism has a prominent role in NBP due to our paradigm shifting redefinition of dharmas as social constructs (i.e. in the practice of awareness of awareness or consciousness of dharmas as social constructs). Huayen and social constructionism share a common ground in their metaperspective that grants primacy to the Interpersonal rather than to the BodyMind. Interrelations and interactions through speech and language form the focus of attention. Placing relationships first, individual psyches constituting the binary "you-me" collapse. Crumbling into emptiness, they simultaneously procreate Interbeing. The relational being or social self that thus comes into existence, although abstract and not tangible, is neither an airy concept, nor is it something metaphysical but is "really" there as long as we, the participants, keep on feeding it. As you read this there is something between you and us going on what might be called consensus or disagreement, which defines our relationship rather than assess individuals, you the reader or us the writers.

The priority given to the relational is depicted in Huayen by the metaphor of "Indra's Jewel Net" that has at each crossing a diamond reflecting any change occuring in all other diamonds while at the same time self-mirroring those changes, thus interpenetrating each other incessantly. Change in this matrix can only take place in IDOAS. Not only does this matrix structure apply in the social realm, but we see its structure on the psychological and biological levels as well. The originator of this metaphor was Fatsang (643-712) who in line of Huayen was inspired by the Avatamsaka Sutra (Flower Ornament, a compilation of 39 books made in the 1st-4th c India). Its last book narrates a pilgrim's journey, a tale about 53 teachers of various backgrounds he met on the road, mostly ordinary people like a prostitute from whom he learned bits of wisdom until he arrived at a jewel tower where he learned equanimity/contentment, loving-kindness/friendliness, compassion/forgiveness, and shared-joy/generosity. Before he entered the room of wisdom — that turned out to be an empty space — he saw what the Buddha allegedly had seen when he awakened, which comes down to Fatsang's epiphany. The emphasis is on the ubiquitous interconnectedness in the world of phenomena, empty waves returning to the sea of emptiness, and interpersonal harmony.

The glue to create harmony is appreciative dialogue implying an inquiry into each other's experience and selves. "Self" is in the end a story that is only "real" if agreed upon together. Stories are by definition subjective and momentary. If they are only contextually real, it questions other stories believed to be real like those about "objective" reality and timeless "truths" as endorsed in positivism, rationalism, and the knowledge they produce. A social constructionist and Huayen metavision co-constructs reality in a joint venture resulting in the paradigm shift that there is no self, but a relational self. Even "private worlds," memories, and dreams cannot be solitary or solipsistic as they ensue from a history of Interbeing and through languaging. The power of words cannot be underestimated in fostering harmonious relations; "right speech" appreciating the other is imminent. In the practice of social meditation as well as in social construction we move beyond the self-contained individual and understand that all thinking-feeling-behaving have a relational or narrative meaning. This is called a postmodern view.

The social constructionist's meta-epistemology is that the site of reality construction is located between individuals, implying contextuality, polyvocality and relativity. Reality resides in social agreement. Nobody is able to declare reality and meaning all alone. In this sense individuals are empty of pure private meaning. Thus, there is no self but a social self, a profound view that coincides with the Buddhist understanding of non-self. NBP embraces the social constructionist view as a postmodern version of the Huayen message. Moreover, NBP concurs with the tenets of Appreciative Inquiry (innovated by D. Cooperrider) embedded in Gergen's social constructionism, a method congruent with the Avatamsaka idea that we are the sculptors of our own destinies. Instead of painting the glass half empty, we paint it half full and apply a positive language to transform sufferings in social contexts (organizations and companies). It is not the problem that we try to solve, unwillingly aggravating it by negative languaging, but we act toward aggrandizing the positive by intentionally zeroing in to the wholesome and participants' well-functioning. This is a paradigm shifting approach to modify karma in the social realm.

The emphasis on social action is in line with the Buddhist tenet to be foremost a practice. A compassionate attitude leading to empathically helping others is especially fostered. This quality is symbolized by the celestial bodhisattva Avalokiteshvara (*Kuan Yin*, C; *Kanzeon*, J), typically depicted with many helping arms and hands. It is said the the Dalai Lamas (a Gelukpa institution installed in the early 15th c) are the reincarnated manifestations of enlightened compassion. In Zen the quality of compassion is discerned in Yin compassion that helps to feed (like giving away fish) and Yang compassion that helps to teach people help themselves (like teaching how to fish). NBP highlights the importance of a middle way, neither egotism nor altruism but a learning to help oneself in order to be better able to help others. Such an attitude is based on the initiation of giving, the celebration of life, and solidarity with humankind.

The emphasis on Interbeing enables Buddhist practitioners to resist the criticism that meditation is ultimately narcissistic and self-serving. For many, the sublime state achieved through meditation is an ultimate conjoining of the individual with an erasure of all distinctions between self and other. The achievement of this state brings forth behavior that exemplifies a self-less condition. It is this emphasis on Interbeing and the well-being of all that makes NBP concur with social constructionist theory and practice. For social constructionists all the daily realities, including the self, owe their existence to relationship. Relationship serves as a fundamental origin of all that human beings take to be valuable and worthy. For both NBP and constructionists, then, it is care of relationship that serves as a first priority (see Gergen & Hosking, Ch. 20).

From Religion to the New Buddhist Psychology

An epistemology, that views reality not restricted behind the eyeballs (within the body or the mind alone) but as a social experience as well, is functional in our endeavour to design a transcultural NBP. Considering that reality is made by social-cultural groups and living in a global village wherein the language of psychology rather than of religion is appreciated in the community we write for, we have high hopes that the construction of human beings as BASIC-I.D.s or BioPsychoSocial systems, with an equal emphasis on Interbeing, fills in a missing link in bridging Buddhist and western psychology in designing NBP. Table 2 summarizes the bridging of Mahayana into NBP. This depicts the prominent links between the subdisciplines of western psychology and the sutras, wherein social construction takes a profound and ubiquitous place from dharmas to binaries and other constructs (that we ultimately consider to be pervasively empty).

Table 2

Humans as BioPsychoSocial Beings
in a NBP Beyond Theravada & Mahayana©

Human Being	Applied Specialty	Change agent/target	Buddhist Tradition	Champion Authors	Sutras/ scriptures
Body	Neuro Ψ 3rd person dharmas	Brain/ Genetic Drives	MTN- only Madhya- maka	Nagarjuna Perfection of Wisdom 2^{nd}c	Prajna- paramita 1^{st}c bce-4^{th}c
Mind	Clinical Ψ 1st person binaries	BASIC-I.D. modalities	Mind- only Yogacara	Vasubandhu B-nature 4^{th}c	Tathagata- garba/ B-womb 1^{st}c bce-4^{th}c
Speech	Social Ψ 2nd person constructs	Interbeing/ Relational Being	Huayen Universal Matrix	Fatsang Inter- penetration 7^{th}c	Avatamsaka/ Flower Garland 1st-3^{rd}c

- BASIC-I.D.: Behavior-Affect-Sensation-Imagery-Cognition-Interbeing-Drives
- dharmas: perceivables-imaginables-knowables-memorables & dreams/illusions (as social constructions)
- bce: before common era; c: century
- B-nature: Buddha-nature
- B-womb: Buddha-womb

Human beings are the only animal capable of thinking about themselves and to make a quantum leap to Buddhahood. The Buddhas have provided a teaching that enables to fathom the mind's eye and non-self, and to develop Buddhanature. According to Dogen: "To study the Dharma is to study the self, to study the self is to forget the self, to forget the self is to become one with existence." The latter corresponds with the root meaning of religion (from religare, reconnecting with the ultimate) and of yoga (from yoking, uniting with existence) that we envision as the wave of self returning to the ocean of the ultimate in existence: emptiness. The quote is also a reminder that all conceptual elaborations are a transitional effort. Those who do not view the Dharma foremost as a practice to liberate from emotional suffering but persist in regarding it as metaphysics are hooked to the opium of the intellectuals.

A Dharma that aims to improve karma as an individually tailored approach to purify affect and as a social application to promote interpersonal well-being can be defined as a psychology. Unfortunately, the term psychology was not known in the East. On the other hand, the term Buddh-*ism* that we have avoided here has no equivalent in the East. It is a container term that can mean anything and is anathema to scientific specificity. Using it would have garbled NBP. The same holds for the term enlightenment (instead of awakening) that — also stemming from 19th century's European rationalism — erroneously make people associate the down-to-earth Buddhahood with a weird hoovering in the sky. Such view was invited by Mahayana itself. For more than two millenia the Mahayana conception of upaya suggested a form of spiritual ignition by deifying celestial beings, an unfortunate development that led many to believe that the Dharma is a religion of devotion and worship. The vehicles that sustain an inflated cosmology and a heavenly pantheon are seductive and treacherous for the meek seeking for a god and finding emptiness instead. The use of religion to lure people into the Dharma was a great upaya "trick" that was once functional in reanimating an anemic Dharma. Its ramification is the present unfortunate situation to find the Dharma as a religion. Thus, in many circles it became a religious quest of worship, instead of a genuine psychology to scaffold contentment and social action.

If the Dharma is to be realized as psychological practice, a Theravada and Mahayana that rely on sky-god images and prostrating rituals function as mystifying opium. This is in line with the meaning of *yana* as vehicle, and with Mahayana's own view that its *raison d'être* is to be a provisional means not an end in itself. It seems however that the Dharma has become trapped if not hijacked in deifying practices by too many local cultures. Moving beyond Theravada and Mahayana, a call is made here for a transcultural Neoyana: an applied, evidence-based, and integrated psychology of the Buddha that is grounded in narratives and metaphors of social/clinical/neuropsychology. Such is the NBP that necessarily discards metaphysics or beliefs in god-like creatures and may serve as the third great vehicle and the fourth turning of the wheel in the glorious history of the BuddhaDharma.

Reference List

Aamri, T., & Umaoka, K. (2002). Effects of cognitive control and self-efficacy on depression and anxiety in female university students. *Journal of the Graduate School: Home Economics, Human Life Sciences*, 8, 29-39 (in Japanese)

Abe, M. (1985). *Zen and western thought*. Honolulu: University of Hawaii Press.

Abele, A., & Brehm, W. (1993). Mood effects of exercise versus sports games: Findings and implications for well-being and health. In S. Maes, H. Leventhal, & M. Johnston (Eds.) *International review of health psychology*, Vol. 2 (pp. 53-80). New York: Wiley.

Agras, W.S., Telch, C.F., Arnow, B., & Eldredge, K. (1997). One-year follow-up of cognitive-behavioral therapy for obese individuals with binge eating disorder. *Journal of Consulting & Clinical Psychology*, 65, 343-347.

Aitken, R., Zealley, A., & Rosenthal, S. (1969). Psychological and physiological measures of emotion in chronic asthmatic patients. *Journal of Psychosomatic Research*, 13, 289-297.

Akizuki, R. (1990). *Zen bukkyo toha nani ka* (What is Zen Buddhism?). Kyoto: Hozo kan.

Albee, G.W. (1982). Preventing psychopathology and promoting human potential *American Psychologist*, 37, 1043-1050.

Alexander, F. (1931). Buddhist training as an artificial catatonia. *Psychoanalytic Review*, 18, 129-145.

Anderson, H. (1997). Conversation, language, and possibilities: A postmodern approach to therapy. New York: Harper Collins.

Anderson, H., & Goolishian, H. (1992). The client is the expert: A not knowing approach to therapy. In S. McNamee & K. J. Gergen (Eds.), *Therapy as social construction* (pp. 25-39). London: Sage.

Ando, O. (2003). *Buddhism as psychotherapy: Psychological approach to Zen, meditation and Buddhism*. Tokyo: Hozokan.

Angus, L. and McLeod, J. (Eds.) (2004). The handbook of narrative and psychotherapy. London: Sage.

Anguttara Nikaya, Vols. I-V (1922-1938). (ed. by R. Morris & E. Hardy). London Pali Text Society.

Antonovsky, A. (1979). *Health, stress, and coping: New perspectives on mental and physical well-being*. San Francisco: Jossey-Bass.

Aquino, K., Douglas, S., & Martinko, M.J. (2004). Overt anger in response to victimization: Attributional style and organizational norms as moderators. *Journal of Occupational Health Psychology*, 9, 152-164.

Argyle, M. (1987). *The psychology of happiness*, London: Methuen.

Aristotle (1960). Rhetoric. In L. Cooper (Ed. & Trans.), *The rhetoric of Aristotle*. Englewood Cliffs, NJ: Prentice Hall.

Ariyapala P.G. (2000). *Buddhist Paritta chanting ritual*. Dehiwela: Buddhist Cultural Centre.

Arkowitz, H. (1997). *Integrative theories of therapy*. In P.L. Wachtel & S.B. Messer (Eds), *Theories of psychotherapy: Origins and evolution* (pp. 227-288). Washington, DC:

American Psychological Association.

Aronson, H.B. (1980). *Love and sympathy in Theravada Buddhism.* Delhi: Motilal Banarsidas.

Ashvaghosha, *The Saundarananda or Nanda the Fair.* (ed. & transl. E.H. Johnston; 1928/ 1975). Lahore: Oxford University Press.

Assagioli, R. (1965). *Psychosynthesis: A manual of principles and techniques.* New York: Hobbs.

Astin, A. (1997). Stress reduction through mindfulness meditation: Effect of psychosocial symptomatology, sense of control, and spiritual experiences. *Psychotherapy & Psychosomatic,* 66, 97-106.

Austin, J.H. (1998). *Zen and the brain: Toward an understanding of meditation and consciousness.* Cambridge, MA: MIT Press.

Baer, R. (2003) Mindfulness training as a Clinical Intervention: a Conceptual and empirical Review. *Clinical Psychology: Science & Practice,* 10, 125-143.

Baer, R.A., Smith, G.T., & Allen, K.B. (2004). Assessment of mindfulness by self-report: The Kentucky Inventory of Mindfulness Skills. *Assessment,* 3, 191-206.

Bahrke, M.S., & Morgan, W.P. (1978). Anxiety reduction following exercise and meditation. *Cognitive Therapy and Research,* 2, 323-333.

Balint, M. (1958). The three areas of the mind. *International Journal of Psychoanalysis,* 39, 328-340.

Bandura, A. (1986). *Social foundations of thought and action.* Englewood Cliffs, NJ: Prentice-Hall.

Bandura, A. (2001). Social cognitive theory: An agentive perspective. *Annual Review of Psychology,* 52, 1-26

Bankart, C.P. (2000a). *Building bridges: Applying Eastern wisdom in Western contexts.* Paper presented at the 108th Annual Convention of the American Psychological Association, August. Washington, DC.

Bankart, C.P. (2000b). Qigong in the West: Challenges, hazards, and opportunities. In W. Weidong, Y. Sasaki, & Y. Haruki (Eds.), *Bodywork in psychotherapy in the East.* Delft, NL: Eburon.

Bankart, C.P. (2001). *Releasing the demons: Teaching men to meditate.* Paper presented at the 109th Annual Convention of the American Psychological Association, August. San Francisco, CA.

Bankart, C.P. (2002). Mindfulness as a useful adjunct in therapeutic work with men. *SPSMM Bulletin,* 7, 5-7.

Bankart, C.P. (2003). A Western psychologist's inquiry into the nature of Right Effort. *Constructivism in the Human Sciences,* 8, 63-72.

Bankart, C.P., Dockett, K.H., & Dudley-Grant, G.R. (2003). On the path of the Buddha: A psychologist's guide to the history of Buddhism. In K.H. Dockett, G.R. Dudley Grant, & C.P. Bankart (Eds.), *Psychology and Buddhism: From individual to global community* (pp. 13-44). New York: Kluwer.

Bankart, C.P., Koshikawa, F., Nedate, K., & Haruki, Y. (1992). When East meets West: Contributions of eastern traditions to the future of psychotherapy. *Psychotherapy,* 29, 141-149.

Barber, J.P., & DeRubeis, R.J. (1989). On second thought: Where the action is in cognitive therapy for depression. *Cognitive Therapy and Research,* 13, 441-457.

Barendregt, H.P. (1996). Mysticism and beyond, Buddhist phenomenology Part II. *The Eastern Buddhist, New Series*, 29, 262-287. <www.cs.ru.nl/ henk/BP/bp2.html>

Barendregt, H.P. (1998). Buddhist phenomenology. In Dalla Chiara (Ed.), *Proceedings of the conference on topics and perspectives of contemporary logic and philosophy of science*. Bologna, Italy: CLUEB. < www.cs.kun.nl/~henk/BP/bp1.htlm >

Barendregt, H.P. (2005b). Reflection and its use: From Science to Meditation. In C.L. Harper Jr. (Ed.), *Spiritual Information* (ch. 69). Philadelphia: Templeton Foundation Press. <ftp://ftp.cs.kun.nl/pub/CompMath.Found/reflection.pdf>.

Barendregt, J.T. (1982). *De Zielenmarkt, over psychotherapie in alle ernst*. Amsterdam: Boom.

Bargh, J.A., & Ferguson, M.J. (2000). Beyond behaviorism: On the automaticity of higher mental processes. *Psychological Bulletin*, 126, 925-945.

Barnes-Holmes, D., Cochrane, A., Barnes-Holmes, Y., & Stewart, A. (2004). Offer it up and psychological acceptance: Empirical evidence for your grandmother's wisdom? *Irish Psychologist*, 31, 72-78.

Barret, F.J. & Fry, R.E. (2005). *Appreciative Inquiry, a positive approach to building cooperative capacity*. Chagrin Falls, OH: Taos Institute Publications.

Barton, R. (1999). Psychosocial rehabilitation services in community support systems: A review of outcomes and policy recommendations. *Psychiatric Services*, 50, 525-534.

Batchelor, S. (1990). *The faith to doubt*. Berkeley, CA: Parallax.

Batchelor, S. (1997). *Buddhism without beliefs*. New York: Riverhead Books.

Bates, P., & Staubinger, U. (2000). Wisdom. *American Psychologist*, 55, 122-136.

Bateson, G. (1972) *Steps to an ecology of mind*. New York: Ballantine Books

Bauhofer, U. (1983). *Das Programm der Transzendentalen Meditation in der Behandlung von Adipositas*. Seelisberg, Switzerland: Maharishi European Research University.

Beck, A.T., Epstein, N., & Harrison, R. (1983). Cognition, attitudes and personality dimensions in depression. *British Journal of Cognitive Psychotherapy*, 1, 1-16.

Beck, A.T., Ward, C.H., Mendelson, M., Mock, J., & Erbaugh, J. (1961). An inventory for measuring depression. *Archives of General Psychiatry*, 4, 561-571.

Beck, C.J. (1993). *Nothing special: Living Zen*. New York: HarperCollins.

Beck, J.S. (1995). *Cognitive therapy: Basics and beyond*. New York: Guilford Press.

Bellenir, K. (Ed.). (1997). *Congenital disorders sourcebook*. Detroit: Omnigraphics.

Bennett-Goleman, T. (2001). *Emotional alchemy: How the mind can heal the heart*. New York: Harmony Books.

Benson, H. (1975). *The Relaxation Response*. New York: William Morrow.

Berger, B.G., & Motl, R. (2001). Physical activity and quality of life. In R.N. Singer, H.A. Hausenblas, & C.M. Janelle (Eds.). *Handbook of Sport Psychology* (2nd ed.) (pp. 636-671). New York: Wiley.

Berger, B.G., & Owen, D.R. (1988a). Stress reduction and mood enhancement in four exercise modes: swimming, body conditioning, hatha yoga, and fencing. *Research Quarterly for Exercise & Sport*, 59, 148-159.

Berger, B.G., Friedmann, E., & Eaton, M. (1988b). Comparison of jogging, the relaxation response, and group interaction for stress reduction. *Journal of Sport & Exercise Psychology*, 10, 431-447.

Berman, M. (1981). *The Reenchantment of the World*. Ithaca: Cornell University Press

Berman, M. (1990). *Coming to our senses*. New York: Bantam.

Berridge, K. (2004). Motivation concepts in behavioral neuroscience. *Physiology & Behavior*, 81, 179-209.

Bhattacharya, B. (1976). *Ashvaghosha: A critical study of his authentic Kâvyas, and the apocryphal works, with special reference to his contributions to the classical Sanskrit literature, and his doctrinal standpoint as a Buddhist*. Santiniketan: Santiniketan Press.

Bhikkhu, A.S. (2000). *Meeting the monkey halfway*. York Beach, ME: Samuel Weiser.

Bion, W.R. (1970). *Attention and interpretation*. London: Tavistock.

Birnbaum, R. (1979). *The healing Buddha*. London: Rider.

Birtchnell, J. (1997). Attachment in an interpersonal context. *British Journal of Medical Psychology*, 70, 265-279.

Bishop, S.R. (2002). What do we really know about mindfulness-based stress reduction? *Psychosomatic Medicine*, 64, 71-84.

Bishop, S.R., Lau, M., Shapiro, S., Carlson, L., Anderson, N. D., Carmody, J., et al. (2004). Mindfulness: A proposed operational definition. *Clinical Psychology: Science & Practice*, 11, 230-241.

Bishop, S.R., Segal, Z.V., Lau, M., Anderson, N.C., Carlson, L., Shapiro, S.L., et al. (2003). *The Toronto Mindfulness Scale: Development and validation*. Manuscript under review.

Bisson, J. (1997). Randomised controlled trail of psychological debriefing for victims of acute trauma, *British Journal of Psychiatry*, 171, 78-81.

Blows, M., Srinivassan, S., Blows, J., Bankart, C.P., DelMonte, M., & Haruki, Y. (Eds.). (2004). *The relevance of the wisdom traditions in contemporary society: the challenge to psychology*. Delft, NL: Eburon.

Boadella, D. (1986). *Lifestreams*. London: Routledge.

Bodhi, B. (2000). *Samyutta Nikaya* (II 94-95).

Bodhi, B. (Ed.). (1993). *A comprehensive manual of Abhidhamma*. Kandy: Buddhist Publication Society.

Bodhi, B. (Ed.). (1994). *The Vision of Dhamma: Buddhist writings of Nyanaponika Thera*. (2nd. ed.). Kandy: Buddhist Publication Society.

Bodhi, B. (Ed.). (2000). *A comprehensive manual of Abhidhamma*. Onalaska, WA: Pariyatti Publishing. (Annotated transl. of the *Abhidhammattha Sangaha* by Acariya Anuruddha.)

Bond, A.J., Verheyden, S.L., Wingrove, J., & Curran, H.V. (2004). Angry cognitive bias, trait aggression and impulsivity in substance abusers. *Psychopharmacology*, 171, 331-339.

Bono, J. (1984). Psychological assessment of transcendental meditation. In D.H. Shapiro, & R.N. Walsh (Eds.), *Meditation: Classic and contemporary perspectives* (pp. 209-217). New York: Aldine.

Borg, G. (1998). *Borg's Perceived Exertion and Pain Scales*. Champaign, IL: Human Kinetics.

Boss, M. (1982). *Von der Spannweite der Seele*. Bern: Benteli Verlag.

Brazier, D. (1995). *Zen Therapy*. New York: Wiley.

Briggs, W. (Ed.). (1961). *Anthology of Zen*. New York: Grove Press.

Bronkhorst, J. (1993). *The two traditions of meditation in ancient India*. Delhi: Motilal Banarsidas.

Brown, D.P., & Engler, J. (1980). The stages of mindfulness meditation: A validation study. *Journal of Transpersonal Psychology*, 12, 143-192.

Brown, K.W., & Ryan, R.M. (2003). The benefits of being present: Mindfulness and its role in psychological well-being. *Journal of Personality and Social Psychology*, 84, 822-848.

Brown, K.W., & Ryan, R.M. (2004). Perils and promise in defining and measuring mindfulness: Observation from experience. *Clinical Psychology: Science & Practice*, 3, 242-248.

Bruckner, P. (2000). *L'Euphorie perpetuelle*. Paris: Grasset.

Bruning, N.S., & Frew, D.R. (1987). Effects of exercise, relaxation, and management skills training on physiological stress indicators: A field experiment. *Journal of Applied Psychology*, 72, 515-521.

Bruyn, B. de, & Hakvoort-Koomen, E. (1986). The Dutch WISC-R and it predecessor. *Kind & Adolescent*, 10, 175-182.

Buchheld, N., Grossman, P., & Walach, H. (2001). Measuring mindfulness in insight meditation (Vipassana) and meditation-based psychotherapy: The development of the Freiburg Mindfulness Inventory (FMI). *Journal for Meditation and Meditation Research*, 1, 11-34.

Buddhadasa, B. (1992). *Paticcasamuppada: Practical dependent origination*. Nonthaburi, TH: Vuddhidhamma Fund

Buddhagosa, B. (ca. 450/1999) *Visuddhi Magga, The Path of Purification*. Onalaska, WA: Pariyatti Publishing. (Transl. from the 450 AD original in Pali by Bhikkhu Ñanamoli.)

Burns, D.D. (1982*). Feeling good: The new mood therapy*. New York: Signet Book.

Calle, M., Claassen, I.E.W.M., Veening, J. G., Roubos, E.W., T. Kozicz, T., & Barendregt, H.P. (2005). Opioid peptides, CRF and urocortin in cerebrospinal fluid-contacting neurons in *Xenepus Laevis*. In H. Vaudry, E.W. Roubos, L. Schoofs, G. Flik, & D. Larhammar (Eds.), *Trends in Comparative Endocrinology and Neurobiology*, Ann. N.Y. Acad. Sci. N.Y. Acad. of Science.

Caplan, G. (1964). *Principles of preventive psychiatry*. New York: Basic Books.

Carrington, P. (1984). Modern forms of meditation. In R.L. Woolfolk & P.M. Lehrer (Eds.), *Principles and practice of stress management* (pp. 108-148). New York: Guildford.

Carrington, P., & Ephron, H.S. (1975). Meditation as an adjunct to psychotherapy. In S. Ariety & G. Chrzanowski (Eds.), *New dimensions in psychiatry: A world view*. New York: Wiley.

Carson, J.W., Carson, K.M., Gil, K.M., & Baucom, D.H. (2004). Mindfulness-based relationship enhancement. *Behavior Therapy*, 35, 471-494.

Cartwright-Hatton, S., & Wells, A. (1997). Beliefs about worry and intrusions: The metacognitions questionnaire and its correlates. *Journal of Anxiety Disorders*, 11, 279-296.

Carver, C.S., & Scheier, M.F. (1981). *Attention and Self-Regulation*. New York: Springer.

Castillo, R.J. (1990). Depersonalisation and meditation. *Psychiatry*, 53, 158-168.

Cautela, J.R. (1967). Covert sensitisation. *Psychological Record*, 74, 459-468.

Chalmers, D. (1996). *The conscious mind: In search of a fundamental theory*. Oxford University Press.

Chan, W. (1963). *A sourcebook of Chinese philosophy*. Princeton, NJ: University Press.

Chatterjee, A.K. (1999). *The Yogacara idealism*. Delhi: Motilal Banarsidass.

Chavira, D., & Stein, M. (2002). Combined psychoeducation and treatment with selective serotonin reuptake inhibitors for youth with generalized social anxiety disorder. *Journal of Child and Adolescent Psychopharmacology*, 12, 47-54.

Chen, K.K.S. (1964). *Buddhism in China*. Princeton, NJ: Princeton University Press.

Chine, E.T. (1984). The use of paradox in Buddhism and Taoism. *Journal of Chinese Philosophy*, 11, 375-399.

Chödrön, P. (1997). *When things fall apart: heart advice for difficult times*. Boston: Shambala.

Chödrön, P. (2003). *Start where you are*. Boston: Shambala.

Claxton, G. (1992). *The heart of Buddhism*. Hammersmith: Thorsons.

Claxton, G. (1994). *Noises from the dark room*. Hammersmith: Aquarian.

Cleary, T. (1992). *Rational Zen: The mind of Dogen Zenji*. Boston, MA: Shambhala.

Cleary, T. (2001). *Classics of Buddhism and Zen (Vol. 3)*. Boston, MA: Shambala.

Cleary, T. (Transl.). (1989). *Entry into the realm of reality* (Gandavyuha, the final book of the Avatamsaka Sutra). Boston, MA: Shambala.

Cochran, S.V., & Rabinowitz, F.E. (2000). *Men and depression: Clinical and empirical perspectives*. New York: Academic Press.

Coenen, A.M. (1995). Neuronal Activities Underlying the Electroencephalogram and Evoked Potentials of Sleeping and Waking: Implication for Information Processing. *Neuroscience & Biobehavioural Reviews*, 19, 447-463.

Cohen, J. (1988). *Statistical Power Analysis for the Behavioral Sciences* (2nd ed.). Hillsdale, NJ: Lawrence Erlbaum.

Colom, C., Vitea, E., Martinez-Aran, A., et al. (2003). A randomized trial on the efficacy of group psychoeducation in the prophylaxis of recurrences in bipolar patients whose disease is in remission. *Archives of General Psychiatry*, 60, 402-407.

Colom, F., Vieta, E., Reinares, M., et al. (2003). Psychoeducation efficacy in bipolar disorders: Beyond compliance enhancement. *Journal of Clinical Psychiatry*, 64, 1101-1106.

Coltart, M. (1992). *Slouching towards Bethlehem and further psychoanalytic explorations*. London: Free Association Books. *Constructivism in the Human Sciences*, 8, 151-171.

Conze, E. (1959). *Buddhism: its essence and development*. New York: Harper

Conze, E. (1980). *A short history of Buddhism*. Oxford, UK: Oneworld.

Conze, E. (Transl.). (1975). *The Large Sutra on Perfect Wisdom*. London: University of California Press.

Cooperrider, D.L. & Whitney, D. (1999). *Collaborating for change: Appreciative Inquiry*. San Francisco: Berrett-Koehler.

Corsini, R.J. (2000). *Handbook of innovative psychotherapies*. New York: Wiley.

Corsini, R.J., & Wedding, D. (2000). *Current psychotherapies (6th ed.)*. Belmont, CA: Thomson.

Costa, P.T., Jr., & McCrae, R.R. (1992). *NEO PI-R professional manual*. Odessa, FL: Psychological Assessment Resources.

Coyle, C., & Enright, R. (1997). Forgiveness intervention with post-abortion men. *Journal of Consulting and Clinical Psychology*, 65, 1042-1046.

Crook, J., & Fontana, D. (1990). Space in mind. Shaftsbury: Element.

Csikszentmihalyi, M. (1999). If we are so rich, why aren't we happy? *American Psychologist*, 54, 821-827.

Cuijpers, P.A. (1998). Psychoeducational approach to the treatment of depression: A meta-analysis of Lewinsohn's "Coping with depression" course. *Behavior Therapy*, 29, 521-533.

Cuthbert, B, Kristeller, J.L., Simons, R, & Lang, P.J. (1981). Strategies of arousal control: Biofeedback, meditation, and motivation. *Journal of Experimental Psychology*, 110, 518-546.

Dalai Lama (1999). *Ethics for the new millennium.* New York: Riverhead Books.

Dalai Lama (2000). *Dzogchen.* Ithaca, NY: Snow Lion.

Dalai Lama (2005). *Practicing wisdom.* Boston: Wisdom Publications.

Dalai Lama (1987). *The Buddhism of Tibet.* London: Unwin & Hyman.

Dalai Lama, Benson, H., Thurman, R.A.F., Gardner, H.E., & Goleman, D. (1991). *Mind science: An East-West dialogue.* Boston: Wisdom.

Dam, A. van, Hosman, C., Hoogduin, C., & Schaap, C. (2003). The Coping With Depression course: Short-term outcomes and mediating effects of a randomized controlled trial in the treatment of subclinical depression. *Behavior Therapy*, 34, 381-396.

Damasio, A. *The feeling of what happens: Body and emotion in the making of consciousness.* New York: Harcourt.

Damasio, A.R. (1995) *Descartes' error: Emotion, reason, and the human brain.* New York, Avon.

Damasio, A.R. (1999). *The feeling of what happens: Body and emotion in the making of consciousness.* Harcourt Brace.

Davidson, R.J. (1995). Cerebral Asymmetry, emotion and affective style. In R.J. Davidson & K. Hugdahl (Eds.), *Brain asymmetry.* Cambridge, MA: MIT Press.

Davidson, R.J. & Irwin, W. (1999). The functional neuroanatomy of emotion and affective style. *Trends in Cognitive Sciences*, 3, 11-21.

Davidson, R.J., Kabat-Zinn, J., Schumacher, J., Rosenkranz, M., Muller, D., Santorelli, S.F., et al. (2003). Alteration in brain and immune function produced by mindfulness meditation. *Psychosomatic Medicine*, 65, 564-570.

De Botton, A. (2003). *The art of travel.* London: Penguin.

De Gracia, M., & Marcó, M. (1997). Adaptación y validación factorial de la subjective exercise experiences scale (SEES). *Revista de Psicología del Deporte*, 6, 59-68.

De Silva, P. (1979). *An introduction to Buddhist psychology.* London: Macmillian.

De Silva, P. (1984). Buddhism and behaviour modification. *Behaviour Research & Therapy*, 22, 661-678.

De Silva, P. (1990). Buddhist psychology: A review of theory and practice. *Current Psychology*, 9, 236-254.

De Silva, P. (1998). Buddhist psychology: Theory and therapy. In M.G.T. Kwee, & T.L. Holdstock (Eds.), *Western and Buddhist Psychology: Clinical perspectives* (pp. 125-147). Delft, NL: Eburon

De Silva, P. (2000). Buddhism and psychotherapy: The role of self-control strategies. *Hsin Lai Journal of Humanistic Buddhism*, 1, 169-181.

De Silva, P. (2001). A psychological analysis of the Vitakkasanthana Sutta. *Buddhist Studies Review*, 18, 65-72.

De Silva, P. (2002). Buddhism and counselling. In S. Palmer (Ed.), *Multicultural counselling: A Reader.* London: Sage.

De Silva, P. (2004). Social well-being through mental health. *Hsin Lai Journal of Humanistic Buddhism*, 5, 192-197.

De Silva, P. (2005). Humanistic Buddhism and mental health: Therapy and prevention. In G. Piyadassi, L. Perera & R. Wijetunga (Eds.), *Buddhism in the West*. London: World Buddhist Foundation.

De Silva, P., & Rachman, S. (2004). *Obsessive-Compulsive Disorder: The facts* (3rd ed.). Oxford: Oxford University Press.

De Silva, P., & Samarashinge, D. (1998). Behaviour therapy in Sri Lanka. In T.P.S. Oei (Ed.), *Behaviour Therapy and Cognitive-Behaviour Therapy in Asia*. Glebe, NSW: Edumedia.

De Wit, H.. (2000). Working with existential and neurotic suffering. In Y.Haruki & K.T. Kaku (Eds.), *Meditation as health promotion: A lifestyle modification approach*. (pp. 19-32). Delft, NL: Eburon.

Deatherage, G. (1975). The clinical use of mindfulness meditation techniques in short term psychotherapy. *Journal of Transpersonal Psychology*, 7, 133-134.

Deikman, A. (1982). *The observing self: Mysticism and psychotherapy*. Boston: Beacon Press.

Del Vecchio, T., & O'Leary, K.D. (2004). Effectiveness of anger treatments for specific anger problems: A meta-analytic review. *Clinical Psychology Review*, 24, 15-34.

DelMonte, M.M. (1984). Physiological responses during meditation and rest. *Biofeedback & Self-Regulation*, 9, 181-200.

DelMonte, M.M. (1981). Suggestibility and meditation. *Psychological Reports*, 48, 699-709.

DelMonte, M.M. (1984a). Response to meditation in terms of physiological, behavioural and self-report measures. *International Journal of Psychosomatics*, 31, 3-17.

DelMonte, M.M. (1984b). Meditation: Similarities with hypnoidal states and hypnosis. *nternational Journal of Psychosomatics*, 31, 24-34.

DelMonte, M.M. (1985). Anxiety, defensiveness and physiological responsivity in novice and experienced meditators. *International Journal of Eclectic Psychotherapy*, 4, 1-13.

DelMonte, M.M. (1987). Constructivist view of meditation. *American Journal of Psychotherapy*, 41, 286-298.

DelMonte, M.M. (1989). Existentialism and psychotherapy: A constructivist perspective. *Psychologia*, 32, 81-90.

DelMonte, M.M. (1990). The relevance of meditation to clinical practice: An overview. *Applied Psychology: An International Review*, 39, 331-354.

DelMonte, M.M. (1995a). Meditation and the unconscious. *Journal of Contemporary Psychotherapy, 25*, 223-242.

DelMonte, M.M. (1995b). Silence and emptiness in the service of healing: Lessons from meditation. *British Journal of Psychotherapy*, 11, 368-378.

DelMonte, M.M. (2000). Non-attachment, dis-identification and dissociation in meditation, Qi-gong and hypnosis: Adaptive or mal-adaptive? In W. Wang W, Y. Sasaki, & Y. Haruki (Eds.), *Bodywork and psychotherapy in the East*. Delft, NL: Eburon.

DelMonte, M.M. (2004). Ways of understanding: Meditation, mysticism and science bridging the gap between East and West. In M. Blows, S. Srinavasan, J. Blows, P. Bankhart, M. DelMonte, & Y. Haruki (Eds), *The relevance of the wisdom traditions in contemporary society: The challenge of psychology* (pp. 1-23). Delft, NL: Eburon.

DelMonte, M.M., & Kenny, V. (1985). An overview of the therapeutic effects of meditation. *Psychologia*, 28, 189-202.

DeLoach, B. (2000). W. James and postmodernism. *Streams of William James, 2*, 1- 5.

Dennett. D. (1991). *Consciousness explained*. Boston: Little.

Derogatis, L.R., Lipman, R.S., Rickels, K. Uhlenhut, E.H., & Covi, L. (1974). The Hopkins Symptom Checklist (HSCL): A self-report symptom inventory. *Behavioral Science*, 19, 1-15.

Derrida, J. (1978). *Writing and difference*. Chicago: University of Chicago Press.

Dhamma, R. (1997). *The first discourse of the Buddha*. Boston: Wisdom Publications.

Dhammananda, K.S. (1987). *What Buddhists believe* (4th ed.). Malaysia: Buddhist Missionary Society.

Dhammananda, K.S. (1995). *Life is uncertain, death is certain*. Malaysia: Buddhist Missionary Society.

Dhammananda, K.S. (Ed.). (1994). *The treasure of the Dhamma*. Malaysia: Buddhist Missionary Society.

Dhammapada. (ed. by S. Sumangala. 1914). London: Pali Text Society.

Dhammapadatthakatha, Vols. I-IV. (ed. by H.C. Norman. 1906-1914). London: Pali Text Society.

Diener, E. (2000). Subjective well-being. The science of happiness and a proposal for a national index. *American Psychologist*, 55, 1, 34-43.

Digha Nikaya, Vol. I-III. (ed. by T.W. Rhys Davids & J.E. Carpenter, 1889-1910). London: Pali Text Society.

Dimidjian, S., & Linehan, M.M. (2003). Defining an agenda for future research on the clinical application of mindfulness practice. *Clinical Psychology: Science and Practice*, 10, 166-171.

Dogen (1994). *Genjo-koan*. In Dogen (1231-1253) (Ed.), Shobogenzo (G. Nishijima & C. Cross, Trans.). Wood Hole, MA: Windbell. (Original work, 1233)

Dorcas, A. (1996). *Qigong: An investigation into the psychological effects of Chinese meditation* (Ph.D. Thesis). University of Hong Kong.

Dowrick, C., Dunn, G., Ayuso-Mateos, J., et al. (2000). Problem solving treatment and group psychoeducation for depression: multicentre randomized controlled trial. Outcomes of Depression International Network (ODIN) Group. *BMJ Clinical Research*, 32, 1450-1454.

DSM IV (2000). *Diagnostic and Statistical Manual of mental disorders* (4th edition), Text Revised. Washington DC: American Psychiatric Association.

Dumoulin, H. (1988). *Zen Buddhism: A history (Vol I, India & China)*. New York.

Durham, R.C., & Turvey, A.A. (1987). Cognitive therapy vs. behaviour therapy in the treatment of chronic general anxiety. *Behaviour Research & Therapy*, 25, 229-234.

Dworkin, B.R., Filewich, R.J., Miller, N.E., Craigmyle, N., & Pickering, T.G. (1979). Barorecepton activation reduces reactivity to noxious stimulation: Implications for hypertension. *Science*, 205, 1299-1301.

Dzongsar Jamyang Khyentse Rinpoche (1996). *Introduction to the Middle Way: Chandrakirti's Madhyamakavatara*. The Khyentse Foundation.

D'Zurilla, T.J. (1986). *Problem-solving therapy: A social competence approach to clinical intervention*. NY: Springer.

Easterlin, B.L., & Cardena, E. (1998). Cognitive and emotional differences between short and long term Vipassana meditation. *Imagination, Cognition & Personality*, 18, 69-81.

Edelman, G. (1987). *Neural Darwinism.* New York: Basic Books.

Ehlers, A., & Clark, D.M. (2000). A cognitive model of posttraumatic stress disorder. *Behaviour Research & Therapy*, 38, 319-345.

Eigen, M. (1986). *The psychotic core.* Northvale, NJ, Jason Aronson.

Ellis, A. (1994*). Reason and emotion in psychotherapy - Revised and updated.* New York: Birch Lane Press.

Endler, N.S., & Parker, J.D.A. (1990). Multidimensional assessment of coping: A critical evaluation. *Journal of Personality and Social Psychology*, 58, 844-854.

Eppley, K.R., Abrams, A.I., & Shear, J. (1989). Differential effects of relaxation techniques on trait anxiety: A meta-analysis: *Journal of Clinical Psychology*, 45, 957-74.

Epstein, M. (1990). Psychodynamics of meditation: Pitfalls on the spiritual path. *Journal of Transpersonal Psychology,* 22, 17-34.

Epstein, M. (1995). *Thoughts without a thinker.* New York: Basic Books.

Epstein, M. (2001). *Going on being: Buddhism and the way of change.* New York: Broadway Books.

Epston, D., White, M., & Murray, K. (1992). A proposal for a re-authoring therapy: Rose's revisioning of her life and commentary. In S. McNamee & K.J. Gergen (Eds.), *Therapy as social construction* (pp. 96-115). London: Sage.

Eriksen, H., & Ursin, H. (2002). Sensitization and subjective health complaints. *Scandinavian Journal of Psychology*, 43, 198-196.

Esterling, B.A., L'Abate, L., Murray, E.J., & Pennebaker, J.W. (1999). Empirical foundations for writing in prevention and psychotherapy. *Clinical Psychology Review, 19*, 79-96.

Fairburn, C.G. (1995). *Overcoming binge eating.* New York: Guilford.

Faure, B. (1993). *Chan insights and oversights: An epistemological critique of the Chan tradition.* New Jersey: Princeton University Press.

Ferarri, M. (2002). Introduction. *Journal of Consciousness Studies*, 9, 1-10

Ferguson, A. (2000). *Zen's Chinese heritage.* Somerville, MA: Wisdom Publications.

Fischer-Schreiber, I., Ehrhard, F., & Diener, M.S (Eds.). (1991). *The Shambhala dictionary of Buddhism and Zen.* Boston, MA: Shambhala.

Fischer-Schreiber, I., Ehrhard, F., Friedrichs, K., & Diener, M.S. (1989). *The encyclopedia of Eastern philosophy and religion. Boston,* MA: Shambala.

Flavell, J. H. (1979). Metacognition and cognitive monitoring: A new area of cognitive-developmental inquiry. *American Psychologist*, 34, 906-911.

Follette, V.M., Palm, K.M. & Rassmussen-Hall, M.L. (2004). Acceptance, mindfulness and Trauma. In Hayes, S.C., Follette, V.M., & Linehan, M.M. (Eds.), *Mindfulness and acceptance.* New York: Guilford.

Fonagy, P., Steele, M., Steele, H., Higgitt, A., & Target, M. (1994). The theory and practice of resilience. *Journal of Child Psychology and Psychiatry*, 35, 231-257.

Fontana, D. (1990). Self-assertion and self-transcendence in Buddhist psychology. In J. Crook & D. Fontana (Eds.), *Space in mind: East-West psychology & contemporary Buddhism* (pp. 42-59). Longmead: Element Books

Forward, S. (2002). *Toxic parents.* New York: Bantam Dell.

Franklin, C. (1998). Distinctions between social constructionism and cognitive constructivism. C. Franklin & P.S. Nurius (Eds.), *Constructivism in practice: Methods and challenges* (pp. 57-94). Milwaukee, WI: Families International Inc.

Freeman, A. (1989). *The practice of cognitive therapy.* Tokyo: Seiwa Shoten.

Freeman, A., Pretzer, J., Fleming, B., & Simon, K.M. (1990). *Clinical applications of cognitive therapy.* New York: Plenum.

Freud, S. (1900). *The Interpretation of Dreams.* New York: Basic Books.

Freud, S. (1905). Jokes and their relation to the unconscious. In J. Strachey, A. Freud, A. Strachey & A. Tyson (Trans.), *The standard edition of the complete psychological works of Sigmund Freud. VIII.* London: Hogarth Press.

Freud, S. (1912). *Recommendations to physicians practising psychoanalysis* (Standard Edition). London: Hogarth.

Freud, S. (1930). *Civilisation and its discontents* (Standard Edition). London: Hogarth.

Friedlander, P. (1969). *Plato: An introduction,* (2nd ed.). Princeton, NJ: University Press.

Fujioka, T. (1987). On the therapeutic process of Dosa therapy. *Journal of Japanese Clinical Psychology,* 5, 14-25.

Fukaya, M. (Ed.). (1998). *Kireru mukatsuku - Monogurafu chugakusei no sekai* (Vol. 61). Tokyo: Benesse Educational Research Center Corporation.

Fukui, I. (1998). Development of Depression and anxiety cognition scale (DACS): For construction of cognitive behavioral model of depression and anxiety. *Japanese Journal of Behavior Therapy,* 24, 57-70.

Fukumori, H., & Mirikawa, Y. (2003). Relationship between focusing and mental health in adolescents. *Journal of Japanese Clinical Psychology,* 20, 580-587.

Gabbard, G.O. (1994). *Psychodynamic psychiatry in clinical practice, the DSM IV edition.* Washington DC: American Psychiatric Press.

Galin, D. (1974). Implications for psychiatry of left and right cerebral specialisation. *Archives of General Psychiatry,* 31, 572-583.

Garfinkel, H. (1967). *Studies in ethnomethdology.* Englewood Cliffs, NJ: Prentice Hall.

Geisinger, K.F. (2003). Testing and assessment in cross-cultural psychology. In I.B. Weiner (Ed.), *Handbook of Psychology,* Vol. 10 (pp. 95-118). New York: Wiley.

Gelderloos, P. (1990). In M.G.T. Kwee (Ed.), *Psychotherapy, meditation and health.*(pp. 215-238). London: East-West.

Gelderloos, P., Walton, D., Orme-Johnson, D., & Alexander, C. (1991). Effectiveness of the Transcendental Meditation program in preventing and treating substance misuse: A review. *International Journal of the Addictions,* 26, 293-325.

Gendlin, E. (1986). *Let your body interpret your dreams.* Wilmette: Chiron.

Gergen, K.J. (1983). Zen Buddhism & psychological science. *Psychologia,* 26, 129-141.

Gergen, K.J. (1994). *Realities and relationships: Soundings in social construction.* Cambridge, MA: Harvard University Press.

Gergen, K.J. (1999). *An invitation to social construction.* London: Sage.

Gergen, K.J., & Kaye, J. (1992). Beyond narrative in the negotiation of therapeutic meaning. In S. McNamee & K.J. Gergen (Eds.). *Therapy as social construction* (pp. 166-185). London: Sage.

Gergen, M. (2001). *Feminist reconstructions in psychology: Narrative, gender, and performance.* Thousands Oaks, CA: Sage.

Germer, C.K., Siegel, R.D. & Fulton, P.R. (2005). *Mindfulness and psychotherapy*. New York: Guilford.

Gethin, R. (1998). *The foundations of Buddhism*. New York: Oxford University Press.

Gijsbers van Wijk, C. M. T., & Kolk, A.M. (1996). Psychometric evaluation of symptom perception related measures. *Personality & Individual Differences*, 20, 55-70.

Gilbert, D., & Abdullah, J. (2004). Holiday taking and the sense of well-being. *Annals of Tourism Research*, 31, 103-121.

Gilbert, P. (Ed.). (2005). *Compassion: Conceptualisations, research and use in psychotherapy*. New York: Routledge.

Glasersfeld, E. von (1984). An introduction to radical constructivism. In P. Watzlawick (Ed.), *The invented reality* (pp. 17-40). New York: Norton.

Glasersfeld, E. von (1995). *Radical constructivism: A way of knowing and learning*. London: Falmer Press.

Goddard, L., Dritschel, B., & Burton, A., (1996). Role of autobiographical memory in social problem solving and depression. *Journal of Abnormal Psychology*, 105, 609-616.

Goldberg, D.P . (1978). *Manual of the General Health Questionnaire*. Windsor, UK: Nfer-Nelson.

Goldfried, M. (1971). Systematic desensitization as training in self-control. *Journal of Consulting and Clinical Psychology*, 37, 228-234.

Goleman, D. (1988). *The meditative mind: The varieties of meditative experience*. New York: J.P. Tarcher.

Goleman, D. (2003). *Destructive emotions: How can we overcome them? A Scientific Dialogue with the Dalai Lama*. New York: Bantam Books.

Gombrich, R. (1988). *Theravada Buddhism*. London: Routledge & Kegan Paul.

Gombrich, R. (1990). How the Mahayana began. *Buddhist Forum*, 1, 21-30.

Gombrich, R. (1996). *How Buddhism began*. London: Athlone

Gonzales-Pinto, A., Gonzalez, C., Enjunto, S., et al. (2004). Psychoeducation and cognitive-behavior therapy in bipolar disorder: an update. *Acta Psychologica Scandinavica*, 109, 83-90.

Gotlib, I., & MacLeod, C. (1997). Information processing in anxiety and depression: A cognitive-developmental perspective. In J. Burack & J. Enns (Eds.), *Attention, Development, and Psychopathology*. New York: Guilford.

Gough, H.G., & Heilbrun, A.B. (1983). *The Adjective Check List manual*. Palo Alto, CA: Consulting Psychologist Press.

Gowans, C.W. (2003). *Philosophy of the Buddha*. London: Routledge.

Greenberg, J.S., & Pargman, D. (1989). *Physical fitness: A wellness approach*. Englewood Cliffs, NJ: Prentice Hall.

Greenberg, L.S. (2002). Integrating an emotion-focused approach to treatment in psychotherapy integration. *Journal of Psychotherapy Integration*, 12, 154-189.

Greene, B. (1999). *The elegant universe*. New York: W.W. Norton.

Gremillion, H. (2003). *Feeding Anorexia: Gender and Power at a Treatment Center*. Durham, NC: Duke University Press.

Griffin, D. (2001). Loss as a lifelong regenerative learning process. *Psychodynamic Counselling*, 7, 413-430.

Griffith, B.A., & Graham, C.C. (2004). Meeting needs and making meaning: The pursuit of goals. *Journal of Individual Psychology*, 60, 25-41.

Gross, R.M., & Muck, T.C. (Eds.) (2003). *Christians talk about Buddhist meditation; Buddhists talk about Christian prayer.* New York: Continuum Press.

Grossman, P., Niemann, L., Schmidt, S. & Walach, H. (2004). Mindfulness-based stress reduction and health benefits: A meta-analysis. *Journal of Psychosomatic Research*, 57, 35-43.

Gunaratana, B.H. (2002). *Mindfulness in plain English.* Boston: Wisdom Publications.

Gunaratna, V.F. (1968). *The Satipatthana Sutta and its application to modern life.* Kandy: Buddhist Publication Society

Guruge, A.W.P. (1999). *What in brief is Buddhism?* Monterey Park, CA: Mitram Press.

Gyatso, T., the 14th Dalai Lama. (1997). *The Four Noble Truths.* Hammersmith: Thorsons.

Gyatso, T., the 14th Dalai Lama. (2003). Foreword. In D. Goleman (Ed.), *Destructive emotions and how we can overcome them: A dialogue with the Dalai Lama* (pp. xiii-xv). London: Bloomsbury.

Habermas, T., & Bluck, S. (2000). Getting a life: The emergence of the life story in adolescence. *Psychological Bulletin*, 126, 748-769.

Hadigan, C.M., Walsh, B.T., Devlin, M.J., LaChaussee, J.L., & Kissileff, H.R. (1992). Behavioral assessment of satiety in bulimia nervosa. *Appetite*, 18, 233-241.

Haley, J., (1985). *Conversations with Milton H. Erickson, MD* (Vols. 1-3). New York: Triangle Press.Haley, J. (1994). Zen and the Art of Therapy. Family Therapy Networker, 1, 55-60

Hallahan, M., & Rosenthal, R. (2000). Interpreting and reporting results. In H. Tinsley & S. Brown (Eds.), *Handbook of applied multivariate statistics and mathematical modeling.* San Diego, CA: Academic Press.

Hamilton, M. (1959). The assessment of anxiety states by rating. *British Journal of Medical Psychology*, 32, 50-55.

Hamilton, M. (1960). A rating scale for depression. *Journal of Neurology & Neurosurgery*, 12, 56-62.

Hamilton, S. (2000). *Early Buddhism - The I of the beholder.* Richmond, UK: Curzon.

Hannay, D.R. (1979). *The symptom iceberg.* London: Routledge & Kegan Paul.

Harmon-Jones, E. (2004). On the relationship of frontal brain activity and anger: Examining the role of attitude toward anger. *Cognition and Emotion*, 18, 337-361.

Harner, L (1982). Immediacy and certainty-factors in understanding future reference. *Journal of child language*, 9, 115-124.

Haruki, Y. (1997). Touyoushisou, fukuzatusei no kagaku, soshite ningenkagaku (Eastern philososophies, sciences of complexity, and human sciences). *Human Sciences*, 10, 10-12.

Haruki, Y. (2004). Concepts of self regulation in the East and the West. In M. Blows, S. Srinivasan, J. Blows, P. Bankart, M. DelMonte, & Y. Haruki (Eds.), *The relevance of the wisdom traditions in contemporary society: The challenge to psychology* (pp. 99-114). Delft, Netherlands: Eburon.

Haruki, Y., & Kaku, K.T. (Eds.). (2000). *Meditation as health promotion: a lifestyle modification approach.* Delft, NL: Eburon.

Haruki, Y., & Takase, H. (2001). Effects of the Eastern art of breathing. In Y. Haruki, I. Homma, A. Umezawa, Y. & Masaoka (Eds.), *Respiration and emotion.* Tokyo: Springer-Verlag.

Haruki, Y., Ishii, Y., Kwee, M.G.T., Sakairi, Y., De Silva, P., & Taams, M.K. (2000). The Transcultural Society for Clinical Meditation: An invitation. *Constructivism in the Human Sciences*, 6, 77-88.

Harvey, P. (1990). *An introduction to Buddhism: Teachings, history and practices*. Cambridge: Cambridge University Press.

Harvey, P. (2000). *An introduction to Buddhist ethics*. Cambridge: University Press.

Hasegawa, K. (1987). *Kazokunai paradokkusu* (Paradox and constructivism). Tokyo: Saikoshobo.

Haskel, P. (1984). *Bankei Zen* (ed. by Y. Hakeda). New York:Grove Press.

Hayashi, K. (1988). Examination of depressive tendency of Japanese student. Japanese *Journal of Counseling Science*, 20, 162-169.

Hayes, S.C., Strosahl, K.D., Wilson, K.G., Bissett, R.T., Pistorello, J., Toarmino, D. et al., (2004). Measuring experiential avoidance: A preliminary test of a working model. The *Psychological Record*, 54, 553-578.

Hayes, S.C. (2002). Buddhism and Acceptance and Commitment Therapy. *Cognitive & Behavioral Practice*, 9, 58-66.

Hayes, S.C. (2002). Acceptance, mindfulness, and science. *Clinical Psychology: Science & Practice*, 9, 101-106.

Hayes, S.C. (2004) Acceptance and commitment therapy and the new behavior therapies: Mindfulness, Acceptance, and relationship. In S.C. Hayes, V.M. Follette, & M.M. Linehan (Eds.), *Mindfulness and acceptance* (pp. 1-29). New York: Guilford.

Hayes, S.C., Folette, V.M., & Linehan, M.M. (2004). *Mindfulness and acceptance: Expanding the cognitive-behavioral tradition*. New York: Guilford

Hayes, S.C., Stosahl, K.D., Wilson, K.G. (1999). *Acceptance and Commitment Therapy*. New York: Guilford.

Hayes, S.K. (1992). *Action meditation*. Ohio: Nine Gates Press.

Hayward, J.W., & Varela, F.J. (1992). *Gentle bridges: Conversations with the Dalai Lama on the sciences of mind*. Boston: Shambala.

Heide, F.J., & Borkovec, T.D. (1983). Relaxation-induced anxiety: Paradoxical anxiety enhancement due to relaxation training. *Journal of Consulting & Clinical Psychology*, 51, 171-182.

Heidegger, M. (1927/1962). *Being and time*. Oxford: Blackwell Publishers.

Heidegger, M. (1988). On adequate understanding of Daseinsanalysis. In E. Craig (Ed.), Psychotherapy for Freedom: The Daseinsanalytic way in psychology and psychoanalysis. *The Humanistic Psychologist*, 16, 75-98.

Hendricks, C.C. (1975). Meditation as discrimination training: a theoretical note. *Journal of Transpersonal Psychology*, 7, 144-146.

Heppner, P.P., & Peterson, C.H. (1982). The development and implication of a personal problem-solving inventory. *Journal of Counseling Psychology*, 29, 66-75.

Herrigel, E. (1953). *Zen in the art of archery*. New York: Pantheon.

Hetherington, M., & Rolls, B. J. (1988). Sensory specific satiety and food intake in eating disorders. In B.T. Walsh (Ed.) *Eating behavior in eating disorders* (pp. 141-160). Washington, DC: American Psychiatric Press.

Hodge, R. & Kress, G. (1988). *Social Semiotics*. Cambridge: Polity Press.

Hofstadter, D. (1979). *Gödel, Escher, Bach*. New York: Basic Books.

Hogan, B.E., & Linden, W. (2004). Anger response styles and blood pressure: At least don't ruminate about it. *Annals of Behavioral Medicine*, 27, 38-49.

Hohmann, G.W. (1966). Some effects of spinal cord lesions on experienced emotional feelings. *Psychophysiology*, 3, 143-156.

Hollon, S.D. (2003). Does cognitive therapy have an enduring effect? *Cognitive Therapy and Research*, 27, 71-75.

Holmes, D. S. (1984). Meditation and somatic arousal reduction: A review of the experimental evidence. *American Psychologist*, 39, 1-10.

Holmes, D.S. (1987). The influence of meditation versus rest on physiological arousal: a second examination. In M.A. West (Ed.), *The Psychology of Meditation* (pp. 81-103). Oxford: Clarendon Press.

Holmes, J. (1997). Attachment, autonomy, intimacy: Some clinical implications of attachment theory. *British Journal of Medical Psychology*, 70, 231-248.

Hoover, T. (1980). *The Zen experience*. New York: The New American Library.

Hoshikawa, T. (1992). Application of Dosa therapy to a case with hyperventilation syndrome. In G. Naruse (Ed.), *Rinsho-Dosahou no riron to chiryo* (pp. 179-187). Tokyo: Shibundo.

Hosking, D.M. (2005). Bounded entities, constructivist revisions and radical re-constructions. Special issue on Social Cognition: *Cognitie*, Creier, Comportament/Cognition, *Brain, Behavior*, IX (4), 609-622.

Hu, S. (1961). The development of Zen Buddhism in China. In W. Briggs (Ed.), *Anthology of Zen* (pp. 7-31). New York: Grove Press

Hubble, M.A., Duncan, B.L., & Miller, S.D. (Eds.). (1999). *The heart and soul of change: What works in therapy.* Washington, DC: APA.

Huberty, C., & Petoskey, M. (2000). Multivariate analysis of variance and covariance. In H. Tinsley & S. Brown (Eds.), *Handbook of applied multivariate statistics and mathematical modeling.* San Diego, CA: Academic Press.

Humphreys, C. (1968). *Concentration and meditation: A manual of mind development.* New York, Penguin.

Hut, P., & R.N. Shepard, R. N. (1996). Turning "the hard problem" upside down & sideways. *Journal of Consciousness Studies*, 3, 313-32.

Ihlebæk, C., Eriksen, H.R., & Ursin, H. (2002) Prevalence of Subjective Health Complaints (SHC) in Norway. *Scandinavian Journal of Publicic Health*, 30, 19-29.

Ingram, R.E., Miranda, J., & Segal, Z.V. (1998). *Cognitive vulnerability to depression.* New York: Guilford.

Ishitani, J. (1995). Warai (Laughter). In Shisou no kenkyukai (Ed.), *Shinpan tetsugaku ronri yougo jiten* (pp. 407-408).

Iverson, G.R. (2003). Knowledge as a numbers game. In Gergen, K.J. and Gergen, M. (Eds.), *Social Construction:* A Reader. London: Sage.

Jackson, R. (1986). Dharmakirti refutation of theism. *Philosophy East & West*, 36, 315-348.

Jacobson, E. (1974). *Progressive relaxation.* Chicago: University of Chicago Press.

Jacobson, N.P. (1983). *Buddhism and the contemporary world: Change and self correction.* Carbondale: Southern Illinois University Press.

James, W. (1890). *The principles of psychology.* Cambridge, MA: Harvard University Press.

James, W. (1902). *Varieties of religious experience. A study in human nature.* New York: Random House.

Jamgon Mipham Rinpoche (1999). Seminary transcripts. Halifax: Vajradhatu Publications.
Jamgon Mipham Rinpoche (2000). Seminary transcripts. Halifax: Vajradhatu Publications.
Jayasuriya, W.F. (1963). *The psychology and philosophy of Buddhism.* Malaysia: Buddhist Missionary Society.
Jevning, R., Wallace, R., & Beidebach, M. (1992). The Pysiology of meditation: a review. A wakeful hypometabolic integrated response. *Neuroscience & Biobehavioral Review,* 16, 415-424.
Jin, P. (1992). Efficacy of Tai Chi, brisk walking, meditation, and reading in reducing mental and emotional stress. *Journal of Psychosomatic Research,* 36, 361-370.
Johansson, R.E.A. (1969). *The psychology of nirvana.* London: Allen & Unwin.
John, O.P., & Srivastava, S. (1999). The Big Five trait taxonomy: History, measurement, and theoretical perspectives. In L. A. Pervin, & O. P. John (Eds.), *Handbook of personality* (2nd ed.) (pp. 102-138). New York: Guilford.
Jong, K. de (2000). *Outcome Questionnaire* (thesis), University of Amsterdam, Netherlands.
Judd, L.J. (1997). The clinical course of unipolar major depressive disorders. *Archives of General Psychiatry,* 54, 989-991.
Jung, C. (1958). Psychological commentary on the Tibetan book of the great liberation. In *Psychology and religion* (transl. R.F. Hull, Vol.3, Collected Works). New York: Pantheon Books.
Kabat-Zinn, J. (1982). An out-patient program in behavioral medicine for chronic pain patients based on the practice of mindfulness meditation: Theoretical considerations and preliminary results. *General Hospital Psychiatry,* 4, 33-47.
Kabat-Zinn, J. (1987). Four-year follow-up of a meditation-based program for the self regulation of chronic pain: Treatment outcomes and compliance. *The Clinical Journal of Pain,* 2, 159-173.
Kabat-Zinn, J. (1990). *Full Catastrophe Living.* New York, NY: Delacorte Press.
Kabat-Zinn, J. (1993). Mindfulness meditation: Health benefits of an ancient Buddhist practice. In D. Goleman & N. Gurin (Eds.), *Mind/Body Medicine* (pp. 259-275). New York: Consumer Reports Books.
Kabat-Zinn, J. (1994). *Wherever you go, there you are:* Mindfulness meditation in everyday life. New York: Hyperion.
Kabat-Zinn, J. (1996). Mindfulness meditation: What it is, what it isn't, and its role in health-care and medicine. In Y.Haruki, Y.Ishii, & M. Suzuki (Eds.). *Comparative and psychological study of meditation* (pp. 161-170). Delft, NL: Eburon.
Kabat-Zinn, J. (2003). Mindfulness-Based Stress Reduction (MBSR). In M.G.T. Kwee, & M.K. Taams (Eds.), *Special issue: A tribute to Yutaka Haruki. Constructivism in the Human Sciences,* 2, 73-106.
Kabat-Zinn. J. (2003) Mindfulness-based interventions in context: past, present, and future. *Clinical Psychology: Science and Practice,* 10,144-156.
Kabat-Zinn, J. (2005). *Coming to our senses: Healing ourselves and the world through mindfulness.* New York: Hyperion.
Kabat-Zinn, J., Massion, A.O., Kristeller, J., et al. (1992). Effectiveness of a meditation based stress reduction program in the treatment of anxiety disorders. *American Journal of Psychiatry,* 149, 936-943

Kalupahana, D.J. (1976). *Buddhist philosophy: A historical analysis.* Honolulu: University of Hawaii Press.

Kalupahana, D.J. (1987). *The principles of Buddhist Psychology.* Albany, NY: State University of New York Press.

Kalupahana, D.J. (1995). *Ethics in Early Buddhism.* Honolulu: University of Hawaii Press.

Kalupahana, D.J. & Kalupahana, I. (1982). *The way of Siddhartha.* Boulder, Co: Shambhala.

Kanaya, O. (1993). *Chugoku shisou wo kangaeru: Mirai wo hiraku dentou* (Considering Chinese philosophy: Opening a future by tradition). Tokyo: Chuo Kouron Shinsha.

Kaplan, H.I., & Sadock, B.J. (1996). *Pocket handbook of clinical psychiatry* (2nd ed.). Baltimore: Williams & Wilkins.

Kaplan, H.J. & Sadock, B.J. (2003). *Synopsis of psychiatry - behavioral sciences/clinical psychiatry.* Baltimore, MA: Williams & Wilkins

Kashiwagi, S. (1997). Evaluation and representation of personality: The Big Five traits approach. Tokyo: Yuhikaku.

Kawamoto, H. (2000). *Otopoieshisu2001: Hibi aratani mezameru tameni* (Autopoiesis 2001: For awakening day by day). Tokyo: Shinyosha.

Kawano, R. (2005). *Anger management and cultivating altruistic spirit of Mahayana to Japanese college students through eight sacred paths.* Paper presented at the 5th International Congress of Cognitive Psychotherapy, Gothenburg, Sweden.

Kazarian, S., & Evans, D.R. (Eds.). (1998). *Cultural clinical psychology.* New York: Oxford University Press.

Kazdin, A. (1984). *Behavior modification in applied settings* (3rd ed.). Homewood, IL: The Dorsey Press.

Kelly, G.A. (1955). *The psychology of personal constructs.* New York: Norton.

Kendler, K.S., Thornton, L.M., & Gardner, C.O. (2000). Stressful life events and previous episodes in the etiology of major depression in women: An evaluation of the "kindling" hypothesis. *American Journal of Psychiatry*, 157, 1243-125.

Keown, D. (2003). *A dictionary of Buddhism.* Oxford: Oxford University Press.

Keown, D. (Ed.) (2000). *Contemporary Buddhist ethics.* London: Curzon Press.

Kepner, J. (1987). *Body process: A Gestalt approach to working with the body in psychotherapy.* New York: Gardner Press.

Kessler, R.C., McGonagle, K.A., Zhao, S., Nelson, C.B., Hughes, M., Eshlerman, S., et al. (1994). Lifetime and twelve-month prevalence of DSM-III-R psychiatric disorders in the United States: Results from the National Comorbidity Study. *Archives of General Psychiatry*, 51, 8-19.

Khong, B. S. L. (2003). Role of responsibility in Daseinanalysis and Buddhism. In K.H. Dockett, G.R. Dudley-Grant, & C.P. Bankart (Eds.), *Psychology and Buddhism: From individual to global community* (pp. 139-159).New York: Kluwer.

Khong, B.S.L. (1999). *Coping with change: The Buddhist response.* Paper presented at the 107th Annual Convention of the American Psychological Association, Boston, Massachusetts.

Khong, B.S.L. (2003a). Buddhism and psychotherapy: Experiencing and releasing dis-ease. *Constructivism in the Human Sciences*, 8, 37-56.

Khong, B.S.L. (2003b). Role of responsibility in Daseinsanalysis and Buddhism. In K.H. Dockett., G.R. Dudley-Grant., & C. P. Bankart (Eds.), *Psychology and Buddhism: From individual to global community* (pp. 139-159). New York: Kluwer.

Khong, B.S.L. (2003c). The Buddha teaches an attitude not an affiliation. In S.R. Segall (Ed.), *Encountering Buddhism: Western psychology and Buddhist teachings* (pp. 61-74). New York: State University of New York Press.

Khong, B.S.L. (2004). Minding the mind's Business. *The Humanistic Psychologist, 32,* 257-279.

Kirk, R. (1996). Practical significance: a concept whose time has come. *Educational & Psychological easurement,* 56, 746-759.

Kishimioto, K. (1985). Self-awakening psychotherapy for neurosis: Attaching importance to oriented thought, especially Buddhist thought. *Psychologia,* 28, 90-100.

Kitagawa, J.M. (1984). Paradigm change in Japanese Buddhism. *Japanese Journal of Religious Studies,* 11, 115-142.

Kitamura, S. (1991). *Jiga no shinri: zokko* (Psychology of ego: an ongoing study). Tokyo: Kawashima-shoten.

Kloppenborg, R. (1989). *De leraar van de wereld, trainer van mensen. De wijze van onderricht van de Boeddha zoals beschreven in de boeddhistische kanonieke geschriften.* Utrecht: Utrechtse Theologische Reeks.

Kloppenborg, R. (1995). Female stereotypes in Early Buddhism: The women of the Therîgâthâ. In R. Kloppenborg & W. J. Hanegraaff (Eds.), *Female stereotypes in religious traditions.* Leiden: Brill.

Kohn, M.H. (Trans). (1991). *The Shambala dictionary of Buddhism and Zen.* Boston, MA: Shambala.

Kolk, A.M., Hanewald, G.J.F.P., Schagen, S., & Gijsbers van Wijk, C. (2003). A symptom perception approach to common physical symptoms. *Social Science & Medicine* (57, 2343-2354).

Konno, Y (1977). *An application of Dosa-control-therapy to children with hyperactivity problem.* Proceedings of the 41st Annual Meeting of the Japanese Society of Psychology, 1098-1099.

Kopp, S.B. (1972). *If you meet the Buddha on the road. Kill him!* New York: Bantam

Kornfield , J. (1993). *A path with heart.* New York: Bantam Books.

Kornfield, J. (2000). *After the ecstasy, the laundry.* New York: Bantam Books.

Korzybski, A. (1933). *Science and sanity: An introduction to non-aristotelian systems and general semantics.* Englewood, NJ: Institute of General Semantics.

Koshikawa, F. (1994). *Toyo no muga to seiyo no jiga* ("Non-self" in the East and Ego in the West). Paper presented at the open symposium sponsored by the Japan Society of Personality Psychology.

Koshikawa, F. (1996). *Jiritu kunren-ho to Jikan-ho* (On Autogenic training and Jikan ho). Paper presented at the Hasemura symposium sponsored by Toyo teki gyoho kenkyu kai, Hasemura, Japan.

Koshikawa, F. (1998). *A technique of self-awareness in the East.* Paper presented at the International Symposium "Psychotherapy and Eastern Thought" of the Asia Division of the World Council for Psychotherapy; 1st AWCP Congress, May 1st, 1998, Beijing, China.

Koshikawa, F. (2000). A technique of self-awareness in the East. Y. Sasaki, & Y. Haruki (Eds.), *Bodywork and Psychotherapy in the East* (pp. 195-203). Delft, NL: Eburon.

Koshikawa, F. (2000a). Muga ni tsuite (On non-self). In T. Takuma, O. Suzuki, K. Shimizu, & Y. Matsui (Eds.), *Seikaku no henyo to bunka* (Transformation of characteristics and culture). Tokyo: Brain-shuppan.

Koshikawa, F. (2000b). A technique of self-awareness in the East. In W. Wang, Y. Sasaki, & Y. Haruki (Eds.), *Bodywork and Psychotherapy in the East* (pp. 195-203). Delft, NL: Eburon.

Koshikawa, F. (2000b). Muga ni tsuite (On non-self). In T. Takuma, O. Suzuki, K. Shimizu, & Y. Matsui (Eds.), *Seikaku no henyo to bunka* (Transformation of characteristics and culture). Tokyo: Brain-shuppan.

Koshikawa, F., & Ichii, M. (1996). An experiment on classifications of meditation methods: on procedures, goals and effects. In Y. Haruki, Y. Ishii, & M. Suzuki (Eds.), *Comparative and Psychological Study on Meditation.* (pp. 212-238). Delft, NL: Eburon

Koshikawa, F., Arai, S, & Takanashi, E. (1997). *Muga no sokutei kanosei ni tsuite* (On possibilities for measurement of muga). Proceedings of the 6th Annual Meeting of the Japan Society of Personality Psychology (p. 50).

Koshikawa, F., Ishii, Y., Sakata, T., & Akutagawa, N. (2002). *Effectiveness of jikan-ho in reducing stress and increasing accessibility to positive memory.* Paper presented at the 7th Conference of the Transnational Network for Physical, Psychological & Spiritual Well-being "The Relevance of the Wisdom Traditions in Contemporary Society: the Challenge to Psychology", Wollongong, Australia.

Koshikawa, F., Ishii, Y., Sakata, T., Akutagawa, N., & Williams, J.M.G. (2004). Effectiveness of the Jikanho in reducing stress and increasing accessibility of positive memories. In M.Blows, S.Srinivasan, J.Blows, P.Bankart, M.DelMonte, & Y.Haruki (Eds.), *The relevance of the wisdom traditions in contemporary society: the challenge to psychology* (pp. 223-233). Delft, NL: Eburon.

Koshikawa, F., Kubozono,Y., Ishii,Y., & Haruki, Y. (2000). *Effectiveness of the jikan-ho (a Japanese self-awareness technique on stress reduction).* International Journal of Psychology, Abstracts of the XXVII International Congress of Psychology (p. 78).

Koshikawa, F., Kuboki, A., & Ishii, Y. (2006). A cognitive-behavioral approach based on Shikanho: A Zen-Based Cognitive-Behavioral Approach. (This book, Chapter 11).

Kraft, K. (Ed.). (1988). *Zen: Tradition & transition.* London: Rider.

Kretschmer, W. (1962). Meditation techniques in psychotherapy. *Psychologia*, 5, 76-83.

Krishnamurti, J. (1991). *Meeting life: Writing and talks on finding your path without retreating from society.* San Francisco: Harper.

Kristeller, J. (2003). Finding the Buddha/finding the self. In S. Segall (Ed.), *Encountering Buddhism: Western psychology and Buddhist teachings.* Albany, NY: SUNY.

Kristeller, J.L. (2003). Mindfulness, wisdom, and eating: Applying a multi-domain model of meditation effects. *Constructivism in the Human Sciences*, 8, 107-118.

Kristeller, J. (2004). Meditation: Multiple effects, a unitary process? In M. Blows, S. Srinivasan, J. Blows, C.P. Bankart, M. DelMonte, & Y. Haruki (Eds.), *The relevance of the wisdom traditions in contemporary society: The challenge to psychology* (pp. 21-37). Delft, NL: Eburon.

Kristeller, J., & Hallett, C.B. (1999). An exploratory study of a meditation-based intervention for binge eating disorder. *Journal of Health Psychology*, 3, 357-363.

Kristeller, J., Quillian-Wolever, R., & Sheets, V. (2004). Mindfulness meditation: mechanisms and effectiveness in treating binge eating disorder. Paper presented at *Society of Behavioral Medicine Annual* Meetings (March 27), Baltimore, MD.

Kristeller, J.L., & Hallett, B. (1999). Effects of a meditation-based intervention in the treatment of binge eating. *Journal of Health Psychology*, 4, 357-363.

Kristeller, J.L., & Johnson, T. (2003). *Cultivating loving-kindness: A two-stage model of the effects of meditation on empathy, compassion, and altruism.* Paper presented at the conference Works of Love: Scientific and Religious Perspectives on Altruism, June. Villanova, PA.

Kristeller, J.L., & Johnson, T. (2005). Cultivating loving kindness: A Two-stage model of he effects of meditation on empathy, compassion, and altruism. *Zygon*, 40, 391-407.

Kristeller, J.L., & Rodin, J. (1989). Identifying eating patterns in male and female undergraduates using cluster analysis. *Addictive Behaviors*, 14, 631-642.

Kristeller, J.L., Schwartz, G.E., & Black, H. (1982). The use of Restricted Environmental Stimulation Therapy (REST) in the treatment of essential hypertension: Two case studies. *Behavior Research & Therapy*, 20, 561-566.

Kubota, N. (1991). The psychotherapeutic treatment for an obsessive-compulsive neurotic client by Motor Action Training. *Journal of Japanese Clinical Psychology*, 9, 17-28.

Kubota, N. (2000). *An analysis of the therapeutic process of Dosa Therapy. Unpublished doctoral dissertation.* Michigan State University, USA.

Kuyken, W., & Brewin, C. R. (1995). Autobiographical memory functioning in depression and reports of early abuse. *Journal of Abnormal Psychology*, 104, 585-591.

Kwee, M.G.T. (1982). Psychotherapy and the practice of General Semantics. *Methodology & Science, 15,* 236-256.

Kwee, M.G.T. (Ed.). (1990a). Psychotherapy, meditation and health: A cognitive behavioural approach. London : East-West Publication.

Kwee, M.G.T. (1990b). Cognitive and behavioral approaches to meditation. In M.G.T. Kwee (Ed.), *Psychotherapy, meditation and health: A cognitive-behavioural approach* (pp. 36-54). London: East-West.

Kwee, M.G.T. (1996). A multimodal systems view on psyche, affect, and the basic emotions. In M.G.T. Kwee & T.L. Holdstock (Eds.). *Western and Buddhist psychology: Clinical perspectives* (pp. 221-268). Delft, NL: Eburon.

Kwee, M.G.T. (1996). Traveling in the footsteps of Hotei towards the 21st century. In M.G.T.Kwee & T.L.Holdstock (Eds.), *Western and Buddhist Psychology* (pp. 175-214). Delft, NL: Eburon.

Kwee, M.G.T. (1998). On consciousness and awareness of the BASIC-I.D. In M.M. DelMonte, & Y. Haruki (Eds.), *The embodiment of mind* (pp. 21-42). Delft, NL: Eburon.

Kwee, M.G.T. (2003). NeoZEN: A deconstructing process into non-self. In M.G.T. Kwee & M.K. Taams (2003) (Eds.), *Special issue: A Tribute to Yutaka Haruki. Constructivism in the Human Sciences*, 8, 181-203.

Kwee, M.G.T., & Lazarus, A.A. (1986). Multimodal therapy: The cognitive-behavioural tradition and beyond. In W. Dryden & W. Golden (Eds.), *Cognitive-behavioural approaches to psychotherapy* (pp. 320-356). London: Harper & Row

Kwee, M.G.T. & Holdstock, T.L. (Eds.). (1996). *Western and Buddhist psychology: Clinical perspectives.* Delft, NL: Eburon.

Kwee, M.G.T., & Ellis, A. (1997) Can Multimodal and Rational Emotive Behavior Therapy be reconciled? *Journal of Rational-Emotive & Cognitive-Behavior Therapy*, 15, 95-133.

Kwee, M.G.T., & Ellis, A. (1998). The interface between Rational Emotive Behavior Therapy and Zen. *Journal of Rational-Emotive & Cognitive-Behavior Therapy,* 16, 5-44.

Kwee, M.G.T., Ishii, Y., & Sakairi, Y. (2001). Clinical meditation: Fundamentals and principles. *Constructivism in the Human Sciences*, 6, 95-112

Kwee, M.G.T., & M.K. Taams (2002). The NeoZen of Kaku-san: A constructivistic synthesis of Zen in post Y2K-West. *Constructivism in the Human Sciences*, 7, 173-205.

Kwee, M.G.T., & M.K. Taams (Eds.). (2003). Special issue: A tribute to Yutaka Haruki. *Constructivism in the Human Sciences*, 8, 2, 1-265.

Kwee, M.G.T., & M.K. Taams (2006). Buddhist Psychology and Positive Psychology. In A. Delle Fave *Dimensions of well-being: Research and intervention* (pp. 565-582). Milano, Italy: Franco Angeli.

Laird, J.D. (1974). Self-attribution of emotion: The effects of expressive behavior on the quality of emotional experience. *Journal of Personality and Social Psychology*, 29, 475-486.

Lambert, M.J., Hansen, N.B., Umpress, V., Lunnen, K., Okiishi, J., Burlingame, G.M., & Reisinger, C. (2001). *Administration and scoring manual for the OQ-45.2*. American Professional Credentialling Services LLC

Lambert, M.J., Okiishi, J.C., Finch, A.E., & Johnson, L.D. (1998). Outcome assessment: From conceptualization to implementation. *Professional Psychology: Research and Practice*, 29, 63-70.

Landers, D.M., & Arent, S.M. (2001). Physical Activity and Mental Health. In R.N. Singer, H.A. Hausenblas, & C.M Janelle (Eds.), *Handbook of Sport Psychology* (2nd ed.) (pp. 740-765). New York: Wiley.

Landers, D.M., & Petruzzello, S.J. (1994). Physical activity, fitness, and anxiety. In C. Bouchard, R.J. Shephard, & T. Stephens (Eds.), *Physical activity, fitness, and health: International proceeding and consensus statement* (pp. 868-882). Campaign IL: Human Kinetics

Langer, E.J. (1989). *Mindfulness*. Cambridge: Perseus.

Latour, B. (1987). *Science in Action*. Cambridge, MA: Harvard University Press.

Lau, M.A., Segal, Z.V., & Williams, J.M.G. (2004). Teasdale's differential activation hypothesis: Implications for mechanisms of depressive relapse and suicidal behaviour. *Behaviour Research and Therapy*, 42, 1001-1017

Law, B.C. (1946). *Ashvaghosha*. Calcutta: Royal Asiatic Society.

Lazar, S.W., Kerr, C. E., Wasserman, R.H., Gray, J.R., Greve, D.N., Treadway, M.T. et al. (2005). Meditation experience is associated with increased cortical thickness. *Neuroreport*, 16, 1893-1897.

Leary, D. (Ed.). (1990). *Metaphors in the history of psychology*. Cambridge: Cambridge University Press.

Ledoux, J. (1996). *The emotional brain*. New York: Touchstone.

Ledoux, J. (2002). *Synaptic self*. New York: Viking.

Lehmann, D., Strik, W.K., Henggeler, B., Koenig, T., & Koukkou, M. (1998) Brain electric microstates and momentary conscious mind states as building blocks of spontaneous thinking: I. Visual imagery and abstract thoughts. *International Journal of Psychophysiology*, 29, 1-11.

Lehrer, P., Sasaki, Y., & Saito, Y. (1999), Zazen and cardiac variability. *Psychosomatic Medicine*, 61, 812-821.

LeShan, L. (1983). *How to meditate*. Boston: Little Brown.

Levine, M. (2000). *The positive psychology of Buddhism and yoga*. Mahwah, NJ: Lawrence Earlbaum.

Libet, B. (2004). *Mind-Time*. Cambridge, MA: Harvard University Press.

Linehan, M. (1993). *Skills training manual for treating borderline personality disorder.* New York: Guilford Press.

Linehan, M.M. (2003). Mindfulness, willingness, radical acceptance in psychotherapy: Seminar workbook. Behavioral Tech, LLC.

Linehan, M.M. (1993a). *Cognitive-behavioral treatment of borderline personality disorder.* New York: Guilford.

Linehan, M.M. (1993b). *Skills training manual for treating borderline personality disorder.* New York: Guilford.

Linehan, M.M., Armstrong, H., Suarez, A., et al. (1991). Cognitive-behavioral treatment of chronically parasuicidal borderline patients. *Archives of General Psychiatry*, 48, 1060-1064.

Ling, T. (1981). *The Buddha's philosophy of man.* London: J. M. Dent.

Lipchik, E. (1999). Theoretical and practical thoughts about expanding the solution-focused approach to include emotions. In W.R. Ray & S. de Shazer (Eds.), *Evolving brief therapy: In honor or John Weakland* (pp. 157-177). Galena, IL: Geist & Russell.

Liu, M.W. (1985). The mind-only teaching of Ching-ying Hui-Yuan: An early interpretation of Yogacara in China. *Philosophy East & West*, 35, 351-375.

Lloyd, K., & Bhugra, D. (1993). Cross-cultural aspects of psychotherapy. *International Review of Psychiatry*, 5, 291-304.

Lopez, D. (1995). *Buddhism in practice.* Princeton: Princeton University Press.

Lopez, D.S. (2001). *Buddhism: An introduction and guide.* London: Penguin.

Lowen, A. (1976). *Bioenergetics.* London: Conventure.

Lutz, A., Greischar, L. L., Rawlings, N. B., Ricard, M., & Davidson, R. J. (2004). Long term meditators self-induce high-amplitude gamma synchrony during mental practice. *Proceedings of the National Academy of Science*, 101, 16369-16373

Lyubomirsky, S., & Nolen-Hoeksema, S. (1995). Effects of self-focused rumination and negative thinking and interpersonal problem solving, *Journal of Personality and Social Psychology*, 69, 176-90.

Lyubomirsky, S., Caldwell, N.D., & Nolen-Hoeksema, S. (1998). Effects of rumination and distracting responses to depressed mood on retrieval of autobiographical memories, *Journal of Personality and Social Psychology*, 75, 166-77.

Ma, S.H., & Teasdale, J.D. (2004). Mindfulness-based cognitive therapy for depression: Replication and exploration of differential relapse prevention effects. *Journal of Consulting and Clinical Psychology*, 72, 31-40.

MacFarland, B.H. (1985). Psychiatric Disorders in Primary Care. *Archives of General Psychiatry*, 42, 583-590.

MacLeod, C., & Rutherford, E. (1998). Automatic and strategic cognitive biases in anxiety and depression. In K. Kisner (Ed.). *Implicit and explicit mental processes.* London: Erlbaum. Macmillan.

Maha Niddesa, Vols. I-III. (ed. by L. de la Vallee Poussin & E.J. Thomas, 1916-1917). London: Pali Text Society.

Maharishi Mahesh Yogi. (1963/1995). *The science of being and art of living.* New York: Penguin Books.

Mahoney, M.J. (1983). *Stream of consciousness: A therapeutic application* (Motion picture]. Keystone Heights, FL: PsychoEducational Resources.

Mahoney, M.J. (1985). Psychotherapy and human change processes. In M.J. Mahoney & A. Freeman (Eds.), *Cognition and psychotherapy* (pp. 3-48). New York: Plenum Press

Mahoney, M.J. (1988). Rationalism and constructivism in clinical judgment. In C. Turk & P. Salovey (Eds.), *Reasoning, inference, and judgment in clinical psychology* (pp. 155-181). London: Collier Macmillan Publishers.

Mahoney, M.J. (1991). *Human change processes: The scientific foundations of psychotherapy.* New York: Basic Books.

Mahoney, M.J. (2003). *Constructive psychotherapy: Practices, processes, and personal* revolutions. New York: Guilford.

Majjhima Nikaya, Vols. I-III. (ed. by V. Treckner & R. Chalmers. 1888-1902). London: Pali Text Society.

Majjhima Nikaya. In K.S. Dhammananda (Ed.). (1994), *The treasure of the Dhamma.* Malaysia: Buddhist Missionary Society.

Marlatt, G.A. (2002). Buddhist philosophy and the treatment of addictive behavior. *Cognitive & Behavioral Practice*, 9, 44-50.

Marlatt, G.A., & Gordon, J.L. (1985). *Relapse prevention: Maintenance strategies in the treatment of addictive behaviors.* New York: Guilford.

Marlatt, G.A., & Kristeller, J.L. (1999). Mindfulness and meditation. In W.R. Miller (Ed.), *Integrating spirituality in treatment: Resources for practitioners* (pp. 67-84). Washington DC: American Psychological Association.

Martin, P. (2000). *The Zen path through depression.* New York: HarperCollins.

Mascaro, J. (1962). *The Bhagavad Gita.* London: Penguin.

Matthews, B. (1983). *Craving and salvation.* Waterloo, Ontario: Wilfred Laurier University Press.

McAuley, E., & Courneya, K.S. (1994). The Subjective exercise experiences scale (SEES): Development and preliminary validation. *Journal of Sport & Exercise Psychology*, 16, 163-177.

McGee, D., Browne, I., Kenny, V., McGennis, A., & Pilot, J. (1984). Unexperienced experience: A critical reappraisal of the theory of regression and traumatic neurosis. Irish *Journal of Psychotherapy*, 3, 7-19.

McLeroy, K.R., Green, L.W., Mullen, K.D., & Foshee, V. (1984). Assessing the effects of health promotion in worksites: A review of the stress program evaluations. *Health Education Quarterly*, 11, 379-401.

McNamee, S., & Gergen, K.J. (1999). *Relational responsibility, resources for sustainable dialogue.* Thousand Oaks, CA: Sage.

McQuaid, J.R., & Carmona, P.E. (2004). *Peaceful mind: Mindfulness and Cognitive Behavioral Psychology to Overcome Depression.* Oakland: New Harbinger.

McWilliams, S.A. (1984). *Construing and Buddhist Psychology*, Constructs, 3(1).

Meares, A. (1978). Vivid visualisation and dim visual awareness in the regression of cancer in meditation. *Journal of the American Society of Psychosomatic Dentistry and Medicine, 25*, 85-88.

Menninger, K., Mayman, M., & Pruyser, P. (1963). *The Vital Balance. The Life Process in Mental Health and Illness.* New York: Viking.

Merriam-Webster online dictionary. (2005-2006). Retrieved January 5, 2006, from www.m-w.com

Meyer, T.J., Miller, M.L., Metzger, R.L., & Borkovec, T.D. (1990). Development and validation of the Penn State Worry Questionnaire. *Behaviour Research & Therapy*, 28, 487-495.

Mikulas, W. (1990). Mindfulness, self-control and personal growth. In M.G.T. Kwee (Ed.), *Psychotherapy, meditation and health: A cognitive-behavioural approach* (pp. 151-165). London: East-West.

Mikulas, W. (2000). Behaviors of the mind, meditation, and health. In Y.Haruki & K.T. Kaku (Eds.), *Meditation as health promotion: A lifestyle modification approach* (pp. 32-49). Delft, NL: Eburon.

Mikulas, W.L. (1981). Buddhism and behavior modification. *Psychological Record*, 31, 331-342.

Mikulas, W.L. (1983). Thailand and behavior modification. *Journal of Behavior Therapy & Experimental Psychiatry*, 14, 93-97.

Mikulas, W.L. (2002). *The integrative helper.* Pacific Grove, CA: Brooks/Cole.

Milindapañha (ed. by V. Trencker. 1886). London: Pali Text Society.

Miller, J.J. (1993). The unveiling of traumatic memories and emotions through mindfulness and concentration meditation: Clinical implications and three case reports. *Journal of Transpersonal Psychology*, 25, 169-180.

Miller, J.J., Fletcher, K., & Kabat-Zinn, J. (1995). Three-year follow-up and clinical implications of a mindfulness meditation-based stress reduction intervention in the treatment of anxiety disorders. *General Hospital Psychiatry*, 17, 192-200.

Miller, T.R. (1991). The psychotherapeutic utility of the five-factor model of personality: A clinician's experience. Journal of Personality *Assessment*, 57, 415-433.

Miura, I., & Fuller Sasaki R. (1965). *The Zen koan.* New York: Harvest Book.

Miyashita, K. & Ohno, H.(Eds.). (2003). *Kireru seishonen no kokoro.* Kyoto, Japan: Kitaoji Shobo.

Miyashita, K. (2001). Kireru hiko no mechanizm (2001). *Pychological World*, 14, 9-12.

Mizumo, K. (1982). *Buddhist sutras.* Tokyo: Kosei Publishing.

Molina, S., & Borkovec, T.D. (1994). The Penn State Worry Questionnaire: Psychometric properties and associated characteristics. In G. C. L. Davey & F. Tallis (Eds.), *Worrying: Perspectives on theory, assessment, and treatment* (pp. 265-283). Chichester, UK: Wiley.

Moncayo, R. (2003). The finger pointing at the moon: Zen practice and the practice of Lacanian psychoanalysis. In J.D. Sanfran (Ed*). Psychoanalysis and Buddhism: An unfolding dialogue.* New York: Wisdom.

Moore, R.G. (1996). It's the thought that counts: The role of intentions and meta awareness in cognitive therapy. *Journal of Cognitive Psychotherapy*, 10, 255-269.

Moore, R.G., Hayhurst, H., & Teasdale, J.D. (1996). *Measure of awareness and coping in autobiographical memory: Instructions for administering and coding.* Unpublished manuscript, Department of Psychiatry, University of Cambridge.

Moore, R.G., Watts, F.N., & Williams, J.M.G. (1998). The specificity of personal memories in depression. *British Journal of Clinical Psychology*, 27, 275-276.

Mori, H., Hasegawa, K., Ishikuma, T., Shimada, H., & Sakano, Y. (1994). Development of irrational belief scale (JIBT-20). *Human Science Research*, 3, 43-58 (in Japanese).

Mori, M. (1969). *"Mu" no shisou: Rousoushisou no keifu* (Philosophy of "nothingness": The history of Taoism). Tokyo: Koudansha.

Mulder, N. (1994*). Into Thai society.* Amsterdam: Pepin.

Murphy, M., & Donovan, S. (1997). *The physical and psychological effects of meditation: A review of contemporary research with a comprehensive bibliography 1939-1996.* Sausolito, CA: Institute of Noetic Sciences.

Murphy, M., & Donovan, S. (1999). *The physical and psychological effects of meditation.* Sausalito: Institute of Noetic Sciences.

Myers, D. (2000). The funds, friends and faith of happy people, *American Psychologist,* 55, 1, 56-67.

Nagura, Y., & Hashimoto, T. (1999). Effects of ruminative response styles on mental maladjustment. *Japanese Journal of Health Psychology,* 12, 1-11.

Nakajima, H. (2000). A Spiritual Dimension to Health in the 21st. Century: Why Now? In Y. Haruki & K.T. Kaku (Eds.), *Meditation as Health Promotion: A Lifestyle Modification Approach* (pp. 96-106). Delft, NL: Eburon.

Nakamura, S. (1992). Zen practice and meditation. In M. Blows, & S. Srinivasan.(Eds.), *Perspectives on relaxation and meditation* (pp. 99-109). Melbourne: Spectrum.

Namkhai Norbu, C.R. (1984). *Dzog Chen and Zen.* Nevada City, CA: Blue Dolphin.

Nan, H.C. (1995). *The story of Chinese Zen.* Boston, MS: Tuttle.

Nanamoli Bhikku (1975). *The path of purification - Visuddhimagga of Bhadantacariya Buddhaghosa* (3rd ed.). Kandy: Buddhist Publication Society.

Nanamoli, B. (Transl.). (1975). *Buddhagosha's Visuddhi Magga* (3rd ed.). Kandy, SL: Buddhist Publication Society.

Naruse, G. (1973). *Psychological rehabilitation.* Tokyo: Seishin-shobo.

Naruse, G. (1985). *Theory of Dosa Training.* Tokyo: Seishin-shobo.

Naruse, G. (1992). *Task achieving methods and experiential theory in psychotherapy. Research Report,* 28, 1-24. Fukuoka, Japan: Kyushu Women's University.

Natsoulas, T. (1998). On the intrinsic nature of states of consciousness: James's ubiquitous feeling aspect. *Review of General Psychology,* 2, 123-152.

Natsoulas, T. (1999). An ecological and phenomenological perspective on consciousness and perception: Contact with the world at the very heart of the being of consciousness. *Review of General Psychology,* 3, 224-245.

Neimeyer, R.A. (1987). An orientation to personal construct therapy. In R.A. Neimeyer & G.J. Neimeyer (Eds.), *Personal construct therapy casebook* (pp. 3-19). New York: Springer.

Neimeyer, R.A. (2000a). Narrative disruptions in the construction of self. In R.A. Neimeyer & J.D. Raskin (Eds.), *Constructions of disorder: Meaning-making frameworks for psychotherapy.* Washington, DC: American Psychological Association.

Neimeyer, R.A. (2000b). The language of loss: Grief therapy as a process of meaning reconstruction. In R.A. Neimeyer (Ed.), *Meaning reconstruction & the experience of loss* (pp. 261-292). Washington, DC: American Psychological Association.

Nelson, K.D., & Fivush, R. (2004). The emergence of autobiographical memory: A social cultural development theory. *Psychological Review,* 111, 486-511.

Nettippakarana (Ed. by E. Hardy. 1902). London: Pali Text Society.

Nideffer, R.M. (1976). Test of attentional and interpersonal style. *Journal of Personality & Social Psychology,* 34, 394-404.

Nieuwenhuizen, C. van (1998). *Quality of life of persons with severe mental illness: An instrument.* Amsterdam: Thesis Publishers.

Nieuwenhuys, R. (1985) *The Chemoarchitecture of the Brain*. Berlin: Springer.

Nieuwenhuys, R. (2000). Comparative aspects of volume transmission, with sidelight on other forms of intercellular communication. In L.F. Agnati, K. Fuxe, C. Nicholson, & E. Syková (Eds.), *Volume Transmission Revisited* (ch. I.4). Oxford: Elsevier.

Nino, A.G. (1997). Assessment of spiritual quests in clinical practice. International *Journal of Psychotherapy*, 2, 193-212.

Nishida, K. (1987). *Last writings: Nothingness and the religious worldview* (D.A. Dilworth, Trans.). Hawaii, Honolulu: University of Hawaii Press. (Original work, 1946)

Nishida, K. (1988). *A study of good* (V. H. Viglielmo, Trans.). New York : Greenwood Press. (Original work, 1911)

Nishida, K. (1989). Zettai mujunteki jikodouitsu (Absolute-contradictory self-identity). In Ueda S. (Ed.), *Nishida Kitaro tetsugaku ronshu III* (pp. 7-84). Tokyo: Iwanami shoten. (Original work published 1939)

Nishida, K. (1994). Koui no sekai (The world of action). In Ueda S. (Ed.), *Nishida Kitaro tetsugaku kouenshu* (pp. 169-218). Kyoto: Toeisha. (Original work, 1934)

Noerholm, V., Groenvold, M., Watt, T., Bjorner, J.B., Rasmussen, N.A., & Bech, P. (2004). Quality of life in the Danish general population — Normative data and validity of WHOQOL-BREF using rasch and item response theory models. *Quality of Life Research*, 13, 531-540.

Nolen-Hoeksema, S., & Morrow, J. (1991). A prospective study of depression and distress following a natural disaster: The Roma Prieta earthquake. *Journal of Personality and Social Psychology*, 61, 115-121.

Noll, D.E. (2004). A place for compassion in the business world. *The Business Journal*, February, 20, 13.

Novaco, R.W. (1996). Anger treatment and its special challenges. *NCP Clinical Quarterly*, 6. <http://www.ncptsd.org/publications/cq/v6/ns/novaco.html>

Nuechterlein, K., Edell, W., Norris, M., & Dawson, M. (1988). Attentional vulnerability indicators, thought disorder, and negative symptoms. *Schizophrenia Bulletin*, 12, 408-426.

Nyanaponika Thera (1986). *The power of mindfulness: An inquiry into the scope of bare attention and the principal sources of its strength*. Kandy, Sri Lanka: Buddhist Publication Society.<www.geocities.com/CapeCanaveral/Runway/5787/wheel121.htm>

Nyanaponika Thera (1998). *Abhidhamma studies, Buddhist explorations of consciousness and time*. Sommerville, MA: Wisdom.

Nyanaponika, Thera (1992). *The heart of Buddhist meditation*. Kandy: Buddhist Publication Society

Nyanatiloka, T. (1970). *Buddhist dictionary: Manual of Buddhist terms and doctrines* (3rd ed.). Taipei: The Corporate Body of the Buddha Educational Foundation.

O'Connell, D., & Alexander, C.N. (Eds.). (1994). *Self recovery: Treating addictions using Transcendental Meditation and Maharishi Ayurveda*. Binghamton, NY: Hawroth Press.

O'Donoghue, J. (1997). *Anam Cara: Spiritual wisdom of the Celtic world*. London: Bantam.

Obayashi, M.K. (2005). A study on "kireru" from the Survey of Life Conditions among Junior and Senior High School Students. *Journal of the National Institute of Public Health*, 54 (2).

Ogawa, Y. (1992). A case of psychosomatic problem. In G. Naruse (Ed.), *Rinshodosaho no riron to chiryo* (pp. 202-213). Tokyo: Shibundo.

Ohno, K. (1978). Children with cerebral palsy and difficulty in motor control. In K. Ohno, K, & S. Murata. (Eds.), *Care and training for children with cerebral palsy: Practice of Dosa training* (pp. 9-35). Tokyo: Keiotsushin.

Okamoto, S. (1976). *Muga no shinrigaku* (Psychology of non-self). Tokyo: Asakura hoten.

Olivier, J., Huxley, P., Priebe, S., & Kaiser, W. (1997). Measuring the quality of life of severe mentally ill people using the Lancashire Quality of Life Profile. *Social Psychiatry and Psychiatric Epidemiology*, 37, 76-83.

Orme-Johnson, D.W. (2000). An overview of Charles Alexander's contribution to psychology: Developing higher states of consciousness in the individual and the society. *Journal of Adult Development*, 7, 199-215.

Osgood, C.E. (1952). The nature and measurement of meaning. *Psychological Bulletin, 49,* 197-237.

Papageorgiou, C., & Wells, A. (2000). Treatment of recurrent depression with attention training. *Cognitive & Behavioral Practice*, 7, 407-413.

Papañcasudani. Vols. I-V. (ed. by J.H. Woods, I.B. Horner, & D. Kosambi (1922-1938). London: Pali Text Society.

Parikh, S., Kusumakar, V., & Haslam, D. (1997). Psychosocial intervention as an adjunct to pharmacotherapy in bipolar disorder. *Canadian Journal of Psychiatry*, 42, 745-785.

Pennebaker, J.W. (Ed.). (1995). *Emotion, disclosure, & health*. Washington, DC: American Psychological Association.

Pensa, C. (2002). *L'intelligenza spirituale*. Roma: Ubaldini.

Perera, G.A. (2000). *Buddhist Paritta chanting ritual*. Dehiwela: Buddhist Cultural Centre.

Perls, F.S., Hefferline, R.F., & Goodman, P. (1973*). Gestalt therapy: Excitement and growth in the human personality*. London: Penguin.

Peterman, A.H., Fitchett, G., Brady, M.J., Hernandez, L., & Cella, D. (2002). Measuring spiritual well-being in people with cancer: the functional assessment of chronic illness therapy-spiritual well-being scale (FACIT-Sp). *Annals of Behavioral Medicine*, 24, 49-58.

Petruzzello, S.J., Landers, D.M., Hatfield, B.D., Kubitz, K.A., & Salazar, W. (1991). A meta-analysis on the anxiety-reducing effects of acute and chronic exercise. Outcomes and mechanisms. *Sports Medicine*, 11, 143-182.

Pharmacy Times (2002). Top 10 drugs of 2001. *Pharmacy Times*, 68, 105.

Pierrakos, J. (1987). *Core Energetics: Developing the capacity to love and heal*. Mendocino, CA: Life Rhythm Publications.

Pirsig, R, (1974). *Zen and the art of motorcycle maintenance: An inquiry into values*. London: The Bodley Head.

Podvoll, E.M. (1991). *The seduction of madness: Revolutionary insights into the world of psychosis and a compassionate approach to recovery at home*. San Fransisco: Harper Perennial.

Post, R.M. (1992). Transduction of psychosocial stress into the neurobiology of recurrent affective disorder. *American Journal of Psychiatry*, 149, 999-1010.

Powers, J. (Transl.). (1994). *Wisdom of Buddha: The Sandhinirmocana Sutra*. Berkeley: Dharma Publishing.

Pradhan, A.P. (1986). *The Buddha's system of meditation.* Vols. I-III. London: Oriental University Press.

Price, A.F., & Wong, M.L.(Trans.). (1990). *The Diamond Sutra and the Sutra of Hui-Neng.* Boston: Shambala.

Punnaji, B. (1978). *Buddhism and psychotherapy.* Buddhist Quarterly, 10, 44-52.

Puriso, B. (1999). Mind Training. *Buddhism Today,* 14, 6-14.

Quine, W.V.O. (1960). *Word and object.* Cambridge: MIT Press.

Rabkin, J.G., & Klein, D.F. (1987). The clinical measurement of depressive disorders. In A. Marsella, R. Hirschefeld, & M. Katz (Eds.), *The measurement of depression.* New York: Guilford.

Rachman, S. (1978). An anatomy of obsessions. *Behaviour Analysis & Modification,* 2, 253-278.

Rachman, S., & Hodgson, R. (1980). *Obsessions and compulsions.* Englewood Cliffs, NJ: Prentice-Hall.

Radloff, L.S. (1977). The CES-D scale: A self-report depression scale for research in the general population. *Applied Psychological Measurement,* 1, 385-401.

Ragsdale, E.S. (2003). Value and meaning in Gestalt psychology and Mahayana Buddhism. In K.H. Dockett, G.R. Dudley-Grant, & C.P. Bankart (Eds.), *Psychology and Buddhism: From individual to global community* (pp. 105-124). New York: Kluwer.

Rahula, W. (1967). *What the Buddha taught.* London: Gordon Fraser.

Rahula, W. (1974). *What the Buddha taught.* New York: Grove Press.

Rahula, W. (1978). *What the Buddha taught.* (rev. ed.). London: Gordon Fraser.

Rahula, W. (1996). *Gems of Buddhist wisdom.* Kuala Lumpur, Malaysia: Buddhist Missionary Society.

Ramel, W., Goldin, P., Caroma, P., & Mc Quaid, J. (2004). The effects of mindfulness meditation on cognitive processes and affect in patients with past depression. *Cognitive Therapy & Research,* 28, 433-455.

Ray, R. (2000). *Indestructible Truth.* Boston: Shambhala Publications.

Reese, E. (2002). Social factors in the development of autobiographical memory: The state of the art. *Social Development,* 11, 124-142.

Reibel, D.K., Greenson, J.M., Brainard, G.C., & Rosenzweig, S. (2001). Mindfulness based stress reduction and health-related quality of life in a heterogeneous patient population. *General Hospital Psychiatry,* 23,183-192.

Reich, W. (1972). *Character analysis.* New York: Farrar, Straus, & Giroux.

Reid, G.B., & Nygren, T.E. (1988). The Subjective Workload Assessment Technique. In P.A. Hancock, & N. Meshkati (Eds.), *Human Mental Workload* (pp. 185-218). Amsterdam: Elsevier.

Rhys Davids, C.A.F. (1900). *A Buddhist manual of psychological ethics.* (Transl. of Dhammasangani). London: Royal Asiatic Society.

Rhys Davids, T.W. & Stede, W. (Eds.). (1921-1925). *The Pali Text Society's Pali English Dictionary.* London: Pali Text Society.

Rice, L.N., & Greenberg, L.S. (1984). Patterns of change: Intensive analysis of psychotherapy process. New York: Guilford.

Richards, J.C., Alvarenga, M., & Hof, A. (2000). Serum lipids and their relationships with hostility and angry affect and behaviors in men. *Health Psychology,* 19, 393-398.

Rodin, J. (1981). The current state of the internal-external hypothesis: What went wrong? *American Psychologist*, 36, 361-372.

Roemer, L., & Orsillo, S.M. (2002). Expanding our conceptualization of and treatment for generalized anxiety disorder: Integrating mindfulness/acceptance-based approaches with existing cognitive-behavioral models. *Clinical Psychology: Science & Practice*, 9, 54-68.

Roger, D., Jarvis, G., & Najarian, B. (1993). Detachment and coping: The construction and validation of a new scale for measuring coping strategies. *Personality & Individual Differences*, 15, 619-626.

Rosen, J.C., & Weines, A.N. (1979). Changes in medical problems and use of medical services following psychological intervention. *American Psychologist*, 35, 420-431.

Roth, S., & Epston, D. (1996). Developing externalizing conversations: An exercise. *Journal of Systemic Therapies*, 15, 5-12.

Rozin, P., Fischler, C., Imada, S., Sarubin, A., & Wrzesneiwski, A. (1999). Attitudes to food and the role of food in life in the U.S.A., Japan, Flemish Belgium and France. *Appetite*, 33, 163-80.

Rubin, J.B. (1996). *Psychotherapy and Buddhism: Toward an integration.* Plenum Press. New York.

Rush, A. (1999). Strategies and tactics in the management of maintenance treatment for depressed patients. *Journal of Clinical Psychiatry*, 60, 21-26.

Sabbe, B.G., Hulstijn, W., Hoof, J.J.van, & Zitman, F.G. (1997). Depressive retardation and treatment with fluoxetine: Assessment for the motor component. *Journal of Affective Disorders*, 43, 53-62.

Saddhatissa, H. (1970). *Buddhist ethics.* London: Allen & Unwin.

Saddhatissa, H. (1971). *The Buddha's Way.* London: Unwin.

Safran, J.D. (Ed.) (2004). *Psychoanalysis and Buddhism: An unfolding dialogue.* Boston, MA: Wisdom.

Sakairi, Y. (1992). Effects of Transcendental Meditation for reducing anxiety of Japanese businessmen. In M. Blows, & S. Srinivasan (Eds.). *Perspectives on relaxation and meditation* (pp. 163-175). Melbourne: Spectrum.

Sakairi, Y. (1998). What does meditation change?: Measurement of cognitive styles. In M.M. DelMonte, & Y. Haruki (Eds.), *The embodiment of mind: Eastern and Western perspectives* (pp. 57-66). Delft, NL: Eburon.

Sakairi, Y. (1999). *Meiso-ho no fuan teigen koka ni kansuru rinsho shinrigaku-teki kenkyu* (Clinical psychological study on the effects of anxiety reduction by meditation. Doctoral Dissertation (Tsukuba University, Japan).

Sakairi, Y. (2002). *Development of a scale for measuring cognitive styles modified by meditation.* Paper presented at the 7th International Conference of Physical, Psychological, and Spiritual Wellbeing, Sydney, Australia.

Sakairi, Y. (2004). Development of a scale for measuring cognitive styles modified by meditation. *Journal of Human Sciences*, 16, 35-44 (in Japanese).

Sakamoto, S. (2000). Self-focus and depression: The three-phase model. *Behavioural and Cognitive Psychotherapy*, 28, 45-61.

Sakamoto, S., Kijima, N., & Tomoda, A. (2002). The association of self-preoccupation to self-reported duration and severity of depressive episodes. *Psychological Reports*, 90, 861-868.

Sampson, E.E. (1993). Celebrating the other, a dialogic account of human nature. Boulder, CO: Westview.

Samyutta Nikaya. In K.S. Dhammananda (Ed.), (1994). *The treasure of the Dhamma.* Malaysia: Buddhist Missionary Society.

Samyutta Nikaya. Vols. I-V. (ed. by L. Feer 1884-1898). London: Pali Text Society.

Sapolski, R.M. (1998). *Why zebras don't get ulcers: An updated guide to stress, stress related disease, and coping* (1st ed.). New York: W.H. Freeman

Sapolski, R.M. (2004). *Why zebras don't get ulcers: An updated guide to stress, stress related disease, and coping* (3rd ed.). New York: W.H. Freeman.

Sarbin, T. (Ed.) (1984). *Narrative psychology: The storied nature of human conduct.* New York: Praeger.

Sato, K. (1951). *Jinkaku shinrigaku* (Psychology of personality). Tokyo: Sogen-sha.

Satonaka, T. (Ed.). (2004). *Ichinichi Ippunhan no eigo joku* (English Jokes for half a minute a day). Tokyo: Takarajima-sha.

Schatzberg, A.F., Posener, J.A., DeBattista, C., et al. (2000). Neuropshychological deficits in psychotic versus non-psychotic major depression and no mental illness. *American Journal of Psychiatry*, 157, 1095-1100.

Schimmel-Spreeuw, A., Linssen, A., & Heeren, T. (2000). Coping with depression and anxiety: Preliminary results of a standardized course for elderly depressed women. *International Psychogeriatry*, 12, 77-86.

Schneider, R.H., Staggers, F., Alexander, C.N., Sheppard, W., Rainforth, M., Kondwani, K. et al. (1995). A randomized controlled trial of stress reduction for hypertension in older African-Americans. *Hypertension*, 26, 820-827.

Schultz, J., & Luthe, W. (1959). *Autogenic training: A psychophysiologic approach in psychotherapy.* New York: Grune & Stratton.

Schumann, H.W. (1989). *The Historical Buddha.* London: Arkana Books.

Schwartz, G.E. (1973). Biofeedback as therapy: Some theoretical and practical issues. *American Psychologist*, 28, 666-673.

Schwartz, G.E. (1975). Biofeedback, self-regulation, and the patterning of physiological processes. *American Scientist*, 63, 314-324.

Schwartz, G.E. (1979). The brain as a health care system: A psychobiological framework for biofeedback and health psychology. In G. Stone, N. Adler, & F. Cohen (Eds.), *Health Psychology.* San Francisco: Jossey-Bass.

Schwartz, G.E. (1983). Disregulation theory and disease: Applications to repression/cerebral disconnection/cardiovascular disorder hypothesis. *International Review of Applied Psychology*, 32, 95-118.

Schwartz, J.M. (1997). Obsessive Compulsive Disorder. *Science & Medicine*, 4, 14-23.

Schwartz, J.M. (1998). Neuroanatomical aspects of cognitive-behavioral therapy response in obsessive-compulsive disorder: An evolving perspective on brain and behavior. *British Journal of Psychiatry*, 173, 38-44.

Schwartz, J.M.S., & Begley, S. (2002). *The mind and the brain: Neuroplasticity and the power of mental force.* New York: Regan.

Saussure, F. de (1983) *Course in general linguistics.* Trans. R. Harris. London: Duckworth.

Segal, Z.V., Gemar, M., & Williams, S. (1999). Differential cognitive response to a mood challenge following successful cognitive therapy or pharmacotherapy for unipolar depression. *Journal of Abnormal Psychology*, 108, 3-10.

Segal, Z.V., Teasdale, J.D., & Williams, J.M.G. (2004). Mindfulness-Based Cognitive Therapy: Theoretical rationale and empirical status. In S.C. Hayes, V.M. Follette & M.M. Linehan (Eds.), *Mindfulness and acceptance* (pp. 45-65). New York: Guilford.

Segal, Z.V., William, J.M.G., & Teasdale, J.D. (2002). *Mindfulness-Based Cognitive Therapy for depression: A new approach to preventing relapse.* New York. Guilford Press.

Segal, Z.V., Williams, J.M.G., Teasdale, J.D., & Gemar, M. (1996). A cognitive science perspective on kindling and episode sensitization in recurrent affective disorder. *Psychological Medicine*, 26, 371-380.

Segerstrom, S., Tsao, J., Alden, L., & Craske, M. (2000). Repetitive thought as a concomitant and predictor of negative mood. *Cognitive Therapy & Research*, 24, 671-688.

Seisdedos, N. (2002). STAI: Cuestionario de ansiedad estado-rasgo, manual (6ª ed.). Madrid: Tea Ediciones.

Seligman, M.E.P., & Csikszentmihalyi, M. (2000). Positive Psychology: An introduction. *American Psychologist*, 55, 5-14.

Selver, Ch. (1957. Sensory Awareness and total functioning. *General Semantics Bulletin*, 20/21, 5-17.

Shafii, M. (1973a). Silence in the service of the ego: Psychoanalytic study of meditation. *International Journal of Psychoanalysis*, 54, 431-443.

Shafii, M. (1973b). Adaptive and therapeutic aspects of meditation. *International Journal of Psychoanalytic Psychotherapy*, 2, 364-382.

Shapiro, D. (1980). *Meditation: Self-regulation and altered states of consciousness.* New York: Aldine Publishing.

Shapiro, D. (1982). Overview: Clinical and physiological comparison of medication and other self-control strategies. *American Journal of Psychiatry*, 139, 267-274.

Shapiro, D. (1992). A preliminary study of long-term meditators: Goals, effects, religious orientation, cognitions. *Journal of Transpersonal Psychology*, 24, 23-39.

Shapiro, D.H., & Walsh, R.N. (Ed.). (1984). *Meditation: Classic and contemporary perspectives.* New York: Aldine.

Shapiro, F. (1997). *EMDR: The breakthrough therapy.* New York: Basic Books.

Shapiro, S.L., Schwartz, G.E., & Bonner, G. (1998). Effects of mindfulness-based stress reduction on medical and premedical students. *Journal of Behavioral Medicine*, 21, 581-599.

Sharf, R. S. (2000). *Theories of psychotherapy and counseling: Concepts and Cases* (2nd ed.). Belmont, CA: Thomson.

Shaw, M. (1987). William James and Yogacara philosophy: A comparative inquiry. *Philosophy East and West*, 3, 223-244

Sheppard, J.L. (1992). East meets West: Six techniques of relaxation/meditation. In M. Blows, & S. Srinivasan (Eds.), *Perspectives on relaxation and meditation* (pp. 21-54). Melbourne: Spectrum.

Sheppard, L.C., & Teasdale, J.D. (2001). Disfunctional thinking in major depressive disorder: A deficit in metacognitive monitoring? *Journal of Abnormal Psychology*, 109, 768-776.

Shevrin, H., & Dickmann, S. (1980). The psychological unconscious: A necessary assumption for all psychological theory? *American Psychologist*, 35, 421-434.

Shibahara, S. (2000). *Investigation of the body work and the body-awareness.* Masters thesis, Waseda University.

Shields, S.A., & Simon, A. (1991). Is awareness of bodily change in emotion related to awareness of other bodily processes? *Journal of Personality Assessment*, 57, 96-109.

Shimizu, R. (1992). An application for a depressed patient with anxiety disorder. In G. Naruse (Ed.), *Rinshodosaho no riron to chiryo* (pp. 223-233). Tokyo: Shibundo.

Shinohara, K., Kotaka, M., & Miura, T. (2002). *A study of daily experience related to the control of attention.* Paper presented at Japan Ergonomics Society (Kansai Branch), Kanazawa, Japan.

Shou-Yu, L., & Wen-Ching, W. (1996). *Tai Chi Chuan: 24 & 48 postures with martial applications.* Washington: YMAA Publication Center.

Silvia, P.J., & Phillips, A.G. (2004). Self-awareness, self-evaluation, and creativity. *Personality and Social Psychology Bulletin*, 8, 1009-1017.

Simons, A.D., Garfield, S.L., & Murphy, G.E. (1986). Cognitive therapy and pharmacotherapy for depression for depression: Sustained improvement over one year. *Archives of General Psychiatry*, 43, 43-50.

Sinclair, J. (2004). *Collins COBUILD English Language Dictionary (New digital edition).* London: Collins.

Singh, R., & Oberhummer, I. (1980). Behavior therapy within a setting of Karma Yoga. *Journal of Behavior Therapy & Experimental Psychiatry*, 11, 135-141.

Skevington, S.M., Lotfy, M., & O'Connell, K.A. (2004). The WHO's WHOQOL-BREF Quality Assessment: Psychometric properties and results of the intern field trial. A report from the WHOQOL group. Quality of Life Research, 13, 299-310.

Smith, H. (1991). *The illustrated world religions: A guide to our wisdom traditions.* San Francisco: Harper.

Snelling, J. (1991). *The Buddhist handbook. The complete guide to Buddhist schools, teaching, practice, and history.* Rochester, VM: Inner Traditions.

Sole-Leris, A. (1986). *Tranquility and Insight.* London: Rider.

Song, T. (1998). *History of Qi-gong.* Paper presented at the 5th Conference of the Transnational Network for the Study of Physical, Psychological and Spiritual Well-being. Beijing, China.

Soons, P.H.G.M. (2004). *Mensbeeld en praktijk van Rationeel-Emotieve Therapie Psychosynthese en Advaita Vedanta* (Unpublished Master's Thesis). Rotterdam, NL: Erasmus University (Faculty of Philosophy).

Speca, M., Carlson, L., Goodey, E., & Angen, M. (2000). A randomized, wait-list controlled clinical trial: The effect of a mindfulness meditation-based stress reduction program on mood and symptom of stress in cancer patients. *Psychosomatic Medicine*, 62, 613-622.

Sperry, L. (2001). *Spirituality in clinical practice: Incorporating the spiritual dimension in psychotherapy and counseling.* New York: Brunner-Routledge.

Stapp, H. (1993). *Mind, matter and quantum mechanics.* Heidelberg: Springer.

Stcherbatsky, T. (1923). *The central conception of Buddhism.* Delhi: Motilal Banarsidas.

Sternberg, R. J. (1998). A balance theory of wisdom. *Review of General Psychology*, 4, 347-365.

Sternberg, R. J. (Ed.). (1990). *Wisdom: Its nature, origins, and development.* Cambridge: Cambridge University Press.

Strack, F., Martin, L.L., & Stepper, S. (1988). Inhibiting and facilitating conditions of the human smile: a nonobtrusive test of the facial feedback hypothesis. *Journal of Personality and Social Psychology*, 54, 768-77.

Strand, B.H., Dalgard, O.S., Tambs, K., & Rognerud, M. (2003). Measuring the mental health status of the Norwegian population: A comparison of the instruments SCL-25, SCL-10, SCL-5 and MHI-5 (SF-36). *Nordic Journal of Psychiatry, 57*, 113-118.

Suedfeld, P., & Kristeller, J.L. (1982). Stimulus reduction as a technique in health psychology. *Health Psychology*, 1, 337-357.

Sugamura, G. (2003). Kouseishugi, touyoushisou, soshite ningenkagaku (Constructivism, Eastern philosophies and human sciences: From hierarchical to heterarchical knowledge). *Human Science Research*, 12, 29-48

Sugiura, Y. (2004). Detached mindfulness and worry: A meta-cognitive analysis. *Personality & Individual Differences, 37*, 169-179.

Sugiura, Y., & Tanno, Y. (2000). Self-report inventory of obsessive-compulsive symptoms: Reliability and validity of the Japanese version of the Padua Inventory. *Archives of Psychiatric Diagnostics & Clinical Evaluation*, 11, 175-189.

Sugiura, T., & Sugiura, Y. (2004*). The effects of cognitive resilience on depression: Cognitive self-regulation skills, self-efficacy, and optimism.* Poster presented at the World Congress of Behavioral and Cognitive Therapies 2004, Kobe, Japan.

Sugiura, T., & Umaoka, K. (2003). The relationship between Cognitive Control and depression in female university students. *Japanese Journal of Health Psychology*, 16, 31-42.

Sugiura, T., Sugiura, Y., & Umaoka, K. (2003). Correlates of cognitive control: Personality traits, meta-cognitions, and coping styles. *Journal of the Graduate School: Home Economics, Human Life Sciences*, 9, 13-23.

Suler, J. R. (1993). *Contemporary psychoanalysis and eastern thought.* State University of New York Press.

Sumangalavilasini. Vols. I-III. (ed. by T.W. Rhys Davids, J.E. Carpenter, & W. Stede, 1886-1932). London: Pali Text Society.

Sumedho, A. (1992). *The Four Noble Truths.* Hertfordshire: Amaravati Publications.

Sutta Nipata (ed. by D. Anderson & H. Smith, 1913). London Pali Text Society.

Suzuki, D.T. (1956). Zen Buddhism. New York: Doubleday.

Suzuki, D.T. (1963). *The essentials of Zen Buddhism: An anthology of the writings of D.T. Suzuki.* London: Rider.

Suzuki, D. T. (1964). *An introduction to Zen Buddhism.* New York: Grove Press. (Original work, 1914).

Suzuki, D. T. (1972). *Living by Zen.* York Beach, ME: Samuel Weiser. (Original work, 1950)

Suzuki, K. (1990). *Satori no boken* (The adventure of enlightenment). Tokyo: Sogen-sha.

Szasz, T.S. (1972). A psychologist's experience with Transcendental Meditation. *Journal of Transpersonal Psychology*, 3, 135-140.

Taft, C.T., Murphy, C.M., King, D.W., Musser, P.H., & DeDeyn, J.M. (2003). Process and treatment adherence factors in group cognitive-behavioral therapy for partner violent men. *Journal of Consulting and Clinical Psychology*, 71, 812-820.

Takai, N. (2000). Investigation about the self-acceptance and the lifestyle. Japanese *Journal of Self Psychology*, 1, 57-71.

Takizaki, N., & Koshikawa, F. (2000). *Development of the Japanese version if the Reflec-tion-Rumination Questionnaire (RRQ)*. Poster presented at the 64th Congress of the Japanese Psychological Association. Kyoto: Japan.

Tambs, K., & Moum, T. (1993). How well can a few questionnaire items indicate anxiety and depression? *Acta Psychiatrica Scandinavica*, 87, 364-367.

Taylor, W.J., Myers, J., Simpson, R.T., McPherson, K.M., & Weatherall, M. (2004). Quality of life of people with rheumatoid arthritis as measured by the World Health Organisation Quality of Life Instrument, short form (WHOQOL-BREF): Score Distribution and Psychometric Properties. *Arthritis & Rheumatism*, 15, 350-357.

Teasdale, J.D. (1988). Cognitive vulnerability to persistent depression. *Cognition & Emotion*, 2, 247-274.

Teasdale, J.D. (1997a). Assessing cognitive meditation of relapse prevention in recurrent mood disorders. *Clinical Psychology and Psychotherapy*, 4, 145-156.

Teasdale, J.D. (1997b). The relationship between cognition and emotion: The mind-in place in mood disorders. In D.M. Clark & C.G.Fairburn (Eds.), *Science and practice of cognitive behaviour therapy* (pp. 67-93). Oxford: University Press.

Teasdale, J.D. (1999). Emotional processing, three modes of mind and the prevention of relapse in depression. *Behaviour Research & Therapy, 37* (Suppl. 1), S53-S77.

Teasdale, J.D. (1999). Metacognition, mindfulness and modification of mood disorders. *Clinical Psychology and Psychotherapy*, 6, 146-155.

Teasdale, J.D. (2000). Mindfulness-Based Cognitive Therapy in the prevention of relapse and recurrence in major depression. In Y. Haruki & K.T. Kaku (Eds.), *Meditation as health promotion: A lifestyle modification approach* (pp. 3-18). Delft, NL: Eburon.

Teasdale, J.D., & Barnard, P.J. (1993). *Affect, cognition and change: Remodeling depressive thought*. Hillsdale, NJ: Erlbaum.

Teasdale, J.D., & Cox, S.G. (2001). Dysphoria: self-devaluative and affective components in recovered depressed patients and never depressed controls. *Psychological Medicine*, 31, 1311-1316.

Teasdale, J.D., Hayhurst, H., Pope, M. et al. (2002). Metacognitive awareness and prevention of relapse in depression: empirical evidence. *Journal of Consulting & Clinical Psychology*, 70, 275-287.

Teasdale, J.D., Segal, Z., Williams, J.M. (1995). How does Cognitive Therapy prevent depressive relapse and why should attentional control mindfulness training help? *Behaviour Research & Therapy*, 33, 25-39.

Teasdale, J.D., Segal, Z.V., Williams, J.M.G., Ridgeway, V.A., Soulsby, J.M., Lau, M.A. (2000). Prevention of relapse/recurrence in major depression by Mindfulness-Based Cognitive Therapy. *Journal of Consulting & Clinical Psychology*, 68, 615-623.

Telch, C.F., Agra, W.S., & Linehan, M.M. (2001). Dialectical behavior therapy for binge eating disorder. *Journal of Consulting & Clinical Psychology*, 69, 1061-1065.

Tellnes, G., & Bjerkedal, T. (1989). Epidemiology of sickness certification: A methodological approach based on a study from Buskerud county in Norway. *Scandinavian Journal of Social Medicine*, 17, 245-51.

Terwiel, B.J. (1977). *Boeddhisme in de praktijk*. Amsterdam: Van Gorcum.

Thanisarro, B. (Transl.). (1996). *The wings to awakening: An anthology from the Pali Canon*. Barre: Dhamma Dana Publications.

Thera, N. (1999). *The four sublime states*. Penang, Malaysia: Inward Path.

Thich Nhat Hanh (1976). *The Miracle of Mindfulness*. Boston: Beacon Press.

Thich Nhat Hanh (1998). *The heart of the Buddha's teaching.* Berkeley: Parallex Press.

Thich Nhat Hanh, T. (1999). *Interbeing: Fourteen guidelines for engaged Buddhism.* Parallax Press.

Thomas, S.P. (2003). Men's anger: A phenomenological exploration of its meaning in a middle class sample of American men. *Psychology of Men & Masculinity, 4,* 163-175.

Thurman, R., & Wise, T. (1999). *Circling the sacred mountain: A spiritual adventure through the Himalayas.* New York: Bantam Books.

Tirch, D. (1993). Nothing in mind: Prajnaparamita and neural network theory. *Insights & Perspectives, 1, 4-6.*

Todorov, T. (1996). *L'homme Dépaysé.* Paris: Editions du Seuil.

Tolle, E. (1999 *The power of now.* Novato, CA: New World Library.

Tophoff, M. (2000). Zen Buddhism and the way of Sensory Awareness. In Y. Haruki & K.T. Kaku (Eds.), *Meditation as health promotion* (pp. 114-132). Delft, NL: Eburon.

Tophoff, M. (2003) *Chan Buddhism: Implication of awareness and mindfulness training for managerial functioning.* Destelbergen, Belgium: Cartim Bvba.

Trapnell, P.D., & Campbell, J.D. (1999). Private self-consciousness and the five-factor model of personality: Distinguishing rumination from reflection. *Journal of Personality and Social Psychology, 76,* 284-304.

Treynor, W., Gonzalez, R., & Nolen-Hoeksema, S. (2003). Rumination reconsidered: A psychometric analysis. *Cognitive Therapy and Research, 27,* 247-259.

Troisi, A., & D'Argenio, A. (2004). The relationship between anger and depression in a clinical sample of young men: The role of insecure attachment. *Journal of Affective Disorders, 79,* 269-272.

Trungpa, Chogyam. In Gimian, C.R. (Ed.) (1999). The Essential Chogyam Trungpa. Boston, MA: Shambhala Publications.

Trungpa, Chogyam (1996). *Shambhala: The Sacred Path of the Warrior.* Boston, MA: Shambhala Publications.

Tsuchiya, K. (1997). *Ware warau, yueni ware ari* (I laugh, therefore I exist). Tokyo: Bungeishunju.

Tsuchiya, K. (1998). *Ningen wa warau ashi dearu* (A man is a laughing reed). Tokyo: Bungeishunju.

Tsuru, M. (1982). Change in Dosa process and in social behavior of schizophrenic patients. In G. Naruse (Ed.), *Sinri-rehabilitation no tenkai.* Fukuoka, Japan: Sinri rehabilitation kenkyujo.

Tulving, E. (1983). *Elements of Episodic Memory.* Oxford University Press.

Turner, E.E., & Rejeski, J.W. (1997). Psychological benefits of physical activity are influenced by the social environment. *Journal of Sport & Exercise Psychology.*

Turvey, T. (1997) Clinical outcomes of an adult clinical psychology service 1988-1995. Paper presented to BPS Clinical Psychology Section Conference.

Ueda, S. (2002). *Jugyu-zu wo ayumu: Shin no jiko eno michi* (Ten Bull Pictures to follow: A way to the real self). Tokyo: Daihorin-kaku.

Urbanowski, F.B., & Miller, J.J. (1996). Trauma, psychotherapy, and meditation. *Journal of Transpersonal Psychology, 28,* 31-48.

Vaihinger, H. (1924). *The philosophy of "as if": A system of the theoretical, practical and religious fictions of mankind.* New York: Routledge. (Original work, 1911)

Vajiranana, P. (1978). *Buddhist meditation in theory and practice* (2nd ed.). Kuala Lumpur: Buddhist Missionary Society.

Van der Does, W. (2002). Cognitive reactivity to sad mood: structure and validity of a new measure. *Behavior, Research and Therapy*, 40, 105-120.

Van der Kolk, B., & Fisher, R. (1995). Dissociation and the fragmentary nature of traumatic memories: Overview and explanatory study. *Journal of Traumatic Stress*, 8, 505-525.

Van der Kolk, B.A., McFarlane, A.C., & Van der Hart, O. (1996). A general approach to treatment of Posttaumatic Stress Disorder. In B.A. van der Kolk, A.C. McFarlane, & L. Weisaeth (Eds.), *Traumatic Stress*. New York: Guilford.

Van Waning, A. (2002). A mindful self and beyond — sharing in the ongoing dialogue of Buddhism and psychoanalysis. In P. Young-Eisendrath & S. Muramoto (Eds.) *Awakening and insight: Zen Buddhism and psychotherapy* (pp. 93-105). New York: Brunner-Routledge.

Varela, F.J., Thompson, E., & Rosch, E. (1993). *The embodied mind*. Cambridge, MA: MIT Press.

Victoria, B.D. (2003). *Zen war stories*. New York: RoutledgeCurzon.

Vinaya Pitaka. Vols. I-V. (ed. by H. Oldenberg, 1879-1889). London: Pali Text Society.

Visuddhimagga. Vols. I-II. (ed. by C.A.F. Rhys Davids, 1920-1921). London: Pali Text Society.

Von der Malsburg, C. (1994). The correlation theory of brain function. In E. Domany, J.L. van Hemmen, & K. Schulten (Eds.), *Models of Neural Networks II*, 95-119. Berlin: Springer.

Vos, F., & Zuercher, E. (1964). *Spel zonder snaren*. Deventer: Kluwer.

Wada, S. (1996). Construction of the Big Five scales of personality trait terms and concurrent validity with NPI. *The Japanese Journal of Psychology*, 67, 61-67.

Waddell, N. (2001). *Wild ivy: The spiritual autobiography of Zen master Hakuin*. Boston: Shambala.

Walen, S.R., DiGiuseppe, R., & Dryden, W. (1992). *A practitioner's guide to Rational Emotive Therapy*. New York: Oxford University Press.

Walsh, R. (1996). Toward a psychology of human and ecological survival: psychological approaches to contemporary global threats. In B.W. Scotton, A.B. Chinen & J.R. Battista (Eds.) *Textbook of transpersonal psychiatry and psychology* (pp. 396-405). New York: Basic Books.

Wang, S. (2005). A conceptual framework for integrating research related to the physiology of compassion and the wisdom of Buddhist teachings. In P. Gilbert (Ed.), *Compassion: Conceptualisations, research and use in psychotherapy*. New York: Routledge.

Wang, W. (1998). Study of the psychology and the behavioral science of Qigong. In M. DelMonte & Y. Haruki (Eds.), *The embodiment of mind: Eastern and western perspectives*. Delft, NL: Eburon.

Warrenburg, S., Critis-Christoph, P., & Schwartz, G.E. (1981). *Biobehavioural etiology and treatment of hypertension: A comparative outcome study of stress management and diet change approaches*. Paper presented at the NATO Symposium on Behavioural Medicine, Greece.

Watanabe, S. (1958). *Nihon no Bukkyo* (Japanese Buddhism). Tokyo, Japan: Iwanami.

Watkins, E. (2004). Adaptive and maladaptive ruminative self-focus during emotional processing. *Behaviour Research & Therapy*, 42, 1037-1052.

Watkins, E., & Teasdale, J.D. (2001). Rumination and overgeneral memory in depression: Effects of self-focus and analytic thinking. *Journal of Abnormal Psychology*, 110, 353-357.

Watkins, E., & Teasdale, J.D. (2004). Adaptive and maladaptive self-focus in depression. *Journal of Affective Disorders, In Press, Corrected Proof.*

Watkins, E., Teasdale, J.D., & Williams, R.M. (2000). Decentring and distraction reduce overgeneral autobiographical memory in depression. *Psychological Medicine*, 30, 911-920.

Watson, B. (1993). *The Zen teachings of master Lin-chi.* Boston, MA: Shambhala.

Watts, A. (1966). *The book on the taboo against knowing who you are.* New York: Vintage Books.

Watts, A.W. (1957). The way of Zen. New York: Pantheon.

Watzlawick, P. (Ed.). (1984). *The invented reality: How do we know what we believe we know? (Contributions to constructivism).* New York: Norton.

Wegner, D.M. (1994). *White bears and other unwanted thoughts: Suppression, obsession, and the psychology of mental control.* Guilford Press.

Wegner, D.M., & Zanakos, S. (1994). Chronic Thought Suppression. *Journal of Personality*, 64, 615-640.

Wegner, D.M. (2002). The illusion of conscious will. Cambridge: MIT Press.

Weisbecker, I. (2002). MBSR and sense of coherence among women with fibromyalgia. *Journal of Clinical Psychology in Medical Settings*, 4, 297-307.

Weissman, A., & Beck, A.T. (1978, November). *The Dysfunctional Attitudes Scale.* Paper presented at the annual meeting of the Association for the Advancement of Behaviour Therapy, Chicago, IL.

Wells, A. (1990). Panic disorder in association with relaxation induced anxiety: An attentional training approach to treatment. *Behaviour Therapy*, 21, 273-280.

Wells, A. (1999). A metacognitive model and therapy for generalized anxiety disorder. *Clinical Psychology and Psychotherapy*, 6, 86-95.

Wells, A. (2002). GAD, metacognition, and mindfulness: An information processing analysis. *Clinical Psychology: Science & Practice*, 9, 95-100.

Wells, A., & Matthews, G. (1994). *Attention and emotion.* Hove: Laurence Erlbaum.

Wells, G.L., & Petty, R.E. (1980). The effects of head movements on persuasion. *Basic & Applied Social Psychology*, 1, 219-230.

Welwood, J. (1983). On psychotherapy and meditation. In J. Welwood (Ed.), *Awakening the heart* (pp. 43-54). Boston: Shambhala.

Wenzlaff, R.M., Rude, S.S., Taylor, C.J., Stultz, C.H., & Sweatt, R.A. (2001). Beneath the veil of thought suppression: Attentional bias and depression risk. *Cognition and Emotion*, 15, 435-452.

West, M.A. (Ed.). (1987). *The psychology of meditation.* Oxford: Clarendon Press.

West, W. (1994). Post-Reichian therapy. In D. Jones. (Ed.), *Innovative therapy: A handbook* (pp. 131-145). Philadelphia: Open University Press.

White, M., & Epston, D. (1990). *Narrative means to therapeutic ends.* New York: Norton.

Wiens, S., Mezzacappa, E.S., & Katkin, E.S. (2000). Heartbeat detection and the experience of emotions. *Cognition and Emotion*, 14, 417-427

Wilber. K. (1986). The spectrum of development. In K. Wilber, J. Engler, & D.P. Brown (Eds.), *Transformations of consciousness* (pp. 65-105). Boston: Shambhala.

Wilfley, D.E., Welch, R.R., Stein, R.I., Spurrell, E.B., Cohen, L.R., Saelens, B.E., et al. (2002) A randomized comparison of group cognitive-behavioral therapy and group interpersonal psychotherapy for the treatment of overweight individuals with binge-eating disorder. *Archives of General Psychiatry*, 59, 713-721.

Wilkins, A., Shallice, T., & McCarthy, R. (1987). Frontal lesions and sustained attention. *Neuropsychologia*, 25, 359-365.

Williams, J.M. (1996). Autobiographical memory in depression. In D. Rubin (Ed.). *Remembering our past: studies in autobiographical memory*. Cambridge: University Press.

Williams, J.M.G. (2004) Experimental Cognitive Psychology and Clinical Practice: autobiographical memory as a paradigm case. In J Yiend (Ed), *Cognition, Emotion and Psychopathology*. Cambridge: CUP.

Williams, J.M.G., Barnhofer, T., Crane, C., & Beck, A.T. (in press c). Problem solving deteriorates following mood challenge in formerly depressed patients with a history of suicidal ideation. *Journal of Abnormal Psychology*.

Williams, J.M.G., Duggan, D.S., Crane, C., & Fennell, M.J.V. (in press b). Mindfulness and acceptance strategies, cognitive reactivity, and the self management of suicide risk. *Journal of Clinical Psychology*.

Williams, J.M.G., Teasdale, J.D., Segal, Z.V., & Kabat-Zinn, J. (in press a). *Mindfulness and the Transformation of Emotion: working wisely with unhappiness and depression.* New York: Guilford.

Williams, J.M.G., Teasdale, J.D., Segal, Z.V., & Soulsby, J. (2000). Mindfulness-Based Cognitive Therapy reduces overgeneral autobiographical memory in formerly depressed patients. *Journal of Abnormal Psychology*, 1, 150-155.

Williams, J.M.G., Watts, F.N., MacLeod, C., & Mathews, A. (1997). *Cognitive psychology and emotional disorders* (2nd ed.). Chichester, UK: Wiley.

Williams, J.W. (1998). A structured interview guide for the Hamilton Depression Rating Scale. *Archives of General Psychiatry*, 45, 742-747.

Williams, P. (1989). *Mahayana Buddhism*. London: Routledge.

Wittgenstein, L. (1953). *Philosophical investigations*. Trans. G. Anscombe. New York: Macmillan.

Wittgenstein, L. (1978). *Philosophical investigations*. Oxford: Blackwell. (Original work, 1953)

Wolpe, J.A. (1958). *Psychotherapy by reciprocal inhibition*. Stanford: Stanford University Press.

Wolpe, J. (1976). Behavior therapy and its malcontents: II. Multimodal eclecticism, cognitive exclusivism and "exposure" empiricism. *Journal of Behavior Therapy and Experimental Psychiatry*, 7, 109-116.

Wolpe, J., & Lazarus, A.A. (1966). *Behavior therapy techniques*. New York: Pergamon.

Wong, E. (1997). *Taoism*. Boston: Shambala.

Wong, M. (1969). *The sutra of Hui-neng*. Berkeley, CA: Shambala.

Woolfolk, R.L. (1975). Psychophysiological correlates of mediation: A review. *Archives of General Psychiatry*, 32, 1326-1373.

Wright, A.F. (1969). *Buddhism in Chinese history*. New York: Atheneum.

Wu, J.C.H. (2003). *The golden age of Zen*. Bloomington, IN: World Wisdom.

Yapko, M.D.(1997). *Breaking the patterns of depression*. New York: Doubleday.

Yatomi, Y., Liang, J., Krause, N., & Akiyama, H. (1993). CES-D ni yoru nihon-rojin no yokuutu shojyo no sokutei: So no insi kozo ni okeru bunka-sa no kento [Measuring depressive symptoms among Japanese elderly by CED-D: Cultural differences in the factor structure]. *Social Gerontology, 37*, 37-47.

Young-Eisendrath, P., & Muramoto (Eds.). (2002). *Awakening and insight — Zen Buddhism and psychotherapy*. New York: Brunner-Routledge.

Zajonc, R.B. (1984). On the primacy of affect. *American Psychologist, 39,* 117-123.

Zeig, J. (Ed.). (1985). *Experiencing Erickson: An introduction to the man and his work.* New York: Brunner/Mazel.

Zuercher, E. (1984). Beyond the Jade Gate: Buddhism in China, Vietnam and Korea. In H. Bechert & R. Gombrich (Eds.), *The world of Buddhism* (pp. 215-252). London: Thames & Hudson.

Zung, W. (1965). A self-rating depression scale. *Archives of General Psychiatry, 12,* 65-70.

Contributors

Richard R. Amodio, Ph.D., is the Director of the Center for Integrative Psychotherapy at the Medical Center and a Clinical Assistant Professor of Psychiatry at the Boston University School of Medicine. Email: Richard.Amodio@med.va.gov

C. Peter Bankart, Ph.D. is the Director of Student Counseling and Professor of Psychology at Wabash College, and the author of *Talking Cures: A History of Western and Eastern Psychotherapies,* and *Freeing the Angry Mind,* and co-editor of *Psychology and Buddhism: From Individual to Global Community,* and of *The Relevance of the Wisdom Traditions on Contemporary Society: The Challenge to Psychology.* Email: Bankartp@Wabash.edu

Henk P. Barendregt, Ph.D., Professor in the Foundations of Mathematics and Computer Science at Radboud University Nijmegen. He is the recipient of the Spinoza Award and a member of Academia Europaea, the Koninklijke Hollandsche Maatschappij der Wetenschappen, and the Royal Dutch Academy of Sciences. Email: henk@cs.ru.nl

Aaron T. Beck, M.D. is the President of the Beck Institute for Cognitive Therapy and Research, and Professor Emeritus of Psychiatry at the University of Pennsylvania. Among his many significant works are *Cognitive Therapy of Depression*, *The Integrative Power of Cognitive Therapy,* and *Cognitive Therapy in Clinical Practice.* Email: abeck@mail.med.upenn.edu

Michael DelMonte, Ph.D., is a Principal Clinical Psychologist in St. Edmundsbury Hospital in Lucan, County Dublin, and co-edited *The Embodiment of Mind: Eastern and Western Perspectives.* Email: pmdelmo@gofree.indigo.ie

Danielle Duggan is a doctoral student at Oxford University. danielle.duggan@psychiatry.oxford.ac.uk

Kenneth J. Gergen, Ph.D., is the President of the Taos Institute and the Mustin Professor of Psychology at Swarthmore College. His major books include *The Saturated Self, Realities and Relationships,* and *An Invitation to Social Construction.* Email: kgergen1@swarthmore.edu;

Fabio Giommi, Ph.D. is a cognitive therapist and a researcher at Radboud University Nijmegen. Email: F.Giommi@cs.ru.nl

Tenzin Gyatso is also known as the 14th Dalai Lama, the spiritual and temporal leader of the Tibetan people. His Holiness was awarded the Nobel Peace Prize on December 10, 1989, the highest of his numerous international awards. Among his many significant writings are *Ethics for the New Millennium, The Heart of Compassion,* and *The Universe in a Single Atom: The Convergence of Science and Spirituality.* Email: tcrc@gov.tibet.net

Jane Henry is a Psychologist at the Open University, U.K. She chairs their Creativity, Innovation and Change masters program. Her publications include *Parapsychology, Research into Exceptional Experience*, and *Creativity and Perception in Management*, Email: j.a.henry@open.ac.uk

Dian M. Hosking, Ph.D., is a Professor at the University of Utrecht, School of Business. She is the co-author of *A Social Psychology of Organizing — People, Processes, and Contexts* and co-editor of *Management and Organization: Relational Alternatives to Individualism*. Email: d.hosking@usg.uu.nl

Yasutomo Ishii is a Professor at the Department of Psychology, Graduate School of Letters, Arts and Sciences, Waseda University, Tokyo, and the Vice-President of the Society for Mind-Body Science. Email: ishiiy@waseda.jp

Yoshinori Ito is an Assistant Professor at the University of the Ryukyus, Faculty of Education, Japan. Email: gitoku@edu.u-ryukyu.ac.jp

James W. Jones, Psy.D., Ph.D., Th.D is a Distinguished Professor of Religion and Adjunct Professor of Clinical Psychology at Rutgers University. His major works include, *Contemporary Psychoanalysis and Religion, Religion and Psychology in Transition*, and *Terror and Transformation: The Ambiguity of Religion*. Email: jwj@rci.rutgers.edu

Rieko Katsukura, is a Clinical Psychologist at the Department of Cognitive Behavioral Therapy, National Center Hospital for Mental, Nervous and Muscular Disorders, Tokyo. Email: ghee@qf7.so-net.ne.jp

Rika Kawano, Ph.D., is a Research Fellow at the Advanced Research Center for Human Sciences, Waseda University, Tokyo. Email: kawanori@kurenai.waseda.jp

Belinda S. L. Khong, Ph.D., is a Practicing Psychologist and Lecturer at the Department of Psychology of Macquarie University, Sydney, Australia. Email: bkhong@psy.mq.edu.au

Fusako Koshikawa, Ph.D., is a Professor at the Department of Psychology, Waseda University, Tokyo, and a licensed Clinical Psychologist. Email: kfusako@waseda.jp

Herman Kyosen K. Kief is a Psychiatrist, Hypnotherapist, and Zen meditation teacher. Email: kief0002@planet.nl

Jean L. Kristeller, Ph.D., is Professor of Psychology at Indiana State University and Director of the Center for the Study of Health, Religion, and Spirituality at ISU. Email: pykris@isugw.indstate.edu

Ayako Kuboki is a student at the Graduate School in Psychology at Waseda University, Tokyo. Email: aya-aoba@fuji.waseda.jp

Noriko Kubota, Ph.D., is a Psychotherapist and teaches psychology at Otsuma Women's University in Tokyo. Email: kubotano@otsuma.ac.jp

Maurits G.T. Kwee, Ph.D., Clinical Psychologist, is co-founder of the Transcultural Society for Clinical Meditation and serves as its President. He edited *Psychotherapy Meditation & Health* and co-edited *Western & Buddhist Psychology*, and *Meditation as Health Promotion*. Email: dr.k.t.kaku@planet.nl

Kaneo Nedate, Ph.D., is a Professor of Psychology at the Faculty of Human Sciences, Waseda University, Saitama, Japan. Email: k.neda@gaea.ocn.ne.jp

Miguel Quintana Santana is currently a Postgraduate Researcher at the Institute of Health and Sport Sciences, University of Tsukuba, Japan. Email: miguelqscanarias@yahoo.es

Padmal de Silva is a Senior Lecturer in Psychology at the Institute of Psychiatry, King's College, University of London. He is the co-author of *Obsessive-compulsive Disorders: the Facts* and co-edited *Obsessive-compulsive Disorders: Theory, Research and Treatment*. Email: spjtpds@iop.kcl.ac.uk

Michael de Vibe, M.D., is a Specialist in Family Medicine and Family Therapy in Norway. He is the President of the International Society for Holistic Health. Email: mdevibe@frisurf.no

Paul H.G.M. Soons, Ph.D., is a practicing Clinical Psychologist and Psychotherapist at the Department of Medical Psychology of Sint Anna Hospital, Geldrop. He is currently also an Associate Professor at the Department of Health Psychology of the University of Tilburg, Netherlands. Email: p.soons1@chello.nl

Genji Sugamura is a Doctoral Candidate at Waseda University and a Research Fellow of the Japan Society for the Promotion of Science. Email: sugamura@constructivism123.com

Yoshinori Sugiura, Ph.D. is an Associate Professor at the Faculty of Arts, Shinshu University, Asahi, Matsumoto City. Email: ysugiur@shinshu-u.ac.jp

Masao Suzuki, Ph.D. is a Professor of Psychology at Waseda University at Tokorozawa, Japan. Email: masaosuz@waseda.jp

Marja K. Taams, Psy.D., is a Clinical Psychologist in private practice and an executive board member of the Transcultural Society for Clinical Meditation. She co-edited a Special Issue on *Clinical Buddhist Meditation* in Constructivism in the Human Sciences. Email: dr.k.t.kaku@planet.nl

Dennis D. Tirch, Ph.D., is the Director of Education of the American Institute for Cognitive Therapy. He serves as an Adjunct Assistant Professor at the Ferkauf Graduate School of Psychology, Albert Einstein Medical School. Email: drdennis@mac.com

Michael M.Tophoff, Ph.D., is a Clinical Psychologist who also conducts management seminars and the Director of *Personal Resource Consultants*. Email: michael@tophoff.nl .

Paul J.C.L. van der Velde, Ph.D., Assistant Professor, Department of Theology and Religious Studies at Radboud University Nijmegen. Email: P.vdVelde@theo.ru.nl

Adeline van Waning, M.D., Ph.D. is a Psychiatrist at the Psychoanalytic Institute, Amsterdam, and board member of the Psychotherapy and Buddhism Foundation in the Netherlands. Email: adelinevanwaning@planet.nl

E. Scott Warren is a Psychotherapist in private practice in Dallas, Texas. He is currently completing his Ph.D. in Counselor Education and Philosophy at the University of North Texas and serves as an Assistant Adjunct Professor at the University of Dallas. Email: scott@lifetreecounseling.com

J. Mark G. Williams, Ph.D., is Professor of Clinical Psychology and the Wellcome Principal Research Fellow at the Oxford University Department of Psychiatry. Email: mark.williams@psychiatry.oxford.ac.uk

Printed in the United Kingdom
by Lightning Source UK Ltd.
123346UK00001BA/44/A